THE CRAFTS SUPPLY SOURCE BOOK

A comprehensive shop-by-mail guide
for thousands of craft materials.

MARGARET A. BOYD

REVISED FOURTH EDITION

BETTERWAY BOOKS
CINCINNATI, OHIO

ACKNOWLEDGMENTS

My appreciation to all the companies that responded with materials for this new edition. Their information helped me to provide more comprehensive listings.

A special thank-you to Patti DeLette Boyd, my dear daughter-in-law, whose assistance throughout this year has been the basis for joyful steps to completion of this work.

To my family and friends—bless you for your love and understanding.

Library of Congress Cataloging-in-Publication Data

Boyd, Margaret Ann
    The crafts supply sourcebook / Margaret A. Boyd.—4th ed.
        p.   cm.
    Includes index.
    ISBN 1-55870-441-8 (pb)
    1. Handicraft—United States—Equipment and supplies—Directories. 2. Handicraft—Canada—Equipment and supplies—Directories. I. Title.
TT12.B683   1994
680'.28—dc20   94-20392
                                                      CIP

Edited: Argie J. Manolis
Production editor: Katie Carroll
Interior and cover design: Clare Finney
Cover photography: Pamela Monfort Braun/Bronze Photography

In memory of my creative grandmothers,
Johanna Pribyl and Elizabeth Jane Munnerlyn.

GUIDE TO THE LISTINGS IN THIS BOOK

The listings in this book are divided into three sections: general arts, crafts and hobbies; needlecrafts, sewing and fiber arts; and resources. Within these sections are more than sixty categories to help you easily locate the supplies you need.

Most suppliers listed here are retailers serving the hobbyist or professional craftsperson. Many also offer wholesale prices to legitimate businesses; when this is the case, there will be a note following the "Discounts" heading. A few of the suppliers listed are manufacturers and sell wholesale only. They are listed here so you will be able to contact them to find a retailer that carries their supplies.

The listings include all available contact information: name of business or catalog, mailing addresses, and phone and fax numbers and e-mail addresses when provided by the company. This contact information is followed by a list of supplies available following the "Offers" heading. When available, the listing will also include how you can get more information. Often a company requests a SASE (self-addressed stamped envelope). SASEs should be no. 10 business-sized envelopes. When the business asks for a large SASE, include a large, manila envelope with double the postage. Be sure you also include a specific request for the information you need.

If a store location is available in addition to the mail order services provided, the listing will include the address of that location and, when provided, the hours during which the location is open to the public. Finally, any discounts offered, as well as any credit cards accepted, are included if the company provided them.

Listings in *The Craft Supply Sourcebook* are free. They are not advertisements, and the author and publisher are not endorsing the businesses listed here. Our aim is to provide you with a number of possibilities so you can make choices that are right for your own business or hobby.

The listings were compiled and verified by mail by the author. Most listings were also checked over the phone by the publisher prior to publication. We have tried to be as accurate as possible; still, the craft supply market is constantly changing, so companies listed may go out of business or make changes in the merchandise they offer. The publisher cannot be responsible for any losses resulting from using this book, such as the cost of postage for mail that is returned to sender.

Comments and contributions are welcome for future editions. May your days be full of the light of creative expression!

Margaret A. Boyd
P.O. Box 6232-FW
Augusta, GA 30906

Contents

Introduction vi

SECTION I: GENERAL ARTS, CRAFTS AND HOBBIES

Art Instruction 2

Artist's Supplies, Graphics and Printing....................5

Basketry and Seat Weaving........................10

Bead Crafts 14

Ceramics 19

Clock Making...28

Construction—Full-Size Structures 30

Construction—Full-Size, Operating Vehicles...........33

Doll and Toy Making—Rigid 36

Fishing Items 46

Frames and Picture Framing 48

Furniture Making and Upholstery...........................50

General Craft Supplies 52

Glass Crafts and Stained Glass 57

Indian and Frontier Crafts....................................60

Jewelry Making and Lapidary 62

Kite Making..73

Leather Crafts 75

Metalworking 78

Miniature Making, Miniatures & Dollhouses...........80

Model Making—Aircraft 88

Model Making—General 92

Model Making—Railroad 99

Mold Crafts 103

Nature Crafts 106

Oddities...110

Paints, Finishes and Adhesives 111

Paper Crafts and Paper Making 112

Photography...114

Rubber Stamping and Stamp Making....................120

Scientific Supplies and Equipment 127

Scrimshaw 128

Sculpture and Modeling 129

Sign Making 131

Taxidermy..134

Tole and Decorative Crafts 135

Tools and Equipment—Multipurpose 141

Wine and Beer Making 144

Wood Carving..146

Woodworking 148

SECTION II: NEEDLECRAFTS, SEWING AND FIBER ARTS

Batik and Dyeing 160

Clothing and Accessories...................................161

Costumes—Ethnic, Historic, Special Occasion......165

Doll, Toy and Clothes Making—Soft....................169

Embroidery and Cross-Stitch 174

Fabric Decorating 179

Fabrics and Trims...183

General Needlecraft Supplies...............................191

Home Decorating 196

Knitting and Crochet......................................199

Lace Making..208

Macrame 209

Needlepoint..210

Outdoors and Outerwear 211

Quilting..213

Rug Making 218

Sewing 224

Spinning and Weaving 232

Yarns—Multipurpose 243

SECTION III: RESOURCES

Associations..247

Books and Booksellers....................................250

General Craft Business....................................252

Publications 254

Supportive Materials and Aids.............................266

Index..273

INTRODUCTION

The fourth edition of this sourcebook includes hundreds of new and exciting supply sources, as well as updated information on the sources included in previous editions. These wonderful companies provide materials that inspire us to even more creatively innovative craft design and work.

Behind every catalog are dedicated business professionals who share their wares and often their experience as well. The literature offered on inquiry may include technical hints that help us avoid pitfalls and produce more satisfying results with greater ease. Often the value of what we can learn far outweighs the cost of the literature.

With that in mind, I urge you to explore your areas of interest and other areas, too—they can lead to new pathways of creation. Whatever you create, enjoy!

Margaret A. Boyd

General Arts,
Crafts and Hobbies

Art Instruction

Also see Artist's Supplies, Graphics and Printing, Books and Booksellers, Publications and Associations.

ART VIDEO LIBRARY
P.O. Box 68
Ukiah, OR 97880
(541) 427-3024

Offers: Over 1,000 art instruction videos for sale or rent. Members may rent videos at low cost and elect to apply rent to purchase. Videos cover acrylics, oils, watercolors, pastels, drawing, color, anatomy, perspective, still life, landscapes, air brushing and portraits. Instructors include Carter, Demeres, Sargent, Burton, Kelly, Jenkins, Palluth, Blackman, Graham, Flannery, Pike, Marchenko, Boyle, Vilppu, Lee, Pitard and Harris.
For Further Information: Free catalog.

ART-VIDEO PRODUCTIONS, INC.
P.O. Box 941
Woodland Hills, CA 91365
(818) 884-6278

Offers: 250 videotapes on color, figure, composition, anatomy, perspective, watercolor painting, portrait and landscape painting, still life and more.
For Further Information: Free brochure.

BOB ROSS TV ART CLUB
P.O. Box 946
Sterling, VA 20167
(703) 803-7200

Offers: A membership in this painting association allows discounts on videos, books and supplies, plus a newsletter subscription and notification of artists' seminars, demonstrations, classes and workshops. Also offers color how-to painting projects from Bob Ross and other national artists. Among mentioned artists: Gary Jenkins, Bob Ross, Priscilla Hauser and Dorothy Dent.
For Further Information: Send SASE.

WM. BLACKMAN PRODUCTIONS
2369 Magda Circle
Thousand Oaks, CA 91360
(805) 495-5076

Offers: Over 40 oil instructional painting videos. Subjects include animals, clowns, florals, seascapes, landscapes, exotic birds, barns and others. Also offers books.
For Further Information: Free brochure.

CARTOONERAMA
P.O. Box 854
Portland, ME 04104
(207) 773-5040

Offers: Cartoon correspondence course with professional instruction.
For Further Information: Free brochures.

TONY COUCH
5840 Musket Ln.
Stone Mt., GA 30087
(800) 491-7870

Offers: 10 art instruction workshop videos on painting and drawing, given by Tony Couch.

CREATIVE CATALYST PRODUCTIONS
P.O. Box 225
Albany, OR 97321

Offers: Instructional videos including watercolor portraits, watercolor and floral painting.
For Further Information: Send SASE for list.
Accepts: MasterCard, Visa

DEMBER ARTS
P.O. Box 8093
Van Nuys, CA 91409

Offers: Instructional art videos covering basic and advanced airbrushing, photo retouching, watercolor, rendering various media and hi-tech rendering (finished, conceptual and cutaway). Also offers demonstrations of mural techniques (materials, paints, airbrush, masking, scaffolding and transferring); plus instructional books.
For Further Information: Send SASE.

DESKTOP IMAGES
P.O. Box 10908
Burbank, CA 91505
(818) 841-8980

Offers: Four instructional videos on caricature drawing for beginner to advanced. Gag ideas book.

For Further Information: Write or call for free brochure.
Accepts: MasterCard, Visa

FLORA & COMPANY MULTIMEDIA
4801 Marble Ave. NE
Albuquerque, NM 87110
(505) 255-9988

Offers: Silkscreen instruction video, adapted to the home workshop, demonstrating techniques for reproducing patterns on fabric, wood, paper, plastics and other flat surfaces; a workbook is included.
For Further Information: Send SASE.
Accepts: American Express

FRED MAITLAND HINES
R.R. 2, Box 675
Johnson, VT 05656
(802) 635-2004

Offers: Marine painting master course on video, with marine artist.

BEEBE HOPPER
731 Beech Ave.
Chula Vista, CA 91910
(619) 420-8766

Offers: Instruction books in decorative arts (featherstroke technique), painting wildfowl and landscapes.
For Further Information: Send SASE.

JURAK
15 Tech Cir.
Natick, MA 01760

Offers: Airbrush instructional videos for starting, painting wild cats and portraits.
For Further Information: Send SASE for list.

DAVID A. LEFFEL
P.O. Box 278
Sanbornton, NH 03269
(603) 934-3222

Offers: Art videotapes covering still life and portraits with palette and brush techniques.
For Further Information: Send SASE.
Accepts: MasterCard, Visa

LILIEDAHL PUBLICATIONS
11814 Coursey Blvd., #498
Baton Rouge, LA 70816
(504) 769-8586

Offers: Art instructional videos including realist and old master methods; oil painting and others.
Accepts: MasterCard, Visa

M-M VIDEOS
P.O. Box 158
Freehold, NY 12431

Offers: Drawing instruction video by Stanley Maltzman demonstrating the techniques of landscape drawing, location through finished picture, techniques, rendering, composition and materials for the beginner and intermediate (56 minutes).
For Further Information: Send SASE.

MAJIC OF MAINE
1065 Riverside Dr.
Auburn, ME 04210
(207) 782-5650

Offers: Instructional videos of painting wildlife into landscapes (bear, fish, birds, moose and deer). Offers sales and rentals. Video production service.
For Further Information: Free brochure.
Store Location: At above address.
Discounts: Sells wholesale.

NORTH LIGHT ART SCHOOL
1507 Dana Ave.
Cincinnati, OH 45207

Offers: Home-study art course from professionals including a series of basic studies, perspective, techniques for pencil, color, painting and others.
For Further Information: Write.

NORTH LIGHT BOOKS
1507 Dana Ave.
Cincinnati, OH 45207
(513) 531-2222

Offers: Art instruction books, covering painting portraits, florals. Offers instruction in landscapes, nature, textures, flowers, weather, animals, people, urban settings and wildlife. Covers techniques for basics, such as color, light and values, acrylics, watercolors, oils, airbrush, screen printing and silk fabrics. Drawing and pastel titles are also available.
For Further Information: Write.

PAINTER'S CORNER, INC.
108 W. Highway 174
Republic, MO 65738
(417) 732-2076

Offers: Instructional, step-by-step books and videos by Dorothy Kent, covering landscape painting and other subjects (oil and acrylic).
For Further Information: Send SASE.

PERFECT PALETTE
P.O. Box 25286
Milwaukee, WI 53225

Offers: Over 36 instructional videos for all skill levels in acrylics, watercolors, faux finishes, oils, pen and ink, fabric painting and others.

For Further Information: Send large SASE for color catalog.

SIGNILAR ART VIDEOS
P.O. Box 278
Sanbornton, NH 03269
(603) 934-3222

Offers: Instructional painting videos by Ken Davies on sharp focus still life and trompe l'oeil, including subject selection, lighting, drawing, painting and perspective. Videos by David A. Leffel cover methods and techniques in portrait painting and still life, including background and design after the style of Rembrandt. Videos by Bruno Lucchesi demonstrate sculpture, including portraits, reclining figures, firing and patina.

For Further Information: Send SASE.

Accepts: MasterCard, Visa

V.E.A.S. PRODUCTIONS
316½ S. Main St.
Royal Oak, MI 48067
(810) 584-2020
Fax: (810) 584-2020

Offers: "Learn the Art of . . ." videos, with instructional programs on mural painting, gold leafing, sign lettering, airbrushing, photo retouching, glass etching and others.

For Further Information: Send SASE.

Discounts: Sells wholesale to mail order catalog distributors.

Artist's Supplies, Graphics and Printing

Also see Paints, Finishes and Adhesives, Tole and Decorative Crafts, Books and Booksellers, Publications, Associations and other specific categories.

AIKO'S ART MATERIALS IMPORT
3347 N. Clark St.
Chicago, IL 60657
(312) 404-5600

Offers: Oriental art supplies including brushes, inks and papers. Also carries Japanese handmade paper (for printing, painting, collage, restoration, crafts, bookbinding), homespun (Kizuki), solid colors, textured with fiber, plus Masa, Hsho and Torinoko paper, designed (paper on paper), stencil designed, metallics and gossamer types. Fabric dyes and equipment are also available.
For Further Information: Catalog, $1.50.

ALEXANDER ART CORP.
P.O. Box 3729
Salem, OR 97302
(503) 362-7939

Offers: Specially formulated oil paints (extra thick), personally designed brushes (by Bill Alexander, as seen on TV), instructional videos (techniques, hints and tips) and books. Publishes a bimonthly newsletter.
For Further Information: Free supply catalog.
Accepts: MasterCard, Visa

ART EXPRESS
P.O. Box 21662
Columbia, SC 29221
(800) 535-5908

Offers: Art supplies in known brands such as Holbein, Grumbacher, Canon-Talons, Artograph, Winsor & Newton and Low Cornell. Carries paints, papers, canvas, inks, pastels, equipment and accessories.
For Further Information: 80-page catalog, $3.50.
Discounts: Wholesale and school discounts.

ART SUPPLY WAREHOUSE
5325 Departure Dr.
Raleigh, NC 27604

Offers: Artist's supplies including Holbein products and hard-to-find items. Also offers a full line of oils and watercolors for professionals, others.
For Further Information: Free catalog.
Discounts: Savings up to 60 percent.
Accepts: MasterCard, Visa

ARTISAN/SANTA FE, INC.
717 Canyon Rd.
Santa Fe, NM 87501
(800) 331-6375

Offers: Artist's supplies including Holbein products and hard-to-find items. Full line of oils and watercolors for professionals also available.

THE ARTIST'S CLUB
P.O. Box 8930
Vancouver, WA 98668
(800) 845-6507

Offers: Unpainted wood decorations, including Christmas ornaments and decorations, spring bunnies, watering cans, others. Also offers painting projects, paints, brushes, tools and instruction books.
For Further Information: Free catalog.
Accepts: MasterCard, Visa

ASW EXPRESS
5325 Departure Dr.
Raleigh, NC 27604
(800) 995-6778

Offers: Full line of artist's supplies including paints, inks, canvas, papers, brushes, frames; supplies for airbrushing and silk painting; and more.
For Further Information: Free catalog.

BADGER AIR-BRUSH CO.
9128 W. Belmont Ave.
Franklin Park, IL 60131
(847) 678-3104

Offers: Airbrushes (large cup gravity feed) for painting and finishing, in sets/outfits. Carries Air-Opaque paints in 35 non-toxic colors and 8 pearlescents that are intermixable—lightfast, waterproof, non-bleed paints for airbrushes, paint brushes and technical pens.
For Further Information: Catalog, $1.50.

DICK BLICK
P.O. Box 1267
Galesburg, IL 61402
(309) 343-6181

Offers: Extensive art supplies (including known brands), papers, paint mediums, canvas, painters' supplies and graphic arts materials. Carries supplies/equipment for intaglio, screen process, etching, block printing, lithography, laminating, dry mounting, signmaking, air brushing, picture framing, woodworking, sculpture and ceramics. Also carries adhesives, tapes, tools, easels, furniture, books, videos and computer software.
For Further Information: Catalog, $5.
Accepts: American Express, Discover, MasterCard, Visa

STAN BROWN'S ARTS & CRAFTS, INC.
13435 NE Whitaker Way
Portland, OR 97230
(503) 257-0559 or (800) 547-5531
Fax: (503) 252-9508

Offers: Artists' supplies—a full line of paints, brushes, papers, canvas and other material, including known brands and books.
For Further Information: Catalog, $2.50.

CHATHAM ART DISTRIBUTORS, INC.
P.O. Box 3851
Frederick, MO 21705
(800) 822-4747
Fax: (301) 631-0108

Offers: Decorative art supplies, including painting surfaces, tools, paints and brushes. Also carries books.
For Further Information: Write for catalog.

CHEAP JOE'S ART STUFF
374 Industrial Park Dr.
Boone, NC 28607
(800) 227-2788

Offers: Artist's supplies, such as papers (known brands) and a line of art supplies at reduced cost including professional colors (oils, watercolors, acrylics and others).
For Further Information: Free catalog.

CHROMA, INC.
205 Bucky Dr.
Lititz, PA 17543
(717) 626-8866 or (800) 257-8278

Offers: Jo Sonja's acrylics and mediums, archival oils and mediums, paints for all surfaces, all grades.
For Further Information: Call or write.

CONRAD MACHINE CO.
1525 S. Warner
Whitehall, MI 49461
(616) 893-7455

Offers: Etching and lithography presses (2 sizes), Convertible Press (hand-driven model) and optional accessories. Carries table and floor model presses, plus re-manufacturered presses in 12″ to 36″ sizes.
For Further Information: Free catalog. Request trade-ins list.
Discounts: Quantity; sells wholesale.

DIXIE ART & AIRBRUSH SUPPLIES
2612 Jefferson Hwy.
New Orleans, LA 70121
(800) 783-2612

Offers: Artist's supplies, including brushes, canvases, papers, paints (oils, acrylics, watercolors), mediums and sets. Carries Grumbacher, Winsor & Newton, Liquitex, Strathmore and Tara. Open stock of pastels.
Store Location: At above address.

FLETCHER-LEE & CO.
P.O. Box 007
Elk Grove Village, IL 60009
(708) 766-8888

Offers: Liquitex watercolors (professional grade), watercolor sets and others at savings.
For Further Information: Send SASE.
Accepts: MasterCard, Visa

FRAME WEALTH INC.
Rd. 2, Box 261-7
Orega, NY 13825
(800) 524-8582

Offers: Wood frames in ready made and custom sizes. Also offers length molding, framing tools and hardware, metals.
For Further Information: Call or write.

GRAPHIC CHEMICAL & INK CO.
728 N. Yale Ave.
P.O. Box 27
Villa Park, IL 60181
(708) 832-6004 or (800) 465-7382

Offers: Printmaking supplies. Block printing line includes linoleum and wood blocks, brayers and cutting tools. Lithographic line includes gums, asphaltum, tusche and rollers (rubber, KU Leather, composition, NuClear). Carries litho stones in many sizes, KU Leather and composition, inks, a variety of papers and other supplies.
For Further Information: Write.

GRAPHIC MEDIA CO.
13916 Cordary Ave.
Hawthorne, CA 90250
(800) 408-6242

Offers: Art supplies in a wide range of name brands, including Grumbacher, Winsor & Newton, Liquitex, Mountblanc, Waterman,Parker, Pelikan, 3M, Letraset and others.
For Further Information: Catalog, $5 (refundable).
Discounts: "20 to 60 percent."

GRUMBACHER
100 North St.
P.O. Box 68
Bloomsbury, NJ 08804
(609) 655-8282

Offers: Full lines of artist's supplies, including brushes for artists and signpainters, Golden Edge synthetic brushes, and other tools and equipment.
For Further Information: Contact your dealer or send SASE.

HK HOLBEIN, INC.
P.O. Box 555
Williston, VT 05495
(800) 682-6686

Offers: A variety of artists' colors—oils, oil sets, pastel/blend brushes, watercolors, acrylics, Aeroflash inks and acrylic gouache.
For Further Information: Catalog and color charts, $6.

THE ITALIAN ART STORE
84 Maple Ave.
Morristown, NJ 07960
(800) 643-6440

Offers: European artist's supplies—colors, oils, acrylics, watercolors and others.
For Further Information: Free catalog.

JERRY'S ARTORAMA
117 S. 2nd St.
P.O. Box 1105
New Hyde Park, NY 11040
(516) 328-6633

Offers: Full line of artist's supplies, reducing lenses and opaque projectors in a variety of models, picture frames, air brushes.
For Further Information: Catalog, $2.

KALISH BRUSHES
43 Parkside Dr.
E. Hanover, NJ 07936
(800) 322-5254

Offers: Line of Kolinsky brushes from Ireland, including watercolor and long-handled oil and acrylics styles in a full range of shapes.
For Further Information: Write or call.

JOE KUBERT ART & GRAPHIC SUPPLY
37A Myrtle Ave.
Dover, NJ 07801
(201) 328-3266
Fax: (201) 328-7283

Offers: Artist's, cartoonist's, and graphic art materials, including boards, papers (art, parchments, drafting, etching, rag, others), paints, finger paints, brushes, palettes, pens, crayons, chalk, pencils, pastels, airbrushes, airbrush sets, calligraphy pens/inks, drafting materials/equipment and Pantographs. Also carries mat/paper cutters, projectors, easels, canvas, stretcher strips, graphic and printing supplies, frisket, grids, films, Letraset letters, tapes, film, waxers, light boxes, projectors, furniture, plus etching, block printing and silkscreen supplies and equipment, tools, knives and books.
For Further Information: Catalog, $4.
Store Location: At above address. Hours: M,T,Th,F, 10-6. W, 10-7:30. Sat, 9-4.
Discounts: Professionals, teachers and institutions.

NAPA VALLEY ART STORE
1041 Lincoln Ave.
Napa, CA 94558
(707) 257-1810 or (800) 648-6696 for orders.
Fax: (707) 257-1111

Offers: Artist's supplies including Winsor & Newton watercolor papers and blocks, watercolor series and others. Also offers Grumbacher and Rembrandt supplies and Sennelier pastels.
For Further Information: Free catalog.
Accepts: MasterCard, Visa

NEW YORK CENTRAL ART SUPPLY
62 3rd Ave.
New York, NY 10003
(800) 950-6111

Offers: Fine arts supplies including colors (oils, watercolors, acrylics, sets), markers, pens, pastels, brushes and pencils. Also carries over 150 types of canvas (widths up to 197 inches), supplies, tools and accessories for silkscreen, woodcut, etching and lithography. Stocks handmade papers by Fabriano, Arches and others, plus marbling supplies and other supplies and equipment.
For Further Information: Call or write.
Discounts: Quantity, sells wholesale.

OTT'S DISCOUNT ART SUPPLY
102 Hungate Dr.
Greenville, NC 27858
(800)356-3289

Offers: A full range of pencils, charcoal, artist's papers and other materials.
For Further Information: Free catalog.

PAASCHE AIRBRUSH CO.
7440 W. Lawrence Ave.
Harwood Heights, IL 60656
(708) 867-9191

Offers: Airbrushes, including gravity feed and siphon single and double action models; airbrush sets for paints, varnish, lacquers and others. Accessories, air compressors, sprayers, equipment and supplies for air etching/spraying are also available. Also offers an air etching video. Manufacturer.
For Further Information: Free literature.
Discounts: Call for current discounts.

PEARL
308 Canal St., Dept. CSS
New York, NY 10013
(212) 431-7932 or (800) 221-6845
Fax: (212) 431-6798

Offers: Extensive artist's supplies (including known brands). Carries paints—oils, acrylics, watercolors, gouache, egg temperas, encaustics, vinyl matte, lettering enamel, gold leaf, specialty paints and various mediums. Also carries paint accessories, and tools, including sculpture, wood carving, framers, others. Also offers airbrushes and printmaking supplies, studio accessories, easels, mannequins, silk paint and dyes, equipment, furniture, others. Provides international mail order. We special order anything.
For Further Information: Write for list. Fine art catalog, $1.
Store Location: 16, coast-to-coast.
Discounts: Quantity; teachers, institutions and professionals; large order discounts negotiable.
Accepts: American Express, Discover, MasterCard, Visa

PENTEL OF AMERICA, LTD.
2805 Columbia St.
Torrance, CA 90503
(310) 320-3831

Offers: An extensive line of pens, including porous, markers, projection, white, ceramic tip, correction and permanent pens. Also offers drafting pencils, erasers and Roll'N Glue adhesive.
For Further Information: Contact your dealer or send SASE.

PERMA COLOR
226 E. Tremont
Charlotte, NC 28203
(704) 333-9201

Offers: Dry pigments in standard pearlescents, bronze powders, iridescents, Rabbitskin glue, gesso-primed panels, Kolinsky sable brushes. Specialty items, including talc, kaolin, gums, binders, gesso and graphite.
For Further Information: Send SASE.
Discounts: Quantity; teachers and institutions; sells wholesale to legitimate businesses and professionals.

PIXATION
1741 N. High Country Dr.
Orem, UT 84057
(801) 235-9500

Offers: Color photograph printing service on canvas for ready-paint, and final image sizes to 32″ × 48″ on primed cotton duck, with border for stretching.
For Further Information: Send SASE for details.

PRINTMAKERS MACHINE CO.
P.O. Box 71
Villa Park, IL 60181
(800) 992-5970
Fax: (708) 832-6064

Offers: Presses, including Sturges and etching presses, printmaker combination and lithopresses and etching presses.
For Further Information: Call.

REX GRAPHIC SUPPLY
P.O. Box 6226
Edison, NJ 08818
(201) 613-8777

Offers: "The Creator" table for graphic artists and draftsman. The table has a melamine top, steel base (enamel finish), dual position foot rest, rear stabilizing bar and built-in floor levelers; it's adjustable for height and angle and comes in 2 sizes.
For Further Information: Send SASE.

SAX ARTS & CRAFTS
P.O. Box 510710
New Berlin, WI 53151
(414) 784-6880

Offers: Artist's supplies (known brands), including a line of paints, brushes, palette knives, boxes, organizers, trays, markers, pens. Also carries sumi supplies, airbrush kits/accessories and compressors, paints, inks, canvas, stretchers, tools, easels, boards, plus a full line of papers, boards, mats and cutters. Also offers frames, framing tools and supplies, knives, scissors, adhesives, paper cutters, waxers, glue guns, tapes, punches and pencils. Carries artists' aids, such as mannequins and models. Drafting items, calligraphy and lettering tools, light boxes, mounting presses, film, projectors, photography supplies, magnifier lamps and furniture are also available. Stocks block printing supplies and presses, offset printing kits and presses, etching, lithography and screen printing items/kits, T-shirt printing machines, photo and speed screen supplies, videos (art, craft), film strips and books.

For Further Information: Catalog, $5 (refundable).
Discounts: Quantity.
Accepts: American Express, Discover, MasterCard, Visa
See Also: General Craft Supplies

ROBERT SIMMONS, INC.

2 Corporate Dr.
Cranberry, NJ 08512
(609) 655-5252

Offers: Brushes for watercolors, oils and acrylics, plus brushes for crafts, artwork, ceramics, hobbies and lettering. Styles available include Priscilla Hauser tole decorative brushes and ceramic brushes, such as Mary Gilbertson, Marc Bellaire and Helen Altieri types. Also offers Fabric Master brushes—design book, base coaters (flat, round) and scrubbers (nylon). Bamboo brushes, brushes for plaster crafts and china painting, brush roll pack sets in most sizes and styles, and books are also available. Manufacturer.
For Further Information: Contact your dealer or write.

DANIEL SMITH, INC.

4150 1st Ave. S.
P.O. Box 84268
Seattle, WA 98124
(800) 426-6740

Offers: Line of artist's supplies, including paints, metallic finishes, brushes, canvas, papers, books and others.
For Further Information: Catalog, $5 (refundable)
Store Location: At above address.

UTRECHT MANUFACTURING CORP.

33 35th St.
Brooklyn, NY 11232
(718) 768-2525 or (800) 223-9132

Offers: Professional artists' colors, stretchers, paper converters and other major brand art supplies, such as papers, colors, brushes, canvases and others.
For Further Information: Free catalog.
Store Location: 10, coast-to-coast.

VERILUX

P.O. Box 2937
Stamford, CT 06906
(800) 786-6850
Fax: (203) 921-2427

Offers: "Instant Sun" full spectrum studio lighting for accurate evalutation of color intensity, value and hues across the entire visible spectrum.
For Further Information: Call or write.

WILD WOMAN ARTWORKS

34 Glen Rd.
P.O. Box 93
Sparta, NJ 07871

Offers: Frame mats in double, ready and custom size on acid-free stock.
For Further Information: Price list, $2.
Discounts: Below list.

WINSOR & NEWTON

P.O. Box 1396
Piscataway, NJ 08855
(908) 562-0770

Offers: Artist's brushes, including the Sceptre 6-brush series that blends synthetic fibers with genuine sable. Offers other brushes for a variety of mediums. Manufacturer only. Does not sell to individuals.
For Further Information: Contact dealer or send SASE.

Basketry and Seat Weaving

Also see Batik and Dyeing, Indian and Frontier Crafts, Nature Crafts and Knitting and Crochet

ACP INC.
P.O. Box 1426
Salisbury, NC 28145
(704) 636-3034

Offers: Basketry supplies including reed, raffia, cane, cane binder, spline, seagrass, fiber rush and prewoven cane. Also carries basket hoops, kits (egg, berry and square handle) for wall, miniature, homestead, wine, other types of baskets in 23 styles. Tools available include awls, cutters. Also stocks dyes, brushes, and over 50 basketry books.
For Further Information: Catalog, $1.
Store Location: At above address.
Discounts: Teachers, institutions and professionals; sells wholesale to legitimate businesses.
Accepts: MasterCard, Visa

ADIRONDACK SEATWEAVERS
337 Old Trail Rd.
Fonda, NY 12068
(518) 829-7241

Offers: Basketry and seat-weaving supplies, including chair and binder cane and webbing. Reed types available include flat, oval, round and smoked. Also carries slab rattan, seagrass, fiber rush and paper twist. Carries kits and a full line of tools, Napier and reed dyes, hoops, 25 handles, frames, Shaker tape, feet and books.
For Further Information: Send $1.
Discounts: Quantity; teachers and institutions.
Accepts: MasterCard, Visa

ALLEN'S BASKETWORKS
P.O. Box 82638
Portland, OR 97202
(503) 238-6384

Offers: Basketry supplies (domestic and imported) and 3 basic basket kits. Also carries reeds (round, flat, half round and oval), rattan, poles, cane, raffia, pine needles, seagrass, fiber rush (paper), "Richard's bean twine," generic papers, fiber core, basket feet, hoops, many handles, wood strips, bases, wire, hearts and dyes. Tools available include awls, pliers and scissors.

For Further Information: Catalog, 45¢.
Store Location: At above address.
Discounts: Sells wholesale.

BASKET BEGINNINGS
25 West Tioga St.
Tunkhannock, PA 18657
(800)82-FIBER

Offers: Basket and fiber art products, including natural, hand gathered, hand-dyed materials, Irish waxed linen, and a line of unusual beads.
For Further Information: Free catalog. Material samples set, $4; waxed linen samples, $2.
Accepts: American Express, MasterCard, Visa

THE CANING SHOP
926 Gilman St., Dept CSS
Berkeley, CA 94710
(510) 527-5010 or (510) 544-3373
Fax: (510) 527-7718

Offers: Basketry and chair caning supplies including cane and webbing, spline, Danish seat cord, rawhide and rubber webbing, Shaker tapes, reed splint, fiber rush, Hong Kong grass, ash splint, braided raffia, willowsticks and reed. Also carries rattan poles, Kooboo and whole rattans, pine needles, hickory and palm bark, paper rush, jute roving, date palm stalks, pressed fiber seats, basket kits and hoops. Tools available include awls, chisels, clamps, knives, clippers, shears, sliver grippers and cutters. Gourds and a gourd crafting book, videos, books, Ukranian egg decorating supplies, books and videos are also available.
For Further Information: Catalog, $2 (refundable).
Discounts: Quantity; teachers and institutions.
Accepts: Discover, MasterCard, Visa

CONNECTICUT CANE & REED CO.
134 Pine St.
P.O. Box 762
Manchester, CT 06045
(860) 646-6586

Offers: Basketry supplies, including a full line of Nantucket basket molds (purse ovals, fruit basket, Shaker style, bushel, pushbottom and hardwood) and Nantucket accessories (rims, rivets, bolts, pins, ears, handle, bases, ribs and weavers). Also carries a variety of basket kits. Materials available include

seagrass, reeds, handles, ash and oak splints and dyes. Books are also available.
For Further Information: Free catalog.

COUNTRY BASKETS
90 Polikoff Rd.
Ashley Falls, MA 01222
(413) 229-2655

Offers: Basketmaking kits including Nantucket style and others. Basket supplies.
For Further Information: Send SASE for catalog.

COUNTRY SEAT, INC.
R.D. 2, Box 24A, Dept. CSS
Kempton, PA 19529

Offers: Basketry and chair seating supplies including oval and other reeds, hoops, handles, basket kits, and over 100 instructional books.
For Further Information: Send $1 + large SASE.
Discounts: Quantity.
Accepts: Discover, MasterCard, Visa

FRANK'S CANE & RUSH SUPPLY
7252 Heil Ave.
Huntington Beach, CA 92647
(714) 847-0707

Offers: Basket and seat-weaving supplies, including 5 rattans and shredded rattan, poles, cane and binder cane, cane webbing, reed spline, fiber and wire rush, Danish cord, sugar palm, raw coconut fiber, fiber wicker and braids, round reeds, oriental sea grass and coir, rice straw, raffia and sisal. Also has woodware, cutting tools, accessories, basket and furniture kits, upholstery supplies include cords, strips, tools, edgings, polyfilament and brass hardware. Tools include awls, wire twisters, cutters, staple guns, templates and calipers.
For Further Information: Free catalog.
Discounts: Quantity; sells wholesale to legitimate businesses.
Accepts: American Express, Discover, MasterCard, Visa

GH PRODUCTIONS
521 E. Walnut St., Dept CS
Scottsville, KY 42164

Offers: Basket making and chair bottoming supplies, including flat and round reed and cane; basket kits; waxed linen thread, Shaker tape, basket handles, tools and others. Also offers books.
For Further Information: Free catalog.

GRATIOT LAKE BASKETRY
Star Rt., Box 16
Mohawk, MI 49950
(906) 337-5116
Fax: (906) 337-4260

Offers: Basketry supplies, including white pulute, maple, black walnut, cherry, 6 types of reeds, ash splint, red oak, poplar, seagrass, cane bindings, slab and chair rattan and cane webbing, birch, cedar, elm bark, honeysuckle, black ash. Also carries spline tools, kits, dyes, handles, hoops and embellishments. Florida materials include grapevines and philodendron sheaths. Also has patterns and books.
For Further Information: Free catalog and newsletter.
Discounts: Quantity; teachers and institutions.

GREAT AUNT VICTORIA'S WICKER
R.R. #1
Waubaushene, Ontario L0K 2C0
Canada

Offers: Basket kits, round and flat reed, seagrass, dyes and books.
For Further Information: Send SASE.
Store Location: 115 Coldwater Rd., Waubaushene, Ontario

THE HERB BASKET
613 Revere Ct.
Sykesville, MD 21784
(410) 549-9264

Offers: Basketmaking material including reed, ash splint, pine needles, oak hoops, handles, kits, dyes, patterns and books. Catalog also lists teachers.
For Further Information: Catalog, $4.
Discounts: Quantity; teachers and institutions.

JAM CREATIONS
1900 W. Wardlow Rd., Box 764
Highland, MI 48357
(313) 887-5045

Offers: Patterns for basket making. Books, including *Tribute*—23 patterns for all levels, and *Tole Sampler*, beginning to intermediate basket weaving and painting patterns.
For Further Information: Send SASE for price list.

JOHN MCGUIRE
398 S. Main
Geneva, NY 14456
(315) 781-1251

Offers: Basketry supplies including Nantucket and Shaker style kits, wooden and resin molds, Nantucket, cane, reed, cherry, hickory, white oak rims, cherry bases, oak staves, bone decorations. Also offers black ash, cedar, bear grass, round and flat reed, splint cutting machines, table-top shave-horses, drawknives, cutters, nippers, handles, dyes, books. Also holds classes.

For Further Information: Send large SASE for 32-page catalog.

Store Location: Two outlets, in Geneva, NY and Penn Yan, NY.

Discounts: Quantity.

THE NORESTA CANE & REED

320 Western Ave.
Allegan, MI 49010
(616) 673-3249

Offers: Basketry supplies including press cane, hank cane, rush, splint, wicker, flat and round reeds, hoops, handles, dyes, basketry tools and books. Holds classes.

For Further Information: Catalog, $2.

Discounts: Sells wholesale.

NORTH CAROLINA BASKET WORKS

P.O. Box 1438
Sanford, NC 27331
(800) 338-4972

Offers: A distinctive selection of basketry kits, plus a complete line of supplies, including reeds, other naturals, and a large selection of handmade white oak handles. Also carries Nantucket and Shaker hardwood molds—accurate reproductions; rental is available on selected molds.

Discounts: Quantity.

OZARK BASKETRY SUPPLY

P.O. Box 599
Fayetteville, AR 72702
(501) 442-9292

Offers: Supplies including basketry kits, tools, chair canes, handles, hoops, materials, chair seating supplies, dyes—low priced. Carries over 100 books.

For Further Information: Catalog, $4.

Discounts: Sells wholesale.

Accepts: MasterCard, Visa

PACIFIC WEAVE

3008-16th Ave. W.
Seattle, WA 98119
(206) 285-9171

Offers: Basket making supplies, including handed reed, raffia and vine rattan. Also offers naturals, including cedar and birch bark, pine needles, sweet grass and bear grass. Basket kits also available. Also offers classes.

For Further Information: Free catalog.

H.H. PERKINS CO.

10 S. Bradley Rd.
Woodbridge, CT 06525

Offers: Natural strand cane in 8 widths, plastic cane, coils. Also offers fiber splint and rust, Hong Kong grass, and reed— flat, flat oval, round, ash. Kits, including kits for bench, bar stools, ladder back chairs, rockers and others. Reed, cane and fiber brush kits available. Also offers Nantucket basketry supplies, raffia in natural colors, Danish cord, macramé cord, cane webbing, stains, finishes, dyes, basketry and hand caning tools. Basket kits, handles, hoops, basket bases, videos and books also available.

For Further Information: Free catalog.

Accepts: Discover, MasterCard, Visa

PLYMOUTH REED & CANE SUPPLY

1200 W. Ann Arbor Rd.
Plymouth, MI 48170
(313) 455-2150
Fax: (313) 455-9984

Offers: Basketmaking supplies including natural weaving products, handles, hoops, tools, Old Village Collection basketry kits, chair seating materials, dyes, stencils and books.

For Further Information: Write.

Store Location: At above address.

Discounts: Wholesale prices available.

Accepts: Discover, MasterCard, Visa

ROYALWOOD LTD.

517-CSS Woodville Rd.
Mansfield, OH 44907
(419) 526-1630 or (800) 526-1630

Offers: Basketry supplies including Irish waxed linen, a line of reed and other naturals, hoops, handles, dyes, accessories, basketry kits, brown ash, tools and molds.

For Further Information: Catalog, $2.

Store Location: At above address.

Discounts: Quantity.

V.I. REED & CANE

Rt. 5, Box 632
Rogers, AR 72756
(501) 789-2639 or (800) 852-0025
Fax: (501) 789-2639

Offers: Over 25 basketry kits, instructions and sets for mail, flower, Cape Cod, tray, "tulip," bushel, Easter, heart and other baskets. Also carries reeds, cane and cane webbing, raffia, handles, wood hoops and others.

For Further Information: Catalog, $2.

Discounts: Quantity discounts; allows discounts to legitimate businesses.

Accepts: American Express, Discover, MasterCard, Visa

VICTORIAN VIDEO PRODUCTIONS
P.O. Box 1540
Colfax, CA 95713
(916) 346-6184
Fax: (916) 346-8887

Offers: Instructional videos, including basketry demonstrating techniques for splint, Appalachian egg and melon-type baskets with handle decoration choices. Offers 19 other craft videos.
For Further Information: Free catalog.
Discounts: Allows discounts to schools and libraries; sells wholesale to legitimate businesses.
Accepts: Discover, MasterCard, Visa

VIRGINIA BASKET SUPPLY
Rt. 71, Box 26
Glenville, WV 26351
(304) 462-7638

Offers: Basketry materials, including cattails, elm, bark, yucca and natural dyes.
For Further Information: Write.

WALTERS BASKET WILLOW CROFT
Mountain Rd.
Washington Island, WI 54246
(414) 847-2276

Offers: Basketry materials include English basket willow

(imported from Bristol, England) and propagated root, which comes with instructions for growing your own materials.
For Further Information: Send SASE.
Discounts: Coupons and quantity discounts available.

MARTHA WETHERBEE BASKET SHOP
171 Eastman Hill Rd.
Sanbornton, NH 03269
(603) 286-8927

Offers: Basketmaking kits, including Nantucket and Shaker styles and others. Materials, including splint and others. Nantucket, tatting and Shaker molds, handles, rim nails, clips, linings and lining patterns. Also offers books and holds classes.
For Further Information: Send SASE with inquiry. Catalog, $2.
Store Loclation: At above address.
Accepts: MasterCard, Visa

WOVEN SPIRIT BASKETRY
820 Albee Road W., Casey Key Plaza
Nokomis, FL 34275
(941) 485-6730

Offers: Full line of basketmaking supplies, equipment and books.
For Further Information: Catalog, $2 (refundable).
Store Location: At above address.

Bead Crafts

Also see General Craft Supplies, Indian and Frontier Crafts, Jewelry Making and Lapidary, Miniature Making and related categories.

ALICE'S STAINED GLASS

7015 N. 58th Ave.
Glendale, AZ 85301
(602) 939-7260

Offers: Hand-crafted glass beads, glass beadmaking supplies, videos and books.
For Further Information: Send SASE.
Store Location: At above address.

ART TO WEAR

5 Crescent Pl. S.
St. Petersburg, FL 33711
(813) 867-3711

Offers: Bead stringing (jeweler's) tools such as pliers, tweezers, scissors, pin vises and awls. Also carries bead boards, needles, tips, crimps, tigertails, cable chains, foxtails, boullion wire, needle cards, silk cones, spool cord kits and jewelry findings. Beads include sterling, 13K, gold-filled types, semi-precious gemstone beads and cultured and freshwater pearls. Carries designer bead kits and books.
For Further Information: Catalog, $1.
Discounts: Sells wholesale to dealers.

BALLY BEAD CO.

2304 Ridge Rd.
Rockwall, TX 75087
(800) 543-0280

Offers: Jewelry making supplies, including gemstones, fetishes, Heishi, old coins and other ethnic items. Beads include Austrian and Czech crystal types, antique silver, seed, 14K gold-filled, sterling and plated types. Designer jewelry parts, angel parts, jewelry chains, ethnic and Santa Fe looks, and others. Beading supplies and classes also available.
For Further Information: Catalog, $4.95 (refundable).
Accepts: Discover, MasterCard, Visa

BEAD BOPPERS

11224 Meridian E.
Puyallup, WA 98373
(201) 848-3880 or (800) 944-2980

Offers: Full line of beads including glass seed; findings, charms, tools. Also offers leather supplies and books.
For Further Information: Catalog, $2.50 (refundable).

BEAD BROKER

P.O. Box 3278
Austin, TX 78764
(512) 472-4490

Offers: A line of beads in wide range of types, sizes and colors.
For Further Information: Catalog, $3.

THE BEAD DIRECTORY

P.O. Box 10103-CB
Oakland, CA 94610

Offers: Directory listing over 400 bead sellers, glass, beadmaking suppliers, beadmakers, bazaars, sources, classes. Includes color section, coupons.
For Further Information: Write.
Discounts: Sells wholesale.

THE BEAD SHOP

177 Hamilton Ave.
Palo Alto, CA 94301

Offers: Line of beads and bead kits and sampler boxes including exotics, ancient, "jeweled," gemstone, metal and glass beads. Also carries charms, findings, threads and other supplies.
For Further Information: Write.
Discounts: Sells wholesale.

BEAD LADY DESIGNS

P.O. Box 1060
Freeland, WA 98249
(360) 678-6085

Offers: Maple 3-in-1 bead loom, adjustable and interchangeable, with up to 12″ × 36″ work surface; basic, deluxe and super deluxe sets in a variety of sizes for double weft or heddle bead weaving. Frame or tapestry loom. Holds loom beading classes.
For Further Information: Write.

BEADA BEADA

4262 N. Woodward
Royal Oak, MI 48073
(810) 549-1005 or (800) 826-5697

Offers: Beads in stone, glass, pearls, 14K, gold-filled, sterling silver and base metals.

For Further Information: Free catalog.
Discounts: Sells wholesale.

BEADS FROM AROUND THE WORLD

152 S. Montezuma
Prescott, AZ 86303

Offers: Beads, including antique glass, seed, druks, rondells, antique glass; Czech glass styles; unusual components and findings. Also offers books.
For Further Information: Catalog, $4.
Store Locations: Minneapolis, St. Louis and El Paso.

BEADWORKS

139 Washington St.
South Norwalk, CT 06854
(800) 232-3761
Fax: (203) 852-9034

Offers: Contemporary beads from areas worldwide—over 2,000 styles, sizes and colors.
For Further Information: See your dealer, or send SASE.
Store Location: At above address. Hours: M,T,W,F, 10:30-5:30. Th, 10:30-7. Sat. 10-6. Sun 12-5.

BEADZIP

2316 Sarah Ln.
Falls Church, VA 22043
(703) 849-8463

Offers: Beads, including glass, from areas worldwide—India, Czech, Peking, others. Also offers American Studio and African trade beads; seed beads, crystals, Bali silver, brass, copper, precious metal and plate, heishi, amber, enamel, cloisonne, porcelain, gemstones, bone, shell, wood, cinnabar and others. Jewelry findings, stringing materials, tools, supplies and books also available.
For Further Information: Catalog with design ideas, $5 (refundable).

BOONE TRADING COMPANY

562 Coyote Rd.
Brinnon, WA 98320
(360) 796-4330

Offers: Antique glass trade beads (strung), including circa 1800s "white hearts," translucent red/white center, blue smalls, jade green or medium blue glass. Carries padre beads (3/8" turquoise round, circa 1500s) and Russian blues (3/8" faceted opaque blue, circa 1800s).
For Further Information: Catalog, $1.
Discounts: Quantity; sells wholesale to businesses.

BOVIS BEAD CO.

P.O. Box 13345
Tucson, AZ 85732
(520) 318-9512
Fax: (520) 318-0023

Offers: Rare antique beads from areas worldwide, including religious, traders and merchants of antiquities. Other items include ceramic beads from Mexico, Peru and Guatemala and Navajo sterling beads. Also carries malachite, garnet, azurite and other gemstone beads in a wide array of sizes, colors and types. Beading supplies available include needles, cords and jewelry findings. Books are also available.
For Further Information: Illustrated catalog, $10 (refundable).

CANYON RECORDS & INDIAN ARTS

4143 N. 16th St.
Phoenix, AZ 85016
(602) 266-4823

Offers: Beads in a variety of types and sizes—seeds, recailles, bugles, crow, hexagon, metal and bone. Also carries threads, quills, furs, shells, feathers, findings and shawl fringes.
For Further Information: Write for craft list.

CARAVAN BEADS

449 Forest Ave.
Portland, ME 04101
(207) 761-2503
Fax: (207) 874-2664

Offers: Beads, including sterling silver beads from the Holy Land, glass, crystal, wood, bone, horn, gemstone, ceramic, cloisonne, seed; African types; and others. Metal casting, findings and tools are also available.
For Further Information: Call or fax for photo sheet and price list.
Discounts: Sells wholesale to stores, wholesalers and designers.

CENTER FOR THE STUDY OF BEADWORK

P.O. Box 13719
Portland, OR 97213
(503) 248-1848
Fax: (503) 248-1011

Offers: Beadwork books, resources and a newsletter. Books include authentic techniques and data, specific tribal and regional beading, patterns and data.
For Further Information: Catalog and sample newsletter, $2.50.

COCHRAN'S CRAFTS
845 Willow Rd.
Lancaster, PA 17601
(717) 392-1687

Offers: Brass, silver and nickel-plated beads, including plain, fluted, swirl, bone hairpipe, F Czech and Japanese seed beads, antique trade beads. Sinew, findings, nymo thread, over 100 books of bead research and instructions.
For Further Information: Catalog, $1.

COLUMBINE BEADS
2723 Loch Haven Dr.
Ijamsville, MD 21754
(800) 638-6947 or (301) 865-5047
Fax: (301) 865-1016

Offers: Imported Japanese square, magmata, triangle and foil beads; Czech specialty beads, double and triple cuts. Newsletter and club available.
For Further Information: Catalog, $3.
Discounts: Sells wholesale.

DIANE'S BEADS
1803 W. Main St.
Medford, OR 97501
(503) 779-5139

Offers: Beads, including seed in 11/0 and 14/0, crow, pony, trade beads, Czech glass, stone and metal. Also offers charms, supplies, looms and books.
For Further Information: Catalog, $4.
Discounts: Sells wholesale.

DISCOUNT BEAD HOUSE
P.O. Box 186
The Plains, OH 45780
(800) 793-7592

Offers: Line of designer beads in large quantity lots.
For Further Information: Catalog, $2.
Discounts: Sells wholesale.

DOUBLE JOY BEADS
7121 E. Shauraro Dr.
Scottsdale, AZ 85254
(602) 998-4495
Fax: (602) 443-9540

Offers: Line of solid copper beads and jewelry findings.
For Further Information: Write or call.

FIREFLY EMBROIDERIES
P.O. Box 304
Davisburg, MI 48350
(800) 447-6218

Offers: Beaded embroidery kits with glass beads, sequins, pattern, needles and fabric in a variety of designs for clothing, jewelry and accessories. Also offers Pinzazz beaded stick pin kits and Razzmatazz beaded barrette kits.
For Further Information: Catalog, $2.

FRANTZ BEAD COMPANY
E. 1222 Sunset Hill Rd.
Shelton, WA 98594
(360) 426-6712
Fax: (306) 427-5866

Offers: Line of beads including Italian glass, Thai/Khmer silver and components; Patricia Frantz handmade glass beads. Indian bone, horn and glass beads also available.
For Further Information: Set of color catalogs, $6. Free beadmaker supply catalog.

THE FREED CO.
415 Central NW
P.O. Box 1802
Albuquerque, NM 87102
(505) 247-9311

Offers: Beads, including collector types, gemstones (coral, amber, ivory and others), clay, wood, glass, cinnabar, metal, cloisonne and oddities. Also carries fetishes, netsuke, sequins, appliqués and milagros.
For Further Information: Send SASE for list.

GAMEPLAN/ABSTRACT
2233 McKinley Ave.
Berkeley, CA 94703
(510) 549-0993

Offers: 14 instructional videos on polymer clay crafting by Tony Hughes, including Beginning Workshop, Bead Shapes and Mixing Media. Also offers videos on recreating turquoise, lapis, bone, jade, amber and coral.
For Further Information: Free catalog.

THE GARDEN OF BEADIN'
P.O. Box 1535
Redway, CA 95560
(800) BEADLUV
Fax: (707) 923-9160

Offers: Beads, including bugles, glass seed in full range of colors and sizes; crow, pony, hex, crystal and other gemstone colors; Czech drops, crystal faceted, glass and crystal.

Carries wood, Venetian, satin glass and pseudo trade types.
For Further Information: Catalog, $2.
Discounts: Quantity discounts; sells wholesale.
Accepts: MasterCard, Visa

HANSA
3039 Lyndale Ave. S.
Minneapolis, MN 55408
(612) 821-1072

Offers: Venetian glass beads and hand-formed beads, including millefiori, chevron, fiorato, floral, foil and lamp.
For Further Information: Catalog, $3.

JOPPA GLASSOWORKS, INC.
P.O. Box 202
Warner, NH 03278
(603) 456-3569
Fax: (603) 456-2138

Offers: Line of mandrel glass beads in a wide range of colors and sizes.
For Further Information: Color catalog, $5.

MANGUM'S WESTERN WEAR
P.O. Box 362
Blackfoot, ID 83221
(208) 785-9967

Offers: Seed beads (down to size 24); will match color swatches.
For Further Information: Catalog, $1.

MORING LIGHT EMPORIUM
P.O. Box 1155
Paonia, CO 81428
(970) 527-4493

Offers: Glass beads, including crow, pony, 11/0 and 14/0 seed beads, bugles, chevrons, metal and bone. Also offers beading thread, needles and books.
For Further Information: Free catalog.

THE NAME GAME
505 S. Beverly Dr. #123
Beverly Hills, CA 90212
(310) 284-3434

Offers: Line of letter and symbol beads of wood in English, Greek and Hebrew.
For Further Information: Send SASE.
Discounts: Sells wholesale.

NEW MEXICO BEAD AND FETISH
323 Romero NW, Suite 11
Albuquerque, NM 87104
(505) 243-2600
Fax: (505) 244-3180

Offers: Hand-carved beads and fetishes, including heishi, shell, horn. Also offers jewelry findings and jewelry.
For Further Information: Color catalog, $4.

ORNAMENTAL RESOURCES, INC.
P.O. Box 3010
Idaho Springs, CO 80452
(800) 876-ORNA

Offers: Complete lines of glass beads, including faceted, cut, foiled, decorated, fancy, metal, ceramic, plastic, bone, stone, shell, bugles, pony, seed beads in all sizes. Collectors' beads, metal stampings, chains, appliqué materials, rhinestones, studs, sequins, glass jewels, tassels, buckles and buttons. Also offers beading tools and supplies and design assistance. $25 minimum order.
For Further Information: Catalog, $15 (with one year's supplements), or call or write.

OUT ON A WHIM
121 E. Cotati Ave.
Cotati, CA 94931
(707) 644-8343

Offers: Japanese and Czech seed beads in more than 500 colors. Also offers beads in Austrian crystal, semi-precious stones and others. Jewelry findings and supplies also available.
For Further Information: Free catalog.

PROMENADE'S LE BEAD SHOP
1970 13th St.
Boulder, CO 80302
(303) 440-4807

Offers: Full line of beadwork supplies (for beaded jewelry, trim on clothing and other). Also carries beading kits, threads, needles and bead instruction booklets for earrings, clothing and other articles.
For Further Information: Catalog, $2.50 (refundable).

SHIPWRECK BEADS
2727 Westmoor Ct. SW
Olympia, WA 98502
(360) 754-2323

Offers: Full line of beads: glass, metal, wood, plastic, antique types and others.
For Further Information: Catalog, $4.
Discounts: Sells wholesale.

L.C. SMITH'S BEADS
P.O. Box 176
Medford, OR 97501
(503) 772-0432
Offers: Beads, glass rod and bead-making supplies, jeweler's tools and books, bead display trays.
For Further Information: Catalog, $2.

TOUCH THE EARTH
30 S. Main St.
Harrisonburg, VA 22801
(540) 932-6289

Offers: Beads, including trade beads (chevrons, ovals, white hearts and Hudson Bay), faceted (lead crystal and colors), crow, abalone discs, pink conch beads, metal (hawk bells, mellon, solid brass, fluted) and bone hairpipe. Also carries glass strung beads, fancies (lined, pearls 3-cut, bugles), jewelry findings such as surgical steel, plated and sterling ear wires, clips and parts, needles, nymo thread and supplies. Stocks finished items as well.
For Further Information: Catalog, $2.

UNIVERSAL SYNERGETICS
P.O. Box 2840
Wilsonville, OR 97070
(503) 625-2323

Offers: Seed beads (11/0-22/0), bugles, findings, threads, beading supplies.

For Further Information: Catalog, $2 plus 52¢ postage.
Discounts: Sells wholesale.

WESTCROFT BEADWORKS
139 Washington St.
South Norwalk, CT 06854
(203) 852-9108

Offers: Over 1,500 different beads including plastics, acrylics, glass types, wood, metal and others in a variety of sizes and shapes.
For Further Information: Catalog, $7.95 ($5 refundable).
Discounts: Sells wholesale.

WORLD BEADS USA
BEADWORKS CANADA
126 W. Third Ave.
Vancouver, British Columbia V5Y 1E9
Canada
(604) 876-6637
Fax: (604) 876-3317

Offers: Line of beads, including seed and other glass types, metallic, semi-precious and more. Also offers findings, leather, FIMO and books.
For Further Information: 62-page color catalog, $10.

Ceramics

Also see Artist's Supplies, General Craft Supplies, Sculpture and Modeling, and Doll and Toy Making—Rigid. And note the many custom services available in this chapter.

AEGEAN SPONGE CO., INC.
4722 Memphis Ave.
Cleveland, OH 44144
(216) 749-1927
Fax: (216) 749-2110

Offers: Natural and synthetic sponges and a variety of tools. Ceramic supplies available include Christmas tree lights and sets, strobe and other bulbs, clocks, music boxes, turntables, touch banks, "twinkle-tone" and liquid gold.
For Further Information: Write for supply catalog.

AFTOSA
1034 Ohio Ave.
Richmond, CA 94804
(510) 233-0334

Offers: Supportive items including votive chimneys, lamp kits, candles, mini-lamp kits and shades, stoppers, dispenser pumps and wire whips. Also carries jewelry findings for pins and earrings, plus wax resist.
For Further Information: Free catalog.
Accepts: MasterCard, Visa

AIM KILNS
350 SW Wake Robin
Corvallis, OR 97333
(800) 647-1624
Fax: (503) 758-8051

Offers: Doll kiln (designed by doll makers for doll makers), 15 amps, cone 10, 8-inch square, with shut off infinite switch.
For Further Information: Write or call.
Discounts: Sells wholesale to established distributors.

ALBERTA'S MOLDS, INC.
P.O. Box 2018
Atascadero, CA 93423
(805) 466-9255

Offers: Full line of ceramic molds including classic, early

American, novelty/holiday figures, animals, music box carousels and dinnerware.
For Further Information: Catalog, $6.

AMERICAN ART CLAY CO., INC.
4717 W. 16th St.
Indianapolis, IN 46222
(317) 244-6871

Offers: AMACO ceramic supplies and glazes. Clays include firing, nonfiring, modeling and other types. Electric kilns include cone 10 gas models and others. Potter's wheels include a rehabilitation model and electric types. Also offers custom decal supplies to make your own ceramic decals, including a handbook, screen bed, light post, clamp light with photo flood, hinges, screen, foam, plate glass, acetate, squeegees and film packet, plus an instructional video. Manufacturer.
For Further Information: Contact your dealer, or send SASE.

ANN'S CERAMICS
282 St. Martins Rd.
Vine Grove, KY 40175
(502) 828-2906

Offers: Line of Alberta bisque Christmas ornaments, plus others.
For Further Information: Send 35¢ and a large SASE for list.

ARNEL'S, INC.
2330 SE Harney St.
Portland, OR 97202
(503) 236-8540

Offers: Arnel's molds for ceramics including over 65 mugs with decorative fronts, boxes (ring, powder, tissue, cigarette, flowered egg and others), cornucopias, plates, bowls, cups, serving dishes, wall plaques, 2 chess sets, animals, pedestals, kitchen ware, Christmas items, and religious and other figures.
For Further Information: Color catalog, $5.

ART DECAL CO.
1145 Loma Ave.
Long Beach, CA 90804
(213) 434-2711

Offers: Custom ceramic decals with complete art service.

Minimum order of 125; food-safe colors available.
For Further Information: Send SASE with inquiry.

ATLANTIC MOLD CORP.

55 Main St.
Trenton, NJ 08620
(609) 581-0880
Fax: (609) 581-0467

Offers: Molds for figurines (children, historical, doll parts, birds, animals and others), Christmas items (nativity, angels, candles, dishes, Santas), and Easter and other holiday designs. Also offers spaceman/craft molds, decoratives, plaques, vases, clocks, containers, beer steins, emblems, chess sets, planters, platters, casseroles, cookie jars, bathroom items and bases. Accessories available include lamp parts, sets, Lanshire clock movements, Lucite lights. Manufacturer.
For Further Information: Contact your dealer; color catalog, $6.50.
Accepts: MasterCard, Visa

AV PRODUCTIONS

P.O. Box 1796
Troy, MI 48099
(810) 879-1884

Offers: Over 40 titles of educational and how-to videos, including videos on ceramics, pottery, dollmaking and quilting, for all levels, beginning to advanced.
For Further Information: Write.
Accepts: MasterCard, Visa
Discounts: Series discounts available.

BLUE DIAMOND KILN

P.O. Box 172
Metairie, LA 70004
(504) 835-2035
Fax: (504) 838-0359

Offers: "Freedom Vent" ceramic kiln feature that requires no outside venting and consumes contaminants inside the firing chamber. Freedom Vent can also be added to a present kiln. Other kiln models also available.
For Further Information: Catalog, $1.

BRICKYARD CERAMICS & CRAFTS

4721 W. 16th
Speedway, IN 46224
(317) 244-5230 or (800) 677-3289

Offers: Parts for kilns and wheels from Amaco, Brent, Reward, Skutt, Duncan and Paragon molds, glazes, tools and crafts.
For Further Information: Write or call.

BRYNE CERAMICS

95 Bartley Rd.
Flanders, NJ 07836
(201) 584-7492

Offers: Stoneware slip in 5 colors for kilns with cones 6 to 10, plus other slips, clays (earthware, raku, reduction, black and grogged), porcelains, glazes and marbleizers. Equipment available includes wheels, kilns and tools.
For Further Information: Free brochures.

C.A.I.-MING

P.O. Box 601
Citrus Heights, CA 96511
(916) 989-1922

Offers: Programmed instruction in ceramics. Allows you to become a certified ceramics teacher through the mail. Available to teachers, dealers and distributors and duly sponsored by prospective teachers. Program provides written and audiotaped instruction, manual and techniques; non-product oriented. Continuing Education Units are also available.
For Further Information: Call or write.

CHARLES A. CASPER

Rt. 1, Box 379
May, TX 76857

Offers: Native American peace pipe kits, pipe bowl molds and wooden stems. Authentic native pot and ostrich egg molds.
For Further Information: Send five 32-cent stamps for prices.

CER CAL, INC.

626 N. San Gabriel Ave.
Azusa, CA 91702
(818) 969-1456
Fax: (818) 334-6639

Offers: Custom decals, complete art service, color matching, sheet runs, gold and combination colors.
For Further Information: Send SASE.

CERAMIC BUG SUPPLIES

17220 Garden Valley Rd.
Woodstock, IL 60098
(815) 568-7663

Offers: Ceramic bug slip marbleizer and 20,000 ceramic molds.
For Further Information: Send SASE.
Store Location: At above address.

CERAMIC CREATIONS

144 Hollyvale Dr.
Houston, TX 77060
(713) 448-2515
Fax: (713) 448-1675

Offers: Ceramic bisque and greenware, including Native American, holidays, country items, angels, cherubs, cookie jars, teapots, canisters and others.
For Further Information: Catalog, $5.95.
Discounts: Quantity.

CERAMIC RESTORATION

2015 N. Dobson Rd.
P.O. Box 59
Chandler, AZ 85224

Offers: Instruction for restoration of damaged porcelains, ceramics and collectibles. Restoration video with detailed examples also available. Also offers a selection of professional supplies.
For Further Information: Send large SASE.

CERAMICORNER, INC.

P.O. Box 1206
Grants Pass, OR 97526

Offers: Decals in over 800 designs, including floral, kitchen verses, labels, and others in traditional motifs.
For Further Information: CeramiCorner color decal catalog, $6; Matthey Florals color catalog, $8.

CLAY MAGIC, INC.

21201 Russell Dr.
P.O. Box 148
Rockwood, MI 48173
(313) 379-3400

Offers: Ceramic molds (whimsical/fantasy) for holidays (Halloween, Christmas and others), plus wreaths, containers, lanterns and other items.
For Further Information: Catalog, $8.

CORONET CHINA & DECAL CO., INC.

12 N. School Ln.
Lancaster, PA 17603
(717) 394-1212
Fax: (717) 394-3889

Offers: Full line of color decals in classic florals, mug wraps, quotes and verses, delicate subjects and seasonal in most design traditions.
For Further Information: Catalog, $7; $10 outside U.S.

CREATIVE CERAMICS

9815 Reeck
Allen Park, MI 48101
(800) 438-2700

Offers: Line of ceramic supplies in known brands.
For Further Information: Write or call.
Store Location: At above address. Hours: M-F, 8:30-4:15.
Accepts: MasterCard, Visa

CREATIVE CORNER

P.O. Box 121
Canistota, SD 57012
(605) 296-3261

Offers: Over 2,900 items in bisque ware, including vases, covered dishes, mugs/cups and other dinnerware, fruits, bookends and canisters. Animal figures include rabbits, squirrels, dinosaurs, and domestic animals. Offers holiday items for Christmas, Halloween and others, plus trees and lights, Southwestern and Native American pieces, line of animal figures, pilgrims, angels, others. Also offers Duncan paints, brushes, kilns and accessories. Has bisque items, including holiday pieces. Holds Duncan classes.
For Further Information: Catalog, $5.
Discounts: Sells wholesale to businesses.

CRIDGE, INC.

P.O. Box 210
Morrisville, PA 19067
(215) 295-3667
Fax: (215) 736-8634

Offers: Full line of porcelain jewelry blanks, plus ornaments, findings and inserts.
For Further Information: Free catalog.
Discounts: Quantity.

CUSTOM CERAMIC MOLDS

P.O. Box 1553
Brownwood, TX 76804
(915) 646-0125

Offers: Molds for ceramics, including jewelry, Indian thunderbird, desert cactus, buffalo, Indian fetish bear, chili pepper and Indian pot jewelry. Carries large chili peppers for Ristras pepper strings, Indian pots and peace pipe bowls.
For Further Information: Brochure, $5.

LOU DAVIS WHOLESALE

N3211 Highway H N.
Lake Geneva, WI 53147
(800) 748-7991 or (414) 248-2000

Offers: Ceramic supplies/equipment, including Kemper and Alcraft tools, Paasche airbrushes, adhesives, flan, clock parts, kiln accessories, desk pens and LCD clocks. Accessor-

ies include stoppers, lamp parts and bulbs, carousel bases, rods and parts. Carries gold, lusters, paints, brushes and finishes, plus musical movements and keys, jewelry findings and magnets.
For Further Information: Free catalog.

DEBCOR
513 W. Taft Dr.
South Holland, IL 60473
(708) 333-2191

Offers: Art/ceramic furniture, including drying and damp cabinets, kiln carts, kiln stands, wedging boards and clay carts. Also offers graphic arts furniture—write for details.
For Further Information: Free catalog.
Discounts: Sells wholesale.

DONGO MOLDS
P.O. Box 9
Morriston, FL 32668
(352) 528-5385

Offers: Over 150 molds for aquariums, terrariums and other items for medium to large tanks. Offers custom mold making from specifications.
For Further Information: Catalog, $3.

DONNA'S MOLDS
P.O. Box 145
West Milton, OH 45383
(513) 947-1333

Offers: Molds including traditional, whimsical, holiday and novelty figures and sets.
For Further Information: Catalog, $7.50; SASE for flyer.

DURALITE, INC.
15 School St.
P.O. Box 188
Riverton, CT 06065
(860) 379-3113
Fax: (860) 379-5879

Offers: Rapid replacement coils and electric elements for all brands/types of kilns and furnaces, plus straight wire and continuous coil. Also offers design services.
For Further Information: Write for brochure and price list.
Discounts: Quantity.

ENGELHARD CORP.
101 Wood Ave. S. CN-770
Iselin, NJ 08830
(908) 205-5000

Offers: Hanovia overglaze products, including lusters, metallics, opal and mother of pearl (for ceramics, china and glass). Also offers Cerama-Pen gold or platinum applicator. Manufacturer.
For Further Information: Contact your dealer; free technique sheets.

EVENHEAT KILN, INC.
6949 Legion Rd.
Caseville, MI 48725
(517) 856-2281
Fax: (517) 856-4040

Offers: Line of kilns (variety of sizes and types), kiln accessories, supplies and parts.
For Further Information: Free brochure.

FASH-EN-HUES
118 Bridge St.
Piqua, OH 45356
(513) 778-8500
Fax: (513) 778-9647

Offers: Instructional videos, including videos on the use of translucent colors on bisque and Flemish gold techniques.
For Further Information: Send SASE.

FAVOR-RITE MOLD CO.
516 Sea St.
Quincy, MA 02169
(617) 479-4107
Fax: (617) 376-2533

Offers: Molds for ceramics—Aficana, Fash-en Hues and Olde Town mold lines.
For Further Information: Catalog, $3.50.
Store Location: At above address. Hours: M-Th, 9-4 and 7-9. F, 9-2. Sat, 10-2.

GARE, INC.
165 Rosemont St.
P.O. Box 1686
Haverhill, MA 01832
(508) 373-9131

Offers: Molds, including traditional figures, "The Sophisticates" (1920s stylized figures), holiday designs (including Christmas Windows series) and others. Also offers texture glazes, stains, fired colors, tools, brushes and kilns.
For Further Information: Offers a variety of catalogs and publications. Write or call.

GHA, THE JEWELRY MOLD CO.
P.O. Box 200262
Austin, TX 78720

Offers: Ceramic jewelry molds, photo frames, vases, night lights and shades.

For Further Information: Catalog, $7.50 (refundable).
Discounts: Sells wholesale.

GOLDLINE CERAMICS
3024 Gayle St.
Orange, CA 92665
(714) 637-2205

Offers: 1,500 personal name decals, hobo style in black.
For Further Information: Send SASE for list.

HILL DECAL CO.
5746 Schutz St.
Houston, TX 77032
(281) 449-1942

Offers: Custom decal service from your artwork, photo or sketch, or complete art services for glass, china and ceramics.
For Further Information: Write or call.

HOLLAND MOLD, INC.
P.O. Box 5021
Trenton, NJ 08638
(609) 392-7032
Fax: (609) 394-0101

Offers: Molds including holiday items and sets, historical figures, wild animals, birds, eggs, steins, mugs, bowls, serving pieces, canisters, candlesticks, picture frames, plaques (marriage, birth, graduation, others), clocks, lamp bases, pedestals, bells and boxes. Custom mold service available. Write for information.
For Further Information: Mold catalog, $7.
Discounts: Offered to those qualified. Schedule included in catalog.
Accepts: MasterCard, Visa

JAY-KAY MOLDS
P.O. Box 2307
Quinlan, TX 75474
(903) 356-3416

Offers: Plaster molds for the ceramic industry, ranging from Southwest pieces to usable items.
For Further Information: Color catalog, $5.50
Discounts: Distributorships and other discounts available.

K-CERAMIC IMPORTS
732 Ballough Rd.
Daytona Beach, Fl 32114
(904) 252-6530
Fax: (904) 257-5486

Offers: Line of imported European decals in range of designs, including hard-to-find.
For Further Information: Ceramic transfers color catalog, $10.

KELLY'S CERAMICS, INC.
3016 Union Ave.
Pennsauken, NJ 08110
(609) 665-4181

Offers: Molds, including Gare, Atlantic, Dona, Holland, Iandola, Duncan, Kimple, Nowell, Provincial, Trenton, Scioto, New Ocean State, Ceramichrome, Mayco, plus White Horse and Clay Magic. Gare distributor.
For Further Information: Send SASE for a flyer or reply.
Accepts: MasterCard, Visa

KEMPER ENTERPRISES
Box 696, 13595 12th St.
Chino, CA 91710
(909) 627-6191
Fax: (909) 627-4008

Offers: Painters of ceramics, china glass and tole; Fluid Writer pens. Paint line includes wipe out tool, spatter brush, dot designer stamps, swizzle stick, rose sticks, paint knife, assorted cleaners and brush and tool caddy.
For Further Information: Call or contact your dealer.

LAGUNA CLAY CO.
14400 Lomitas Ave.
City of Industry, CA 91715
(818) 330-0631

Offers: Line of ceramic supplies, including clays, glazes, deco products for screen, brush and decal printing. Also offers kilns, potter's wheels, videos and books. Consulting service available.
For Further Information: Comprehensive catalog.
Store Location: At above address.
Discounts: Quantity; sells wholesale through national network of distributors.

LAMP SPECIALTIES, INC.
P.O. Box 204
Westville, NJ 08093
(800) CALL-LAMP

Offers: Electronic music boxes with Touch-Me (including blinking lights or harmony types) and multi-tunes. Also carries carousels, lamp-making parts (including kits and shades), sheet decals, foil leafing, gold leaf, clock parts (including fit-ups, quartz and electric), brushes (known brands), and Paasche and Badger airbrushes. Carries electrical items, such as tree kits, cord sets, bulbs and strobes. Overglazes, tools, pouring and cleaning items and accessories such as chenille, felt, stoppers, magnets, trims and findings are also available.
For Further Information: Catalog, $5.
Discounts: Quantity; sells wholesale to legitimate businesses.
Accepts: Discover, MasterCard, Visa

LEHMAN

P.O. Box 46

Kentland, IN 47951

(800) 348-5196

Fax: (219) 474-6014

Offers: Slip handling equipment, such as Paint Safe drying table, Trim'N Clean tools, STK-1 slip testing kit, slip-doppe, and original and jumbo stencil pencils. Manufacturer.

LILY POND PRODUCTS

351 W. Cromwell, Suite 105

Fresno, CA 93711

(209) 431-5003

Fax: (209) 431-6718

Offers: Lil' Pumper ⅓ HP pump—heavy-duty and operates on 1 to 5 gallons of slip. Also offers Lil' Puddle table and Big Puddle mix/pour and reclaim machine with mixer, plus others.

For Further Information: Send SASE.

MARJON CERAMICS

3434 W. Earl Dr.

Phoenix, AZ 85017

(602) 272-6585

Offers: The instructional video, *Mold Making*, with Bill Anderson (creating molds step-by-step) and a complete mold-making kit (mold box, textbook, tools and supplies). Order the video and kit together for savings.

For Further Information: Send SASE.

Accepts: MasterCard, Visa

MARYLAND CHINA CO.

54 Main St.

Reisterstown, MD 21136

(410) 833-5559

Offers: Over 850 white porcelain blanks: tableware, giftware, novelty, souvenir items, white and gold banded dinnerware, coffee and beer mugs, promotional items, ashtrays and trivets, bells, plaques, desk accessories and others.

For Further Information: Contact your dealer or send SASE.

MAYCO COLORS

4077 Weaver Ct. S.

Hilliard, OH 43026

(618) 876-1171

Offers: Ceramic colors, finishes, glazes (Satina matte colors, exotics and others), stoneware glazes, lead-free glazes and crystal patterned. Also offers bisque colors and underglazes, non-firing opaque stains, translucents, metallics, non-fired

pearl, stain kits, sealers, accent glazes and wax resist. Manufacturer.

For Further Information: Catalog, $7.95.

MCRON CERAMIC MOLDS

2660 NE Seventh Ave.

Pompano Beach, FL 33064

(954) 784-7707

Fax: (954) 784-7505

Offers: Ceramic molds, including McRon, Bil-Mar and Vicki's brands.

For Further Information: Color catalog, $8 (continental U.S. only).

Accepts: Discover, MasterCard, Visa

MINNESOTA CLAY USA

8001 Grand Ave. S.

Bloomington, MN 55420

(612) 884-9101, (800) 252-9872

Offers: Clays including Rainbow Air-Dry Clay (no firing needed), clay bodies, stonewares and porcelains, glazes (liquid and dry), chemicals, stains, lusters, overglazes, plaster and pouring tables. Also offers kilns and kiln parts, the products of Creative Industry, Skutt, Cress, Amaco, Brent, Lehman, Ohaus and others.

For Further Information: Free catalog.

Store Location: At above address.

Discounts: Quantity; teachers and institutions; sells wholesale to legitimate businesses.

MR. & MRS. OF DALLAS

1301 Ave. K

Plano, TX 75074

(214) 881-1699

Fax: 423-2092

Offers: White porcelain and ceramic blanks in white, gold trimmed and colors, including mugs, plates, tiles, small boxes, cups, Christmas ornaments, piggy bank and others. Also offers china decorating supplies.

For Further Information: Free catalog.

NATIONAL ARTCRAFT CO.

7996 Darrow Rd.

Twinsburg, OH 44087

(800) 793-0152

Fax: (800) 292-4915

Offers: A ceramic supplies catalog that shows ceramic and china paints brushes, tools, studio equipment, cleaning and smoothing materials, kilns and firing equipment. A musical and clock movement catalog offers a wide selection of tunes and clock inserts. An electrical/lamp supply catalog and general craft catalog offers a range of craft supplies including

glitters, miniature novelties, jewelry parts, cements, display items and more.
For Further Information: Each catalog, (please sepcify) $1 (refundable).
Discounts: Quantity.

NOWELL'S MOLDS
1532 Pointer Ridge Place
Bowie, MD 20716
(301) 249-0846

Offers: Molds for ceramics, including whimsical shadowbox plaques—3 molds make over 20 combinations, including window seat, rocking chair and oval shadowbox. Also carries molds for bears, rabbits, dogs, oil lamps, table lamps, bells, boots, bonnets, parasols, ballet dancers, vases, pitchers, bowls, cat picture frames, grapevine wreaths, bicycles and others. Sizes vary from ½" to 3". Carries Super Brute ¾" disc magnets (3 times as strong as ordinary).
For Further Information: Card catalog, $6.
Discounts: Quantity.
Accepts: MasterCard, Visa

OLYMPIC ENTERPRISES, INC.
P.O. Box 321
Campbell, OH 44405
(216) 746-2726
Fax: (216) 746-1156

Offers: Line of ceramic decals, including holiday and angel designs, florals, inspirational, borders and others. Also offers brushes.
For Further Information: 94-page color catalog and brush catalog, $12.

EDWARD ORTON JR. CERAMIC FOUNDATION
6991 Old 3C Highway
P.O. Box 460
Westerville, OH 43082
(614) 895-2663
Fax: (614) 895-5610

Offers: Pyrometric products, including self-supporting cones, pyrometric bars, others to measure heat treatment, indicate or control kiln shut-off and monitor firings, plus kiln ventilation systems and firing supplies.
For Further Information: See your dealer or write for catalog.
Discounts: Sells wholesale to legitimate businesses.

PARAGON INDUSTRIES, INC.
2011 S. Town E. Blvd.
Mesquite, TX 75149
(214) 288-7557 or (800) 876-9328

Offers: Full line of ceramic kilns, china painting kilns, heat-treating and knife-making furnaces, glass-fused jewelry kilns and kiln accessories. Manufacturer. Sells to consumers only if there is no area dealer.
For Further Information: Free catalog.

R-MOLDS
18711 St. Clair Ave.
Cleveland, OH 44110
(216) 531-9185

Offers: Line of ceramic molds including dinnerware, Mammy and other canister sets, vases, baskets, kitchen accessories and more.
For Further Information: Color catalog, $7.50.
Accepts: MasterCard, Visa

CAROL REINERT CERAMICS
1100 Grosser Rd.
Gilbertsville, PA 19525
(610) 367-4373
Fax: (610) 367-4373

Offers: Ceramic molds by Dona's Molds, Scioto, Nowell, Georgie's Bulldog, Starlight, Catskill, Gator, Kimple, and more. Manufactures Fairieland, Fairy Princess products. Also carries Dona's Hues, Kimple stains, Royal brushes, music boxes, decals, electrical supplies, plastic lights and others.
For Further Information: Send SASE or call for list.

RIVER VIEW MOLDS
2141 P. Ave.
Williamsburg, IA 52361
(319) 668-9800
Fax: (319) 668-9600

Offers: Line of molds including holiday designs, figures and others.
For Further Information: Color catalog, $7.

ROCKING B MANUFACTURING
3924 Camphor Ave.
Newbury Park, CA 91320
(805) 499-9336

Offers: Music boxes including Sankyo movement, mini, mobile, electronic Touch-Me, bank slot and Touch-Me with blinking lights, Waggie Arm and accordion sleeve movements. Accessories available include turntables, keys and extenders.
For Further Information: Send SASE for catalog.
Discounts: Quantity; teachers and institutions; sells wholesale to legitimate businesses.

RYNNE CHINA CO
222 W. Eight Mile Rd.
Hazel Park, MI 48030
(800) 468-1987

Offers: Full and complete line of china blanks—plates,

bowls, cups, saucers, creamers, sugar bowls, serving dishes and others. Also offers gold-rimmed items. Manufacturer.
For Further Information: Free catalog.

SCHOOLHOUSE CERAMICS
3860 Columbia Rd.
North Olmsted, OH 44070
(216) 777-5155

Offers: Line of bisque with many popular breeds of dogs and cats.
For Further Information: Send SASE for pictures of specific breeds.

SCIOTO CERAMIC PRODUCTS, INC.
2455 Harrisburg Pike
Grove City, OH 43123
(614) 871-0090

Offers: Molds, including classical, whimsical, contemporary, traditional, fantasy, holiday, Western and other motifs, plus cherubs and other angels, animals, fowl, figures, villages, creches and Christmas ornaments. Also offers vases, planters, pots, pedestals, scenes, bird feeders, 2 chess sets and others.
For Further Information: Mold catalog, $5 plus $2 postage.
Discounts: Sells wholesale to legitimate businesses.

SCOTT PUBLICATIONS
30595 Eight Mile Rd.
Livonia, MI 48152
(810) 477-6650 or (800) 458-8237
Fax: (810) 477-6795

Offers: Instructional books and videos.
For Further Information: Send SASE for list.
Discounts: Sells wholesale to legitimate businesses.

SIOUX CERAMIC SUPPLY
P.O. Box 655
Mandan, ND 58554
(701) 663-3682

Offers: Mold-making kit—"How to Make Your Own Molds"—and materials and instructions for making 2-piece molds. Book: *Advanced Mold Making*.
For Further Information: Send SASE.

SKUTT CERAMIC PRODUCTS
2618 Steele St.
Portland, OR 97202
(503) 231-7726

Offers: Electric kilns, featuring multi-sided models in modular-section construction, stainless steel jackets, reversible fire-brick bottom slabs; cone 1 to cone 10 models. Also offers cone 6 portable, supersized models, Enviro-Vent for kilns

(vents fumes outdoors), kiln furniture, accessories and parts, plus Potter's tools and aids. Manufacturer.
For Further Information: Write.

STAR STILTS CO.
P.O. Box 367
Feasterville, PA 19053
(215) 357-1893
Fax: (215) 953-8263

Offers: Stilts products including napkin ring, star tree, rods (setter for beads, buttons, trinkets and others), bell type, junior shelves, high stilts (5 sizes), element retaining stables and others.
For Further Information: Contact your dealer, or write for free catalog.

SUGAR CREEK INDUSTRIES, INC.
P.O. Box 354
Linden, IN 47955
(317) 339-4641

Offers: Pouring room equipment, including over 60 items such as pouring machines (from a 4 gallon Flow Baby to a basic 125 gallon unit), pumps (immersion red heads, reversible/external), mixers and reclaimers (from 1 gallon porcelain to 200 gallons), tables (4′ through 16′ in 6 sizes) and the Spraymaster booth for greenware, airbrush and other uses.
For Further Information: Free catalog.

TAMPA BAY MOLD CO.
2724 22nd St. N.
St. Petersburg, FL 33713
(813) 823-3784

Offers: Original molds in a full line of traditional designs, bisque and technical sheets.
For Further Information: Catalog, $5.

TBR, INC.
824 Maxine NE
Albuquerque, NM 87123
(505) 292-0041
Fax: (505) 299-4425

Offers: Porcelain blanks and jewelry findings; Southwestern and Native American motif style decals.
For Further Information: Color catalog, $5.

TRENTON MOLD
329 Whitehead Rd.
Trenton, NJ 08619
(609) 890-0606

Offers: Molds, including dog figurines (55 popular breeds),

other animals, holiday items, figures, plaques, vases, pitchers and others.
For Further Information: Color catalog, $6.

VITO'S CERAMIC SUPPLY
1920 Main St.
Tewksbury, MA 01876
(508) 851-4232

Offers: Ceramic bisque from the molds of a variety of manufacturers. Also offers Mayco paints and Gare brushes.
For Further Information: Send SASE for list.
Discounts: Quantity.

VITREX CERAMICS, LTD.
P.O. Box 888
Tonawanda, NY 14150
Additional address:
5365 Munro Ct.
Burlington, Ontario L7L 5M7
Canada
(905) 637-8137

Offers: Line of ceramic molds including Art Deco lamps, vases, figurines, picture frames, pedestals, dogs, eagles, jaguar, others.
For Further Information: Catalog, $7.

WESTWOOD CERAMIC SUPPLY
14400 Lomitas Ave.
City of Industry, CA 91715
(818) 330-0631

Offers: Casting clay bodies in earthenware, stoneware and porcelain (50 pounds and up). Also offers special clay formulas, low-fire clays, raku, high/low-fire casting bodies, chemicals, colors and finishes (including metallics, texture and other glazes, and lusters), Egyptian paste, Engobe stains, and equipment (of known brands such as Kemper, Kingspin, Ohaus, Cress, Olympic and others). Books are also available. Manufacturer, distributor.
For Further Information: Catalog, $5.

WISE SCREENPRINT, INC.
1015 Valley St., Dept. CSS
Dayton, OH 45404
(513) 223-1573

Offers: Custom ceramic and glass decals from customer's rough sketch, photo or artwork. Complete art services, design and technical assistance are available.
For Further Information: Free color card, price list and samples.

YOZIE MOLD CO.
Rd. 1, Box 415
Dunbar, PA 15431
(412) 628-3693

Offers: Line of ceramic molds, designs include Art Deco, Judaic, dogs, others. Jewelry molds and findings also available.
For Further Information: Color mold catalog, $12; jewelry mold catalog, $6.50.
Accepts: MasterCard, Visa.

ZEMBILLAS SPONGE CO., INC.
P.O. Box 24
Campbell, OH 44405
(216) 755-1644
Fax: (216) 755-0828

Offers: Mediterranean silk sponges in a variety of sizes, plus imported ceramic decals in a wide assortment of traditional motifs.
For Further Information: Catalog, $7.50.

ZIP MANUFACTURING
13584 East Manito Rd.
Pekin, IL 61554
(309) 346-7916

Offers: Zip porcelain and stoneware slips in 40 colors.
For Further Information: Send SASE for price list.
Discounts: Quantity.

Clock Making

AMERICAN MINERAL GIFT
326 Steel Rd.
Feasterville, PA 19053
(215) 364-1114

Offers: Mini-quartz clock movements (3 shaft sizes). Jewelry eye glass frame chains. Gift items.
For Further Information: Free catalog.
Discounts: Quantity.

B&J
14744 Manchester Rd.
Ballwin, MO 63011
(314) 394-4567
Fax: (314) 394-4567

Offers: Line of clock kits (clock movements with hands and numbers, polished/drilled agate clock faces and clear Lucite stands), desk clock kits and large models (with 5″ to 6½″ faces). Carries quartz clock movements—Seiko, battery with ⁵⁄₁₆″ or ¹¹⁄₁₆″ shaft (with hour, minute and second hands, hangers, hardware, numbers/dots).
For Further Information: Catalog, $3 (refundable).
Discounts: Quantity.

CREATIVE CLOCK
P.O. Box 565
Hanson, MA 02341
(617) 293-2855

Offers: Clock components, movements and others; any related accessories.
For Further Information: Free catalog.

DECOR TIME
P.O. Box 277698
Sacramento, CA 95827
(916) 362-4777, (800) 487-2524

Offers: Full line of clock parts, dials, quartz motors and accessories. Also carries epoxy, resin, pen sets and others.
For Further Information: Free catalog.

EMPEROR CLOCK CO.
Emperor Industrial Park
Fairhope, AL 36532
(334) 928-2316

Offers: Clock kits, including grandfather, mantel and wall models in cherry or oak with solid brass West German movements and dials. Also carries furniture kits and assembled clocks.
For Further Information: Color catalog, $1.

HASKELL'S
48 Main St.
Oakland, ME 04963
(207) 465-2940

Offers: Clock kits, parts and accessories, plus books.
For Further Information: Catalog, $6 (refundable).

KLOCKIT
P.O. Box 636, Dept. CSS
Lake Geneva, WI 53147
(800) 556-2548
Fax: (414) 248-9899

Offers: Clock kits (quartz or quartz Westminster chime movements), including wooden gears, shelf, schoolhouse or Alpine steeple models. Also carries wood blanks for clocks in various shapes, stitchery clocks, country wood kits (easy), desk clocks, wall clocks and jumbo watches. Grandfather, grandmother, and cypress clocks, desk sets, contemporary wood/brass, time and weather, mantel, banjo/cloth, gallery, nautical, carriage, time zone, cottage, carriage/moving moon, 400-day crystal and wood and regulator types are also available. Parts available include chimes, hardware, fit-ups, movements, pendulums, wood shapes, brass nameplates, plus lamp items.
For Further Information: Free catalog.
Accepts: Discover, MasterCard, Visa

KUEMPEL CHIME
21195 Minnetonka Blvd.
Excelsior, MN 55331
(800) 328-6445

Offers: Redi-Hut traditional and contemporary clock kits, including grandfather, wall and mantel types of walnut, cherry or oak with German tabular bell and chime rod, one and three-tune Westminster, Whittington and St. Michael styles. Handcrafted and brass clock pendulums, handpainted moonwheels also available.
For Further Information: Catalog, $2.

MURRAY CLOCK CRAFT LTD.
512 McNicoll Ave.
Willowdale, Ontario M2H 2E1
Canada
(416) 499-4531

Offers: Clock plans and kits for grandfather, grandmother, wall and shelf models. Also carries battery, weight and spring-driven movements and dials.
For Further Information: Catalog, $2 (refundable).

PRECISE CLOCK, INC.
8107 Braeburn Lane
Orland Park, IL 60462
(708) 403-0515

Offers: Clock fit-ups and mini-quartz movements, plus many styles of dials and hands.
For Further Information: Write or call for brochure.
Discounts: Sells wholesale.

PRECISION MOVEMENTS
4283 Chestnut St., P.O. Box 689
Emmaus, PA 18049
(610) 967-3156, (800) 533-2024
Fax: (610) 967-2827

Offers: Full line of clock-making needs, including clock hands, dials, bezels, quartz movements, and a variety of clock styles and accessories.
For Further Information: Write or call for color catalog.
Discounts: Quotations upon request.

PSMC, INC.
P.O. Box 5099
Oroville, CA 95966
(916) 589-1840
Fax: (916) 589-2042

Offers: Clock-making parts, including quartz motors (SPD, NSN, Rhythm, Takane)—5 mini and standard sizes, 4 pendulum types, 7 chimes/double chimes, 30 fit-ups, LCDs, alarms and reverse motors. Carries over 50 number sets, over 180 painted dials, over 60 starbursts, over 50 styles of hands, plus dials and bezel dial combinations.
For Further Information: Free catalog.

SCHOOL OF CLOCK REPAIR
6313 Come About Way
Awendaw, SC 29429
(803) 928-3489

Offers: Instructional videos on clock repair, a comprehensive home-study course. Also carries clock-making tools.
For Further Information: Free catalog.

STEEBAR
P.O. Box 463
Andover, NJ 07821

Offers: Clock kits, and over 2,000 clockmaking products, including components, parts, plans, epoxy resin and others.
For Further Information: 64-page color catalog, $3 (refundable).

TURNCRAFT CLOCKS, INC.
P.O. Box 100
Mound, MN 55364
(612) 471-9573

Offers: A complete line of clock movements, dials, clock fit-ups. Also offers hardware and parts, including pendulums (regular and mini-size), chimes, movements, dials, hands, decoratives and others. Woodworking plans for over 150 clocks also available.
For Further Information: Catalog, $2.
Accepts: Discover, MasterCard, Visa

VILLAGE ORIGINALS
24140 Detroit Rd.
Cleveland, OH 44145
(800) 899-1314
Fax: (216) 835-9060

Offers: Quartz movements—regular, miniature, pendulum and electronic chime, plus clock accessories and parts.
For Further Information: Free catalog.

YANKEE INGENUITY
P.O. Box 113
Altus, OK 73522
(405) 477-2191

Offers: Line of battery clock movements in a variety of styles and sizes, plus accessory items.
For Further Information: Free catalog.
Discounts: Quantity.

Construction—Full-Size Structures

Includes Houses, Barns, Garages, Shops, Docks, Studios, Shelters, Gazebos, Saw Mills, Tepees.
Also see Miniature Making, Model Making, Tools and Equipment, Woodworking and related categories.

ASHLANDBARNS
990CSS Butler Creek
Ashland, OR 97520
(541) 488-1541

Offers: Blueprints of 94 barns, craft shops, garages and storage areas.
For Further Information: Catalog, $2 (refundable).

BARTON'S BARNWOOD
RR 3
Carp, Ontario K0A 1L0
Canada
(613) 839-5530

Offers: Weathered barn siding, old flooring, hand-hewn beams and other barn material by the square foot.
For Further Information: Send SASE.

BETTER BUILT CORP.
789 Woburn St.
Wilmington, MA 01887
(508) 657-5636
Fax: (508) 658-0444

Offers: Portable Sawmill, a one-man band sawmill that cuts 20″ diameter logs into lumber ⅛″ to 9″ in thickness. Instructional video available.
For Further Information: Write for brochure.

BROWN ENGINEERING
P.O. Box 40
West Point, CA 95255
(209) 293-4816

Offers: Lumberjack chain saw sawmills with power-feed; cut forward and reverse.
For Further Information: Send SASE.

CARLISLE RESTORATION LUMBER
HCR 32, P.O. Box 566-C
Stoddard, NH 03464
(603) 446-3937 or (800) 595-9663

Offers: Wide plank flooring and paneling in Eastern white pine, Southern long leaf heart pine and a variety of hardwoods.
For Further Information: Send SASE.

CLASSIC COLONIAL HOMES
P.O. Box 31
Historic Old Deerfield, MA 01342
(800) 413-9111

Offers: Colonial home plans with classic exteriors and modern interiors, including saltboxes, capes, colonials, gambrels and carriage sheds.
For Further Information: Study folio, $14.
Accepts: MasterCard, Visa

CONKLIN'S
RD 1
P.O. Box 70
Susquehanna, PA 18847
(717) 465-3832

Offers: Authentic antique barnwood and hand-hewn beams, old flooring, plus Pennsylvania flagstone and wall stone.
For Further Information: Send $1.
Discounts: Sells wholesale.

DESIGN WORKS, INC.
11 Hitching Post Rd.
Amherst, MA 01002
(413) 549-4763

Offers: Model designing kit (cardboard) that aids in visualizing designs before building or adding to a home. Includes miniature siding, roofing, brick, stone, decking, windows, doors and skylights. Also offers floor plan grids, scale ruler roof-slope calculator and appliance cut-outs; reusable, peel/stick furniture, fixtures, windows, doors and walls for layout design of home or office.
For Further Information: Send SASE.
Discounts: Quantity; teachers, institutions and professionals.

EBAC LUMBER DRYERS
106 John Jefferson Rd., Suite 102
Williamsburg, VA 23185
(800) 433-9011
Fax: (804) 229-3321

Offers: Lumber dryer system (construct kiln, and Ebac supplies this drying equipment) for drying green lumber.
For Further Information: Write or call.

FOLLANSBEE DOCK SYSTEMS
State St.
Follansbee, WV 26037
(304) 527-4500, (800) 223-3444 (except WV)

Offers: Dock products including heavy galvanized wood dock hardware, hinges, pipe and pile holders, ladders, dock boxes, power systems, boarding steps, uprights, fasteners, accessories, floating and stationary docks and float drums (foam-filled), plus swim float kits.
For Further Information: Write or call.

GRANBERG INTERNATIONAL
P.O. Box 70425
Richmond, CA 94807
(800) 233-6499
Fax: (510) 237-1667
E-mail: granberg@aol.com

Offers: Portable chain saw lumber mill attachment (clamps to chain saw) that makes lumber from rough logs for furniture, beams, decks, cabins, etc.
For Further Information: Write.

GREATWOOD LOG HOMES, INC.
P.O. Box 707
Elkhart Lake, WI 53020
(414) 876-3378

Offers: Traditional full log or insulated log home kits, with R-40 roof system of white cedar or pine.
For Further Information: Free booklet. Plan book (100 models), $8.95.

THE IRON SHOP
400 Reed Rd.
P.O. Box 547
Broomall, PA 19008
(610) 544-7100

Offers: Oak and metal stair kits (to-be-assembled) with hardware, handrail kit, in-between spindle kits and rail kits for enclosed landings.
For Further Information: Write or call for free brochure.
Accepts: American Express, Discover, MasterCard, Visa

KEY DOME
P.O. Box 430253
South Miami, FL 33143
(305) 665-3541

Offers: Dome home plans for 14′ to 50′ domes in a variety of shape combinations.
For Further Information: Plans/how-to book, $7.

LINDAL CEDAR HOMES
P.O. Box 24426
Seattle, WA 98124
(800) 345-0096

Offers: Full line of plans for contemporary homes including A-frames, modified A-frames, houses for full-time use, vacation homes, and one- and two-story models.
For Further Information: Catalog with 266 pages of plans, $20.

OREGON DOME, INC.
3215 Meadow Lane
Eugene, OR 97402
(800) 572-8943
Fax: (541) 689-9275

Offers: Geodesic dome plans in a variety of design arrangements.
For Further Information: Catalog, price and planning set, $12.
Store Location: At above address. Hours: M-F, 8-5.

PANTHER LODGES
P.O. Box 32-SS
Normantown, WV 25267
(304) 462-7718

Offers: Tepees, tepee poles and other pre-1840 products.
For Further Information: Catalog, $2 (refundable).

SALTER INDUSTRIES
P.O. Box 183
Eagleville, PA 19408
(610) 631-1360

Offers: Metal spiral staircases, in install-it-yourself kit form for 3½′ to 6′ diameters, adjustable to any height; oak and brass options available. Manufacturer.
For Further Information: Free brochure.
Accepts: MasterCard, Visa

SANDY POND HARDWOODS, INC.
921 A Lancaster Pike
Quarryville, PA 17566
(717) 284-5030 or (800) 546-9663

Offers: Lumber and flooring in tiger and bird's eye maple,

curly cherry, flame birch, and quilted western maple. 15 b.f. minimum. Ships UPS or common carrier.
For Further Information: Call for price list and color brochure.

SHELDON DESIGNS

759 State Rd.
Princeton, NJ 08540
(609) 683-4625

Offers: Plans and blueprints for small cabins, polebarns and sheds.
For Further Information: Catalog, $4 (refundable).

SHELTER SYSTEMS

P.O. Box 67
Aptos, CA 95001
(415) 323-6202

Offers: Instant dome shelters, many quick-assemble models.
For Further Information: Catalog, $1.

STEEL MASTER

(800) 888-4606
Offers: Steel buildings, 4 size you-build models, $25' \times 36'$ to $50' \times 120'$. Manufacturer.
For Further Information: Call.

TIMBERLINE GEODESICS

2015 Blake St.
Berkley, CA 94704
(415) 849-4481 or (800) DOME-HOME
Fax: (510) 849-3265
E-mail: Info@domehome.com

Offers: Prefabricated dome home kits (pre-cut and pre-drilled, with heavy-duty steel connector system); as complete kit, strut framing kit (all but pre-cut plywood), connector kit (with lumber cutting instructions) in a variety of dome sizes/design combinations.
For Further Information: Catalog/video, $22. Free brochure.

TROY-BUILT MANUFACTURING CO.

102nd St. 9th Ave.
Troy, NY 12180
(518) 233-4500

Offers: Greenhouse kit (to-be-assembled with hand tools) with over 50 sq. ft. of usable space beneath a $7\frac{1}{2}'$ peak; includes glass (with double-strength glazing) and aluminum frame, with sliding door and built-in rain gutter.
For Further Information: Write.

VINTAGE WOOD WORKS

Highway 34
P.O. Box 2265
Quinlan, TX 75474
(903) 356-2158
Fax: (903) 356-3023

Offers: Victorian and country gingerbread trims for buildings (solid wood), including brackets (for openings), porch turnings, gable decorations, spandrels and doorway embellishments in a wide range of styles and sizes.
For Further Information: 50-page illustrated catalog, $2.

VIXEN HILL

Elverson, PA 19520
(610) 286-0909

Offers: Gazebo kits. Offers a wide selection of architecturally authentic gazebos, pre-engineered for easy assembly by the non-carpenter. Available in a variety of styles and sizes.
For Further Information: 20-page color catalog, $4.

WOOD MIZER PRODUCTS

8180 W. 10th St.
Indianapolis, IN 46214
(317) 271-1542 or (800) 553-0219

Offers: Portable sawmills with remote hydraulic log handling, capacities to 32″ in diameter by 33″ long; includes bandsaw cutting head. Solar Dry Kiln and Vacu-Kiln also available.
For Further Information: Catalog, $2; demonstration video, $10.
Accepts: MasterCard, Visa

Construction—Full-Size, Operating Vehicles

Includes Cars, Boats, Hovercraft, Trailers, Go-Carts, Tractors. Also see Model Making, Tools and Equipment and related categories.

A-1 RACING PARTS, INC.
770 Rt. 28, P.O. Box 4
Middlesex, NJ 08846
(908) 968-2323

Offers: For cars—Mustang II/Pinto-type struts, heavy-duty strut rods (production struts made from 1″ stock, originals were ¾″), with same angle as Ford D5FZ3468 units, includes strut bushings and retainers.
For Further Information: Send SASE or call with inquiry.
Accepts: MasterCard, Visa

ARIZONA Z CAR
2043 E. Quartz St.
Mesa, AZ 85213
(602) 844-9677

Offers: Manufactures racing and performance parts for Datsun 240, 260 and 280. Examples include limited slip differentials, cams, pistons, rods, racing brakes and suspensions, and a line of fiberglass racing body parts.
For Further Information: Catalog, $2.

BERNIE BERGMANN, VW ENGINE SPEC.
340 N. Hale Ave.
Escondido, CA 92029
(619) 747-4649
Fax: (619) 740-8522

Offers: Car parts including both single and dual carbureted, single/dual carbureted engines for sedans, Baja, Rail and others. Also carries hydraulic lifters, unleaded heads, shuffle pins and others.
For Further Information: Photo products display, $2.

CLARKCRAFT
16-45 Aqualane
Tonawanda, NY 14150
(716) 873-2640

Offers: Boat kits/plans/patterns, over 250 designs, 68″ to 70′ models in plywood, fiberglass or steel, including powerboats, inboards, outboards, jets, cruisers, sports fishers, hydro-planes, houseboats, runabouts, sailboats, motorsailers, multihulls, kayaks and canoes (over 35 models). Kit materials include hardware, fastenings, master rigging, sails, plywood, fiberglass, foams, resins, glues, polyesters, mats, cloth, others, depending on type. Books also available.
For Further Information: Catalog, $3, bulk mail; $5, first class.

CLASSIC INSTRUMENTS, PK
P.O. Box 1216
Crooked River Ranch, OR 97760
(541) 548-1940

Offers: Original instruments for classic vehicles, including speedometers, indicators for oil pressure, petrol, battery voltage and water temperature, programmable electric instruments, electric senders, lighting and matching quartz clocks.
For Further Information: Information and catalog, $2.
Discounts: Factory direct . . . at below dealer cost.

CLASSIC ROADSTERS, LTD.
Division of Leisure Industires, Inc.
1617 Main Ave.
Fargo, ND 58103
(800) 373-9000

Offers: Automobile kits including Classic Roadsters—reproductions of The Marlene, '65 Mercedes, 500K and Sebring Austin-Healey. Reproduction kits for the Jaguar, MG and 4-passenger Mercedes. Cars are equipped with V-8 power.
For Further Information: Information on you-assemble kit, or brochure.
Accepts: MasterCard, Visa

E&B MARINE
201 Meadow Rd.
Edison, NJ 08817
(800) BOATING

Offers: Boating products—a full line of parts, accessories, kits and others. Carries everything for boating, sailing and fishing.
For Further Information: Call or write for catalog.

EAGLE COACH WORK, INC.
760 Northland Ave.
Buffalo, NY 14211
(716) 897-4292

Offers: Replica car kits for the Jaguar SS100 and XK120G

sports cars. Both cars are built on custom-engineered steel chassis—bolt to Ford Pinto or Mustang II running gear.
For Further Information: Color brochure, $3.

EVA SPORTSCARS
Pleasant Corners
Vankleek Hill, Ontario K0B 1R0
Canada
(613) 678-3377

Offers: The Beva sports car kit, with Toyota drive train/parts, MIG welded space frame chassis with mounting brackets for all components, tilting front body section, fiberglass body and wet weather equipment.
For Further Information: Send $3.

EVERETT-MORRISON MOTORCARS
5137 W. Clifton St.
Tampa, FL 33634
(813) 887-5885

Offers: Replica 427SC Cobra car kits (Mustang or Pinto components bolted on 4" round tube frame kit) including Cobra bodies, body frame kits, optional Jaguar front and rear end, and optional Corvette suspension.
For Further Information: Product literature, $5.
Discounts: Factory direct.

GENNIE SHIFTER CO.
930 S. Broadmoor Ave.
West Covina, CA 91790
(626) 337-2536
Fax: (626) 338-9444

Offers: Street and racing hot rod parts including gas pedals with splined shaft, new stealth gas pedals, column dress-up, Gennie shifter and hand brakes for GM, Ford and Mopar. Rear mount shifter, boot kits, brake pedal pads, Lo-Line hand brakes, Gennie hood props, throttle cables, kick-down cables. Headlight bars, brake cables and flushmount mini antenna kits are available. Billet aluminum mirrors are also stocked.
For Further Information: Send SASE.

GLEN-L MARINE
P.O. Box 1804 CR
Bellflower, CA 90707
(310) 630-6258

Offers: Boat kits, plans and full-size patterns in over 250 designs for sailboats, power and fishing boats, canoes, kayaks, skiboats, runabouts, work boats, pontoons, houseboats, and boats designed for kids. Models are 7' to 55', made of wood, steel, aluminum or fiberglass. Also offers boat builder supplies, including epoxy resins, fiberglass materials, marine fastening, glues, instructional videos and books.
For Further Information: 176-page catalog, $5.
Accepts: MasterCard, Visa

GOLDEN WEST MOTORSPORT, INC.
27732 Industrial Blvd.
Hayward, CA 94545
(415) 783-7555

Offers: Cobra replica car kits, rolling chassis and turnkey cars, plus replicas from ERA, NAF and contemporary "award winning" sports convertibles. Also offers Gran Sport 'Vette and Daytona Spyder replicas.
For Further Information: Catalog, $5.

KEN HANKINSON ASSOCIATES
P.O. Box 272
Hayden Lake, ID 83835
(208) 772-5547

Offers: Boat plans and kits for hundreds of models from world-famous designers—powerboats, inboards, outboards, rowboats and sailboats in a wide variety of types and sizes.
For Further Information: Catalog, $6 (includes 8 dinghy plans).

HARRIS ENGINEERING
P.O. Box 885192
San Francisco, CA 94188
(415) 469-8966

Offers: Kit cars—Countach SRT 9000 body kits, round tube space frames for Countach or Cobra, plus any suspension or drive train equipment. Also carries equipment for V8-ZF/ Porsche, V6 Transverse and Fiero.
For Further Information: Information package, $5.

JAMESTOWN DISTRIBUTORS
28 Narragansett Ave.
P.O. Box 348
Jamestown, RI 02835
(800) 423-0030
Fax: (800) 423-0542

Offers: A line of boatbuilding and woodworking supplies.
For Further Information: Free catalog.
Store location: Highway 27 and 21 Gardens Corner, Rt. 1, P.O. Box 375, Seabrook, SC 29940.
Discounts: Commercial discounts available.

KART WORLD
1488 Mentor Ave.
Painesville, OH 44077
(216) 357-5569

Offers: Go-carts—kits, engines and parts. Also has kits, engines and parts for minicars and minibikes.
For Further Information: 88-page catalog, $3.

MARAUDER & CO.
Rt. 2
Potomac, IL 61865
(217) 569-2255

Offers: Marauder kits for replicas of sports cars, including McLauren, Chevron, B16, Contach, Ferrari 512M, Pantera, Lola GT MKII, and others. Services include conversions, including conversions of real Lola T70s to Lola MKIIIB; also restoration of cars.
For Further Information: Catalog and complete information, $12.

POLI-FORM INDUSTRIES
15 Grove St. #101
Watsonville, CA 95076
(408) 722-4418

Offers: Kit cars from individual parts to complete kits, including '27 Track Roadster kit using molded fiberglass parts, and Ford bodies including the '15 Roadster, '19 Speedster, '27 Roadster, '27 four-door touring car, '29 Roadster, '29 Highboy and '34 3-Window Coupe. Full line of bodies, fenders, aprons, dashes and other parts for '26 to '34 Fords and Chevrolets. Also stocks hoods, grills, fuel tanks, radiators, frames and custom windowshield posts.
For Further Information: Catalog, $3.

REDLINE ROADSTERS
30251 E. Acre Place
Orange, CA 92669
(714) 771-0533

Offers: Donor car parts for Sebring, Speedster, Cobra, Corvette, VW-based or whatever car is being built. Donor parts are rebuilt, with new bushings and bearings—reconditioned arms, rack and pinions, springs, differentials, custom power steering units, motors, trannys—all built to specification. Custom kit building to any step of completion.
For Further Information: Send SASE or call with inquiry.

ROWAN REPLICARS
P.O. Box 2133
Salisbury, NC 28145
(704) 636-7020

Offers: Car component kits for the 427 SC Cobra, including heavy-duty frames, one-piece molded bodies with hinged doors, hoods and trunks, and extra features to aid the assembler.
For Further Information: Color brochure, $2.

SEVTEC, INC.
P.O. Box 846
Monroe, WA 98272
(206) 794-7505

Offers: Hovercraft plans, for crafts that fly over land, sea or air, with 3 to 160 HP, including surface skimmers for single place, cruisers, utility cars for cruising or fishing.
For Further Information: Information package, $4 (refundable).

SPORTSCRAFT
P.O. Box 640
Meeker, OK 74855
(405) 279-3835

Offers: Airboats—hovercraft plans, kits, propellers, engines and other supplies and accessories, plus wind machines.
For Further Information: Catalog, $3.

STREET SPECIALTIES
2560 S. Hairston Rd.
Decatur, GA 30035
(770) 981-4143

Offers: Custom kit car assembly service for any model, from crate to turnkey. Also offers kit car accessories, aero packages and lowering kits.
For Further Information: Call or write.

SUN RAY PRODUCTS CORP.
8017 Ranchers Rd. NE
Fridley, MN 55432
(612) 780-0774

Offers: Bradley GT parts—original equipment replacements, including doors, windows, gaskets, wiring harnesses and other items, some of limited quantity.
For Further Information: Free parts list.

TEXAS DORY BOAT PLANS
P.O. Box 720
Galveston, TX 77553

Offers: Standardized boat plans, including exact reproductions of original plans on 17″×22″ paper. Boats include dories, including sailing types, power, dory/skiff, oars/sail and others. Also offers skiffs, trollers, sampans, sailers.
For Further Information: Send SASE.

Doll and Toy Making—Rigid

Also see Ceramics, Miniature Making, Model Making, Woodworking and related categories.

ADOPT-A-DOLL
1041 Lincoln Ave.
San Jose, CA 95125
(408) 298-DOLL

Offers: Doll supplies, greenware and bisque kits; accessories for Playhouse, Seeley, Global, Jean Nordquist, Kemper, Virginia La Vorgna, Connie Lee Finchum Patterns and Royal.
For Further Information: Call.
Store Location: At above address.
Discounts: Sells wholesale.

AIM KILNS
350 SW Wake Robin
Corvallis, OR 97333
(800) 647-1624, (800) 222-5456 (in CA)

Offers: AIM Doll Kiln, 8″×8″×9″ deep, 120V, to cone 10 with kiln-sitter shut-off and infinite switch; an optional timer is available. Other kilns sizes 6″×6″ to 35″ diameter; automatic models; also shelves, cones and replacement parts.
For Further Information: Free literature.
Discounts: Sells wholesale.

THE AMERICAN COASTER
7106 Lake Rd.
Montrose, MI 48457
(810) 639-7004

Offers: Early American coaster wagon kits and full-scale blueprints for farm and flat wagons, wheelbarrows, sleds, scooters and others. Wood and rubber wheel kits including Amish-made, steam bent handles and hounds; metal parts. Also offers completed unpainted wagons.
For Further Information: Brochure, $1.

& EVERYTHING NICE
1108 First Ave.
Toms River, NJ 08757
(908) 349-8859

Offers: Originally designed doll bodies and costume patterns. Also offers soft-fired porcelain greenware.

For Further Information: SASE and $3.50 payable to Catherine Horan.
Store Location: At above address.
Discounts: Quantity.

ANNE'S DOLL THINGS
P.O. Box 371
West Linn, OR 97068
(503) 656-9556

Offers: Handcrafted glass doll eyes from England, all styles. Also offers doll teeth.
For Further Information: Send stamp for catalog.

BALDWIN FINE PORCELAIN
4886 Hercules, Suite H
El Paso, TX 79904
(800) 414-9876
Fax: (915) 751-9821

Offers: "Heirloom" doll-making kits for 9″ to 60″ dolls. Also carries supply packets (eyes, lashes, wigs, body patterns/stringing and other items).
For Further Information: Send large SASE for list.
Store Location: At above address. Hours: M-F 8-4:30.
Discounts: Quantity.
Accepts: MasterCard, Visa

TOM BANWELL DESIGNS
16424 Glenko Rd.
Rough & Ready, CA 95975
(916) 432-1464
Fax: (916) 432-5302

Offers: Instructional video, "The Art of Resin Dollmaking," which covers resin casting and rubber mold making.

BARBARA'S PLAYHOUSE
25393 Huntwood Ave.
Hayward, CA 94544
(510) 786-0668
Fax: (510) 786-6578

Offers: Doll crafting supplies, including waxes, vinyl kits, glass and acrylic eyes and other body parts. Doll Artworks molds, stands and armatures also available. Carries over 70 styles of wigs; mohair and others. Doll accessories and playhouses also available.
For Further Information: Call.
Discounts: Sells wholesale.
Accepts: MasterCard, Visa

BELL CERAMICS

P.O. Box 120127
Clermont, FL 34712
(904) 394-2175

Offers: Doll molds for over 200 modern and antique reproduction styles. Carries the Gold Marque Artist Series and others, plus porcelain and composition slip, dry and pre-mixed china paints, wigs, patterns, eyes and other items.
For Further Information: Catalog, $8.

JOANN BENTSON

15612 Erin Lane
Orland Park, IL 60462
(708) 403-0270

Offers: Doll blanks, painted kits, eyes, wigs and patterns for antique reproductions and modern dolls. Carries milette to 30" sizes.
For Further Information: Catalog, $3.

BOBEL BROS.

5134 Simpkins Rd.
Whites Creek, TN 37189
(615) 876-6714

Offers: Kits for child's wagon, including a set of wheels, plans and metal parts. Aluminum wagon wheels, 10 spoke, 9" to 11" in diameter for ⅜" axle.
For Further Information: Write.
Discounts: Quantity.

BROWN HOUSE DOLLS

3200 N. Sand Lake Rd.
Allen, MI 49227
(517) 869-2833

Offers: Over 230 doll clothing pattern designs (in several sizes) including those of antique vintage, babies, toddlers and known dolls. Also carries doll accessories patterns.
For Further Information: Catalog, $2 ($3 foreign).
Accepts: Discover, MasterCard, Visa

CAMPVILL HILL CRAFTS

94 Campville Hill Rd.
Harwinton, CT 06791
(203) 485-1253

Offers: Doll furniture plans and kits, including rocking chair, wagon and shoo fly, and cradle. Also offers finished pieces.
For Further Information: Send large SASE.

CANADIAN CRAFT SUPPLIES

Don Park Rd., #2
Markham, Ontario L3R 2V2
Canada
(905) 477-3655

Offers: Porcelain, composition slip (in large quantities), accessories, Opti-visors, brushes, paints, pellets, silica sand and other supplies.
For Further Information: Catalog, $8 Canadian. Does not ship to U.S.
Store Location: At above address. Hours: M-F, 9-5.
Discounts: Sells wholesale.

CARVERS' EYE COMPANY

P.O. Box 16692, Dept. 80
Portland, OR 97216
(503) 666-5680

Offers: Glass or plastic eyes, noses, joints, growlers and eye glasses for teddy bears and dolls and others.
For Further Information: Send $2.
Discounts: Sells wholesale.

CHICAGO LATEX PRODUCTS, INC.

1030 Morse Ave.
Schaumburg, IL 60193
(708) 893-2880

Offers: Non-toxic, one-part Latex, including natural or neoprene for casting, sculpting or coatings. Latex can be used for dolls, puppets, figurines, displays and more.
For Further Information: Call or write.

COLLECTIBLE DOLL

4216 6th NW
Seattle, WA 98117
(206) 781-1963

Offers: Instructional video—*Painting Reproduction Antique Dolls*, with Jean Nordquist. Also carries China paints and over 170 rare, classic molds, plus eyes, wigs, kilns, books.
For Further Information: Send SASE for further details, or $9 for complete catalog.

COLORADO DOLL FAIRE

116 E. Foothillls Pkwy.
Fort Collins, CO 80525
(970) 226-3655

Offers: Composition doll repair kit. Craze Control restores minor crazing cleans; Care-Repair flesh-tinted compound fills cracks, rebuilds fingers and toes and resurfaces chips.
For Further Information: Send SASE or call.

CREATE AN HEIRLOOM

West St.
P.O. Box 1068
Berlin, MA 01503
(508) 838-2130

Offers: Porcelain doll kits and accessories. Large variety of porcelain doll heads, including The Nativity Grouping, Three Wise Men, Victorian Carolers, Mr./Mrs. Claus, fairy sets, or-

naments, heads, ballerina legs, angels, Black angels, Black Santa porcelain sets. Victorian, traditional smiling and Old World Santa sets.
For Further Information: Catalog, $1.
Store Location: At above address.
Discounts: Quantity.

CREATIONS BY ERLINE
4045 Transport St.
Palo Alto, CA 94303
(510) 830-0381
Fax: (415) 494-6235

Offers: Line of doll sculpting supplies. Also offers an instructional video and dollmaking seminars.
For Further Information: Send SASE or call for supplies list and calendar of seminars.

CREATIVE PAPERCLAY CO.
1800 S. Robertson Blvd., Suite 907
Los Angeles, CA 90035
(800) 899-5952
Fax: (310) 839-6330

Offers: Creative Paperclay, an air-hardening, lightweight material for doll heads and other parts. Also carries kits, molds and books.
For Further Information: Send SASE.
Discounts: Teachers and institutions; sells wholesale to legitimate businesses.

CR'S CRAFTS
P.O. Box 8-61CB
109 Fifth Ave. W.
Leland, IA 50453
(515) 567-3652
Fax: (515) 567-3652

Offers: Extensive lines of dollmaking supplies, including painted designer porcelain sets and heads, pre-sewn and composition bodies, patterns, wigs, hair, eyes and eyelashes. Mauerhan and Glorfix doll supplies, including vinyl dolls, vinyl and wool doll parts, clay dollmaking supplies. Carries fabrics, furniture, wicker, stands, clothing, shoes, accessories, patterns and books.
For Further Information: 136-page catalog, $2 U.S., $4 Canada (U.S. funds).
Store Location: At above address.
Discounts: Quantity.
Accepts: Discover, MasterCard, Visa

DEAR DOLLY
1602 Edgewater Dr.
Orlando, FL 32804
(407) 839-2041

Offers: Doll-making porcelain bisque and greenware, plus a line of supplies, books and patterns.

For Further Information: Send SASE.
Store Location: At above address.

DIANA'S TREASURES, INC.
P.O. Box 206
219 E. Aspen
Fruita, CO 81521
(907) 858-7552
Fax: (907) 858-3915

Offers: Vinyl doll kits including Aiesha, Baby Me, Charleen, Helena, Katie and Nikki, and others. Playhouse products. Doll clothes patterns. Also doll accessories, clothes, furniture.
For Further Information: Call.
Store Location: At above address.
Discounts: Sells wholesale.
Accepts: MasterCard, Visa

THE DOL-LEE SHOP
3160 Flying Horse Rd.
Colorado Springs, CO 80922
(719) 591-5609

Offers: Doll greenware of past times, including Kays Klowns, Bell, Jan Garnett and Donna RuBert. Also carries cloth body patterns and pre-made bodies.
For Further Information: Send double postage SASE for list.

THE DOLL ADVENTURE
2129 S. U.S. Highway 1
Jupiter, FL 33477
(407) 575-4292
Fax: (467)743-1978

Offers: Doll supplies and parts, including composition bodies, eyes, bisque kits and greenware, armatures and pellets of Playhouse, Maimie, Connie Lee Finchum, Byron, Vee's Victorian, Bell, Karl, Judith Howe and others.
For Further Information: Send SASE.
Store Location: At above address. Hours: T-Sat, 10-4.
Discounts: Sells wholesale.
Accepts: MasterCard, Visa

DOLL ANNEX
2609 E. Business 98
Panama City, FL 32401
(904) 769-1707

Offers: Doll supplies, bisque and kilns for Playhouse, Bell, Kemper, Byron, Brown House, Doll Emporium and others.
For Further Information: Send SASE for list.
Store Location: At above address.
Discounts: Sells wholesale.
Accepts: MasterCard, Visa

DOLL GALLERY, INC.
1137 Susan Rd.
Columbia, SC 29210
(803) 798-7044

Offers: Doll supplies for Playhouse, Kemper, Global, Seeley and others.
For Further Information: Free catalog.

THE DOLL HOUSE
17535 Highland
Tinley Park, IL 60477
(708) 532-4797

Offers: Doll kits—soft-fired or painted bisque for antique and modern reproduction dolls.
For Further Information: Price list, $1.50.

DOLL MAJIK!
106 S. Martin Ln.
Norwood, PA 19074
(610) 522-1704

Offers: Over 950 porcelain doll kits, including modern reproductions, softfire, unpainted or painted bisque ware. Also offers finished dolls.
For Further Information: Call or write for price list.
Accepts: MasterCard, Visa

DOLL SCULPTING VIDEOS
22930 SW Schmeltzer
Sherwood, OR 97140
(503) 628-2098

Offers: Doll-making instruction videos by Lewis Goldstein on head- and mold-making, hands and feet, fashion doll mold-making, working with Cernit and Sculpey, full bodies and miniatures.
For Further Information: Send SASE for list.
Accepts: MasterCard, Visa

THE DOLLMAKERS
505 S. Myrtle Ave.
Monrovia, CA 91016
(818) 357-1091

Offers: Complete line of doll supplies. Also offers finished dolls in clay, wax and porcelain. Bears also available. Holds classes.
For Further Information: Send SASE.

DOLLS AND TREASURES
127 Ridgewood Village Center
Garland, TX 75041
(214) 271-8996 or (800) 222-7073

Offers: Doll greenware, molds and bisque kits, products of Kemper, Bell, Byron, Jean Nordquist, Brown House and others.
For Further Information: Send SASE.
Store Location: At above address. Hours: M-Sat, 9-6.

DOLLS, BEARS & SURPRISES
3743 E. Indian School Rd.
Phoenix, AZ 85018
(602) 956-8648

Offers: Full line of doll supplies, glass eyes, composition bodies, and a doll repair service. Also carries antiques and reproductions.
For Further Information: Send SASE for list.

DOLLS, ETC.
P.O. Box 410
Maud, TX 75567
(903) 585-2475
Offers: Doll molds, bisque and line of supplies for porcelain dollmaking.
For Further Information: Send large SASE for price list.

DOLLSPART SUPPLY CO.
8000 Cooper Ave., Bldg. #28
Wendale, NY 11385
(718) 326-4587

Offers: Full and complete line of doll-making supplies, including kits for baby, fashion, ethnic and other dolls, plus doll parts, bodies, heads, hands, feet, eyes, wigs, ceramic supplies and paints, doll shoes, clothing, costumes, hats and stands. Also carries elastic cordrubber loops, doll sewing notions and trims.
For Further Information: Free color catalog.
Accepts: Discover, MasterCard, Visa

DOLLY DELITES
35 King Ridge
Cloverdale, CA 95425
(707) 894-2180

Offers: Doll supplies, patterns and tools from Kemper, Heinz-Scharff, Carlisle, Doll Emporium, Jean Nordquist, San A Flex, Marx, Seeley's, Virginia La Vorgna, Dove, Connie Lee Finchum, Judith Howe and Masterpiece. Also carries doll pellets and other supplies.
For Further Information: Send SASE for list.
Store Location: At above address. Hours: M-F, 8:30-4:30
Discounts: Sells wholesale.
Accepts: MasterCard, Visa

THE FIBER STUDIO
P.O. Box 637 CSS
Henniker, NH 03242
(603) 428-7830

Offers: Lambskins for doll making—Tibetan, Lincoln, Kal-

gon and Pearl. Also offers mohair, wool, alpaca, flax, others.
For Further Information: Send SASE for price list. Doll hair samples, $7.
Discounts: Sells wholesale.

FLORA MULTIMEDIA & CO.
4801 Marble Ave., NE
Albuquerque, NM 87110
(505) 255-9988

Offers: Instructional video, "How to Build and Perform a Punch & Judy Show," with instructions on puppet making, stage construction and presentation. Over 100 original videos for recreational programs.
For Further Information: Send SASE.

FUN STUF
P.O. Box 999
Yuma, AZ 85366

Offers: Line of porcelain and vinyl doll kits in a variety of sizes.
For Further Information: Send SASE for list.

ADOLA GALLOWAY
3430 Walhalla Highway
Six Mile, SC 29682
(864) 868-2285

Offers: Doll kits, bisque, painted kits and others.
For Further Information: Price list, $2.

GLASS HOUSE
P.O. Box 278
Woonsocket, SD 57385

Offers: Line of doll eyes including sleeping, movable with lashes and others for a variety of doll types and sizes, and for toys.
For Further Information: Free catalog.

GLOBAL DOLLS CORP.
1903 Aviation Blvd.
Lincoln, CA 95648
(916) 645-3000

Offers: Manufacturer and wholesaler of doll wigs in mod-acrylic, mohair and human hair, plus doll molds. Also has doll supplies and accessories.
For Further Information: Send SASE.
Discounts: Sells wholesale.

GNOMEBODIES & SOMEBODIES
42 Mitchell St.
Norwich, NY 13815
(607) 334-8375

Offers: Human hair weft for doll wigmaking in 2 lengths.

For Further Information: Sample cards, $5.
Discounts: Sells wholesale.

GOLDENWEST MANUFACTURING, INC.
P.O. Box 1148
Cedar Ridge, CA 95924
(916) 272-1133
Fax: (916) 272-1070

Offers: Casting resin and silicone rubber for molds and other suppliers. Also offers how-to information on making decorative cast reproductions for dolls and wall plaques.
For Further Information: Send SASE.

GOOD-KRÜGER DOLLS
1842 William Penn Way
Lancaster, PA 17601
(717) 687-7208

Offers: Doll molds for heads and hands, including Hard Lessons and Simple Pleasures, 15″ soft-body types that share the same hand mold and body pattern. Also carries Loreli doll molds.
For Further Information: Send SASE.

HAMILTON EYE WAREHOUSE
P.O. Box 450-MB
Moorpark, CA 93021
(805) 529-5900

Offers: Doll eyes made of hollow blown glass and acrylics; also solid glass paperweights (antique-look). Eyes are available in over 8 colors, 2mm to 30mm sizes, each pair matched.
For Further Information: Catalog, $1.
Discounts: Quantity discounts of up to 50 percent.

HANDCRAFT DESIGNS
63 E. Broad St.
Hatfield, PA 19440
(215)855-3022

Offers: Cernit modeling compound in 3 flesh tones and colors. Also offers air-dry clays by LaDoll, Premier and Crafty.
For Further Information: Send 55¢ for color catalog and price sheet.

HAUS OF DOLLS
3009 Abingdon Rd.
Abingdon, MD 21009
(410) 515-2555

Offers: Doll supplies from Playhouse, Monique, Kemper, Global, Seeley and Judith Howe.
For Further Information: Send SASE for list.
Store Location: At above address.
Discounts: Quantity; sells wholesale.
Accepts: MasterCard, Visa

HEARTWARMERS

P.O. Box 517
Lennox, SD 57039
Fax: (605) 647-5047

Offers: Over 1,500 doll kits (bisque, soft-fired, painted antique-to-modern types), in a variety of sizes.
For Further Information: Catalog, $7.

HEAVENLY DOLLS

114 S. K St.
Tulare, CA 93274
(209) 688-1829

Offers: Known dolls in kit, soft fire or blank forms. Kits include painted porcelain, eyes, lashes, wig, sewn bodies. Also offers doll molds, supplies.
For Further Information: Mold and supply list, $1.
Accepts: MasterCard, Visa

HEIRLOOM TOYS

8393 Strato Dr.
Sandy, UT 84093
(801) 562-2546

Offers: Barbie-size doll house kits and wood furniture.
For Further Information: Send SASE and $1 for brochure/coupons.

HELLO DOLLY

6550 Mobile Highway
Pensacola, FL 32526
(800) 438-7227
Fax: (904)944-7062

Offers: Doll greenware for over 1,500 modern dolls and reproductions, soft-fire or bisque. Also carries doll finishing supplies.
For Further Information: Free list.
Discounts: Sells wholesale.

HUSTON'S

7960 U.S. Rt. 23
South Chillicothe, OH 45601
(614) 663-2881

Offers: Over 200 handmade porcelain doll kits (and dolls) plus old-fashioned girls, babies and others.
For Further Information: Catalog, $2.

IRENE'S DOLLS

4716 64th St.
Lubbock, TX 79414
(806) 792-9114
Fax: (806)792-8244

Offers: 300 doll kits (greenware to finished, with instructions).

For Further Information: Send large SASE for list; photocopied picture, $6 plus $2.90 shipping and handling.
Discounts: Quantity; supply.

JENNELL'S DOLL HOUSE

Rt. 9, Box 939
Tool, TX 75143
(903) 932-4894

Offers: Porcelain doll kits from Doll Artworks and others.
For Further Information: List, $4.

KAIS, INC.

11943 Discovery Ct.
Moorpark, CA 93021
(805) 523-8985
Fax: (805) 523-9170

Offers: Doll-making supplies, including eyes, wigs (modacrylic or mohair for new release dolls), porcelain slip and China paint, plus leather shoes and other accessories.
For Further Information: Send SASE for list.

KEMPER DOLL SUPPLY

Box 696, 13595 12th St.
Chino, CA 91710
(909) 627-6191
Fax: (909) 627-4008

Offers: Top quality wigs, eyes, eyelashes, socks, hosiery and underwear, connectors, pates, bear joints, elastic cord, *S* hooks, buttons, doll-mates, pellets, teeth, stands, shoes, vinyl dolls, angel wings, eye setting wax, sanders, detailing tools, mini finger tool, doll stringing tools, eye sizers and tool caddy.

LES FRENCH WIGS

P.O. Box 620223
Littleton, CO 80162
(303) 979-1929

Offers: Imported French human hair antique and modern style doll wigs, in large selection of sizes and colors.
Discounts: Quantity; sells wholesale.

LIFETIME CAREER SCHOOLS

101 Harrison St.
Archbald, PA 18403
(717) 876-6340

Offers: Doll repair/restoration home-study course, plus courses on dressing antiques, other aspects of doll repair and restoration for business or hobby.
For Further Information: Free booklet.

LUCI'S DOLLS
8083 Bell St.
Weelsburg, OH 45694
(614) 574-2068

Offers: Porcelain reproductions of known dolls in blank or painted kit forms (or complete). Kits include painted porcelain parts, body pattern, preset eyes, lashes. Doll wigs and clothes also available.
For Further Information: Send large SASE for complete list.
Accepts: MasterCard, Visa

MA'S BODY SHOP
1628 Eifert Rd.
Holt, MI 48842
(517) 694-9022

Offers: Composition bodies for dolls—finished or straight from the mold, in a variety of sizes and types. Also repairs dolls.
For Further Information: Send SASE for price list.

MASTERPIECE EYE CO., INC.
3603 Johnston St.
Lafayette, LA 70503
(318) 988-9881
Fax: (318) 988-9884
Offers: Line of soft "glass" eyes by Eveline Frings of Germany.
For Further Information: Color charts and brochure, $5 and large SASE.
Accepts: All major credit cards.

MAYBELLE'S DOLLWORKS
140 Space Park Dr.
Nashville, TN 37211
(615) 831-0661

Offers: Doll molds and supplies from Playhouse, Bell, Kemper, Monique, Global, Brown House, Sugar Creek, Royal and others. Carries Paragon kilns, plus armatures, pellets, tools, equipment and porcelain prop—in bulk or blanket.
For Further Information: Catalog, $7.50.
Store Location: At above address.
Discounts: Sells wholesale.
Accepts: American Express, Discover, MasterCard, Visa

JANICE NAIBERT
16590 Emory Lane
Rockville, MD 20853
(301) 774-9252
Fax: (301) 924-1725

Offers: French human-hair doll wigs (for antique and con-

temporary dolls). Also carries leather shoes and cotton socks. Trims and accessories at wholesale only.
For Further Information: Send large SASE for list.
Discounts: Trade.

PEARL MOON FIBERS
597 Black Brook Rd.
Goffstown, NH 03045
(603) 774-4104

Offers: Doll hair materials, including mohair and cotswold sheep hair in wefted or loose fibers. Natural or dyed sheepskins, lambskins, deerskins and handspun yarns, wool stuffing also available.
For Further Information: Catalog, $2.
Store Location: At above address.
Accepts: MasterCard, Visa

PERFECT TOUCH
P.O. Box 2422
Brenham, TX 77834
(409) 836-6012

Offers: Modeling and sculpting tools for dolls and miniature dolls that can be used with Sculpey, FIMO, Cernit.
For Further Information: Catalog, $3 (refundable).

PIPPIN'S HOLLOW
7996 Darrow Rd.
Twinsburg, OH 44087
(216) 963-6011
Fax: (800) 793-0152

Offers: Porcelain doll kits, wigs, pates, wire frames, hookups and stringing items, wires, hooks and connectors. Also carries accessories, acrylic and animal eyes, whiskers, doll teeth, pellets, Friendly Plastic, fiberfill, plus baby sounds, cries and growlers. Stocks fabric and composition bodies, Cernit model compound, FIMO, Evenheat kilns, Kemper and Narco tools, Seeley China colors and kits. Cleaning items, adhesives, stands, music movements and parts, containers and display cases are also available.
For Further Information: Catalog, $2 (refundable).
Discounts: Quantity.

PLEASURE CRAFTS
Rt. 2, Dept. B
P.O. Box 1485
Mannford, OK 74044

Offers: Woodcraft patterns for performing action animated toys. Also offers patterns for decorative folk arts, gadgets, household accessories.
For Further Information: Write.

PROVINCIAL CERAMIC PRODUCTS, INC.
140 Parker Ct.
Chardon, OH 44024
(216) 286-1277
Fax: (216) 286-1280

Offers: Line of doll molds, porcelain, China paint, kilns, doll eyes, wigs and shoes.
For Further Information: Doll mold catalog, $6.50; doll pattern catalog, $6.95.
Store Location: At above address. Hours: M-F, 8-4:30.
Discounts: Quantity; teachers and institutions; sells wholesale to businesses.

KAREN RAUM'S FANTASY DOLLS
202 Ridgeview Lane
Boulder, CO 80302
(303) 499-8998

Offers: Doll-making supplies, including mohair wig-making items, silks and other fabrics, purse handles, patterns, books, accessories and other items.
For Further Information: Catalog, $3.75.
Accepts: MasterCard, Visa

REJA DOLLS
517 Hartford Rd.
Manchester, CT 06040
(203) 742-9090
Fax: (203) 742-1461

Offers: Doll supplies, including kilns, molds, greenware, fabrics, trims and patterns. Brands include Playhouse, Kemper, IMSCO, Brown House, Global, La Sioux, Karl, Monique, Connies, Dollspart, Wee 3 and others. Also carries notions.
For Further Information: Catalog, $2.
Store Location: At above address.
Discounts: Sells wholesale.
Accepts: MasterCard, Visa

BRYNN RIORDAN
P.O. Box 42
Tuppers Plains, OH 45783
(614) 667-6802

Offers: Technical assistance in vinyl doll production (client list includes Klowns by Kay, Johannes Zook, Connie Walser Derek and others).
For Further Information: Free consultation.

RIVENDELL, INC.
125C N. Lake St.
Madison, OH 44057
(216) 428-0042

Offers: Dolls, doll parts and supplies by Wee3, Kemper,

Playhouse, Virginia La Vorgna, Global, Judith Howe, Kais, Sugar Creek Scharff, Langnickell, Bell Research, European Colours, Kaiser, Orton and others. Also carries doll clothes and patterns.
For Further Information: Catalog, $6.
Discounts: Sells wholesale.
Accepts: Discover, MasterCard, Visa

ROMAN'S
9733 Palmetto Ave.
Fontana, CA 92335
(909) 823-1100

Offers: Doll-making molds, cloth bodies and patterns.
For Further Information: Mold catalog, $4.50; pattern catalog, $4.50.
Accepts: MasterCard, Visa

SANDCASTLE CREATIONS
124 SE First St.
Newport, OR 97365
(541) 265-2499

Offers: Doll wig-making kit (5 shades), cleaned and combed mohair.
For Further Information: Send for samples and price list. Free doll dress list.
Discounts: Quantity.
Accepts: Discover, MasterCard, Visa

G. SCHOEPFER, INC.
460 Cook Hill Rd.
Cheshire, CT 06410
(203) 250-7794
Fax: (203) 250-7796

Offers: Eyes for dolls, including round and oval paperweight, Glastic, Glastic Realistic and Lifetouch series eyes in full range of sizes and colors.
For Further Information: Send SASE or call for catalog.

SCOTT PUBLICATIONS
30595 Eight Mile Rd.
Livonia, MI 48152
(810) 477-6650

Offers: Magazines and books for the ceramicist, dollmaker, doll collector and miniature enthusiast.
For Further Information: Free catalog.

SEELEY DOLL CENTER
2200 Charleston Dr.
Aurora, IL 60506
(630) 892-3081

Offers: Complete line of porcelain doll-making supplies.
For Further Information: Send SASE.

SHEAR DELIGHT FIBERS
3033 Mattson Pl.
Coos Bay, OR 97420
(541) 264-7828

Offers: Alpaca, wool, mohair, flax for doll hair.
For Further Information: Catalog and samples, $2.50.
Discounts: Sells wholesale.

JEWEL SOMMARS
958 Cambridge Ave.
Sunnyvale, CA 94087
(408) 732-7177

Offers: Instructional video (Beta or VHS) entitled *Delightful Dolls—Collecting and Making*, which demonstrates techniques for portrait, original and reproduction dolls, and offers expert instruction in sculpting, molds, casting, finishing, wigs, eyes, costume making and more.
For Further Information: Send SASE.

SOUTH FORTY FARMS
1272 16½ Rd.
Fruita, CO 81521
(303) 858-3687

Offers: Mohair for doll wigs—colors or natural shades, in all stages of preparation.
For Further Information: Send SASE.

STANDARD DOLL SUPPLY HOUSE, INC.
2383 31st St.
Long Island City, NY 11105
(718) 721-7787
Fax: (718) 274-4231

Offers: Doll-making supplies, including China doll kits (old fashioned, pincushion, character and *Gone With the Wind* characters), porcelain bisque kits (reproductions), and bisque doll heads and parts. Also carries body patterns, doll stands, covers, accessories, voices, squeakers, music boxes, eyes, wigs, magnifiers, patterns, books, laces, notions and other supplies. Offers vinyl undressed dolls, doll shoes.
For Further Information: Catalog, $3.
Discounts: Quantity.
Accepts: American Express, MasterCard, Visa

T.L.C. DOLL HOSPITAL
2479 Sheridan Blvd.
Edgewater, CO 80214
(303) 233-3006

Offers: Line of doll parts, mechanicals and accessories. Professional doll restoration services.
For Further Information: Send SASE.

TALLINA'S DOLL SUPPLIES, INC.
15791 SE Highway 224
Clackamas, OR 97015
(503) 658-6148

Offers: Doll-making kits, bodies, eyes, lashes, wigs and other extensives supplies for collectors and crafters.
For Further Information: Catalog, $1.

TDI DOLL CO.
P.O. Box 690
Cave Creek, AZ 85331
(602 488-1030

Offers: Line of mechanical doll parts and accessories. Over 70 porcelain doll heads from 1″ to 6″. Professional doll restoration services.
For Further Information: Write.

TM PORCELAIN CO.
108 N. Henry St.
Bay City, MI 48706
(517) 893-3526

Offers: Doll molds, porcelain slip, China paint, body frames, wigs and beard specialty items. Lambskins include—Lincoln, Kalgon, Icelandic and alpaca. Also carries suede leather, rabbit furs and plates. Stocks supplies, equipment and patterns by Connie, Monique, Kemper, La Sioux, Karl, Royal, Brown House and others. Carries Blue Diamond high fire kilns, and offers a custom mold service.
For Further Information: Catalog, $7.50.
Discounts: Sells wholesale.
Accepts: MasterCard, Visa

TOTAL NONSENSE CERAMICS
9330 B Mira Mesa Blvd.
San Diego, CA 92126
(619) 695-3071

Offers: Doll greenware and supplies by Bell, Connie Lee Finchum, Seeley's, Playhouse and others.
For Further Information: Send SASE for list.
Store Location: At above address.
Accepts: MasterCard, Visa

THE ULTIMATE COLLECTION, INC.
12773 W. Forest Hill Blvd., Suite 107
West Palm Beach, FL 33414
(407) 790-0137
Fax: (407) 790-0179

Offers: Artist doll molds including baby heads—Sweetness (eyes open), Serenity (eyes closed), plus hands and patterns. Also offers 11″ baby, others.
For Further Information: Catalog, $6.
Accepts: Discover, MasterCard, Visa

VAN DYKE'S
P.O. Box 278
Woonsocket, SD 57385
(800) 843-3320

Offers: Doll restoration products, including eyes (for all purposes), plus modeling, casting and filling materials.
For Further Information: Catalog, $1.

VICKIE'S ANGUISH ORIGINAL MOLDS
1704 SE Morrison St.
Topeka, KS 66605
(913) 673-4812

Offers: Doll head and hand molds (and body and clothing patterns) including those for 19″ baby Cuddle-bug, Elizabeth, Rachel, with darker skin (head only can be used on Phylis dolls), Melody (head only 8″ in circumference) with darker skin, the 25″ Phylis doll (head circumference 8½″) with light skin and open crown head. Hand and foot molds are available.
For Further Information: Mold list and photo, send $3 and large SASE.
Accepts: MasterCard, Visa

VICKI'S ORIGINAL DESIGNS
2100 East 85th St. N.
P.O. Box 363
Valley Center, KS 67147
(316) 755-1504

Offers: Original porcelain doll molds from 5¼″ to 11½″. Also offers lady fashion dolls by Vici Hamilton.
For Further Information: Catalog, $7; pattern catalog, $7.

WEE WORLD OF DOLLS, INC.
112 W. Tarrant Rd.
Gardendale, AL 35071
(205) 631-9270

Offers: Porcelain doll kits and a line of supplies for antique and modern dolls by Playhouse, Seeley, Bell, Brown House, Monique and others.
For Further Information: Send SASE for list.
Store Location: At above address. Hours: M, T, Th, F, 9-4.
Discounts: Sells wholesale.

WEEFOKE EMPIRE
619 4th St.
Bremerton, WA 98337
(360) 792-9293

Offers: Line of collectible dolls, furniture.
For Further Information: Send SASE.

WESTBANK DOLL SUPPLY, INC.
5006 Belle Terre Rd.
Marrero, LA 70072
(504) 347-4903
Fax: (504) 341-3421

Offers: Full line of dollmaking supplies by Seeley, Bell, Playhouse, Global, Monique, Kais, Masterpiece Eyes, La Vorgna paints, Jayne Houston, Real Eyes, others. Finchum and Doll Emporium patterns also available. Also offers classes, soft-fire dolls, cut and beveled eyes on soft-fire.
For Further Information: Send SASE for newsletter. Steeley's catalog, $9.50; Bell's catalog, $8.
Store Location: At above address.
Discounts: Sells wholesale.
Accepts: MasterCard, Visa

WOODEN MEMORIES
Rt. 1, Box 87
Bear Lake, PA 16402
(814) 489-3002

Offers: Wood rocking animals patterns in full scale, including 1 rocking burro with 14″ high seat and rocking Clydesdales with 20″ seat height. Also an 8-reindeer herd, 12″ and 18″ sizes. Other patterns also available.
For Further Information: Catalog, $1.

YESTERDAY'S CHILDREN
1723 Portland Ave.
Savanna, IL 61074
(815) 273-3964
Fax: (815) 273-4468

Offers: Doll supplies including wigs, eyes, eyelashes, stands and others. Carries patterns by Jean Nordquist, Yesterday's. Also carries Virginia LaVorgna China paints. Brands available include Playhouse, Kemper, Monique, Global, La Sioux, Seeley and Bell.
For Further Information: Catalog, $5.
Discounts: Sells wholesale.
Accepts: Discover, MasterCard, Visa

YESTERDAY'S CHILDREN PATTERN COMPANY
413 Harvey St.
Des Plaines, IL 60016
(847) 635-3049

Offers: Over 350 easy-sew patterns for doll clothes, antique to country styles, for 8″ to 36″ dolls. Fabrics, notions and lace are also available.
For Further Information: Catalog, $4.
Discounts: Sells wholesale.

Fishing Items

THE ANGLERS ART
P.O. Box 148
Plainfield, PA 17081
(717) 243-9721
Fax: (717) 243-8603

Offers: Full line of books on fly fishing, including crafting of items and many others.
For Further Information: Free catalog.

ANGLER'S WORKSHOP
P.O. Box 1044
Woodland, WA 98674
(360) 225-9445
Fax: (360) 255-8641

Offers: Rod building and fly tying kits, blanks, components, tying materials, rods, reels, lines, rod guides and tops and other fishing products.
For Further Information: Write for free catalog, or send $1 for first class mail.

CUSTOM TACKLE SUPPLY
2559 Hwy. 41 South
Shelbyville, TN 37160
(615) 684-6164
Fax: (615) 684-1755

Offers: Custom fly rod building components, including fly blanks, cork rings, fly grips, reel seats, rod tubes and bags, guides, threads, glues, finishes, accessories and more.
For Further Information: Call or write for catalog.
Discounts: Sells wholesale to businesses with sales tax number, license.

EGGER'S
P.O. Box 1344
Cumming, GA 30128

Offers: Fly tying supplies, tools, net kits and more.
For Further Information: Free catalog.

FEATHER CRAFT FLY FISHING
8307 Manchester Rd.
P.O. Box 19904
St. Louis, MO 63144
(800) 659-1707

Offers: Line of fly tying patterns, components and other products.

For Further Information: Free bulletin catalog.
Store Location: At above address.

JANN'S
P.O. Box 89
Maumee, OH 43537
(419) 868-8288

Offers: Materials/accessories for tackle building, including lure making, fly tying and rod building.
For Further Information: Free catalog.

JERRY'S TACKLE
604 12th St.
Highland, IL 62249
(800) 500-6585

Offers: Line of components for lures, jigs, feathers and fur for fly tying and rod building. Also offers KT products water-based paints and glitter finishes.
For Further Information: Free catalog.

MIDLAND TACKLE
66 Rt. 17
Sloatsburg, NY 10974
(914) 753-5440

Offers: Fishing rod building equipment, lure parts, molds and others.
For Further Information: Free catalog.
Store Location: At above address. Hours: M-Sat, 9-5.

NORTH COUNTRY OUTFITTERS
2 Central Square, Box 300
New Boston, NH 03070
(603) 487-3388 or (800) 331-8558

Offers: Fly tying components and supplies including feathers, threads, tools and other products.
For Further Information: Free catalog.

ON THE FLY
3628 Sage Dr.
Rockford, IL 61114
(815) 877-0090

Offers: Fly tying materials and components for salt, cold and warm water use. Also offers fly fishing tackle and other products.
For Further Information: Free catalog.

SHOFF TACKLE
P.O. Box 1227
Kent, WA 98035
(206) 852-4760

Offers: Rod guiding supplies for custom builders, including products of G Loomis, Sage, St. Croix blanks and others.
For Further Information: Free catalog.

THE TACKLE SHOP
P.O. Box 830369
Richardson, TX 75083

Offers: Supplies/accessories for lures, including skirts, blades, worms, bulk plastics and others.
For Further Information: Free catalog.

Frames and Picture Framing

Also see General Craft Supplies, Artist's Supplies, Woodworking, General Needlecraft Supplies, Quilting and other related categories.

AMERICAN FRAME CORP.
400 Tomahawk Dr.
Maumee, OH 43537
(800) 537-0944
Fax: (419) 893-3553

Offers: Laminated frame sections, metal frames, section pairs and custom cut frames. Also carries hardwood section frames, Plexiglas, matboards and foam core.
For Further Information: Free catalog.
Store Location: At above address. Hours: M-F, 9-4.
Accepts: American Express, Discover, MasterCard, Visa

DOCUMOUNTS
3709 W. 1st Ave.
Eugene, OR 97402
(800) 769-5639
Fax: (503) 686-1954

Offers: Full assortment of wood picture frames in a variety of sizes, styles and colors, plus bevel-edged mats.
For Further Information: Call.

THE FLETCHER-TERRY CO.
65 Spring Lane
Farmington, CT 06032

Offers: Picture-framing tools—FrameMaster stapler (fires flat points), FrameMate unit (flat framers, points or brads into molding), matboard cutters, glass, and stained glass cutters.
For Further Information: Send SASE.

FRAME FIT CO.
P.O. Box 8926
Philadelphia, PA 19135
(215) 332-0683 or (800) 523-3693
Fax: (800) 344-7010

Offers: Custom aluminum frames in sectional pairs-4 profiles and 6 finishes each. "Evolution" line of composite molding in a variety of profiles and colors
For Further Information: Call, write or fax.
Discounts: Quantity.

FRAME STRIPS
P.O. Box 1788
Cathedral City, CA 92235
(619) 328-2358

Offers: Framestrips, clear self-adhesive channel for mounting, framing and attaching; good for changeable artwork, signs and others.
For Further Information: Write for free samples.

FRANKEN FRAMES
609 W. Walnut St.
Johnson City, TN 37604
(800) 322-5899

Offers: Picture frames custom made to order. Also offers custom depth golds, linen liners, custom cut mats, hardware.
For Further Information: Write for catalog.
Discounts: Wholesale prices.

GRAPHIC DIMENSIONS LTD.
2130 Brentwood St.,
High Point, NC 27263
(910) 887-3700 or (800) 221-0262
Fax: (910) 887-3773

Offers: Picture frames in a full line of modern metals, lacquered styles and classic woods, plus frames with linen, burlap or suede liners. Other styles include rustic, traditional, contemporary, Oriental, European.
For Further Information: Free color catalog.

IMPERIAL PICTURE FRAMES
P.O. Box 598
Imperial Beach, CA 91933
(800) 423-2620

Offers: Frames in many styles, types and sizes.
For Further Information: Free color catalog.
Discounts: Sells wholesale.

THE METTLE CO.
P.O. Box 525
Fanwood, NJ 07023
(908) 322-2010 or (800) 621-1329

Offers: Aluminum picture frame sides in 47 colors and a variety of sizes and widths, plus other metallic and color finished styles and custom cuts.
For Further Information: Send SASE for list.

Discounts: Quantity.
Accepts: Discover, MasterCard, Visa

STU-ART

2045 Grand Ave., Dept. CSS
Baldwin, NY 11510
(516) 546-5151

Offers: Mats/picture frames. Mats include conservation types, ready-mats and hand-cut beveled. Frames include aluminum, wood; frame sections, and pre-assembled aluminum and wood frames in a variety of sizes. Also carries plastic picture saver panels and shrink wrap.
For Further Information: Free catalog and mat samples.

TENNESSEE MOULDING & FRAME CO.

1188 Antioch Pike
Nashville, TN 37211
(800) 821-5483

Offers: Picture frames, a full line, including 450 choices of metals and woods, including oaks, pines, poplar, painted colors/metallics, soft-shades, art deco look, gilded and others. Also carries designer molding, Crescent mat board (63 colors), foam center and newsboards, black core and simulated fabrics, plus oversizes, barrier papers and museum boards.
For Further Information: Call or write for full-color catalog.

WORLD FRAME DISTRIBUTORS

107 Maple St.
Denton, TX 76201
(817) 382-3442

Offers: Frames—traditional, ready-made types and sizes, plus gallery-style, ornately crafted frames, supplies and canvas.
For Further Information: Free brochure and price list.

Furniture Making and Upholstery

Also see Basketry and Seat Weaving, Miniature Making, Paints, Finishes and Adhesives, Woodworking and other related categories.

DESIGNER FURNITURE PLANS

179 Davidson Ave., Dept. 6
Somerset, NJ 08873
(908) 469-6200

Offers: Furniture construction plans, including kids' size and other home furnishings.
For Further Information: $2 for kids' size furniture catalog. $3 for catalog of other home furnishings. $4.50 for both catalogs—includes 55 designs.

EAGLE WOODWORKING

1130 East St.
Tewksbury, MA 01876
(800) 628-4849
Fax: (508) 640-1501

Offers: Dovetailed drawers of ½″ maple, assembled and custom-sized width and depth, for cabinets.
For Further Information: Write.

EMPEROR CLOCK CO.

Emperor Industrial Park
Fairhope, AL 36532
(334) 928-2316

Offers: Furniture kits—traditional-style cabinets, chests, tables, chairs, and others in cherry or oak. Also carries grandfather and other clock kits, movements and dials.
For Further Information: Color catalog, $1.

FURNITURE DESIGNS, INC.

1827 Elmdale Ave.
Glenview, IL 60025
(847) 657-7526

Offers: More than 200 professionally designed full-size furniture plans in Early American, American Chippendale, Queen Anne, and Arts and Crafts (Mission) styles, including rolltop desks, cradles, dining and poker tables, chairs, buffets, china hutches; curio, gun and corner cabinets; chests, beds, dressers, chests of drawers, spinning wheels, children's furntiure, rocking horses, Adirondack and English furniture, others.
For Further Information: Catalog, $3.
Discounts: Teachers and institutions; sells wholesale to businesses.

J&L CASUAL FURNITURE CO.

P.O. Box 208
Tewksbury, MA 01876
(508) 851-4514

Offers: Full line of PVC pipe furniture kits, plans and supplies.
For Further Information: Send SASE.

OWEN PUBLISHING CO.

Battle Ground, WA 98604
(360) 887-8646

Offers: Starter guide to PVC furniture making (indoor and outdoor), including chairs, tables, love seats, couches, chaise lounges, swing sets, recreation items, children's items, wood stackers and others. Includes plans and diagrams. Also carries cushion patterns, data on PVC furniture, how-to videos and more.
For Further Information: Write.

QUALITY UPHOLSTERY

75 Diggs Blvd.
Warner Robins, GA 31093
(912) 922-8911

Offers: Upholstery instructional video by German craftsmen.
For Further Information: Send SASE.

SHAKER WORKSHOPS

P.O. Box 8001
Ashburnham, MA 01430
(800) 840-9121
Fax: (508) 827-9900

Offers: Shaker kits for rockers, dining chairs, tables, beds, pegboards and pegs. Also carries dolls, oval boxes and custom-made furniture.
For Further Information: Catalog and tape samples, $1.

TERRY CRAFT
12 Williams Ct.
Shelby, OH 44875
(419) 342-4609

Offers: Adirondack chair kit with instructions, including an optional leg rest.
For Further Information: Send SASE.

THE ROUDEBUSH CO.
P.O. Box 348
Star City, IN 46985
(800) 847-4947

Offers: Buckboard bench kit with authentically designed steel springs that give, metal arms and backrails; comes with complete hardware and instructions. Also carries precut and drilled red oak.
For Further Information: Write.
Accepts: MasterCard, Visa

V.U.E.
P.O. Box 128-CSS
El Verano, CA 95433
(800) 635-3493

Offers: Instructional/training videos on upholstery, slip covering and auto/marine recovering (car, truck and boat seats). Carries tools and upholstery supplies.
For Further Information: Free brochure.
Store Location: 17421 Sonoma Highway, El Verano CA.
Discounts: Quantity.
Accepts: American Express, MasterCard, Visa

VAN DYKE'S
P.O. Box 278
Woonsocket, SD 57385
(800) 843-3320

Offers: Furniture components, including fiber and leather seats, table and posterbed parts, Queen Anne legs, rolltop desks, and chair and piano stool kits/parts. Also carries cane web, cane, rush and reeds. Carries wood turnings and wood carvings, such as gingerbread, filigrees and others. China cabinet glass, plywood, spring straps, metal tacking straps, fastener strips, Klinch-It tool, zippers and chains, heavy-duty sewing machines, rubber webbing, hemp and jute webbing, cord, super steamer, threads, clips, helicals, torsion, rocker springs, and a variety of fabrics and trims are available. Tools include awls, pinking machines, stuffing irons, stretchers, punches, nippers, mallets, staple guns and shears, plus fasteners and kits. Videos and hardware (brass, wood, cast iron) are also available.
For Further Information: Catalog, $1.
Discounts: Quantity.

General Craft Supplies

Also see specific art/crafts chapters, Books and Booksellers, Publications and Associations.

Browse through this sourcebook for unexpected, unusual and often valuable items for your personal creative expression.

ALPEL PUBLISHING
P.O. Box 203-CSS
Chambly, Quebec J3L 4B3
Canada
(514) 658-3514
Fax: (514) 658-3514

Offers: *Catalogue of Canadian Catalogues* a directory of 900 mail order sources in 110 categories, including crafts, graphics, needlecrafts, woodworking and others. Also offers "Duplicate" reusable grid for enlarging miniature patterns, and sewing pattern books.
For Further Information: Brochures and 20 sample patterns, $2.
Discounts: Teachers and institutions; sells wholesale to legitimate businesses and professionals.

AMERICAN ART CLAY CO., INC.
4717 W. 16th St.
Indianapolis, IN 46222
(317) 244-6871

Offers: Craft supplies, including Friendly Plastic, Friendly Clay, Sculptamold and Claycrete for modeling. Also carries jewelry accessories and findings, metallic acrylics, translucent paints and glitters, phosphorescent paints, Batikit cold water fabric dyes, metallic and other wood finishes.
For Further Information: Free catalog and literature.
Discounts: Sells wholesale through distributors only.

THE ART STORE
935 Erie Blvd. E.
Syracuse, NY 13210
(315) 474-1000

Offers: Surface design supplies and equipment for screen printing, papermaking, marbling, gold leaf, airbrush, modeling, batik, silk painting and dyeing. Also carries beads and jewelry findings and others.
For Further Information: Complete list, $3.

ART VIDEO LIBRARY
P.O. Box 68
Ukiah, OR 97880
(541) 427-3024

Offers: Craft instructional videos available to members for sale or rent at low cost on payment of a yearly fee at low cost (rental can apply to purchase). Videos demonstrate paints, color, candy making, stencil, theorem, bronzing, soft-sculpture dolls, cake decorating, tole, stained glass, sculpting, plaster, waste and other molds, bas relief, bronze casting, etching and engraving. Also offers videos on sewing basics, including knits, lingerie, jeans, embroidery, teddy bears and others.
For Further Information: Free catalog.

DICK BLICK
P.O. Box 1267
Galesburg, IL 61402
(309) 343-6181

Offers: Videos, books, and a complete line of artist's supplies. Crafts: Paints, markers, art and specialty papers, and wearable art supplies. Supplies and equipment for: Airbrushing, sign making, wood carving, printing, modeling, stencils, resin, plaster, mâché, molding and casting, enameling, jewelry making and basketry. Also carries ceramic clays, equipment, kilns, tools and glazes, metal punch and leather supplies, power tools, stitchery and fabric decorating supplies, wood ware and boxes. Group value packs are available.
For Further Information: Catalog, $5.
Accepts: American Express, Discover, MasterCard, Visa

BOLEK'S CRAFT SUPPLYS, INC.
P.O. Box 465
330 N. Tuscarawas Ave.
Dover, OH 44622
(216) 364-8878

Offers: Decorative items, including silk and ribbon roses, Styrofoam shapes, fillable ornaments, twisted paper ribbon, Spanish moss and more. Wood doll heads, plastic doll cones, angel sets and other supplies also available.
For Further Information: Catalog, $1.50.
Accepts: MasterCard, Visa

BOUTIQUE TRIMS, INC.
21200 Pontiac Trail
South Lyon, MI 48178
(810) 437-2017
Fax: (810) 437-9436

Offers: AG and AS jewelry findings and charms, woodenware, stencils, paint and art supplies, silk flowers, floral supplies and dried materials. Also offers resin figures, papier-mâché and others.
For Further Information: Metal findings catalog, $3.
Discounts: Quantity; teachers, institutions and professionals.

BOYD'S
P.O. Box 6232-C
Augusta, GA 30916

Offers: Resin-It Crafting Instruction, including art work on paper for jewelry, magnets and other items with resin surface and finishing.
For Further Information: Formulas, booklet and Resin-It brochure/sample, $7.

BRIAN'S CRAFTS UNLIMITED
1421 S. Dixie Freeway, Dept. CSS
New Smyrna Beach, FL 32168
(904) 672-2726
Fax: (904) 426-0350

Offers: Wearable art supplies including T-shirts, ribbon roses, pens (markers, transfer, others) and Art Deco, and other paints and glitters. Carries stamps, inks and tints. Also offers beads and floral supplies including wreaths, moss, grapevine novelties and dried flowers. Also carries doilies, fabric yo-yos, muslin dolls, resin faces, Friendly Plastic, rhinestones, lace, pins, foam, feathers, chenille, felt, adhesives, macrame accessories, wood beads and blocks, rings, ribbon, paper twist, wood items and cross-stitch supplies. Bargain grab bags are available.
For Further Information: Catalog, $1 (refundable); Canada, $2.
Accepts: Discover, MasterCard, Visa

MARTIN R. CARBONE, INC.
2519 Bath St.
Santa Barbara, CA 93105
(805) 682-0465

Offers: The Carbone Cutter foam cutting machine, for polystyrene and other lightweight plastics; cuts foam up to 12″ thick; cutting wire works by melting a fine cut through the material. Also offers box-making kits.
For Further Information: Send SASE.

CHARLOTTE'S HOBBIES & CRAFTS
782 Shield Rd.
Hemmingford, Quebec J0L 1H0
Canada
(514) 247-2590
Fax: (514) 247-3661

Offers: Line of "Knorr" craft supplies and kits. Selection of imported gift items, including paper napkins and doilies.
For Further Information: Catalog, $5.

CHESTER BOOK CO.
4 Maple St.
Chester, CT 06412
(203) 526-9887

Offers: Line of quality books in variety of arts, crafts and neelecrafts including Japanese, African and other ethnic crafts; pattern and project books, ceramics, fabric and fiber arts, dyeing, glass, basketmaking, jewelrymaking, metal working, paper crafting, furniture making and others.
Accepts: MasterCard, Visa

CRAFT CATALOG
P.O. Box 1069
Reynoldsburg, OH 43068

Offers: Craft supplies, including pine brooms, grapevine wreaths, decoratives, ribbons, florals, plush and others. Paints, glues, finishes, stencils, brushes and cross-stitch products also available.
For Further Information: Catalog, $2.

CRAFT KING
P.O. Box 90637, Dept. CSS
Lakeland, FL 33804
(942) 648-2969
Fax: (941) 648-2972

Offers: Over 6,000 art/craft supplies, including paints, papers, canvas board, Ceram tole kits, wood shapes, plastic canvas, macrame, doll-making items, wood, wearable art, trims including rhinestones, sequins, buttons, felt and pompoms. Also carries music box movements, adhesives, foam, glue guns, modeling and floral items, iron-on transfers, jewelry findings, beads, lampshades and supplies for rag baskets. Miniatures available include sports figures, teddies, trees, vehicles, hats, holiday items and flowers. Naturals include wreaths, baskets, raffia, excelsior and moss. Books are also available.
For Further Information: Free introductory catalog.
Discounts: Sells wholesale to legitimate businesses.

CRAFT MAKERS
3958 Linden Ave.
Dayton, OH 45432
(800) CRAFTS-5

Offers: Decorative items, including holiday ornaments and

products, ribbons and shredders, doll parts and accessories, stands, glues, paints and others.
For Further Information: Catalog, $2.

CRAFTS UNLIMITED
1421 S. Dixie
New Smyrna, FL 32168

Offers: Supplies for jewelrymaking and macrame. Also offers basic supplies and decoratives, including florals, wood items, Styrofoam, muslin, paints, glues and others.
For Further Information: Catalog, $1 (refundable).

CREATIVE CRAFT HOUSE
P.O. Box 2567
Bullhead City, AZ 86430
(520) 754-3300

Offers: Full lines of pinecone and seashell projects, plus other natural materials—pods, cones, foliages and Christmas materials. Also carries jewelry findings and parts, dollmaking items, party and wedding favors, and animal and doll parts. Miniatures, beads, novelties, conchos, foil and mirrors are also available.
For Further Information: Catalog, $2.
Discounts: Quantity.

CRYSBI CRAFTS, INC.
17514 S. Ave. 4E
Yuma, AZ 85365
Additional address:
RR #3
High River, Alberta T1V 1N3
Canada

Offers: Craft supplies, including dried and preserved florals and moss, raffia, excelsior, wheats, grasses, flax, nests, wreaths, floral supplies. Line of baskets, wicker products and craft kits also available. Decorative items include laces, paper twist, doll hair, eyes, pompoms, bells, Styrofoam, buttons, ribbons, beads, magnets, birds, plush animals, hats, twists, chenille, glitter, felt, mop heads, doll furniture and more.
For Further Information: Catalogs, $2
Discounts: Quantity.

LOU DAVIS WHOLESALE
N3211 City Rd. H. North
Lake Geneva, WI 53147
(414) 248-2000 or (800) 748-7991

Offers: Brand name craft and ceramic supplies, including music movements in more than 200 tunes, chalks, paints, spray finishes, air brushes and compressors, clock movments, dollmaking supplies, lamp parts and accessories, brushes, magnets, glitter, abrasives, adhesives and cleaning tools.
For Further Information: Free catalog.
Accepts: Discover, MasterCard, Visa

DISCOUNT ARTS AND CRAFTS
9015 US 19 N.
Pinellas Park, FL 34666
(813) 572-1600

Offers: Arts and crafts supplies including canvas, paints, miniatures, wood products and macrame cords. Also offers decoratives, including paper twists, pompoms; cross-stitch items and others. Closeout books also available.
For Further Information: Catalog and closeout flyer, $2.

DOVE BRUSH MFG., INC.
280 Terrace Rd.
Tarpon Springs, FL 34689
(813) 934-5283
Fax: (813) 934-1142

Offers: Full art brush line covering dollmaking, ceramics, decorative painting, crafts and more; including "Mid-Night Dove" brushes and specialty brushes-½" feather edge by Jill MacFarlane and others.
For Further Information: Full brush catalog, $2.50; Mid-Night price list, send SASE.

DOVER PUBLICATIONS, INC.
31 E. 2nd St.
Mineola, NY 11501

Offers: Craft and needlecraft books. Carries a series of copyright-free design books, including clip art (holiday designs, borders, layout grids, old-fashioned animals, transportation, patriotic, sport, wedding, humorous, nautical and alphabets); designs from various eras, including Japanese, Chinese, Art Nouveau, Early Arabic and Mayan designs; stencil books; and folk designs. Also carries books on stained glass, calligraphy, costumes, art, silk screen, bookbinding, paper, beads, jewelry, basketry, marionettes, leather, tole, miniatures, dollhouses, and 39 cut/use stencils. Needlecraft books include 79 plus quilting, appliqué, knitting/crochet, lace, many embroidery patterns, needlepoint and many charted doll-making books.
For Further Information: Free catalog.

ENTERPRISE ART
P.O. Box 2918, Dept. 810
Largo, FL 34649
(800) 366-2218
Fax: (800) 366-6121

Offers: Line of craft kits, beads, jewelry making supplies, doll products, angel-making parts, hard-to-find items, patterns and books.
For Further Information: Basic supply catalog, $4.

FACTORY DIRECT CRAFT SUPPLY
440 Conover Dr.
P.O. Box 16
Franklin, OH 45005
(513) 743-5855 or (513) 743-5500 (outside continental U.S.)
Fax: (800) 269-8741

Offers: Decorative items, including cotton crochet doilies, laces, Styrofoam, wood shapes and beads, mop heads, plush animals and parts, doll hair, hats, vinyl doll heads and sets, jute, notions and more. Chipwood box sets and pocket bibles also available.
For Further Information: Catalog, $2.
Accepts: Discover, MasterCard, Visa.

KAREN'S CRAFTING ACCESSORIES
Box 25909
Colorado Springs, CO 80936

Offers: Craft accessories including jewelry findings, fabric, buttons, charms, button assortments, rubber stamps, paper punches, yo-yos, cookie cutters, wire ribbon and other products.
For Further Information: Catalog, $1.

KIRCHEN BROS.
P.O. Box 1016
Skokie, IL 60076
(708) 647-6747

Offers: Doll Baby parts and animal parts. Also carries fashion dolls and crochet patterns and accessories, pre-painted wood and tin items, baskets, wreaths, paints, brushes, craft kits (holiday items, ornaments and others). Other items offered include burlap, felt, "fur," foam, various trims, Shrink Art, magnets, miniatures, novelties, small mirrors, butterflies and quilling papers and tools. Naturals include cones, brooms, mats, wreaths, corn husks, wheat, feathers and baskets. Also stocks books.
For Further Information: Catalog, $1.50 (refundable).
Discounts: Sales and quantity prices.
Accepts: Discover, MasterCard, Visa

JOE KUBERT ART & GRAPHIC SUPPLY
37A Myrtle Ave.
Dover, NJ 07801
(201) 328-3266

Offers: Artist's and graphics materials (major brands), papers (rice types and others), boards, markers, paints, sets, adhesives, airbrushes and compressors. Also carries silk screen supplies, kits and equipment, plus magnifiers, lamps, clays, cartoonist supplies (including inks, pen nibs and brushes, vinyl letters and frames). Offers custom framing. Wire/sculpting tools and books are also stocked.
For Further Information: Catalog and flyers, $7.
Store Location: At above address. Hours: M-F, 10-6. Sat, 9-4.

MFD ENTERPRISES, INC.
222 Sidney Baker S., Suite 205
Kerrville, TX 78028
(210) 896-6060

Offers: MagEyes magnifiers, including visor style, 2½× and 4× lenses, interchangeable, cushioned headband, swings when not in use.
Discount: Sells wholesale.

NATIONAL ARTCRAFT CO.
7996 Darrow Rd.
Twinsburg, OH 44087
(800) 793-0152

Offers: Three catalogs offer a broad range of hard-to-find craft products. A 112-page general craft catalog includes studio display items, cements and glues, jewelry parts, brushes, fountain pumps, doll glasses, novelty items, rhinestones, desk pens, miniatures. A 40-page musical/clock movment catalog includes a large selection of tunes and clock insert styles. Also offers a 32-pate electrical/lamp catalog.
For Further Information: Catalogs, $1 each.
Discounts: Quantity.

NANCY NEALE TYPECRAFT
Box 40
Roslyn, NY 11576
(516) 612-7130
Summer address:
Steamboat Wharf Rd.
Bernard, ME 04612

Offers: Antique and old wood printing type (letters, numbers, punctuation, in 1″ to 5″ sizes, in a variety of styles. Most type is in English, some in German and Hebrew [inquire]; sold by 100 plus lots. Type can be used for printing, as ornaments, for collages, for nameplates, door knockers, inlaid wood patterns, etc.) Also carries old copper and zinc engravings, metal dingbats, printer's galleys, initials and others. Provides assistance and assembling instructions on request.
For Further Information: Free catalog.

PATTERNCRAFTS, INC.
P.O. Box 25639
Colorado Springs, CO 80936-5639
(800) 456-1239

Offers: Instructional videos on folk art, tole painting, quilting, kids' crafts, naturals, ribbon crafts, floral arranging, calligraphy, cake decorating, etching/mirror removal, fabric painting and others. Also carries over 600 craft patterns—country, unusual, "critters," sweatshirt, decorating, Christmas boutique, paper cutting, dolls, cookie cutters, no-sew, folk art, wood, seasonal motifs and gift ideas, accessories and others.
For Further Information: Catalog, $2.

POLYFORM PRODUCTS CO.

1901 Estes Ave.
Elk Grove, IL 60007-5415
(847) 427-0020

Offers: Super Sculpey, a ceramic-like sculpturing compound for miniatures, plaques, jewelry and sculpture. It's workable until baked in a home oven at 275 degrees; it can be molded by hand, and later sanded, drilled, painted, engraved, carved, antiqued, glazed or bronzed. Thirty colors are available.
For Further Information: Contact dealer or write.

PRIME PUBLISHING, INC.

1954 1st St.
P.O. Box 663, Dept. FWL56
Highland Park, IL 60035

Offers: Directory with over 400 free or postage-only offers in crafts, ceramics, sewing, quilting, tole and decorative painting and needlecrafts, includes booklets, patterns, kits, home decor ideas, samples, project sheets and newsletters.
For Further Information: Directory, $3.

S&S ARTS & CRAFTS

P.O. Box 513
Colchester, CT 06415
(800) 243-9232, Dept. 2007
Fax: (800) 566-6678

Offers: Low-cost/group projects, including arts, crafts, beads, toys, scraps, mosaics, multi-cultures, naturals, metals/tools, papers, clays, paints, woods, jewelry, decoupage, masks, costumes and educational projects. Also carries sticks, chenille, shapes, puzzles, blocks, rubber stamps, science items, novelties, papers, paints, foam, ribbons, sand, beads and looms. Projects for modeling, plaster, papier mâché, stencil and baking crystals are available. Also offers leathercraft tools, sets, lacings and kits, plus wood items and kits, basketry supplies, tools, games and musical instruments.
For Further Information: Free catalog.
Store Location: 75 Mill St., Colchester, CT.
Discounts: Quantity.
Accepts: American Express, Discover, MasterCard, Visa

SAX ARTS & CRAFTS

2405 S. Calhoun Rd., P.O. Box 51710
New Berlin, WI 53151
(414) 784-6880

Offers: A variety of supplies (known brands), including a full line of enameling products—kits, enamels, tools, aids, class pack, copper forms and others. Also carries tooling metals, weaving looms and aids, yarns, weaving kits, rug/craft yarns, embroidery/crewel threads, rug hook frames and aids, canvas, hoops, burlap, felt and soft sculpture and string art items. Indian beading, beads, feathers, macrame, basketry and batik supplies, fabric paints, airbrush kits and inks, stencil films, trims, foam, mosaics, stained glass kits, etching and beveled glass supplies and supplies for decoupage, jewelry making, leather, casting, plastics, wood and metal working are also available.
For Further Information: Catalog, $4 (refundable).
Discounts: Quantity; sells wholesale to legitimate businesses.

WOOD-N-CRAFTS, INC.

P.O. Box 140
Lakeview, MI 48850
(800) 444-8075
Offers: Decorative craft supplies including toy parts, stuffing, raffia, excelsior, straw hats, miniatures, wooden parts, beads, trims, accessories. Also offers hardware, glues, paints and more.
For Further Information: Free catalog.
Discounts: Sells wholesale.

Glass Crafts and Stained Glass

Also see General Craft Supplies, Bead Crafts, Ceramics and other related categories.

ALICE'S STAINED GLASS
7015 N. 58th Ave.
Glendale, AZ 85301
(602) 939-7260

Offers: Glass beadmaking tools, supplies, videos and books. Also offers handmade glass beads.
For Further Information: Send SASE.
Store Location: At above address.
Discounts: Quantity; sells wholesale.

ANYTHING IN STAINED GLASS
1060 Rt. 47 S.
P.O. Box 444
Rio Grande, NJ 08242
(609) 886-0416

Offers: Full lines of Worden and Bradley forms/patterns, Weller irons, Morton Works, Glastar and Inland routers, Willard and Canfield solder, Fry metals, Armour etching, BE level clusters, Toyo and Fletcher cutters, Diebel Foilers, Northern hardwoods, McNeil frames.
For Further Information: Free catalog.
Store Location: At above address.
Discounts: Quantity; sells wholesale to legitimate businesses and professionals.

C&R LOO, INC.
1085 Essex Ave.
Richmond, CA 94801
(510) 232-0276

Offers: Flashed color/clear glass in over 20 combinations, plus double flashes on clear and color
For Further Information: Contact dealer or send SASE.

COVINGTON ENGINEERING CORP.
715 W. Colton Ave.
P.O. Box 35
Redlands, CA 92374
(909) 793-6636

Offers: Glass machinery, including a glass beveling system, a 2-station unit with polisher, horizontal glass lap, sphere cutting cups and glass smoothing beveler. Also offers a glass lap kit, diamond mini-lap, arbors (for vertical glass units), belt sanders/polishers, web sanders, large sphere maker, cutter cups and supplies. Trim saws/cutters, arbors and accessories, lathes (engraver/cutter), Koolerant pumps, water and drain items are also available.
For Further Information: Send SASE for list.

CREEK-TURN, INC.
Rt. 38
Hainesport, NJ 08036
(609) 265-1170

Offers: Glassmold mix for mold making, kiln fired glass, antique reproductions, Tiffany style lamps, dimensional glass, draping, and slumping. Also offers self-stacking slumping molds (no shelves needed), glass separator, mold release, mold makers' clays, a line of glass fusing kilns and firing kilns, plus kiln lids with elements. Glass crafting tools and complete instructions are also available.
For Further Information: Write or call.

EASTERN ART GLASS
P.O. Box 341-703
Wyckoff, NJ 07481
(201) 847-0001

Offers: Glass etching and mirror removing kits and a glass engraving course. Carries rotary engraving power tools (to carve or engrave on glass, plastic, metal, wood). Supplies available include stencils, mirrors and slab glass. Glass etching and mirror decorating video course also available.
For Further Information: Catalog, $2 (refundable).
Accepts: American Express, Discover, MasterCard, Visa

FRANKLIN ART GLASS
222 E. Sycamore St.
Columbus, OH 43206
(614) 221-2972

Offers: Stained glass tools including metal running pliers, glazing hammers, lead nippers, breaker-groziers, breakers and other pliers. Carries foil, lead, two-in-one patterns and other shears.
For Further Information: Send SASE for list.

FRANTZ BEAD COMPANY

1222 Sunset Hill Rd.
Shelton, WA 98584
(360) 426-6712
Fax: (360) 427-5866

Offers: Glass crafting for beadmaking and lampworking, including Moretti glass rods, diachronic and milefiori, bullseye and borosilicate diachronic glass. Also offers Chameleon and Northstar colored borosilicate. Annealing kilns, controllers, tools, supplies, books and videos on beadmaking, borosilicate lampworking, marble making and more also available.
For Further Information: Send SASE.

GLASS CRAFT, INC.

626 Moss St.
Golden, CO 80401
(303) 278-4670

Offers: Line of glass-blowing equipment, tools, supplies and books.

THE GLASS WORKBENCH

318 S. Main
St. Charles, MO
(800) 746-2002

Offers: Full extensive line of stained glass supplies, tools and equipment. Also offers classes.
For Further Information: Call about mail order catalog.
Store Location: At above address.

HOTGLASS

213 S. Whisman Rd.
Mountain View, CA 94041
(800) 9HOTGLASS

Offers: Large selection of glass, tools and supplies for fusing and beadmaking. Also offers fusing, casting and beadmaking kilns and Latticino machine.
For Further Information: Free fusing or beadmaking catalog.

HOUSTON STAINED GLASS SUPPLY

2002 Brittmore St.
Houston, TX 77043
(713) 690-8844
Fax: (713) 690-0009

Offers: Over 6,000 products for stained glass crafting, including 1,200 colors of glass and 800 beveled glass designs and shapes.
For Further Information: Contact your glass supplier.

ED HOY'S STAINED GLASS DISTRIBUTORS

1620 Frontenac Rd.
Naperville, IL 60563
(630) 420-0890

Offers: Glass crafting supplies, including glass bevels

(shapes, clusters, color, mirror, panel and engraved), painted/fired shapes, gems, marbles, nuggets, jewels. Carries colored sheets including antiques, glashed, streakies, crackles, mirror, Oceana, textures, art, Bullseye, cathedral, Spectrum and others. Also carries scraps, fusing kilns, clay molds and supplies, fusing supplies and tools, plus fusible glass, fusing kits and projects, glass paints, brushes and stains. Tools available include circle and other cutters, pliers, shears, engravers, soldering irons, tools to bend foil, glass drills, burnishers, grinders, routers, belt sanders and saws. Also offers projectors, foil, came, channel, chemicals and Lamp forms and bases.
For Further Information: Contact dealer or send SASE.
Discounts: Sells wholesale to businesses.

HUDSON GLASS CO., INC.

219 N. Division St., Dept. CS-6
Peekskill, NY 10566
(800) 413-2964
Fax: (800) 999-FAXIT

Offers: Stained glass supplies from Glastar, Inland, Morton, Worden, Reusche, Venture, Quicksilver, Ungar, Weller, McNeil, Diamond, Fletcher, Armour, Bullseye, Kokomo, Carolyn Kyle, Armstrong and others. Carries glass fusing and etching supplies, stained and other types glass, crystals, chemicals, foils, patterns, tools and equipment, electrical parts, box accessories and books.
For Further Information: Catalog, $3 (refundable).
Store Location: At above address.
Discounts: Based on dollar volume. Sells wholesale to legitimate businesses.

JAX CHEMICAL CO., INC.

78-11 267th St.
Floral Park, NY 11004
(718) 347-0057

Offers: Stained glass, lamps and lighting fixtures, hardware, Master Metal finishing solutions. Also offers antiques and statues.
For Further Information: Send SASE.

MYTHICAL REFLECTIONS

360 S. Hwy. 17/92
Longwood, FL 32750
(407) 767-5510
Fax: (407) 767-8830

Offers: Stained glass, supplies, tools and equipment.
For Further Information: Free catalog.
Discounts: Monthly sales.

PARAGON INDUSTRIES, INC.

2011 S. Town E. Blvd.
Mesquite, TX 75149
(800) 876-4328

Offers: Glass fusing kiln with digital temperature controller.

For Further Information: Free catalog.
Discounts: Sells wholesale to legitimate businesses.

PRAIRIE DESIGNS OF CALIFORNIA

Box 886
Brisbane, CA 94005
(415) 468-5319
Fax: (415) 468-6634

Offers: Art glass patterns in Prairie style for windows and lamps, based on the designs of Frank Lloyd Wright (but not authentic Wright designs).
For Further Information: Catalog, $2.

PREMIUM PRODUCTS OF LOUISIANA, INC.

2008 Johnston St.
Lafayette, LA 70503
(318) 234-1642

Offers: Beveled glass and mirrored products of all shapes, sizes and colors. Custom beveling and mirror resilvering, tempering and insulating glass available.
For Further Information: Send SASE.

RAYER'S BEARDEN S.G. SUPPLY, INC.

4101 E. Kellogg
Wichita, KS 67200
(800) 228-4101

Offers: Full line of stained glass supplies for all levels, beginning to professional. Also offers Tiffany lamps, entryways and more. Classes and workshops available.
Store Location: At above address.

SETH ROSEN STUDIO

19 Curtis Lane
Dennis, MA 02638
(508) 385-5413

Offers: Line of mirrors, $1/16''$ and $1/8''$ thickness.
For Further Information: Price list, $1.
Discounts: Quantity.

THE STAINED GLASS SUPERSTORE

8740-18 Cherry Lane
Laurel, MD 20810
(301) 953-1740

Offers: Full line of stained glass and glass supplies, tools and equipment. Also offers glass fusing and beadmaking supplies and equipment.
Store Location: At above address.

UNITED ART GLASS, LTD.

1032 E. Ogden Ave., #128
Naperville, IL 60563
(630) 369-8168

Offers: Supplies/equipment including bevels, engraved, star, faceted, mirror, color, clusters, jewels, nuggets and marbles. Glass includes Bulleye, Chicago Art, Cotswold, Emaille, flashed, Flemish, antique Kokomo, Oceana, Waser, Wissmach, mirror, plate and others. Carries chemicals and tools, including 10 cutters, lead cames, shears, engravers, flexible shafts, glass drills, foiling machines, Foilomatic guide rollers and Glastar tools, Morton Surface systems (cutting shops), routers, saws, soldering irons and etching items. Metal lamp bases, fusing projects, fusing kilns, packs, equipment, Badger spray guns, paints. Kiln firing items and patterns for lamp forms also available. Also offers repairs and restorations.
For Further Information: Catalog, $5.
Discounts: Quantity.

V.E.A.S., INC.

P.O. Box 278
Troy, MI 48099
(800) 584-2020

Offers: Instructional video on Glass Erasing (a controlled form of sandblasting)—can also be used for wood, plastic or metal—program teaches techniques for professional results, for mirror decorating, monogramming and other projects, plus embellishing on glass. Also offers videos for gold leafing on glass.
For Further Information: Send SASE for brochure.
Discounts: Sells wholesale.
Accepts: MasterCard, Visa

WHITTEMORE-DURGIN

P.O. Box 2065
Hanover, MA 02339
(617) 871-1743 or (800) 262-1790
Fax: (617) 871-5597

Offers: Stained glass including French and German antique, cathedral types (in sheets and by the pound), antique, opalescent, clear beveled, jewels and others. Carries stained glass kits with tools, tool and supplies kits, Suncatcher kits, lampshade maker kits. Tools available include glass cutters, pliers, lead straighteners, soldering irons, glass grinders and accessories. Also offers lead came, copper foil, brass channel and banding, lamp parts, decorative chains, hinges, metal lamp bases, lead castings, patterns and books.
For Further Information: Catalog, $2.
Store Location: 825 Market St., Rochland, MA 02370. Hours: M, 8-8. T-F, 8-4:30. Sat, 8-12.
Discounts: Quantity.

Indian and Frontier Crafts

Also see Basketry and Seat Weaving, Bead Crafts, Leather Crafts and General Needlecraft Supplies.

BUFFALO TIPI POLE CO.
3355 Upper Gold Creek
Sandpoint, ID 83864
(208) 263-6953

Offers: Tipis (variety of sizes) and tipi poles.
For Further Information: Catalog, $2.

CHARLES A. CASPAR
Rt. 1
P.O. Box 379
May, TX 76857
(915) 643-2388

Offers: Peace pipe kits, molds, wooden stems and Indian pot molds.
For Further Information: Send large envelope and 4 stamps.

CRAZY CROW TRADING POST
P.O. Box 874
Pottsboro, TX 75076
(903) 786-9059
Fax: (903) 786-9059

Offers: Beads, bone hairpipe, chevrons, tihe cones, tacks and nails. Also offers knife blades and knife-making supplies, mandallas, rosettes, beaded strips and shawl fringes. Kits including breast plates, chokers, war bonnets, moccasins, bead looms, shawls, bustles, knives, fans, and roaches, all with illustrated instructions. Native American clothing patterns, accessories, hats, war bonnets, porky roaches, sinew, claws, teeth, quills, hides and furs, feathers, broadcloth, German silver work and 18th and 19th century clothing also available.
For Further Information: Catalog, $3.
Discounts: Quantity.

EAGLE FEATHER TRADING POST
168 W. 12th St.
Ogden, UT 84404
(801) 393-3991

Offers: American Indian costume kits, including single feather, beaded pouch, 17 chokers, 4 headdresses, bustles, necklaces, bandoliers, breastplates, bell sets and medicine pouches. Authentic clothing patterns are available for war shirts, frontiersmen's shirts, leather dresses and others. Beads available include bugle, striped pony, wood and large holed beads; faceted glass and plastic, tile loose seed and trade beads. Conchos, tin cones and cowrie shells also available. Stocks scissors and glue, punches, awls, cutters, chisels, buckle blanks, fringes, blankets and books.
For Further Information: Catalog, $3.
Store Location: At above address.
Discounts: Quantity; teachers and institutions; sells wholesale to legitimate businesses.

EARTHWORKS
33 N. Uncompahgre Ave.
Montrose, CO 81401
(970) 240-2111

Offers: Tipis—buffalo hide reinforced, mildew/flame retardant, in a variety of sizes.
For Further Information: Brochure, $1.

GREY OWL INDIAN CRAFT CO., INC.
13205 Merrick Blvd.
P.O. Box 340468
Jamaica, NY 11434
(718) 341-4000

Offers: Over 4,000 Native American and craft items, including costume kits and parts (roaches, headdresses, others), beading and beads (trade, seed, cut beads, crow, pony, brass), bone hairpipes, elk teeth, tin cones, feathers, shawl fringe, leathers (cowhide and others), furs, bones, skins, animal parts, blankets, videos and books.
For Further Information: Catalog, $3.
Store Location: At above address.
Discounts: Quantity; teachers and institutions; sells wholesale to businesses.
Accepts: American Express, Discover, MasterCard, Visa

THE INDIAN STORE
123 S. Beach Blvd.
Anaheim, CA 92804
(714) 828-3050
Fax: (714) 828-5765

Offers: Native American kits, including leather, necklace and jewelry, beads and beading supplies, feathers, books.
For Further Information: Free brochure.

Store Location: At above address.
Accepts: American Express, Discover, MasterCard, Visa

PANTHER PRIMITIVES

P.O. Box 32-55
Normantown, WV 25267
(304) 462-7718

Offers: Tipi poles, lacing pins, instruction books (also ready-made items for store booths), waterproof canvas and cottons by the yard, frontier clothing kits and patterns, bead kits, plus beads, looms and supplies. Stocks bone choker kits, 15 flags (historical), tinware, oak kegs, wood buckets, metal tinder boxes, candle molds, quills, quillwork kits and finished items.
For Further Information: Catalog, $2 (refundable).
Discounts: Sells wholesale to legitimate businesses.
Accepts: Discover, MasterCard, Visa

SWEET MEDICINE

P.O. Box 30128
Phoenix, AZ 85046
(602) 788-3840
Fax: (602) 788-4801

Offers: Feathers, leather, beads, crystals, animal bones gourds; also Pendleton blankets and more.
For Further Information: Call or send $3 for catalog.
Discounts: Sells wholesale to legitimate businesses.

WAKEDA TRADING POST

P.O. Box 19146
Sacramento, CA 95819
(916) 485-9838

Offers: Native American crafts and garment patterns for au- thentic, early American fur hats, shirts, pants, leggings, breechclouts, dresses, capotes, coats and accessories. Costume kits include chokers, war bonnets, quillwork, moccasins, fans, hair roaches, breechclouts. Carries shawls and metallic fringes, trade cloths, wool, calico, blankets, beads (seed, pony, iris, luster, crow, tile, others), bead supplies, looms, mirrors, brass nails, tin cones, buckles, metal spots, bells. Naturals available include sweet grass, ropes, sage, gourds and cedar. Also carries hides, furs including sheep, beaver, coyote, red fox, ermine, plus tails. Carries leathers for garment buckskins, thongs, straps, rawhide, latigo. Porcupine quills and teeth are also available.
For Further Information: Catalog, $2.
Discounts: Quantity; sometimes sells wholesale to legitimate businesses.
Accepts: MasterCard, Visa

WESTERN TRADING POST

P.O. Box 9070
Denver, CO 80209
(303) 423-9446

Offers: Beads (metal, brass, wood, bone, hairpipe, seed, tile, others), beading supplies, looms, cones, feathers, conchos, jewelry findings, bells (sheep, dance, sleigh, sets), buckles, shells, buttons, blanks. Carries animal parts, including buffalo horns, bladders and skulls, claws, teeth, porcupine hair, pheasant skins, ermine, horse tails and leather (latigo, rawhide, buckskin, white deer, others). Dance accessories include chainette fringewool trade cloth. Patterns available for Indian and frontier garments. Kits include beading, feather headdresses and feather bonnets. Books also available.
For Further Information: Catalog, $3.
Discounts: Quantity.
Accepts: Discover, MasterCard, Visa

Jewelry Making and Lapidary

Also see General Craft Supplies, Bead Crafts, Indian and Frontier Crafts, Metalworking, Tools and Equipment and other related categories.

A.A. CLOUET
369 W. Fountain St.
Providence, RI 02903
(401) 272-4100

Offers: Fasteners, ear nuts, clutch backs, clip pads, disks, guards, cushions, jewelers staples, elastic barbs and others.
For Further Information: Send SASE for list.

ACKLEY'S
3230 N. Stone Ave.
Colorado Springs, CO 80907
(719) 635-1153

Offers: Lapidary and silversmithing supplies, rough rock. Jewelry findings include ear wires, beads, chains, mountings.
For Further Information: Catalog, $1 (refundable).

ALETA'S ROCK SHOP
1515 Plainville Ave. NE
Grand Rapids, MI 49505
(616) 363-5394

Offers: Rocks, cutting and tumbling. Lapidary equipment includes machines and tumblers. Carries findings, tools and silversmith supplies.
For Further Information: Catalog, $1.50 (refundable). Free rock list.
Store Location: At above address. Hours: T-Sat, 10-6.

ALPHA FACETING SUPPLY, INC.
1225 Hollis St.
P.O. Box 2133
Bremerton, WA 98310
(360) 377-5629 or (800) 257-4211

Offers: Over 15,000 items for casting, jewelry making, faceting, wax casting and display. Carries equipment for lapidary, beading, faceting and prospecting.
For Further Information: Supply catalogs, $5.
Discounts: Quantity; institutions and professionals; sells wholesale to businesses.
Accepts: American Express, Discover, MasterCard, Visa

APACHE CANYON MINES
P.O. Box 530
Baker, CA 92309

Offers: Gem-grade turquoise, in untreated rough or stones.
For Further Information: Free price lists and information sheets.
Discounts: Sells wholesale.

APL TRADER, INC.
P.O. Box 1900
New York, NY 10185
(718) 454-2954 or (800) 5APLTRA
Fax: (718) 454-8990

Offers: Faceted gemstones—emeralds, rubies, sapphires, amethysts, citrines, peridots, rhodolites, topaz, tourmalines and others. Also offers cabochons, pearls, beads and diamonds.
For Further Information: Price list, $1 or call or fax.
Discounts: Sells wholesale.

ARA IMPORTS
P.O. Box 41054
Brecksville, OH 44141
(216) 838-1372
Fax: (216) 838-1367

Offers: Jewelry findings, including precious and semi-precious beads, plus pearls and corals.
For Further Information: Catalog and price list, $1.

ARE, INC.
Rt. 16
P.O. Box 8
Greensboro Bend, VT 05842
(802) 533-7007
Fax: (802) 533-7008

Offers: Gold, gold-filled, s/s and silver solder findings. Also offers craft metals, including brass, copper, pewter, casting alloys and others. Also offers an extensive line of tools, supplies and equipment for jewelry making, casting and working.
For Further Information: Catalog, $3 (refundable).

ARIZONA GEMS & MINERALS, INC.
22025 N. Black Canyon Hwy.
Phoenix, AZ 85267
(602) 951-0032
Fax: (602) 991-1005

Offers: Beads (Austrian types, metal, plastic, glass, s/s, gold filled, 14K, others), beading and bolo supplies, cabochons, charms, chains, crystals and jewelry findings. Equipment includes grinding wheels, silversmithing, buffing wheels and jewelry making tools. Also offers a line of display cases.
For Further Information: 160-page catalog, $4 (refundable).
Store Location: At above address.
Discounts: Quantity; sells wholesale to legitimate businesses.
Accepts: American Express, Discover, MasterCard, Visa

ARTGEMS EXPORTERS, INC.
P.O. Box 12610
Scottsdale, AZ 85267
(602) 951-0032
Fax: (602) 991-1005

Offers: Gemstone beads, including garnet, amethyst, tourmaline, citrine, moonstone, peridot, lapis, aquamarine, labradorite, opal, crystal, topaz and others. Also offers tumbled chips, beggar beads, points, donuts, spheres and agate items.
For Further Information: Free color catalog.

ART TECH CASTING CO.
P.O. Box 54
Scottsville, NY 14546
(716) 889-9187

Offers: Casting services—gold, sterling and bronze—for one-of-a-kind or production run, from professionals.
For Further Information: Write.

AUSTRALIAN OPAL IMPORTS
P.O. Box 44208
3170 Tillicum Rd.
Victoria, British Columbia V9A 7H7
Canada
(604) 385-1639
Fax: (604) 381-2306

Offers: Australian opals, rough and cut, black and boulders, doublets, triplets, cameos, calibrated, freeform and opal matrix.
For Further Information: Free price list.

B&J ROCK SHOP
14744 Manchester Rd.
Ballwin, MO 63011
(314) 394-4567
Fax: (314) 394-7109

Offers: Faceted gemstones, including assorted amethyst and others. Carries quartz crystals, amethyst crystal clusters, bead stringing supplies, gemstone beads (14K, s/s and others) and big earring mountings. Also carries quartz clock movements and kits.
For Further Information: 50-page catalog, $3 (refundable).
Store Location: At above address.
Discounts: Quantity.

BADALI: JEWELRY AND PROSPECTING SUPPLIES
100 S. Fort Lane
Layton, UT 84041
(801) 546-4086

Offers: Instructional video (VHS)—*Making Gold Nugget Jewelry*, with Paul J. Badali, covers design, tools, crafting items and mounting for the beginner through advanced silversmith or jeweler. Carries gold panning sand with directions, gold samples and jewelry findings (s/s, gold filled). Also offers gold pans, sluices and equipment. Runs gold prospecting classes.
For Further Information: Send large SASE for catalog.
Discounts: Quantity; sells wholesale.

BEADBOX, INC.
10135 E. Via Linda
Scottsdale, AZ 85258
(800) BEADBOX

Offers: Beads from 30 countries, exotics and unusuals, in a line of sizes/shapes, plus beading kits for jewelry, others.
For Further Information: Color catalog, $3.
Accepts: MasterCard, Visa

BEADNIKS
1104 E. 200 S.
Salt Lake City, UT 84102

Offers: Art Deco style beaded earring kits, others.
For Further Information: Details, $1.

BOMBAY BAZAAR
P.O. Box 770727
Lakewood, OH 44107
(216) 521-6548

Offers: Lapidary/jewelry-making supplies, including Crystalite equipment and supplies, Diamond saw blades, Raytech and Covington equipment, Rock Rascal gemmaker, saws and arbor, Graves/Raytech machines (faceting and units). Genie and Titan units, Foredom mini and other power tools and tumblers. Carries hand tools including 18 tweezers, Eastwing line. Rough facet material, synthetics, preforms, cabochons and faceted gemstones are also available.
For Further Information: Catalog, $1.50.

BOURGET BROS.

1636 11th St.
Santa Monica, CA 90404
(800) 828-3024
Fax: (310) 450-2201

Offers: Lapidary/jewelry equipment/tools—full lines to cast, weld, drill, enamel, plate, engrave, others. Carries furnaces, saws, flexible shafts, magnifiers, files, torches, tumblers and metals (s/s, gold and gold-filled, copper in sheets, wires, channels, bezels and fancies). Also carries jewelry findings, wires, threads—full lines. Beads include turquoise, amber, gemstones, cabochons and synthetics. Stocks pearls, metal and s/s coil types, s/s button covers, chains, mounts and books.
For Further Information: Tool/jewelry catalog; lapidary catalog.
Store Location: At above address.
Discounts: Quantity.
Accepts: MasterCard, Visa

COVINGTON ENGINEERING CORP.

P.O. Box 35
Redlands, CA 92373
(714) 793-6636

Offers: Lapidary/glass equipment, including lapidary machines (mills, carvers, combos, drum units, gem shops, grinders, slab saws, laps, sanders, sphere makers, tumblers, others), glass machines (bevelers, carving tools, coolerant systems, drills, engravers, laps, polishers, sanders, saws, smoothers, grinders, others), equipment/supplies (adhesives, beading items, dressers, drill bits, drums, Eastwing and jewelry tools), plus motors, templates and grinding wheels.
For Further Information: Free catalog.
Accepts: Discover, MasterCard, Visa

CRAFT SUPPLIES 4 LESS

13001 Las Vegas Blvd. S.
Las Vegas, NV 89124
(702) 361-3600

Offers: Glass beads from areas worldwide including grab bag assortments (crystal, antique, handmade, mosaic, trade, unusuals). Other beads include metal, plastic, acrylic. Carries jewelry findings, rhinestones, pewter and metal charms, beading supplies, FIMO, Sculpey, tools, adhesives, Friendly Plastic, kits and books.
For Further Information: Catalog, $4 (with filigree sample).
Store Location: At above address.
Accepts: MasterCard, Visa

CROOKED-RIVER

413 Main St.
P.O. Box 129
La Farge, WI 54639
(608) 625-4460

Offers: Watch parts and faces for jewelry making. Unbaked, patterned polymer clay also available.
For Further Information: Send SASE for catalog.
Discounts: Quantity; sells wholesale to legitimate businesses.

DAWN FOR NEW DIRECTIONS

P.O. Box 2034
Simi Valley, CA 93062
(805) 584-2567

Offers: Gemstones, including ruby, sapphire, emerald, tanzanite, amethyst, garnet, peridot, star sapphire, moonstone, topaz, sunstone, tourmaline, others.
For Further Information: Free list.
Accepts: MasterCard, Visa

DENDRITICS, INC.

223 Crescent St.
Waltham, MA 02154
(800) 437-9993

Offers: Pocket-sized professional electronic gem scales ($5'' \times 3'' \times 1''$) to weigh $50.50 \times .01$ karats or $100.00 \times .01$ karats.
For Further Information: Call.

DIAMOND PACIFIC TOOL CORP.

2620 W. Main St.
Barstow, CA 92311
(800) 253-2954
Fax: (619) 255-1077

Offers: Jewelers' tools and supplies, diamond lapidary equipment, Vanguard saw blades, Foredom power tools, Eastwing tools, Rockhound products and others.
For Further Information: Free catalog.
Store Location: At above address.
Discounts: Sells wholesale to legitimate businesses.

DISCOUNT AGATE HOUSE

3401 N. Dodge Blvd.
Tuscon, AZ 85716
(520) 323-0781

Offers: Cutting rocks from areas worldwide, lapidary machinery, accessories, sterling silver and smithing supplies and jewelry findings.
For Further Information: Send for rough rock list.
Store Location: At above address.

Discounts: Sells wholesale.
Accepts: MasterCard, Visa

EARTH ART
127½ St. Paul St.
Burlington, VT 05401
(802) 658-8750 or (800) 656-8750

Offers: Beads, including semiprecious types, glass, crystal, turquoise, bone, chips and others.
For Further Information: Free catalog.

EASTGEM, LTD.
P.O. Box 7454
North Brunswick, NJ 08902
(908) 545-9726

Offers: Cut gemstones—cabachons and faceted, plus custom cutting service and appraisals.
For Further Information: Free price list.
Discounts: Quantity; teachers and institutions.

EBERSOLE LAPIDARY SUPPLY, INC.
11417 W. Highway 54
Wichita, KS 67209
(316) 722-4771

Offers: Lapidary equipment and supplies, plus jewelers' supplies, mountings, cabs, and other gemstones and beads.
For Further Information: 130-page catalog, $5 (refundable).

ELOXITE CORP.
806 10th St., Dept. 40
Wheatland, WY 82201
(307) 322-3050
Fax: (307) 322-3055

Offers: Jewelry mountings—full line of buckles and inserts, bracelets, pendants, bolos, others, plus jewelry making tools and supplies, 5 tumblers, clock parts and movements, display boxes, racks and earring displays. Beads include gemstone, seed, others. Books available.
For Further Information: Catalog, $1.
Store Location: At above address.
Discounts: Quantity; sells wholesale to legitimate businesses.
Accepts: MasterCard, Visa

ENGRAVING ARTS
4200 N. Highway 101
Laytonville, CA 95454
(707) 984-8203

Offers: Branding irons for leather and woodworkers. Jewelry dies for embossing, coining, striking, blanking, trim dies.

For Further Information: Free brochure.
Store Location: At above address. Hours: M-F, 8-5.

DAVID H. FELL & COMPANY, INC.
6009 Bandini Blvd.
City of Commerce, CA 90040
(213) 722-9992 or (800) 822-1996
Fax: (213) 722-6567

Offers: Sheet (all karats, platinum, silver) all gauges, shaped wire—round, half round, triangle, bezel, flat, square all karats, all gauges. 14K tubing, 14K rod stock, discs. Gold, sterling fine silver, platinum, palladium casting grain or pieces, alloys and solders. Variety of karat gold colors. Pattern sheet—photo etched on sterling fine silver, 10K, 14K, and 18K, all gauges. 400 patterns, including gallery sheet and ribbon sheet. Refining services, fast turnaround. Technical services.
For Further Information: Free catalogs; specify Product, Pattern Sheet or Refining Schedule.
Store Location: 550 South Hill St., Suite 550, Los Angeles, CA 90013. Call ahead.
Accepts: MasterCard, Visa

FOB VILLAGE ORIGINALS
7256 Cross Park Dr.
North Charleston, SC 29418
(803) 760-3050

Offers: Brazilian and Uruguayan amethyst, agates, tumbled stones and others.
For Further Information: Free catalog.
Discounts: Quantity.

GABRIEL'S
P.O. Box 222
Unionville, OH 44088
(216) 428-6163

Offers: Cabochons and shapes (including hard-to-find)—teardrops, wedges, triangles, others in a variety of materials. Jewelry-making video rentals and one-of-a-kind stones on approval also available.
For Further Information: Free catalog.
Accepts: American Express, MasterCard, Visa

GEMCO INTERNATIONAL
Howard Bank Building
P.O. Box 833
Fayston, VT 05673
(802) 496-2770
Fax: (802) 496-5619

Offers: Gem facet rough—ruby, tsavorite, emerald, kunzite, hiddenite, aquamarine, tourmaline, sapphire, golden beryl, imperial topaz, rhodolite garnet, Malaya rhodolite, almandite

garnet, amethyst, citrine, gilson emerald opal, facet opal, peridot and melee. Gemstones may also include beryl, spinel, rubellite, Kashan ruby, others.
For Further Information: Free catalog.

THE GEMMARY
P.O. Box 2560
Fallbrook, CA 92088
(619) 728-3321

Offers: Out of print and rare books on gemology, jewelry (history and making), mineralogy and mining.
For Further Information: Catalog, $2.

GEMSTONE EQUIPMENT MANUFACTURING
750 Easy St.
Simi Valley, CA 93065
(805) 527-6990

Offers: Lapidary equipment, including slant cabbing machine, also available as a kit in 4 models, 5 vibratory tumblers, bench rollaway sand blasters, saws (4″, 6″ and 10″ trim, 8″ dynamotrim and drop saw) and saw blades. Also carries diamond products—6 carving points, blades, discs, points, dressers, files, 9 compounds, plus stone and metal finishing kits, router bevelers, sculpture router, super buffer and plastic gold pans.
For Further Information: Write or call.

GLOBE UNION INTERNATIONAL, INC.
1237 American Pkwy.
Richardson, TX 75081
(214) 669-8181, (800) 765-5339
Fax: (214) 669-8639

Offers: Gemstone beads and chips, including rose quartz, aventurine, jaspers, unakite, hematite, black quartz, onyx, dyed fossil, agate, tiger eye, carnelian, malachite, lapis, amethyst, others, plus color-treated quartz.
For Further Information: Free catalog.

A. GOODMAN
949 Beaumont Ave.
P.O. Box 667
Beaumont, CA 92223
(800) 382-3237

Offers: Lapidary instruction videos covering lost wax casting, meet-point faceting carving techniques, crystal and mineral energy, jewelry design, handcrafting, faceting, forming, plating, sphere making, emerald cutting, soldering, faceting, plus videos on opal, bead stringing, gemstone carving and lapidary basics.
For Further Information: Send SASE for list.
Discounts: Sells wholesale to legitimate businesses.
Accepts: MasterCard, Visa

GRAVES, CO.
1800 N. Andrews Ave.
Pompano Beach, FL 33069
(954) 960-0300
Fax: (954) 960-0301

Offers: Gemstone cutting and polishing equipment, lapidary equipment, including Cab-Mate (grinds, polishes, sands, rock vise, electric preformer), saws, cabochon preforms, metal polisher, cabaret unit, crowner, spool polisher, 6-wheeler unit, faceting preforms and faceting machine.
For Further Information: Write for free catalog and nearest dealer.

GRIEGER'S
P.O. Box 93070
Pasadena, CA 91109
(800) 423-4181
Fax: (818) 577-4751

Offers: Jewelry-making/lapidary supplies, equipment, tools and accessories. Jewelry-making supplies include kits, display items (cases, boxes, trays, stands), and jewelry findings (in 14K, s/s, filled, others)—a full line—plus gemstone beads, baroque chip necklaces, chains, cabochons, stones (large variety—diamonds, pearls). Carries beading supplies and accessories. Also carries a full line of hand and power tools for lapidary, jewelry making, silversmithing and lost wax casting. Scales, casting metals, s/s sheet and wires, gold-filled and 14K wires, gold sheet, clock parts and books are available.
For Further Information: Free catalog.
Discounts: Quantity; sells wholesale to legitimate businesses.
Accepts: American Express, Discover, MasterCard, Visa

GRYPHON CORP.
12417 Foothill Blvd.
Sylmar, CA 91342
(818) 890-7770

Offers: Diamond band saw (cuts glass, tile, minerals) and abrasive miter saw for cutting most metal up to ¾″ crossection. Manufacturer.
For Further Information: Free catalog.

T.B. HAGSTOZ & SON, INC.
709 Sansom St.
Philadelphia, PA 19106
(800) 922-1006

Offers: Metals: Gold, silver, gold filled, platinum, pewter, copper, bronze, brass, nickel silver. Carries jewelry tools and equipment, waxes, accessories. Brands available include GFC, Vigor, Dremel, Foredom, Kerr, Af USA. Findings: 14K, sterling, gold-filled, base metals. Solders: Gold, silver, plati-

num, soft. Wire-wrapping and bead-stringing supplies are also available.
For Further Information: Catalog, $5 (refundable).
Accepts: MasterCard, Visa

HEAVEN & EARTH
R.R. 1, Box 25
Marshfield, VT 05658
(800) 348-5155

Offers: Metaphysical gems and minerals, including moldavite, tanzanite, phenacite, sugilite, larimar, charoite, iolite, garnet, amethyst, opal and many others.
For Further Information: Call or write for free catalog and periodic newsletter.

HONG KONG LAPIDARIES, INC.
2801 N. University Dr.
Coral Spring, FL 33065
(305) 755-8777
Fax: (954) 755-8780

Offers: Semi-precious stone beads in 100 colors and 100 or more different sizes and shapes.
For Further Information: Catalog, $3 (refundable).
Discounts: Quantity.

HOPE-FRANKLIN, INC.
1201 Iron Springs Rd., #3-4
Prescott, AZ 86301
(602) 778-2739

Offers: Jewelry mountings for all cuts of stones. Jewelry findings in 14K white and yellow gold. 14K gold-filled, sterling silver and plated base metal.
For Further Information: Catalog, $2 (includes $3 coupon for first order).
Store Location: At above address.
Discounts: Quantity; sells wholesale to legitimate businesses; large order discounts.
Accepts: American Express, Discover, MasterCard, Visa

HOUSE OF ONYX
120 Main St.
Greenville, KY 42345
(800) 844-3100
Fax: (502) 338-9605

Offers: Genuine gemstones, beads, cut gems—may include white and blue sapphire, blue topaz, amethyst, emerald, aquamarine, garnet and others. Also has solid gold and some supplies.
For Further Information: Free monthly catalog.
Discounts: 15 percent discount on large orders.
Accepts: MasterCard, Visa (U.S. zip codes only)

HUBERS
20012 Enadia Way
Canoga Park, CA 91306
(800) 424-8237

Offers: Jewelry findings in 24K, gold-filled and sterling; beads, clasps, ear wires, chains, wire, and snap-in gem mounts in gold-filled and sterling.
For Further Information: Send SASE for list.

JAY'S OF TUCSON
6637 S. 12th Ave.
Tucson, AZ 85706
(520) 294-3397 or (800) 736-6381
Fax: (520) 294-3397

Offers: Beads and bead stringing supplies, including bolo tie parts, findings, Native American products, others.

ESTHER KENNEDY, F.G.A.
P.O. Box 220014
Charlotte, NC 28222

Offers: Gemstones, amethyst, to zircon. Also offers jewelry findings in 14K, sterling, gold filled earrings, pendants and clasps.
For Further Information: Send SASE for prices.
Discounts: Sells wholesale.

KINGSLEY NORTH, INC.
910 Brown St.
P.O. Box 216
Norway, MI 49870
(906) 563-9228 or (800) 338-9280
Fax: (906) 563-7143

Offers: Lapidary tools, equipment and supplies: Diamond tools, saws, tumblers, soldering torches, gauges, cutters, gravers, pliers, screwdrivers, gripper and clamp, plus third hand, pick-hammer, jewelry waxer kit, machine super kit, Flex shaft equipment, electroplating items and rolling mills. Gemstones include jaspers, quartz, agate, hematite, obsidian, others. Jewelry findings available include necklaces, earrings, ring and pendant mountings, bolos, chains and others.
For Further Information: Free catalog.
Store Location: At above address. Hours: M-F, 8-5. Sat, 9-12.
Discounts: 10-20 percent below list price.
Accepts: Discover, MasterCard, Visa

KNIGHT'S
P.O. Box 411
Waitsfield, VT 05673
(802) 496-3707

Offers: Gem roughs—emerald, tourmaline, black star sapphire, jade, star garnets, amethyst, opal, topaz, cat's eye, tur-

quoise, snowflake jade, smoky quartz, India star ruby, moonstone, chrysoprase, lapis lazuli, peridot.
For Further Information: Free price list.
Discounts: Sells wholesale.

KRONA INTERNATIONAL
P.O. Box 9968
Colorado Springs, CO 80932
(719) 597-8779
Fax: (802) 496-5619

Offers: Faceted gemstones—emerald (Brazilian, Colombian), amethyst, andalusite, aquamarine, citrine, enstatite, helidor, hiddenite, iolite, kunzite, moonstone, morganite, rubelite, tsavorite, and many rare, unique types.
For Further Information: Free lists.

LANEY CO.
6449 S. 209 E. Ave.
Broken Arrow, OK 74014
(918) 355-1955

Offers: Gold metal letter cutouts (computer/laser) in Old Timer and trophy styles. Wire available round and half, square, dome, rectangle, triangle, fancy and channel. Metal sheets, solders, fluxes, nickel pickle, leaves, bezel cups, ring shanks, beads, bolos, buckle backs and squash blossoms also available.
For Further Information: Free catalog.
Discounts: Quantity; teachers and institutions; sells wholesale to legitimate businesses.

LAPCRAFT, INC., U.S.A.
195 W. Olentangy St.
Powell, OH 43065
(614) 764-8993

Offers: Diamond tools—pre-forming/diamond grinding wheels, drilling/diamond drills, core drills, faceting/diamond discs, carving/diamond points, polishing/diamond powders.
For Further Information: Free catalog.

LAPIDABRADE, INC.
8 E. Eagle Rd.
Havertown, PA 55408
(215) 789-4022
Fax: (612) 871-1178

Offers: Full range of jewelry findings and tools, lapidary equipment, tools and supplies.
For Further Information: Findings Catalog, $4; Jewelry Makers Tool Catalog, $2; Lapidary Equipment & Supply Catalog, $2. (All catalogs refundable.) Bonus coupons also available.
Discounts: Sells wholesale.

LJ BOOK & VIDEO SELLERS
60 Chestnut Ave., Suite 201
Devon, PA 19333

Offers: Instructional videos on gemstone carving, glass bead making, beading, wire-craft for beginners and advanced, design, jewelry finishing, soldering, metalsmithing and opal cutting. New titles monthly.
For Further Information: Send SASE for list.

LORTONE, INC.
2856 NW Market St.
Seattle, WA 98107
(206) 789-3100

Offers: Rotary tumblers in 13 models, 1½ to 40 lb. capacity, plus other lapidary equipment.
For Further Information: Send SASE for catalog.

MAXANT INDUSTRIES
P.O. Box 454, Dept. CDT
Ayer, MA 01432
(508) 772-0576

Offers: Lapidary equipment and supplies—saws (4″ to 16″), grinders, sanders, polishers, automatic cabachon maker, others.
For Further Information: Catalog, $1.

METALLIFEROUS
34 W. 46th St.
New York, NY 10036
(212) 944-0909
Fax: (212) 944-0644

Offers: Metals—titanium, bronze, fine silver, brass, copper, nickel silver, s/s, niobium, pewter, aluminum—sheet, wire, circles, rod, tube, stampings, machined parts, hoops, findings, solders, casting alloys. Carries enameling shapes and supplies, plus tools.
For Further Information: Catalog, $5 (refundable).
Store Location: At above address. Hours: M-F, 8:30-6. Sat, 10-3.

MINNESOTA LAPIDARY SUPPLY CORP.
2825 Dupont Ave. S.
Minneapolis, MN 55408
(612) 872-7211
Fax: (612) 871-1178

Offers: Lapidary equipment—rock cutting and polishing: Diamond saw blades, sanding belts and grinding wheels, diamond wheels and belts. Diamond products, tumbling grit.
For Further Information: Free catalog. Bonus coupons.
Discounts: Institutions; sells wholesale to legitimate businesses.

MOUNTAIN-MARK TRADING

268 SW 31st St.
Fort Lauderdale, FL 33315
(954) 525-6310 or (800) 346-3691
Fax: (954) 525-6311

Offers: Blue pectolite (Caribbean) rough, slabs, cabochons, carvings.
For Further Information: Free catalog, price list.

NATURE'S TREASURES

1163 E. Ogden Ave., Suite 705-324
Naperville, IL 60563

Offers: Line of Baltic amber pieces with fossils and insect inclusions from Russia and Lithuania.
For Further Information: Call or send SASE with inquiry.
Discounts: Sells wholesale.

NCE ENTERPRISES

107 W. Van Buren, Suite 207
Chicago, IL 60605
(312) 663-9738
Fax: (312) 663-9446

Offers: Gemstone: Facet and cabbing rough from areas worldwide, by piece or kilo.
For Further Information: Send SASE for price list.
Accepts: MasterCard, Visa

NGRAVER CO.

67 Wawecus Hill Rd. J.
Bozrah, CT 06334
(203) 848-8031

Offers: Hand-engraving, flexible shaft machines, gravers and liners, rotary handpieces, engravers blocks, chasing hammers, engravers pencils, electric etchers, graver sharpeners, sharpening stones, plus practice mediums, magnifiers, fixtures, punches, Florentine tools, others.
For Further Information: Catalog, $1 (refundable).

O'BRIEN MANUFACTURING

2081 Knowles Rd.
Medford, OR 97501

Offers: Wood and glass jewelry display and wall cases with velvet covered bottoms in a range of sizes.
For Further Information: Free brochure.

OPITMAGEM

P.O. Box 1421
San Luis Obispo, CA 93406
(800) 543-5563

Offers: Faceted and cabochon gemstones, including sapphire (colors), ruby, garnet, amethyst, topaz, tanzanite, tsavorite, aquamarine, citrine, peridot, opal, star sapphire. Also offers synthetic stones.
For Further Information: Write for list.
Accepts: American Express, MasterCard, Visa

OPTIONAL EXTRAS

P.O. Box 1421
Burlington, VT 05402
(802) 658-0013
Fax: (802) 864-5030

Offers: Jewelry supplies: Beads (glass, crystal, ceramic, metal, bugles, seed, others). Carries findings, cords, adhesives, starter kits and books.
For Further Information: Catalog, $2.

ORNAMENTAL RESOURCES, INC.

P.O. Box 3010
Idaho Springs, CO 80452
(303) 279-2102

Offers: Beads—full line of types, styles, sizes and shapes. Carries brass stampings, charms, plus jewelry findings, parts, tools and supplies, rhinestones and books.
For Further Information: Catalog, $25 (with year's supplements/discounts).

PARSER MINERALS CORP.

P.O. Box 1094
Danbury, CT 06813
(203) 744-6868

Offers: Rare and unusual gemstone cutting materials (rough): From Brazil—watermelon tourmaline, andalusite, jacobina amethyst, rutilated quartz, water clear topaz, rose quartz crystal, blue (indicolite) tourmaline. Others include rhodochosite (Argentina), wine red garnet (India), Labradorite moonstone and apatite (Madagascar), iolite (Tanzania). Diamonds.
For Further Information: Send SASE for list.

PDI, INC.

4500 E. Speedway Blvd. #50
Tucson, AZ 85712
(800) 238-2307
Fax: (520) 881-2862

Offers: "The Little Dipper" dip electroplating combination unit and Maestro electroplating professional pen sets with solutions, tools, timer, instructions.
For Further Information: Call.

THE PERUVIAN BEAD CO.

1601 Callens Rd.
Ventura, CA 93003
(805) 642-0952

Offers: Pre-Colombian collection of beads—contemporary

ethnic types in a variety of sizes/styles in s/s and brass, designed/manufactured in U.S.
For Further Information: Send for catalog.

PIONEER GEM CORP.
P.O. Box 1513
Auburn, WA 98071
(206) 833-2760

Offers: Cabachons: Opals, black opal, malachite, paua shell, jade, lapis, sapphires, others. Carries bulk bags mixed, plus faceted gemstones: Citrine, amethyst, emerald, lapis, opal, ruby, sapphires, blue topaz, others.
For Further Information: Catalog/price list, $5 (6 times yearly).
Discounts: Quantity; teachers and institutions; sells wholesale to legitimate businesses; large order discounts.

PUEBLO TRADING
P.O. Box 1115
Zuni, NM 87327
(505) 782-5555

Offers: Tibetan turquoise cabochons (calibrated and free form), polished nuggets (drilled, undrilled, by pound), beads (rondels, rounds), lapidary supplies.
For Further Information: Send SASE for list.
Store Location: 1173 Highway 53, Zuni, NM. Hours: Daily, 9-6.

RAINBOW OPALS & GEMS
138 E. Grand River Ave.
Williamston, MI 48895
(517) 655-5815
Fax: (517) 655-4678

Offers: Gemstones, including opals in fiery rough, colored and doublets and others. Custom opal cutting services, jewelry repair and stone setting.
For Further Information: Free price list.

REACTIVE METALS STUDIO, INC.
P.O. Box 890
Clarkdale, AZ 86324
(520) 634-3434
Fax: (520) 634-6734

Offers: Titanium, shakudo, shibuichi, and mokume-gane sheet and wire. Also offers findings, fusion findings, beads, miniature nuts and bolts and Sparkie welders.
For Further Information: Free catalog.
Discounts: Quantity.

RIVER GEMS AND FINDINGS
6901 Washington St. NE
Albuquerque, NM 87109
(505) 345-8511

Offers: Lines of over 2,500 beads, over 5,000 gemstones,

over 7,500 jewelry findings and parts in a variety of sizes, styles and types for jewelry making, fashions, other.
For Further Information: Catalog, $10.

ROUSSELS
107-100 Dow
Arlington, MA 02174

Offers: Jewelry supplies: Neckchains, variety of ear wires, others, plus polybags.
For Further Information: Wholesale catalog, 50¢.

ROYAL FINDINGS, INC.
301 W. Main St.
P.O. Box 92
Chartley, MA 02712
(800) 343-3343
Fax: (800) 458-7423

Offers: Jewelry findings: Complete line of precious metal findings for Sparkie Midget Welder. Friction ear nuts, ball earrings, diamond settings, pendants, beads (rondels, corrugated), Karat Katch, lobster claws, bead clasps, Omega ear clips including Easy Loc and others.
For Further Information: Write or call for complete catalog.

SHIPWRECK BEADS
2727 Westmoor Ct. SW
Olympia, WA 98502
(360) 754-2323

Offers: Beads: Czech glass, gemstone, metallics, crystal, seed, wood, bone, buffalo horn, plastic, antique, trade and others, plus beading supplies and tools, jewelry findings and books.
For Further Information: Catalog, $4.
Store Location: At above address.
Discounts: Quantity; sells wholesale to legitimate businesses and professionals.
Accepts: MasterCard, Visa

SILVER ARMADILLO
40 Westgate Pkwy.
Asheville, NC 28806

Offers: Line of jewelry parts, beads, lapidary and rockhound equipment, minerals, others.
For Further Information: Catalog, $5 (refundable).
Store Location: At above address.

SMITH EQUIPMENT
Watertown, SD 57201
(800) 328-3363

Offers: The Little Torch welding torch (works with any fuel gas), with temperatures to 6,300 degrees (solders, melts,

welds, brazes), lightweight hand-held model, with flexible hose.
For Further Information: Call for free brochure.

SOUTHWEST AMERICA
1506-C Wyoming Blvd. NE
Albuquerque, NM 87112
(505) 299-1856
Fax: (505) 299-1856

Offers: Beads: Ornamental and ethnic (old, new) seed, bugles (including antique) in a variety of colors.
For Further Information: Brochure, $1.50.
Store Location: At above address. Hours: M-F, 10-5. Sat, 10-4.

SPARKLING CITY GEMS
P.O. Box 905-CSS
Kingsville, TX 78364
(512) 296-3958

Offers: Precious and semi-precious gems, minerals and crystals, from alexandrite to zircon.
For Further Information: 40-page gem list, $3.
Accepts: MasterCard, Visa

STARR GEMS, INC.
220 West Drachman St.
Tuscon, AZ 85705
(520) 882-8750 or (800) 882-8750
Fax: (520) 882-7947

Offers: Jewelry findings and chains in silver and 14K gold, plus jewelery supplies, tools. Carries sterling concha stampings, E-Z Mount settings, beads and how-to books.
For Further Information: Catalog, $3.50 (refundable).

STONE AGE INDUSTRIES, INC.
P.O. Box 383
Powell, WY 82435
(307) 754-4681 or (800) 571-4681

Offers: Full line of Covington lapidary equipment, motors, commercial equipment, plus Eastwing tools, Foredom flexible shafts and brand tumblers. Carries gemstone rough and slaps from India, Brazil, Mexico, Africa, U.S. and petrified palmwood, picture rock and others.
For Further Information: Catalog, $1.50.
Discounts: Quantity; sells wholesale to legitimate businesses.
Accepts: MasterCard, Visa

TIMBERLINE
P.O. Box 367
Carlsbad, CA 92008
(619) 438-5370
Fax: (619) 438-1828

Offers: Wax patterns and casting in over 2,500 styles, includ-

ing rings, charms, pendants, overlays, findings.
For Further Information: Catalog, $3.

TRIPP'S MFG.
1406 Frontage Rd.
P.O. Box 1369
Socorro, NM 87801
(800) 545-7962
Fax: (505) 835-2848

Offers: Jewelry-making supplies: Easy mounts in 14K gold and sterling including pendants, ladies' and men's rings in plain and fancy shapes, plus rings and other mountings. Line of chains: Gold filled, 14K, s/s and findings. Carries sterling castings, synthetic stones, natural faceted gemstones, including peridot, garnet, ruby, others.
For Further Information: Free catalog.
Discounts: Quantity.
Accepts: American Express, MasterCard, Visa

TSI
101 Nickerson St.
P.O. Box 9266
Seattle, WA 98109
(206) 282-3040, (800) 426-9984
Fax: (206) 281-8701

Offers: Full line of lapidary and jewelry-making tools and findings, equipment, supplies, plus beads and beading supplies.
For Further Information: Free catalog.
Store Location: At above address. Hours: M-Sat, 9-5:30.
Discounts: Quantity; teachers, institutions and professionals; sells wholesale to businesses.

UNITED STATES PEARL CO., INC.
4805 Old Hickory Blvd.
Hermitage, TN 37076
(615) 391-0920 or (800) 248-3064

Offers: Freshwater pearls: American, Chinese, Japanese, also Japanese cultured pearls, mother-of-pearl.
For Further Information: Send SASE for list.

UNIVERSAL WIRECRAFT CO.
P.O. Box 20206
Bradenton, FL 34203
(914) 745-1219

Offers: Solderless wirecraft supplies: 14K gold and sterling silver wire, gold-filled wire (in square, round and half round; gauges 24 to 16 on some), by 1 oz. and 3 oz. coil. Carries gold plate and silver-filled square and round wires, by 3 oz. coils and up. Wirecraft tools: Round, flat and chain-nose pliers, side cutters, pin vise, iron ring mandrel. Carries a variety of cabochons, including onyx, goldstone, hematite, amethyst, agates, tigereye, others. Also carries gemstone beads, books.

For Further Information: Send large SASE for price list.
Discounts: Quantity, sells wholesale.

VIBRA-TEK COMPANY
1844 Arroya Rd.
Colorado Springs, CO 80906

Offers: Vibra-Tek rock polishers in regular or magnum units in 3 and 8 lb. capacities.
For Further Information: Send SASE.

WATCH PARTS
1001 N.E. 36th St. #5E
Pompano Beach, FL 33064

Offers: Line of watch parts, including bulk miscellaneous collections, dials in matched pairs, all sizes of gears and others.
For Further Information: Send SASE for list.

Kite Making

Also see Fabrics and Trims, Outdoors and Outerwear and other related categories.

BFK
2500 E. Imperial Hwy., 122B
Brea, CA 92621
(714) 529-6589
(714) 529-6152

Offers: Over 50 kite models (3 feet to 21 feet), including kits by Action, Flexifoil, Jordan Air, Skyward, Crystal, Highflyers, Rainbow, Advantage, AFC, Renegade, Gayla Wind, Peter Powell, Revolution, Wolfe, Force 10, Shanti, Moran Precision, others
For Further Information: Free catalog.

BOISE KITES
1122 E. Hays St.
Boise, ID 83712
(208) 344-2844

Offers: Variety of kite kits.
For Further Information: Call or write for information.

FLYING THINGS
130 SE Highway 101
Lincoln City, OR 97367
(503) 996-6313

Offers: Kite accessories and kits; major brands.
For Further Information: Write for catalog.
Discounts: Factory direct prices.

GOODWIN'S KITES
3333 Wallingford Ave. N.
Seattle, WA 98103
(206) 632-6151

Offers: *Goodwin's Guide to Kitemaking*, supplies, including supplies and information for kite or banner making or flying.
For Further Information: Contact a dealer or call.
Discounts: Sells wholesale.

GREAT WINDS KITE CO.
402 Occidental Ave. S.
Seattle, WA 98104
(206) 624-6886

Offers: Kite kits, including those for beginners and advanced

flyers. Materials include Tyvek and others. Carries Frustrationless Flyer to be colored, made of waterproof plastic paper, requires minimal assembly. Custom printing of kites.
For Further Information: Send SASE.

GRIZZLY PEAK KITEWORKS
1305 Alvarado Rd.
Berkeley, CA 94705
(510) 644-2981

Offers: Kite-making materials—full line including known brands; carries finished kites.
For Further Information: Free catalog.
Accepts: MasterCard, Visa

HANG-EM HIGH FABRICS
1420 Yale Ave.
Richmond, VA 23224
(804) 233-6155

Offers: Kite kits, fabrics/materials: Ripstop nylon, polyester and dacron. Carries adhesives, fiberglass and carbon spars, poles, webbing, dihedrals, line, fiberglass and aluminum couplings, caps, swivels, tapes, spools, eyelet tools and others.
For Further Information: Free catalog.
See Also: Outdoors and Outerwear

HIGH FLY KITE COMPANY
P.O. Box 2146
Haddonfield, NJ 08033
(609) 429-6260

Offers: Kites and kite kits—over 75 fabric styles, 26 stunt kites in a variety of sizes and color combinations. Supplies include over 10 types of reels and handles, 100-plus building items, and over 10 colors/types of ripstop material.
For Further Information: Free catalog.

INTO THE WIND
1408 Pearl St.
Boulder, CO 80302
(800) 541-0314
Fax: (303) 449-7315

Offers: Kite kits: Over 56 sport and other kites. Carries kite-making supplies and tools, packs, wind meters, lighting systems, plus a full range of line, accessories and spare parts for sport (and other) kites.
For Further Information: Free catalog.

JACKITE, INC.

2868 West Landing Rd.
Virginia Beach, VA 23456
(804) 426-5359
Fax: (804) 426-7190

Offers: Jackite kite kits, which depict a bird (osprey or eagle) in flight; beating wings are made of Tyvek, poles are fiberglass or bamboo.
For Further Information: Write.

KALABASH KITES

(800) 576-5462

Offers: Wide variety of kite materials and accessories for 1-, 2-, 4-line and power types.
For Further Information: Call for free color catalog with kite rating chart.

KITE SAILS

3555 Jubilant Place
Colorado Springs, CO 80917
Phone: (719) 596-2332

Offers: Instructional video, "Stunt Kite Basics: Build Your Own Stunt Kite," a guide through the construction of an 8' stunt kite, including materials list and pattern layout.
For Further Information: Send SASE.

KITE STUDIO

5555 Hamilton Blvd.
Wescosville, PA 18106
(215) 395-3560 or (800) KITE-991

Offers: Line of kitemaking and flying books, including *The Complete Rokkaku Kite Chronicles & Training Manual* (reprinted material from *Kitelines* magazine), and plans and drawings for the 6 foot Sanjo Rokkaku kite, and more.

For Further Information: Catalog, $2.
Store Location: At above address.

KITELINES

P.O. Box 466
Randallstown, MD 21133
(410) 922-1212

Offers: Reprints of articles important for kite crafting: (1) "Mastering Nylon," by G. William Tyrrell, Jr. (fabric types, tools, hot/cold cutting, seams, hems, edging, design transferring and coloring; source list, $1 ppd.); (2) "New American Tradition: Kite Festivals!" by Valerie Govig (guidance in festival organizing, beginning to end; includes "Figure Kiting," by Red Braswell, $3 ppd.).
For Further Information: Send SASE for book list.

THE UNIQUE PLACE/WORLD OF KITES

525 S. Washington Ave.
Royal Oak, MI 48067
(810) 398-5900

Offers: Kite accessories (for Oriental, sport, custom, fine art, stunters, fighters), plus lines, reels. Over 250 kites.
For Further Information: Write.

WIND UNDER YOUR WINGS

11046 W. Derby Ave.
Wauwatosa, WI 53225
(414) 461-3444

Offers: Stunt kite kits and spare parts including those for Shadow and Team Spirit models; includes carbon graphite and ripstop nylon sails.
For Further Information: Write for brochure; send SASE for list.
Accepts: MasterCard, Visa

Leather Crafts

Also see General Craft Supplies, Indian and Frontier Crafts, Fabrics and Trims and other related categories.

BERMAN LEATHERCRAFT
25 Melcher St., Dept. CSS
Boston, MA 02210
(617) 426-0870

Offers: Leathers: Pigskin, sheepskin, cowhide suede splits, deerskin, elk, antelope, rabbit, garment cowhide, bat leathers—by skins. Carries latigo, crepe, English kip, wallet leathers, calfskin in assortments. Also carries belt blanks, a full line of buckles, leather kits and garment leathers in smooth, sueded, unusuals, including cowhide, calfskin, others. Tools: Knives, edgers, gauges and shears, cutters, anvils, strippers, plus stamping/sewing tools. Carver kits, finishes, hardware, accessories and books also available.
For Further Information: Catalog, $3 (refundable).
Discounts: Large order discounts.

C.S. OSBORNE & CO.
146 Jersey St.
Harrison, NJ 07029
(201) 484-3621

Offers: Leather crafting tools: Snap setters (snaps), edgers, pliers, hot glue guns, shoe and other hammers, punches, rawhide hammers and mallets, punches, scratch compasses, nippers, creasers, gauges, gasket cutters, splitting machines, knives, shears, pincers, grommet dies (and grommets), hole cutters, awl hafts and awls, modeler tools, chisels, eyelet setters, space markers, embossing wheel carriages, needles. Carries upholstery repair kits, sail and palm thimbles and others. Manufacturer.
For Further Information: Write for free catalog and name of nearest dealer.

CAMPBELL BOSWORTH MACHINERY CO.
720 N. Flagler Dr.
Fort Lauderdale, FL 33304
(305) 463-7910 or (800) 327-9420

Offers: Leather machines and hand tools for splitting, plus airbrushes and compressors, overlocks, embossers, new/used and reconditioned machinery, heavy-duty sewing machines, hot stamping and cut-out units, hand/kick presses. Line of hand tools includes punches, shears, measurers, cutters, modeling and edging tools, awls, others, plus jewels, rivets and snap setters.
For Further Information: Free catalog.

FEIBING COMPANY, INC.
516 S. 2nd St.
Milwaukee, WI 53204
(414) 271-5011 or (800) 558-1033

Offers: Leather dyes: 27 colors (mixable/range of shades). Also carries paints and Rosolene finish. Manufacturer.
For Further Information: Send SASE.

HORWEEN LEATHER CO.
2015 N. Elston Ave.
Chicago, IL 60614
(312) 772-2026

Offers: Leathers: Latigo, Chromexcel, waxed flesh, horse fronts, side leathers and shell cordovan.
For Further Information: Write for catalog/swatches.

LAVINA INTERIORS
170 Boston Post Rd.
Madison, CT 06443
Phone: (203) 245-0885

Offers: Gilt edged handcrafted English leather in 5 colors, for desk, tabletop or similar use.
For Further Information: Color brochure, $3.

THE LEATHER FACTORY, INC.
P.O. Box 50429
Fort Worth, TX 76105
(817) 496-4874

Offers: Full line of leathers for seating, harness, tooling and lining, plus garment leathers. Specialty leathers include remnant packs, exotics, upholstery, moccasin chap sides and others. Carries belt/strap embossing machines/design rolls, hand-sewing supplies and tools including full line of punches, hammers, stamps and strippers, cutters (also sold in sets). Dyes, stains, finishes, adhesives, buckles, accessories and kits, starter sets, moccasins and books are also available.
For Further Information: Catalog, $3.
Store Location: Over 20 warehouses nationwide.
Discounts: Teachers and institutions; sells wholesale to businesses.

LEATHER UNLIMITED

7155 Highway B., Dept. CSS96
Belgium, WI 53004
(414) 994-9464
Fax: (414) 994-4099

Offers: Wide array of leather kits. Leather includes splits, oak, deerskin, sheepskin, hair-on hides, cycle leather and chamois. Tanning kits, leather pieces and belts also available. Also offers findings, including buckles, conchos, snaps, others. Zippers, thread, beads, dyes, books and finished items available.
For Further Information: 64-page catalog, $2 (refundable).
Discounts: Quantity discounts; sells wholesale to businesses.
Accepts: MasterCard, Visa

M. SIEGEL CO., INC.

120 Pond St.
Ashland, MA 01721
(508) 881-5200

Offers: Leathers: Cowhide vesting, garment, luxury garment (deer, suedes, lambskin, others), plus bag, belt, wallet, tooling, sandal (buffalo, calf, kip, horse and pigskin). Specialty leathers include chrome moccasin sides, shearling, plus saddlery and briefcase leathers. Carries close-out lots (inquire), full line of buckles in brass, nickel/brass and other metals, plus bag closures/fasteners, and a full line of tools and supplies.
For Further Information: Send SASE.
Store Location: At above address.
Discounts: Quantity.

MID-CONTINENT LEATHER SALES CO.

1539 S. Yale Place
Tulsa, OK 74136
(800) 926-2061

Offers: Leathers: Saddle (skirting, latigo, others), rawhide, tooling (sides, strap sides, shoulders, others), plus chap and garment leathers (sides, splits, deerskin), lacing and stirrup leather. Carries conchos, snaps, grommets, inserting dies, buckles, rings, rigging plates, fasteners and zippers. Threads available include nylon, waxed linen, Nytex. Also offers complete line of C.S. Osborne tools. Conditioners and finishes also available.
For Further Information: Free catalog.

PILGRIM SHOE & SEWING MACHINE CO.

21 Nightingale Ave.
Quincy, MA 02169
(800) 343-2202
Fax: (617) 773-9012

Offers: New, used and rebuilt shoe and leather machines, sewing machines, eyelet setters, patchers, clickers, skivers, splitters, cementers, trimmers, 5-in-1 bench cutters, others, plus needles and awls for all machines. Machine parts: Singer, U.S.M., Landis, American, Fortuna, Puritan, Consew, Union Special, Adler, Autosoler, Geneva, Jupiter, United Shoe Machine, Besser, D.N. Machines, Pfaff, Juki and others, plus obsolete and hard-to-find parts.
For Further Information: Free parts catalog or send SASE with inquiry.

POCAHONTAS LEATHER

P.O. Box 253
Garrettsville, OH 44231
(330) 527-5277

Offers: Deer and elk skins (lots by the foot and up), tannery deep-Scotchgarded for water and soil resistance and pre-stretched for honest, useable footage.
For Further Information: Send SASE for price list.

S-T LEATHER CO.

P.O. Box 78188
St. Louis, MO 63178
(314) 241-6009
Fax: (314) 241-8428

Offers: Leathers: Specialty types, including calf, upholstery and suede. Carries a line of garment leathers and furs, suede and scraps. Kits/patterns include moccasins, accessories, bags. Carries snaps, grommets, rivets, laces, dyes, acrylics, finishes, and a line of hand tools including a variety of punches and chisels: Midas tools, modelers and sets. Buckles and books also available.
For Further Information: Write or call for catalog.
Discounts: Quantity.

SAV-MOR LEATHER & SUPPLY

1626 S. Wall St.
Los Angeles, CA 90015
(213) 749-3468

Offers: Leathers: Sandal, scrap, garment types, belt blanks (odd lots), leathers. Also carries buckles, wallet and bag kits, tools and Fiebing dyes.
For Further Information: Catalog, $2.
Discounts: Sells wholesale.

SOLMON BROTHERS

12331 Kelly Rd.
Detroit, MI 48224
(313) 571-9466

Offers: Industrial sewing machines (for leather, other); buys, sells, trades, repairs. Carries machine parts. Attachments made.
For Further Information: Send SASE.

TANDY LEATHER CO.

P.O. Box 791, Dept. TCS96SB
Fort Worth, TX 76101

Offers: Kits for handbags, fringed bag, dream catchers, Native American style items, wood and leather bootjack and others. Complete selection of leathers, including tooling, garment and exotics like pigskin, deerskin, cowhides (smooth and suede), sheepskin, embossed belt blanks, buckles, bolo tie slides, lace, beads, jewelry findings, accessories, pre-cut fringe, and synthetic horsehair. Also offers leatherworking tools, dyes, finishes, group project packs, patterns and books.
For Further Information: Catalog, $3.
Discounts: Quantity on regularly stocked items, wholesale to qualified buyers.

VETERAN LEATHER CO.

204 25th St.
Brooklyn, NY 11232
(718) 768-0300

Offers: Leathers: Grained cowhide, splits, skivers, chrome and kip sides, English morocco, sueded cowhide splits, others; sells remnants by the pound. Sells belt blanks. Tools available include stamps, rivets, punches, cutters, fasteners, lacing and stitching types, eyelet setters, others. Buckles, leather kits for handbags, dyes, laces and sewing items also available.
For Further Information: Write for catalog.
Discounts: Quantity.

WEAVER LEATHER, INC.

P.O. Box 68
Mt. Hope, OH 44660
(216) 674-1782, (800) 6-WEAVER
Fax: (216) 674-0030

Offers: Leather hides: Chap, suede, strap, skirting, harness, bridle, latigo, others. Hardware includes snaps, loops, rings, dees, buckles, others. Also carries leather crafting tools, thread, nylon webbing, poly rope, oils and dyes.
For Further Information: Free catalog.
Discounts: Quantity.

WORLD TRADING, INC.

121 Spencer Plain Rd.
Old Saybrook, CT 06475
(860) 339-5962

Offers: Imported leathers: Kangaroo, buffalo, calfskins and exotics (ostrich, elephant, shark). Also carries lizardskins and snake skins (rattlers, pythons, others).
For Further Information: Send SASE for list.

Metalworking

Also see Jewelry Making and Lapidary, Miniature Making, Model Making and Sculpture and Modeling.

AMERICAN ART CLAY CO., INC.
4717 W. 16th St.
Indianapolis, IN 46222
(317) 244-6871

Offers: Metal enameling—3 kilns and glass/metal enameling colors, over glaze colors and range of supplies.
For Further Information: Free information packet.
Discounts: Sells wholesale.

ATLAS METAL SALES
1401 Umatilla St.
Denver, CO 80204
(800) 662-0143

Offers: Silicone bronze: Sheets and plate (1/16″ to 3/8″ thicknesses), rods, rectangles, circles, plus thin-gauge strips, ingots (1/2-20 lbs.)

COUNTRY ACCENTS
P.O. Box 437
Montoursville, PA 17754

Offers: Pierced tin working kits and materials. Also offers finished panels.
For Further Information: Color catalog, $5.

EAST WEST DYE CO.
5238 Peters Creek Rd. NW
Roanoke, VA 24019
(540) 362-1489
Fax: (540) 362-7425

Offers: Anodized aluminum as wire, sheets, tubing, beads and other components. Carries dyes and sealers, gloves and books. Offers custom anodizing and dyeing service.
For Further Information: Catalog, $5 (refundable).
Discounts: Quantity; sells wholesale to legitimate businesses.

EDMUND SCIENTIFIC
101 E. Gloucester Pike, Dept. 16A-C911
Edscorp. Bldg.
Barrington, NJ 08007
(609) 547-8880

Offers: Technical and scientific products, including some for metal crafting or useful aids: Electroplating kits, 6 submersible pumps, compressors and over 20 small motors. Carries a wide array of miniature tools: Dremel Moto-Tools, pin vises, drills, hammers, jeweler's drill presses, mini-torches and table saws. Engraver's tools, wire benders. 30-plus magnifiers and loupes, diffraction grating and others also available.
For Further Information: Write for catalog.

EXTRA SPECIAL PRODUCTS CORP.
P.O. Box 777
Greenville, OH 45331
(513) 548-9388 or (800) 648-5945
Fax: (513) 548-9580

Offers: House of Copper line of die-cut copper shapes (to punch, bend, burnish, antique, paint, use as trims, window decorations, tree ornaments, candle trims, quilt templates, applique templates, wreath decorations, others), and a booklet with over 24 projects.
For Further Information: Contact your dealer, or write for catalog.

NONFERROUS METALS CO.
P.O. Box 2595
Waterbury, CT 06723
(203) 274-7255
Fax: (203) 274-7202

Offers: Wire, including brass, copper, black annealed, galvanized, in a variety of gauges.
For Further Information: Send SASE.

PYRAMID PRODUCTS
85357 American Canal Rd.
Niland, CA 92257
(619) 354-4265

Offers: Small and large foundry furnaces for home or foundry, including chamber, lid, motor, components and accessories (in complete, short sets or commercial units) for casting gold, silver, aluminum, brass, bronze, gray iron. Also good for lost wax casting and glass blowing. Carries ingots: Fluxing aluminum and alloy, and brass.

For Further Information: Catalog, $2.
Store Location: At above address.
Discounts: Teachers and institutions.

SCHAIFER'S ENAMELING SUPPLIES

1012 Fair Oaks Ave. #170
South Pasadena, CA 91030
(800) 525-5959

Offers: Copper enameling supplies, including Thompson enamels and American Metalcraft copper shapes.
For Further Information: Call or write.

SHELTECH

4207 Lead Ave. SE
Albuquerque, NM 87108
(505) 256-7073

Offers: Custom RT Stamping dies made of heat-treated tool steel for cutting parts from sheet metal. Blanking service with dies.
For Further Information: Send SASE.

WOOD-MET SERVICES

3314 Shoff Circle, Dept. CSS
Peoria, IL 61604
(306) 637-9667

Offers: Over 700 plans to build home workshop machines/equipment for wood and metal work: Universal clamping system, metal spinning, metal lathe, 9 wood turning chisels, miter arm for bandsaw and router, electric band sander, photographic equipment, air compressor, drill press items, router and bandsaw items, shop metal benders, welding and hand tools, fixtures, wood lathe items, sander with power feed, circular saw items, power rasps, 6 tools for grinding wheels, milling machine and metal shaper items. Investing cast equipment. Also offers circular saws, wood jointer, belt sander items and woodworker's kits and sets.
For Further Information: Catalog, $1.
Discounts: Quantity; sells wholesale to legitimate businesses.

Miniature Making, Miniatures & Dollhouses

Also see Model Making, Paints, Finishes and Adhesives, Tools and Equipment and specific categories of interest.

JOAN ADAMS
2706 Sheridan Dr.
Sarasota, FL 34239
(941) 924-8185

Offers: Miniature needlepunch rug sets of 22 mesh canvas in a variety of designs.
For Further Information: Send SASE for new designs; catalog, $2.75.

AMERICAN CRAFT PRODUCTS
3150 State Line Rd.
North Bend, OH 45052
(513) 353-3390

Offers: Dollhouse windows and doors, ready-to-finish and install, scaled to fit standard dollhouse openings. Styles include tall Victorian, traditional, French and colonial. Both working and non-working windows and ½″ scale available.
For Further Information: Catalog, $3.

GINA C. BELLOUS
3629 Helms Ave.
Culver City, CA 90232
(310) 836-8065

Offers: Dollhouse dolls in porcelain blanks, molds and painted kits. Also offers painted faces and portrait dolls.
For Further Information: Catalog, $3 and large SASE.

BODKIN CRAFT
130 Patricia Ave., Lot 2Q
Dunedin, FL 34698
(813) 736-4103

Offers: Miniature lazy Susan plans, instructions.
For Further Information: Write.

BRAMSCH VIDEO GROUP
P.O. Box 515165
St. Louis, MO 63151
(314) 638-3404
Fax: (314) 638-3161
Website: http://ww.TWEB.COM/INFOSTATION

Offers: Video library of 7 workshops (65 hours of instruc-

tion) on polymer casting, oven bake modeling clay, and more.
For Further Information: Call or write.
Accepts: MasterCard, Visa

BRODNAX PRINTS
3870 W. Beverly Dr.
Dallas, TX 85209
(214) 528-7773
Fax: (214) 528-2290

Offers: Dollhouse ¼″ scale flooring papers in larger sheet sizes and colors; wallpapers in over 200 designs, in ½″ and ¼″ scale, including "Angel Pigs" and others.
For Further Information: Color catalog sheets, $1.
Discounts: Sells wholesale.

CAT'S PAW
336 Candlewood Lake Rd.
Brookfield, CT 06804

Offers: 1″ scale miniature trunk kits in 16 styles, with trunk hardware. Also offers other 1″ scale doll accessories.
For Further Information: Catalog, $2.
Accepts: MasterCard, Visa

CIR-KIT CONCEPTS, INC.
32 Woodlake Dr., SE
Rochester, MN 55904
(800) 676-4252

Offers: Complete line of wiring kits and lamps including the deluxe wiring kit (for 10- to 12-room dollhouses) and others.
For Further Information: Catalog, $3, or see your dealer.

CONCORD MINIATURES
400 Markley St.
P.O. Box 99
Port Reading, NJ 07064
(800) 888-0936

Offers: Over 200 pieces of Concord miniature furniture and accessories—mahogany furniture, some ½″ scale items, plus baby's, children's and teen's bedroom pieces and others. Manufacturer.
For Further Information: Catalog, $7.50.

CRISS-CROSS
P.O. Box 324
Wayne, NJ 07474
(201) 835-9339

Offers: Plans (in 1″ to 1′ scale, with full-size cutting details, hints, assembly views and photos) for replicas of Peddlers wagons (of late 1800s), like the one at Longstreet Farm Museum, Homdel, NJ, plus plans for the Concord stage coach and Conestoga covered wagon. Miniature wheel-making plans also available.

For Further Information: Catalog, $1.
Accepts: MasterCard, Visa

DEE'S DELIGHTS, INC.
3150 State Line Rd.
North Bend, OH 45052
(513) 353-3390

Offers: FIMO modeling compound in a variety of colors (oven-bakes). Also offers more than 2,000 miniature and dollhouse-related items.
For Further Information: Contact dealer, or send SASE for information.
Discounts: Sells wholesale to legitimate businesses.

THE DEPOT DOLLHOUSE SHOP
215 Worchester Rd., Rt. 9
Framingham, MA 01701
(508) 872-5444

Offers: Full line of scale miniatures, including ⅜″ cabinet grade dollhouses from known manufacturers, also offers a children's line of dollhouses and furniture, plus handcrafted accessories for all rooms, by established artisans.
For Further Information: Call or write.

DESIGN TECHNICS MINIATURES
9548 Walmer
Overland Park, KS 66212

Offers: House plans in 1″ scale, kitchen and bathroom sink kits, and Dollhouse Builders Handbook. Also offers a 1920s cast-metal stove, refrigerator, modern tub and toilet in ¼″ scale.
For Further Information: Write.

DESIGNS BY JUDI
Rt. 2
P.O. Box 204
Scotland Neck, NC 27874

Offers: Miniature scale buttons in a variety of styles. Also offers over 200 doll clothes patterns plus dolls.
For Further Information: Catalog, $2.

DIAMOND "M" BRAND MOLD CO.
15081 91st St.
Hinsdale, IL 60521
(708) 323-5691

Offers: 1″ scale miniature molds (poured in ceramic) including 3-mold Victorian bath set (claw tub, pedestal sink, water-closet toilet). Other molds, for tea sets, variety of pots, vases, and country accessories, plus dolls and various items of furniture and fireplaces. Factory direct.
For Further Information: Catalog, $3 ($5 foreign).

DIMINUTIVE SPECIALTIES
10337 Ellsworth Dr.
Roscoe, IL 61073
(815) 623-2011

Offers: Nite-Lite Boxes (holds miniatures) for any occasion; miniature photos. Full line of miniatures.
Accepts: American Express, MasterCard, Visa

THE DOLLHOUSE FACTORY
157 Main St.
P.O. Box 456
Lebanon, NJ 08833
(908) 236-6404 or (800) DOLL-HOUSE

Offers: Over 8,000 miniatures products: 50-plus 1″-scale dollhouse kits/plans, stores/buildings kits, ½″-scale dollhouse kits and furniture. Also offers display items and scale furniture kits by X-acto, Realife, Shenandoah, others. Carries needlework Shadowbox kits, a full line of building hardware, plus windows and other components, FIMO, stencils, decals, wallpapers, carpet, cords, finishing materials, electric lighting items, hand/power tools, magnifiers, landscape supplies.
For Further Information: Catalog, $5.50.
Store Location: At above address.
Discounts: Sells wholesale to legitimate businesses.
Accepts: MasterCard, Visa

DUCKWORK'S WOODCRAFTS
7736 Ranchview Lane
Maple Grove, MN 55311

Offers: Plywood in 1/32″, 1/16″ and ⅛″ stocks; in even-density material (12″ × 15″ squares).
For Further Information: Catalog, $2.

LIGIA DURSTENFELD
2315 Caracas St.
La Crescenta, CA 91214
(818) 248-8058

Offers: Scale enameled miniatures, including bowls, Fabrege eggs/silver, flower arrangements, other flowers, Oriental screens (enamel on copper) and others. Will custom enamel miniatures to specification.
For Further Information: Catalog, $2 and SASE (refundable).
Discounts: Some dealers' discounts available.

DWYER'S DOLL HOUSE
1944 Warwick Ave.
Warwick, RI 02889
(401) 738-3248

Offers: Complete line of dollhouses and all accessories.
For Further Information: 800-page color catalog, $25.
Accepts: MasterCard, Visa

ELECT-A-LITE, INC.
P.O. Box 865
West End, NC 27376
(800) EAL-KITS

Offers: Scale dollhouse lighting system kits and accessories (copper tape wiring system, fabricated for shadow boxes, for from 3- to 5-room dollhouses to the largest 9- to 12-room models); complete with patented connectors, parts and instructions.
For Further Information: Contact dealer, or send SASE for information.

THE ENCHANTED DOLL HOUSE
Rt. 7A
Manchester Center, VT 05255
(802) 362-3030
Fax: (802) 362-4223

Offers: Miniatures, dollhouses, miniatures kits and room settings workshop materials, plus kits and books. Many handmade or exclusive by renowned artisans.

ENGLAND THINGS
15 Sullivan Farm
New Milford, CT 06776
(860) 350-4565

Offers: Line of miniature building kits, including houses, tollhouse, Victorian factory, clapboard shop and others. Also offers finished buildings.
For Further Information: Brochures, $5 and large SASE.

FANTASY CRAFT
933 E. Carson Lane
Pomona, CA 91766
(909) 591-8252

Offers: Contemporary and Southwestern room box and house kits—unassembled or assembled, plus finishing kits.
For Further Information: Catalog, $5 (refundable with first $50 order).

FERN VASI DOLLS
P.O. Box 16164
Newport Beach, CA 92659

Offers: Kits, including Raggedy Ann, Raggedy Andy, rein-

deer wallhanging, Mammy/Southern Bell "flip doll."
For Further Information: Call.
Discounts: Sells wholesale.

FERNWOOD MINIATURES
12730 Finlay Rd. NE
Silverton, OR 97381
(503) 873-2397

Offers: ½"-scale miniature furniture kits of basswood, including Colonial, Early American, Shaker, Victorian, Empire, Craftman, Southwestern, country pieces. Offers dressers, stands tables, chairs, desks, cabinets, beds, wardrobes and more.
For Further Information: Send large SASE for catalog.

THE FIELDWOOD CO., INC.
P.O. Box 6
Chester, VT 05143
(802) 875-4127

Offers: "Precious Little Things" handcrafted scale miniature accessories, including food (artichokes in a pewter bowl, apples, baked goods, meats, vegetables in wicker basket, filled Mason jars, hand-blown glass and others. Also offers furnishings and accessories in 1" and ½" scales.
For Further Information: 32-page color catalog, $3.50.
Discount: Sells wholesale.

FRED'S DOLLHOUSE & MINIATURE CENTER
Rt. 7, RE 2
P.O. Box 2134
Pittsford, VT 05763
(802) 483-6362

Offers: Complete line of scaled building materials, dollhouse kits, furniture and accessories. Also offers custom service, including replicas of homes, remodeling, wiring and wallpapering of dollhouses.
For Further Information: 92-page catalog, $5.

L. FREEMAN
Box 1168
Nederland, CO 80466

Offers: Real adobe dollhouse builder's kit, in Old Santa Fe style with adobe bricks. Can also be used as a night-light or incense burner. Kit includes multi-mold, reinforcements, adobe mix, and plans for three projects, with data on designing adobes.
For Further Information: Send SASE.

GINGERBREAD HOUSE OF MINIATURES
2170 Lawndale Dr.
Greensboro, NC 27408
(910) 273-2831

Offers: Marklin trains, miniatures, plus a custom finishing service—inside and outside of dollhouses. Also Goebel miniatures.

For Further Information: Call or write.
Store Location: At above address.
Accepts: MasterCard, Visa

GREENBERG'S GREAT TRAIN, DOLLHOUSE & TOY SHOWS

7566 Main St.
Sykesville, MD 21784
(410) 795-7447

Offers: Full line of miniature goods, including dollhouses. Books, including *Finishing Touches—Creating Miniature Building Components*, also carried.
For Further Information: Send SASE.

J. HERMES

P.O. Box 4023
El Monte, CA 91734
(818) 287-3141

Offers: Miniatures—½" scale wallpapers and floor papers in 100 designs and color combinations, plus smaller ¼" scale wallpapers and projects (breakaway box kit and others). Also carries miniature gift wrap.
For Further Information: Catalog, $4; smaller-scale swatch book, $2.

HIS & HER HOBBYS

15 W. Busse Ave.
Mt. Prospect, IL 60056
(847) 392-2668

Offers: Miniature dollhouse kits (and built), furniture kits, lighting, moldings, siding, staircases, roofing, landscaping, hard and soft wood selections and hardware. Miniatures include furniture, figures, others. Custom dollhouse modeling and wiring services.
For Further Information: Send SASE for list.

HOUSE OF CARON

10111 Larryln Dr.
Whittier, CA 90603
(310) 947-6753
Fax: (310) 943-5103

Offers: Miniature doll molds by Parker-Levi, Keni, Paulette Stinson, Mystic, Theresa Glisson, Ayanna, House of Caron molds. Carries doll clothes patterns, books, doll-making supplies, tools, doll props and accessories.
For Further Information: Illustrated price lists, $3.
Discounts: Quantity.

THE HOUSE OF MINIATURES

3890 Oakcliff Industrial Ct.
Atlanta, GA 30340
(800) 679-9090

Offers: Members of this society receive miniature furniture kits monthly with no obligation to buy. Furniture kits include classic Chippendale styles, Queen Anne and other traditional styles, scaled ¹/₁₂ of full-size originals; with hardwoods and solid brass fittings.
For Further Information: Send SASE.

INNOVATIVE PHOTOGRAPHY

1724 NW 36th
Lincoln City, OR 97367
(541) 994-9421

Offers: Framed miniature photos of old masters, impressionist and modern paintings by Da Vinci, Rembrandt, Boticelli, Van Gogh, Degas, Gainsborough, Picasso, Marin, Pollack and others, plus Gutmann babies, Eisley, C.B. Barber, J.W. Carries Victorian photos—framed or in folders, stereoview cards, diplomas, certificates, postcards, color maps (U.S., world, states, antique), postcard and hanging display racks and others. Will do custom reduction of any photos.
For Further Information: Catalog, $3.

JACQUELINE'S

463 Crestmont
Oakland, CA 94607

Offers: Dollhouse-making catalog: Plans, building supplies, accessories, dolls, others.
For Further Information: Catalog and newsletter, $3 (refundable).

JANNA JOSEPH DESIGNS

P.O. Box 1262
Denedin, FL 34697
(813) 784-1877

Offers: Line of scale miniature doll molds.
For Further Information: Catalog, $5.

KARIN'S MINI GARDEN

2905 9th St. NW
Albuquerque, NM 87107
(505) 883-4561

Offers: Miniature garden items: Variety of indoor and outdoor plants (in containers), cacti, succulents and arrangements, plus other realistic items.
For Further Information: Catalog, $3.50 (refundable).

KILKENNY MINIATURES
791 Kamechameha Hwy.
Punaluu, Oahu, HI 96717

Offers: Original ultra-fine glitter kits, including 1"-scale romantic and holiday items.
For Further Information: Large SASE for catalog.

BETTY LAMPEN
2930 Jackson St.
San Francisco, CA 94115
(415) 674-1114

Offers: Miniature knitting pattern books—sweaters for teddies, people.
For Further Information: Send SASE for list.

LITTLE GOODIES
P.O. Box 1004
Lewisville, TX 75067
(214) 625-9303

Offers: Over 95 pre-cut paper flower kits (1" to 1' scale): Marigolds, hollyhocks, lilies of the valley, violets, lilies, carnations, irises, tulips, poppies, dandelions, rose bushes, ivy and others.
For Further Information: Catalog, $2 (refundable).
Discounts: Sells wholesale to legitimate businesses.

LITTLE HOUSE OF MINIATURES ON CHELSEA LANE
615 Sycamore St.
Waterloo, IA 50703
(319) 233-6585

Offers: Over 20,000 miniature items, including dollhouse and furniture kits, dolls, wallpapers and other decorator components, electric wiring and building supplies and others.
For Further Information: Catalog, $18 (refundable).
Store Location: At above address.

LITTLE RED HOUSE AT BEAUVAIS CASTLE
141 Union St.
Manchester, NH 03108
(603) 625-8944

Offers: Over 6,000 miniatures and accessories of known brands—furniture, figures, components, others. Specializes in doll house electrification.
For Further Information: 300-page catalog, $5.

A LITTLE SOMETHING FOR EVERYONE
6203 S. Dover St.
Littleton, CO 80123

Offers: Southwestern abode kits and other items.
For Further Information: Catalog, $2.

M.G. LIGHTHOUSE
22 Felton St.
New Bedford, MA 02745
(508) 995-6283

Offers: 1"-scale lighthouse kit, including 4 levels with central stairway and front opening. Electrical kit for lighthouse and miniature furniture also available.
For Further Information: Send SASE.
Accepts: MasterCard, Visa

MARYDOLL'S MOLDS
1335 S. Oakland St.
Aurora, CO 80012
(303) 752-0468

Offers: Line of original miniature doll molds in 1" scale.
For Further Information: Color brochure, $3 and large SASE.
Accepts: MasterCard, Visa

MASTERPIECES IN MINIATURE
Ruth L. Mazar
13083 Drummer Way
Grass Valley, CA 95949
(916) 268-1429

Offers: Handcrafted, scaled miniatures in 1", ½" and ¼" scales, including oil paintings, peteco brass picture lights, artists' furniture and assorted household accessories. "Instant Age" weathering liquid for wood/painted surfaces also available. Also carries "Tips and Techniques for the Miniaturist" video.
For Further Information: Catalog, $3.
Discounts: Sells wholesale to store-front shops.

MICROSCALE INDUSTRIES, INC.
P.O. Box 11950
Costa Mesa, CA 92627

Offers: Line of miniature model decals for 1" scale, traditional and other periods. Also carries general purpose decals and model finishing products.
For Further Information: See your dealer, or catalog, $4.

MINI GRAPHICS
2975 Exon Ave.
Cincinnati, OH 45241

Offers: Lines of miniature wallpapers, variety of fabrics, carpeting, others. Miniature needlecraft book (needlepoint, cross stitch for rugs, bedspreads, wallpaper paste). Also offers "How to Wallpaper a Dollhouse" booklet.
For Further Information: 92-page catalog, $6.

THE MINIATURE CORNER, TEXAS

13080 Veterans Memorial Dr.
Houston, TX 77014
(800) 928-0899
Fax: (713) 444-5032

Offers: Dreamland Babies human figures (1″ and ½″ scales) kits, wigs and dresses.
For Further Information: Send SASE and $4 (refundable) for brochure.

MINIATURE IMAGE

P.O. Box 465
Lawrenceburg, IN 47025
(800) 942-9076

Offers: Scale dollhouses, dollhouse kits and basic building supplies, scale miniatures including furniture kits and finished accessories, including hard-to-find items. Carries reference and how-to books, others.
For Further Information: Full catalog, $30 (refundable).
Accepts: American Express, MasterCard, Visa

MINIATURE LUMBER SHOPPE

812 Main St.
Grandview, MO 64030

Offers: Line of ¼″ and ½″ scale building kits and components, and furniture kits.
For Further Information: Catalog, $2.50.

MINIATURE MAKER'S WORKSHOP

4515 N. Woodward Ave.
Royal Oak, MI 48073
(810) 549-0633

Offers: Magic Mitre miniature mitering kit (for door, window and picture frames, other uses).
For Further Information: Send SASE.
Store Location: At above address. Hours: T-Sat, 10-5.

MINIATURE WOOD PRODUCTIONS

140 B Vivian Rd.
Belton, MO 64012

Offers: Miniature windows, doors, moldings and other building components in 1″ scale.
For Further Information: Catalogs, $2.

MY SISTER'S SHOPPE, INC.

1671 Penfield Rd.
Rochester, NY 14625
(716) 381-4037

Offers: Collection of scale dollhouses and miniatures (authentic detailed reproductions, and/or whimsical in style) including Laura's Linens English coordinated bedding ensembles in florals and stripes, plus English country gifts (soaps, fragrances, geraniums in pitcher/bowl, lace pillows, luggage, potpourri jar) and others.
For Further Information: Catalog, $2.

JOSEPH F. NOCERA MINIATURES

P.O. Box 1387
Forestville, CA 95436
(707) 544-0462

Offers: Dollhouse kits, including Southwestern house in adobe style with fireplace, maple plank floor, door and windows, redwood arbor front, brick patio and clear plastic top in 2 sizes. One room log cabin with loft, fireplace, chimney, ladder, veranda, windows, door, wooden floor and open back also available.
For Further Information: Photos and catalog, $3.

NOONMARK

6224 Sycamore Ave. NW
Seattle, WA 98107

Offers: Extra-thin micro glass in bulk size or custom cut to specification.
For Further Information: Send large SASE for information.

NORTHEASTERN SCALE MODELS, INC.

99 Cross St.
P.O. Box 727
Methuen, MA 01844
(508) 688-6019

Offers: Model-building components and laser-cut items: Precision scale basswood structural shapes, dollhouse molding, carving blocks, decking, strips and sheets. Also offers hardware and model railroad kits.
For Further Information: Catalog, $1.
Store Location: At above address.
Discounts: Sells wholesale to legitimate businesses.

OAKRIDGE HOBBIES

P.O. Box 247
Lemont, IL 60439
(708) 257-0909

Offers: Large selection of 1″-scale doll house kits, building components, lighting, trims, figures and landscaping. Also offers glues, paints, hard-to-find items of many manufacturers, how-to books.
For Further Information: Catalog, $3 (refundable).

JOY PARKER

P.O. Box 34
Midland, Ontario L4R 4K6
Canada

Offers: Porcelain doll kits, including exclusives. Clothing

patterns, knitting patterns, yarns, needles, fabrics, trims, mohair, viscose. Also videos.
For Further Information: Catalog, $3 (refundable).

DON PERKINS MINIATURES
1708 59th St.
Des Moines, IA 50322
(515) 279-6639

Offers: Cords for miniature wicker work: White linen, by the half-pound spool (or pound); (natural linen spool) or quarter-pound spools of 3-cord (for ½-scale work).
For Further Information: Send SASE for price list.

PINOCCHIO'S MINIATURES
465 Main St.
Frankenmuth, MI 48734
(517) 652-2751 or (800) 635-4603

Offers: Line of dollhouses, miniatures and supplies of known manufacturers.
For Further Information: 800-page catalog, $18, plus $4.50 shipping and handling.

POSY PATCH ORIGINALS
P.O. Box 52173
Atlanta, GA 30355

Offers: Plant and flower kits in 1″ and ½″ scales, including trees, orchids, geraniums, bonsai, Christmas greenery, others.
For Further Information: Photo brochure, $2 and large SASE (refundable).
Discounts: Sells wholesale.

BARBARA J. RAHEB
30132 Elizabeth Ct.
Agoura Hills, CA 91301
(818) 991-3109

Offers: Miniature books: Over 350 selections of abridged and unabridged editions of well-known favorites, classics, reproduced antique books, masterpieces (professionally typeset, illustrated, handsewn, hardbound with titled decorative spines and cover designs stamped in 23K gold). Books are limited, numbered, fully readable editions in 1″ scale.
For Further Information: Catalog, $5.
Discounts: Sells wholesale.

GOLD AND BETTY RIMER
515 Crystal Ave.
Findlay, OH 45840
(419) 423-3261

Offers: Handcrafted scale miniatures including furniture (hutch, cabinet, dry sink, others). Custom-made miniatures by special request (send picture or good description).
For Further Information: Price list, $2.50.

RONDEL WOOD PRODUCTS
63 U.S. Highway 1
Nobelboro, ME 04555
(207) 563-6693

Offers: Wood wagon and carriage kits at 1/12 scale: Blueprints, patterns and components.
For Further Information: Brochure, $3.

SCIENTIFIC MODELS, INC.
340 Snyder Ave.
Berkeley Heights, NJ 07922
(908) 464-7070

Offers: Real life miniature dollhouse furniture kits with pre-cut basswood parts, brass hardware, and supplies to finish, available in various styles, including traditional and country.
For Further Information: Color catalog, $1.

SHARON E. RUSSELL
P.O. Box 2124
Chino, CA 91708
(909) 591-6383

Offers: Wicker furniture kits (1″ and ½″ scales) and finished furniture.
For Further Information: Brochure/price list, $1 and large SASE.

THE SIDE DOOR
P.O. Box 573
Dennisport, MA 02639
(508) 394-7715

Offers: Bisque dollhouse/doll kits, patterns, dressed dolls, trims, accessories.
For Further Information: Illustrated brochure, $3.

SMALL HOUSES
8064 Columbia Rd.
Olmstead Falls, OH 44138
(216) 235-5051

Offers: Full line of dollhouses and components: Furniture, wallpapers, carpet, building supplies and accessories.
For Further Information: Call.

PHYLLIS STAFFORD
939 North St.
P.O. Box 157
Suffield, CT 06078
(860) 668-2391

Offers: Scale miniature carpet kits, including design reproductions (from seventeenth century) on 42 silk gauze mesh

with DMC floss; also offers *Our Lady of Czestochowa* design kit. Has finished carpets.
For Further Information: Send large SASE and $2.

RON STETKEWICZ
HCR 1
P.O. Box 61B
Cairo, NY 12413
(518) 622-8311

Offers: Miniature brass hardware: Hinges, drawer pulls, lock plates, screens, others.
For Further Information: Catalog, $6 (refundable).

LINDA TAYLOR
2228 Leif Ave.
Muskegon, MI 49441
(616) 795-2334

Offers: Stuffed bears and bunnies kits (1″ tall when seated); others.
For Further Information: Send large SASE for brochure.

THE VICTORIAN CRAFTSMAN, LTD.
P.O. Box 234
New York, NY 10276
(212) 673-0369

Offers: Kits for miniature reproductions of Persian style rugs, including work in petite point or cross-stitch with charts, canvas, mesh or linen, DMC floss, color picture, backing. Also offers kits in 30-, 33- and 36-count for runners and larger, simple to intricate designs.
For Further Information: Color catalog, $6 (refundable).
Accepts: All credit cards

VICTORIAN TIMES
2310 Monument Blvd.
Pleasant Hill, CA 94523

Offers: Kits for scale miniature buildings, including a Country Victorian store (large building with a 2-bedroom flat and balcony upstairs).
For Further Information: Contact your dealer, or send SASE.

VILLAGE MINIATURES
P.O. Box 142
Queenston, Ontario L0S IL0
Canada
(416) 262-4779

Offers: Miniatures: Wallpaper and floor coverings, electrical wiring, doors, windows, stairways. Also offers dollhouses, kits and plans, porcelain doll kits, specialized lumber, landscaping materials, mini holiday decorations, handmade accessories. Carries Dremel and X-acto tools and others.
For Further Information: First-time catalogs, $5 ($4 after).

W & D MINI HOMES
1005 Nota Dr.
P.O. Box 1654
Bloomington, IN 47401
(812) 332-2499

Offers: American Indian scale miniatures (of clay, fiber, wood, etc.), including a variety of clothing, costumes, pottery, baskets, blankets, rugs, figures, paintings, others.
For Further Information: Brochure, $1 and SASE (double postage).

WALDEN WOODS DESIGNS
4604 Wilson Ave.
Signal Mountain, TN 37377

Offers: Collection of 42-count cross stitch kits, framed pictures, rugs, quilts and others.
For Further Information: Color catalogs, $2 (refundable).

WARLING MINIATURES
22453 Covello St.
West Hills, CA 91307
(818) 340-9855
Fax: (818)999-6020

Offers: Miniatures (1″ and ½″) wicker furniture kits of Victorian to modern styles, including chairs, rockers, tables, sofas, baskets, others.
For Further Information: Send large SASE.

PETER WESTCOTT
6256 N. 85th St.
Scottsdale, AZ 85250
(502) 922-1547

Offers: Furniture pattern books in 1″ scale, including Southwestern, Mission, Shaker, Art Deco, Chippendale, modern and other styles.
For Further Information: Send $2 and large SASE.

Model Making—Aircraft

Also see Miniature Making, Model Making—General, Model Making—Railroad and other related categories.

ASTRO FLIGHT, INC.
13311 Beach Ave.
Marina Del Rey, CA 90292
(310) 821-6242

Offers: Electronic speed controls, digital battery chargers and electric motors for model airplanes, cars and boats.
For Further Information: Send SASE.

BALSA USA
P.O. Box 164
Marinette, WI 54143
(800) BALSA US

Offers: Balsa wood sticks, sheets, carving blocks and custom shapes. Also offers spruce, bass wood dowels, birch and poplar plywood. Flying radio-control model airplane kits, music wire, adhesives, modeling knives, saws and other hobby products also available.
For Further Information: Send SASE.
Accepts: Discover, MasterCard, Visa

BYRON ORIGINALS, INC.
P.O. Box 279
Ida Grove, IA 51445
(712) 364-3165

Offers: Kits for 28 model R/C aircraft: Biplanes, classics, aerobatics, warbirds, ducted fan jets, others. Plus Christen Eagle, F-4U-1 Corsair, P-51 Mustang, G-17S Staggerwing, F-16 Fighting Falcon, Glasair RG, F-15 Eagle, others.
For Further Information: Catalog, $5.

CARLSON ENGINE IMPORTS
814 E. Marconi Ave.
Phoenix, AZ 85022

Offers: Glow and diesel model engines, including Aurora, AE, AM, AME, CS, Cipolla, Elphin, Jin Shi, KMD MK-17, Letmo, Marz, MDC, Merco, Meteor, Model A, MVVS, MP Jet, Paw, Silver Swallow, Stas's, Pfeffer and Phittecyh brands.
For Further Information: 20-page catalog, $1.

CHEETAH MODEL
14725 Bessemer St.
Van Nuys, CA 91411
(818) 781-4544

Offers: Model aircraft—slope acrobatic, combat gliders including super model (wingspan 64") and Cheetah (wingspan 48"), both with "unbreakable fuselage."
For Further Information: Send SASE.
Discounts: Sells wholesale.

CLEVELAND MODEL & SUPPLY CO.
9800 Detroit Ave.
Cleveland, OH 44102
(216) 961-3600

Offers: Model aircraft (C-D) plans (for giant scale models, R/C, electric, rubber, or gas powered) for early bird, warbirds, commercial and racers, private models, homebuilts, jets and others.
For Further Information: Catalog and price list, $2; price list, $1.

CS FLIGHT SYSTEMS
31 Perry St.
Middleboro, MA 02346
(508) 947-2805

Offers: Electrical flight equipment from over 40 manufacturers including materials for lightweight building and covering. Carries Piza/Robe, Hobby Lobby and ACE RC.
For Further Information: Discount catalog available with electric flight information, $7 (U.S.), $8.50 (Canada), $10 (foreign).
Discounts: Quantity; sells wholesale.
Accepts: MasterCard, Visa

D & J ELECTRONICS
1236 Marigold St. NW
Hartville, OH 44632
(216) 877-1445

Offers: Full line of RCD RXs and products for upgrading, plus frequency changes and focus series R/C systems repair service for most R/C systems.
For Further Information: Call or send SASE.
Accepts: Discover, MasterCard, Visa

DGA DESIGNS
16 Main St.
Phelps, NY 14532
(315) 548-3779
Fax: (315) 548-4099

Offers: Model aircraft—Jet Pilot Kit (pilot bust with modern jet helmet, face mask, oxygen hose, weight 12 oz.), 9 other pilot styles and sizes, 1:8 scale, 1:7 scale, others.
For Further Information: Contact your dealer, or catalog, $2.

DON'S HOBBY SHOP, INC.
1819 S. Broadway
Salina, KS 67401
(913) 827-3222
Fax: (913) 827-0472

Offers: R/C engines: Webra, Moki, YS, ASP, MVVs, others, plus Sig kits, JR servos, JR and Futaba radio systems, others. Also offers a line of RC cars and accessories.
For Further Information: Send SASE for list.
Store Location: At above address. Hours: M-F, 10-6, Sat, 10-5.
Discounts: Quantity; sells wholesale.
Accepts: MasterCard, Visa

FRANK'S HOBBY HOUSE
19401 N. Cave Creek Rd.
Phoenix, AZ 85024
(602) 992-3495

Offers: Kits and supplies by Acc, Airtronics, Altech, Bru-Line, Cox, Du-Bro, Ernst, Futaba, Goldberg, Great Planes, Hobbico, JR, Lanier, Magnum, McDaniel, Midwest, Moki, Panavise, RCD, R/C Sports, Robart, SIG, Webra, YS, Zenoah, others.
For Further Information: Send SASE.
Store Location: At above address.
Accepts: Discover, MasterCard, Visa

GM PLASTICS
7252 Industrial Park Blvd.
Mentor, OH 44060
(216) 953-1188

Offers: Model R/C aircraft kits (machine cut parts, sheeted foam wing design, solid balsa tail feathers, one-piece ABS cowl, plans, instructions, hardware, decals).
For Further Information: Contact your dealer or send SASE.
Accepts: MasterCard, Visa

HERRILLS EXECUFORM
P.O. Box 7853
Laguna Niguel, CA 92607
(714) 495-0705

Offers: Model aircraft vacform kits in 1:72 scale, including

Abrahms, Beech, Bell, Bellanca, Canadair, Cessna, Consol, Convair, Curtiss, Douglas, Fairchild, Gen, Avia, Grumman, Hughes, Howard, Lockheed, Martin, Northrop, North American, Republic, Ryan, Seversky, Spartan, Stinson, Timm, Vultee, Waco.
For Further Information: Send SASE for catalog.

HOBBIES & HELIS INTERNATIONAL
201 S. 3rd St. & Rt. 309 N.
Coopersburg, PA 18036
(610) 282-4811

Offers: Model helicopter kits including Hirobo, X-Cell, Kalt, Kyosho, others. Also offers beginner packages/kits. Parts available include rotor blades, fuselages, motors, R/Cs and others. Tools: Blade balancer, flybar lock, paddle gauges, piston head lock, link pliers, others.
For Further Information: HHI or TSK catalog, $5 each (specify).

HOBBYLAND
1810 E. 12th St., Unit C
Mishawaka, IN 46544

Offers: Model aircraft by Tamiya and Monogram.
For Further Information: Write for aircraft and armor sales flyer.

HOBBY SHACK
12480 Bandilier Circle
Fountain Valley, CA 92708

Offers: Model R/C aircraft kits, ARF models and others, by Two Tee, Parma International, others. Models include hydro-racing boat, Tamiya Grasshopper II Racer and others. Carries supplies, parts including silk-like material in 2-meter and 5-meter rolls, 11 colors, and Miller deluxe airbrush spray set. Carries Pacer products, R/C model car kits and combos.
For Further Information: Free 96-page Sport Flyer catalog.
Accepts: MasterCard, Visa

INDOOR MODEL SUPPLY
P.O. Box 5311
Salem, OR 97304

Offers: Ultra-light indoor type En Pierance rubber-powered flying model kits, supplies and books; also gliders, helicopters and 13" scale models. Also offers supplies, including indoor balsa, coverings, cements, winders, tools for model crafting.
For Further Information: Illustrated catalog, $2.

INNOVATIVE MODEL PRODUCTS
P.O. Box 4366
Margate, FL 33063
(305) 978-9033

Offers: Model aircraft kits: Thunderbolt P-47, Mustang P-

51D, Hawker Hurricane, other propeller models. Carries dummy radials, PFM adhesive, others.
For Further Information: Catalog, $5.
Accepts: MasterCard, Visa

JOHNSON'S CUSTOM MODELS
P.O. Box 296
Aguanga, CA 92536
(909) 767-2414

Offers: Custom built kits (by Johnson, or others) from framing, ready-to-cover or ready-to-fly.
For Further Information: Call or write for prices.

K & B MANUFACTURING
2100 College Dr.
Lake Havasu City, AZ 86403
(520) 453-3030
Fax: (520) 453-3559

Offers: K & B model aircraft and marine engines, fuels, glow plugs, fiberglass cloth, super epoxy resin and primer, micro-balloon filler, super epoxy thinner and paints.
For Further Information: Send SASE.

LENCRAFT
P.O. Box 770
Springville, CA 93265

Offers: Aircraft kits, including hard-to-find models, decals and accessories by all WWI, Huma, Italeri, Matchbox, Pioneer, Vacuforms, Hasegawa, Model Decal, Xtra Color, Esoteric, Frog, Novo, Minicraft, REvell, KP, Falcon, Blue Rider, Fujimi, Airfix, Aeroclub, D.B. Conv., Meikraft, Heller and Rareplanes. Free search service for wanted kits.
For Further Information: Send large SASE for list. Hot sheet mailing also available.

MIDWEST PRODUCTS CO., INC.
400 S. Indiana St.
P.O. Box 564
Hobart, IN 46342
(800) 348-3497

Offers: Micro-cut woods: Balsa, basswood, hardwoods, carving blocks. Model aircraft kits—R/C including trainer (50″ wingspan) Aero-Star. Others. Manufacturer.
For Further Information: See your dealer or write for free catalog.

MINIATURE AIRCRAFT USA
2324 N. Orange Blossom Trail
Orlando, FL 32804
(407) 422-1531

Offers: Model aircraft kits—X-Cell Quick-Silver competi-tion helicopter, epoxy-fiberglass, with rear gyro mounting kit, torque rail rotor drive. Others.
For Further Information: Send SASE.

MTA HOBBIES
4172 Pacific Coast Highway, Suite 102
Torrance, CA 90505
(310) 375-0773

Offers: Helicoptor kits by Hirobo, Kyosho, Miniature Aircraft, TSK, others. Parts include engines, combos, bodies, mufflers, others. Also carries hand tools and sets.
For Further Information: Send SASE for list.
Discounts: 10-15 percent discount on all Heli parts.
Accepts: MasterCard, Visa

NORTHWEST HOBBY SHOP
P.O. Box 44577
Tacoma, WA 98444
(206) 531-8111

Offers: Model aircraft kits including super sport, aeromaster, others, plus starter packages, electric packages, and fiberglass foam kits with wood and hardware. Accessories include firewall mounts, spinners, nylon racing wheels, axles, racing accessories, props, blues, others.
For Further Information: Send SASE.
Accepts: MasterCard, Visa

OLD TIME PLAN SERVICE
P.O. Box 90310
San Jose, CA 95109
(408) 292-3382

Offers: Model aircraft plans. Lists available include Old Timer/Free Flight Nostalgia, $2; Rubber Power/Control Line/Radio Control, $2; Flying Scale A-K, $2.50; Flying Scale L-Z, $2.50.
Accepts: Visa.

PECK-POLYMERS
P.O. Box 710399
Santee, CA 92072
(619) 448-1818

Offers: Model aircraft kits, a variety of rubber power, CO_2, and electric models, plus model aircraft building plans. Carries parts including electric motors, such as "super lightweight" R/C and FSystems, CO_2 engines, others.
For Further Information: Catalog, $2.

PRECISION ENTERPRISES UNLIMITED
P.O. Box 97
Springfield, VT 05156

Offers: Model aircraft kits, including PP Aero kits, Maintrack Models, Dynavector, others.
For Further Information: Complete catalog listing, $3.

QUADROTECH
3148 Kingston Rd., Suite 202
Scarborough, Ontario M1M 1P4
Canada
(416) 931-5564

Offers: Aircraft kits, including Extra 260 (70″ wingspan R/C), Laser 200, 1:20 size aircraft—extra 3005, 70″ wingspan, Extra 260 71.5″ wingspan, Ultimate biplane and others..
For Further Information: Send $1.

R/C MODELER
P.O. Box 487
Sierra Madre, CA 91025
(818) 355-1476

Offers: Over 875 model plans: Scale aircraft, fun-fly ships, sailplanes, boats, others.
For Further Information: Catalog, $5.

ROSEMONT HOBBY SHOP
Lamar Center
7720 Main St., Suite 5
P.O. Box 996
Foglesville, PA 18051
(610) 398-0210

Offers: 1:72 scale aircraft and other kits, Meikraft injected kits. Other aircraft kits from 1919 to modern, all scales, plus armor, WWI to present, all scales.
For Further Information: Catalog, $2 (refundable).
Discounts: Sells wholesale.
Accepts: Discover, MasterCard, Visa

SHELTON'S HOBBIES
2135 Old Oakland Rd.
San Jose, CA 95131
(800) 228-3237 or (800) 822-1688 (CA)

Offers: Model products, name brand, 4 to 8 channel systems and servos, plus aircraft parts, components, supplies. Carries R/C model car kits and combos, parts and radios.
For Further Information: Free 136-page catalog.
Accepts: MasterCard, Visa

SIG MANUFACTURING CO., INC.
401-7 Front St.
Montezuma, IA 50171
(515) 623-5154

Offers: Model aircraft kits (balsa, plywood)—classic, biplanes, stunts, sports, multiwing, miliatary, racers, trainers, gliders, others. Includes models for flying confined area, and for 2- to 9-channel radio equipment. Carries beginners' models, and a variety of scale sizes. Also carries aircraft parts, kit plans, balsa, spruce, plywood, dowels, glues, wire, fuel, engines and metal sheets, including aluminum and brass. Also offers several weights of silk, silray, ply span tissue, nylon, polyester, plastic and flight foam. Stocks paints for foam, ARF models, casting materials, including resin, fiberglass and control lines. Services include vacuum molding, silk screening, custom decals, laser cutting, wire bending, and composition and printing.
For Further Information: Contact a dealer, or catalog, $3.
Accepts: MasterCard, Visa

SKYTECH MODELS
2373 N.W. 185th, #290
Hillsboro, OR 97124

Offers: Model aircraft kits, including aerial aircraft carriers, the U.S.S. Macon and U.S.S. Akron. Kits feature 24″ fiberglass hull, brass outriggers, props and other details, decals and history with photos and instructions in 1/400 scale.
For Further Information: Send SASE.

DON SMITH
2260 N. Dixie Highway
Boca Raton, FL 33431
(305) 796-6800

Offers: Scale R/C aircraft plans: Messerschmitt, Henschel, Lavochkin, Heinkel, Hawker Sea Furn, Curtis R3C2, others. Cowls, canopies.
For Further Information: Send $1.

SUPERIOR AIRCRAFT MATERIALS
12020 Centralia
Hawaiian Gardens, CA 90716
(310) 865-3220

Offers: Balsa wood: sticks, wide sheets, "superlite," planks, others. Carries bargain balsa and birch plywood.
For Further Information: Send SASE for catalog.

WESCRAFT
P.O. Box 188
Aguanga, CA 92536
(909) 767-2414

Offers: Giant-scale R/C aircraft kits, including B-17G, P-51D, PBY 5A, HR-1, B-24J, A-20; Tsunami; Unlimited and Racer. All kits with fiberglass fuselages, foam wing cores and foam tail assemblies.
For Further Information: Call or send SASE.

Model Making—General

Also see Miniature Making, Model Making—Aircraft, Model Making—Railroad and other related categories.

A.J. FISHER, INC.
1002 Etowah Ave.
Royal Oak, MI 48067
(810) 541-0352

Offers: Model ship and yacht fittings to scratch build a competitive R/C model yacht in the 36/600, 1 meter, 50/800 or 10 rater class. Kits of Great Lakes and ocean-going vessels available, plus model building plans and books.
For Further Information: Illustrated catalog, $3.

ACE R/C
116 W. 19th St.
P.O. Box 472
Higginsville, MO 64037
(816) 584-7121, (800) 322-7121

Offers: Model products utilizing Amazing Hinges of latex rubber. Surfaces can be butt-fitted; hinge tension pulls the surfaces together. Others.
For Further Information: Catalog, $3.

AEROSPACE COMPOSITE PRODUCTS
14210 Doolittle Dr.
San Leandro, CA 94577
(510) 352-2022
Fax: (510) 352-2021

Offers: Composite materials: Vacuum bagging supplies, carbon fiber laminates, Rohacell (light, rigid foam in 3 thicknesses), carbon or Kevlar mat, glass cloth, carbon fiber (tape, ribbon) fabric tapes. E-Z lam epoxy laminating resin. Also offers kelvar, carbon woven fabrics.
For Further Information: Send SASE for complete listing.
Accepts: American Express, Discover, MasterCard, Visa

AMERICA'S HOBBY CENTER, INC.
146 W. 22nd St.
New York, NY 10011
(212) 675-8922

Offers: Model R/C aircraft, boat and car kits, parts and supplies in known brands for systems (Airtronics, Futaba, Challanger, Cannon), motors (Enya, O.S. Technopower, G-Mark,

K & B, Cox, OS, Royal). Also offers kits, starter kits, kits combos with engines or systems for airplanes, boats, ships, cars. Carries Tamiya cars/accessories, glider accessories, retracts, batteries, plugs and engine starters, R/C model car kits/combos: Futaba, Tamiya, Marui, others. Also carries radios, parts, power tools (Dremel, Miller—sprayer set), Taig micro lathe and accessories. Aero Publishers books available.
For Further Information: R/C models catalog, $2.50; airplane catalog, $2.50.

APC HOBBIES
Box 122
Earlysville, VA 22936
(804) 973-2705

Offers: Model kits, including 2,000-plus old and out-of-production kits and new kits including by Tamiya, Aoshima, Commanders $\frac{1}{35}$, Mb $\frac{1}{350}$, scale ships and Bandai $\frac{1}{24}$ and others.
For Further Information: APC Full Line catalog, $4.50; old kit lists, $3 each.

APPLIED DESIGN CORP.
P.O. Box 3384
Torrance, CA 90510
(310) 375-4120

Offers: Tools for model building, etc.: mini hand belt sander (adjustable tension), mini sandpaper strips, T-bar aluminum sanding block (2 sizes), Ruff Stuff adhesive sheet sandpapers (3 grains), mini compact hacksaw (10″ handles wood, plastic, metal and hardened music wire). Others.
For Further Information: Catalog, 50¢.

ARCHER'S HOBBY WORLD
15432 Alsace Circle
Irvine, CA 92714
(714) 552-3142

Offers: Plastic model kits for aircraft, ships, military vehicles by: Ace, Airfix, Arc, Bandai, Crown, Detail Master, DML, ESCI, Fujini, Glencoe, Masegama, Keller, Hobbycraft, IMAI, Italeri, Johan, Lindberg, LS, Matchbox, Mikro, Inicraft, Mitsowa, Model Tech, Monogram, MPC, Pegasus, Pioneer, Red Star, Revell, Skywave, Supermodel, Yaksts, Tamaya, Testors, Trimaster, Union, Verlinden, Williams Bros., WK Models. Vacuform kits by: Airframe, Air Vac, Combat, Contrail, Elliott, Execuform, Falcon, Formaplane, Joystick, Rareplanes, Wings. Also carries decals, finishes, tools, modeling supplies, books. Minimum order, $10.

For Further Information: Catalog, $5.00 (U.S.); $6 overseas.

AUTO-ETCH
P.O. Box 12921
Philadelphia, PA 19108

Offers: Auto-Etch top photo-etching machine to design and create parts.
For Further Information: Packet, $2.

BENSON HOBBY PRODUCTS
7119 N. Chimney Rock Place
Tucson, AZ 85718

Offers: Model electronic accessories for electric R/C, wide range of products.
For Further Information: Send SASE for brochure.

BLUEJACKET SHIP CRAFTERS
P.O. Box 425
Stockton Springs, ME 04981
(800) 448 5567

Offers: Over 35 fine-scale ship model kits in a wide variety of materials for all levels and interests, with pre-carved wooden hulls, plank-on-frame construction or fiberglass and cast resin, static display and R/C models, available with laser-cut wood parts, etched brass details and case Britannia fittings.
For Further Information: Catalogs, $3.

CENTRAL MODEL MARKETING
P.O. Box 772
Aurora, CO 80040
(800) 962-2010

Offers: R/C cars, boats and planes.
For Further Information: Catalog, $1.
Accepts: MasterCard, Visa

CLEVELAND MODEL & SUPPLY CO.
9800 Detroit Ave.
Cleveland, OH 44102
(216) 961-3600

Offers: Model aircraft (C-D) plans (for giant scale models, R/C, electric, rubber or gas powered) for early birds, warbirds, commercial and racers, private models, homebuilts, jets, others: Supermarine, Boeing, Beech, Piper Cubs, Fokker, Lindbergs, Waco Taper-Wings, Bristol, Lock Air Express, Curtiss, others.
For Further Information: Pictorial catalog and price list, $2 ($3 outside the U.S.).

ERIC CLUTTON
913 Cedar Lane
Tullahoma, TN 37388
(615) 455-2256

Offers: P.A.W. diesels for model aircraft, .049 to .35, RC and STD, plus Davies-Charlton diesels (English-made) including Dart .03, Merlin .045, Spitfire .06, Sabre .09.
For Further Information: Lists, $1.

CONCEPT RESEARCH AND DEVELOPMENT, INC.
Siegecraft Division
1003 S. Christensen Rd.
Medical Lake, WA 99022
(509) 244-0106

Offers: Miniature functional catapults and ballista kits, parts and accessories. Also carries preassembled models.
For Further Information: Brochure, $2 U.S. (refundable).

D & J HOBBY & CRAFTS
96 San Tomas Aquino Rd.
Campbell, CA 95008
(408) 379-1696

Offers: Complete lines of model materials: Imported aircraft, ships and armor kits, fantasy miniatures and games, mini-tanks and GHQ micro armor, scratch building supplies, and materials by Humbrol, Polly S, Floquil, plus Paasche airbrushes and parts. Decals, books and magazines are available.
For Further Information: Send SASE with specific inquiries.
Store Location: At above address. Hours: M, T, W 10-6. Th, F, 10-4. Sat, 12-5:30. Sun, 10-5:30.

DIAMOND ENTERPRISES
P.O. Box 537
Alexandria Bay, NY 13607
(613) 475-1771
Fax: (613) 475-3748

Offers: Live steam model train kits—complete Wilesco & Mamod line. Also offers kits for tractors, marine craft, cars and trucks, plus stationary engines and accessories, including a wide array of parts. Service department.
For Further Information: Catalog, $5.95 (refundable).

DISCOUNT HOBBY CENTER
P.O. Box 370
Utica, NY 13503
(315) 733-3741

Offers: Full range of model kits, including Revell, DML, Italeri, Heller, Monogram, Hobby Craft, Tamiya, Minicraft, Testor and others. Also offers Badger airbrushes, Testor brushes and paints, including acrylics and enamels.

For Further Information: Catalog, $5.
Accepts: MasterCard, Visa

THE DROMEDARY

6324 Belton Rd.
El Paso, TX 79912
(915) 584-2445

Offers: Model ship builder supplies—full lines of tools, rigging and fittings, ship kits (U.S. and plank-on-frame imported), plus a variety of woods, and others.
For Further Information: Catalog, $6 ($7 outside the U.S.).
Accepts: MasterCard, Visa

EVERGREEN SCALE MODELS

12808 NE 125th Way
Kirkland, WA 98034

Offers: Styrene products for model building: Board and batten, $3/16''$ and $1/4''$ square strips, larger telescoping tubing, wide-spaced clapboard, others. Handbook: Tips/techniques.
For Further Information: Contact dealer, or $2 for handbook.

FORMULA 1

5 Keane Ave.
Islington, Ontario M9B 2B6
Canada
(416) 626-5781

Offers: Scale model classic racing and other cars by Tamiya, Fujimi, Hasegawa, Protar, Lemans Miniatures, Gunze, Modelers' and others.
For Further Information: Free price list.
Accepts: American Express, MasterCard, Visa

GALASTIC TRADE COMMISSION

10185 Switzer
Overland Park, KS 66202
(913) 492-2169

Offers: Over 1,000 science fiction models from Robotech, Star Trek, Thunderbirds, Star Wars, SF3D, Galctiza, Starblazers, Macross and others.
For Further Information: 28-page catalog, $3.
Discounts: Sells wholesale.

GREAT PLANES MODEL MANUFACTURING

P.O. Box 9021
2904 Research Rd.
Champaign, IL 61826
(217) 398-6300 or (800) 637-7660
Fax: (217) 398-1104

Offers: Model kits, including R/C cars, boats, airplanes, helicopters and accessories; model railroading, plastics, die-cast, roadracing and rockets. Tools, building supplies, activity crafts and science products also avaiable. Carries publications, books and over 300 hobby lines, including the following brands: Great Planes (their own), Kyosho, O.S. Engines, Hobbico, Top Flite, U.S. AirCore, SuperTigre, DuraTrax, Heli-Max, DuraPlane, Flitecraft, Milt Video.
For Further Information: Call or write with inquiry.

HOBBY HOUSE, INC.

30991 Smile Rd.
Livonia, MI 48150
(313) 425-9720

Offers: Complete line of supplies, including R/C planes, boats and cars, plastic models, trains in all scales, kites, dollhouses, diecasts, steam engines, science supplies.
For Further Information: Send SASE for list.
Store Location: At above address. Hours: M-Sat, 10-8. Sun, 12-5.
Accepts: MasterCard, Visa

HOBBY LOBBY INTERNATIONAL, INC.

5614 Franklin Pike Circle
Brentwood, TN 37027
(615) 373-1444

Offers: Model boat/ship items, including unusuals: Electric flight props, fast scale offshore racing cat, 400-watt electric flight motor, l-meter racing sailboat, 3-meter electric soarer, 4' steam launch, wood-colored old-timer props, electric flight propulsion systems and others.
For Further Information: Free catalog ($2 outside the U.S.).

INTERNATIONAL HOBBY SUPPLY

P.O. Box 426
Woodland Hills, CA 91365
(818) 886-0423

Offers: Over 12,000 items, including a line of plastic model kits from most known manufacturers and a large selection of accessories, decals and books. Also offers science fiction items.
For Further Information: 300-page catalog, $5 ($12.50 in Canada and Mexico).
Accepts: MasterCard, Visa

I/R MINIATURES, INC.

P.O. Box 89, Dept. Y
Burnt Hills, NY 12027
(518) 885-6054

Offers: Over 1,000 miniature model soldier kits, including 54mm and 76mm scale. Also offers Christmas and literary figures, soldiers of most conflicts worldwide, from the ancient world to Vietnam.

For Further Information: Send SASE; illustrated catalog, $6.

Discounts: Sells wholesale to legitimate businesses.

K & S ENGINEERING
6917 W. 59th St.
Chicago, IL 60638
(312) 586-8503

Offers: Metal products for model building, etc.: Aluminum tube (8 sizes), round brass tube (20 sizes), copper tube (4 sizes), soft brass fuel tubing, rectangular brass tube (4 sizes), brass strips (20 sizes), square brass tube (7 sizes), brass angles, channel and solid brass rods (many sizes), sheet metal ($4'' \times 10''$), brass (4 thicknesses), tin, aluminum (3 thicknesses), .025 copper, soldering tools (4 models with 30, 60 or 100 watt capacity).

For Further Information: Catalog.

THE KIT BUNKER
2905 Spring Park Rd.
Jacksonville, FL 32207

Offers: Line of aircraft, armor, ships and figures kits (old and new). Also purchases kits, small or large quantity.

For Further Information: Send $1 and SASE with double postage for list.

LIGHTSHEET
319 Main Dunstable Rd.
Nashua, NH 03062
(800) 595 7146

Offers: Neon lighting from paper-thin, flexible electronic material, trims to any size/shape for scale models. Also science fiction props, miniatures and others.

For Further Information: Send SASE.

MICRO-MARK
340-2015 Snyder Ave.
Berkeley Heights, NJ 07922

Offers: Hard-to-find modeler's tools (hand and power types): Saws, including miter cutoff type, Dremel motoshop attachments, Moto-Tool and holders, flexible shaft, drill press attachments, table shaper, disc/belt sander and rotor attachments for Moto-Tools, plus jeweler's drill press, Mini-Vac micro cleaner, Miter-Rite tools, nippers, tweezers, brushes, file sets, mini bolt cutters, knife blades and sets. Carries Badger airbrush sets and compressors. Others.

For Further Information: 80-page catalog, $1 ($2 outside U.S.).

Accepts: American Express, Discover, MasterCard, Visa

MODEL EXPO, INC.
P.O. Box 1000
Mt. Pocono, PA 18344
(717) 839-2080

Offers: Historic ship model kits (from Europe): Replicas (many over 4' long) with walnut and mahogany planking, fittings and details in bronze, brass and rare hardwoods—large-scale plans, step-by-step instructions and all materials included. Models include clipper and other sailing ships like the Bluenose II (replica of the last of the tall schooners). Instructional video, *You Take the Helm*, shows how to build the Bluenose, step by step.

For Further Information: Catalog, $1.

Accepts: MasterCard, Visa

MODEL SHIPWAYS
P.O. Box 1000
Mt. Pocono, PA 18344

Offers: Line of ship model kits of historically accurate scale, including replicas of known sailing ships and others. Kits of solid hull or plank on bulkhead types with Britannia metal fittings, laser cut wooden parts, plans and instructions are available for craftspeople at all levels. Among the ships replicated are Bluenose, Colonial Schooners and Phantom. Also offers team towboat, whaleboat and other boats. Cutting and shaping tool sets and an electric plank bender are also available.

For Further Information: Free catalog.

NK PRODUCTS
P.O. Box 94
Landing, NJ 07850

Offers: Model diorama accesories at 1:35 scale (a variety of buildings, walls, fences, vehicles, others).

For Further Information: Catalog, $1.75.

OMNI MODELS
P.O. Box 708
Mahomet, IL 61853
(800) 342-6464

Offers: R/C model car kits and combo deals, plus parts, accessories and electronics by: Advanced, Airtronics, Aristocraft, Associated, Astro Flight, B & B, Bolink, Cox, Dean's, Dynaflite, Futaba, Higley's, KO Propo, Leisure, Losi, McAllistor, MRC, MRP, Novak, Paragon, Parma, Proline, Protec, Ram, Robart, Royal, Sanyo, Schumacher, Tekin, Traxxas, Trinity, Twister, Varicom, World Engines, Yokomo, others.

For Further Information: Send SASE for list.

Accepts: MasterCard, Visa

PACIFIC FRONT HOBBIES
11804 N.E. 138th St.
Lorland, WA 09034
(206) 821-2564
Fax: (206) 821-9034

Offers: Scale ship model kits, including imported and domestic resin and injected types of Kobo-Hiyu, Navalworks, Waveline, Pitroad, Corsair Armada, Doc-Modell, P & I, MB, Iron Shipwright, Classic Warships and others. Full line of detail parts, paints, accessories, plans and books also available.
For Further Information: Catalog, $5 ($6 outside U.S.).
Accepts: MasterCard, Visa

PHOENIX MODEL CO.
P.O. Box 15390
Brooksville, FL 34609
(904) 754-8522
Fax: (904) 754-1882

Offers: Scale model kits, including cars, ships, planes, trucks, motorcycles. Kits from Protar, Airvix, Revell, Nagano, Heller, Arii, Airfix, Revell Germany, Monogram and Matchbox are available.
For Further Information: Catalog, $3.

PLASTRUCT
1020 S. Wallace Place
City of Industry, CA 91748

Offers: Over 1,500 different scratch building model parts and kits, including plastic scale model parts and others.

CHRIS ROSSBACH
RD 1, Queensboro Manor
Gloversville, NY 12078
(518) 725-4446

Offers: Antique model ignition engines and parts: Precision cast timers, original cylinder heads, point sets, drive washers, spark plugs, tanks. Wide range of engines.
For Further Information: Catalog, $5 ($8 outside the U.S.).

ROYAL PRODUCTS CORP.
790 W. Tennessee Ave.
Denver, CO 80223
(303) 778-7711

Offers: Model R/C products—Head Start systems including heavy-duty starter (standard or jumbo, for engines up to 1:4 scale), power panels, 12V fuel pump (fills or drains model or diesel fuel), locking socket (lock-on battery clip, even fits 4-cycle plugs). Other model aircraft and accessories.
For Further Information: Contact your hobby dealer, or catalog, $4.

SARATOGA SOLDIER SHOP & MILITARY BOOKSTORE
831 Rt. 67, #40
Ballston, NY 12020
(518) 885-1497

Offers: Pewter soldier kits, including 54mm scale Civil War and figures from other eras. Also offers modeler's aids, paints and books.
For Further Information: Catalog, $6.

SATELLITE CITY
P.O. Box 836, Dept. I.O.F.
Simi Valley, CA 93062
(805) 522-0062

Offers: Glues for wood, plastic, rubber, fiberglass or Kevlar—instant and penetrating odorless types.
For Further Information: Send SASE for free tip booklet and fiberglassing instructions.

RENE D. SERRAO
Box 30, Site 3, R.R. 5
Armdale, Nova Scotia B3L 4J5
Canada

Offers: Plans of America's Cup J Boats, ¾″ to 1′ scale; plans of America's Cup 12 metros, drawn 1″ to 1′ scale.
For Further Information: Send SASE.

SMALL WORLD
1100 W. Chester Pike #C22
Westchester, PA 19382

Offers: Science fiction and horror model kits of resin and vinyl from Biliken, Halcyon, Horizon, Lunar Models, Screamin' and others.
For Further Information: Illustrated catalog, $2.50; $4 outside U.S (refundable).

SPAULDING TRADING AND SHIPPING
W290 Co. Rd. Q
Mindoro, WI 54644
(608) 857-3932
Fax: (608) 857-3624

Offers: Model truck kits in ¼ and ⅕ scales, current and discontinued kits, diecast and plastic models, resin parts and truck books.
For Further Information: Catalog, $1.
Accepts: MasterCard, Visa

TECH-TOYS
370 Rt. 46 W.
Parsippany, NJ 07054
(201) 227-7012

Offers: R/C model car customizing parts in a variety of scales

for on and off road cars, trucks and boats—specializes in 1:4 and 1:6. Carries finishing materials and equipment, electronics by: A & L, Advance, Airtronics, Astroflight, Badger, Blue Ribbon, Bolink, Buds, Goldberg, Champion, Cobra International, Composite, Cox, CRP, Custom, Dahms, Deans, Delta, Dremel, Dubro, Duratrax, Floquil, Fox, Futaba, Higley, Houge, JG, K & B, KO Propo, Lavco, M&M, Marui, MCS, MIP, Monogram, Panaconic, Paragon, PDI, Cut, Pro-Shop, Raceco, Race, Sanyo, Tekin, Thorp, Universal, Ungar.
For Further Information: Call or send SASE with inquiry.
Accepts: MasterCard, Visa

TELEFLITE CORP.
11620 Kitching St.
Moreno Valley, CA 92557
(909) 242-0500

Offers: Model rocket motors—you-build (using a rock tumbler and simple handtools), finished product gives 40 lbs. of thrust. Electric igniter from household materials.
For Further Information: Brochure and sample igniter, $2.

32ND PARALLEL
P.O. Box 804
Pismo Beach, CA 93448
(805) 481-3170

Offers: Scale model submarines, 3 models in 1:32 scale with a variety of ballast control systems and options, including working torpedos. Models available from hull kit only, to complete kits with all required parts (less radio) to operate submerged.
For Further Information: Color catalog, $3.

TOWER HOBBIES
P.O. Box 9078
Champaign, IL 61826

Offers: Model R/C equipment, kits and supplies/parts for model cars, boats, planes, tanks, engines, radios, accessories by over 300 manufacturers, including ACE R/C, Astro-flight, Dave Brown, Cox, Cressline, Davey Systems, Dremelools, Du-Bro, Future Flight airplane, Flitecraft Models, Futaba (servos, sticks), Carl Goldberg model kits, Great Planes airplane kits, Guillows, Hobbico, Hot Stuff, K & B, Kyosho (aircraft kits, chargers), Master Airscrew, K J Miller, Milt Video, Royal (starter, fuel pump), Sanyo, Supertiger, Top Flite aircraft. Tower Hobbies: Charger, hydrometer, voltmeter, fuel pump, battery, fuels, tools, balsa assortment, heatgun, sealing iron. Others.
For Further Information: Catalog, $3.

THE TOY SOLDIER CO.
100 Riverside Dr.
New York, NY 10024
(212) 799-6348

Offers: Model toy soldiers of plastic and lead. Includes 600 figures from U.S. and foreign manufacturers, dating 1900 to the present (15mm to 70mm scales). Lead soldiers by Authenticast, Bastion, Benbros, Britains, Charbens, Cherilea, Citadel, Crescent, Dorset, Games Workshop, Grenadier, Heritage USA, Herrings, Imperial, Marlborough, Mignot, Minifigs, Ral Partha, S.A.E. Steadfast, Taylor & Barrett Timpo, Trophy, Tunstill, Wend-Al. Plastic soldiers by: Airfix, Atlantic, Auburn, Blue Box, Charbens, Cherilea, Crescent, Deetail, Elastolin, ESCI, Eyes Right, Giant, Hillco, Ideal, Marx, Merton, MPC, Rel, Remsea, Starlux, Superior, Swoppet, Timpo, others.
For Further Information: Send SASE for sample of monthly list; lead or plastics catalog, $7.50 each (specify lead or plastic).

TWELVE SQUARED
P.O. Box 21547
Eagan, MN 55121

Offers: Model aircraft kits—B-1, Bell, Northrop, Heinkel with injected kits and conversions: 1/144 scale and 1/72 scale models kits. Carries model stands for aircraft. Others.
For Further Information: Send SASE for illustrated catalog.

UNIVERSAL HOVERCRAFT
1204 3rd St.,
P.O. Box 281
Cordova, IL 61242

Offers: Plans for model hovercrafts, including air cushion vehicles that move inches above any surface, in a variety of types. Also offers full-size hovercraft plans.

VANGUARD MODEL MARINE
P.O. Box 708, Station B
Ottawa, Ontario K1P 5P8
Canada

Offers: Ship drawings for Canadian warships and government vessels of many types.
For Further Information: Catalog, $2.

VANTEC
460 Casa Real Placa
Nipomo, CA 93444
805-929-5055

Offers: Radio control (18-channel) for boats, subs, robots, quarter scale, plus 6 servo channels for control surfaces, electric drive motors, proportional functions, and 8 momentary on-off functions for guns, torpedos, horns, cranes, sub diving pumps; has 4-key on/key off channels for lights, etc.
For Further Information: Specifications, $2.
Accepts: MasterCard, Visa

VINYLWRITE CUSTOM LETTERING

16043 Tulsa St.
Granada Hills, CA 91344
(818) 363-7131

Offers: Model service, including custom lettering—pre-spaced, pre-aligned, custom computer cut in 3M premium cast vinyl, 2 mil thin. Choose from vertical or horizontal text in custom lengths, available in 15 colors and 6 typestyles, including military block, slanted or upright text, ½-inch to 12 inches high.
For Further Information: Write or call for sample.

UNIVERSAL HOVERCRAFT

1204 3rd St.,
P.O. Box 281
Cordova, IL 61242

Offers: Plans for model hovercrafts, including air cushion vehicles that move inches above any surface, in a variety of types. Also offers full-size hovercraft plans.

WINGS 'N THINGS

1073 Main St.
Manchester, CT 06040
(203) 533-1412

Offers: Extensive line of plastic and resin model kits, modeling accessories, Badger and Pasche airbrushes, decals, scratch building materials, vinyl Science Fiction figures and books.
For Further Information: Catalog, $3 (refundable).
Accepts: MasterCard, Visa

ZONA TOOL COMPANY

P.O. Box 502
Bethel, CT 06801

Offers: Berna Assemblers Clamping System, which aids in the multiple clamping of model parts for assembly, gluing of miniatures, and similar uses. Also offers razor saws.
For Further Information: Send SASE.
Discounts: Sells wholesale.

Model Making—Railroad

Also see Miniature Making, Model Making—General and other related categories.

AMERICA'S HOBBY CENTER, INC.
146 W. 22nd St.
New York, NY 10011
(212) 675-8922

Offers: Model railroads, HO and N gauge: Locomotives, cars, coaches (ready-to-run) by Riverossi, Bachmann, MDC, Athearn, International Hobbies, Atlas, Con-Cor, others. Automatic switches, track, crossings, switch machines, couplers, switches, MRC power packs, dual packs also available.
For Further Information: Free catalog.

NOEL ARNOLD
84 Twin Arch Rd.
Washingtonville, NY 10992
(914) 496-5185

Offers: Model railroads—from 200 manufacturers, including locomotives, deisels, cabooses, and a variety of car types, are available in kits and as parts and accessories, plus layout structures and materials.
For Further Information: Send $1 and large SASE for newsletter.

ASHLANDBARNS
990CSS Butler Creek
Ashland, OR 97520
(541) 488-1541

Offers: Blueprints of 94 barns, craft shops, garages, and storages, including model and full-sized. Cast weathervanes, posts and mailbox signs also available.
For Further Information: Catalog, $5.

CABOOSE HOBBIES
500 S. Broadway
Denver, CO 80209
(303) 777-6766

Offers: Model railroad items in all scales and gauges.
For Further Information: Send SASE.

CENTRAL VALLEY
1203 Pike Lane
Oceano, CA 93445
(805) 489-8586

Offers: Model railroad kits in HO scale black, styrene plastic: Pratt truss bridges, bridge tie sections, girders, fences, railings, steps, ladders, end beams and brake shoes (detailed).
For Further Information: Contact dealer or send SASE.

CON-COR
1025 Industrial Dr.
Bensenville, IL 60106
(708) 595-0210
Fax: (708) 595-0924

Offers: Model railroad car kits (metal) including 40' sliding door boxcars (of the 1940s to the 1960s), including Santa Fe, Southern Pacific, Baltimore & Ohio, Conrail, Southern Railway, SOO Line. N-gauge locomotives—Great Northern, Heavy Pacific, Berkshire, Streamlined Hudson (with tender). Other cars and coaches available.
For Further Information: Contact your dealer or send SASE for list.

DESIGN PRESERVATION MODELS
P.O. Box 66
Linn Creek, MO 65052
(573) 346-1234
Fax: (573) 346-6700

Offers: Model kits, including buildings and other structures for towns and villages, and others.
For Further Information: Color catalog, $1.50 or 5 stamps.

GREEN FROG PRODUCTIONS LTD.
200 N. Cobb Pkwy, Suite 138
Marietta, GA 30062
(770) 422-2220
Fax: (770) 422-2467

Offers: 10 videotape series of instruction, "Building a Model Railroad," which includes designing, benchwork construction, laying track, wiring building structures, and tips on rolling stock, scenery, adding realism and railroad operation.
For Further Information: Send SASE.

H&B PRECISION CARD MODELS

2026 Spring Branch Dr.
Vienna, VA 22181
(703) 281-0813
Fax: (703) 281-0813

Offers: Paper model kits for railroad buildings, in HO and N scale including buildings, city blocks from German cities in N and Z scale, Australian HO and N scale model train accessories and others.
For Further Information: Send SASE.

HOBBY SURPLUS SALES

P.O. Box 2170CS
New Britain, CT 06050
(203) 223-0600

Offers: Model railroad items including Lionel, American Flyer, HO, N-gauge, LGB. Carries full lines of train repair parts. (Also has other models—R/C, plastic and wood—and model accessories.)
For Further Information: 128-page catalog, $3.

INTERNATIONAL HOBBIES

10556 Combie Rd., Suite 6327
Auburn, CA 95602
(916) 268-8715

Offers: Selection of British model railroad kits in HO and O scale including steam, diesel, rolling stock, road vehicles and structures. Ready to run model in HO. Also equipment, videos, books and more.
For Further Information: Illustrated catalog, $4.
Accepts: American Express, MasterCard, Visa.

INTERNATIONAL HOBBY CORP.

413 E. Allegheny Ave.
Philadelphia, PA 19134
(215) 426-ATSF

Offers: Model railroad structures/buildings: IHC carnival series (HO-scale carousel and ferris wheel, plus motorizing kits), HO-scale 5-pack gingerbread houses in HO-, N- or O-scale kits. O-scale Pola, HO- and N-scale building kits (block of buildings, antique shop/home, old-time bank, brewery, 3 buildings, pickle factory). HO- and O-scale model trains, kits by Rivarossi. Model trees—over 15 types—by IHC. Others.
For Further Information: Contact dealer, or order catalogs. IHC catalog ($4.98), Preiser catalog ($14.98), parts catalog/Scratch Builders Bible, ($14.98), parts price list ($1.98), ROCO ($7).

LOCOMOTIVE WORKSHOP

9 Rt. 520
Englishtown, NJ 07726
(908) 536-6873

Offers: Model railroad economy 0-6-0 kits in O-scale brass,

plus scale and highrail. Also carries a wide range of O-scale kits of Athearn, Lobaugh and Loco Works parts for steam operation.
For Further Information: Send large SASE for current newsletter.

MAINLINE AND SIDING

392 Morrison Rd.
Columbus, OH 43213
(614) 755-5401
Fax: (614) 755-5402

Offers: Wood model series of more than 40 structures, including prototypes of the Pennsylvania oil industry in the 1900s—main building and loading platform, oil storage vats/shed, oil well derricks with cast metal pumps; barrels and Jordon truck and others.
For Further Information: Catalog, $1 (Please specify N or HO scale).

MAINLINE HOBBY SUPPLY

15066 Buchanan Trl. E.
Blue Ridge Summit, PA 17214
(717) 794-2860
Fax: (717) 794-5594
Offers: Model railroad structures, parts, figures, scenery, tools, videos and books.
For Further Information: Send SASE for newsletter.
Store Location: At above address.
Accepts: American Express, Discover, MasterCard, Visa

DONALD B. MANLICK, MMR

2127 S. 11th St.
Manitowoc, WI 54220
(414) 684-8688

Offers: Line of DM custom decals in HO, N, O and S scales.
For Further Information: Send large SASE with double postage.

MANTUA INDUSTRIES

P.O. Box 10
Woodbury Heights, NJ 08097
(609) 853-0300

Offers: HO gauge model railroad engines, rolling stock and sets, including a series of steam and diesel locomotives. Vintage cars include combines, passenger, box, horse, water, log and cabooses. Also carries freight cars, train sets and signals: sporting goods and games
For Further Information: Contact dealer, or catalog, $2.

MINIATRONICS

561 Acorn St.
Deer Park, NY 11729
(516) 242-6464
Fax: (516) 242-7796

Offers: Electronics, including clear and colored incandescent lamps, micro mini connectors, blinker, flasher and standard LEDs, neon-like signs, power distribution blocks, terminal blocks, mini slide and toggle type switches.
For Further Information: Send SASE.
Accepts: American Express, Discover, MasterCard, Visa.

P & D HOBBY SHOP

31902 Groesbeck
Fraser, MI 48026
(810) 296-6116

Offers: Model railroad components, including conversion for Weaver RS-3, early Weaver RS units and RS-4/5 conversion kits. Parts and parts kits with components and instructions and RS and FA parts are available. Parts include windshield wipers, headlights, flag pole holders, market lights, stacks, steam vents, grills, horns, marker lights, fans, others. Carries O-scale model railroad locomotives and cars (40' box cars, others).
For Further Information: O-scale list, send SASE with triple postage.
Accepts: MasterCard, Visa

RAIL GRAPHICS

1183 N. Lancaster Circle
S. Elgin, IL 60177
(708)742-5404
Fax: (708) 742-5407

Offers: Custom decals from submitted artwork in sets for two model railroad cars; dimensional data for all eras; computerized art and text services. Sizes for all scales.
For Further Information: Send large SASE for free sample.

RAILS 'N SHAFTS

P.O. Box 300
Laurys Station, PA 18059
(610) 261-0133
Fax: (610) 261-7962

Offers: Books on America's railroads, including B&O Steam, Canadian national railways, Chessie, C & NW power, Chicago's trains, Colorado rail, North Shore, diesel locomotive rosters, electric locomotive plans, Grand Trunk Western Guide to Tourist Railroads, Pennsylvania, Kansas City Southern, Katy railroad, Lehigh and New England, MR Cyclopedia, Milwaukee electrics and rails, N&W, New York Central, Grand Central, Norfolk & Western, Old Dominion, passenger trains, cabooses, Mexican railroads, Red Arrow, St. Clair,

Santa Fe Trails, Seaboard, Southern Pacific, trolleys, traction classics, Union Pacific and others.
For Further Information: Send SASE for catalog.
Accepts: American Express, Discover, MasterCard, Visa

REALISTIC BACKDROPS

P.O. Box 873
Baldwinsville, NY 13027

Offers: Scenic backdrops including sky in real colors with whispy clouds or clear blue sky.
For Further Information: Send SASE for catalog.

THE RED CABOOSE

23 W. 45th St. Downstairs
New York, NY 10036
(212) 575-0155
Fax: (212) 575-0272

Offers: Model railroad trains and accessories, including American and foreign prototypes, in N, HO and other scales by Kadee, Atlas, Rivarossi, Mantua, Stewart, Bachmann, Peco, Marklin, Shinohara, Walthers, Kibri, Vollmer/Faller, Fleischman and European trains in all scales. Carries Paasche airbrush sets. Custom services include layout building, repairs and restoration.
For Further Information: Call with specific inquiry.
Accepts: American Express, Discover, MasterCard, Visa

CHARLES RO SUPPLY COMPANY

P.O. Box 100
662 Cross St.
Malden, CA 92148
(617) 321-0090
Fax: (617) 321-6459

Offers: Model railroad kits including Lionel buildings, and others. Trackside accessories, track and switches, cork road bed, metal boulevard lights, transformers, car kits, track and other products. Trains from many manufacturers.
For Further Information: Lionel catalog, $3. Send SASE for O-gauge price list.
Accepts: Discover, MasterCard, Visa.

STANDARD HOBBY SUPPLY

P.O. Box 801
Mahwah, NJ 07430
(201) 825-2211
Fax: (201) 512-0882

Offers: Model railroad products from Atlas, Boser Mfg., CAboose Industries, Kadee, Athearn, IHC, Peco, Model Power, Proto Power, Rivarossi, Bachmann, Shinohara, Cooch Ent., Tomar, Heljan, Stewart and others—for train kits, detail and structures kits, buildings, electronics, scenics, mini-scenes, tree kits, ballast, vehicles, and others. Badger airbrushes, Dremel tools, Floquil paints and other finishing products.

For Further Information: Catalog, $3; foreign $4 (U.S. funds).
Accepts: Discover, MasterCard, Visa

THE TRAIN MASTER LTD.
P.O. Box 5208
Albany, NY 12205
(518) 489-4777

Offers: N-scale model railroad items, including kits and cars (freight, passenger and box), turntables, locomotives, track, switches and many other parts, model structures and scenery, of major manufacturers: Acme, AMM, Aim, AMI, Arbour, B-R, Bachmann, Bowser, Brawa, Caboose Ind., DMK, EKO, Gloor, Green Max, Faller, Cork, Heljan, Herpa, Kadee, Kato, Kibri, Labelle, Lifelike, Magnuson, Midwest, ML, MLR, Model Dynamics, Model Rectifier, MZZ, MJ Int., Roco, Walthers, others.
For Further Information: N-scale price list/catalog, $2 ($1 refundable).

TRAINTOWN OF CANADA
323 - 9632 Cameron St.
Burnaby, V3J 1M2
Canada

Offers: HO-scale cork roadbed, Atlas track, couplers and many other products.
For Further Information: Send large SASE for bulletin of specials.

TRAIN WORLD
751 McDonald Ave.
Brooklyn, NY 11218
(800) 541-7010
Fax: (718) 972-8514

Offers: Model railroad trains, including LGB collectors' cars, power packs and electronics, box cars and gondolas. Carries over 90 buildings, replacement parts, starter sets with track and transformer, locomotives, street cars, passenger and freight cars, accessories, and electrical items. Also carries Aristo Craft G-scale model buildings, Mantua locomotives and cars, plus Lionel releases, engines and cabooses, rolling stock, operating cars including classics, standard gauge classics, collector sets, cars and others. Bowser and Rivarossi trains are available including locomotives, cars, kits and sets. Athearn cars, MRC power packs, plus various operating accessories are also available.

For Further Information: Send SASE for list.
Accepts: MasterCard, Visa

VALLEY MODEL TRAINS
91 Market St., Suite 32, Bldg. 10
Wappingers Falls, NY 12590
(914) 297-7511

Offers: Model railroad building kits in all scales (Z to LBG) and by most manufacturers, including Design Preservation Models series 2 kits for buildings, stores, garages, packing houses and others. Also offers Faller buildings and others. Carries HO scale model automobiles including Cadillac, Buick, Bentley models, Rolls Royce Silver Cloud, Volvo, Mercedes and others.
For Further Information: Send SASE with 55¢ postage for newsletter and list.

WOODLAND SCENICS
P.O. Box 98
Linn Creek, MO 65052
(573) 346-5555

Offers: Model scenics, including all formulated to coordinate colors, turf, and a variety of foilage and lichen in realistic colors. Carries decals—model graphics for letters, lines, numbers (any scale), dry transfers with authentic advertising, posters, signs and railroad heralds (full color).
For Further Information: Contact your dealer or send 4 stamps for catalog.

WORLD OF TRAINS
10518 Metropolitan Ave.
Forest Hills, NY 11375
(718) 520-9700

Offers: Model railroad trains, kits, accessories and parts by Gargraves (track), Lionel (trains, track), LGB locomotives, caboose and cars (passenger, platform gondola, box, flat, hopper, tank, others), plus Bachmann steam locomotives and diesels (HO), Atlas (HO trackage), Bachmann N-scale locomotives and N-Gauge locomotives, HO- and N-gauge powerpacks, and Bachmann N-scale buildings. Also offers transformers and tracks, pre-war and post-war trains and accessories. Buys train collections (old Lionel, American Flyer, M.P.C. and store inventories). Repairs all 027.0 and standard gauges.
For Further Information: Catalog, $3.
Accepts: Discover, MasterCard and Visa

Mold Crafts

Includes Cake, Candles, Concrete, Paper, Plaster, Plastics. Also see Ceramics, Metalworking, Sculpture and Modeling and related categories.

AMERICAN ART CLAY CO., INC.
4717 W. 16th St.
Indianapolis, IN 46222
(317) 244-6871

Offers: Molding and modeling supplies including Sculptamold (clay/plaster/papier-mâché), instant papier-mâché, claycrete, casting compound, Flexwax carving wax and Superdough modeling compound. Carries modeling tools, Mix A Mold (mix powder with water to make reproduction molds in minutes; fill with casting medium), CreaStone (stone-like material for casting), and Rub 'N Buff wood finishes.
For Further Information: Free information packet.

BARKER COMPANY
15106 10th Ave. SW
Seattle, WA 98166
(800) 543-0601

Offers: Candle-making supplies: Dyes, waxes, additives, releases, glaze, metal and plastic candle molds in a variety of shapes and sizes. Honeycomb and smooth beeswax sheets also available.
For Further Information: Catalog, $2.

CANDLECHEM CO.
P.O. Box 705
Randolph, MA 02368
(508) 586-0844

Offers: Line of candle-making chemicals, scents, dyes, pigments, perfume and essential oils and others.
For Further Information: Free catalog.
Discounts: Sells wholesale to legitimate businesses.

CASTCRAFT
Box 17000
Memphis, TN 38187

Offers: Line of moldmaking and casting materials and supplies.
For Further Information: Free information packet.

CASTINGS
P.O. Box 298
Eastsound, WA 98245
(360) 376-3266
Fax: (360) 376-3280

Offers: Casting equipment and supplies for creating toy soldiers, Civil War figures/horses, cannons and weapons, cowboys, Indians, and cavalry men, plus action soldiers of WWI and WWII, aircraft, medieval horses/riders, Napoleonic foot soldiers, artillery and riders/horses. Also offers a German marching band mold, carousel molds, chess set molds (fantasy, Waterloo and King Richard's Court) and winter village molds (carolers, Santa, snowman, skaters, boy and girl on sleds, street lamp). Carries paint kits for mold sets, complete introductory starter kits, casting metals and instruction booklets. Small vulcanizer for silicone rubber mold making from a master in an hour in the kitchen oven.
For Further Information: Product information, $1.
Discounts: Quantity.

CASTOLITE
4915 Dean
Woodstock, IL 60098
(815) 338-4670

Offers: Liquid plastics for casting, coating, fiberglassing, reproducing and embedding, plus additives and fillers.
For Further Information: Catalog, $3.

CEMENTEX LATEX CORP.
121 Varick St.
New York, NY 10013
(212) 741-1770 or (800) 782-9056
Fax: (212) 627-2770

Offers: Natural latex molding compounds: High solids type with medium viscosity (brushable or sprayable) to cast plaster, Portland cement and some waxes; also carries a pre-vulcanized type. Stocks latex for casting hollow articles (pour into plaster mold—when used with filler, very hard articles may be obtained), plus 2-part RTV polysulfide rubber for flexible molds (pourable for casting plaster, cement and others). Manufactures and compounds natural and synthetic latex materials.
For Further Information: Send SASE.

CHICAGO LATEX PRODUCTS, INC.
1030 Morse Ave.
Schaumburg, IL 60193
(708) 893-2880
Fax: (847) 658-7246

Offers: Latex for molding, sculpture, mâché, casting, coatings and adhesives, including one-part natural or neoprene type, for figurines, displays, dolls and others.
For Further Information: Call or write.

COASTAL ENTERPRISES
60 Bretonian Dr., Suite MB
Brick, NJ 08723
(908) 477-7948

Offers: Lead soldier molds and mold-making and casting supplies—full line. Also offers castings, collectibles and hard to find items.
For Further Information: Lists, $1.

COOKIE MOLD CARVER
Box 25
Belleville, IL 62222
(618) 233-7689

Offers: "Edible Art" molds including holiday and others. Also offers Springerle presses, cookie stamps and collectibles.
For Further Information: Catalog, $1 (refundable).

CRAFT TIME
211 S. State College Blvd., #341
Anaheim, CA 92806

Offers: Plastercraft figures—a full line, ready-to-paint, many with instructions and color guide—including adults, children, houses, scenery, animals, others.
For Further Information: Catalog, $2 (refundable).

CREATIVE PAPERCLAY CO.
1800 S. Robertson Blvd., Suite 907
Los Angeles, CA 90035
(310) 839-0466

Offers: Paperclay modeling material, molds for masks, doll heads, others, plus kits and books.
For Further Information: Send SASE.
Discounts: Teachers and institutions; sells wholesale to legitimate businesses.

ESSENTIALS & SUCH
4746 W. Jennifer Ave., Suite 107
Fresno, CA 93722
(209) 277-4747
Fax: (209) 277-9755

Offers: Candlemaking products, including waxes, wicks, dyes, colors, scents, others. Also offers sealant, containers, bottles, droppers and bags.
For Further Information: Call or write for catalog.
Discounts: Sells wholesale.

KEMPER MANUFACTURING CO.
13595 12th St.
Chino, CA 91710
(909) 627-6191

Offers: Cake and candy-making decorator sets. Tools: Flower and leaf cutting, rollers, mini ribbon sculpting, detail carving, bud-setter, others.
For Further Information: Contact dealer or write.

KATHRYN LUNA
24796 Sunstar Ln.
Dana Point, CA 92629

Offers: Metal and other molds for beeswax, chalkware, chocolate or papier mâché; in holiday and other designs.
For Further Information: Catalog, $2 (refundable).

MAXANT INDUSTRIES
P.O. Box 454, Dept. CDT
Ayer, MA 01432
(508) 772-0576

Offers: Candlemaking tanks, including double wall water jacketed, electrically heated for pouring into molds or for dipping.
For Further Information: Send SASE.

POURETTE MFG. CO.
1418 N.W. 53rd
P.O. Box 17056
Seattle, WA 98107
(206) 789-3188
Fax: (206) 789-3640

Offers: Full line of candlemaking supplies, including metal, plastic, specialty and other molds, waxes, scents, colors, additives, glass containers and books.
For Further Information: Free catalog.
Discounts: Sells wholesale.

SWEET CELEBRATIONS
7009 Washington Ave., S.
Edina, MN 55439
(800) 328-6722
Fax: (612) 943-1688

Offers: Line of cake and candy making molds, tools, pans, accessories, ornaments and books.
For Further Information: Free catalog.

VAN DYKE'S
P.O. Box 278
Woonsocket, SD 57385
(800) 843-3320

Offers: Molding: Plaster, Hydro-cal, Hydrostone, rock putty, resin putty, Sculpall. Also offers polymer finish kit, scenery resin, fiberglass cloth, chopped strand mat, strands, polyester resin, talc, whiting, color paste and gel wax. Fillers: Granulated cork, paper pulp. Mold-making materials: Silicone rubber, polymold, latex, epoxy putty sticks, plastic resin dyes. Flocking gun, adhesive, airbrush sets, compressors, spray guns, booth, finishes, glues, Dremel Moto-Tool sets, woodworking and upholstery tools and materials also available.
For Further Information: Catalog, $1.

Discounts: Quantity.
Accepts: MasterCard, Visa

WILTON ENTERPRISES
2240 W. 75th St.
Woodridge, IL 60517
(708) 963-7100

Offers: Cake and candy decorating materials, supplies, tools and equipment including cake pans, sheets, specialty shapes, accessories, special occasion supplies, bags for decorating, cookie cutters and other cutters, cake novelties, decorating sets and icing colors. Also offers candy-making molds and supplies.
For Further Information: Contact your dealer or send SASE.

Nature Crafts

Also see General Craft Supplies, Basketry and Seat Weaving, Miniature Making, Model Making, Fabrics and Trims and other related categories.

ART BY GOD
3705 Biscayne Blvd.
Miami, FL 33137
(306) 573-3011

Offers: Ostrich eggs, by six-and-up lots.
For Further Information: Send SASE for price list.

ATLANTIC SPICE CO.
P.O. Box 205
North Truro, MA 02652
(800) 316-7965
Fax: (508) 487-2550

Offers: Full line of herbs, spices and potpourri ingredients.
For Further Information: Free catalog.
Discounts: Quantity; sells wholesale.

CADILLAC MOUNTAIN FARM
4481 Porter Gulch Rd.
Aptos, CA 95003
(408) 476-9595

Offers: Dried flowers, herbs, exotics, supplies.
For Further Information: Send SASE for list.
Discounts: Sells wholesale.

THE CANING SHOP
926 Gilman St.
Berkeley, CA 94710
(510) 527-5010

Offers: *The Complete Book of Gourd Craft*, a guide to gourd crafting which includes 22 projects, 55 techniques and 300 designs. Also includes color photographs of the work of over 120 contemporary artists and covers wood burning; carving; inlay and painting techniques. Carries a full line of basketry materials.
For Further Information: Send SASE.
Store Location: At above address.
Accepts: MasterCard, Visa

DODY LYNESS CO.
7336 Berry Hill Dr.
Palos Verdes Peninsula, CA 90275
(310) 377-7040

Offers: Publications on dired floral arranging and potpourri crafting. Eight volumes of excerpts from former publication *The Flora-Line* with articles on designing dried florals.
For Further Information: Send SASE for list.

DOROTHY BIDDLE SERVICE
HC01
P.O. Box 900
Greeley, PA 18425
(717) 226-3239
Fax: (718) 226-0349

Offers: Flower drying/arranging supplies/equipment: Preservatives, floral clays, foam, picks, pins, wires, tapes, snips, flower presses, holders, beach pebbles, marble chips, moss, adhesives, silica gel. Also carries garden tools, accessories and books.
For Further Information: Catalog, 50¢.
Discounts: Quantity; teachers and institutions; sells wholesale to legitimate businesses.

EVERLASTINGS
20220 U.S. 6
Milford, IN 46542
(219) 831-5763

Offers: Line of dried flowers, preserved greens and ferns in bunches. Also carries heather ti trees, hydrangea and peonies.
For Further Information: Send SASE for price list.

FLORAL DECOR
P.O. Box 215
Wauna, WA 98411
(206) 857-3041

Offers: Mossy forest products. These are all natural products made from moss- and lichen-covered branches, harvested from local forests and hand crafted into variety of styles of wreaths, arches, hearts, topiaries and other shapes.
For Further Information: Catalog, $1.

THE GINGER TREE
245 Lee Rd. #122, Dept. CSS
Opelika, AL 36801
(334) 745-4864

Offers: Full line of potpourri and fragrance crafting supplies,

dried flowers, fixatives, oils. Also books, information sheets and packaging supplies.
For Further Information: Catalog, $1.
Discounts: Sells wholesale to businesses with tax ID.

HERB SHOPPE
199 N. Madison Ave.
Greenwood, IN 46142
(317) 889-4395

Offers: Bulk herbs, potpourri supplies, essential oils, herb bunches and wreaths, others.
For Further Information: Catalog and newsletter, $3 (refundable).

HERBALLY YOURS
Box 3074
Kamloops, B.C. V2C 6B7
Canada
(604) 554-4344
Fax: (604) 554-4331

Offers: Full line of oils, including essential, specialty and fragrance types. Also offers muslin draw string bags and gift items.
For Further Information: Send SASE for list.

HOFFMAN HATCHERY
P.O. Box 129
Gratz, PA 17030
(717) 365-3694

Offers: Eggs (blown): Goose, guinea, duck, turkey, quail, pheasant   variety of sizes.
For Further Information: Send SASE for price list.

J & T IMPORTS DRIED FLOWERS
143 S. Cedros, # F
Solana Beach, CA 92075
(619) 481-9781

Offers: Dried/preserved flowers/naturals: Pepper grass, capsia, baby's breath, eucalyptus, pennyroyal, moss, raffia, lycarpodium, larkspur, straws, branches, wreaths, natural twig products, herbs. Also carries floral supplies, decoratives, ribbons and others.
For Further Information: Send SASE for list.
Discounts: Quantity; teachers and institutions; sells wholesale to legitimate businesses.

JURGEN CRAFT PRODUCTS
14700 172nd Dr. SE #1
Southeast #1
Monroe, WA 98272
(800) 735-7248

Offers: "Flower Preserve" preservative, craft glue.
For Further Information: Call or write.

LILY OF THE VALLEY
3969 Fox Ave.
Minerva, OH 44657
(216) 862-3920

Offers: Over 740 species of herbal plants, dried herbs—perennials, scented species, everlastings, rare and unusuals (including passion vine, carob), others.
For Further Information: Plant and product list, $1 (refundable).
Store Location: At above address.
Discounts: Quantity; sells wholesale to legitimate businesses.

LONG CREEK PRODUCTS
P.O. Box 900
Dallas, NC 28034
(800) 542-8734

Offers: Supplies for making natural wreaths including straw, birdseed, pine, moss, potpourri, others. Also carries excelsior, pine needles, straw bales. Adhesives, pick machines and glue guns also available.
For Further Information: Call for product list.
Accepts: MasterCard, Visa

MEADOW EVERLASTINGS
16464 Shabbona Rd.
Malta, IL 60150
(815) 825-2539

Offers: 30-plus dried flower/plants and pods: unusuals and teasels, thistle, yarrow, sea holly, nigella, poppy pods, natural wreaths, plus arches, bunches, swags, bouquets. Carries 18 herbal potpourri ingredients, blends, oils, others.
For Further Information: Catalog, $2 (refundable).
Store Location: At above address. Hours vary.
Discounts: Quantity.

NATURE'S FINEST
P.O. Box 10311, Dept. CSS
Burke, VA 22009

Offers: Over 150 dried flowers, herbs and spices; 30 potpourris and bath potpourris. Over 200 essential oils, fixatives, reviving solutions, herb bead kits, spice necklace kits; also bags. baskets and bottles..
For Further Information: 34-page catalog and 16-page price list $2.50 (refundable).
Discounts: For wholesale, send resale number.

NATURE'S HERB CO.
1010 46th St.
Emeryville, CA 94608
(510) 601-0700

Offers: Over 350 bulk spices and herbs, plus potpourri ingre-

dients in bulk quantities; all products milled and blended in-house. Also has bulk teas and powdered botanicals, and bulk gelatin capsules, and packaged teas and spices.
For Further Information: Write or call for free catalog.
Discounts: Sells wholesale to businesses with resale license.

NATURE'S HOLLER
RR 1
P.O. Box 29-AA-CS
Omaha, AR 72662
(501) 426-5489

Offers: Naturals: wild grapevine curls, bulk, wreaths (variety) buttonbush balls, teasel, cone flowers, sycamore bark/balls, sweetgum, cockleburrs, magnolia. Pods available include okra, milkweed, lotus pods. Also offers moss, lichens, wheat, acorns, hickory nuts, bamboo, dried flowers, and a variety of cones, driftwood and slabs. Carries woodware, puzzles, shelves, cutouts, finished and unfinishedd.
For Further Information: Catalog, $2.
Discounts: Quantity.

NORTHWIND FARM PUBLICATIONS
R.R. 2, Box 246
Shevlin, MN 56676
(218) 657-2478

Offers: Directory of over 1,100 sources and resources for supplies, gardens, greenhouse, shop, nursery, seeds/plants, festivals, publications, classes.
For Further Information: Send SASE.

OUR NEST EGG
205 S. 5th
Mapleton, IA 51034
(712) 882-1940

Offers: Natural eggs: ostrich, rhea, emu, goose, duck. Egg decorating materials: line of pearl and metal ornaments/findings. Tools: markers, cutters, drills, marker-units. Supplies: braids, ribbons, rhinestones, mirrors, adhesives, finishes, miniatures, hinges, hinge rings, brass tubes and rods. Carries 65-plus egg stands and books.
For Further Information: Catalog, $4.

PRAIRIE RANCH
P.O. Box 1338
Yelm, WA 98597
(360) 458-5262

Offers: Emu feathers, oil products, llama and alpaca wool.
For Further Information: Sample feathers and details, $2.50.

SAN FRANCISCO HERB CO.
250 14th St.
San Francisco, CA 94103
(800) 227-4530
Fax: (415) 861-4440

Offers: Full line of herbs, potpourri including allspice, apple pieces, cedarwood chips, chamomile, cinnamon, coriander, feverfew, ginger root, hibiscus, lavender, lemon verbena, oak moss, orange peel, pine cones, rosebuds, rosemary, rose hips, sage, sassafras, statice flowers, yarrow, others. Also offers 4 potpourri mixes, 29 mix recipes, 6 simmering potpourri recipes, 7 sachet recipes. Carries 24 fragrance oils: frankincense, exotic spices, floral bouquet, and others. 60-plus botanicals also available.
For Further Information: Free catalog.
Discounts: Sells wholesale.

SHAW MUDGE AND CO.
P.O. Box 1375
Stamford, CT 06904
(203) 327-3132 ext. 205
Fax: (203) 324-6104

Offers: Complete line of fragances for gift manufacturing and processing. Custom design and stock compounds available. Manufacturer.
For Further Information: Contact your dealer, or send SASE.

SIMPLY DE-VINE
654 Kendall Rd.
Cave Junction, OR 97523

Offers: 15 grapevine wreaths: teardrops, heart, oval, matted back, others. Carries baskets, bundles and cane wreaths. Manufacturer. Special orders service.
For Further Information: Catalog, $1 (refundable).
Discounts: Quantity.

SUNFEATHER HERBAL SOAP CO.
HCR 84, Box 60
Potsdam, NY 13676
(315) 265-3648
Fax: (315) 265-2902

Offers: Soapmaking kits, bulk soaps, supplies and books.
For Futher Information: Color catalog, $2.

TEXTILE ENTERPRISES, INC.
216 Main St.
P.O. Box 154
Whitesburg, GA 30185
(404) 834-2094

Offers: Dried and painted floral products, Spanish moss, excelsior, wreaths, others. Floral supplies: foams, wires, tapes,

pins. Natural materials: variety of cones, pods, lotus, grapevine. Wreaths: statice, twig, wheat, wood based, gypsophia, others. Bells, beads, novelties, baskets.
For Further Information: Catalogs, $5.
Store Location: At above address.
Discounts: Quantity; sells wholesale to legitimate businesses.

TOM THUMB WORKSHOPS
P.O. Box 357
14100 Lankford Hwy.
Mappsville, VA 23407
(804) 824-3507

Offers: Dried flowers, including herbs on stems, cockscomb, hydrangeas, lavender, pepper berries, tallow berries and mini-rosebuds. Cones and pods, including hemlock, bakuli, cedar, eucalyputus, acorns, lotus, nigella. Potpourri, including blackberry, royal lavendar, woods, roses and others. How-to literature for bath salts, lotions, creams. Plastic bags, cellophane and cloth bags, boxes, lotion bottles, cream jars. Mosses, wreaths, raffia, wire. Full line of herbs, spices, essential and fragance oils. Books.
For Further Information: Catalog, $1.
Store Location: At above address.
Discounts: Quantity.
Accepts: MasterCard, Visa

THE ULTIMATE HERB & SPICE SHOPPE
111 Azalea
P.O. Box 395
Duenweg, MO 64841
(417) 782-0457

Offers: Over 500 bulk herbs/spices, 70 potpourri blends, plus supplies.
For Further Information: Catalog, $2.
Store Location: At above address.

VAL'S NATURALS
P.O. Box 832
Kathleen, FL 33849
(941) 858-8991

Offers: Dried miniature roses, pepper berries and other naturals.
For Further Information: Free catalog and price list.
Discounts: Sells wholesale.

WEST MOUNTAIN GOURD FARM
Rt. 1
P.O. Box 1049
Gilmer, TX 75644
(903) 734-5204

Offers: Gourds in a wide range of shapes and sizes, cleaned and ready-to-paint or craft.

Oddities

BALLOONS
P.O. Box 215
Cedar, MN 55011
(612) 753-6588

Offers: Balloon decorating instruction for special events.
For Further Information: Write for free brochure.

PTNA
333 Westlake Ave. No.
Seattle, WA 98109
(206) 622-7850
Fax: (206) 628-3162

Offers: Full line of theater, stage and studio supplies including scenic paints, fabrics, hardware, books and materials. Thermoplastics, including nontoxic workable fabric-form, sheets, and pellets for molding and free-form sculpture are also available. Colors include golf leaf, bronzing powders, fiber dyes, flourescence and others. Also carries makeup material and tools, books on making theater props and masks, scenic design, lighting and more.
For Further Information: Free catalog.

SPAULDING & ROGERS
Rt. 85, New Scotland Rd.
Voorheesville, NY 12186
(518) 768-2070

Offers: Full line of tattooing equipment and supplies, including tattooing machines with shaders, needles and outliners. Also carries power packs, parts, needle jigs, ultrasonic cleaners, autoclaves, sterilizers, medical supplies, eye loupes, lamps, ink mixers, skin markers, hectograph pencils and stencil cutters. A line of colors, including cosmetic types, inks and glow sets are also available. Also offers over 2,600 design sets, including figures, animals, cartoons, seaside, religious, emblems, fantasy, Indian, Egyptian and others. Carries videos and books. Manufacturer.
For Further Information: 3 catalogs, $12.
Store Location: At above address.

Paints, Finishes and Adhesives

Also see Artist's Supplies, Tole and Decorative Crafts, and categories throughout the book.

ART ESSENTIALS OF NEW YORK LTD.
3 Cross St.
Suffern, NY 10901
(800) 283-5323

Offers: Gold leaf, genuine and composition, sheets and rolls (22K patent, 23K patent, 22 and 23K glass type, white gold, French pale gold, lemon gold, gold metal or composition types). Also offers silver leaf. Supplies: gilding size and gilding knife, burnishing clay, and other tools and brushes. Carries technical books.
For Further Information: Free catalog.
Discounts: Quantity; teachers, institutions and professionals.

BENBOW CHEMICAL PACKAGING, INC.
935 E. Hiawatha Blvd.
Syracuse, NY 13208
(315) 474-8236
Fax: (315) 478-1307

Offers: Fezandie & Sperrle dry pigments for artist's colors.
For Further Information: Free price list.

CREATEX COLORS
14 Airport Park Rd.
East Granby, CT 06026
(203)653-5505, (800) 243-2712

Offers: Createx colors—non-toxic, water-based liquid dyes, textile paints, airbrush colors, marble colors and others. Manufacturer.
For Further Information: Free catalog.

CRESCENT BRONZE POWDER CO.
3400 N. Avondale Ave.
Chicago, IL 60618
(800) 445-6810

Offers: Metallic pigment colors (86) including over 28 gold shades. Phosphorescents, metallic paints and lacquers, plus glitters, diamond dust, glass tinsel, beads, bronze liquids (heat resistant) and finishes. Foil and epoxy-coated foil, concrete finishes; aluminum paints, primers, clears and sealers; screen ink colors. Manufacturer.

For Further Information: Contact a dealer, or request free color card.

DELTA TECHNICAL COATINGS, INC.
2550 Pellissier Place
Whittier, CA 90601
(213) 686-0678

Offers: Ceramcoat acrylics, fabric colors and fabric paints; Stencil Magic stencils and paints; and Home Decor stains and finishes. Also offers tempera poster markers, Shiva acrylics and Paintstik oil (solid form).
For Further Information: Contact your dealer, or send SASE.

THE DURHAM CO.
54 Woodland St.
Newburyport, MA 01950
(508) 465-3493 or (800) 462-1009

Offers: Gold leaf (hand-beaten) including XX deep patent, glass and surface types.
For Further Information: Send SASE.

GOLD LEAF & METALLIC POWDERS, INC.
74 Trinity Place, Suite 1200
New York, NY 10006
(212) 267-4900

Offers: Gold leaf—22K and 23K patent gold, glass gold, roll gold. Metallic powders.
For Further Information: Send SASE.

SEPP LEAF PRODUCTS, INC.
381 Park Ave. S.
New York, NY 10016
(212) 683-2840

Offers: August Ruhl gold leaf (carat leaf) in variety of shades, plus LeFranc oil size and Gilder's tips. Also offers the instructional video; *Gold Leaf Basics*, with Kent H. Smith.
For Further Information: Contact your dealer or request free catalog. Write for technical data.

U.S. BRONZE POWDERS, INC.
Rt. 202
P.O. Box 31
Flemington, NJ 08822
(908) 782-9096

Offers: Metallic pigments and paints, silver lining paste, others.
For Further Information: Send SASE.

Paper Crafts and Paper Making

Also see General Craft Supplies, Artist's Supplies, and categories throughout the book.

BEE PAPER CO.
P.O. Box 2366
Wayne, NJ 07474

Offers: Aquabee plotter paper—for check plots, charts, graphs, etc., available in grades from economy bond to 100 percent rag vellum. Sold by sheets or rolls or cut to specifications.
For Further Information: Send SASE.

THE BOOKBINDER'S WAREHOUSE
31 Division St.
Keyport, NJ 07735
(908) 264-0306
Fax: (908) 264-8266

Offers: Line of bookbinding materials, including parchment, papers, vellum, leather, book cloth. Also has finishing tools and equipment, books and more.
For Further Information: Free catalog.

MARTIN C. CARBONE, INC.
2519 Bath St.
Santa Barbara, CA 93105
(805) 963-1606
Fax: (805) 682-2352

Offers: Boxmaking systems, including kits for cardstock or corrugated cardboard boxes in all sizes up to 21″ deep. Scoring tablet allows you to make envelopes, displays, portfolios, models, and other items. Also has adhesives and a bookbinding system.
For Further Information: Call or send SASE.

COLOPHON BOOK ARTS SUPPLY, INC.
3046 Hogum Bay Rd. N.E.
Olympia, WA 98516
(360) 459-2940
Fax: (360) 459-2945

Offers: Line of paper marbling and bookbinding supplies, equipment and books.
For Further Information: Free catalog.

GERLACHS OF LECHA
P.O. Box 213
Emmaus, PA 18049

Offers: Paper-cutting supplies: variety of papers, scissors, pattern packets and other designs.
For Further Information: Catalog, $2.25.

GOLD'S ARTWORKS, INC.
2100 N. Pine St.
Lumberton, NC 28358
(800) 356-2306

Offers: Line of papermaking products including kits, molds, deckles, cotton pulp and pigments.
For Further Information: Free catalog.

GOOD STAMPS—STAMP GOODS
30901 Timberline Rd.
Willits, CA 95490
(707) 459-9124

Offers: Blank paper goods (14 colors) in business cards, postcards, giant tall and regular greeting cards (scored), book marks, envelopes, stationery. Also offers mixed scrap bag, "Stamper's Sampler," cut-out greeting cards (hearts, stars, trees) with envelopes and tags.
For Further Information: Send SASE for paper swatch book.
Discounts: Quantity.

LAKE CITY CRAFT CO.
Rt. 2
P.O. Box 2009
Highlandville, MO 65669
(417) 725-8444

Offers: Quilling kits (papers, patterns for standard-size frames), including Honeycomb Posies, Magnetic Charmers, Hearts, Christmas motifs, quotes, announcements, alphabet sampler, floral bouquets and mini-designs. Papers: Over 25 colors and assortments, including parchment paper. Carries mini-shadowbox frames, quilling tools and accessories, plus miniature (1″ scale) furniture and accessories kits.
For Further Information: Color catalog, $2.
Discounts: Sells wholesale to legitimate businesses.

MAGNOLIA

2527 Magnolia St.

Oakland, CA 94607

(510) 839-5268

Fax: (510) 893-8334

Offers: Line of papermaking supplies, books and handmade papers. Holds classes.

For Further Information: Call or write for catalog.

JOHN NEAL, BOOKSELLER

1833 Spring Garden St.

Greesboro, NC 27403

(910) 272-6139

Fax: (910) 272-9015

Offers: Book-arts books on bookbinding, paper crafting, calligraphy, lettering, layouts, marbling and others. Also offers supplies, including calligraphy and other pens and lettering, brushes, inks, gouache, gold leaf, fine papers, tools and light boxes.

For Further Information: Free catalog.

Discounts: Runs sales.

QUILL-IT

P.O. Box 1304-CSS

Elmhurst, IL 60126

(630) 834-5371

Offers: Quilling papers (full line of colors, widths), kits, tools, fringers, miniature containers, shadow box and other frames, books.

For Further Information: Catalog, $1 (refundable).

SAX ARTS & CRAFTS

P.O. Box 510710

New Berlin, WI 53151

(414) 784-6880

Offers: Arts/crafts supplies. Paper-making: kits, vat, molds, felts, cotton linters, unbleached abaca pulp, methylcellulose, retention aid (for colors). Papers (in known brands): drawing, construction (regular and large), sulphite, Color Kraft, backgrounds, plus plates, bags, Origami packs and papers; features include fadeless colors, corrugation, borders, doilies, precut puzzle sheets, fluorescents, gummed, neons, flint, cellophanes (and colors), crepe and streamers, metallics, tissue (and pomps squares kits), Mod Podge art paper tape, velour, printing types, etching. Offers 11 rice papers—3 pads, 2 assortments—plus boards, scratchboards and books.

For Further Information: Catalog, $5 (refundable).

Discounts: Quantity; teachers and institutions; sells wholesale to businesses with retail licenses.

Accepts: American Express, Discover, MasterCard, Visa

SIMPLY ELEGANT DESIGNS

2248 Obispo Ave., Suite 206

Signal Hill, CA 90806

Offers: Quilling and paper cutting supplies silhouettes, iron-ons, papers and tools, and design books.

For Further Information: Catalog, $1 (refundable).

TWINROCKER HANDMADE PAPER

P.O. Box 413

Brookston, IN 47923

(317) 563-3119

Fax: (317) 563-8946

Offers: Line of papermaking supplies, including 20 fibers, ready to use pulps, pigments, sizing, and books. Personal consultation available.

For Further Information: Free supplies catalog.

Photography

Also see Artist's Supplies and other related categories.

A&I CAMERA CLASSICS LTD.
2 World Financial Center
New York, NY 10281
(800) 786-4695
Fax: (212) 786-0825

Offers: Cameras/equipment: Canon, Nikon, Olympus, Pentax, Konica, Minolta, Nikon, Yashica, Leica, Polaroid, others. Books, collectible cameras from Alpa to Zeiss available.
For Further Information: Send SASE for list.
Store Location: At above address.
Accepts: American Express, Discover, MasterCard, Visa

AAA CAMERA EXCHANGE, INC.
43 7th Ave.
New York, NY 10011
(212) 242-5800

Offers: Camera outfits: beginner—with camera, lens, film, tripod, gadget bag, strap, flash; Dream Kit and Deluxe SLR outfits—with choice/selection of cameras (Canon, Minolta, Fujica, Pentax, Olympus, Ricoh, Yashica). Cameras—these brands, and also Chinon, Mamiya, Konica, others. I.D. cameras: Polaroids, Shackman, Beatti. Lenses: Leitz, Minox, Nikon, Minolta, Canon, Sigma, Soligor, Tamron, others.
For Further Information: Send SASE or call for list.
Accepts: American Express, MasterCard, Visa

ABE'S CAMERAS & ELECTRONICS
1957-61 Coney Island Ave.
Brooklyn, NY 11223
(718) 645-0900

Offers: Cameras: Canon, Nikon, Minolta, Pentax, Olympus. Auto focus cameras: Nikon, Olympus, Pentax, Canon, Minolta, Fuji, Ricoh. Lenses and flashes: Vivitar, Tokina, Sigma, Canon, Tamrac, Minolta, Telesor, others. Video camcorders by Panasonic, Sony and JVC, plus Slik tripods and others.
For Further Information: Send SASE or call for list.
Store Location: At above address.
Accepts: Discover, MasterCard, Visa

ALBUMS INC.
P.O. Box 81757
Cleveland, OH 44181-9986
(216) 243-2127

Offers: Albums for weddings, studio and portrait photographers, plus plaques and a line of frames in a variety of styles and sizes (products of Holson, Topflight, Camille, Sureguard, Pro-Craft, Yankee Plak, Lacquer-Mat, Marshall's).
For Further Information: Free wholesale catalog.
Accepts: MasterCard, Visa

B&H PHOTO
119 W. 17th St.
New York, NY 10011
(212) 807-7474 or (800) 221-5743

Offers: Still cameras/equipment/accessories: Hasselblad, Bronca, Rollei, Pentax, Mamiya, others. Also offers studio lighting, strobe and tungsten lights, lenses, filters, papers, aids, copy systems and underwater photo equipment. Known brands in used equipment also available.
For Further Information: Free catalog.
Discounts: Quantity.
Accepts: MasterCard, Visa

BACKDROP OUTLET
1524 Peoria Ave.
Chicago, IL 60608
(312) 842-6550

Offers: Line of backgrounds and glamour backdrops and accessories (hand-painted muslin and canvas types), plus stools and other accessories.
For Further Information: Free catalog.

BOGEN PHOTO CORP.
565-E Crescent Ave.
Ramsey, NJ 07446
(201) 818-9500
Fax: (201) 818-9177

Offers: Line of darkroom products including dry-mount presses, proof printers, easels and others.
For Further Information: Send SASE.

BROMWELL MARKETING
3 Allegheny Center, #111
Pittsburgh, PA 15212
(412) 321-4118

Offers: Cameras, equipment and supplies for large format:

view cameras, lenses, tripods, and a full line of accessories and specialty items.
For Further Information: Free catalog.

CALUMET
890 Supreme Dr.
Bensenville, IL 60106
(800) CALUMET
Fax: (708) 860-7105

Offers: Line of wet-side and dry-side darkroom items, including those manufactured by teh company and other brands—Zone IV, Gravity Works and more; for any size darkroom.
For Further Information: Catalog, $5.

CAMBRIDGE CAMERA EXCHANGE, INC.
7th Ave. & 13th St.
New York, NY 10011
(212) 675-8600

Offers: Cameras and equipment in known brands: Agfa-Gevaert, Bronica, Cambron, Canon, Casio, Chinon, Exakta, Fuji, Hassclblad, Kodak, Konica, Leica, Lindenblatt, Mamiya, Praktica, Ricoh, Rollei, Topcon, Vivitar, Contax/Yashica, Polaroid, Passport, other imaging equipment, plus 4×5 and 8×10 cameras. Stocks lenses, flashes, exposure meters, tripods, darkroom equipment and used cameras.
For Further Information: Free catalog.
Discounts: Sells wholesale.
Accepts: American Express, Discover, MasterCard, Visa

CAMERA WORLD OF OREGON
500 SW 5th & Washington
Portland, OR 97204
(503) 227-6008

Offers: Cameras and accessories by: Canon, Fuji, Chinon, Nikon, Ricoh, Minolta, Konica, Pentax, Olympus, Yashica, Tamron, others. Video camcorders by: Sony, Panasonic, Chinon, Canon, Hitachi, Olympus, Minolta, Nikon, Quazar, JVC, RCA, Magnavox, Pentax. Camera lenses by Sigma, Tokina, Vivitar and others. Carries flashes, light meters, others.
For Further Information: Send SASE or call for list.
Accepts: MasterCard, Visa

CENTRAL CAMERA CO.
230 S. Wabash Ave.
Chicago, IL 60604
(312) 427-5580

Offers: Cameras/equipment: Nikon, Pentax, others including shutter and SLR's. Carries Ilford papers and film, Metz flash/accessories, Bogen tripods, others.
For Further Information: Send SASE for list.
Store Location: At above address.

CPM, INC.
10830 Sanden Dr.
Dallas, TX 75238
(214) 349-9799
Fax: (214) 503-1557

Offers: Darkroom equipment, including water pressure and temperature controls, filters, faucets, sinks and drains, cabinets, exhaust and air cleaning units. Also safelights and blackout material; accessories and more.
For Further Information: Delta 1 catalog available.

DARKROOM AIDS COMPANY
3449 Lincoln Ave.
Chicago, IL 60657
(312) 248-4301

Offers: New and used darkroom products, including print dryers and drying cabinets, sinks, archival print washers, parts for discontinued equipment; and others.
For Further Information: Send SASE.

DELTA 1 CUSTOM PHOTO MANUFACTURING
10830 Sanden Dr.
Dallas, TX 75238
(214) 349-9779 or (800) 627-0252

Offers: Line of darkroom and studio products and accessories.
For Further Information: Call for free catalog.

DIAL-A-PHOTO, INC.
P.O. Box 5063
Jacksonville, FL 32247
(904) 398-8175

Offers: Dial-A-Photo computer system for all cameras, films. Pocket-sized system helps predict shots in a variety of conditions.
For Further Information: Send SASE.
Accepts: American Express, MasterCard, Visa

DORAN ENTERPRISES
2779 S. 34th St.
Milwaukee, WI 53215
(414) 645-0109
Fax: (414) 645-1744

Offers: Over 100 models of darkroom products, including sheet and roll film processors, agitator, washers, safelights, fans and louvers, easels, dryers, cutters, rollers, trays, film tanks, accessories and more.
For Further Information: Free catalog.

EXECUTIVE PHOTO & SUPPLY CORP.
120 W. 31st St.
New York, NY 10001
(212) 947-5290 or (800) 223-7323

Offers: Cameras and accessories for Nikon, Minolta, Canon, Pentax, Yashica, Leica, Fuji, Konica, Polaroid passport models, EW Marine underwater equipment, Mamiya, Hasselblad, others. Lenses, including Tokina, Sigma, Pentax, Canon, Nikon, Ed-IF, others. Also flashes, tripods, projectors/viewers, studio kits, stands, reflectors, darkroom equipment/supplies, enlarger outfits, film, papers and chemicals.
For Further Information: Write for catalog.

FOCUS CAMERA, INC.
4419-21 13th Ave.
Brooklyn, NY 11219
(718) 436-6262

Offers: Cameras and equipment: Nikon, Hanimex, Contax, Yashica, Konica, Canon, Olympus, Pentax, Vivitar, others. Lenses: Vivitar, Kiron, Sunpak, Sigma, Tokina, Polaroid, Tamron, Canon, Nikon, Metz, others. Also offers carousels, flashes, digital flashes, meters, camera cases and gadget bags, Bogen and Slik tripods, others.
For Further Information: Send SASE or call for list.
Accepts: American Express, Discover, MasterCard, Visa

FRANKLIN DISTRIBUTORS CORP.
P.O. Box 320
Denville, NJ 07834
(201) 267-2710

Offers: Line of archival storage materials for slide, negative and print storage including Perma-Saf pages of polypropylene for file cabinet, with hanging bars inserts into channels made for hanging pages.
For Further Information: Free catalog.

FREE TRADE PHOTO
4718 18th Ave., Suite 127
Brooklyn, NY 11204
(718) 435-4141

Offers: Cameras/accessories/equipment: Canon, Nikon, Pentax, Maxxum, Leica, Olympus, Minox, Minolta. Carries Rokunar SP studio systems, studio lighting, darkroom accessories and others.
For Further Information: Send SASE for list.

FREESTYLE
5120 W. Sunset Blvd.
Los Angeles, CA 90027
(800) 292-6137
Fax: (800) 616-3686

Offers: Darkroom supplies/accessories: Stainless tanks/

reels, thermometers, film loaders, filters, polarizers, mount boards. Film: Black-and-white by Ilford, Arista, Kodak, Ortho Litho. Carries color and black-and-white papers, film.
For Further Information: Send SASE or call for list.
Accepts: MasterCard, Visa

FUJI PHOTO FILM, U.S.A., INC.
555 Taxter Rd.
Elmsford, NY 10523
(914) 789-8100

Offers: Fuji film and cameras in a variety of sizes/types.
For Further Information: Contact dealer, or write for information.

GARDEN STATE CAMERA
101 Kuller Rd.
Clifton, NJ 07011
(201) 742-5777

Offers: Cameras/equipment/accessories: Nikon, Canon, Sigma, Yashica, Pentax, Tokina, Wamron, Samyang, Sunpak, Vivitar, Olympus, Minolta, Konica, others. Carries special camera outfits for beginners and professionals. Buys cameras.
Store Location: At above address.
Accepts: American Express, Discover, MasterCard, Visa

LIGHT IMPRESSIONS
439 Monroe Ave.
P.O. Box 439
Rochester, NY 14603

Offers: Photography supplies: archival storage and display products, studio and darkroom equipment, photography gear. Wide range of fine art photography books, from classics to most recent, and hard-to-find titles.
For Further Information: Free catalog.
Store Location: At above address.
Discounts: Quantity.

MAMIYA AMERICA CORP.
8 Westchester Plaza
Elmsford, NY 10523
(914) 347-3300

Offers: Mamiya photographic equipment—a variety of cameras, interchangeable lenses, others.
For Further Information: Contact your dealer, or send SASE.

MERIT ALBUMS, INC.
19338 Business Center Dr.
Northridge, CA 91324
(818) 886-5100

Offers: Wedding albums and others in a variety of styles and sizes. Also carries proof books, photo mounts and folios by Topflight, Leathermark, Tap, Holson, Camille and Dimension.

For Further Information: Free wholesale catalog.
Accepts: MasterCard, Visa

MINOLTA CORP.

101 Williams Dr.
Ramsey, NJ 07446
(201) 825-4000

Offers: Minolta cameras and accessories in a variety of types, including a sports action card set camera for continuous autofocus and others.
For Further Information: Contact your dealer, or write for information.

NEW YORK INSTITUTE OF PHOTOGRAPHY

211 E. 43rd St.
New York, NY 10017
(212) 372-7050

Offers: Photography home study course—30 lesson program covering both the basics and advanced, professional aspects of photography. Includes a mini-course in video techniques, with training materials, cassette tape communication, and individual attention and constructive criticism to enhance learning.
For Further Information: Free *Career Guide* and catalog.

NIKON CONSUMER RELATIONS

19601 Hamilton Ave.
Torrance, CA 90502
(310) 516-7124

Offers: Photographic equipment, including full line of cameras, some with 5-segment Matrix Metering, plus synchronized, cybernetic, rear-curtain fill-flash and other advanced systems. Stocks speedlight and other flashes.
For Further Information: Contact your dealer, or write.

NRI SCHOOL OF PHOTOGRAPHY

4401 Connecticut Ave. NW
Washington, DC 20008
(202) 244-1600

Offers: Photography and video production home-study course for professional training in still and video photography. Includes instruction in studio, darkroom equipment and techniques for equipment use. Critiques and communication from professional instructors (of the McGraw-Hill Continuing Education Center).
For Further Information: Free catalog.

PATTERSON

21 Jet View Dr.
Rochester, NY 14624

Offers: Over 100 darkroom products, including complete line of tanks, trays, reels, tongs and others.
For Further Information: Write for brochure.

PHOTO SCOPE

5745 Plauche Ct.
New Orleans, LA 70123
(504) 834-6171

Offers: Black-and-white photo finishing; complete services for all sizes.
For Further Information: Write or call for free start-up kit.

PHOTO-THERM

110 Sewell Ave.
Trenton, NJ 08610
(609) 396-1456

Offers: Darkroom equipment, including film processor E6C41, black and white, temperature baths and modular controls in a variety of models of high precision type; reasonable cost.
For Further Information: Write or call for catalog.

PHOTOGRAPHERS' FORMULARY CO.

P.O. Box 950
Condon, MT 59826
(406) 754-2891 or (800) 922-5255

Offers: Full and complete line of photographic chemicals for processing and printing. Cyanotype and Van Dyke kits for transfer of negative images onto fabric.
For Further Information: Send SASE for list.

PHOTOGRAPHER'S WARE HOUSE

P.O. Box 3365
Boardman, OH 44513

Offers: Photographic lighting equipment: home studio lighting kits, professional starter kits (strobes, umbrellas/adapters, stands), others. Also offers strobe lights and umbrella outfits, light boxes, soft boxes, slaves, reflectors, others.
For Further Information: Send SASE for list.

PHOTOGRAPHY BOOK CLUB

P.O. Box 2003
Lakewood, NJ 08701

Offers: Photography books at savings for members. When choosing an introductory title at token cost, members agree to purchase more books in the first year of membership. Club bulletins are sent 15 times yearly; card to be returned if selection is declined.

For Further Information: Send SASE.

THE PIERCE CO.

9801 Nicollet
Minneapolis, MN 55420
(612) 884-1991

Offers: Photography studio products: Painted backgrounds (25 including scenics), photography supplies, photo albums and mounts, drapes, printed forms, poly bags, toys, others.

For Further Information: Catalog, $1 (refundable).

PNTA

333 Westlake Ave. N.
Seattle, WA 98109
(206) 622-7850 or (800) 622-7850

Offers: Stage, studio and photography supplies including thermoplastics, paint, fabrics, studio draperies, scenery, hardware, dyes, makeup, color filters, lighting gubo patterns, lights, dimming and control, and others. Also sells trade show booths and rents lighting, special effects, scenery, draperies and platforms.

For Further Information: Free catalog and samples.

SHOOTERS OF USA LAB

P.O. Box 8640
Rolling Meadows, IL 60008
(708) 956-1010

Offers: Professional developing/printing service for prints, photo business cards, greeting cards, "blow-up" color enlargements (16″ × 20″ and up) and other enlargements.

For Further Information: Send SASE for list.

Discounts: Quantity.

SMILE PHOTO AND VIDEO, INC.

29 W. 35th St.
New York, NY 10001
(212) 967-5900 or (800) 516-4218
Fax: (212) 967-5912

Offers: Cameras/accessories by Canon, Nikon, Minolta, Ricoh, Nikonos (underwater equipment), Fujica, Yashica, Konica, Olympus, Nikon, Pentax, others. Also offers lenses, cases and studio accessories, including lights, booms, stands, copy systems, lighting assemblies, reflectors, copy stand, umbrellas and slide projectors. Videos, electronics and office equipment also available.

For Further Information: Send SASE or call.

Accepts: Discover, MasterCard, Visa

SPEEDOTRON CORP.

310 S. Racine Ave.
Chicago, IL 60607
(312) 421-4050
Fax: (312) 421-5079

Offers: Speedotron Fresnel spotlights, including 8″ focusing unit with built in flash tube, and 14″ sport that accepts any major electonic flash light unit. Also has accessories, other light units and power supplies.

For Further Information: Contact your dealer, or send SASE.

THOMAS INSTRUMENT CO., INC.

1313 Belleview Ave.
Charlottesville, VA 22901
(804) 977-8150
Fax: (804) 977-8151

Offers: Duplex Super Safelight, a darkroom light with monochromatic light source and special filters to give soft light. Others.

For Further Information: Contact dealer, or call/write for details.

VC PHOTOGRAPHIC ART SUPPLIES

7506 New Jersey Ave.
Hudson, FL 34667
(813) 863-2738
Fax: (813) 862-3567

Offers: Photographic products, including black-and-white negative and transparency retouching material, hardware items, chemicals and others.

For Further Information: Catalog available.

WALL STREET CAMERA

82 Wall St.
New York, NY 10005
(212) 344-0011

Offers: Camera equipment by Bronica, Hasselblad, Rollei, Pentax, Mamiya, Canon, Leica. Press/view cameras: Omega, Sinar, Nagaoka. Also offers lenses and light meters (known brands), plus zoom outfits by Olympus and Minolta. Video camcorders and darkroom outfits (enlarger plus accessories) also available. Allows trade-ins of cameras for new models.

For Further Information: Call.

Discounts: Below list prices.

Accepts: MasterCard, Visa

F.J. WESTCOTT CO.

P.O. Box 1596
1447 Summit St.
Toledo, OH 43603
(419) 243-7311

Offers: Portable fabric darkroom unit with blower and wall pockets for film and items.

.For Further Information: Send SASE.

ZONE VI STUDIOS, INC.
Newfane, VT 05345
(802) 257-5161
(800) 225-8638

Offers: Photographic specialties: Zone VI camera—hand-crafted field camera with extensions/removable bellows, lenses to 360mm, a mahogany body with brass fittings, plus a case. Also offers archival print washers, tripods and cases, compensating enlarging metronomes, view camera lenses by Schneider, and 4 × 5 camera outfits, modified meters and cold light enlarger timer. Carries print flatlevers, cold light heads, stabilizers, developing timers, drying screens, paper, chemicals, easels, film washers, darkroom tanks, reels, over-sized proofers, magnifiers and books.
For Further Information: Free catalog.

Rubber Stamping and Stamp Making

Also see General Craft Supplies, Artist's Supplies, Paints, Paper Crafts and Paper Making and Fabric Decorating.

ACEY DEUCY
P.O. Box 194
Ancram, NY 12502

Offers: Rubber stamp designs including Ugly Ties or Dumb Hats postal stamps, goddess and Santa collections. Has unmounted stamps at half price.
For Further Information: Catalog, $1.50.

ALL NIGHT MEDIA, INC.
P.O. Box 10607
San Rafael, CA 94912
(415) 459-3013

Offers: Rubber stamp designs, including cartoons Stamp-A-Face, sets. Other designs include Winnie the Pooh, teddies, animal designs (and sets), Stamps-On-Wheels, Global Cow, cats, fish, shells, waves, teacher's stamps, messages, birthday, nature, fantasy, musical, country, borders, flowers, classic and love motifs. Also carries bookplates. Wholesale only.
For Further Information: Send SASE for list.

ANNE-MADE DESIGNS
P.O. Box 697
Erwin, TN 37650

Offers: Decorative rubber stamps: whimsical and folk art images, others. Has unmounted stamps at very low cost.
For Further Information: 226-page catalog and card of unmounted stamps, $8.

ART IMPRESSIONS
P.O. Box 20085
Salem, OR 97307
(503) 393-2014

Offers: Original rubber stamps designs including over 1,300 name stamps in 12 designs, plus special occasions and others, both mounted and unmounted.
For Further Information: Catalog, $4.
Discounts: Wholesale welcome, send copy of business license.
Accepts: MasterCard, Visa

THE ARTERY
1411 N. 25th St.
Boise, ID 83702
(208) 336-2783

Offers: Kite designs—full line from areas worldwide. (And kite jewelry.)
For Further Information: Write.
Discounts: Sells wholesale.

BIZARRO
P.O. Box 1292
Rumford, RI 02828
(401) 231-8777
Fax: (401) 231-4770

Offers: Design rubber stamps: sports figures, map of U.S., alphabet stamp sets, others. Supplies include embossing powders and rainbow stamp pads. Also offers *How to Use Rubber Stamps* books.
For Further Information: Catalog, $3.
Discounts: Sells wholesale.

VICTORIA CHRISTIE DESIGNS
9140 Fairway Dr.
Kelseyville, CA 95451
(707) 277-7470

Offers: Rubber art stamps in an array of animals, whimsical characters, hearts, and others. Also carries unmounted stamps, stamping supplies, including ink pads, embossing colors and other materials.
For Further Information: Catalog, $1 (refundable).

CIRCUSTAMPS
P.O. Box 250
Bolinas, CA 94924
(415) 868-1470

Offers: Scaled images in rubber stamps (to be used with one another) of an array of circus performers in action: Clowns, trapeze artists, lion tamers, Oriental acrobats, jugglers, stilt walkers, band/action animals. Also offers animal bases and animal wagon and cage (in parts). Unmounted stamps sold at half price. Scissors for rubber and vulcanizing services for beginning rubber stamp companies.
For Further Information: Catalog, $1.

CO-MOTION RUBBER STAMPS
2711 E. Elvira Rd.
Tucson, AZ 85706

Offers: Artistic rubber stamps including Southwestern (saguaro cactus, Indian pottery and designs), teddy bear, penguins, others. Techniques video.
For Further Information: Catalog, $5 (refundable).
Discounts: Sells wholesale.

DELAFIELD STAMP CO.
P.O. Box 56
Delafield, WI 53018
(414) 646-8599

Offers: Over 400 rubber stamp designs: Holiday (Halloween, Christmas, others), seasonal, others. Also offers stamping accessories, ColorBox items, DSC Art greeting cards.
For Further Information: Catalog and supplement, $4.
Discounts: Sells wholesale.
Accepts: MasterCard, Visa

DIVA RUBBER
P.O. Box 849
Montara, CA 94037

Offers: Rubber stamps by Susan Newell, Vivian Jean, Roger Jones, Anne Norcia—unmounted only.
For Further Information: Catalog $1.50 (refundable). Send SASE for flyer.

DOUBLE D RUBBER STAMPS, INC.
P.O. Box 1
Olivia, MN 56277
(320) 826-2288

Offers: Sign language alphabet rubber stamps and over 900 other designs.
For Further Information: 2 catalogs, $5 (refundable).
Discounts: Wholesale, send copy of resale permit or license.
Accepts: Discover, MasterCard, Visa

EMBOSSING ARTS CO.
P.O. Box 626
Sweet Home, Or 97386
(541) 928-9898

Offers: Line of art rubber stamps, embossing materials, stencils and paper items.
For Further Information: Retail catalog, $3.

EMERALD CITY STAMPS
Box 43187
Cincinnati, OH 45243

Offers: Hundreds of creative rubber stamps, including people, animals, nature, places, geometric and graphic designs,
vehicles, paraphernalia, food, word stamps and others. Unmounted stamps also available.
For Further Information: Catalog, $2.

EXQUISITE IMAGES
4188 Piedmont Ave.
Oakland, CA 94611
(510) 601-6847

Offers: Rubber stamps from over 70 companies, stampers' supplies and accessories. Also offers brass stencils, storage and display cases. Holds classes and demonstrations.
For Further Information: Send SASE for list.
Accepts: MasterCard, Visa

FRUIT BASKET UPSET
P.O. Box 23129
Seattle, WA 98102
(800) 263-1900

Offers: Rubber stamp images, including over 100 new designs and 4 new alphabets.
For Further Information: Catalog, $3 (refundable).

GOOD IMPRESSIONS
P.O. Box 33 RB
Shirley, WV 26434
(304) 758-4252

Offers: Rubber stamp images: People, plants, borders, animals, fantasy, cupids, birds, silhouettes, quilting motifs, food, buildings, holiday, alphabets, sign language. Also offers Letter Lock personal stamps—banner and 250-piece alphabet set. Banner slogans, quotations also available.
For Further Information: Catalog, $1.

GOOD STAMPS—STAMPS GOOD
30901 Timberline Rd.
Willits, CA 95490
(707) 459-9124

Offers: Rubber stamps in a variety of designs, including holiday, rainbows, Pot o' Gold, clover, leprechaun, sunrise, clouds, rabbits, ducks, broken egg (pair), 13 heart motifs and others. Blank paper goods are also available.
For Further Information: Catalog, $3.

GRAPHIC RUBBER STAMP CO.
11250 Magnolia Blvd.
North Hollywood, CA 91601
(818) 762-9443

Offers: Rubber stamp designs: circus, sheep, photographic, castles, borders, people, telephones, bicycles, flowers, Hollywood, dancers, sports, trees, animals, fantasy, quotations, alphabets, transportation, Native American, spiritual, cartoons, others. Also offers embossing powders (kit available), stamp

pads, glitter, paper items, printing kits and techniques video.
For Further Information: Catalog 1 (displaying 3,000 stamps), $4; Catalog 2 (displaying 900 stamps), $3.50.
Store Location: At above address.
Discounts: Quantity; sells wholesale to legitimate businesses.

GUMBO GRAPHICS
1320 N.W. Northrup St.
Portland, OR 97209
(503) 226-9895

Offers: Over 2,000 rubber stamp images and sets, including reproductions, bizarre items, animals, fish, plants, Indians, abstracts, children, women, men, bugs, birds, beasts, dragons, others.
For Further Information: Catalog, $2.

A LA ART STAMP CRAFTERS
37500 N. Industrial Pkwy.
Willoughby, OH 44094
(216) 431-9001

Offers: Original hand-drawn art rubber stamps—decorative imagery, Mother Goose designs, fantasy, animals, landscapes, bears and toys, others.
For Further Information: Catalog, $3 (refundable).
Discounts: Sells wholesale.

HIPPO HEART
P.O. Box 4460
Foster City, CA 94404
(415) 347-4477

Offers: Rubber stamp designs including mini motifs, animals, birds, borders/corners, fantasy, foods, flora, holidays, sports, leisure, quotes, people, seashore, transportation, teachers, skies, others. Wholesale only.
For Further Information: Catalog, $2.

INKADINKADO
60 Cummings Park
Woodburn, MA 01801
(617) 338-2600

Offers: Rubber stamps, paper products and unusual craft items.
For Further Information: Write or call for free catalog.

INKERS-A-WAY
P.O. Box 6247
San Mateo, CA 94403

Offers: Original art rubber stamps, mounted and unmounted, including scene building, cartoon-like images of people, kids, animals, cars, trucks, and planes. Also offers people/occupations as well as postal, address and message frames. Interact-

ive sets featuring foreground to horizon depth of streets, parks, toy trains and the ocean. Movie theater and holiday themes and stamps designed for laminating are also available.
For Further Information: Catalog, $2 (refundable).
Discounts: Inquire regarding wholesale.
Accepts: MasterCard, Visa

JACKSON MARKING PRODUCTS
Brownsville Rd.
Mt. Vernon, IL 62864
(618)242-1334 or (800) 851-4945
Fax: (800) STAMP-FAX

Offers: Rubber-stamp-making equipment: Precision rubber stamp presses (Mazak and Standard Foundry), hand press and stamp die-cutting machines, and hot stamping and laminating equipment. Also offers mount strip (6 styles), matrix board, stamp gum, cushions, pads and inks, solutions, self-inkers, racks, 64 type styles and handles. Services: Photo engraving of artwork, matrix board molding, rubber die molding.
For Further Information: Free brochure.
Discounts: Quantity.

ED JACOBS
7316 San Bartolo St.
Carlsbad, CA 92009
(619) 438-5046

Offers: Your name custom designed on a Chinese seal. Chinese seals, also known as "chops," are used to stamp names or insignias. Known to be carved from many materials, now manufactured in photo polymer resin fused to the base of replicas of authentic Chinese figures.
For Further Information: Write or call.
Discounts: Quantity.

JUDI KINS RUBBER STAMPS
17832 S. Hobart Blvd.
Gardena, CA 90248
(310) 515-1115

Offers: Rubber stamp images (original designs): Seal and heart, ducks, monkey hanging from balloon, elephant, water drops, rabbits, others. Custom stamp service, from customer's designs.
For Further Information: Catalog, $5.
Discounts: Sells wholesale.

KLEAR COPY DESIGN RUBBER STAMPS
55 7th Ave. S.
New York, NY 10014
(212) 243-0357

Offers: Design rubber stamps: Beetle, elephant, lion head, other animals, drinks on tray, pocket watch, period images, historical locales and costumes, antiquities, unusuals (Spam, luggage, coins, bottles), Palmer Cox's Brownie. Also offers

Christmas designs, ornate alphabets, cupids.
For Further Information: Catalog, $2 (refundable).

L.A. STAMPWORKS

P.O. Box 2329
North Hollywood, CA 91610-0329
(818) 761-8757

Offers: Art rubber stamps: Popeye characters in action, balloon quotes, air mail, animals, circle motifs, Art Nouveau, florals, scenes, people (dancers, mermaids, kids, flappers, 30s ladies, old-timers, silhouettes), holiday themes, teacher's, zodiac, cartoon, borders, others.
For Further Information: Catalog, $5.
Discounts: Sells wholesale.

LASTING IMPRESSIONS

198 Greenwood Ave.
Bethel, CT 06801
(203) 792-3740

Offers: Rubber stamps in floral, holiday, nature and miscellaneous designs. Also offers accessories, original rubber stamp of the month club.
For Further Information: Send SASE.
Discounts: Sells wholesale.

LOVE YOU TO BITS

P.O. Box 5748
Redwood City, CA 94063
(415) 367-1177

Offers: Over 250 original rubber stamp designs: whimsical holiday motifs, quotes and signs, Christian stamps, stamps in Spanish, animals, flowers, cartoon creatures, others. Has unmounted stamps at half price.
For Further Information: Catalog, $7.
Discounts: Sells wholesale.

LOVING LITTLE RUBBER STAMPS

1 Federal St.
Newburyport, MA 01950
(508) 465-9954

Offers: Over 1,500 rubber stamp designs—originals and oldies: Special occasion, holiday, quotes, people, money, food, seashore, ecology, buildings, sports, animals, vintage motifs, hands, borders, signs, others.
For Further Information: Catalog, $2.

MAINE STREET STAMPS

P.O. Box 14
Kingfield, ME 04947
(207) 265-2500

Offers: Line of rubber stamps, embossing power and stamp pads.
For Further Information: Catalog, $2.

MEDIAESCAPE INC.

P.O. Box 24107
Denver, CO 80224
(303) 758-8232

Offers: Rubber stamps of the Jewish tradition—full range, "from reverence to pure silliness," including animals, ark, people, quotes, others. Catalog has design tips.
For Further Information: Catalog, $2 (refundable).
Discounts: Sells wholesale.

LOUIS MELIND CO.

P.O. Box 1112
Skokie, IL 60076-8112
(847) 581-2500
Fax: (800) 782-2542

Offers: Art stamp making supplies including stamp gum, wood and plastic mounts in popular hourglass shape, cushion, adhesive, matrix; vulcanizes and indexing ink. Production of rubber dies from artwork—submit samples and quantities for quote (must be original artwork or licensed for your use). Stationery seals and embossers with custom or stock artwork.
For Further Information: Call or write for free catalog (Mention *Crafts Supply Sourcebook*.)
Discounts: Quantity.
Accepts: American Express, MasterCard, Visa

MOE WUBBA

P.O. Box 1445
San Luis Obispo, CA 93406
(805) 547-IMOE

Offers: Stamp designs including "classical," fantasy, quotes, cartoon, others.
For Further Information: Stamp album, $2 (refundable).
Discounts: Sells wholesale.

MOSTLY ANIMALS

P.O. Box 2355
Oakdale, CA 95361
(800) 830-0611
Offers: Interactive art stamps for craft/hobby industry, along with related kits and tools—stamp-o-graph, scoreboard and stamp-o-round.
For Further Information: Call or write.
Discounts: Dealer support program and volume discounts.

MUSEUM OF MODERN RUBBER

3015 Glendale Blvd., Suite 100C
Los Angeles, CA 90039
(213) 662-1133

Offers: Wood-mounted rubber stamps in a variety of original images, including funny people, Old West, art masterpieces, words/sayings, and holidays.

For Further Information: Catalog, $3.
Discounts: Sells wholesale.

NAME BRAND
P.O. Box 34245
Bethesda, MD 20827
(301) 299-3062

Offers: Calligraphic rubber stamps—We've Moved, Handmade By, Thank You, Junk Mail, others. Custom stamps (addresses, monograms, names) and logos available.
For Further Information: Catalog, $3.50 (refundable).
Discounts: Sells wholesale.

100 PROOF PRESS
Rt. 1
Box 136
Eaton, NY 13334
(315) 684-3547

Offers: Over 4,000 rubber stamp images: holiday, people, crowds, hands, bicycles, ethnic, vintage, elves, Native American, dancing, soldiers, photographic, sports, cosmic, dolls, toys, angels, fantasy, animals, birds, transportation, food, alphabets and others.
For Further Information: Catalog, $4 (refundable).

PEACE RESOURCE PROJECT
P.O. Box 1122
Arcata, CA 95521
(707) 822-4229

Offers: Artistic rubber stamps with peace motifs and slogans: "Peace" in several languages, "Create Peace"/Picasso Dove Face, "Wage Peace," "Let Peace Begin With Me" and others. Also offers peace buttons, stickers, T-shirts, and a list of peace and environmental organizations.
For Further Information: Write for catalog.
Discounts: Quantity.

PIPE DREAMS
P.O. Box 275
Erving, MA 01344
(508) 544-7334

Offers: Graphic rubber stamps, including Victorian, teacher, country, angels, names, holiday and other subjects.
For Further Information: Send large SASE for list of subjects
Discounts: 10 percent discount with mention of the *Craft Supply Sourcebook*. Wholesale available to qualified businesses.

POSH IMPRESSIONS
875 E. Birch St.
Brea, CA 92621
(714) 529-9933

Alternate Address: 4708 Barranka Pkwy.
Irvine, CA 92714
(714) 651-1145

Offers: Exclusive rubber stamps of over 40,000 images, plus sticker rolls and unlimited accessories. Also offers classes, videos, others.
For Further Information: Catalog, $4.
Discounts: Sells wholesale; lifetime 10 percent discount through 500 Club.

PRINT PLAY
P.O. Box 4252
Portland, OR 97208
(503) 274-8720

Offers: Individual words rubber stamp collection to help children learn to read and write. Also offers a wide selection of animal and bird tracks.
For Further Information: Free catalog.

RED BEANS & RUBBER STAMPS
41 Timberline Dr.
Warrensburg, MO 64093
(816) 747-6596

Offers: Line of African-American rubber stamp images for the ages in a variety of designs.
For Further Information: Catalog, $1.50 (refundable).

RED HOT RUBBER, INC.
363 W. Glade Rd.
Palatine, IL 60067
(847) 991-6700

Offers: Line of rubber stamps, including foods, birthday, western, Halloween, Valentine's Day, Easter, Christmas, greetings and others. Unmounted stamps also available.
For Further Information: Catalog, $2 (refundable).
Discounts: Sells wholesale.

REMARKABLE RUBBER STAMPS
P.O. Box 2004
Snoqualmie, WA 98065
(206) 888-9559

Offers: Rubber stamps in a wide variety of designs.
For Further Information: Catalog, $2.50.
Discounts: Wholesale available to businesses.

RUBBER DUCK STAMP CO.

P.O. Box 416
Medford, OR 97501
(541) 734-7390

Offers: Rubber stamps, including ducks, rabbits, teddy bears, Easter baskets, flowers, others. Assorted die cuts. Supplies: pads, inks, wood blocks.
For Further Information: *Ducklog*, $2.50 (½ refundable).
Discounts: Sells wholesale.

RUBBER POET

P.O. Box 218-CS
Rockville, UT 84763

Offers: Petroglyph and southwest cactus motifs; repeatable rubber stamp fabric designs, including contemporary, geometric, others.
For Further Information: Catalog, $2.50 (refundable).

RUBBER RAILROAD STAMP WORKS

P.O. Box 11801
Eugene, OR 97440
Offers: Line of rubber stamps of great American railroads and regional lines.
For Further Information: Catalog, $2 (refundable).
Discounts: Sells wholesale.

RUBBERSTAMPEDE

P.O. Box 246
Berkeley, CA 94701
(510) 420-6800

Offers: Rubber stamp designs (mostly original): Plants/trees, flowers, cartoon characters, dinosaurs, fantasy, Noah's ark, people, holiday, slogans, quotations and greetings. Includes animals, both domestic and wild (15 cats, 58 teddies, others). Also offers 17 roller stamps: borders, footprints, teddies, cat tracks, others. Carries Face Case (parts to mix), love kit motifs, Posh Impression stamps (variety of companies), art maker sets, wrapping papers, ink pads, inks. Wholesale only.
For Further Information: Send SASE.

SOUTH WESTAMPS

3445 N. 19th Ave.
Phoenix, AZ 85015
(602) 274-2282

Offers: Rubber stamps: Close Encounters, holiday motifs, Premium and Economounts, custom stamps, rubber plates. Has unmounted, grab-bag specials. Also offers custom stamps, vulcanizing and wood mounting services. Holds classes.
For Further Information: Pieces catalog, $4.

STAMP ADDICTION

3230 E. Flamingo Rd.
Las Vegas, NV 89121
(702) 434-3405

Offers: Precia Prints rubber stamps: Holiday, fantasy, quotes, animals, others.
For Further Information: Catalog, $3 (refundable).
Accepts: MasterCard, Visa

STAMP ANTONIO

1931 NW Military Highway
San Antonio, TX 78213
(210) 342-6217

Offers: Rubber stamps with contemporary Texas/Western motifs, quotes and others produced by over 50 companies.
For Further Information: Flyer, $1 and large SASE with double postage.
Accepts: Discover, MasterCard, Visa

A STAMP IN THE HAND CO.

20630 S. Leapwood Ave., Suite B
Carson, CA 90746
(310) 329-8555

Offers: Rubber stamps from favorite companies, many in hand-carved eraser designs: hearts, paper dolls, tree with hearts, animals. Carries custom stamps, paper, cards.
For Further Information: "Kat-A-Log" and supplements, $3.75.

STAMP OF EXCELLENCE, INC.

1105 Main St.
Canon City, CO 81212
(719) 275-8422

Offers: Line of rubber stamps including special occasion (designs, quotes): holiday, birthday, baby, bridal, party, Valentine's, springtime flowers. Other subjects include kitchen, mail, "frames," classroom, notecard, Oriental, Native American, cosmic, fantasy, scenic, animals, others. Has unmounted angels and spiritual quotes, and a full line of supplies.
For Further Information: Catalog, $3; angel flyer $1.
Store Location: At above address.
Discounts: Quantity; sells wholesale to legitimate businesses.
Accepts: American Express, Discover, MasterCard, Visa

THE STAMP PAD CO., INC.

P.O. Box 43
Big Lake, MN 55309
(612) 263-6646 or (800) 634-3717

Offers: Rubber stamps in over 1,600 original art stamp designs. Also offers name stamps, paper products and stamping accessories.

For Further Information: Catalog, $3 (refundable with first order).
Accepts: Discover, MasterCard, Visa

STAMPENDOUS!
1357 S. Lewis St.
Anaheim, CA 92805
(800) 869-0474

Offers: Original design rubber stamps, including "Handcrafted by" and other phrases, plus bears, rabbits and other "creative" figures in action. Mini-stamp sets supplies.
For Further Information: Catalog, $3.
Accepts: MasterCard, Visa

STAMPINKS UNLIMITED
P.O. Box 97
Shortsville, NY 14548

Offers: Artistic rubber stamps, including peace motifs/slogans—"Wage Peace" and globe, peace dogs, peace (in several languages, including Chinese character), others. Also offers E. Robin Allen's carousel/stylized designs and Cindy Pacileo's motifs, including zoo and other animals. Carries mail art, stars, hearts, other animals, birds, old structures, slogans, cathedrals, trees. Also carries greetings and postcard designs. Unmounted stamps at half price. Custom stamp service available.
For Further Information: Catalog and supplement, $2.50.
Discounts: Sells wholesale.

STAMPOURRI
P.O. Box 3434
La Habra, CA 90632
(310) 69-STAMP
Fax: (714) 526-4344

Offers: Artistic rubber stamps: teacher stamps in English and Spanish, holidays, angels, inspirational, thanks, party, spring, borders, Americana, primitive, gardening, floral, folk art; over 150 designs by artist Lisa Hindsley. Sets: Bible, Noah's ark, animals, others. Also offers templates and paper products (cards, bookmarks, others).
For Further Information: 35-page catalog, $3 (refundable).
Discounts: Wholesale available.

STEWART-SUPERIOR CORP.
1800 W. Larchmont Ave.
Chicago, IL 60613
(312) 935-6025 or (800) 621-1205

Offers: Rubber stamp manufacturing equipment/supplies: vulcanizers, stamp gum, matrix, imprinted stamp pads, ce-

ments, daters, seals, photopolymers, acrylic mounts, inks (over 100 colors), cushions, molding, brushes, bottles, sign makers, others.
For Further Information: Send SASE with inquiry.

TOOMUCHFUN RUBBERSTAMPS
2200 Coolidge Rd., Suite 14
East Lansing, MI 48823
(517) 351-2030

Offers: Rubber stamp motifs, including special occasions and other stamps "for celebrating"—candles, sun face designs, etc. Unmounted stamps half price.
For Further Information: Catalog, $4.
Discounts: Sells wholesale.
Accepts: MasterCard, Visa

UNCLE REBUS STAMP CO.
P.O. Box 334
Rutherford, CA 94573

Offers: Line of rubber stamp designs. Most designs are hieroglyphic rebus puzzle stamps, and letter/picture combinations.
For Further Information: Catalog, $1.

VISUAL IMAGE PRINTERY
1215 N. Grove St.
Anaheim, CA 92806
(714) 632-2441

Offers: Rubber stamp designs including Forest Folk, and other fantasy characters (wizards, dragons, castle, fairies, trees, others). Also offers foiling kits, stamping cubes, sparkles holographic sticker sheets, watercolor pencils.
For Further Information: Catalogs, $3.
Discounts: Sells wholesale.
Accepts: MasterCard, Visa

ZUM BALI BALI RUBBER STAMPS
P.O. Box 610187
Newton Highlands, MA 02161
(617) 965-1268
Fax: (617) 965-6158

Offers: Original art work, including pattern, Judaica, New England, lighthouses, whimiscal animals, birds, eraser carved images, sports, strong graphic design, architecture, postoids. Also carries interactive sets, including Design Your Own Jerusalem, bicycle kit, Cubist guitar set. Unmounted stamps also available.
For Further Information: Catalog, $2.50 (refundable).
Discounts: Sells wholesale; non-profit organizations.

Scientific Supplies and Equipment

ADVANCE SCIENTIFIC
2345 S.W. 34th St.
Ft. Lauderdale, FL 33312
(305) 327-0900 or (800) 524-2436
Fax: (954) 327-0903

Offers: Line of laboratory chemicals, instruments, supplies and glassware.
For Further Information: Call.

AMERICAN SCIENCE & SURPLUS
3605 Howard St.
Skokie, IL 60076
(847) 982-0870

Offers: Surplus/unusual items: laboratory equipment/supplies/kits, fiber optics and electrical items, lighting, wires, cords, bottles, jars, boxes, tool sets, solders, hemostats, airbrushes, jewelry, military items, and scientific kits and items. Electronics: magnetics, oscillators, lighting, clocks, motor building, rocketry, telegraphy items, hydroponics, solar energy, transducers, solenoids, AC/DC motors. Science novelties: kaleidoscopes, mirrors, magnifiers, "wonder" and gravity items. Also offers magnets and bunsen burners.
For Further Information: Catalog.
Store Location: At above address.
Discounts: Quantity.

ANALYTICAL SCIENTIFIC
11049 Bandera Rd.
San Antonio, TX 78250
(210) 684-7373

Offers: Scientific-related products: chemicals, a variety of equipment, glassware, experiments/projects and books.
For Further Information: Catalog, $3 (refundable).

EDMUND SCIENTIFIC
Dept. 16A-C911, Escorp Bldg.
Barrington, NJ 08007
(609) 574-8880

Offers: Technical/scientific products: kits for mini hot-air balloons and steam engines, microscope accessories, optics, ES lens, diffraction grating, kaleidoscopes, science subjects, 16 microscopes and pocket models, eyepieces, prisms, alcohol lamps, tubing, goggles, pH paper, clocks, timers, scales/balances, 35-plus magnifiers, loupes and electroplating kits. Also offers pencils and drawing sets, plastic bottles, dispensers, fiber optics fibers, light guides, helium-neon laser and others. Solar-related items include panels, cells, photovoltaics, trackers, others. Carries magnets, mirror film, modeling items, motors, fans, components, Dremel tools, measuring items, projectors, light boxes, steam-driven models, jeweler's items, papers.
For Further Information: Write for catalog.

PYROTEK
P.O. Box 1
Catasauqua, PA 18032
(717) 256-3087

Offers: Experimenters' chemicals, plans and supplies for making homemade rockets and fireworks; hobby cannon fuse, paper tubing and others. Laboratory glassware and other products.
For Further Information: Catalog, $3.

SOUTHERN OREGON SCIENTIFIC
1000 SE "M" St., Unit A
Grants Pass, OR 97526
(541) 955-8073
Offers: Laboratory chemicals and a variety of glassware.
For Further Information: Catalog, $2.

Scrimshaw

Also see Jewelry Making and Lapidary, Tools and Equipment and other related categories.

BOONE TRADING CO.
562 Coyota Rd.
Brinnon, WA 98320
(360) 796-4330

Offers: Raw materials, including fossil walrus ivory (teeth in 3 sizes), tusks, tips, polished pieces, scrap chip tusks. Elephant materials include scrap, tusk tips, slabs, sections, whole and hollow tusks. Also offers mammoth ivory, jewelry blanks, polished slabs, belt buckle blanks, scrimshaw kits, simulated stag, amber and ivory (with some original material/resin), stag antler burrs, crowns, rosettes and sheep horns. Carries books, animal skins, trade beads, ancient coins, others.
For Further Information: Send SASE for list.
Discounts: Quantity; sells wholesale to businesses.
Accepts: MasterCard, Visa

ALAN ZANOTTI
20 Braunecker Rd.
Plymouth, MA 02360
(508) 746-8552

Offers: Ivory (legal from estates), bone material, fossil ivory, horns, skulls.
For Further Information: Send SASE for list.

Sculpture and Modeling

Also see Ceramics, Metalworking, Mold Crafts and Woodworking.

AMERICAN ART CLAY CO., INC.
4717 W. 16th St.
Indianapolis, IN 46222
(317) 244-6871

Offers: FIMO modeling material for home oven firing of small items, miniatures, jewelry and other sculpting. Available in 36 bright colors. Sculptamold modeling compound, clays, others.
For Further Information: Contact your dealer, or send SASE.

BRI METAL FABRICATORS
72 Knowlton St.
Bridgeport, CT 06608
(203) 368-1649

Offers: Metal sculpture service: flame cutting, press forming, shearing, machining, plasma cutting, roll forming, welding and finishing.
For Further Information: Send SASE or call.

BRYANT LABORATORY, INC.
1101 5th St.
Berkeley, CA 94710
(415) 526-3141

Offers: Patina chemicals (solvents, acids and dry chemicals for art needs) including silver nitrate, chloride and sulfide, borax, calcium carbonate, eucalyptus oil, gold chloride, mercury, talc, preservatives, others. Lab items: alcohol lamps, beakers, bottles, filters, bunsen burners, cylinders, clamps, flasks, hydrometers, droppers, funnels, petri dishes, slides, stirrers, test tubes, tubing, others. Books are also available.
For Further Information: Write for price list and formulas.
Discounts: Quantity; teachers and institutions.

THE COMPLEAT SCULPTOR, INC.
90 Van Dan
New York, NY 10013
(212) 243-6074 or (800) 9-SCULPT
Fax: (212) 243-6374

Offers: Complete line of materials, including tools and supplies for stone, metal, clay, resin and other sculpture work. Also offers support services, including casting, patination, stone finishing, basing and photography.
For Further Information: Free catalog.

DESIGN CONSULTING SERVICE
41355 Covelo Rd.
Willits, CA 95490
(707) 984-8394

Offers: Low shrink wax for electro-plated molds. Also offers custom rooting of vinyl heads.
For Further Information: Call or write.

DICK BLICK
P.O. Box 1267
Galesburg, IL 61402
(309) 343-6181

Offers: Full line of art/sculpture and other materials and equipment: soapstone, alabaster, stone sculpture tool sets. Modeling: instant papier-mâchés, Sculptamold, plastercraft gauze, plaster of Paris (and molds), Sculpey, modeling clays, plasticolor. Clays: Mexican pottery, Marblex, Westwood ovencraft, others. Also offers Egyptian paste, earthenware and other kitchen-fired clays, plus glazes, ceramic and modeling tools/sets and aids.
For Further Information: Catalog, $5.
Accepts: American Express, Discover, MasterCard, Visa

DODD: MARBLE & GRANITE
P.O. Box 2721
North Hill, CA 91393
(818) 891-1909 or (800) 2-SCULPT

Offers: Stones for sculpting including marble, granite, alabaster, limestone, sandstone, onyx, soapstone, steatite, serpentine, travertine, lapis, sodalite, and others, to 5 tons. Tools include chisels, mallets, rasps, rifflers, turning pins, grinding machines, discs and burrs, bits, diamond saws and others. Supplies include bases, polishing compounds, expoxies and others, videos and books also available.
For Further Information: Free list; request in writing only.
Discounts: Quantity buyers, schools and professional groups and trade.

DURHAM
P.O. Box 804
Des Moines, IA 50304
(515) 243-0491

Offers: Durham's Rock Hard Water Putty: molds, carves, sculpts, models or casts (no firing).
For Further Information: Send large SASE for handcraft booklet.

THE ROBERT FIDA STUDIO
1100 Storey Blvd.
Cheyenne, WY 82009
(307) 635-5056

Offers: *The Sculptor's Studio* video series with Robert Fida covers moldmaking and casting, including casting with concrete, plaster, hydrostone, hydrocal, pewter, bronze, pecan shell, marble. Also covers gold leafing, finishing techniques for concrete and plaster, shrinking castings, marketing for the visual artist and other topics.
For Further Information: Send SASE for list.

GAMEPLAN/ARTRANCH
2233 NcKinley Ave.
Berkeley, CA 94703
(510) 549-0993

Offers: Instructional videos on working with polymer clay, including a foundation course and surface techniques, mokume gane, embellishments, molds/stamps/tools, and recreating materials, including lapis, bone, ivory, jade, amber and coral.
For Further Information: Free catalog.

MONTOYA/MAS INTERNATIONAL, INC.
435 Southern Blvd.
West Palm Beach, FL 33405
(407) 832-4401

Offers: Carving stones (imported), line of marble bases (many sizes/colors), over 1,600 sculpture tools (including hard-to-find), clays and waxes. Services available include art foundry, casting, mounting, repairs and restoration.
For Further Information: Catalog, $3.
Store Location: At above address.
Discounts: Quantity; teachers and institutions; sells wholesale to legitimate businesses.

PAUL KING FOUNDRY
92 Allendale Ave.
Johnston, RI 02919
(401) 231-3120

Offers: Custom services, including sculptural and architectural castings, lost wax and French sand processes, bronze, plus aluminum and other non-ferrous metals.
For Further Information: Write or call with inquiry.

PREMIER WAX CO., INC.
3327 Hidden Valley Dr.
Little Rock, AR 72212
(501) 225-2925

Offers: Microcrystalline waxes (for sculpting and casting): Victory, available in 3 colors, and Be Square types. Sold in 10 pound lots and up.
For Further Information: Send SASE or call.

SCULPTURE STUDIO & FOUNDRY
1150 Clare Ave.
West Palm Beach, FL 33401
(407) 833-6950

Offers: Art casting services: enlargements to any size, mold making, bronze casting with ceramic shell, resin and stone casting, patina.
For Further Information: Send SASE or call with inquiry.

STEATITE OF SOUTHERN OREGON, INC.
2891 Elk Lane
Grants Pass, OR 97527
(503) 479-3646

Offers: Sculpturing stone, including soapstone in white, greens, dentrites, black/white, standard cuts, blocks. Orders must be more than 1 lb. Carving booklet also available. Other stones, include chlorite, alabaster, anhydrite, catlinite. Hard stones, marble in a variety of colors, limestone and travertine onyx are also available. Also offers line of sculpting tools by Trow & Holden, Alpha Professional and other brands.
For Further Information: Send SASE for prices.
Discounts: Sells wholesale.

TALLIX
175 Fishkill Ave.
Beacon, NY 12508
(914) 838-1111

Offers: An enlarging studio with a scraping technique that enables enlargements with detail. Enlarges sculpture to any size and any degree of finish.
For Further Information: Send SASE or call for price quotes.

TROW AND HOLDEN CO.
P.O. Box 475
Barre, VT 05641
(800) 451-4349
Fax: (802) 476-7025

Offers: Line of stone sculpting and cutting tools: 5 pneumatic carving tools, pneumatic stone carving sets, soft stone hand carving sets, mallets, carbide tip chisels, rippers, chisels (machine, splitter, clean-up, double blade, marble lettering, 4-point, 9-point, marble tooth and cutting types), and carver's and other drills.
For Further Information: Free catalog.

Sign Making

Also see Artist's Supplies, Paints, Finishes and Adhesives, and Tole and Decorative Crafts.

ART ESSENTIALS OF NEW YORK LTD.
3 Cross St.
Suffern, NY 10901
(914) 368-1100
Alternate address: 508 Douglas Ave.
Toronto, Ontario M5M 1H5
Canada

Offers: Gold leaf (genuine and composition) in sheets and rolls (variety of shades/karats), plus glass-type gold leaf. Also offers silver leaf and supplies, such as gilding size, knives, burnishing clay, and other tools and brushes. Books are also available.
For Further Information: Send SASE for product lists.

BARCLAY LEAF IMPORTS, INC.
21 Wilson Terrace
Elizabeth, NJ 07208
(908) 353-5522
Fax: (908) 353-5525

Offers: Line of gold and metal leaf and supplies for professionals and beginners (including introductory packages).
For Further Information: See your dealer or send SASE.
Discounts: Distributors.

DICK BLICK
P.O. Box 1267
Galesburg, IL 61402
(309) 343-6181

Offers: Arts/crafts/graphics and sign-making supplies including airbrushes, paints, banners, sign blanks, sign cloth. Also offers sandblaster units, supplies and equipment (for gold leafing, pinstriping, screen printing), plus books on lettering and other topics.
For Further Information: Catalog, $5.
Accepts: American Express, Discover, MasterCard, Visa
See Also: Artist's Supplies and General Craft Supplies

THE CUTAWL CO.
16 Stony Hill Rd.
Bethel, CT 06801
(203) 792-8622

Offers: Cutawl machine (with knife, chisel and saw blades that cut curves, logos or patterns—blades swivel 360 degrees)—cuts most sign and display materials including Lexan, Plexiglas, Lucite, Fome-Cor, Gatorfoam, plywood, particle board, stencil board, vinyl, cloth, others.
For Further Information: Free catalog.

THE DURHAM CO.
54 Woodland St.
Newburyport, MA 01950
(508) 465-3493 or (800) 462-1009

Offers: Gold leaf (hand beaten), including XX deep patent, glass and surface types.
For Further Information: Send SASE.

GEMINI INC.
103 Mensing Way
Cannon Falls, MN 55009
(507) 263-3957

Offers: Letters of vacuum formed plastic, injection-molded plastic, cast aluminum, cast bronze, flat cut-out plastic and metal types, and edge trim gemlite letters. Also offers aluminum and bronze plaques, custom metal cut-outs, custom formed plastic, and videos and manuals.
For Further Information: Free catalog.

GOLD LEAF & METALLIC POWDERS, INC.
74 Trinity Place, Suite 1200
New York, NY 10006
(212) 267-4900

Offers: Genuine metallic leaf: Gold (variety of shades/karats), palladium, silver leaf and composition leaf products, including gold, bronze, copper, variegated and others. Also offers patinating and gilding supplies and accessories, restoration aids and others.
For Further Information: Send SASE.

HARTCO
1280 Glendale-Milford Rd.
Cincinnati, OH 45215
(513) 771-4430

Offers: Sandmask stencils: vinyl (for sandblasting raw or treated wood, plastic or glass), pin-feed stencil materials, etching tapes and others.
For Further Information: Send SASE.

HAYNES SIGN CO.
Highway 27 S.
Murrells Inlet, SC 29576
(803) 651-0700

Offers: Instructional video on sign painting from veteran painter; includes step-by-step directions, techniques.
For Further Information: Send SASE.

PETER HORSLEY PUBLICATIONS
115 Riverbirch Cresent SE
Calgary, Alberta T2C 3M1
Canada
(403) 279-0227
Fax: (403) 279-1785

Offers: Self-study course in neon crafting. The course is clearly written with photos and diagrams, complete technical information, basic electricity, design and selling, manufacturing and service/repair. A course in servicing electric signs and a course for inventors are also available. Also supplies source data and sign books, including books about the manufacture of neon signs and engineering sign structures.
For Further Information: Send for free sample lesson.

EARL MICH CO.
806 N. Peoria St.
Chicago, IL 60622
(312) 829-1552

Offers: Sign letters, both vinyl and reflective types (computer prespaced or individual die cut), for producing computer digitized logos, punched materials, universal symbols, alphabet sheets, screen printing, police and fire decals, plastic dimensional letters, static lettering. Also offers magnetic sheeting, letters and signs, prespacing tapes, vinyl and reflective material (in sheets, striping, rolls) and other die-cut sign graphics—over 100 colors/type styles.
For Further Information: Write or call.
Accepts: MasterCard, Visa

MULLER STUDIOS SIGN CO.
59 Ringe Rd.
Union, CT 06076
(203) 974-2161

Offers: Sign blanks—constructed of Simpson Signal M.D.O., with mahogany frames and waterproof glue. A variety of stock sizes and shapes (including old-tavern, oval, round, rectangular, other old-world looks). Custom wood signs built to specifications.
For Further Information: Write or call.

NUDO PRODUCTS, INC.
2508 S. Grand Ave. E.
Springfield, IL 62703
(800) 826-4132

Offers: White-wood sign panel (smooth vinyl surface, fac-

tory laminated to exterior plywood) for hand/screen lettering or vinyl letters (flame resistant), available in a variety of sizes and other substrates. Also offers fiberglass surfaced sign panels.
For Further Information: Write or call for sample.

RAYCO PAINT CO.
6100 N. Pulaski Rd.
Chicago, IL 60646
(800) 421-2327

Offers: Banner blanks—drill cloth with nylon rope top/bottom, can be lettered on two sides if latex coated—available in 14 sizes, to 4'×40'. Full line of screen process, sign and painter's supplies and equipment.
For Further Information: Write or call for catalog.

SEPP LEAF PRODUCTS, INC.
381 Park Ave. S.
New York, NY 10016
(212) 683-2840

Offers: August Ruhl gold leaf, glass gold, patent gold, palladium leaf, karat gold in a variety of shades and roll gold. Also offers gilder's tips, LeFranc oil size and an instructional video—*Gold Leaf Basics*, with Kent H. Smith. Technical data service available—write.
For Further Information: Free catalog.
Discounts: Sells wholesale to legitimate businesses.

SIGN-MART
410 W. Fletcher
Orange, CA 92665
(714) 998-9470 or (800) 533-9099

Offers: Blank vinyl banner material: 3' times any length, hemmed and grommeted, for lettering or silkscreen, in 12 colors.
For Further Information: Send SASE.

T.J. RONAN PAINT CORP.
749 E. 135th St.
Bronx, NY 10454
(718) 292-1100
Fax: (718) 292-0406

Offers: Japan color paints used for striping, stenciling, and making antiquing or graining glazes and stains. Paint can also be used for specialty and scenic painting, for aging, faux finishes and glasing. Paints come in 33 colors.
For Further Information: Contact your dealer or send SASE.

TARA MATERIALS INC.
P.O. Box 646
Lawrenceville, GA 30246
(404) 963-5256

Offers: Vinyl banner cloth in three types, including Taravyn

9 oz., reinforced for use with vinyl paints or inks and pressure sensitive graphics; Taravynall 10 oz. reinforced cloth, coated on one side to accept paint, ink, enamel and pressure sensitive graphics; and Taracloth III, smooth moisture-resistant polyflax fabric, triple-coated for paints and pressure sensitive graphics. Also offers Tyvek, Tygerag and Taracloth banner cloth. Manufacturer.
For Further Information: Write.

TIP SANDBLAST EQUIPMENT
7075 Rt. 446
P.O. Box 649
Canfield, OH 44406
(216) 533-3384 or (800) 321-9260

Offers: Combination sandblaster and paint units, accessories, and 3M Buttercut resist material, available by the yard or roll.
For Further Information: Free catalog.

TRADEMARK SIGN SYSTEMS
4 Hall Rd.
Ithaca, NY 14850
(800) 423-6895

Offers: Carving and sandblasting blanks: Old growth redwood with vertical grain, splined glue joints, matched boards ready to finish.
For Further Information: Color brochures.
Discounts: Sells wholesale to dealers.

LEO UHLFELDER CO.
420 S. Fulton Ave.
Mt. Vernon, NY 10553
(914) 664-8701

Offers: Gold leaf—quality Florentine gold, XX deep patent, glass, surface gold, roll gold. Also offers gold size (quick and slow forms). Importers.
For Further Information: Send SASE.

WENSCO SIGN SUPPLY
2910 Schoeneck Rd.
Macungie, PA 18062
(215) 966-3555

Offers: Complete line of sandblasting sign supplies (to sandblast wood, glass, stone, brick, others): Sandblast machines, air compressors, tape masking materials. Also offers Sign-Life products, automatic letter-cutting machines, hoods, nozzles, and other parts and supplies. Has custom sandblasting service.
For Further Information: Send SASE.

YARDER MANUFACTURING CO.
708 Phillips Ave.
Toledo, OH 43612
(419) 476-3933

Offers: Sign blanks—steel and aluminum in stock sizes with factory-to-you pricing.
For Further Information: Send SASE.

Taxidermy

DAN CHASE TAXIDERMY SUPPLY CO.
13599 Blackwater Rd.
Baker, LA 70714
(504) 261-3795

Offers: Full and complete line of taxidermy supplies and over 500 instructional videotapes on subjects related to taxidermy.
For Further Information: Free catalog.

MCKENZIE TAXIDERMY SUPPLY
P.O. Box 480
Granite Quarry, NC 28072
(800) 279-7985

Offers: Full line of taxidermy supplies, including deer and animal forms.
For Further Information: Free catalog.

VANDYKE'S
P.O. Box 278
Woonsocket, SD 57385
(800) 843-3320

Offers: Taxidermy kits for beginners, instructional videos and handbooks. Also offers advanced/professional supplies, a full line for taxidermists and tanners.
For Further Information: Free booklet.

Tole and Decorative Crafts

Also see General Craft Supplies, Artist's Supplies, Miniature Making, Paints, Finishes and Adhesives, Fabric Decorating and other related categories.

ADVENTURES IN CRAFTS
Yorkville Station
P.O. Box 6058
New York, NY 10128
(212) 410-9793
Fax: (212) 410-9793

Offers: Decoupage products, including prints, (animals, flowers, Oriental, Goodey's Ladies, Anton Pieck, others) and black-and-white prints (botanicals, borders, birds, animals) and decoupage kits designed by Dee Davis. Also offers wood products, including a line of boxes, lap desks and screens (3 and 4 panels). Gilding supplies available include Dutch metal gold/silver leaf. Carries epoxy and other adhesives, sizing, box hardware, papers, decoupage scissors, brayer, burnisher, tools, finishes and books.
For Further Information: Catalog, $3.50.

B&B PUBLISHING, INC.
P.O. Box 420268
Kissimmee, FL 34742
(407) 870-2121

Offers: How-to decorative painting videos and books by Maureen McNaughton and Linda Wise.
For Further Information: Free brochure.
Discounts: Sells wholesale to legitimate businesses.

BARCLAY LEAF IMPORTS, INC.
21 Wilson Terrace
Elizabeth, NJ 07208
(908) 353-5522

Offers: Gold leaf, including introductory packages, line of professional supplies. Also offers metal leaf.
For Further Information: Send SASE.

BEAR WOODS SUPPLY CO., INC.
P.O. Box 40
Bear River, Nova Scotia B0S 1B0
Canada
(902) 467-3703

Offers: Unfinished wood ware, including candle cups, hold-
ers, sticks, Shaker pegs, other pegs, wheels, toys (cargo and people, yo-yos, bells, animals, bowling pins), kitchen items, miniatures, line of boxes and shapes, spindles, bars, knobs, beads, game pieces, spools, finials, dowels, others.
For Further Information: Free catalog.
Discounts: Quantity; sells wholesale to legitimate businesses.
Accepts: MasterCard, Visa

BRIDGEWATER SCROLLWORKS
Rt. 1
P.O. Box 585
Osage, MN 56570
(218) 573-3094

Offers: Wood cutouts—over 1,000 shapes, including hearts, animals, flowers, figures, others. Custom cutting service.
For Further Information: Catalog, $5 (refundable).
Discounts: Quantity.

CAPE COD COOPERAGE
1150 Queen Anne Rd.
Chatham, MA 02633
(508) 432-0788

Offers: Barrel staves—sanded, ready-to-decorate/paint—and hinged-top chests and boxes.
For Further Information: Send SASE for list.

CRAFTS JUST FOR YOU
2030 Clinton Ave.
Alameda, CA 94501
(800) 272-3848
Fax: (510) 521-4789

Offers: Over 6,000 products in lines of paints, brushes, precut wood, stencils, tole books and more.
For Further Information: Catalog, $5.

CRANBERRY PAINTER
P.O. Box 1495
Buzzards Bay, MA 02532
(508) 759-4623

Offers: Decorative painting pattern packets, 12-plus motifs (including some to personalize with names/dates/events), and pen and ink supplies. Also offers books and videos.
For Further Information: Brochures, $1 (refundable).

CUPBOARD DISTRIBUTING

114 S. Main St.
P.O. Box 148
Urbana, OH 43078
(513) 652-3338

Offers: Woodenwares, including miniatures, carousel horses and other animals, jointed animals, pull toys, spools, candles, sticks, cups, holders, eggs, fruit, boxes, gameboards, shapes, signs, wheels, pegs, dowels, knobs, school items. Also offers jewelry, including necklace kits, patterns, beads, findings, bells and cord, plus resin figures, hardware, paints, brushes and others.
For Further Information: Catalog, $1.
Accepts: Discover, MasterCard, Visa

CUSTOM WOOD CUT-OUTS UNLIMITED

P.O. Box 518
Massillon, OH 44648
(330) 832-2919

Offers: Wood cut-outs in a wide array of shapes and sizes, plus custom wood cutting services.
For Further Information: Catalog, $2 (refundable).
Accepts: MasterCard, Visa

DESIGNS BY BENTWOOD, INC.

P.O. Box 1676
Thomasville, GA 31799
(912) 226-1223

Offers: Bentwood products for painting, including boxes— pie, bonnet, bride's, cheese, tine, purse, paint, pantry and others. Also offers scoops, piggins, sifter, wastebaskets and canisters.

DUX' DEKES DECOY CO.

RD 2
P.O. Box 66
Greenwich, NY 12834
(518) 692-7703 or (800) 553-4725

Offers: Over 100 patterns of carved decoy blanks, including swan, goose, duck, loon, shorebirds and wading blanks (miniature to full-size white pine or basswood). Also offers cork decoy kits and paint kits for usable hunting decoys.
For Further Information: Write.
Discounts: Sells wholesale.
Accepts: MasterCard, Visa

EASY LEAF

947 N. Cole Ave.
Los Angeles, CA 90038
(213) 469-0856

Offers: Line of genuine gold leaf and composition metal leaf

in a variety of shades, karats and types. Also offers gold leaf accessories and supplies. Manufacturer.
For Further Information: Free catalog.

THE ELBRIDGE COMPANY

7108 Conser
Overland Park, KS 66204
(913) 384-6188

Offers: Manucturers of ready-to-paint wooden lamps and lamp shades, including lightweight in several sizes. Also offers other wood products.
For Further Information: Call or write.
Discounts: Sells wholesale to distributors.

CHARLOTTE FORD TRUNKS

P.O. Box 536
Spearman, TX 79081
(806) 659-3027

Offers: Trunk repair/restoration supplies: hinges, lock sets, other hardware, finishes, linings. Also offers how-to books to help restore, refinish, line and decorate all kinds of trunks.
For Further Information: Illustrated catalog, $3.

FORTÉ INDUSTRIES INC.

P.O. Box 276
Stephenson, MI 49887
(906) 753-2317

Offers: Wood cut-outs and unassembled kits including miniatures, wall units, collector boxes, shadowboxes, basket covers, Christmas shapes. Also offers basswood lumber in 3 widths.
For Further Information: Catalog, $1.

THE GATSONIAN DETAIL

Rt. 2, Box 48
Chillicothe, MO 64601
(816) 646-0015

Offers: Pecan resin ready-to-paint figurines, including angels, Santas, bears, bunnie, ornaments, gingerbread, villages and others.
For Further Information: 40-page color catalog, $4.

GODIN ART, INC.

RR1
352 German School Rd.
Paris, Ontario N3L 3E1
Canada
(519) 448-1244

Offers: Cast waterfowl carvings including life-size drakes (canvas back, buffinhead, others) by Pat Godin. Also offers

blending brushes, waterfowl pattern books and instructional videos.
For Further Information: Call or write.

GOLD LEAF & METALLIC POWDERS, INC.
74 Trinity Place, Suite 1807
New York, NY 10006
(212) 267-4900

Offers: Genuine and composition gold leaf in a variety of karats and shades, plus silver, palladium, copper and aluminum leaf, supplies for patinating and gilding and restoration aids.
For Further Information: Send SASE.

HERITAGE CRAFT STUDIO, INC.
1592 Major Oaks Rd.
Pickering, Ontario L1X 2G9
Canada
(905) 427-6666
Fax: (905) 427-3822

Offers: Line of folk art pattern packets and folk art, tole and decorative painting books.
For Further Information: Packet catalog and book catalog, $5 each (refundable).
Discounts: Sells wholesale.

HERITAGE SAW CO.
11225 6th St. E.
St. Petersburg, FL 33706
(813) 367-7557

Offers: Line of woodenware, paints, brushes, books, plus folk art painting tools and supplies.
For Further Information: Catalog, $2.
Discounts: Sells wholesale.

HOFCRAFT
P.O. Box 72
Grand Haven, MI 49417
(800) 828-0359

Offers: Tole art supplies, including a full line of paints (Priscilla, Permanent Pigment, Shiva), dyes, brushes and handcrafted wood items, plus books.
For Further Information: Catalog, $4.
Accepts: Discover, MasterCard, Visa

HOME CRAFT EXPRESS, INC.
P.O. Box 24890
San Jose, CA 95154
(800) 301-7377
Fax: (800) 528-4193

Offers: Decorative painting products, including paints, brushes and supplies by Delta, JoSonja, Loew Cornell, De-

coArt, Robert Simmons, Blair Satin Tole, Designs From the Heart Sealer, White Lightning and others. Also offers paper mache items, painting videos and books.
For Further Information: Free catalog.

HOUSTON ART & FRAME, INC.
10770 Moss Ridge Rd.
Houston, TX 77043-1175
(713) 868-2505
Fax: (713) 462-1783

Offers: Decoupage materials, gold leaf, decorative painting accessories, chaco paper, gessoed masonite and super film.
For Further Information: Send for free product listing

JENNINGS DECOY CO.
601 Franklin Ave. NE
St. Cloud, MN 56304
(800) 331-5613
Fax: (602) 253-9537

Offers: Decoy painting kits including blanks, eyes, paints, patterns. Custom casting available.
For Further Information: Free catalog.
Accepts: MasterCard, Visa

K&S TOLE & CRAFT SUPPLY
1556 Florence St.
Aurora, CO 80010
(303) 364-3031

Offers: Known lines of decorative painting supplies, including paints, acrylics, watercolors, oils, fabric dyes and paints, mediums, sealers. Also offers brushes, wood turnings and cutouts, canvas, drawing materials and tole. Clock and music box works and books are also available.
For Further Information: Send SASE for catalog packet.

LAILA'S
22 Strathearn Ave, Units 1 & 2
Bramalea, Ontario L6T 4L8
Canada

Offers: Full line of decoupage prints by a variety of artists in traditional, classics, florals, animals, birds and others. Books also available.
For Further Information: Color catalog, $20, or send SASE with inquiry.

THE MAGIC BRUSH, INC.
P.O. Box 530
Portal, AZ 85632

Offers: Pattern/instruction books for decorative painting, by Sherry C. Nelson, MDA, including how to paint realistic

birds, butterflies and animals on wood, reverse glass or canvas; carries design/pattern packets.
For Further Information: Send four 32¢ stamps for catalog.

MANOR HOUSE DESIGNS

85 Great Lake Dr.
Annapolis, MD 21403-3725
(410) 268-9782

Offers: Precut stencils (mylar, acetate) of wreaths, potted flowers, topiaries, tabletop, trompe l'oeil, bird cages and others—detailed cut. Precut stencils for wall murals.
For Further Information: Stencil catalog, $5.
Discounts: Sells wholesale to legitimate businesses.

NEW ENGLAND COUNTRY DESIGNS

20 Hatheway Rd.
Ellington, CT 06029
(860) 871-0033

Offers: Pattern packets for New England homes in wood and acrylic (miniature collectibles), with instructions, drawings, photos, wood.
For Further Information: Catalog, $1.
Discounts: Sells wholesale.

ORNAMENTS UNLIMITED

7416 Bay Shore Dr. West 190
Muskego, WI 53150
(800) 762-3556
Fax: (414) 679-1578

Offers: Birch ply cutout ornaments and others, in ⅛" or ¼" birch plywood. Custom cutting service for original patterns.
For Further Information: Call or write.
Discounts: Sells wholesale. Distributor prices available.

P.C. ENGLISH

Thornburg, VA 22565
(800) 221-9474

Offers: Carved waterfowl blanks (with eyes and color painting patterns) of mallards, wood and goldeneye ducks.
For Further Information: Write for catalog.

PLAID ENTERPRISES

P.O. Box 7600
Norcross, GA 30091
(770) 923-8200

Offers: Acrylic paints, stencils, plaster, faux finish kits, fabric painting, glues and finishes, publications. Manufacturer.
For Further Information: Send SASE.

RAINBOW WOODS

20 Andrews St.
Newnan, GA 30263
(770) 251-4195

Offers: Unfinished hardwood turnings and shapes, including dowels, wheels, axles, candle cups, hearts, napkin rings, eggs, Shaker pegs, boxes, checkers, fruit, balls, knobs, spindles, thimbles and others in wide array of sizes. Jewelry findings.
For Further Information: Free catalog.
Discounts: Quantity; sells wholesale to legitimate businesses.

BARNEY ROBERTI, DAUGHTERS AND SONS

174 Matthew Run Rd.
Youngville, PA 16371

Offers: Wood parts and wood stenciled shapes in country and modern styles, including animals, others.

S&G, INC.

P.O. Box 805
Howell, MI 48844
(517) 546-9240
Fax: (517) 546-9720

Offers: Line of windchimes, preprimed and ready-to-print metal in four sizes. Also offers windchime patterns.
For Further Information: Call or send SASE.
Discounts: Sells wholesale to dealers.

SANDEEN'S SCANDINAVIAN ART, GIFTS & NEEDLECRAFT

1315 White Bear Ave.
St. Paul, MN 55106
(612) 776-7012 or (800) 235-1315

Offers: Tole-making and folk art supplies including wood items, paints, patterns and instructional books. Also offers Norwegian rosemaling, Swedish Dala painting and Bavarian Bauernmalere.
For Further Information: Catalog, $2 (refundable).
Accepts: American Express, MasterCard, Visa

SAWDUST AND PAINTINGS

382 E. Rialto Ave.
San Bernardino, CA 92408
(909) 381-3885

Offers: Unfinished wood products—shapes, wheels, others.
For Further Information: Catalog, $2 (refundable).
Store Location: At above address.
Discounts: Sells wholesale to legitimate businesses.

JACKIE SHAW STUDIO

13306 Edgemont Rd.
Smithsburg, MD 21783
(301) 824-7592

Offers: 100 videos/books, including *View It 'N Do It* decorative painting lessons by Jackie Shaw, Ardi Hansen, Nancy Michael, Sherry Gunter, others. Subjects include angels, wildflowers, birds/butterflies, animals, simple strokes and faux finishes. Pattern books include subjects such as folk art, wood, fabric painting, tin punch, stenciling, others. Also carries brushes, kits.
For Further Information: Contact your dealer; catalog, $1.
Discounts: Sells wholesale to legitimate businesses.

STENCIL HOUSE OF N.H., INC.

P.O. Box 16109
Hooksett, NH 03106
(603) 625-1716

Offers: Over 200 stencils (from mylar) designs: Reproductions, children's, florals, traditional, others—for hard surfaces and fabrics. Also offers Paintstiks, acrylics, stencil adhesives, brushes, cleaners and floor cloths. Services include custom designing and stenciling information.
For Further Information: Catalog, $2.50 (refundable).
Discounts: Sells wholesale to legitimate businesses.

SURMA

11 E. 7th St.
New York, NY 10003
(212) 477-0729
Fax: (212) 473-0439

Offers: Line of Ukranian egg decorating kits, dyes and other supplies.
For Further Information: Free catalog.

SWISS BOX, LTD.

P.O. Box 26063
Shawnee Mission, KS 66225
(913) 663-1158

Offers: Wood cutout shapes with music mechanism to create music boxes, including angel, rabbit, Christmas tree, fish, heart and other designs.
For Further Information: Brochure, $1 and SASE.

TOFT'S TOLE HOUSE

P.O. Box 249X21
Waynesville, MO 65583
(573) 774-5651

Offers: Patterns, pole people using landscape timbers.
For Further Information: Catalog, $2

TRAFTON THOMPSON PUBLISHING

P.O. Box 9068
Amarillo, TX 79105

Offers: Ready to paint "Works of Art" wood cutout kits in country designs by known artists, including Elaine Thompson, Rosemary West, Susie Saunders and others. Designs include "Cottontail Cousins," "Tree Top Villages" and others.
For Further Information: Free catalog.
Discounts: Sells wholesale to retail stores.
Accepts: MasterCard, Visa

TREASURES

P.O. Box 9
Huntsville, OH 43324
(513) 686-4191

Offers: Plans/cutting patterns for furniture pieces and home accessories (as shown in books by Jo Sonja, Helan Barrick, Pat Clarke, Folk Art Finish and others) in all shapes full size, plus kits. (Also has assembled items.)
For Further Information: Catalog, $3.
Discounts: Quantity; teachers and institutions; sells wholesale to legitimate businesses.

VIKING FOLK ART PUBLICATIONS

1317 8th St. SE
Waseca, MN 56093
(507) 835-8043

Offers: Pattern/instructional books for decorative painting, including transparent flowers (acrylics and bronzing powder), traditional and country designs, for all levels of ability. Also offers decorated dimensional frames and sweatshirt designs for fabric dyes.
For Further Information: Contact your dealer or send SASE for list

VIKING WOODCRAFTS, INC.

1317-8th St. SE
Waseca, MN 56093
(507) 835-8043
Fax: (507) 835-3895

Offers: Ready-to-paint decorative items, including wood items, ash baskets, metal shapes and others. Also carries Jo-Sonja paints, accessories and more.
For Further Information: 700-page catalog available

WESTERN WOODWORKS

1142 Olive Branch Lane
San Jose, CA 95120
(408) 997-2356

Offers: Wood items, including Native American hardwoods for decorative painting— lamp bases and many others.

For Further Information: Free catalog.
Accepts: MasterCard, Visa

WHITE PINE DESIGNS, INC.
Rt. 1
P.O. Box 99
Roland, IA 50236
(515) 388-4601

Offers: Raw wood boxes: pantry, recipe, jewelry, trunks, tissue. Also offers doll toys and furniture.
For Further Information: Catalog, $3.
Discounts: Sells wholesale.

SHIRLEY WILSON'S LADYBUG ART CENTER
P.O. BOX 4159
Springfield, MO 65808
(417) 883-4708

Offers: Decorative painting instruction/pattern books: traditional and country designs, including country kids, florals, whimsical animals, how-to lettering book, still lifes, angels, nautical scenes and more.
For Further Information: Contact your dealer, or send SASE for list.
Accepts: MasterCard, Visa

WIZARDS OF WOOD
5250 Bonsai Ave.
Moorpark, CA 93021
(805) 523-3181
Fax: (805) 523-2708

Offers: Line of unfinished wood clocks in fret work and other shapes. Also offers paintable watches, clock movements and pattern packets.
For Further Information: Send SASE.
Accepts: All major credit cards

THE WOOD CELLAR
114 Creek Rd.
Mt. Laurel, NJ 08054
(800) 303-5895
Fax: (609) 273-1117

Offers: Custom personalized wood cutting service from customer's pattern.
For Further Information: Call or write.

WOOD TO PAINT
P.O. Box 70
Mound, MN 55364

Offers: Line of pre-cut wood kits, furniture, shelves and wood cutouts. Also offers stenciling and painting supplies, hardware items and books.
For Further Information: Catalog, $2.
Accepts: Discover, MasterCard, Visa

THE WOODEN HEART
Rt. 11
P.O. Box 2260
Elizabethton, TN 37643
(423) 543-5602

Offers: Wood design packets for birdhouses, plates.
For Further Information: Send SASE with 2 stamps for catalog.
Discounts: To shops or studios with small minimum order.

WORDEN'S WORLD OF CRAFTS, INC.
3359 N. Federal Highway
Pompano Beach, FL 33064
(954) 941-0326

Offers: Paper tole kits (75 designs)—traditional and classic motifs, florals, others.
For Further Information: Free catalog.

Tools and Equipment—Multipurpose

Also see specific arts, crafts and needlecrafts categories.

ARTOGRAPH, INC.
2838 Vicksburg Lane N.
Minneapolis, MN 55447
(612) 553-1112

Offers: Artograph opaque projectors (transfers, enlarges or reduces photos, designs or patterns for tracing), including compact models and others plus floor stands. Manufacturer.
For Further Information: Contact your dealer, or write.

BLUE RIDGE MACHINERY & TOOLS, INC.
P.O. Box 536
Hurricane, WV 25526
(304) 562-3538
Fax: (304) 562-5311

Offers: Machinery/tools, including lathes, milling machines, and hand and power tools by Unimat, Compact, Maximat, Myford, Sherline, Atlas, Jet and many other manufacturers. Also offers machine shop supplies and accessories.
For Further Information: Free catalog.
Discounts: Sells wholesale to legitimate businesses.

BRANDMARK
462 Carthage Dr.
Xenia, OH 45434
(513) 426-6843

Offers: Branding irons in solid brass, with convenient torch heating. The first line of each brand reads "Handcrafted by" and is followed by a custom-made second line of up to 20 letters and spaces maximum. The brands feature ¼″ letters with line borders. Also offers an electric model.
For Further Information: Send SASE for details.
Accepts: MasterCard, Visa

CARDINAL ENGINEERING
Rt. 1
P.O. Box 163
Cameron, IL 61423
(309) 342-7474

Offers: You-Build Wood-Met Plans: clamp and spin tools, lathes, turning chisels, saws, routers, air compressors, sanders, drill presses, boring heads and bars, pantographs, gas-fired furnaces and many accessories. Also offers hand tools, drills, measuring items, magnifiers, aluminum and stainless steel, tool steel, brass, music wire and copper tubes. Books are also available.
For Further Information: Catalog, $2.
Accepts: MasterCard, Visa

THE DAN-SIG CO.
P.O. Box 2141
Memphis, TN 38101
(901) 525-8464

Offers: Dazor line of magnifier lamps in a variety of styles and types, including floating arm pedestal and a floating arm model on rollers. Also offers replacement lamps and bulbs.
For Further Information: Contact your dealer, or send SASE. Send phone number in query.

DREMEL, INC.
4915 21st St.
Racine, WI 53406
(414) 554-1390

Offers: Power tools, attachments and accessories, including redesigned Moto-Tool high-speed rotary tools, shaft attachments and drill presses, plus 2-speed scroll saws, disc/belt sanders, table saws, engravers, attachments and over 165 bits for over 10 applications. Manufacturer.
For Further Information: Contact your dealer or write.

THE FOREDOM ELECTRIC CO.
16 Stony Hill Rd.
Bethel, CT 06801
(203) 792-8622

Offers: Flexible shaft rotary power tools, 21 handpieces and accessories tools to cut, grind, buff, polish, sand and deburr. Also offers bench lathes (variable speeds), hand-piece holders, and power tools and accessories for crafts, jewelry making. Manufacturer.
For Further Information: Contact your dealer or write for free catalog.

HARBOR FREIGHT TOOLS
3491 Mission Oaks Blvd.
Camarillo, CA 93012
(805) 388-2000

Offers: Full line of power and hand tools, equipment and accessories by Porter-Cable, Goodyear, Powerwinch, Black

& Decker, Stanley, Makita, SK, Skil, Hanson, Industrial, Eastern, Ryobi, Chicago Pneumatic, Campbell Hausfeld, Homelite, Milwaukee, Empire, Vise-Grip, Quincy, others. Usuals, and automobile tools, trailers, dollys, shop cranes, carts, pumps, generators and welding equipment.
For Further Information: Write for catalog.
Store Location: At above address.
Accepts: American Express, Discover, MasterCard, Visa

HTC
P.O. Box 839
Royal Oak, MI 48068
(800) 624-2027

Offers: Line of mobile bases for most tool brands/models, including out and infeed roller systems, tool tables and stands, oscillating sanders, portable miter/table saws, shop accessories and jig/fixture items.
For Further Information: Write or call for free catalog.

MICROSTAMP CORP.
2770 E. Walnut St.
Pasadena, CA 91107
(818) 793-9489

Offers: Trace Mark micro-marking system (for permanent identification of cameras, most metals, plastics, other smooth firm surfaces). The imprint is virtually invisible, but legible under a magnifying glass.
For Further Information: Send SASE.

NORTHERN
P.O. Box 1219
Burnsville, MN 55337
(612) 894-9510

Offers: Full and complete lines of hand and power tools, parts and equipment including sandblasters, drills, a variety of saw models, gas engines, generators, hydraulic parts, welders and welding sets, winches and jacks, air compressors and air tools, saws, sanders and drill bits. Also offers Pro-Max chainsaws, log splitters, Sawzall kits, portable MIG welder and torches (including pen/pocket), welders, pressure washers, hole shooters (industrial drill use) and drill presses. Carries workbench kits, tool boxes and others.
For Further Information: Free catalog.

NOVA TOOL CO.
6678 Sierra Lane
Dublin, CA 94568
(510) 828-7172

Offers: Branding irons for hard and soft woods with solid brass heads and deep cut letters. The first line says "Hand-crafted by," and the second line consists of up to 20 characters and spaces of choice. Also offers a 3-line model iron.

For Further Information: Free brochure.
Accepts: Discover, MasterCard, Visa

PARAGRAPHICS CORP.
1455 W. Center St.
Orem, UT 84057
(801) 225-8300, (800) 624-7415

Offers: Paragrave hi-tech engraving system (with thin, ultra-high speed drill in Parapak). It engraves glass, metal, wood and other hard surfaces. Also offers high-pressure sandblasting system, with easy-to-use stencil system that works on virtually any hard surface. Demonstration video available.
For Further Information: Send SASE.
Accepts: Discover, MasterCard, Visa

REX GRAPHIC SUPPLY
P.O. Box 6226
Edison, NJ 08818
(201) 613-8777

Offers: "The Creator" table for draftsmen, artists and graphic artists. The table has a white melamine top, heavy gauge tubular steel base (enamel finish), dual-position foot rest, rear stabilizing bar and built-in floor levelers. It's adjustable for height and angle and comes in 2 size models.
For Further Information: Send SASE or call.

SMITHY
P.O. Box 1517
Ann Arbor, MI 48106
(800) 476-4849

Offers: Lathe/mill/drill 3-in-1 machine shop (multi-use for any shape or size work in metal, wood or plastic).
For Further Information: Write or call.

TESTRITE INSTRUMENT CO., INC.
135 Monroe St.
Newark, NJ 07105

Offers: Wide selection of lightweight, American-made Stanrite metal artists' easels. Display and presentation easels, Seerite light boxes, Rollrite brayers, and Seerite opaque projectors, lighting and magnifiers. Desk accessories also available.
For Further Information: Free art and office products catalog.

THE TOOL CRIB OF THE NORTH
P.O. Box 1716
Grand Forks, ND 58206
(800) 582-6704

Offers: Power tools by Smart, Freud, Skil, Davis, Performax, Biesemeyer, DeWalt, Powermatic, Black & Decker, Elu, Delta, AEG, Makita, JET, Milwaukee, Accu-Miter, Jorgen-

sen, Panasonic, Ryobi, Bosch, Porter-Cable and others.
For Further Information: Buyer's Guide, $3.
Accepts: Discover, MasterCard, Visa

ULTRAVISION
5645 Cote des Neiges
Montreal, Quebec H3T 1Y8
Canada
(514) 344-3988

Offers: Magnifiers in a variety of models, including 3 clip-ons, Optivisor and other headband types, stand (flexi), hand, Magnistitch with mount or clamp, loupes and linen testers. Also offers Big Eye and other illuminated/lamp magnifiers.
For Further Information: Free catalog.
Discounts: Quantity.

Wine and Beer Making

BEER & WINE HOBBY

P.O. Box 3104
Wakefield, MS 01880

Offers: Line of wine- and beer-making supplies and equipment.
For Further Information: Free catalog.

THE BREWERY

1304 Quincy
Minneapolis, MN 55413
(800) 781-8529

Offers: Beginner's kits for home brewing.
For Further Information: Free catalog

THE CELLAR HOMEBREW

14411 Greenwood Ave. N.
Seattle, WA 98133
(206)365-7660 or (800) 342-1871
Fax: (206) 365-7677

Offers: Full line of equipment and supplies for beer and wine making. Products include mini-brewery kits, yeast, malt extracts, fresh hops, brewing equipment—fermenters, brew kegs, controllers, additives, bottling equipment, bottles. Wine-making products include ingredients, kits, supplies, fermentation items, hydrometers, barrels, crushers, presses, pumps, filters, bottling equipment and bottles. Also offers soda pop extracts, dispensers, glassware, videos, books.
For Further Information: Free catalog.
Store Location: At above address.
Discounts: Quantity.
Accepts: American Express, Discover, MasterCard, Visa

GENERATIONS BREWING

(800) 715-8442

Offers: Line of home brewing equipment, ingredients, recipes and instructions.
For Further Information: Call.

GREAT FERMENTATIONS

87 Larkspur St.
San Rafael, CA 94901

Offers: Line of home brew supplies, "pub quality."
For Further Information: Free catalog

KRAUS

P.O. Box 7850
Independence, MO 64054

Offers: Wine- and beer-making supplies, including fruit presses, crushers, siphons, tubing, hops, malted barley grains, malt extracts, yeasts, heading powders, brewing salts, gypsum, concentrates. Extracts include liqueur, wine, soda pop. Also offers food grade containers, fermenters, fruit presses, grape crushers, hydrometers, wine filter kits, filters, brushes, pitters, sieves, funnels, cappers, labels, bottle capping and corking machines and corks.
For Further Information: Free illustrated catalog.
Accepts: MasterCard, Visa

O'BRIENS CELLAR SUPPLIES

P.O. Box 284
Wayne, IL 60184
(312) 289-7169

Offers: Beer- and wine-making supplies. Wine-making products include additives, concentrates, neutralizers, tannin, nutrients, oak chips, equipment sets, pressure and other barrels, bags, cloths, transferring items, vinometer, balance scales, presses, kits, corkers and cappers. Beer-making products include malt extracts, 16 kits, malt syrups, additives, brewing enzymes, malt grains, grain mills, hops, screw caps, corks, crowns and stoppers. Books are also available.
For Further Information: Free catalog.
Discounts: Quantity.
Accepts: MasterCard, Visa

SEMPLEX

P.O. Box 11476
Minneapolis, MN 55411
(612) 522-0500

Offers: Wine- and beer-making supplies/equipment: nutrients, clarifiers, filters, yeasts, filter kits, stoppers, bungs, spigots, hand-corking machines, fermentation locks, hydrometers, vinometers, bags, funnels, winebases, bottle cappers, bottles, chemicals, beer yeasts and hops, barley, over 160 malt extracts and T. Noirot extracts.
For Further Information: Free illustrated catalog
Accepts: American Express, Discover, MasterCard, Visa

SPECIALTY PRODUCTS INTERNATIONAL

P.O. Box 784
Chapel Hill, NC 27514
(919) 929-4277

Offers: Beer- and wine-making supplies: kits, ingredient

packs, bottle capper sets, fermenters, siphon units, hydrometers, enzymes, tannin, descalers/sterilizers, malts. Books are also available.
For Further Information: Free catalog.

WILLIAM'S
P.O. Box 2195
San Leandro, CA 94577
(800) 759-6025
Fax: (510) 895-2745

Offers: Line of beer-making supplies: yeast, hops, malts, bottles, equipment, caps, others.
For Further Information: Free catalog and newsletter.

Wood Carving

Also see General Craft Supplies, Construction—Full-Size Structures, Doll and Toy Making—Rigid, Furniture Making and Upholstery, Frames and Picture Framing, Woodworking and other related categories.

BUCK RUN CARVING SUPPLIES
781 Gully Rd.
Aurora, NY 13026
(315) 364-8414

Offers: Detail Master woodburners, Foredom power tools, Miller wildfowl study bills, pewter-cast feet, Kuzalls and Ruby carvers, High-Tech grinders, paints, brushes, others. Books and videos are also available.
For Further Information: Catalog, $2 (refundable).

COXE BLOCKS
555 Redfern Lane
Hartsville, SC 29550
(800) 354-4262

Offers: Carving blocks in over 10 standard sizes (tupelo, juniper). Does custom sawing from patterns or for special sizes.
For Further Information: Send for price sheet.
Discounts: Sells wholesale.
Accepts: MasterCard, Visa

GREGORY D. DORRANCE CO.
1063 Oak Hill Ave.
Attleboro, MA 02703
(508) 222-6255
Fax: (508) 222-6648

Offers: Decoy carving blanks and wood. Supplies include power tools for carving, wood burners, study casts, Ashley Isles chisels, cast feet and eyes, diamonds, texturing stones, brushes, and Paasche and Badger airbrushes. Art supplies include Grumbacher, Liquitex, Jo-Sonja, Winsor & Newton, Robert Simmons. Also offers over 300 books, cane and reproduction hardware.
For Further Information: Write.
Store Location: At above address.

FLEX EYES
5000 Krystal Dr.
Milton, FL 32571
(904) 994-6122

Offers: Eyes for carvers and taxidermists—nonbreakable, painted, adjustable, flexible, with finished front eyeball. Also offers waterfowl and fish eyes.
For Further Information: Write.
Accepts: MasterCard, Visa

GILMER WOOD CO.
2211 N.W. St. Helens Rd.
Portland, OR 97210
(503) 274-1271
Fax: (503) 274-9839

Offers: Over 100 species of rare and exotic woods in logs, planks and squares. Also offers turning, cutlery and musical instrument woods.
For Further Information: Call or write.

HIGHWOOD BOOKSHOP
P.O. Box 1246MB
Traverse City, MI 49685
(616) 271-3898

Offers: Decoy and fish carving books on painting, design, carving techniques, reference, patterns. Outdoor magazines, back issues.
For Further Information: Send 62¢ postage for book catalog.
Accepts: MasterCard, Visa

JANTZ SUPPLY
P.O. Box 584-CS
Davis, OK 73030
(800) 351-8900

Offers: Knife making supplies, including over 100 blades and blade kits (with handle material, fittings, instructions). Also offers tools (by Dremel, Baldor, Starrett and others), abrasives and polishing equipment.
For Further Information: Catalog, $3.
Accepts: Discover, MasterCard, Visa

JENNINGS DECOY CO.
601 Franklin Ave. NE
St. Cloud, MN 56304
(320) 253-2253
Fax: (612) 253-9537

Offers: Over 1,400 products for carvers: basswood, tupelo, butternut cutouts and cut-out kits—wildfowl, Santas, others.

Also offers eyes, other accessories, patterns, cork decoy kits and books.
For Further Information: Free catalog.

J.H. KLINE CARVING SHOP
Forge Hill Rd.
P.O. Box 445
Manchester, PA 17345
(717) 266-3501

Offers: Over 1,400 patterns of precut wood blanks, Foredom tools, glass eyes, woodburning units, bits, carvers, sanders, abrasives, cast bills and feet.
For Further Information: Catalog, $1 (refundable).

MDI WOODCARVERS SUPPLY
228 Main St.
Bar Harbor, ME 04609
(800) 866-5728

Offers: Selection of both traditional hand-carving tools and complete selection of power carving supplies.
For Further Information: Write.
Accepts: Discover, MasterCard, Visa

MOUNTAIN WOODCARVERS, INC.
P.O. Box 3485
150 E. Riverside Dr.
Estes Park, CO 80517
(800) 292-6788
Fax: (970) 586-5500

Offers: Hand-carving tools from Austria, Germany, Switzerland and the U.S., including power carver and burner tools. Also offers basswood roughouts, including animals, suns/moons, angels, people, frontier designs, Christmas designs, religious designs and others. Blanks and pewter bird feet, videos, extensive selection of wood carving books also available. Holds classes.
For Further Information: Free catalog.

RAZERTIP INDUSTRIES
P.O. Box 1258
Martensville, Saskatchewan S0K 2T0
Canada
(306) 931-0889
Fax: (306) 242-6119

Offers: Detail burning unit for very fine detail on wood, leather, plastics, and wax, with over 40 pen and tip styles and custom tip slaps. Bird carvings and artist's supplies also available.
For Further Information: Write.
Accepts: MasterCard

RITTER CARVERS, INC.
1559 Dillon Rd.
Maple Glen, PA 19002
(215) 997-3395 or (800) 242-0682

Offers: Carving supplies for basswood, white cedar, tupelo and hardwoods. Also offers carving cutouts, cast pewter feet, glass eyes and other accessories, diamonds, carbides, Jo-Sonja colors. Tools: Foredom chisels, detailers.
For Further Information: Free catalog.
Store Location: At above address.

G. SCHOEPFER, INC.
460 Cook Hill Rd.
Cheshire, CT 06410
(800) 875-6939

Offers: Eyes for decoys, birds, fish: basic glass, lead crystal, machine glass lenses, others.
For Further Information: Send SASE for price list.
Discounts: Quantity.
Accepts: American Express, MasterCard, Visa

WOOD CARVERS SUPPLY, INC.
P.O. Box 7500
Englewood, FL 34295

Offers: Carving supplies, including woods, kits, hand and power carving tools, carving knives and books.
For Further Information: Catalog, $2.

WOOD N' THINGS, INC.
601 E. 44th St., #3
Boise, ID 83714
(208) 375-9663

Offers: Carving supplies by Foredom and Auto Mach, including gouges, burners, knives, glass eyes, woods and over 300 books.
For Further Information: Free catalog.
Accepts: American Express, Discover, MasterCard, Visa

Woodworking

Also see General Craft Supplies, Construction—Full-Size Structures, Doll and Toy Making—Rigid, Furniture Making and Upholstery, Frames and Picture Framing, Tools and Equipment, Wood Carving and related categories.

ACME ELECTRIC
P.O. Box 14040
Grand Forks, ND 58208
(701) 746-6481

Offers: Power tools, including Delta woodworking machines (Unisaw, sanders, router/shapers, saws, tilting arbors, others), and Powermatic saw units and others. Also offers nailers, drills, jointing systems, jigsaws, cross cutter and miter saws, sanders, shapers, lathes, jointers, routers and saw bosses.
For Further Information: Catalog, $3.
Accepts: Discover, MasterCard, Visa

ADAMS WOOD PRODUCTS
974 Forest Dr.
Morristown, TN 37814
(423) 587-2942
Fax: (423) 586-2188

Offers: Stock wood legs in maple, cherry, oak, mahogany, walnut in a variety of styles and sizes.
For Further Information: Free brochure

ADJUSTABLE CLAMP CO.
437 N. Ashland Ave.
Chicago, IL 60622
(312) 666-0640
Fax: (312) 666-2723

Offers: Jorgensen, Pony and Adjustable clamps, clamping accessories, vises, miter boxes and related fine tools for woodworking, furniture repair, you-do projects and maintenance.
For Further Information: Full-line catalog, $1. Product pamphlet free.
Discounts: Sells wholesale to dealers and distributors.

ADVANCED MACHINERY
P.O. Box 312
New Castle, DE 19720
(800) 322-2226

Offers: Full line of scroll saw blades, accessories and im-
provements for almost any scroll saw, plus Hegner precision scroll saws. Also offers lathes, lathe duplicators, jet clamps, workbenches, Felderr systems and others.
For Further Information: Write.

WILLIAM ALDEN COMPANY
27 Stuart St.
Boston, MA 02116
(800) 249-8665 or (617) 426-3430 (outside U.S.)

Offers: Power tools and equipment including by Hitachi, De-Walt, Porter-Cable, Delta and others.
For Further Information: Free catalog.

ARMOR
P.O. Box 445
East Northport, NY 11731
(516) 462-6228

Offers: Wood products: balls, pegs, cradles, cups, toy wheels, axle pegs, door harp parts, cutouts, pins, others. Woodworking plans: swinging cradle, Adirondack chair, rocking horse, traditional furniture (desks, ice boxes, shelves, cabinets, chairs, spinning wheel, dry sinks, stools, children's items, lamps, clocks, pool and soccer tables, others). Also offers clocks and lamp parts, tools, hardware, furniture trim, dollhouse kits and components, stencils, other craft supplies.
For Further Information: Free catalog.
Accepts: MasterCard, Visa

AVIATION INDUSTRIAL SUPPLY CO.
3900 Ulster St.
Denver, CO 80207
(303) 355-2391

Offers: Tools and equipment including Bosch, Poter Cable (saws, drills, sanders, routers, trimmers), Hitachi saws, others.
For Further Information: Write or call for prices.
Accepts: MasterCard, Visa

BADGER HARDWOODS OF WISCONSIN
N. 1517 Highway 14
Walworth, WI 53184
(800) 252-2373 or (414) 275-9855
Fax: (414) 275-9855

Offers: Aromatic cedar, ash, aspen, basswood, birch, butter-nut, cherry, mahogany, hickory, hackberry, hard and soft maple, nothern white pine, poplar, red elm, red oak quartersawn, red and white oak, walnut, others.

For Further Information: Free catalog.

Discounts: Special prices on 20 b.f. bulk packs of lumber.

Accepts: MasterCard, Visa

BOGERT & HOPPER, INC.

P.O. Box 119
Northport, NY 11768
(516) 261-6173 or (800) 338-9938

Offers: Wood parts: wheels, axles, Shaker pegs, candle cups, dowels, others.

For Further Information: Free catalog.

BURL TREE

3527 Broadway St.
Eureka, CA 95503
(707) 442-1319 or (800) 785-BURL

Offers: Burlwoods: redwood, maple, buckeye, manzanita, madrone, oak, myrtle, walnut, rhododendron, yew, nutmeg; size or thickness for any/all uses.

For Further Information: Call.

Discounts: Sells wholesale, based on quantity.

CARTER PRODUCTS CO., INC.

437 Spring Ave. NE
Grand Rapids, MI 49503
(616) 451-2928
Fax. (616) 451-4330

Offers: Delta (Rockwell) 14″ and 20″ bandsaw guide conversion kits plus other kits for popular brand saws 14 inches and larger (including Jet, General Grizzly, Grob, Davis, Wells and others).

For Further Information: Free brochure.

CASEY'S WOOD PRODUCTS

P.O. Box 365
Woolwich, ME 04579
(800) 45-CASEY

Offers: Factory seconds woodenware: Shaker pegs, beanpot candle cups (by 100 plus lots), turnings, dowels, novelties in first and second quality. Hardware including small hinges, screws, lazy susan bearings, and others.

For Further Information: Catalog, $1.

THE CAYCE CO.

221 Cockeysville Rd.
Hunt Valley, MD 21030
(410) 771-0213
Fax: (410) 771-0215

Offers: Brand name used power equipment, including banders, jointers; band, table, vertical and other saws; sanders,

shapers, air compressors, tenoner, planers, grinders and others.

For Further Information: Call or write.

Accepts: MasterCard, Visa

CERTAINLY WOOD

11753 Big Tree Rd.
E. Aurora, NY 14052
(716) 655-0206
Fax: (716) 655-3446

Offers: Fine wood veneers in a variety of species. Also offers custom plywood and exotic hardwoods.

For Further Information: Free catalog.

CHERRY TREE TOYS

P.O. Box 369-319
Belmont, OH 43718
(614) 484-4363

Offers: Woodcrafting parts/supplies/kits/plans. Wood parts include pegs, wheels, spindles, knobs, plugs, dowels, others. Also offers door harp parts/accessories, toy wagon kits, whirligigs and musical banks, trains and other vehicles, clock and desk parts, miniature hobby tools and sets, miniature items (including authentic old-time gas pumps, washboards, others), plus hardware, stencils, paints, brushes.

For Further Information: Catalog, $1.

Discounts: Quantity.

Accepts: Discover, MasterCard, Visa

COLONIAL HARDWOODS, INC.

7953 Cameron Brown Ct.
Springfield, VA 22153
(800) 466-5451 or (703) 451-9217
Fax: (703) 451-0186

Offers: Hardwoods (cut to order) in 120 species, veneers, mouldings, wood to 4″ thickness, burls and blocks for turners, hardware, finishes and books.

For Further Information: Send SASE for list.

M.L. CONDON COMPANY, INC.

246 Ferris Ave.
White Plains, NY 10603
(914) 946-4111
Fax: (914) 946-3779

ALBERT CONSTANTINE & SON, INC.

2050 Eastchester Rd.
Bronx, NY 10461
(718) 792-1600

Offers: Woodworking/veneering supplies: kits, 80-plus veneers, veneering tools, marquetry kits, Optivisor, pantograph, chisels, mallets, drawknives, carving tools, woodburners,

planes, spokeshaves, scrapers, sharpeners, saws, cutters, measurers, rasps. Also offers joiners, routers, doweling units, planers, sanders, sprayers, engravers, gilding supplies, stains, finishes, furniture plans (full-sized), carving and decoy kits. Tools: knives, vises, router bits, nailers, woodturning tools. Materials: lumber, turning blocks. Carries clock parts, dollhouse/furniture kits, model kits, toy parts, upholstery tools/supplies, cane, webbing, guitar/dulcimer parts and woods, lamp parts, workbenches and books.
For Further Information: Send for free 128-page catalog.
Accepts: American Express, Discover, MasterCard, Visa

CRAFT SUPPLIES USA
P.O. Box 50300
Provo, UT 84605
(801) 373-0919 or (800) 551-8876

Offers: Woodturning equipment and accessories including full line of pen, pencil, fountain and rollerball pen kits. Woodfast lathes, Henry Taylor tools, Oneway and Nova chucks. Dale Nish workshops offered.
For Further Information: Catalog, free.

CRAFTERS MART
P.O. Box 2342
Greeley, CO 80632
(970) 351-0676

Offers: Wood parts/shapes, including turnings (Shaker pegs, candle cups, balls), wheels, door harp tuning pens, clapper balls, plus harp wire, hangers, others.
For Further Information: Catalog, $2 (refundable).

CRAFTSMAN WOOD SERVICE CO.
1735 W. Cortland Ct.
Addison, IL 60101-4280
(708) 629-3100

Offers: Hardwoods: veneers, marquetry and inlay, turning blocks, boards, lumber, plywood, dowels, pegs, relief carving and moulding. Tools: Dremel, Foredom and others, plus carving sets, upholstery equipment, flexible shaft, power and jigs, others. Also offers hardware, lamp parts, wooden ship models, 11 dollhouse kits, gauges, plans, adhesives, finishes, books and upholstery supplies.
For Further Information: Write for catalog.

CRAFTY CUT-OUTS
1705 Taylor Ave.
Evansville, IN 47714
(812) 471-3092

Offers: Scroll saw patterns—over 150 designs, all occasion. Word cutouts, alphabets.
For Further Information: Send SASE for list.

CROFFWOOD MILLS
RD 1
P.O. Box 14B
Driftwood, PA 15832
(814) 546-2507

Offers: Pennsylvania hardwoods—15 species, over 2,000 sizes, 12 species, to 2″ thick, kiln-dried. Also offers random board and specialty packs, dimension cuts, thin woods. Unique: sapwood cherry or walnut, others.
For Further Information: Free catalog.

CROWN CITY HARDWARE CO.
1047 N. Allen Ave.
Pasadena, CA 91104
(818) 794-1188

Offers: Over 1,000 reproductions of European hardware (restorations, others) for cabinetry, furniture, doors, windows of iron, brass, wood, porcelain—"olde worlde pieces" authentically produced.
For Further Information: Catalog/history, $25.

CROWN PLANE CO.
61 Western Ave.
Bath, ME 04530
(207) 443-4183

Offers: Molding, panel raising, smoothing and jack wooden planes. Also offers chairmakers compass, hollowing plane and travisher.
For Further Information: Call or write.

CUSTOM WOOD CUTOUTS UNLIMITED
P.O. Box 518
Massillon, OH 44648
(216) 832-2919

Offers: Wood cutouts: animals, fowl, birds, holiday/novelty shapes, figures, fish and quotes. Also offers necklace parts, ornaments, racks, toys, child's furniture and stools.
For Further Information: Catalog, $2 (refundable).
Discounts: Quantity; sells wholesale to legitimate businesses.
Accepts: MasterCard, Visa

DEER CREEK PRODUCTS
3038 NW 25th Ave.
Pompano Beach, FL 33069
(954) 978-0597

Offers: Over 500 wood patterns for toys: circus, mermaids, bears, clowns, rockers, playthings, trains, dinosaurs, others. Also offers shelves, signs, ornaments, door stops, weather vanes, kitchen items, decorations, plaques, organizers, tables, chairs, TV trays, lamps, others.
For Further Information: Send SASE for list.

DJ HARDWOODS
317 Nebraska Ave.
Columbia, MO 65201
(800) 514-3449
Fax: (573) 815-9932

Offers: Thinwoods with ¹⁄₁₆″, ⅛″, ¼″ and ⅜″ thicknesses for scroll sawing, crafts, inlays, boxes, segmented turning and other uses. Species range from ash to zebrawood.
For Further Information: Free brochure.

DOYEL ENTERPRISES
P.O. Box 315
Yorba Linda, CA 92686
(714) 666-1770

Offers: Radial arm saw fence system (cuts angles with one saw groove, adjustable to 47 degrees), aluminum. Others.
For Further Information: Send SASE for details.
Accepts: MasterCard, Visa

DREMEL
P.O. Box 1468
Racine, WI 53401
(414) 559-4390

Offers: Line of woodworking machinery, power tools and accessories, kits and sets. Manufacturer.
For Further Information: Write for free brochure.

EAGLE AMERICA CORP.
P.O. Box 1099
Chardon, OH 44024
(216) 286-7429

Offers: Largest selection of American-made router bits, cutting tools, router accessories and woodworking helpers.
For Further Information: Free catalog.
Discounts: Schools, technical institutes, volume users, woodworking clubs, guilds, associations.
Accepts: Discover, MasterCard, Visa

ECON ABRASIVES
P.O. Box 1628
Frisco, TX 75034
(800) 367-4101

Offers: Sandpaper and sander accessories: belts, discs, sheets, wide belts, rolls, flap wheels, pump sleeves, cabinet paper, finish paper, jumbo cleaning sticks, abrasive belts in any size or grit.
For Further Information: Free catalog.

EDUCATIONAL LUMBER CO.
P.O. Box 5373
Asheville, NC 28813
(704) 255-8765

Offers: Over 20 species of hardwoods and softwoods, including Appalachian woods and hard-to-find imported woods—select and project grades.
For Further Information: Write or call for catalog.
Discounts: Quantity.

FARRIS MACHINERY
1206 Pavilion Dr.
Grain Valley, MO 64029
(800) 872-5489

Offers: Woodworking tools for machinery, home workshop wood machining center, saws, planes, molds, mortises; takes up less than 12 sq. ft. of space, runs on 110V AC power.
For Further Information: Free information kit.

FORMBY'S WORKSHOP
825 Crossover Lane
Memphis, TX 38117
(800) FORMBYS

Offers: Formby's products for wood: furniture refinisher dissolves old varnish, lacquer or shellac and conditions the wood.
For Further Information: Free booklet, "Successful Refinishing."

FROG TOOL CO. LTD.
2169 Illinois Rte. 26
Dixon, IL 61021
(800) 648-1270

Offers: Hand woodworking tools: German carving, Swedish carving, hammers, screwdrivers, Japanese sharpening items, doweling jigs, bevelers, cutters, drills, measuring items, planes, drawknives, spokeshaves, musical instrument tools, saws, veneering/turning tools, panovise, woodburning tools, lathes, dowels, table hardware, sanding items, log cabin tools, finishes, workbenches. Also offers books on woodworking and finishing materials.
For Further Information: Catalog, $5.
Discounts: Quantity; sells wholesale to legitimate businesses.
Accepts: MasterCard, Visa

GARRETT WADE CO., INC.
161 Avenue of the Americas
New York, NY 10013
(212) 807-1757 or (800) 221-2942

Offers: Full line of hand tools, including the new advanced precision honing guide (sets micro bevels), "blind nailer" tool (like a positioning jig), scrapers with prepared edges for longer use, multi-angle aluminum gauges, bandsaw blades (including ¹⁄₁₆″ narrow, in raker style, and "cabinetmaker's special" skip-tooth and unset raker), and other scroll and cab-

inet styles. Also offers saw setting gauges, gap filling glue, and other common and unique hand tools.
For Further Information: Free catalog.

GILLIOM MANUFACTURING, INC.
P.O. Box 1018
St. Charles, MO 63302
(314) 724-1812

Offers: Power tool kits (to-construct), including 12″ bandsaws, 18″ bandsaws, 10″ tilt/arbor saws, lathe/drill press combinations, 9″ tilt table saws, 6″ belt sanders, spindle shapers and circular saw tables. Kits include step-by-step plans and all necessary metal parts and components (except wood and motor). Also offers some accessory kits, including a speed reduction kit for cutting steel that fits the 18″ bandsaw. Power tool plans available (individually, or a set at a savings).
For Further Information: Brochure, $2.

GRIZZLY IMPORTS, INC.
2406 Reach Rd.
Williamsport, PA 17701
(717) 326-3806
For West Coast:
P.O. Box 2069
Bellingham, WA 98227
(360) 647-0801

Offers: Shop equipment: Sanders (drum, combo, others), saws (heavy duty, band, others), planers, jointers, shapers, dust collectors, others.
For Further Information: Write or call.
Accepts: MasterCard, Visa

HARRIS ENTERPRISESS
76 Quentin Rd.
Brooklyn, NY 11223
(800) 449-7747

Offers: Line of old-style hand tools including wooden spoke-shave (with adjustable mechanism) and others.
For Further Information: Catalog, $1 (refundable).

HOGUE
P.O. Box 2038
Atascadero, CA 93423
(805) 466-4100

Offers: Exotic woods (cut-off sizes, others): rosewood, gonedlo alves, pau ferro, coco bolo, others. Use for jewelry, inlays, knife handles, parquet tables.
For Further Information: Send SASE.

HOME LUMBER CO.
499 Whitewater St.
Whitewater, WI 53190
(800) 262-5482

Offers: Woodworking tools/equipment by DeWalt, Makita, Bostitch, Ryobi, others.
For Further Information: Send SASE for list.
Accepts: Discover, MasterCard, Visa

HOOD FINISHING PRODUCTS, INC.
East Brunswick, NJ 08816
(800) 229-0934
Fax: (908) 254-6063

Offers: Line of products for wood finishing and refinishing from surface preparation to wood care.
For Further Information: Free catalog.

HORTON BRASSES
Nooks Hill Rd.
P.O. Box 120
Cromwell, CT 06416
(860) 635-4400

Offers: Full line of cabinet and furniture hardware for homes and antiques, including handles, knobs, latches, hinges and slides in many styles (brass, antiqued, others).
For Further Information: Catalog, $4.

HOWEE'S INC.
Rt. 7
P.O. Box 633
Joplin, MO 64801
(417) 623-0656

Offers: Wood turnings, including wheels, pegs, spindles, candle cups, knobs, rings, spools, fruits, hearts, finials, boxes, smokestacks, miniatures, beads, bells, buckets, dolls, bowling pins, dowels. Also offers hardware, hinges, scroll saw blades, sanding and clock making supplies.
For Further Information: Free catalog.
Discounts: Quantity; sells wholesale.

HTC
120 E. Hudson
P.O. Box 839
Royal Oak, MI 48068
(800) 624-2027

Offers: Mobile machine bases (shop on wheels) in a variety of models of welded steel construction.
For Further Information: Free catalog.

INTERNATIONAL TOOL CORP.
2590 Davie Rd.
Davie, FL 33317
(808) 338-3384

Offers: Full line of woodworking equipment/tools in known brands: Porter-Cable, Delta, Airy, Senco, Makita, Skil, Hitachi, Ryobi, Mirka, Milwaukee, Bosch, Freud, DeWalt, Felker, Powermatic.
For Further Information: Send SASE for list.
Accepts: American Express, Discover, MasterCard, Visa

INTERNATIONAL VIOLIN CO.
4026 W. Belvedere Ave.
Baltimore, MD 21215
(800) 542-3538
Fax: (410) 542-3546

Offers: Violin and guitar kits, tools, parts, accessories, tone wood, strings, cases, bows, others. Also offers oil and spirit varnish, pre-carved parts, violins in the white.
For Further Information: Call or write for free catalog.

BOB KAUNE
511 W. 11th
Port Angeles, WA 98362
(360) 452-2292

Offers: Antique and used tools for woodworkers, including scarce, older and ready-to-use hand tools; planes and other edge tools. Specializes in Stanley Tools.
For Further Information: List, $3.50.
Accepts: MasterCard, Visa

KAYNE & SONS CUSTOM HARDWARE
100 Daniel Ridge Rd.
Candler, NC 28715
(704) 667-8868
Fax: (704) 665-8303

Offers: Builders/household/gate hardware, strap hinges, thumblatch sets, locks, fireplace tools/equipment, hand forced and cast brass/bronze hardware finished black, antique polished. Also reproductions, restoration and repair services.
For Further Information: Catalog, $5.

KEYSTONE WOOD SPECIALTIES, INC.
P.O. Box 10127
Lancaster, PA 17605
(800) 233-0289
Fax: (800) 253-0805

Offers: Wood drawers with ½″ or ⅝″ thick sides, available in 10 species, including oaks, maple, cherry, mahogany, poplar, ash, pine, walnut and aromatic cedar. Drawers are avail-

able assembled or unassembled, unfinished or prefinished, with a choice of bottoms.
For Further Information: Call or write.

LEICHTUNG WORKSHOPS
4944 Commerce Pkwy.
Cleveland, OH 44128
(216) 591-9148

Offers: Over 400 hand and power woodworking tools, with unusual/exclusive tools for workbench, cabinetry to sharpen, clamp, dowel, instrument-make, mat, frame. Includes tools for miniature crafting, mini-welding, others. Also offers wood and clock parts, woodburners, paints, brushes, abrasive cords/tapes, blade sharpeners for chain saws and mowers and others.
For Further Information: Free catalog.
Accepts: Discover, MasterCard, Visa

LOBO POWER TOOLS
9034 Bermudez St.
Pico Rivera, CA 90660
(310) 949-3747

Offers: Woodworking equipment including saws, planers, shapers, lathes, jointers, sanders, routers, milling units, tool grinders, others.
For Further Information: Send SASE for list.

MACBEATH HARDWOOD CO.
930 Ashby Ave.
Berkeley, CA 94710
(510) 843-4390
Fax: (510) 843-9378

Offers: Basswood—kiln dried, 1″ through 4″ thicknesses—and Jelutong in clear, KD, rough. Also offers lumber and carving blocks and a variety of other hardwoods.
For Further Information: Send SASE for stock list.

MAFELL NORTH AMERICA, INC.
80 Earhart Dr.
Williamsville, NY 14221
716-626-9303

Offers: Erika pull-push combination radial arm saw unit as table/radial arm saw (and accessories for customizing). Also offers other stationary or timber-framing tools.
For Further Information: Catalog, $1.

MANNY'S WOODWORKERS PLACE
555 Broadway St.
Lexington, KY 40508
(606) 255-5444

Offers: Woodworking books and videos on a variety of top-

ics, including woodturning, carving, carpentry, and furniture making, toymaking and others.
For Further Information: Catalog, $2.

MANZANITA DECORATIVE WOOD
P.O. Box 111
Protrero, CA 91963
(619) 478-5849

Offers: Manzanita burls—full range of sizes, full inventory.
For Further Information: Call, or send SASE with inquiry.
Discounts: Sells wholesale.

MARLING LUMBER CO.
P.O. Box 7668
Madison, WI 53704
(800) 247-7178

Offers: Makita power tools, cordless driver-drill (2-speed, variable speed), 25-piece ratchet set, ⅜″ cordless drill (variable speed), finishing sander, ⅜″ drill and others.
For Further Information: Send SASE or call.
Accepts: MasterCard, Visa

MASTERCRAFT PLANS
P.O. Box 625
Redmond, WA 98073

Offers: Patterns (full-sized) in packets: jigsaw items, birdhouses, shelves, windmills, tool houses, donkeys with carts, garden furniture, gifts and novelties, country crafts, variety designs, others.
For Further Information: Send SASE for catalog.

MLCS, LTD.
P.O. Box 4053
Rydal, PA 19046
(800) 533-9298
Fax: (215) 938-5070

Offers: Woodworking tools, including 1,000 plus carbide-tipped router bits, raised panel door sets, Forster bits, the Router Speed Control, and clamps; other tools and supplies.
For Further Information: Send SASE for catalog.

MEISEL HARDWARE SPECIALTIES
P.O. Box 70
Mound, MN 55364
(612) 479-2138

Offers: Over 850 woodworking project plans, including country, storage and outdoor furniture; kitchen items, intarsia, child's furniture and toys, lamps, music boxes, holiday cutouts, bird feeders and houses, lawn ornaments; woodturnings and parts. Hardware available includes wind chime tubing, parts for music boxes and others.

For Further Information: Catalog, $2.
Accepts: MasterCard, Visa

MIDWEST DOWEL WORKS, INC.
4631 Hutchinson Rd.
Cincinnati, OH 45248
(513) 574-8488

Offers: Dowels, plugs and pegs in a variety of sizes and woods: oak, walnut, hickory, maple, cherry, mahogany, teak. Treated dowels are available.
For Further Information: Write for catalog.
Discounts: Quantity.

E.C. MITCHELL CO.
88-90 Boston St.
Drawer 607
Middleton, MA 01949
(508) 774-1191
Fax: (508) 774-2494

Offers: Flexible sanding/abrasive cords and tapes (for grooves, slots and holes) in 18 sizes.
For Further Information: Send SASE for list.

OAK LEAF WOOD 'N SUPPLIES
210 N. Main
Moweaqua, IL 62550
(217) 768-3202

Offers: Line of bowl blanks and spindle stock in domestic and exotic woods.
For Further Information: Call or write.

PELHAM TOOL, INC.
21 Abendroth Ave.
Port Chester, NY 10573
(914) 937-1771
Fax: (914) 937-1176

Offers: Power tools and equipment, including tools by Hitachi, Black & Decker "Professional," Porter-Cable, Milwaukee, Makita, Bosch, AEG, ITW Paslode, Bostitch and Senco.
For Further Information: Call for prices.
Accepts: Discover, MasterCard, Visa

PENN STATE INDUSTRIES
2850 Comly Rd.
Philadelphia, PA 19154
(215) 676-7609

Offers: Woodworking machines/accessories—line of air guns, dust collectors, planers, sanders, scroll saws, lathes and suplicators, carving and drill tools, grinders, router bits, shaper cutters, speed control units, corner clamps, others.

For Further Information: Free catalog.
Accepts: American Express, Discover, MasterCard, Visa

PERFORMAX PRODUCTS, INC.
12211 Woodlake Dr.
Burnsville, MN 55337
(800) 334-4910

Offers: Power tools: component drum sander, with radial saw attachment or stand alone, plus manual or power feed option conveyor unit and a 22″ drum sander with open end.
For Further Information: Write or call for free brochure.

PORTA-NAILS, INC.
P.O. Box 1257
Wilmington, NC 28402
(910) 762-6334 or (800) 634-9281

Offers: Woodworking machines: dowel mate, ring master, panel template, router arc attachment, router mate, universal router system (3 tools from 1), others.
For Further Information: Contact dealer, or write for brochure.

RB INDUSTRIES, INC.
1801 Vine St.
P.O. Box 369
Harrisonville, MO 64701
(800) 487-2623

Offers: RBI Hawk line of scroll saws including beginner and pro models. Also offers wood, scroll sawblades and pattern books.
For Further Information: Free information kit

RIDGE CARBIDE TOOL CORP.
595 New York Ave.,
P.O. Box 497
Lyndhurst, NJ 07071
(201) 438-8778
Fax: (201) 438-8792

Offers: Custom router bits, shaper cutters, shaper knives, moulder knives and others, including manufactured tools to custom profiles, drawings or wood samples, in RCT-Alloy for natural material of C-3 carbide for man-made material; micro-grain carbide for solid surface material.
For Further Information: 100-page product catalog, $3.

SB POWER TOOLS
4300 W. Peterson Ave.
Chicago, IL 60646
(312) 286-7330

Offers: Power tools: Drills, cordless drill (with 5-position variable torque clutch, 2-speed, with 7.2 volt rechargeable

battery pack), variety of saws, others. Manufacturer.
For Further Information: Send SASE.

SEVEN CORNERS ACE HARDWARE, INC.
216 7th St. W.
St. Paul, MN 55102
(800) 328-0457

Offers: Woodworking equipment/tools/accessories by Milwaukee, Makita, Freud, Biesmeyer, Bosch, Porter Cable, Ryobi, Delta, Jorgensen, DeWalt, Dremel, Hitachi, David White, Senco, others—bench-top, power and hand tools. Also offers ladders (fiberglass, aluminum types), air tools, variety of kits, sets.
For Further Information: Send SASE for list.
Accepts: Discover, MasterCard, Visa

SHOPSMITH, INC.
3931 Image Dr.
Dayton, OH 45414
(513) 898-6070

Offers: Workshop power tools: All-in-one units, scroll saw—20″ variable speed model, with sawdust blower.
For Further Information: Send SASE.

SUN DESIGNS
P.O. Box 6
Oconomowoc, WI 53066
(414) 567-4255

Offers: Design plan books for 55 gazebos (mix and match designs for railings, fascia, etc.), bird houses/feeders, toys, backyard structures, cupolas and bridges, privies. Construction plans, all designs.
For Further Information: Send SASE.
Discounts: Sells wholesale to legitimate businesses.
Accepts: MasterCard, Visa

THE TAUNTON PRESS
63 S. Main St.
P.O. Box 5506
Newtown, CT 06470
(203) 426-8171

Offers: Instructional videos for professionals on Shaker tables, mortise-and-tenon joints, joinery, router jigs, shop tips, wood finishing, tiling, carving (ball-and-claw), chip tips/techniques. Books also available.
For Further Information: Free catalog.
Discounts: Sells wholesale to businesses.

TAYLOR DESIGN GROUP
P.O. Box 810262
Dallas, TX 75381
(214) 484-5570
Fax: (214) 243-4277

Offers: Incra precision positioning fences for the routes table

and table saw for all operations including box joints, dove-tails, and Incra corner post, double and double-double joinery.
For Further Information: Free catalog.

THE TOOL CRIB OF THE NORTH
P.O. Box 14040
Grand Forks, ND 58206
(800) 358-3096
Fax: (800) 343-4205

Offers: Name brand woodworking machinery/power tools/accessories: Wedge, Bosch, Panasonic, Makita, Skil, Freud, Milwaukee, Selta, Englo, Porter Cable, Black & Decker, others.
For Further Information: Buyer's Guide, $3.
Discounts: Quantity.

TOOL FACTORY
P.O. Box 461
Rt. 17
Goshen, NY 10924
(914) 294-1696

Offers: Power tools and equipment by Bosch, Porter-Cable, Milwaukee, DeWalt, Bostitch, Makita, Ryobi, Delta, Duo-Fast, Dremel and others.
For Further Information: Call or write.
Accepts: Discover, MasterCard, Visa

TOOLMARK CO.
6840 Shingle Creek Pkwy.
Minneapolis, MN 55430
(612) 560-8035

Offers: Wood lathe accessories for wood turning including spindle duplicators, duplicator systems, bowl turners, Uni-center systems, woodshavers, steady rests, safety shields.
For Further Information: Free literature and price list.

TOTAL SHOP
P.O. Box 25429
Greenville, SC 29616
Order line: (800) 845-9356

Offers: Total shop multi-purpose machine (converts to 5 basic power tools). Other units: bed jointers, shapers, sanders, planers, saws, dust collectors, others.
For Further Information: Free catalog.

TREMONT NAIL CO.
8 Elm St.
P.O. Box 111
Wareham, MA 02571
(800) 842-0560

Offers: Old-fashioned steel cut nails, 20 types from old patterns: rosehead, wrought-head, others.

For Further Information: Free catalog.
Discounts: Quantity; teachers and institutions; sells wholesale to legitimate businesses and professionals.

TREND-LINES, INC.
375 Beacham St.
Chelsea, MA 02150
(800) 767-9999

Offers: Over 3,000 woodworking tools: saws, routers, planers, bands, jointers, grinders, drills, planer jointers, sanders, mortisers, drill presses, laminate sitters, trimmers, Dremel tools, others. Accessories: sawhorses, supports, airbrushes, nail/spray guns, sand blasters, vises, measuring and carving/turning tools and router bits. Also offers wood sign layout kit, dollhouse kits, project plans, turning items, folding table legs, metal wheels, cedar liners/blocks, finishes.
For Further Information: Free catalog.
Accepts: Discover, MasterCard, Visa

UNICORN UNIVERSAL WOODS
4190 Steeles Ave. W.
Woodbridge, Ontario L4L 3S8
Canada
(905) 851-2308
Fax: (905) 851-8039

Offers: 70 species of lumber, millwork, plywoods, veneers, others. Carving wood, turning blanks, musical instrument woods and others also available.
For Further Information: Free catalog.
Discounts: Sells wholesale.

VAUGHN & BUSHNELL MANUFACTURING CO.
11414 Maple Ave.
Hebron, IL 60034
(815) 648-2446

Offers: Vaughn hand tools, including hammers, picks and axes.
For Further Information: Contact dealer, or send SASE.

VEGA ENTERPRISES, INC.
Rt. 3
P.O. Box 193
Decatur, IL 62526
(800) 222-8342

Offers: Woodworking tools/equipment: saw fences—professional, utility, radial, mitre, others. Lathe duplicators—3 models; lathes—bench, heavy, bowl. Also offers sanders, tenon jigs, mitre gauges, stock feed systems and video tapes.
For Further Information: Call or write.

STEVE WALL LUMBER CO.
Rt. 1
P.O. Box 287
Mayodan, NC 27027
(910) 427-0637 or (800) 633-4062
Fax: (910) 427-9588

Offers: Woodworking machinery including Mini-Max and Delta units, Hawk and planer-molder, others. Also offers lumber (kiln dried rough, sold by board): aromatic red cedar, cherry, red or white oak, hard maple, mahogany, walnut, butternut and others. Craft wood mixtures.
For Further Information: Catalog, $1.
Accepts: MasterCard, Visa

WHOLE EARTH ACCESS
2990 7th St.
Berkeley, CA 94710
(510) 845-3000

Offers: Power tools: Porter-Cable saws, drills, laminate trimmers, routers, removers, sanders. Also offers Skil drill kits, saws, Freud router bits, carving and Forstner bits. Carries Milwaukee drills, sanders, chainsaws, jigsaws, others. Hitachi router, plane, saws, sanders. Makita drills, saws, sanders and Delta shop machinery are also available.
For Further Information: Send SASE for list.

RON WIENER, WOOD CARVER
54 Cottage St.
Jersey City, NJ 07306
(201) 659-5666

Offers: Line of relief wood carvings for cabinets and furniture, including traditional and other designs.
For Further Information: Call for brochure.

WILKE MACHINERY CO.
3230 Susquehanna Trail
York, PA 17402
(717) 764-5000 or (800) 235-2100

Offers: Bridgewood woodworking machinery, including shaper units, planers, jointers, others.
For Further Information: Catalog, $1.

WILLIAMS & HUSSEY MACHINE CO., INC.
Riverview Mill
P.O. Box 1149
Wilton, NH 03086
(800) 258-1380
Fax: (603) 654-5446

Offers: Molder-planer unit (cuts moldings and planes hardwood) with "two-minute" cutter changes—for professionals and hobbyists. Manufacturer.
For Further Information: Free information kit.

THE WINFIELD COLLECTION
112 E. Ellen St.
Fenton, MI 48430
(800) 946-3435

Offers: Full-size country woodcraft patterns: frames, cutouts, self-sitters, swivel leg figures and animals, country scenes, animals, holiday items, candleholder motifs, action toys, racks, stools, boxes, baskets, weather vanes, vehicles, dinosaurs, carousels, others.
For Further Information: Catalog, $1.
Discounts: Sells wholesale.

WOOD MOLDING & MILLWORK PRODUCERS ASSOCIATION
507 1st St.
Woodland, CA 95695

Offers: Booklet: *500 Wood Molding Do-It-Yourself Projects* (for birdhouses, bookshelves, door trims, drawer dividers, planters, others), plus illustrated traditional projects and scores of new ways to use molding.
For Further Information: Copy of booklet, $6.

WOOD-PLY LUMBER CORP.
100 Bennington Ave.
Freeport, NY 11520
(516) 378-2612 or (800) 354-9002
Fax: (516) 376-0345

Offers: Over 60 species of exotic/domestic hardwoods including lumber, plywood, veneers, papers and foil backed, bowl blanks, burls, turning blocks and squares, table top and clock slabs, alabaster, soapstone. Wood and stone carving tools and wood finishes are also available.
For Further Information: Send SASE for list.

WOODARTIST
P.O. Box 80003
Charleston, SC 29416

Offers: Antique birdhouse plans for bluebirds, martins, other birds.
For Further Information: Send SASE for price list.

WOODCRAFT SUPPLY CORP.
210 Wood County Industrial Park
P.O. Box 1686
Parkersburg, WV 26102
(800) 542-9115

Offers: Woodworking tools: sculptor's/carving, punches, adzes, hooks, rasps, files, rifflers, and measuring and layout tools/equipment. Also offers planes, vises, framing tools/equipment, plus tools to dowel, turn, log build, do marquetry and veneering. Carries branding irons and power tools by

Dremel, Delta, Foredom. Specialty: planes, vises, saws, miters, clamps. Also carries glass domes and inserts, clock parts, musical movements, hardware, wood, plans and books.
For Further Information: Free catalog.
Discounts: Quantity; teachers and institutions.
Accepts: American Express, Discover, MasterCard, Optima, Visa

WOODCRAFTS AND SUPPLIES

Oblong, IL 62449
(800) 592-4907
Fax: (618) 592-4902

Offers: Woodworker's supplies, including shaker pegs, candle cups, unfinished minatures and more.
For Further Information: Free catalog.

WOODMASTER TOOLS, INC.

1431 N. Topping Ave.
Kansas City, MO 64120
(800) 821-6651

Offers: Woodmaster power-feed machine (planes/molds/sands) to frame, mold, do casings, tongue and groove. Also offers picture frame patterns and drum sanders.
For Further Information: Free information kit.

THE WOODTURNER'S CATALOG

P.O. Box 50300
Provo, UT 84605
(800) 551-8876
Fax: (801) 374-2879

Offers: Woodturning tools and supplies, including Woodfast wood lathes, Axminster chuck system, Henry Taylor Tools, Sorby Tools, Artisan project kits, Dymondwood, Corian turning squares, Ray Key videos and Dale Nish workshops.
For Further Information: Free catalog.

WOODWORKER'S BOOK CLUB

P.O. Box 12171
Cincinnati, OH 45212-0171
(513) 531-8250

Offers: Each month brings a free issue of the club newsletter, describing the main selection and up to 100 more how-to and reference books for woodworkers. Members have ten days to decide. Write for latest membership opening offer. A free book plus a half-price book with no obligation to buy another is the current offer.
For Further Information: Call for information.

WOODWORKERS SOURCE

5402 S. 40th St.
Phoenix, AZ 85040
(602) 437-4415

Offers: Hardwoods—exotic and domestic—from over 75 species: lumber, plywood, veneers, turning squares and blanks. Collector's hardwoods sample kit (30 woods from worldwide).
For Further Information: Send SASE for list.

THE WOODWORKERS' STORE

4365 Willow Dr.
Medina, MN 55340
(612) 478-8201

Offers: Wood veneers and kits (35 species), tools, inlay/bandings, wood strips, wood trims, moldings, parts, hardware (for furniture), upholstering rush and caning, flexible shaft and carving tools, clock parts, musical movements, finishes. Also offers a variety of hardwood lumber and plans (furniture, dollhouses, toys, others).
For Further Information: Catalog, $2.
Accepts: Discover, MasterCard, Visa

WOODWORKER'S SUPPLY

5604 Alameda Place NE
Albuquerque, NM 87113
(505) 821-0500

Offers: Woodworking machinery: routers, borers, saws, shapers, scrolls, planers, sanders, pantographs, plus wood turning items, cedar lining and veneers, Bosch power tools, laminates, trimmers, drills, router. Porter-Cable routers and others. Also offers hardware, lights, cutters, drawer slides, lock sets, folding table legs, latches, hinges, doweling tools/aids, picture framing guns and Framemate items (miter box, clamps, others). Carries a full line of routers and other bits, plus edge banding systems, joining machines and drill presses.
For Further Information: Free catalog.
Discounts: Quantity.
Accepts: MasterCard, Visa

WOODWORKS

213 Cutting Horse
Fort Worth, TX 76117
(817) 588-5230

Offers: Wood turnings: candle cups, Shaker and other pegs, bean pots, hearts, toy wheels, axle pegs, spindles, door harp parts, eggs, apples, others—most by 100-piece lots. Also offers jewelry findings, hardware and pattern packets.
For Further Information: Free catalog.
Store Location: At above address.
Discounts: Quantity; sells wholesale to legitimate businesses.
Accepts: MasterCard, Visa

Needlecrafts, Sewing
and Fiber Arts

Batik and Dyeing

Also see Artist's Supplies, Fabric Decorating, Fabrics and Trims, General Needlecraft Supplies, Rug Making, Spinning and Weaving and other related categories.

ALJO MANUFACTURING CO.
81 Franklin St.
New York, NY 10013
(212) 226-2878
Fax: (212) 274-9616

Offers: Dyes: direct dyes (for cotton and rayon), acid dyes (for silk, wool, batik, tie-dye, printing), Zymo-Fast vat dyes (for cotton, batik, tie-dye), alcohol/water-base dyes (for hand painting on silk), cold process fiber reactive dyes (for painting on silk, cotton, rayon, wool, batik), acid dyes for nylon (7 fluorescent colors), acetate nylon disperse-type dyes (for nylon, synthetics). Also offers tjanting tools, beeswax, paraffin, plus chemicals/agents.
For Further Information: Free catalog.
Discounts: Quantity; teachers, institutions and professionals.

DHARMA TRADING CO.
P.O. Box 150916
San Rafael, CA 94915
(800) 542-5227

Offers: Fabric dyes: Procion, acid; Deka L., Dupont, Tinfix, Jacquard silk types. Also offers fabric paints. Waxes are also available, including sticky, paraffin, bee's, batik. Also offers resists, including guttas, Deka, Silkpaint water soluble, inko and Presist, tools, fabric markers. Children and adult clothing and accessory blanks and white or natural fabrics, books also available.
For Further Information: Free catalog.
Store Location: At above address.
Discounts: Quantity discounts; sells wholesale to businesses.
Accepts: Discover, MasterCard, Visa

IVY IMPORTS, INC.
6806 Treyler Rd.
Lanham, MD 20706
(301) 474-7347
Fax: (301) 441-2395

Offers: Instructional videos, kits, and books on silk painting, dyeing and related subjects. Also offers services, including fabric finishing, hemming, tie making and custom screening of designs. Books include *The Complete Book of Silk Painting* and *Creative Silk Painting* (silk painting as a fine art) by Diane Tuckman and Jan Janas (North Light Books).
For Further Information: Catalog, $3.
Discounts: Sells wholesale to businesses.

RUPERT, GIBBON & SPIDER, INC./JACQUARD PRODUCTS
P.O. Box 425
Healdsburg, CA 95448
(707) 433-9577 or (800) 442-0455

Offers: Over 50 silk and cotton fabrics, imported silk and cotton scarves. Manufactures Jacquard line of paints and dyes for fabrics; complete line of books and accessories. Also offers Jacquard wood products, easels, frames and stitchery items.
For Further Information: Free catalog, referrals to nearest store.
Discounts: Quantity; sells wholesale to legitimate businesses.

Clothing and Accessories

Also see Costumes—Ethnic, Historic, Special Occasion, Doll, Toy and Clothes Making—Soft, Fabrics, Outdoors and Outerwear, Sewing and related categories.

ALPEL PUBLISHING
P.O. Box 203-CSS
Chambly, Quebec J3L 4B3
Canada
(514) 658-6205

Offers: Patterns/instruction books, including: *Easy Sewing for Infants* (with 70 patterns), *Easy Sewing for Children* (75 patterns for 3- to 10-year-olds), *Easy Sewing for Adults* (78 patterns), and *Easy Halloween Costumes for Children* (60 costumes for 3- to 12-year-olds) all for $16.10. Halloween book includes ideas and patterns for accessories and mini-patterns. "Duplicut" vinyl grid sheets for enlarging patterns are also available. Also offers *Hey Kids, Let's Make Gifts* ($17.50) and *Catalog of Canadian Catalogs* ($16.95).
For Further Information: 20 sample patterns, $5.
Discounts: Quantity.

ARTFUL ILLUSIONS
P.O. Box 278
Ector, TX 75439
(903) 961-2816

Offers: 27 Artwear clothing patterns: designer jackets in a variety of styles, shredded cloth design jackets, Sante Fe blouses and skirts, vests, coats, others.
For Further Information: Catalog, $1.50.
Discounts: Sells wholesale to legitimate businesses.

BARTLEY SOFTWARE, INC.
72 Robertson Rd., Box 26122
Nepean, Ontario K2H 9R6
Canada
(613) 829-6488

Offers: Computer program for designing custom-fitted sewing patterns. Includes design tools, variable seam allowances and printing of patterns to any system compatible printer, with no limit on size or number of patterns.
For Further Information: Call or write for free demo disk.

BONFIT AMERICA, INC.
5959 Truimph St.
Commerce, CA 90040
(800) 768-8008 (consumers) or
(800) 5BONFIT (distributors)

Offers: "Patterner" units: no paper, adjustable for custom fit of clothing and for pleats, darts, yokes, basques, panels, flares. Create skirts, pants, bodices and other men's/women's clothes (elegant, casual, sports, maternity, sleep and bridal wear designs—with storage bag). Designer kits.
For Further Information: Call.
Discounts: Sells wholesale. Call (800) 5BONFIT.
Accepts: American Express, Discover, MasterCard, Visa

BURDA PATTERNS
P.O. Box 67028
Marietta, GA 30066
(800) 241-6887

Offers: Line of fashion patterns, variety of sizes/styles/items.
For Further Information: Send SASE (double-stamped) for mini-catalog.

CARDIN ORIGINALS
15802 Springdale St., #1
Huntington Beach, CA 92649
(714) 897-2437

Offers: Garment patterns, including a rag "fur" coat (all cotton, in one pattern piece). Others.
For Further Information: Catalog, $2.
Discounts: Sells wholesale.

CHARTRU ENTERPRISE
P.O. Box 177
Platteville, CO 80651

Offers: All occasion wallet pattern (with checkbook holder, license pocket, credit card section, coin purse). Also offers accessories and patterns.
For Further Information: Send SASE for details.

CREATE-A-TIE
P.O. Box 3015-CS
Renton, WA 98056
(206) 226-2419

Offers: Clip-on tie and bow-tie patterns in children's through adult sizes (includes 3 tie clips, full-sized pattern). Tie clips.

For Further Information: Send SASE.
Discounts: Quantity; sells wholesale to legitimate businesses.

COCHENILLE DESIGN STUDIO
P.O. Box 4276
Encinitas, CA 92023
(619) 259-1698
Fax: (619) 259-7348

Offers: Computer programs, including Stitch Painter, Stitch Editor, Garment Styler and others. Also offers designer aids, including garment templates yarn inventory cards and others. Books and patterns also available.

DOS DE TEJAS
P.O. Box 1636
Sherman, TX 75091
(903) 893-0064
Fax: (903) 893-0064

Offers: Sewing patterns: tote and garment bags, "chameleon" vest, broomstick skirt, "Hobo walkabout" bags, no-sew hats, applique, recycling and crafts. Charlatan button kits for vintage, classic and ethnic closures; companion hardware to patterns. Also sells instructional videos, including "Appliquick" applique and redesign of sweater projects, and a book on "designer look" sewing.
For Further Information: Catalog, $2.
Accepts: MasterCard, Visa

DOUBLE D PRODUCTIONS
4110 Willow Ridge Rd.
Douglasville, GA 30135
(770) 949-3648

Offers: Square dance apparel patterns—over 60 items, including full skirts, petticoats, tops, others.
For Further Information: Catalog, $1.

ELAN PATTERN CO.
534 Sandalwood Dr.
El Cajon, CA 92021
(619) 442-1167

Offers: Bra patterns and kits, including in colors, in regular and plus sizes, with fitting tips.

LOIS ERICSON
P.O. Box 5222
Salem, OR 97304

Offers: Creative sewing books: *Design and Sew It Yourself* (techniques, drawings), *The Great Put On* (progressive techniques), and *What Goes Around* on belts. Innovative Design & Sew patterns, including vests, ragland jacket, bathrobe

coats, tops, reversible pants, collars, cuffs and links, and jackets for leather, with directions.
For Further Information: Free list.
Discounts: Quantity; sells wholesale to legitimate businesses.

FASHION BLUEPRINTS
2191 Blossom Valley Dr.
San Jose, CA 95124
(408) 356-5291

Offers: Classic ethnic clothing patterns—over 20 designs in blueprint format, multi-sized, for women, men, children—some fashionable today. Patterns include wrap dresses, tunics, pants, jackets, vests, tops, robes, shirts, coats, others—with Oriental, Far Eastern, African, Mexican, European origins. Early American patterns that adapt to today: prairie skirt, gown, apron, shirts.
For Further Information: Catalog, $2.
Discounts: Sells wholesale to businesses.

FASHION TOUCHES
170 Elm St.
P.O. Box 804
Bridgeport, CT 06601
(203) 333-7738

Offers: Service: custom-covered belts and buttons from customer's fabrics, earrings, cuff links, upholstery buttons.
For Further Information: Catalog, $1.25.
Discounts: For teachers and institutions.

FAY'S FASHION FABRICS
155 Webster Dr., #508
Pensacola, FL 32505
(904) 455-2410

Offers: Half-slip instructions—7 styles with fabric.
For Further Information: Send SASE for details.

JACKIE FEARS
2931 St. Johns Ave.
Billings, MT 59102
(406) 656-9829

Offers: Discontinued patterns in popular brands.
For Further Information: Send $5 for complete list or $2 per brand. 50¢ per pattern, plus postage.

FRIENDS PATTERNS
P.O. Box 657
Berthoud, CO 80513

Offers: Amish clothing patterns for men, women and children: Mennonite dresses, other dresses, aprons, bonnets, children's caps, broadfall pants (men's, boys), sack coats, shirts, vests. Patterns for coveralls, overalls and farm coats avail-

able. Also offers Amish dolls and quilt designs.
For Further Information: Illustrated catalog, $1.
Discounts: Wholesale Accounts welcome.

GHEE'S
2620 Centenary Blvd., #2-250
Shreveport, LA 71104
(318) 226-1701
Fax: (318) 226-1781

Offers: Handbag-making supplies: metal frames in a variety of sizes and shapes, magnetic closures, chains, handbag accessories, handbag and vest patterns, notions, and books on fabric manipulation.
For Further Information: Catalog, $1.

GREAT COPY PATTERNS
P.O. Box 085329
Racine, WI 53408
(414) 632-2660

Offers: Great Copy patterns, including 40 designer copies sized EXs to EL. Also offers *Polarfleece Pizzazz* book.
For Further Information: Send large SASE for information.

HARRIET'S
P.O. Box 1363
Winchester, VA 22604
(540) 667-2541

Offers: Patterns and costumes from 1690 to 1910, especially Victorian.
For Further Information: Catalog, $10.

HESSON COLLECTABLES
1261 S. Lloyd
Lombard, IL 60148
(708) 627-3298

Offers: Mail-order catalogs of 1900-1996, including Sears, Montgomery Ward, Penny's, Alden and Spiegel's.
For Further Information: List of more than 1,000 catalogs, $4.

JEAN HARDY PATTERNS
2151 La Cuesta Dr.
Santa Ana, CA 92705
(714) 544-1608

Offers: Men's and women's riding clothes patterns for English, Western and saddle seat riding.
For Further Information: Catalog, $1.

THE KWIK-SEW PATTERN CO.
3000 Washington Ave. N.
Champaign, IL 61826
(612) 521-7651

Offers: Patterns for dance dresses, petticoats, ruffled panties, and Western-style patterns for men.
For Further Information: See your dealer, or send SASE for information.

LACE LAND
P.O. Box 1504
Sugarland, TX 77487
(713) 983-5223

Offers: Laces and bridal laces and motifs; swimsuits and lingerie patterns. Also offers fabrics, including lycra, tricot, stretch laces, others. Underwires, bra cups and others also available.

LOGAN KITS
Rt. 3
P.O. Box 380
Double Springs, AL 35553
(205) 486-7732

Offers: Garment kits (and refills) including patterns/fabric (some elastic) for lingerie items, nightgowns, men's underwear, girl's lingerie. Also offers a master pattern for a baby wardrobe. A variety of fabrics is included with kits.
For Further Information: Brochure, $1.50.
Discounts: Quantity; sells wholesale.

MARY WALES LOOMIS
1487 Parrott Dr.
San Mateo, CA 94402
(415) 345-8012

Offers: *Make Your Own Shoes*, a book with illustrated instructions for making custom fitted ladies' pumps.
For Further Information: Free color brochure.
Discounts: Sells wholesale to legitimate businesses.

PARK BENCH PATTERN CO.
5423 Mary Lane Dr.
San Diego, CA 92115
(619) 286-6859
Fax: (619) 287-0841

Offers: New, imaginative, alternative patterns for comfortable women's clothing that is easy to sew.
For Further Information: Catalog, $3.

PAW PRINTS
19618 Canyon Dr.
Granite Falls, WA 98252
(360) 691-4293

Offers: Jean jackets "Art to Wear" patterns.
For Further Information: Send large SASE for brochure.

THE PLATEAU
616 10th St.
Saskatoon, Saskatchewan S7H 0G9
Canada
(800) 269-1566 or (306) 221-6644
Fax: (306) 477-7175

Offers: "Atelier Plateau Collections" menswear patters. Also offers mail order fabrics.
For Further Information: Call or send SASE.

PREEMIE-YUMS
2260 Gibson Woods Ct. NW
Salem, OR 97304

Offers: Preemie patterns, pre-cut kits and readywear for infants 4 to 6 pounds.
For Further Information: Send $1.50 and large SASE for brochure.

SAF-T-POCKETS
1075 NW Murray Rd., #163
Portland, OR 97229
(503) 643-1968

Offers: Pattern for travel clothing with hidden pockets for safety and convenience.
For Further Information: Send SASE for details.

SEW LITTLE PATTERN CO.
P.O. Box 3613
Salem, OR 97302

Offers: Master sewing patterns (full-size) each with 4 sizes and 16 or more garments—in full, European styling for all bodies, both regular/serger styles. Offers quick/easy playwear—preemies to 12 months, layette or "Cabbage Patch" clothes, toddlers garments with "grow features." Doll patterns are also available.
For Further Information: Catalog, $2 USA; $3 Canada.
Discounts: Quantity; sells wholesale.

SEW SASSY LINGERIE
9009-C South Memorial Pkwy.
Huntsville, AL 35802

Offers: Lingerie materials including tricot with matching lace elastics, sheet slip straps, all over stretch lace, Char-meuse, re-embroidered lace, lightweight knits, specialty plastics; bra accessories, power knit for girdles and bras. Lycra in solids, prints, linings, sheer, cotton types, stretch velvet. Specialty fashion fabrics, knits, interlock prints and solids. Line of patterns from Stretch & Sew and Kwik Sew.
For Further Information: Catalog, $2; $3 out of U.S. (U.S. funds).
Discounts: Quantity prices on bulk orders.
Accepts: MasterCard, Visa.

JANET STAHL
P.O. Box 27035
Concord, CA 94527

Offers: Instructional sewing videos, including Perfect-Fit Pants, "Blazers Made Easy," with methods applicable to other garments, by Janet Stahl, President of the National Fashion Sewing Institute.
For Further Information: Send SASE.

SUITABILITY
P.O. Box 3244
Chico, CA 95927
(800)207-0256

Offers: Equestrian clothing patterns including Western duster, others.
For Further Information: Free catalog.

SUITABLES
P.O. Box 17601
San Antonio, TX 78217

Offers: Instructions for no-sew fabric covered shoes and fabric covered belts, $5.
For Further Information: Send SASE for details.

THE THREAD BARE PATTERN CO.
P.O. Box 1484
Havelock, NC 28532
(919) 447-4081
(800) 4-PATTERN

Offers: Large collar patterns (with appliqués), plus other clothing/accessory patterns.
For Further Information: Catalog, $2 (refundable).

THE THRIFTY NEEDLE
3233 Amber St.
Philadelphia, PA 19134
(800) 324-9927

Offers: Sweater fabric in kits, for cut-and-sew like a T-shirt; in cotton, wool and acrylic.
For Further Information: Catalog, swatches and discount coupons, $2.

Costumes—Ethnic, Historic, Special Occasion

Also see Clothing and Accessories, Doll, Toy and Clothes Making—Soft, Fabrics and Trims and other related categories.

ALPEL PUBLISHING
P.O. Box 203-CSS
Chambly, Quebec J3L 4B3
Canada
(514) 658-6205
Fax: (514)658-3519

Offers: Easy-Sew pattern book: children's traditional costumes (3- to 12-year-olds) and pirates, Peter Pan, robots, others; includes accessories and patterns to be enlarged. Makeup and wigs are also covered. Carries Duplicut wipe-clean, vinyl grid sheets for pattern enlargement.
For Further Information: Free brochure with sample infant's pattern, $1.

ALTERYEARS
3749 E. Colorado Blvd.
Pasadena, CA 91107

Offers: Over 1,400 historical, ethnic and specialty patterns from 48 companies. Also sells over 200 hard-to-find supplies and accessories, complete corsetry supplies, millinery, hoops and bustles, gloves, panniers, clasps and others, and nearly 1,000 costume reference books.
For Further Information: Catalog, $5.

AMAZON DRYGOODS
2218 E. 11th St.
Davenport, IA 52803
(319) 322-6800 or (800) 798-7979
Fax: (319) 322-4003

Offers: Nineteenth-century-inspired products: Over 1,200 historic/ethnic clothes patterns from 1390 to 1950, with emphasis on the 1800s—coats, cloaks, hats, bonnets, gowns, suits, corsets, lingerie, underwear, formal clothes, everyday, work outfits and military uniforms (sizes for most patterns: ladies, 6 to 44-plus, men's 32 to 48-plus). Supplies: hoop wire, boning, stays, ostrich feathers, specialty fabrics (including fancies), uniform wools, tradecloth, veilings. Indian/frontier patterns available.
For Further Information: General catalog, $3. Shoe catalog, $5. Pattern catalog, $7.
Accepts: American Express, Discover, MasterCard, Visa

ARON'S
8974 E. Huntington Dr.
San Gabriel, CA 91775
(818) 285-8544

Offers: Line of square dance and western clothing patterns and accessories.
For Further Information: Western patterns catalog, $1. Square dance patterns catalog, $2.

ATIRA'S FASHIONS
3935 S. 113th St.
Seattle, WA 98168
(206) 767-3357
Fax: (206) 767-4991

Offers: Middle Eastern patterns (men's, women's), plus imported accessories, custom bras for Renaissance look, beaded fringe and dance accessories.
For Further Information: Catalog, $4.
Store Location: At above address.

BAER FABRICS
515 E. Market St.
Louisville, KY 40202
(502) 569-7010 or (800) 769-7776
Fax: (206) 767-4991

Offers: Special bridal collection of fabrics, including taffetas, satins, chiffons, organzas, nettings and laces in a range of colors, plus trims, notions, supplies. Also offers prom and evening wear collection. Also sells Ultrasuede, Ultrasuede light and Ultra-leather in 75 colors. Personal shopper service.
For Further Information: Bridal collection sample set (#11525), $10. Prom and evening wear collection sample set (#12525), $6. Ultrasuede and ultra-leather sample set (#01525), $9.50. Notions and trims catalog, $3.
Discounts: Quantity; teachers, institutions and businesses.

BARLETTA'S
P.O. Box 1749
Wayne, NJ 07474
(201) 696-2369

Offers: Bridal supplies and headpiece materials, including veils, rhinestones, pearls, hats and others.
For Further Information: Catalog, $3.

BALTAZOR'S
3262 Severn Ave.
Metairie, LA 70002

Offers: Bridal/fine hand-sewing supplies: fabrics, laces, bridal accessories, plus lace-making and smocking items.
For Further Information: Catalog, $2.

BEAUTIFUL BRIDE PATTERN CO.
1707 Evansdale Dr.
Toledo, OH 43607
(419) 539-9471

Offers: Bridal veil kits and patterns, fabric to match gowns, and line of supplies.
For Further Information: Catalog, $1.

BIRCH STREET CLOTHING
P.O. Box 6901
San Mateo, CA 94403
(415) 578-9729

Offers: Sewing pattern for 6 Halloween costumes from sweatshirts for children 6 mos. to 10 years: jester, devil, skeleton, others.

BRIDALS INTERNATIONAL
45 Albany St.
Cazenovia, NY 13035
(800) 752-1171

Offers: Imported bridal fabrics and laces for designer look gowns; patterns from major companies.
For Further Information: Catalog, $9.50.
Store Location: At above address.

BRIDES 'N BABES
P.O. Box 2189
Manassas, VA 22110

Offers: Wedding supplies, including you-make bridal gowns and accessories, brides' maids gowns, party favors. Also offers instructions for bridal headpieces (hats, veils, combs, garlands, halos, coronets, cascades, nosegays, corsages, rice roses, others).
For Further Information: Send large SASE for brochure.
Accepts: American Express, MasterCard, Visa

BUCKAROO BOBBINS
P.O. Box 95314
Las Vegas, NV 89193
(702) 384-1885

Offers: Clothing patterns of authentic vintage western style.

DOWERING DESIGNS
68935 233rd St.
Dassel, MN 55325

Offers: Selection of Scandinavian costume patterns—women's, men's, children's multi-sized; 14″ and 18″ dolls. Braid and pewter also available.
For Further Information: Catalog, $1.

FABRIC FANCIES
P.O. Box 50807
Reno, NV 89513
(702) 746-0666

Offers: Catalog #1 is a Bridal Laces catalog and includes fabrics, embroideries, trims, veil kits and others. Catalog #2 offers a variety of bridal silk fabrics. Catalog #3 offers Bridal Elegance (R) patterns in more than 1,000 traditional styles.
For Further Information: Catalog #1, $12. Catalog #2, silk samples album, $10. Catalog #3, 60-page pattern catalog, $10.

FOLKWEAR
The Taunton Press
63 S. Main St.
P.O. Box 5506
Newtown, CT 06470
(203) 426-8171

Offers: 66 folkwear sewing patterns (for men, women, children—multi-sized): ethnic (of Gaza, France, Syria, Turkey, Afghan, Japan, China, Russia, Croatia, Tibet, Hong Kong, Austria, Bolivia, Australia, Morocco, India, Native American, others) and vintage (Edwardian, Victorian, Early American from the 1920s to 1950s).
For Further Information: Catalog, $3.
Discounts: Sells wholesale.
Accepts: MasterCard, Visa

FOREVER TIMELESS
RR1
Hillsburgh, Ontario N0B 120
Canada
(519) 855-6507 or (519) 855-6037
Fax: (905) 274-2610

Offers: Clothing patterns, including Folkwear, Past Patterns, Old World Enterprises, Patterns of History, Mill Farm, Heidi Marsh, Period Impression, D.L. Designs, Harriet's, Attic Copies, Missouri River, Eagle's View and others.
For Further Information: Catalog, $5.50 U.S.; $7.50 Canada.

HARRIET'S TCS-PATTERNS
P.O. Box 1363
Winchester, VA 22604
(540) 667-2541

Offers: 180 plus garment patterns, including men's, women's

and children's, in a variety of day and evening gowns, undergarments, blouses, skirts, coats, trousers, jackets, shirts, hats, and crinolines, circa 1600-1945.
For Further Information: Catalog, $10.

ILLUSIONS OF GRANDEUR
P.O. Box 735B
Cloverdale, CA 95425

Offers: Bridal kits, including headpieces, ringbearer's pillow and veils, pre-cut and ready to assemble, with materials and instructions.
For Further Information: Catalog, $3 (refundable).

MAHAMADON SUMARCH
508 Monroe, Suite 508
Detroit, MI 48226
(313) 965-6620
Fax: (313) 965-0066

Offers: African fabrics, Kuba and Mud cloth, others. Also offers Yosuba bead work, trade beads and other items.
For Further Information: Catalog available.
Discounts: Sells wholesale.

MEDIEVAL MISCELLANEA
6530 Spring Valley Dr.
Alexandria, VA 22312
(703) 642-1740

Offers: Patterns for garments of the medieval era—a variety of gown styles, headgear, others.
For Further Information: Write.
Discounts: Sells wholesale.

MURIELLE ROY & CO.
67 Platto Mill Rd.
Naugatuck, CT 06770
(203) 729-0480
Fax: (203) 720-2101

Offers: Fabrics and trims for performers, including lycras, chiffons, silks, laces, stretch sheer, mesh, velvets, satin and foil. Also offers glitter and metallic lycra, feathers, sequins, beaded fringe and others.
For Further Information: Catalog available.
Accepts: Discover, MasterCard, Visa

NEWARK DRESSMAKER SUPPLY
Dept. CSS
P.O. Box 20730
Lehigh Valley, PA 18002
(610) 837-7500

Offers: Sewing and needlecraft supplies, aids and fabrics. Bridal supplies include pearl buttons, looping, hair boning, appliqués, bands, garters, flowers (garlands, sprays), accessories, veils, fabrics (laces, satins, moire, organza, esprit, nylon net, tulle, illusion). Also offers pressing items, fabric paints, sequins, rhinestones, beads, others.
For Further Information: Free catalog.
Discounts: Quantity; sells wholesale.

PAST PATTERNS
P.O. Box 2446
Richmond, IN 47374
(317) 962-3333
Fax: (317) 962-3773

Offers: Historic garment patterns from 1829 to the present (on brown paper), including authentically styled gowns, blouses, suits, petticoats, nightwear, men's dusters and suits.
For Further Information: Catalog, $4; information flyer free.
Accepts: Discover, MasterCard, Visa

PATTERNS OF HISTORY
816 State St.
Suite CS
Madison, WI 53706
(608) 264-6428

Offers: Patterns for garments of the nineteenth century, including gowns in a variety of styles.
For Further Information: Send for free brochure.

PEGEE OF WILLIAMSBURG
P.O. Box 127
Williamsburg, VA 23187
(804) 220-2722

Offers: Historic patterns, including 1776 lady's dress, girl's dress, lady's cloak, men's and boy's shirt, breeches and waistcoat, men's military/civilian coat, Scarlett O'Hara's Barbecue Party Dress, hoop skirt and Green Velveteen Portieres Dress, Bonnie's blue riding habit, and others. Patterns are replicas of the original, with detailed instructions and illustrations.
For Further Information: Brochure, $2.
Discounts: Sells wholesale to businesses.

PIECES OF OLDE
P.O. Box 65130
Baltimore, MD 21209
(410) 366-4949
Fax: (410) 466-9326

Offers: Patterns for women's accessories, including Victorian drawstring pouch, heart-shaped evening bag, women's lace cardigan sweatshirt and character dolls.
For Further Information: 36-page catalog, $3.

RENEGADE

P.O. Box 7089

Phoenix, AZ 85011

(602) 482-6777

Fax: (602) 482-1952

Offers: Law enforcement holsters.

For Further Information: Send SASE for details.

ROCKING HORSE FARM

Box 735 N

Chardon, OH 44024

Offers: Over 70 historic and vintage clothing patterns for medieval period, 1740 to 1950.

For Further Information: Pattern catalog, $2.

ROSEBAR TEXTILE CO., INC.

93 Entin Rd.

Clifton, NJ 07014

(201)777-0078, (800) 631-8573

Offers: Fabrics, including satins, taffetas, sheers, lamés, jacquards, novelties, linings. Supplies accessory, box, ribbon, tabletop, elegant craft, bridal and evening wear fabrics.

For Further Information: Send SASE for details.

R.L. SHEP

P.O. Box 2706

Fort Bragg, CA 95437

(707) 964-8662

Offers: Out of print books on textiles and costumes. Also carries reprints of Edwardian and Victorian titles for accurate reproduction of period clothing and other use.

For Further Information: Free brochure.

Discounts: Sells wholesale to legitimate businesses.

SPARKLE!

Box 5006

Grand Forks, ND 58206

Offers: Accessories for bridal gowns, including a wide selection of lace trims, appliqués, bodices, sequin/beaded appliques and trims, rhinestones, pearls and other accessories.

For Further Information: 32-page catalog, $5.

THE TAUNTON PRESS

63 S. Main St.

Newtown, CT 06470

(203) 426-8171

Offers: 80 folkwear vintage and ethnic patterns: Algerian suit, Russian Cossack uniform, dresses of Gaza, Afghani Nomad, Syrian, Hong Kong Cheongsam, Austrian Dirndl, Russian settlers and children's prairie. Also offers outerwear of Turkey, Japan, China, Tibet, Bolivia, Seminole, Morocco, Belgium, South Asia, Australia, Hungary, Scotland.

For Further Information: Free catalog.

Discounts: Sells wholesale to legitimate businesses.

THE WHOLE COSTUMER'S CATALOGUE

P.O. Box 207M

2860 Main St.

Beallsville, PA 15313

(412) 632-3242

Offers: A directory of costume resources for craftspeople, costumers, fiber artists and sewers, including a shopping guide to New York, Los Angeles and Philadelphia, books and periodicals, organizations and a wide range of source listings for historical and ethnic clothing and accessories. Also carries fabrics, trims, casting materials, paints and dyes, tools, patterns and many others.

For Further Information: Send SASE.

Doll, Toy and Clothes Making—Soft

Also see Doll and Toy Making—Rigid, Miniature Making, Fabrics and Trims, Knitting and Crochet and other related categories.

ALL ABOUT DOLLS
49 Lakeside Blvd.
Hopatcong, NJ 07843
(201) 770-3228

Offers: Line of soft doll kits, doll blanks and supplies (including plastic armatures for soft bodies, others).
For Further Information: Catalog, $3.
Accepts: American Express, Discover, MasterCard, Visa

ATLANTA PUFFECTIONS
P.O. Box 13524
Atlanta, GA 30324
(404) 262-7437

Offers: Over 75 soft doll patterns including Puff Ima Doorstop Mouse, Nanny and the Twins, others. Supplies (to support patterns).
For Further Information: Color catalog, $1.50; send SASE for brochure.
Discounts: Sells wholesale to legitimate businesses.

BEMIDJI WOOLEN MILLS
Box 277
Bemidji, MN 56601
(218) 751-5166
Fax: (218) 751-4659

Offers: Rockford Red Heel sock, heather brown with red heel, used to make monkeys and other stuffed toys. Available in two sizes.
For Further Information: Call or write for mail-order catalog.

BY DIANE
1126 Ivon Ave.
Endicott, NY 13760
(607) 754-0391

Offers: Fuzzy Friends toy kits/patterns including teddy bears, sea creatures, other wild and domestic animals and hand puppet kits/patterns. Also offers animal eyes, noses and joint sets, glass eyes, armatures.

For Further Information: Catalog, $3.
Discounts: Quantity; teachers and institutions; sells wholesale to legitimate businesses.

MARY CANTRELL
505 Pratt Ave.
Huntsville, AL 35801
(205) 533-4972

Offers: Soft sculpture doll patterns (with clothes) by Miss Martha, plus 17 assorted books. Also offers iron-on transfer eyes.
For Further Information: Send SASE.

CARVERS' EYE CO.
P.O. Box 16692, Dept. 80
Portland, OR 97216
(503) 666-5680

Offers: Glass or plastic eyes, noses, joints, growlers and other merchandise for teddy bears and dolls.
For Further Information: Send $2.
Discounts: Sells wholesale.

CR'S CRAFTS
P.O. Box 8-41 CB
Leland, IA 50453
(515) 576-3652

Offers: Doll and animal patterns, kits, supplies: teddies (and posable bears filled with plastic beads), monkeys, wraparound puppets, dolls (plastic heads). Also offers craft fur, fabrics, fiberfill, animal parts, animal voices (cow, lamb, bear, puppy, bird, cat), cow and other bells, music boxes and doll parts. Others.
For Further Information: 112-page catalog, $2, ($4 Canada).
Discounts: Quantity.

DAR'S QUIET CORNER
1308 Grant
Grand Haven, MI 49417
(616) 846-0247

Offers: Doll body patterns for modern porcelain dolls. Also offers Loc-Line armatures.
For Further Information: Call.

DOLL EMPORIUM PATTERN CO.

1546 S. Wallis Ave.
Santa Maria, CA 93454
(805) 925-2245

Offers: Doll clothing patterns (full-sized) for specific dolls (as released by the artist); multiple designs per pattern.
For Further Information: Contact nearest distributor; catalog, $3.50 (with coupon).

THE DOLLHOUSE FACTORY

157 Main St.
P.O. Box 456
Lebanon, NJ 08833
(908) 236-6404

Offers: Full line of name brand dollhouses and supplies—needlework, wood, lighting, components, accessories, wallpapers, furniture, moldings, hardware, masonry. Kits and tools also available.
For Further Information: Catalog, $5.50.

DOLLS DELIGHT, INC.

P.O. Box 3226
Alexandria, VA 22302
(800) 257-6301

Offers: Doll clothing patterns (for 18″ dolls), plus ready-to-wear items.
For Further Information: Send SASE for list.
Accepts: MasterCard, Visa

THE ENCHANTED ATTIC

Route 5
Box 165AAA, Oakview Addition
El Dorado Springs, MO 64744

Offers: Thirty-eight original cloth doll patterns for various sized lady, children, animal, holiday and ethnic dolls, with their clothing. Two books of traceable faces, with mix and match facial features for creating other doll faces, and instructional materials are also available. Services include custom finished doll faces.
For Further Information: Send $2 for fold-out brochure.
Discounts: Sells wholesale.

FANCYWORK AND FASHION

4728 Dodge St.
Duluth, MN 55804
(218) 525-2442

Offers: Several doll costuming pattern books for 18″ vinyl and porcelain dolls. Authors of *The Best Doll Clothes Book.*
For Further Information: Send SASE for list.
Accepts: MasterCard, Visa

FIBERS & MORE

Box 636
Camas, WA 98607
(260) 834-4426

Offers: Doll hair, in a full range of styles. Also offers knit and handweaving kits.
For Further Information: Doll hair catalog, $3.95, with 135 yarn/fiber samples.
Accepts: MasterCard, Visa

GOLDEN FUN KITS

P.O. Box 6792
Chesterfield, MO 63006
(314) 391-2197

Offers: Soft toy patterns for animals and dolls. Also offers eyes, noses, squeakers, joints, animal voices (growlers, others), musical movements, doll/animal joints, doll pellets.
For Further Information: Catalog, $1.
Discounts: Quantity.

SALLY GOODSPEED

2318 N. Charles St.
Baltimore, MD 21218
(410) 235-6736

Offers: Reprints of 1900-1940 doll pattern designs, quilt, embroidery, applique and paint designs; over 600 Sunbonnet babies and Colonial ladies, many from Corbett's Primer. Also offers Dolly Dingle, Kewpies, Kate Greenaway.
For Further Information: Catalog, $2.95.

HANNILY PATTERNS

427 Chalfonte Dr.
Baltimore, MD 21228
(410) 744-5832

Offers: 36 patterns for dolls, crafts and quilts, including jointed, posable Christmas Angel doll with four wooden wheels, and others.
For Further Information: Brochure, $1.50.

HAPPY HEARTS

653 SW 2nd St., #164
Lee's Summit, MO 64063
(816) 525-2746

Offers: Doll costuming items: feathers (small ostrich plumes, pompoms and boas; marabou and boas; pheasant fluff; peacock). Also offers elegant laces and trims, and an assortment of fabrics and accessories.
For Further Information: Catalog, $2 (refundable).

HEARTFELT
995 East Otero Ave.
Littleton, CO 80122
(303) 795-7541

Offers: Pressed felt doll kits with three-dimensional molded felt mask, body material and pattern. Doll kits include arm, leg and neck joints, painting guide and instructions.
For Further Information: Send SASE.
Discounts: Sells wholesale.

JOAN JANSEN
P.O. Box 85
Monterey Park, CA 91754

Offers: Father Christmas 20" old world Santa doll patterns, free-standing or with legs, in robes. Also offers toy sack that includes 5 toy patterns. Options are indicated.
For Further Information: Doll newsletter, $1

JUDI'S DOLLS
P.O. Box 607
Port Orchard, WA 98366

Offers: Whimsical doll patterns, including "Fiona," a little girl in a three-dimensional form, with detail, and others.
For Further Information: Catalog, $2.50.

JUDY HOLLAWAY
13650 E. Zayante Rd.
Felton, CA 95018
(408) 335-4684

Offers: Contemporary/heirloom reproduction supplies: patterns, imported fabrics, laces, smocking supplies, trims, others. Also offers custom-made dresses.
For Further Information: Catalog, $5.

JOSEPH'S COAT
26 Main St.
Peterborough, NH 03458
(603) 924-6683

Offers: Nineteenth-century heirloom cloth doll kits (by Gail Wilson): snowman, angel, Santa, Pinnochio, Humpty Dumpty, and other dolls and character dolls.
For Further Information: Send SASE for catalog.

LAUREL STREET STUDIO
P.O. Box 409
Milford, NJ 08848
Offers: Rag doll patterns in folk art designs, including cats, boys and girls, 10" to 15" in size.
For Further Information: Catalog, $2.

LITTLE JOYS DOLLS
11910 Meridian E. #166
Puyallup, WA 98373
(206) 845-7912

Offers: "Little Joys" soft sculpture doll kits for natural fiber dolls with choice of skin tone, pre-made wig, wool stuffing and pattern. Also includes option to create own ethnic characteristics.
For Further Information: Color catalog with color selection card, $2.

LORD PERRY HISTORICAL FASHIONS
6041 Sanford Dr.
San Jose, CA 95123

Offers: Historical doll patterns, including patterns of Marie Antoinette, Cleopatra, Nigerian Princess, Madam Pompadour and others. Clothes fit Barbie, Imani and others.
For Further Information: Catalog and price list, $3.

SYLVIA MACNEIL
2325 Main St.
West Barnstable, MA 02668
(508) 362-3875

Offers: Antique fabrics (1860 to 1900): silk taffeta, faille, cottons, woolens, others.
For Further Information: Send SASE for list.

MAGIC CABIN DOLLS
Rt. 2, P.O. Box 39
Westby, WI 54667
(608) 634-2848

Offers: Doll-making (natural fibers) kits/patterns. Also offers skintone cotton knits, accessories and yarns: mohair, wool, llama, boudez.
For Further Information: Free catalog.
Discounts: Quantity.

MAGIC THREADS
Studio 719 P St., #3
Lincoln, NE 68508
(402) 477-6650

Offers: Cloth storybook doll patterns: 15" dolls—elves, Rapunzel, knight, sprite, Raggedy, mermaid, dragon, others. 22" Santas (with quilt/block robes designs). Also offers supplies: fringes, eyes, lamé, others.
For Further Information: Send SASE for brochure.
Discounts: Sells wholesale.

MATERIAL MEMORIES
P.O. Box 39
Springville, NY 14141

Offers: Folk art doll/toy patterns (full-sized): From a 5" Raggedy up to a 15″ guardian angel, plus animals, round bottom-standable dolls, black kids/watermelons, Amish, cherubs, babies, topsy-turvy, others. Birth certificates offered. Also offers curly chenille.

For Further Information: Catalog, $1.
Discounts: Sells wholesale.

MIMI'S BOOKS & PATTERN FOR THE SERIOUS DOLLMAKER

P.O. Box 662
Point Pleasant, NJ 08742
(908) 899-6687
Fax: (908) 714-9306

Offers: Teaching patterns with step-by-step instructions for beginning dollmakers, with variations and advanced techniques for dollmakers at all skill levels. Also offers *Let's Talk About Dollmaking* magazine.
For Further Information: Send SASE for list.

EDWINA L. MUELLER

1 Dogwood Lane
Washington, NJ 07882

Offers: Doll fashion patterns: adaptation of old Patsy doll wardrobe (fits 8″ to 9″ toddler dolls), patterns from Dorita Alice Doll Fashions, patterns for Ginny dolls, Barbie and Ken outfits.
For Further Information: Send SASE for list.

MUFFY'S BOUTIQUE

1516 Oakhurst Ave.
Winter Park, FL 32789
(407) 644-8883

Offers: Patterns by Yesterday's Children (professional, for doll costumes). Also offers Swiss batiste, French laces, silks, trims, silk ribbons, others.
For Further Information: List, $1 and SASE; catalog, $3.50; pattern catalog, $2.50.

PEAR BLOSSOM PATTERNS

P.O. Box 1826
Jacksonville, OR 97530

Offers: Cloth doll patterns, including 23″ country boys and girls, animals including reindeer in 3 sizes, and others.

ELLIS PEEPLES DOLLS

23403 NE 92nd Ave.
Battle Ground, WA 98604

Offers: Line of whimsical cloth doll patterns.
For Further Information: Catalog, $1.

PLAY DOLLS

539 Sargent
Jackson, CA 95642

Offers: Duplicated copies of outdated doll patterns and wardrobes.
For Further Information: Send large SASE for list.

PLATYPUS

P.O. Box 396, Planetarium Station
New York, NY 10024
(212) 874-0753

Offers: Soft doll and animal patterns (full-sizes) in booklets. Doll patterns include 8″ pocket dolls to 24″ mannequin proportional figured; includes boy, girl, jester, mermaid, others. Other patterns available include pocket dolls, platypus, holiday items and soft toys such as trains, animal silhouettes, others. Supplies: muslin, fur, notions. Booklets available.
For Further Information: Catalog with free pattern, $2.
Discounts: Sells wholesale.

BEVERLY POWERS

Box 13
South Lyon, MI 48178

Offers: Over 1,500 antique and commercial out-of-print patterns for doll wardrobes, old cloth dolls and animals.
For Further Information: Catalog, $4.

THE QUILTING B

232 2nd St. SE
Cedar Rapids, IA 52401
(319) 363-1643

Offers: Line of over 35 textured yarns and fibers for Santa beards and doll hair.
For Further Information: Send SASE.

ROBBIE'S DOLL CREATIONS

7102 Longmeadow, #109
Madison, WI 53717
(608) 836-6873

Offers: Molded-face doll supplies (Swiss imported), 100 percent cotton Euro-tricot, 30-plus doll masks.
For Further Information: Catalog, $2.

SEW LITTLE PATTERN CO.

P.O. Box 3613
Salem, OR 97302
(800) 552-5733

Offers: 25 or more folk art patterns for dolls, angels, bunnies, bears and ornaments.
For Further Information: Brochure, $1.
Discounts: Quantity.

SEW SPECIAL
P.O. Box 271646
Dept. CS
Sacramento, CA 95827
(916) 361-2086

Offers: Over 100 original patterns for dolls, holiday decorations in country themes. Also offers hard-to-find supplies, including doll body fabric, hair products, bulk buttons, wooden spools and embellishments.
For Further Information: Catalog, $2.
Discounts: Sells wholesale.

SEW SWEET DOLLS FROM CAROLEE CREATIONS
787 Industrial Dr.
Elmhurst, IL 60126
(708) 530-7175

Offers: Full line of easy-sew cloth doll patterns (full-sized): clowns, kitties, cowboys, little girls (8″ to 43″), little boys and babies and layettes. Also offers Amish, ethnic and other dolls. Animal and other long-legged creatures and critters are available. Supplies include furs, hair wigs, loom tools and fabrics. Books are also available.
For Further Information: Color catalog, $2.
Accepts: Discover, MasterCard, Visa

SOMETHING SPECIAL
502 N. Canal
Carlsbad, NM 88220
(800) 272-6992

Offers: Doll pellets by pound, bisque (flesh shades) and doll-making kits.
For Further Information: Send SASE for list.

SPRINGTIME DESIGN
3000 Topley Ave.
Las Cruces, NM 80005

Offers: Line of animal and doll patterns, including Joy Angel and others.
For Further Information: Pattern catalog, $1 and large SASE.

STANDARD DOLL CO.
2383 31st St.
Long Island City, NY 11105
(718) 721-7787

Offers: Doll-making supplies, including doll parts, body patterns (8″ to 36″), voices/sounds/growlers, line of music boxes, shoes and other accessories, pellets, chenille, fabrics (flesh, others), plus lace and other trims and aids. Mini-zippers and buttons, tags, bags, boxes, magnifiers and books are also available. Carries porcelain and other dolls.
For Further Information: Catalog, $3.
Discounts: Quantity.
Accepts: American Express, MasterCard, Visa

TREASURES FROM HEAVEN
68 N. Broadway Dr., #2
Blackfoot, ID 83221
(208) 785-1166

Offers: Doll clothing for a variety of sizes.
For Further Information: Brochure, $2.

UNICORN STUDIOS
P.O. Box 9240
Knoxville, TN 37940

Offers: Musical movements and voices (full line of tunes, electronic types, windup types): Music, animal and doll voices (12), accessories, mini-light sets, kits, animal and doll parts. Also offers Wyndo cards, instructions and books.
For Further Information: Catalog, $1 (refundable).

VIV'S RIBBONS & LACES
212 Virginia Hills Dr.
Martinez, CA 94553
(516) 944-5042

Offers: Doll sewing/French hand-sewing supplies: silk and other ribbons, ribbon rose maker, old/new French and English cotton laces, plus other laces and trims. Also offers buckles, jewelry findings and books on silk ribbon embroidery, millinery, others.
For Further Information: Catalog, $3.50 (refundable).
Discounts: Quantity; teachers and institutions; sells wholesale to legitimate businesses.
Accepts: MasterCard, Visa

KATE WEBSTER CO.
83 Granite St.
Rockport, MA 01966
(508) 546-6462
Fax: (508) 546-6466

Offers: Doll costuming supplies, including vintage textiles and trims, new ribbons, trims, laces, tulle, fairy wings, parasol and purse frames, hat making supplies, buttons and others.
For Further Information: 50-page color catalog, $3.
Discounts: Quantity.
Accepts: MasterCard, Visa

Embroidery and Cross-Stitch

Also see Bead Crafts, General Needlecraft Supplies, Miniature Making, Needlepoint, Quilting, Sewing and other related categories.

ANGEL STITCH

1588 E. March Lane, #3F
Stockton, CA 95210
(209) 472-7519
Fax: (209) 472-0919

Offers: Supplies for cross-stitch, needlepoint, Brazilian silk ribbon work, and others. Also offers pulled thread and silk and metal embroidery.
For Further Information: Send SASE.

ARTISAN DESIGN

2208 South Elder Circle
Broken Arrow, OK 74012
(800) 747-8263

Offers: Line of needlework stands, including floor, table and portable models, with Lockscroll pinchlock system for secure fabric attachment through tension knobs/scrolling and tightening, in a variety of sizes.

BECAUSE YOU COUNT, INC.

P.O. Box 610
Dora, AL 35062
(800) 605-3003 or (205) 648-2220

Offers: Custom cross stitch kits from personal photos or artwork. Service provides any size patterns using DMC floss and background removal.

BERNADINE'S NEEDLE ART

911 E. Columbia St.
P.O. Box 41
Arthur, IL 61911
(217) 543-2996

Offers: Supplies, pattern kits, threads and ribbon for embroidery, including punchneedle, bullion stitch and silk ribbon; crazy quilt embellishments and punch needles—Igolochkoy to large and other accessories. Patterns include dollhouse rubs, chenille bedspreads and 3-D bullion stitch combined with quilting in rise designs. Also offers silk ribbon embroidery kits and a line of books.
For Further Information: Catalog, $2; $3 in Canada.

CANTERBURY DESIGNS, INC.

P.O. Box 204060
Martinez, GA 30917
(706) 860-1674
Fax: (706) 860-9614

Offers: Over 80 cross-stitch books, leaflets: original and reproduced samplers, scenes, miniatures, holiday motifs, baby, florals, quilts, borders, others.
For Further Information: Call or write.
Discounts: Teachers and institutions; sells wholesale to legitimate businesses.

COHERENT VISUAL

204 N. El Camino Real
Suite E 229N
Encinitas, CA 92924
(619) 944-8973

Offers: Computer program for cross stitch and plastic canvas patterns, including Windows, DOS and Macintosh versions.
For Further Information: Call for free pattern and details.

COMPUCRAFTS

P.O. Box 6326
Lincoln Center, MA 01773

Offers: Cross-stitch design software to create designs manually or automatically from any color picture.
For Further Information: Call or write.

COMPU STITCH

P.O. Box 157
Syracuse, NY 13206
(800) 445-3661

Offers: Custom cross-stitch and needlepoint charts and kits from photos or artwork, including full-color graphs and keychart, printout, and background removal. Other options also available.

CRAFTS BY DONNA

P.O. Box 1456
Costa Mesa, CA 92628
(714) 545-8567

Offers: Supplies/kits for Brazilian embroidery, battenberg lace, trapunto, ribbon embroidery, others.
For Further Information: Catalog, $2.

CRAFTSMEN'S STUDIO

2727 Ring Rd.
Greensboro, NC 27405

Offers: Line of Zweigart fabric in every count, color and kind. Also offers duplicate stitch sweaters, patterns and porcelain buttons.
For Further Information: Catalog, $3.

THE CROSS STITCH

574 Main St.
Harwichport, MA 02646
(508) 432-1669

Offers: Cross stitch patterns in Cape Cod designs and custom framing service.
For Further Information: Call or write for catalog.

DAISY CHAIN

P.O. Box 1258
Parkersburg, WV 26102
(304) 428-9500

Offers: Embroidery fabrics including silk gauze, a ver a soie silk, others. Also offers Balger metallic ribbons, gold- and platinum-plated needles, accessories, charted design cross-stitch books, resource books, needleworker's hand cream.
For Further Information: Catalog, $2.
Discounts: Quantity.

DAVIC COMPUTER SERVICES, INC.

P.O. Box 750141
New Orleans, LA 70715
(800) 231-3480

Offers: "EasyGrapher" computer program for designing needlework charts. Program will cut/paste, copy, rotate or mirror designs. It is IBM PC compatible and prints with HP LaserJet II or graphics printer.
For Further Information: Call.
Discounts: Sells wholesale.
Accepts: MasterCard, Visa

EMBROIDERY MACHINE

P.O. Box 599
Pawtucket, RI 02862
(401) 272-0380

Offers: Automatic punch embroidery tool ("up to 500 stitches a minute"). Use with all punch patterns/materials, it's push button. Spool on the end feeds thread. Available in 3 needle sizes, battery-powered. Also offered as kit. Pattern books are available.
Accepts: MasterCard, Visa

FANCY STITCHES

104 Lakewood Dr.
Battle Creek, MI 49015
(616) 962-6110

Offers: Sampler cross-stitch kits of nineteenth-century family records, including personalized records, genealogy, family, marriage and birth records and others.
For Further Information: Catalog, $2.

FANCYWORK

2708 Slaterville Rd.
P.O. Box 130
Slaterville Springs, NY 14881
(607) 539-6610

Offers: 10,000 cross-stitch books—most all design categories: Country, classic, contemporary, holiday motif, men, women, children, babies, whimsical, Oriental, Western, nautical, early American, flowers, wild and domestic animals, scenes, geometrics and many others in mini to large sizes. Accessories for cross-stitch are also available.
For Further Information: Catalog, $2.75 prepaid. Newsletter, $4 for 6 issues per year.

5 T'S EMBROIDERY SUPPLY

P.O. Box 484
Macedon, NY 14502
(315) 986-8434
Fax: (315) 986-8436

Offers: Line of machine embroidery supplies, including threads, backings, scissors and nippers, Oxford dress shirts, needles and other notions.
For Further Information: Call or write for free catalog.
Accepts: MasterCard, Visa

HH DESIGNS

P.O. Box 183
Eastchester, NY 10709

Offers: Line of candlewick (colonial needlecraft) pillow kits—simple embroidery stitches in a variety of designs. Also offers white work embroidery in square, round and bolster pillow forms.
For Further Information: Catalog, $2.

IN STITCHES

P.O. Box 8014
Blaine, WA 98231
(800) GO TO SEW

Offers: Custom cross-stitch service: hand charting of photos of home, car, logos, others.
For Further Information: Catalog, $1 (refundable).

INTERNATIONAL HOUSE OF BUNKA, INC.

19 Tulane Crescent
Don Mills, Ontario M3A 2B9
Canada
(416) 445-1875
Fax: (416) 444-6705

Offers: Japanese bunka embroidery punch needle supplies, kits, accessories and threads. Also carries teach-yourself starter kits and instruction books. Custom framing service. Holds classes.
For Further Information: Write or call for price lists.
Discounts: Sells wholesale.

JUST NEEDLIN'

611 NE Woods Chapel
Lee's Summit, MO 64064
(816) 246-5102

Offers: Cross-stitch fabrics: Aida (colors), Alice, Alma, Anne, coverner block, Damask, Davos, Fiddlers, Floba, Gloria, Hampton, Hearthside, Hopscotch, Jobelan, Klostern, Linda, linens, Loomspun, Melinda, Monza, Patrice, Rustico, Shenandoah, others. Also offers DMC, Balger, Ginny Thompson and filament threads. Carries perforated papers, projects (with inserts), hoops, scroll frames, magnifiers and other aids, and over 1,200 design chart booklets.
For Further Information: Catalog, $3 (refundable).

KATRINA'S BITS & BOBS

18129 Erik Ct., Suite 328
Canyon Country, CA 91351
(800) 252-1089

Offers: Line of cross-stitch kits, charts, fabrics, threads and accessories, including Anchor, DMC, Zweigart, Charles Craft, Heritage, Lavender & Lace, Teresa Wentzler, Mirabilla and other brands. Search and customizing services available.
For Further Information: Call or send SASE.

KEMP'S KRAFTS

5940 Taylor St.
Coloma, MI 49038

Offers: Plastic canvas/needlework projects for doll furniture.
For Further Information: Send SASE for list.

KREINIK MANUFACTURING CO., INC.

9199 Reistertown Rd., Suite 2098
Owings Mills, MD 21117
(800) 624-1928

Offers: French silk yarns and threads for needlepoint, cross-stitch, embroidered smocking and other; includes Soie d'Alger and other silks, Balger metallics.
For Further Information: Send SASE for sample (specify interest).
Discounts: Sells wholesale.

LJ ORIGINALS, INC.

516 Sumac Place
De Soto, TX 75115
(214) 223-6644
Fax: (214) 223-1431
E-mail: TRNSGRPH@E-TEX.COM
Additional Location: In Montalba, TX
(903) 549-3403
Fax: (903) 549-3506

Offers: "Transgraph X" needleart kit with clear plastic grid overlays which allow craftsperson to convert drawings into charts without hand charting. Available for any needleart of 5 to 25 count per inch; calculates size, reduces and enlarges patterns.
For Further Information: Catalog, $1 (refundable).
Discounts: Quantity; sells wholesale to legitimate businesses.

M&R TECHNOLOGIES, INC.

P.O. Box 9403, Wright Brothers Branch
Dayton, OH 45409
(513) 294-1983

Offers: PC Stitch for Windows software for cross-stitch pattern designs, including patterns to 500 stitches, 64 colors in DMC or other brand colors; draws, copies and more.
For Further Information: Send SASE.

MARILYN'S NEEDLEWORK & FRAMES

4336 Plainfield Ave. NE
Grand Rapids, MI 49505
(616) 364-8411

Offers: Stoney Creek Collection cross-stitch designs/kits, plus a wide selection of fabrics. Also offers Balger blending filaments, fibers, DMC and Anchor Floss.
For Further Information: Catalog, $6.

MARY JANE'S CROSS 'N STITCH, INC.

1948 Keim Ct.
Naperville, IL 60565
(709) 355-0071

Offers: Over 1,200 stitchery books and leaflets, embroidery

fabrics (Aida, linens, others) and variety of fibers and floss.
For Further Information: Catalog and stitchery guide, $7.50 (refundable).

MASTER STITCH DESIGNS, INC.

P.O. Box 6283
Kent, WA 98064
(206) 413-1054
Fax. (206) 432-6511

Offers: MSD CrossStitch Designer V3.0 computer program. Includes paint program, charts and color code legend, with up to 120 colors per image. Includes DMC line prints to laser; Deskjet or dot matrix with stitch counter.

MEISTERGRAM

3517 W. Wendover Ave.
Greensboro, NC 27407

Offers: Monogramming and embroidery equipment and supplies (also training, service and marketing know-how).
For Further Information: Write.

MENS SANA

P.O. Box 530
Naperville, IL 60566

Offers: Line of "Zoids" contemporary designs with optical blending techniques using overdyed fiber colors.
For Further Information: Catalog, 55¢ and large SASE; chart and catalog, $6.

OXFORD CRAFT SOFTWARE

P.O. Box 208
Bonsall, CA 92003
(800) 995-0420

Offers: X-Stitch Designer Gold—software for Microsoft windows.
For Further Information: Call or send SASE.

PANTOGRAMS MANUFACTURING CO., INC.

4537 Dale Mabry Hwy.
Tampa, FL 33611
(813) 839-5697 or (800) 812-1555

Offers: Embroidery and monogramming systems.
For Further Information: Write or call.

ANNE POWELL LTD.

P.O. Box 3060
Stuart, FL 34995
(407) 287-3007

Offers: Counted cross-stitch charts, kits, Glenshee linen, Solingen embroidery scissors, plus antique sewing tools, informative books and gift items for needlecrafters.

For Further Information: Catalog, $5.
Discounts: Sells wholesale to legitimate businesses.

PURE CHINA SILK CO.

Rt. 2
P.O. Box 70
Holdrege, NE 68949
(308) 995-4755

Offers: Silk embroidery threads in 14-yard skeins and multi-strand twist threads in 64 colors for embroidery, cross-stitch, needlepunch, petit point, etc.
For Further Information: Color card, $1.25.
Discounts: Quantity.

RIBBONS & ROSES

13626 Dornock Ct.
Herndon, VA 22071
(703) 435-0150
Fax: (703) 787-7558

Offers: Silk ribbon in over 150 colors in 4 mm to 32 mm widths. Kanagawa silk embroidery threads, Rajmahal art silks, DMC machine embroidery threads and YLI Ultrasheet and Candlelight threads. Also offers Seta-Color dye for silk ribbon, royal stitch embroidery wool and others. Holds classes.
For Further Information: Catalog, $2 (refundable).

ROBISON-ANTON TEXTILE CO.

P.O. Box 159
Fairview, NJ 07022
(201) 941-0500

Offers: Super Luster embroidery floss on 1-lb cones of 6-strand mercerized cotton; available in 228 colors. Specializes in cones for kit manufacturers.
For Further Information: Contact your dealer, or send SASE.

EVA ROSENSTAND

P.O. Box 185
Clovis, CA 93613
(209) 292-2241

Offers: Cross-stitch kits and designs from Denmark in a wide array of traditional and classic designs—people, scenes, flowers, animals, other motifs.
For Further Information: Catalog, $4.50.

SANDEEN'S

1315 White Bear Ave.
St. Paul, MN 55106
(612) 776-7012 or (800) 235-1315

Offers: Scandinavian, Norwegian and Danish Embroidery/handcraft supplies: Swedish kits, Hardanger supplies, brack-

ets, others. Also offers a giftware catalog at no charge.
For Further Information: Needlecraft catalog, $3 (refundable).

SEW ORIGINAL NEEDLEART

6423 Ming Ave. #A
Bakersfield, CA 93309
(805) 832-9276
Fax: (805) 832-0597

Offers: Evenweave fabrics selection, threads (metallics, DMC, others), fibers, stitching aids, kits, books.
For Further Information: Catalog, $3.

STITCH IN TIME

P.O. Box 317
Spring Lake, MI 49456
(616) 847-0063

Offers: Service: Custom color cross-stitch charting from photographs—any subject.
For Further Information: Send SASE for brochure.

THE STRAWBERRY SAMPLER

#7 Olde Ridge Village
Chadds Ford, PA 19317
(610) 459-8580

Offers: Cross-stitch kits (some with framing kits): Samplers, florals, Oriental, Danish, traditional, quotations, holiday motifs, samplers, state; many designs are printed on home accessories. Kits: afghans, pillows. 85 Fabrics: Klostern, Aida, Fiddler, Loomspun, Rustico, Congress, Hardanger, linens, Jobelan, afghan types. Magnifiers, waste canvas. Also offers accessories, framing supplies/kits and design books.
For Further Information: Color catalog, $3.50.
Accepts: MasterCard, Visa

STRINGS 'N THINGS

1228 Blossom Terrace
Boiling Springs, PA 17007
(717) 258-6022

Offers: Threads: Marlitt, silk, metallic, wool, tatting, embroidery/tapestry cottons, cutwork, Pearl cotton, DMC and Baroque (and other) crochet cottons, Persian wool, Balger filaments and braid.

For Further Information: Send SASE.
Discounts: Quantity.

THEO-STITCH

P.O. Box 543
Hopewill, VA 23860
(804) 530-0386 or (800) 336-8846

Offers: Custom cross-stitch patterns and kits from submitted photograph or artwork.
For Further Information: Write or call.

THUMBELINA NEEDLEWORK SHOP

P.O. Box 1065
Solvang, CA 93464
(805) 688-4136

Offers: Full line of counted-thread designs (charts and kits with Aida floss, chart): classics, traditional, other motifs.
For Further Information: Send SASE.

TWILIGHT DESIGNS

2051 Robinwood Dr.
Algonquin, IL 60102
(708) 854-9367

Offers: Custom cross-stitch patterns and kits from photographs and artwork, including color DMC chart and symbols—only chart to 380 × 380 stitches, and optional J & P Coats and Anchor floss numbers.
For Further Information: Call or send SASE.

WONDER PUNCH

10 Pinelands Ave.
Stoney Creek, Ontario L8E 3A5
Canada
(905) 662-8116
Fax: (905) 662-8179

Offers: Needle-punch embroidery accessories in 3 kit sizes, including acrylic metallics, angel hair and needle paks, hot iron-on transfers, rug punching kits including starter, and interchangeable "Side-A-Loop" needle kit for three different yarn thicknesses.
For Further Information: Send for price list and nearest dealer location, or order directly.
Discounts: Sells wholesale to businesses.

Fabric Decorating

Also see Bead Crafts, General Needlecraft Supplies, Batik and Dyeing, Embroidery and Cross-Stitch, Fabrics and Trims and Sewing.

THE ART STORE
935 Erie Blvd. E.
Syracuse, NY 13210
(315) 474-1000

Offers: Fiber arts/crafts supplies and equipment: jacquard textile and silk paints, batik, screen printing, marbling, beads, others.
For Further Information: Complete list, $3.
See Also: General Craft Supplies

ART QUILTERS STUDIO
513 Madison Ave.
Redwood City, CA 94061

Offers: Dyes, textile paints and inks, batik tools, metallic thread, cotton prints, dyeing fabrics, notions and books.
For Further Information: Send large SASE for free catalog. 4″ swatches, $5.

ARTISTICALLY INCLINED, INC.
463 Commerce Park Dr.
Marietta, GA 30060
(770) 419-8176

Offers: "Blank" fashions for decorating, including denim shirts, vests and dresses, 50/50 knit pants sets in 16 colors, including children's, petites, one size and plus sizes.

ATELIER DE PARIS
1543 S. Robertson Blvd.
Los Angeles, CA 90035
(310) 553-6636
Fax: (213) 939-2637

Offers: Lines of products for silk painting and fabric decorating, including 180 colors of Dupont dyes and Rocco all-fabric head-set colors and pearl paints. Also offers silk scarves and ties, panels and jewelry blanks. Findings, marbling supplies and kits, picot stretch frames and stretching pins, brushes, magic applicators, refill markers, steaming and sewing supplies also available.
For Further Information: Send SASE.

BLUEPRINTS-PRINTABLE
1504 #7 Industrial Way
Belmont, CA 94002
(415) 594-2995

Offers: Blueprinting design and print kits, sweatshirts, and T-shirts for cyanotype; clothing and accessory blanks in woven fabric; and fabric yardage, including silks, rayons, cotton sheeting, knits. Also offers accessories, including earrings, ties, scarves, silk notions, findings, others.
For Further Information: Catalog and fabric samples, $3.

BY JUPITER!
7146 N. 58th Dr.
Glendale, AZ 85301
(602) 931-2658

Offers: Fabric fading kit and pictures, fabric transfer gel, over 1,100 brass and silver plated charms and findings.
For Further Information: Catalog, $5.
Discounts: Wholesale available.

COLLINS CREATIONS
Rt. 1
P.O. Box 1562
Streetman, TX 75859
(800) 374-4078

Offers: Ultrasuede appliqué patterns (and instructions) in a variety of designs for surface decorating. Also offers ultrasuede by piece and by yard.
For Further Information: Catalog, $2 (refundable).

COLORCRAFT, LTD.
14 Airport Park Rd.
East Granby, CT 06026
(860) 653-5505

Offers: Createx colors (acrylics), kits, plus glitter powders, adhesives, mediums, "perma seal," marble colors, foils, others. Instructional videos on fabric painting are also available.
For Further Information: Contact your dealer, or write for catalog.
Accepts: MasterCard, Visa

CRAFT INDUSTRIES LIMITED
P.O. Box 38
Somerset, MA 01716
(508) 676-3883
Fax: (509) 676-3980

Offers: Surface decorating colors, including Country Clas-

sics dyes for wool and other fabrics, fabric paints in neon, puff, pearlescents, tie-dye kits, marbling paints.
For Further Information: Send SASE.

DECART, INC.
Lamoille Industrial Park
P.O. Box 309
Morrisville, VT 05661
(802) 888-4217

Offers: Deka line of fabric paints in a full array of colors. Also offers paints for other craft uses and a series of kits. Manufacturer.
For Further Information: See your dealer, or send SASE.

DELTA TECHNICAL COATINGS, INC.
2550 Pellissier Place
Whittier, CA 90601
(213) 686-0678

Offers: Delta fabric dyes, colors, glitter, Shiny and Swell Stuff and Stichless glue, plus Ceramcoat acrylics, Shiva Signa-Tex acrylic paints and Marble-Thix powder (water base) for marbling.
For Further Information: Send large SASE for free color guide.

DESIGNS BY DEBBIE MITCHELL
304 W. Cheryl Ave.
Hurst, TX 76053
(817) 282-6890

Offers: Iron-on transfer designs, including whimsical animals (bears, reindeer, chickens, others), holiday motifs, others; by packets. Books also available.
For Further Information: Catalog, $4.

DHARMA TRADING CO.
P.O. Box 150916
San Rafael, CA 94915
(800) 542-5227

Offers: Fabric paints, Pientex silk inks, Deka-silk and metallics, Texticolor iridescent, Versatex textile paint, dyes. Also offers fabric pens, brushes, jars, gloves, squeeze bottles. Carries T-shirt and other cotton fabrics, T-shirts, T-dresses and pants, silk fabrics, silk and cotton scarves, and a line of dyes and batik products.
For Further Information: Free catalog.
Discounts: Quantity.
Accepts: MasterCard, Visa

EXTRA SPECIAL PRODUCTS CORP.
P.O. Box 777
Greenville, OH 45331
(800) 648-5945 or (513) 548-9388
Fax: (513) 548-9580

Offers: Surface decoratives: Flex-O-Mirro, "Razzles" se-

quin pieces and "grass," Fuzzy Wuzzy iron-on velour sheets, foils, copper sheets, templates, black transfers, jewelry findings and trace-a-shapes.
For Further Information: Free catalog.
Discounts: Teachers, institutions and professionals; sells wholesale to legitimate businesses.

FC&A'S TRANSFER PATTERNS
103 Clover Green
Peachtree City, GA 30269

Offers: Iron-on transfer patterns (for clothing) in country designs, whimsical and other animals, Southwest motifs, 20s, circus clowns, dinosaurs, bows, holiday motifs, others; by packets and collections. Also offers pattern books for quilting, crochet and woodworking.
For Further Information: Send SASE for list.

FLORA MULTIMEDIA & CO.
4801 Marble Ave. NE
Albuquerque, NM 87110
(505) 255-9988

Offers: Silkscreen printing video (with workbook) for home workshop—presents progressive techniques to print on fabrics (and other flat surfaces); includes supply sources data.
For Further Information: Send SASE.
Accepts: American Express

G.H.T.A. CO.
5303 Holly Springs Dr.
Houston, TX 77056
(713) 683-7900

Offers: Cotton and 50/50 blend plain clothing: T-shirts and sweatshirts, leggings, long T-shirts, golf shirts, shorts, others.
For Further Information: Catalog, $2.
Discounts: Sells wholesale.

GRAMMA'S GRAPHICS
20 Birling Gap, Dept. TCSS-P6
Fairport, NY 14450
(716) 223-4309
Fax: (716) 223-4789

Offers: Fabric and paper "Sun Print" kits—fabric images derived by printing photo negatives, objects, stencils, or cutouts on material treated with a light-sensitive solution; sun exposure turns prints blue. Designs are permanent and washable. Also offers untreated cotton print cloth by the yard, refill kits, assembly instructions for heirloom portrait quilt and sun print pillows. Toning instructions for changing to other colors to make line or halftone negatives. Classroom/group sun kits for notecards and gift tags.
For Further Information: Brochure, $1 and large SASE.
Discounts: Quantity; sells wholesale.

IMAGINATION STATION
P.O. Box 2157
White City, OR 97503
(800) 338-3857

Offers: Photographs transferred to fabric: black-and-white, color, sepia. Enlarges, reduces, customized to order (photos returned).
For Further Information: Free brochure.
Accepts: MasterCard, Visa

IVY IMPORTS, INC.
6806 Trexler Rd.
Lanham, MD 20706
(301) 474-7347
Fax: (301) 441-2395

Offers: Visionart instant set silk dyes and the Silk Experience kits. Fabrics: silk, cottons. Also offers Tinfix and Silktint colors, fabric pens, paints, additives, resists, brushes and steamers. Instructional videos with Diane Tuckman and Naomi Barsk; silk painting books are also available.
For Further Information: Contact your dealer, or send SASE. Catalog, $3.
Discounts: Quantity; teachers, institutions and businesses.

CAROLYN KYLE ENTERPRISES, INC.
2840 E. Black Lake Blvd. SW
Olympia, WA 98512
(360) 352-4427 or (800) 428-7402

Offers: Line of stained glass pattern books.
For Further Information: Send SASE.

LAURATEX FABRICS
153 W. 27th St.
New York, NY 10001
(212) 645-7800

Offers: Cotton fabrics prepared for painting and screen painting: Sateen, ottoman, batiste, linens.
For Further Information: Send SASE for information.

M & M TRIMS
91 S. Main Plaza
Wilkes-Barre, PA 18701
(717) 825-7305
Fax: (717) 825-7436

Offers: Swarovski rhinestones, beads, sequins, pearls, mirrors, feathers, appliques, nailheads and others.
For Further Information: Brochure, $1 and SASE.
Discounts: Wholesale available.

PENTEL OF AMERICA, LTD.
2805 Columbia St.
Torrance, CA 90503

Offers: Line of Fabric Fun pastel dye sticks (for natural fabrics). Also offers artist's pastels, watercolors, pens and adhesives.
For Further Information: See your dealer, or send SASE.
Discounts: Quantity.

PHOTOGRAPHER'S FORMULARY CO.
P.O. Box 950
Condon, MT 59826
(800) 922-5255

Offers: Cyanotype and Van Dyke kits for transfer of photo negative images onto fabric. Kit allows 24 8 × 10 images, and chemicals are pre-measured with instructions in blue print or other optional colors. Also offers photographic chemicals.

PRO CHEMICAL & DYE, INC.
P.O. Box 14
Somerset, MA 02726
(508) 676-3838
Fax: (508) 676-3980

Offers: Full line of dyes for silkscreen, handpainting, batik, other, including permanent cold-water types that are washfast. Also offers pigments, marbling items, fluorescents and auxiliaries.
For Further Information: Free catalog.
Discounts: Quantity; sells wholesale.

QUALIN INTERNATIONAL, INC.
P.O. Box 31145
San Francisco, CA 94131
(415) 333-8500

Offers: Silk scarf blanks imported from China, with hand-rolled hems. Also offers scarf assortments and silk fabrics.
For Further Information: Send SASE for list.
Discounts: Quantity.

SILKPAINT CORP.
P.O. Box 18
Waldron, MO 64092
(816) 891-7774

Offers: Silkpaint! resist, Fiber-Etch fiber remover for cotton, linen and rayons, plus silkpaint kits and air-powered resist pens.
For Further Information: Free catalog.
Discounts: Teachers and institutions; sells wholesale to legitimate businesses.
Accepts: MasterCard, Visa

SOHO SOUTH

P.O. Box 1324
Cullman, AL 35056
(800) 280-6520

Offers: Fabric dyes and paints, marbling materials, Czech glass beads, precious metal findings, silk painting and batik supplies.
For Further Information: Free catalog.

SUREWAY TRADING ENTERPRISES

826 Pine Ave., #5
Niagara Falls, NY 14301
(716) 282-4887

Offers: Line of silk fabrics and scarves, French dyes for painting and airbrush.
For Further Information: Free catalog.
Discounts: Quantity; sells wholesale.

TEXTILE COLORS

P.O. Box 887
Riverdale, MD 20738
(800) 783-9265

Offers: FabricArts all-fabric paints and mediums, dyes, sample and other painting kits. Also offers silk and wool fabrics and silk scarves. Carries tools, brushes, accessories, chemicals, cleaners, videos and books.
For Further Information: Catalog and color charts, $2.
Discounts: Quantity; teachers, institutions and professionals.

J. TREAR DESIGNS

2121 Slater St.
Santa Rosa, CA 95404
(707) 523-2840

Offers: All cotton clothing (for painting or dyeing): Fleece, crinkle cotton, sheeting and cotton lycra.

For Further Information: Catalog and swatches, $1.
Discounts: Quantity.

WEB OF THREAD

3240 Lone Oak Rd., Suite 124
Paducah, KY 42003
(502) 554-8185

Offers: Machine embroidery threads, couching braids, cords, ribbons (silk, rayon, metallics, others).
For Further Information: Catalog, $2.

THE WOODEN HEART

Rt. 11
P.O. Box 2260
Elizabethton, TN 37643
(423) 543-5602

Offers: Line of fabric pattern packets: decorative designs (tole-like whimsical and country) including holiday motifs, scenes, rabbits, flowers for dolls.
For Further Information: Send 2 stamps for brochure.
Discounts: Sells wholesale.

YESTERDAYS

P.O. Box 4308
Scottsdale, AZ 85261
(602) 201-5732

Offers: Service: iron-on transfers made from photos, drawings or sketches—full-color up to 11″×17″; for fabric surfaces.
For Further Information: Send SASE.
Accepts: MasterCard, Visa

Fabrics and Trims

Also see most other categories in Section II.

ARISE

6925 Willow St. SW
Washington, DC 20012
(202) 291-0770
Fax: (202) 291-2073
E-mail: ARISEDC@AOL.COM

Offers: Japanese silk kimono-bundle or hand-picked line of other Japanese textiles, including obi, Kasurilyukata, silk, serape and other. Also offers Morrocan, Indonesian, Phillipine, Japanese and Chinese artifacts and furniture.
For Further Information: Send SASE.
Store Location: At above address. Hours: M-Sat, 10:30-6. Sun 11-5.

ASF (ALL SISTERS FABRICS)

4115 Brownsville Rd.
Pittsburgh, PA 15227
(412) 881-6777

Offers: Silks, wools, cottons, others. Also offers buttons and patterns.
For Further Information: Bimonthly swatches, $10 yearly.
Store Location: At above address. Hours: M-Sat, 10-5, Th, 10-7
Discounts: Available

ASLI ARTS

Box 1198
Freeland, WA 98249
(360) 331-4122
Fax: (360) 331-1946

Offers: Indonesian textiles, including ikat weavings from Sumba, Savu, Sumatra, Lomblen and other islands; Bali and Java batik fabrics.
For Further Information: Write for photos and prices.

AVENRICH

900 S. Santa Fe Dr. #C
Denver, CO 80223
(303) 722-3056
Fax: (303) 722-3093

Offers: Line of leather hides, soft drum dyed in variety of colors.
For Further Information: Swatches, $3.

BAER FABRICS

515 E. Market St.
Louisville, KY 40202
(502) 569-7010 or (800) 769-7776
Fax: (502) 582-2331

Offers: Line of fabrics including Ultrasuede, Bengaline faille, catchet lace, chiffon-polyester, cotton lycra, fine bridal satin lining, industrial felts, trunk liner, laminette, nugget cloth, polyester satin, re-embroidered gallcon lace, silk dupioni, stretch nude (Glissnet, lycra, Powernet), theatrical fabrics, and more.
For Further Information: Sewing notion/trims catalog, $3, or $2 per sample set card for specific fabric
Store Location: At above address. Hours: M, 9-9. T-Sat, 9-5:30

BARBEAU FINE FABRICS

1308-A Birch St.
Fort Collins, CO 80521
(970) 221-9697

Offers: Members get 4 mailings yearly of fashion fabric swatches: silks, wools, cottons, others.
For Further Information: Swatch service, $12 yearly (with binder).

SONYA LEE BARRINGTON

837 47th Ave.
San Francisco, CA 94121
(415) 221-6510

Offers: Hand-dyed cotton fabrics, including over 300 solids, variety of patterns.
For Further Information: Swatches, $5.
Accepts: MasterCard, Visa

BATIKS ETCETERA

411 Pine St.
Fort Mill, SC 29715
(800) BATIKS-ETC

Offers: Hoffman "batiks," Indonesian and African wax batiks, cottons, rayons; Roberta Horton stripes and plaids, and others.
For Further Information: Swatches, $5.

THE BINDING STITCH

8 Taunton Ave.
Dennis, MA 02638
(508) 385-2444
Fax: (508) 385-2444

Offers: Dressmaker cotton velveteens (31 colors), needlepoint finishing services, full anchor fibers, blocking kits.
For Further Information: Swatch cards, $10.
Store Location: At above address. Hours: M-F, 9:30-3:30.
Accepts: MasterCard, Visa

BRITEX-BY-MAIL

146 Geary St.
San Francisco, CA 94108
(415) 392-2910

Offers: Fashion fabrics in a variety of domestic/imported cottons, blends, silks, linens, rayons, woolens, knits, spandex, others.
For Further Information: Swatch service available. Specify needs, describing garment/yardage and fiber wanted, price restrictions; for personal consultation include $5.
Store Location: At above address. Hours: M, T, W, Fri, Sat, 9:30-6. Th, 9:30-8.
Accepts: American Express, MasterCard, Visa

SAWYER BROOK DISTINCTIVE FABRICS

P.O. Box 1800
Clinton, MA 01510
(508) 368-3133

Offers: Collection of imported and domestic fabrics—natural cottons and blends, silks, linens, denims, outing flannels, batik fabrics, others.
For Further Information: Send SASE for samples.
Accepts: MasterCard, Visa

THE BUTTON EMPORIUM

P.O. Box 1628
Portland, OR 97207
(503) 228-6372

Offers: Line of studio buttons by American artists including porcelain reproductions of Victorian designs in sterling and brass. Also offers other handcrafted selections, including birds, cats, frogs, angels, hearts, dolphins, eagles, roses in porcelain, pewter, polymer clay and 24K gold inlay; sterling with gemstones.
For Further Information: Catalog, $2.
Accepts: MasterCard, Visa

BUTTON FACTORY

8205 Santa Monica Blvd. Unit # 1-212
West Hollywood, CA 90046
(310) 659-7307

Offers: Line of buttons in wood, metal, plastic, cotton, rubber and aluminum in a variety of sizes.
For Further Information: Catalog and samples on request.

CAROLINA MILLS

P.O. Box V, Highway 76 W.
Branson, MO 65616
(417) 334-2291
Fax: (417) 334-8884

Offers: Polyesters, doubleknits, gabardines, silks, challis, jacquards, crepe de chine, velours, shirting, fleece, lamé, wools and blends, flannel, denim, linings, ultrasuede, lace, tapestries, vinyls, upholstery, calico, Christmas and others. Also offers pillow panels, quilt squares and craft stamps.
For Further Information: Color cards for three fabrics, $2.

CENTURY LEATHER

P.O. Box 256
Wakefield, MA 01880
(617) 245-6171
Fax: (617) 245-1557

Offers: Garment leathers, including French butts, English sides, shoulders, both suedes and smooth-sided types, plus dyes and finishes. Also offers upholstery leather, upholstery tools and accessories.
For Further Information: Catalog and swatches, $1.

CINEMA LEATHERS

1663 Blake Ave.
Los Angeles, CA 90031
(213) 222-0073
Fax: (213) 222-8221

Offers: Line of garment leathers, including suedes and others—lamb, pig, cow, novelties, foils, others.
For Further Information: Send SASE.
Store Location: At above address. Hours: M-F, 8-5.
Discounts: Quantity; sells wholesale to legitimate businesses.

CODE FELT LTD.

P.O. Box 130
Perth, Ontario K7H 3E3
Canada
(613) 267-2464
Fax: (613) 264-0261

Offers: Felt, burlap, vinyl, other fabrics and craft items.
For Further Information: Shade cards, coupon, $3.

Discounts: Quantity; teachers and institutions; sells wholesale to legitimate businesses.
Accepts: MasterCard, Visa

THE COTTON SHOPPE
P.O. Box 3168
Key Largo, FL 33037
(800) 856-4923

Offers: Lines of known-brand fabrics including Hoffman, RJR, Kona Bay and many others. Fabric club offers member specials.
For Further Information: Allows a 600-swatch loaner service without charge. Call and leave your name, address, phone and MasterCard or Visa number and expiration date (used as security deposit until swatches are returned).

D'ANTON LEATHER COMPANY
5530 Vincent Ave., N.E.
West Branch, IA 52358
(319) 643-2568

Offers: Full line of luxury garment leathers: suedes, smooth and fun types in a variety of colors, textures and finishes.
For Further Information: $2 and SASE.
Discounts: Quantity; sells wholesale to legitimate businesses and professionals.

DIMPLES
101 Sunset
Collinsville, IL 62234

Offers: Line of children's fabrics; seasonal selections.
For Further Information: Swatch mailings (1 year), coupon, $5 (Canada, $8).

EVENING STAR DESIGNS
69 Coolidge Ave.
Haverhill, MA 01832
(800) 666-3562

Offers: Line of sewing trims including silk ribbons, Shisha mirrors, stone animal beads, charms, glass and porcelain buttons, sew-on beads, and others. Also offers embroidery threads.
For Further Information: Catalog, $3.

FABRIC GALLERY
146 W. Grand River
Williamston, MI 48895
(517) 655-4573

Offers: Fashion fabrics: imported/domestic silks, wools, cottons. Line of buttons, others.
For Further Information: Swatches service, silk, wool gabardine or cotton shirtings, each $4, or all three for $10.

Store Location: At above address. Hours: M-Sat, 10-5. Th, 10-8.

FABRICS UNLIMITED
5015 Columbia Pike
Arlington, VA 22204
(703) 671-0325
Fax: (703) 671-0324

Offers: Ultrasuede and many other designer fabrics (including Adele Simpson, Calvin Klein, others and exclusives).
For Further Information: Send SASE; ultrasuede color card (over 30 colors), $4
Store Location: At above address. Hours: M, T, W, F, Sat, 10-6. Th, 10-8.
Discounts: Quantity; teachers, professionals and institutions.

FAMOUS LABELS FABRIC OUTLET
2155 E. Burnside
Gresham, OR 97030
(503) 666-3187

Offers: Club plan— members join with yearly fee, receive monthly mailers of swatches of designer sports and active wear fabrics, including rayons, cottons, wools, lycras; knits and wovens.
For Further Information: Sample, $4.
Discounts: Outlet prices.

FASHION FABRICS CLUB
10490 Baur Blvd.
St. Louis, MO 63132
(800) 468-0602

Offers: Club plan—members join with yearly fee and receive monthly swatch kits of designer fabrics including Liz Claiborne, Blassport, Villager, Herman Geist, Leslie Fay, Koret, Jones N.Y., Evan Picone, Polo and others.
For Further Information: Membership, $4.95. (U.S. only).
Accepts: MasterCard, Visa

FAY'S FASHION FABRICS
1155 Webster Dr.
Pensacola, FL 32505
(904) 455-2410

Offers: Line of lingerie fabrics and Kwik-Sew pattern line.
For Further Information: Catalog, samples, coupon, $5.
Discounts: Sells wholesale; Kwik-Sew patterns at discount.

FIELD'S FABRICS
1695 44th SE
Grand Rapids, MI 49508
(616) 455-4570
Fax: (616) 455-1052

Offers: Fabrics: Cuddleskin brushed back satin sleepwear,

Polo cotton interlock, silks, Canton fleece, cotton, washable bridal satins, metallic fabrics, Pendleton wools.
For Further Information: Specify swatch sets, $4 each. Swatches, $10 (refundable) for: Ultrasuede, Facile and Ultraleather in over 75 colors
Store Location: At above address. Hours: M-Sat, 9-9.
Accepts: Discover, MasterCard, Visa

FISHMAN'S FABRICS
1101-43 S. Desplaines St.
Chicago, IL 60607
(312) 922-7250

Offers: Line of designer fabrics including woolens, silks, linens, velvets and cottons.
For Further Information: Call with specific sample request.

J. FLORA
1831 Hyde St.
San Francisco, CA 94109
(415) 824-4636

Offers: Soft suede scraps (for trims, appliqués, crafts) by pound of mixed colors.
For Further Information: Send SASE for list.
Discounts: Quantity.

G STREET FABRICS
12240 Wilkins Ave.
Rockville, MD 20852
(301) 231-8690 or (800) 333-9191
Fax: (301) 231-9155

Offers: Line of known brand fashion fabrics. Also offers portfolio selection service with monthly mailings—over 700 selections yearly. Fabric sample charts on ultrasuede and Ambience Demberg rayon lining. Custom sample service. Fees refundable with orders.
For Further Information: Inquire with SASE.
Store Location: At above address. Hours: M-Sat, 10-9, Sun, 11-6.
Discounts: Professional discounts available.
Accepts: MasterCard, Visa

GLOBAL VILLAGE IMPORTS
3439 NE Sandy Blvd. #263
Portland, OR 97232
(503) 236-9245

Offers: Line of handloomed ikat cottons from Mayan weavers in bright colors and exotic designs.
For Further Information: Swatch pack, $5.
Discounts: Sells wholesale.

GREAT AMERICAN SEWING FACTORY
8 Croton Dam Rd., Dept. CS
Ossining, NY 10562-2822
(914) 941-7444

Offers: Sewing trims, including laces (eyelet, cotton, cluny, flat, ruffled, others), ribbon assortments, Christmas trims, elastics, velcro, appliqués, ribbon roses, pearls, and other trims.
For Further Information: Catalog, $1.

H.E. GOLDBERG & CO., INC.
9050 Martin Luther King Jr. Way S.
Seattle, WA 98118
Fax: (206) 722-0435

Offers: Tanned furs and skins: large/small quantities—fox, beaver, mink, calfskin, lambskin, muskrat, raccoon, rabbit skin, opossum, reindeer, ermine, others.
For Further Information: Catalog, $1.
Accepts: MasterCard, Visa

HERMES LEATHER
45 West 34th St., Room 1108
New York, NY 10001
(212) 947-1153
Fax: (212) 967-2701

Offers: Line of garment leathers/suedes; hides, pig suede, cabretta, others. Custom colors available.
For Further Information: Send SASE for swatch card.
Store Location: At above address. Hours: M-F, 8-5.
Discounts: Sells wholesale to legitimate businesses.

JEHLOR FANTASY FABRICS
730 Andover Park West
Seattle, WA 98188
(206) 575-8250
Fax: (206) 545-8281

Offers: Specialty fabrics: sequined and beaded fabrics, "cracked ice," metallics, brocades, lamés, satins, chiffons, lycra, stretch satin and nude sheers. Trims: rhinestones, glass beads and jewels, sequins, appliqués/trims, fringe, feathers, others.
For Further Information: Catalog, $5.
Store Location: At above address. Hours: M, 10-9. T-Sat, 10-6. Sun, 1-5.
Discounts: Quantity.

JOSEPH'S COAT
26 Main St.
Peterborough, NH 03458
(603) 924-6683
Fax: (603) 827-3630

Offers: Fabrics, including Indonesian ikat, English lawn, Af-

rican kangas, batik. Also offers findings, fasteners, and rare textile books.
For Further Information: Send SASE.

KENNEBEC WOOL & FUR
Route 32
Windsor, ME 04363
(207) 445-4812

Offers: Specializes in sheepskins.
For Further Information: Write or call for price list.

LACE HEAVEN
2524 Dauphin Island Pkwy.
P.O. Box 50150
Mobile, AL 36605
(334) 478-5644
Fax: (334) 450-0489

Offers: Fabrics: lace, lycra, velour, tricots, stretch lace, T-shirt knits, interfacings, flannels, others. Also offers lace inserts, trims and notions.
For Further Information: Catalogs, $3 (refundable).
Store Location: At above address. Hours: T-Sat, 10-4.
Discounts: Quantity.

THE LEATHER FACTORY, INC.
3847 E. Loop 820
P.O. Box 50429
Fort Worth, TX 76105
(817) 496-4414

Offers: Leather skins for garment making: cowhide, deerskin, elk, rabbit, thin velvet suedes, others. Lining leathers: kip, pigskin, others. Exotic leathers: python, cobra, whipsnake skins, embossed splits in alligator lizard and ostrich grains.
For Further Information: Catalog, $3.

LEATHER UNLIMITED CORP.
7155 Country Highway B
Dept. CSS96
Belgium, WI 53004
(414) 994-9464
Fax: (414) 994-4099

Offers: Wide array of leather, kits and products including garment bag, splits, deerskin, sheepskin, chamois, and others. Also offers leather findings, including buckles, conchos, snaps, zippers, thread, dyes, belts, beads and others. Books and finished products also available.
For Further Information: 84-page catalog, $2 (refundable).
Store Location: At above location. Hours: M-F, 7-3.
Discounts: Wholesale.
Accepts: Discover, MasterCard, Visa

LINDA'S SPECIALTY FABRICS
24 Main
Norwich, Ontario N0J 1P0
Canada
(519) 863-2887
Fax: (519) 424-2655

Offers: UltraSuede yardage, squares, scraps. Also offers lycra solids, velvets, prints.
For Further Information: Set of 135-plus swatches, $5. (refundable).

THE MATERIAL WORLD
5700 Monroe St.
Sylvania, OH 43560
(419) 885-5416 or (607) 535-4105

Offers: Line of quality fashion fabrics—imported and domestic silks, wools, cottons, blends, others; coordinated selections from areas worldwide.
For Further Information: Send $7.50 to receive collection of swatches 4 times a year.

MICHIKO'S CREATIONS
P.O. Box 4313
Napa, CA 94558
(707) 224-8546

Offers: Ultrasuede fabrics, by yard and in sized packages. Also offers other similar fabrics. Wholesale only.
For Further Information: Send SASE. Color card with 150 swatches, $10.

MILL END STORE
12155 SW Broadway
Beaverton, OR 97005
(503) 646-3000
Fax: (503) 646-3000
Alternate address:
9701 S.E. McLoughlin Blvd.
Portland, OR 97222
(503) 786-1234
Fax: (503) 786-2022

Offers: Fabrics, including imported cottons, wools, silks; outerwear fabrics, including nylon, packcloth, fleece, rainwear, knits, ribbing. Also offers drapery and upholstery fabrics, polyesters, velvets, velveteen, laces, trims. Patterns, notions, yarns and needlework items also available.
For Further Information: Send SASE for brochure or with inquiry.

MONTEREY, INC.
1725 E. Delavan Dr.
Janesville, WI 53546
(608) 754-8309

Offers: Synthetic furs: shags, shearling, plush, toy animal

types, closeouts, remnants. Also offers stuffings.
For Further Information: Sample package, $5.
Discounts: Quantity.
Accepts: MasterCard, Visa

NATIONAL NONWOVENS

P.O. Box 150
Easthampton, MA 01027
(413) 527-4445

Offers: Perfection brand felt by the piece in assortments or by yard; also offers felt appliqué shapes and letters.
For Further Information: See your dealer, or send SASE for prices.

NATURAL FIBER FABRIC DIRECT

10490 Baur Blvd.
St Louis, MO 63132

Offers: On payment of fee, members in this natural fabrics club receive 4 scheduled mailings of swatches of fashion fabrics from areas worldwide, plus a handbook and illustrated sewing aids catalog. Portfolio of swatches of 24 basic fabrics in stock: cottons, wools, silks. Unscheduled mailings. Members get savings from retail cost.
For Further Information: Send SASE for full details.
Accepts: MasterCard, Visa

CAMELA NISCHKE RIBBONRY

119 Louisiana Ave.
Perrysburg, OH 43551
(419) 872-0073

Offers: French ribbons, including reproductions of seventeenth- and eighteenth-century styles; flower and ornament ribbon kits; instructional videos on holiday ornaments and flowers. Also carries handcrafted bridal accessories.
For Further Information: Call for color catalog.

ON MY GOODKNITS INC.

P.O. Box 8658
Allentown, PA 18105
(610) 439-8862
Fax: (610) 435-7819

Offers: Line of cotton fabrics: interlocks, jerseys, ribs, French terry and fleece in custom colors. Also offers fabric development services, consulting. (Single roll minimums.)
For Further Information: Send SASE for list.

OPPENHEIM'S

120 E. Main St.
North Manchester, IN 46962
(219) 982-6848 or (800) 461-6728
Fax: (219) 982-6557

Offers: Fabrics, (including irregulars): linen-look and many

other cottons, knits, satins, polyester and polycottons, calicos, rug weavers' scraps, faux fur, needlecraft and bridal fabrics, taffetas, muslin netting, cheesecloth. Specialty fabrics: wool remnants, Ultrasuede scraps, Christmas. Also offers trims, stamped goods and quilt blocks, pillow forms, upholstery squares, "thermal suede" lining, rubber sheeting, poly doll cloth, wool mattress pads, polyfill and trims. Carries cut/sew and other sewing projects, plus remnants and package bargains.
For Further Information: Write or call for catalog.
Store Location: At above address. Hours: M-F, 9-5.
Accepts: MasterCard, Visa

ORIENTAL SILK CO.

8377 Beverly Blvd.
Los Angeles, CA 90048
(213) 651-2323

Offers: Fabrics, including crepe, tussah, Jacquard, Georgette, chiffon, China, noil, taffeta, satin, brocade, crepe de chine, satin stripes, silk/rayon velvet, wool and others. Also carries hand embroidered silk shawls.
For Further Information: Send SASE.
Store Location: At above address.

ORNAMENTAL RESOURCES, INC.

P.O. Box 3010
Idaho Springs, CO 80452
(800) 876-ORNA

Offers: Embellishments (many rare/unique): beads, chains, rhinestones, jewels, shells, appliqué, tassels, brass stampings, feathers, findings, supplies. Also offers tools.
For Further Information: Catalog in 3-ring binder, $15 (with a year's supplements).

PELLON DIVISION

119 W. 40th St.
New York, NY 10018
(212) 391-6300

Offers: Pellon Wonder Under transfer fusing material (heat press to fuse to fabrics; has peel-off backing), Pellon CraftBond backing material (fusible), and Pellon Tru-Grid enlarging material.
For Further Information: Contact your dealer, or send SASE.

PHILIPS BOYNE

1646 New Highway
Farmington, NY 11735
(800) 292-2830
Fax: (516) 755-1259

Offers: Fine shirtings: woven fabrics, imported/domestic in cottons, silks, blends, novelties. Also offers yarn dyed in stripes, checks, plaids. Wholesale only.

For Further Information: Sample package, $3 (refundable).
Store Location: At above address. Hours: M-F, 9-5
Accepts: American Express, Discover, MasterCard, Visa

QUALIN INTERNATIONAL, INC.

P.O. Box 31145
San Francisco, CA 94131
(415) 333-8500
Fax: (415) 282-8789

Offers: Silk fabrics (also blanks, scarves, others) of natural white, plus silk painting supplies.
For Further Information: Send SASE for catalog.

THE RIBBON FACTORY

P.O. Box 405
Titusville, PA 16354
(814) 827-6431

Offers: Ribbons in 20 to 100 yard rolls, including satins, grosgrains, tinsels and other specialties. Also offers closeouts and special orders.
For Further Information: Color catalog, $2.

SEW FAR, SEW GOOD

2734 Isabella
Evanston, IL 60201

Offers: Fabrics for girls, boys, infants: knits, wovens, Disney, OshKosh, holiday and other motifs.
For Further Information: Brochure, swatches, $3.

SEW NATURAL

A 521 N. Essex Dr.
Lexington Park, MD 20653
(301) 863-5952

Offers: 100 percent cotton fabrics, including knits, interlock-jersey, French terry, ribs of all weights; wovens—denim, twill, diaper fabric, flannel, chambray. Also offers ultrex, batting—wool and cotton, notions and patterns.
For Further Information: Send $1 for catalog and swatches (refundable).

SPECIALTIES

4425 Cotton Hanlon Rd.
Montour Falls, NY 14865
(607) 594-2021
Fax: (607) 594-2021

Offers: Lingerie fabrics: nylon, tricot, silky and cotton wovens, laces, cotton knits, foundation materials, others. Also offers notions, patterns, threads, accessories and lingerie kits.
For Further Information: Catalog, $2.
Accepts: MasterCard, Visa

STRETCH & SEW FABRICS

P.O. Box 185
Eugene, OR 97440
(800) 547-7717

Offers: Fabrics, including dyed-to-match rib, interlocks, fleeces, others. Line of patterns.
For Further Information: Catalog of patterns, $3.
Discounts: Quantity; teachers and institutions.

SUCH A DEAL TULLE

3515 Sunrise Blvd. #18
Rancho Cordova, CA 95742
Offers: Tulle fabric in 9″ to 108″ widths, with up to 36 colors available.
For Further Information: Send SASE for price list and colors.

SUNFLOWER STUDIO

2851 Road B ½
Grand Junction, CO 81503
(970) 242-3883
Fax: (970) 242-3883

Offers: Traditional natural fiber fabrics (handwoven, hand-dyed)—eighteenth- and nineteenth-century adaptations.

TANDY LEATHER CO.

P.O. Box 791
Fort Worth, TX 76101

Offers: Leather, including garment and exotics—pigskin, deerskin, sheepskin, grain leathers, saddle skirting and others. Also offers fashion accessories, beads, findings, dyes, finishes, garment patterns, kits, leatherworking materials, tools, group project packs and books.
For Further Information: Catalog, $3.
Discounts: By quantity on stocked items; wholesale to qualified buyers

TESTFABRICS, INC.

P.O. Box 420
Middlesex, NJ 08846
(908) 469-6446
Fax: (908) 469-1147

Offers: Fabrics, including specialty types for museums, universities, others.
For Further Information: Free catalog.
Discounts: Sells wholesale.
Accepts: MasterCard, Visa

THAI SILKS
252 State St.
Los Altos, CA 94022
(415) 948-8611
Fax: (415) 948-3426 or (800)722-SILK

Offers: Silk fabrics, including velvets, chiffons, prints, satins, suitings, scarves and others. Silk Fabric Club also available.
For Further Information: Free brochure.
Discounts: Specials for stores, artists, dressmakers.

THREADS AT GINGERBREAD HILL
356 E. Garfield
Aurora, OH 44202
(216) 562-7100

Offers: Fashion fabrics: imported/domestic/designer silks, wools, cottons, synthetics, others.
For Further Information: Swatches 4 times yearly, $8.

L.P. THUR FABRICS
126 W. 23rd St.
New York, NY 10011
(212) 243-4913
Fax: (212) 243-4913

Offers: Line of unique/hard-to-find fabrics: lycra, rayons, cottons, craft, theatrical, costume and designer fabrics, trims, glass beads, buttons, others.
For Further Information: Send SASE for samples.
Store Location: At above address. Hours: M-F, 9:30-5:30. Sat, 12-5.
Discounts: Sells wholesale.

ULTRAMOUSE LTD.
3433 Bennington Ct.
Bloomington Hills, CT 48301
(313) 646-8712

Offers: Ultrasuede scraps in assorted colors, by 8 ounce lots. Other scrap materials.
For Further Information: Send $2 for catalog.

ULTRASCRAPS/D.M. DESIGNS
6626 W. 79th Ave.
Arvada, CO 80003
(800) 431-1032

Offers: Ultrasuede scraps by the pound—assorted colors/sizes. Also offers specially cut package pieces or yardage.
For Further Information: Send SASE for list.

THE UNIQUE SPOOL
407 Corte Majorca
Vacaville, CA 95688

Offers: Line of African and Australian fabrics; African swatches, patterns, notions. Fabric club available.
For Further Information: Send large SASE.

UTEX TRADING
710 9th St., Suite 5
Niagara Falls, NY 14301
(716) 596-7565
Fax: (716) 282-8211

Offers: Couture silk fabrics: prints, crepe de chine, China colors, Thai and Fuji silks, raw silk noil, doupioni organzas, knits, charmeuse, jacquards, crepe satin, twill, boucles, tussah, others—dress/suit weights. Also has a branch office in Toronto, Canada.
For Further Information: White silks, $15; colored silks, $25; complete 3 sets, $55.
Accepts: MasterCard, Visa

General Needlecraft Supplies

Also see General Craft Supplies and specific categories in Section II.

AARDVARK ADVENTURES
P.O. Box 2449
Livermore, CA 94551
(510) 443-2687

Offers: Line of cross-stitch embroidery fabrics: Aida, Congress cloth, Hardanger, Lugana, others. Threads: Natesh rayons, metallics, iridescents and Mettler brand, plus a variety of yarns. Trims: ribbons, braids, buttons, tassels, shisha, diffraction foil, lamé, others. Surface decorating: paints, glitters, silk scarves, needlepoint canvases. Aids: tweezers, scissors, stabilizers, Sculpey, beads, shells, trims, others. Also offers rubber stamps and books.
For Further Information: Catalog, $2 (refundable).
Discounts: Sells wholesale to legitimate businesses.
Accepts: MasterCard, Visa

AMERICAN HANDICRAFTS/MERRIBEE
P.O. Box 2934
Fort Worth, TX 76113
(817) 921-6191

Offers: Needlecraft kits/tools/equipment/supplies: knitting, crochet, cross-stitch, plastic canvas, quilting, others.
For Further Information: Free catalog.

BALTAZOR'S
3262 Severn Ave.
Metairie, LA 70002
(504) 889-0333

Offers: Sewing supplies: fabrics, lace-making supplies, smocking and laces, bridal accessories, others.
For Further Information: Catalog, $2.

SUSAN BATES, INC.
P.O. Box 24998
Greenville, SC 92616
(800) 241-5997 or (803) 234-0337

Offers: Full line of sewing notions and aids, knitting and crochet hooks, crochet tools and accessories.
For Further Information: Contact your dealer, or send SASE.

BECK'S WARP 'N WEAVE
2815 34th St.
Lubbock, TX 79410
(806) 799-0151, (800) 658-6698

Offers: Knitting kits, yarns, tools, weaving and lace-making yarns and items. Also offers books; runs specials.
For Further Information: Catalog, $2.
Discounts: Quantity.
Accepts: MasterCard, Visa

BUFFALO BATT & FELT
3307 Walden Ave.
Depew, NY 14043
(716) 683 4100

Offers: Polyester stuffing in pound bags, Super Fluff bags or bulk rolls. Also offers Ultra Fluff premium and economy fiberfill; Super Fluff quilt batt, crib through king size, up to 2″ loft. Pillow inserts also available.
For Further Information: Brochure and swatches, $1 (refundable).
Discounts: Wholesale prices with quantity.

CRAFT GALLERY
P.O. Box 145
Swampscott, MA 01907
(508) 744-2334

Offers: Needlecraft kits: crewel, silk, mini-rugs, cross-stitch, counted thread, lace-making, embroidery. Complete DMC line available. Also offers threads, machine and hand: machine embroidery, tatting, quilting, plus knitting/crochet yarns and accessories. Carries ribands, lace net, iron-on transfers, shisha, scissors, and a variety of canvases. Fabrics: Aida, Linda, Hardanger, Wool Davos, Herta, Rustico, others. Patterns/books also available.
For Further Information: Catalog, $2.
Discounts: Teachers, institutions and professionals.

CREATIVE CRAFT HOUSE
P.O. Box 2567
Bullhead City, AZ 86430

Offers: Line of trims: braids in a variety of styles and widths, plastic and other beads, rhinestones, naturals.
For Further Information: Send SASE for list.

EARTH GUILD

33 Haywood St.
Asheville, NC 28801
(800) 327-8448

Offers: Materials and tools for knitting, crochet, weaving, spinning, dyeing and beads. Also carries books, anslo surface designs, polymer clay work, basketry, caning, pottery, candlemaking, and wood carving.
For Further Information: Free catalog of starter sets, samples and basic books; Complete 100-page catalog, $3.

BETTE S. FEINSTEIN

96 Roundwood Rd.
Newton, MA 02164
(617) 969-0942
Fax: (617) 969-0942
E-mail: needlewk@Tiac.net

Offers: Hard-to-find needlework books: needlepoint, embroidery, fibers, sewing, dollmaking, textiles, weaving, fashion making, quilt, lace, beadwork. Free search service available.
For Further Information: Catalog, $1.
Accepts: Discover, Mastercard, Visa

GRANNY'S QUILTS SEWING CENTER

4509 W. Elm
McHenry, IL 60050
(815) 385-5107

Offers: Quilting and sewing supplies, including cotton fabrics, patterns, notions, kits, stencils and Viking Pfaff sewing machines. Also offers accessories, books.

HANDWORKS

Rt. 1
P.O. Box 138
Afton, VA 22920
(800) 346-2004

Offers: Line of children's sewing projects, knitting baskets, others.
For Further Information: Send SASE for list.

HARD-TO-FIND NEEDLEWORKBOOKS

96 Roundwood
Newton, MA 02164
(617) 969-0942

Offers: Search service—without charge—for needlework books.
For Further Information: Catalog, $1.

HERRSCHERS

Hoover Rd.
Stevens Point, WI 54481
(800) 441-0838

Offers: Tools/equipment: frames (quilt, scroll, adjustable, tapestry), magnifiers, adjustable dressmaker forms, Fiskars scissors. Kits: cross-stitch, crewel, cloth dolls, crochet, candlewicking, latch hook, needlepoint, quilts, holiday items and thread-its. Also offers stamped table linens and pillowcases, yarns, (DMC and Star floss), fiberfill, fabrics (flour sacking, toweling, flannel, linen, Hardanger, Aida, toweling), towels, canvases, laces, trims.
For Further Information: Free catalog.

HIGH COUNTRY WEST NEEDLEWORK SHOP

114 N. San Francisco St., Suite 201
Flagstaff, AZ 86001
(520) 779-2900

Offers: Handpainted canvases and kits, including southwestern and western, pet and house portraits; custom designing. "Learn to needlepoint" kits, yarns, fibers by Paterna, Appleton, medici, Kreinik also available. Also offers watercolors, overdyes, silks, beads, laces, threads and more.
For Further Information: Catalog subscription, $3.50.
Accepts: MasterCard, Visa

IDENT-IFY LABEL CORP.

P.O. Box 140204
Brooklyn, NY 11214
(718) 436-3126

Offers: Personalized labels on white cotton, woven labels, custom labels and name tapes.
For Further Information: Free brochure.
Discounts: Quantity; institutions.

INTERWEAVE PRESS

201 E. 4th St.
Loveland, CO 80537
(800) 645-3675
Fax: (970) 667-8317

Offers: Needlecraft books: weaving titles and patterns, dyeing, spinning, textiles, yarn guide, knitting, sweaters, care of spinning wheels.
For Further Information: Contact dealer, or free catalog.
Discounts: Sells wholesale to legitimate businesses.

KIYO DESIGN, INC.

11 Annapolis St.
Annapolis, MD 21401
(410) 280-1942
Fax: (410) 280-2793

Offers: Line of fine, heirloom and smocking fabrics; laces,

Delica beads and beaded embroidery supplies, fashion accessories; and other supplies. Also offers sewing and needle art consignments.

For Further Information: Send SASE.

Store Location: At above address.

Accepts: American Express, MasterCard, Visa

LACIS

3163 Adeline St.
Berkeley, CA 94703
(510) 843-7178
Fax: (510) 843-5018

Offers: Extensive threads, ribbons and supplies for lacemaking, embroidery and costume. Lacemaking tools, sew-on purse frames, tatting shuttles and reproduction tools, tassel forms, DMC "Floche" and other cotton threads, Ed mar Brazilian embroidery and Japanese Bunk threads. Selection of period images on silks and other fabrics. Also publisher of over 60 books on needlework and costume and 3,000 titles on textiles and costume in English and foreign languages. Photo transfer service (images or documents to fabric) also available.

For Further Information: Catalog, $5.

Store Location: Separate retail store and gallery at 2982 Adeline St.

Discounts: Wholesale available to needlework industry.

MAGIC NEEDLE

Rt. 2
P.O. Box 172
Limerick, ME 04048

Offers: Crazy quilting items. Ribbons, including "The Magic Needle" silk and hand-dyed silk; "jazz" embroidery type; silk, metal, Japanese and hand-dyed threads. Also offers pre-cut fabrics for embroidery; supplies for tatting, punch embroidery, beading and needlepoint. Persian wool, canvas and other supplies also available. Has a swatch club.

For Further Information: Catalog, $1.

MARY MAXIM, INC.

2001 Holland Ave.
P.O. Box 5019
Port Huron, MI 48061
(810) 987-2000 or (800) 962-9504

Offers: Kits: quilting, cross-stitch, crewel, embroidery, others. Also offers cloth doll supplies, notions, sewing aids, threads, quilting frames and stands, holiday items, stencils, batting and fiberfill, pillow forms and other supplies.

For Further Information: Free 72-page color catalog.

MORNING GLORY PRODUCTS

302 Highland Dr.
Taylor, TX 76574
(800) 234-9105

Offers: Polyester bonded and unbonded batting and cotton quilt batting in three types—bleached and unbleached, feather/downfill, cotton tick. Pillow forms and stuffing also available.

For Further Information: Contact your dealer, or send SASE.

NANCY'S NOTIONS

P.O. Box 683, Dept 32
Beaver Dam, WI 53916
(414) 887-0391
Fax: (414) 887-2133

Offers: Sewing, quilting and serging products: glass locked beads, charted needlework designs and kits, hoops, applique"s, Gosling drapery tapes, shade tapes, reflective tapes and material, machine embroidery and other threads. Also offers rag rug items, quilted clothing patterns and many others, plus instructional videos—many on machine sewing, knitting, cross-stitching, quilting, decorating, rug braiding, weaving.

For Further Information: Free catalog.

Discounts: Quantity; teachers, institutions and professionals; sells wholesale to legitimate businesses.

NEWARK DRESSMAKER SUPPLY

P.O. Box 20730 Dept. CSS
Lehigh Valley, PA 18002
(610) 837-7500

Offers: Needlecraft/sewing items. Threads: Swiss Metrosene, machine rayon, silk, Coats & Clark, elastic, cotton, upholstery, metallics, ribbon floss, overlocks, stretch nylon. Also offers zippers (including doll sized), buckles, bow-tie clips, silk and dry flowers, ribbons, over 50 laces, metallics, bindings, tapes, elastics, buttons. Carries fabrics, appliqués, scissors, cutters, bridal items, veiling, flowers, others. Doll items: heads, eyes, stands, others. Also carries stencils, adhesives, paints, sequins/rhinestones, beads.

For Further Information: Free catalog.

Discounts: Quantity; sells wholesale to legitimate businesses.

Accepts: Discover, MasterCard, Visa

NO STARCH PRESS

1903 Jamestown Ln.
Daly City, CA 94014

Offers: Computer book for needlecrafters which demonstrates ways to use computer to design quilts, cross-stitch and

knitting patterns, and explains how to get free patterns and advice, go online, and more.
For Further Information: Send SASE.

OVERSEAS PUBLISHERS REPRESENTATIVES
1328 Broadway, Suite 645
New York, NY 10001
(800) 666-MAGS

Offers: Line of international books and magazines on fashion, graphics, textiles and others
For Further Information: Free catalog.

PEDDLER'S WAGON
P.O. Box 109
Lamar, MO 64759
(417) 682-3734

Offers: Pre-owned needlework and quilting books and magazines.
For Further Information: Free book search. Send large SASE with inquiry. Next 3 catalogs in each category, $3 (refundable).

S&S ARTS & CRAFTS
P.O. Box 513
Colchester, CT 06415
(800) 243-9232
Fax: (800) 566-6678

Offers: Group bulk-pack supplies: Latchhook, plastic canvas, looper weave and cross-stitch, plus kits, frames and items. Also offers felt, fur, burlap, lace, cords, netting and low-cost projects.
For Further Information: Free catalog.
Discounts: Quantity.

SOURCE MARKETING LTD.
600 E. 9th St.
Michigan City, IN 46360
(219) 873-1000
Fax: (219) 879-6181

Offers: GlissenGloss metallic threads: subdued, antique, shimmer or multi-ply sparkly metallics in a variety of colors for needlepoint, plastic canvas and cross-stitch.
For Further Information: Catalog, $1.
Accepts: MasterCard, Visa

STUDIO BOOKS
P.O. Box 7804
Huntington Beach, CA 92615
(714) 965-3267

Offers: Pre-owned needle and fiber arts books, magazines and leaflets. Freebook search service.
For Further Information: Next 3 book catalogs, $3.

STUDIO WORD PROCESSING, LTD.
5010-50 Ave.
Camrose, AG T4V 0S5
Canada
(403) 672-5887
Fax: (403) 672-9570

Offers: Software Directory for Fiber Artists, which lists 275-plus programs for weaving, knitting, quilting, sewing and needlework. Directory also includes artist profiles and sample printouts.
For Further Information: Call or send SASE.

THE TAUNTON PRESS
63 S. Main St.
P.O. Box 5506
Newtown, CT 06470
(203) 426-8171
Fax: (203) 426-3434

Offers: 80 folkwear patterns in ethnic and vintage styles. Also offers knitting patterns, books, including fabric/fiber sourcebooks and knitting titles, and instructional videos.
For Further Information: Free catalog.
Discounts: Sells wholesale to legitimate businesses.
See Also: Costumes—Ethnic, Historic, Special Occasion

TAYLOR BEDDING MANUFACTURING CO.
P.O. Box 979
Taylor, TX 76574

Offers: Line of fiberfill, batting, pillow forms, others.
For Further Information: Contact your dealer, or send SASE.

TAYLOR'S CUTAWAYS & STUFF
2802 E. Washington St.
Urbana, IL 61801

Offers: Fabrics by the pound: polyester, satin, felt, cottons, blends, silks. Remnants: velour fleece, tricot. Fabric packs: craft velvet, calico, cotton prints, solids. Also offers pre-cut fabric squares, lace, trims, ribbons, buttons, doll and animal parts, eyes, potpourri fragrances, satin ornaments, iron-on transfers and quilt and crochet patterns.
For Further Information: Brochure, $1.
Discounts: Quantity.

TEXTILE REPRODUCTIONS
P.O. Box 48
West Chesterfield, MA 01084
(413) 296-4437
Fax: (413) 296-0036

Offers: Products naturally dyed with vegetable dyes, including embroidery threads, fabrics, trimmings, wool blend felt, silk ribbons, needlecraft tools and books.

For Further Information: Catalog, $4; catalog with samples, $14.

THE UNIQUE SPOOL
407 Corte Majorca
Vacaville, CA 95688

Offers: African fabrics: cotton yardage, swatches, Australian fabrics. Also offers patterns for African wildlife vest (appliqué), Christmas quilt, wall hangings, placemats, caftans, long vest, yo-yo vest, skirts, cloth doll patterns, Christmas patterns. Tube threads and spool insert also available.
For Further Information: Send SASE.

WELLSPRING GALLERY
3333 S. Robertson Blvd.
Los Angeles, CA 90034
(310) 441-4204

Offers: Line of art supplies and books for fiber artists.
For Further Information: Call or send for color catalog.

WOODEN PORCH BOOKS
Rt. 1
P.O. Box 262
Middlebourne, WV 26149
(304) 386-4434
Fax: (304) 386-4868

Offers: Used and out-of-print books (fiber art and related categories): fashion, costume, sewing and dressmaking—garments, pattern design, historica/ethnic costumes, fabric design, Godey's Lady's books, French, bridal, children's, Civil War uniforms, leather and fur, tailoring. Needlework: beaded bags, wig making, embroidery, lace making, crochet, knitting, quilting, dyeing, needlepoint, smocking, and others.
For Further Information: Send $3 for next three catalogs.

WSC
P.O. Box 212
Alamogordo, NM 88311
(505) 437-2934

Offers: Over 150 Indian patterns/kits in crochet, needlepoint, latchhook.
For Further Information: Catalog, $3.
Discounts: Quantity; wholesale to legitimate businesses.
Accepts: MasterCard, Visa

YLI CORP.
P.O. Box 109
Provo, UT 84603
(800) 854-1932

Offers: Silk embroidery products, including ribbons in 185 colors, thread, floss, kits, patterns, needles and silk ribbon, embroidery videos and books. Also offers serging threads, including Wooly Nylon, Candleight metallic yarn, Pearl Crown Rayon, Designer-6, Jean Stitch, Success; metallic, monofilament and lingerie/bobbin thread. Wool embroidery yarn, fabric and books also available.
For Further Information: Catalog, $2.50.

Home Decorating

Also see most other categories where home accessories are listed.

AMERICAN BLIND & WALLPAPER FACTORY
909 North Sheldon
Plymouth, MI 48170
(313) 207-5800
Fax: (313) 207-0947

Offers: Wall coverings—all national brands (traditional, classic, contemporary, florals, textured, embossed, etc.), plus shades and blinds.
For Further Information: Write or call for quote on specific brand; give pattern book name and pattern number.
Accepts: Discover, MasterCard, Visa

COUNTRY HEARTS & STARS
3433 Weymouth Ct.
Marietta, GA 30062
(404) 565-7933

Offers: Fabrics, including a line of homespun checks and plaids.
For Further Information: Catalog, $5 (refundable).

DESIGNER SECRETS
P.O. Box 529
Fremont, NE 68025
(800) 955-2559

Offers: Designer fabrics, wallcoverings, window treatments, bedspreads, furniture accessories.
For Further Information: Catalog, $5 (refundable).

DOBRY ENTERPRESS
P.O. Box 112
Severna Park, MD 21146
(410) 437-0297
Fax: (410) 937-9200

Offers: Instruction books on custom draperies, cloud shades, no-sew drapery swags and jabots.
For Further Information: Free literature.
Discounts: Quantity; teachers and institutions; sells wholesale to legitimate businesses.

FABRIC CENTER
484 Electric Ave.
P.O. Box 8212
Fitchburg, MA 01420
(508) 343-4402
Fax: (508) 343-8139

Offers: Full line of home decorating fabrics.
For Further Information: Free brochure; catalog, $2.

THE FABRIC OUTLET
30 Airport Rd.
West Lebanon, NH 03786

Offers: Most major brands of decorator fabrics, including Waverly and Robert Allen.
For Further Information: Send fabric name, number, yardage.
Accepts: MasterCard, Visa

HANCOCK FABRICS
3841 Hinkleville Rd.
Paducah, KY 42001
(800) 845-8723

Offers: Fabrics, including a line of drapery and upholstery; also fashion and quilting types. Also offers other sewing supplies.
For Further Information: 60-page color catalog, $1.

HOME FABRIC MILLS
882 S. Main St.
Cheshire, CT 06410
(203) 272-3529
Fax: (203) 272-6686

Offers: Decorator fabrics: chintz, wovens, textures, prints, tapestries, jacquards, lace, others. Also offers fire-retardant contact fabrics, trims, accessories. Has three retail locations.
Store Location: At above address. Hours: M, T, W, F, 10-9. Th, Sat, 10-5.
Accepts: MasterCard, Visa

HOMESPUN
P.O. Box 4315 CSS
Thousand Oaks, CA 91359
(805) 381-0741

Offers: Seamless cotton drapery fabrics—10 feet wide, heav-

ily textured selections (for drapes, wall coverings, upholstery, bedspreads, tablecloths, clothing).
For Further Information: Catalog and swatches, $2.
Discounts: Factory direct prices.
Accepts: MasterCard, Visa

INSTANT INTERIORS

P.O. Box 1793
Eugene, OR 97440
(503) 689-4608

Offers: Instant decoration how-to booklets: *Bed Covers, Easiest Furniture Covers, Fabric Space Makers, Table Toppings, Lampshades, Quickest Curtains* and *Pillows and Cushions.*
For Further Information: Contact your dealer, or send SASE for catalog sheets.

IT'S SEW EASY HOME VIDEO

201 W. Genesee St. #167E
Fayetteville, NY 13066
(800) 837-1238

Offers: Instructional video on sewing curtains, drapes and valances, including step-by-step techniques and hints.
For Further Information: Send SASE.
Accepts: MasterCard, Visa

THE LAMP SHOP

Box 3606
Concord, NH 03302
(603) 224-1603

Offers: Line of lampshade making supplies and instruction books.
For Further Information: Catalog, $2.
Discounts: Sells wholesale.

MARJE LOMORIELLO

799 Broadway
Ulster Park, NY 12487

Offers: "Country" window and bed hangings, including handwoven dimities, linens, linsey woolseys, and others.
For Further Information: Brochure and cotton and lines swatches, $8.50.

MARLENE'S DECORATIVE FABRICS

301 Beech St.
Hackensack, NJ 07601
(800) 992-7325

Offers: Major manufacturer's decorator fabrics for draperies, slipcovers, upholstery, including 118" Tergal, voiles and batiste fabrics.
For Further Information: Send SASE with specific inquiry.
Discounts: Quantity.

ON BOARD FABRICS

P.O. Box 14
Edgecomb, ME 04556

Offers: "Table cloth" fabric, including "tavern check" in lobsters, pine trees, sailboats; and "bistro" check fabric.
For Further Information: Catalog, $2.50.

REPCON INTERNATIONAL, INC.

P.O. Box 548
Nixa, MO 65714
(417) 725-2450
Fax: (417) 725-1755

Offers: Create-A-Room products of corrugated cardboard pieces to cover with fabric or paper for decorator room furnishing. These include instructions, Create-A-Headboard, and screen, and nightstand, chest, canopy, valance. Create-A-Magazine Basket, waste basket, toilet tissue toppers, frame and wreath.
For Further Information: Call or send SASE.

ROLLERWALL, INC.

P.O. Box 757
Silver Spring, MD 20918
(301) 680-2510

Offers: Embossed paint rollers for wall patterns (florals, traditional, colonial, contemporary designs).
For Further Information: Send SASE for list.

SHEFFIELD SCHOOL OF INTERIOR DESIGN

211 E. 43rd St.
New York, NY 10017
(212) 661-7270
Fax: (212) 867-8122

Offers: Interior decorator home-study course—taped/printed lessons on color, fabrics, furniture, accessories; individualized taped analyses of student's room designs.
For Further Information: Free illustrated catalog.
Accepts: American Express, Discover, MasterCard, Visa

SILVER'S WHOLESALE CLUB

3001-15 Kensington Ave.
Philadelphia, PA 19134
(800) 426-6600

Offers: Wallcoverings and blinds.
For Further Information: Call or send SASE.
Accepts: MasterCard, Visa

WARM PRODUCTS, INC.

16110 Woodinville-Redmont Rd., # 4
Woodinville, WA 98072
(206) 488-4464 or (800) 234-WARM

Offers: Warm Window insulated fabric, with four layers quilted together for energy saving. Warm & Natural needled cotton batting for quilts, crafts and wearable art, Steam-A-Seam fabric fusing web.

For Further Information: Free brochures.

Discounts: Available for quantity orders.

WITH HEART & HAND
541 South St.
Wrentham, MA 02093
(508) 384-6568

Offers: "Homespun Fabrics" handwoven and authentically reproduced designs with the look of the 1800s.

For Further Information: Shop brochure and 40 samples, $6.50.

Knitting and Crochet

Also see General Needlecraft Supplies, Rug Making, Spinning and Weaving, Yarns and other related categories.

ABBY YARNS 'N KITS
1512 Myers Rd.
Marion, OH 43302
(614) 389-1461
Fax: (614) 386-2120

Offers: Line of yarns from major manufacturers, including Classic Elite, Rowan Tahki, Unique Colors, Hayfield and others.
For Further Information: Call or send SASE.
Accepts: MasterCard, Visa

ALDEA'S
P.O. Box 667
Beaumont, CA 92223
(909) 845-5825

Offers: Machine knitting instructional videos by Alvina Murdaugh covering basics, converting hand to machine knitting, techniques, maintenance, tips, ribber techniques, gifts. Also offers a variety of clothing titles (coats, sweaters, dresses, skirts, pants, others).
For Further Information: Send SASE for list.
Discounts: Sells wholesale.
Accepts: MasterCard, Visa

ALL BRANDS
9789 Florida Blvd.
Baton Rouge, LA 70815
(504) 923-1285 or (800) 866-1261 (for quotes)
Fax: (800) 866-1261

Offers: Knitting machines: Brother, Knitking, Singer Studio, Toyota-Elna Knitcraft, Bond/Baby Knit/Simplicity Bulkys. Also offers all machine accessories. Service contracts available. Buys some products.
For Further Information: Send SASE for brochures (specify product interest and price level).
Accepts: American Express, Discover, MasterCard, Visa

ANNIE'S ATTIC
1 Annie Lane
P.O. Box 212B
Big Sandy, TX 75755
(800) LV-ANNIE
Fax: (800) 88-ANNIE

Offers: Crochet kits/patterns: afghans, scarves/hats, slippers, Pocket Pals, buttons, bows, jewelry, rugs, doilies, bath and flower sets, potholders, layette items, baby outfits, sweaters, collars, fashion and other doll clothes, toys, baskets, others. Also offers plastic canvas kits, yarns, knitting and canvas accessories and instructional videos.
For Further Information: Free catalog.
Store Location: At above address.
Discounts: Quantity; sells wholesale.
Accepts: American Express, Discover, MasterCard, Visa

APOLLO KNITTING STUDIO
2305 Judah St.
San Francisco, CA 94122
(415) 664-2442

Offers: Instructional videos (VHS or Beta) for machine knitting, beginner or advanced, with Nobu Mary Fukuda.
For Further Information: Send SASE for full details.
Store Location: At above address. Hours: T, W, Th, Sat, 9:30-4.

ARNHILD'S KNITTING STUDIO
2315 Buchanan Dr.
Ames, IA 50010
(515) 232-7661

Offers: Rauma (Norwegian) sportweight and fingering wools, Gjestal superwash sport, yarn kits, pewter buttons, clasps, Norwegian patterns, Vadmel kits and wool ribbons.
For Further Information: Catalog, $5. Color cards, $3.50.

AUNTIE KNITS, INC.
212 Rock Rd.
Glen Rock, NJ 07452
(201) 447-1331

Offers: Over 40 sweater kits (yarns by major companies) in a variety of styles, including cardigans, pullovers, vests, others.
Store Location: At above address. Hours: Tues-Sat, 10-5.

BARE HILL STUDIOS/FIBER LOFT
Rt. 111
P.O. Box 327
Harvard, MA 01451

Offers: Natural fiber yarns for machine/hand crochet and knitting: Rowan, Tahki, Elite, Crystal Palace. Also offers mill ends. Exotic fibers: silks, angoras, ribbons.
For Further Information: Yarn samples, $5.25; exotic fiber samples of silks, angoras, ribbon, $2.75.
Discounts: Quantity.

BARKIM, LTD.
47 W. Polk St., Suite 100
Chicago, IL 60605
(312) 548-2211

Offers: Yarns from New England, Canada, Norway, Iceland. Also offers Guernsey wool (England), Rowan kits and yarns, and Shetland and Aran yarns. Carries mini-kits and other patterns.
For Further Information: Catalog and yarn samples, $4 (refundable); send SASE for newsletter.
Accepts: American Express, Discover, MasterCard, Visa

BAY COUNTRY BOUTIQUE
P.O. Box 1612
Carolina Beach, NC 28428
(301) 862-4220

Offers: Knitting yarns and kits, patterns, implements. Also offers a quarterly knitting newsletter, TKGA correspondence course and over 100 books.
For Further Information: Send SASE for list.

BENDIGO WOOLEN MILLS
P.O. Box 27164
Columbus, OH 43227
(614) 236-9112
Fax: (614) 236-8111

Offers: Line of Australian cabled wool yarns for knitting—hand washable.
For Further Information: Send for free shade cards.
Accepts: MasterCard, Visa

BLACK SHEEP WOOLS
P.O. Box 9205
Lowell, MA 01853
(508) 937-0320
Fax: (508) 452-3085

Offers: Brand name yarns—mill ends and discontinued styles.
For Further Information: Samples, $3.
Accepts: MasterCard, Visa

BRAMWELL YARNS, U.S.A.
P.O. Box 8244
Midland, TX 79708
(915) 685-5052

Offers: Bramwell imported yarns, knitting publications, knitting machine accessories.
For Further Information: Write or call for nearest dealer.
Discounts: Sells wholesale.

ANN C. BUSHFIELD
P.O. Box 187
Romney, IN 47981

Offers: Pre-owned books: crochet, knitting and other needlecrafts.
For Further Information: 100-plus-page list, $3 (refundable).

BY SHIRLEY MCKIBBEN
3720 Hood Ct.
Turlock, CA 95380
(209) 668-0550

Offers: Machine knitting instructional videos by Shirley McKibben (5) and others, including repair for Toyota machines.
For Further Information: Send SASE for list.

CARODAN FARM WOOD SHOP
Route 1, Box 127
Stanardsville, VA 22973
(804) 985-7083

Offers: Line of wool yarns in worsted and sport weights in over 20 colors.
For Further Information: Send large SASE for brochure/color card
Accepts: MasterCard, Visa

CHARLES PUBLISHING
P.O. Box 577
Weatherford, TX 76086

Offers: Over 250 crochet, sewing and needlepoint patterns including known characters and creatures, Roadrunner, Coyote, Country Bunny, King Lion, football player, cheerleader, dinosaurs and others.
For Further Information: Send SASE for complete list.

CHARMOR'S
108 S. Division St., Suite 4
Auburn, WA 98001

Offers: Knitting machines: Melrose, Brother, White, Heir-

loom. Yarns: Brown Sheel Wool, Yarn Country. Monthly knitting club.
For Further Information: Send SASE for details.

COLOURFIELDS
Rt. 1, Box 601
Rio Vista, TX 76093

Offers: Handspun yarns in wool, mohair, alpaca and silk; custom colors available.
For Further Information: Sample and details, $3.

COTTON CLOUDS
5176 S. 14th Ave., CS
Safford, AZ 85546
(520) 428-7000 or (800) 323-7888

Offers: Cotton and rayon chenille yarns in solids and variegated; fibers. Knitting machines, books and kits. Also offers spinning wheels and looms.
For Further Information: Catalog and samples, $6.50 ($5 refundable).
Discounts: Quantity; sells wholesale to legitimate businesses and production artists.

CREATE SOMETHING BEAUTIFUL
P.O. Box 1794
Wallingford, CT 06492
(203) 269-9270

Offers: Original sweater kits. Brand name knitting/crochet yarns: Alpaca, cottons, wools, others.
For Further Information: Brochure and over 100 yarn samples, $3.
Accepts: MasterCard, Visa

CREATIVE HANDCRAFTS
79 Elm St.
Danvers, MA 01923
(508) 774-7770

Offers: Hand knitting yarns—variety of types and odd lots. Also offers books.

CUSTOM KNITS & MANUFACTURING
Rt. 1
P.O. Box 16
Lake Park, MN 56554
(218) 238-5882 or (800) 726-4084

Offers: Wood yarn trees: rotating floor model (for 72 cones of yarn) or ceiling model. Also offers yarn plyer, pom-pom maker, cone holder.
For Further Information: Free catalog
Store Location: At above address.

Discounts: Quantity; teachers and institutions; sells wholesale to legitimate businesses.
Accepts: MasterCard, Visa

D'ARGENZIO'S
5613 Berkshire Valley Rd.
Oak Ridge, NJ 07438
(201) 697-1138

Offers: Knitting kits: S.C. Huber, Los Manos, North Island, Prism, Rowan, others. Also offers yarns, knitting machines, instructional videos and books.
For Further Information: Call.
Accepts: American Express, Discover, MasterCard, Visa

DESIGNS BY CYNTHIA WISE
122 Scoville Hill Rd.
Harwinton, CT 06791
(203) 485-9489

Offers: Yarns, including Brown Sheep, On the Inca Trail alpaca, Australian Gaywool Merino and others. Also carries needles, including Clover Bamboo, handcrafted buttons and others.
For Further Information: Color catalog and yarn samples, $2.

DESIGNS BY ROBERTA
28 Bach Dr.
Charlotte Hall, MD 20622

Offers: Crochet booklets: monthly verses, all occasion verses and patterns for holiday trims, frigies, lapel pins, others. Also offers discounted booklets.
For Further Information: Send large SASE for information and free pattern.

DIMITY
389 Dewey St.
Churchville, NY 14428
(716) 293-1468

Offers: Knitting machines by Brother, Knitking, Passap and Studio. Accessories, yarn and books also available.

EARTHSONG FIBERS
Rt. 3, Box 108
Westby, WI 54667
(800) 473-5350

Offers: Natural and organic yarns, fibers, dyes, herbs and essential oils for mothproofing and other uses. Also offers knitting, spinning and weaving equipment, videos and books.
For Further Information: Catalog and quarterly newsletter, $5.

ECONO CRAFT
RFD #1, Box 1440
Palermo, ME 04354

Offers: Antelope 50 percent cotton/50 percent acrylic yarn from France; 4 colors available.
For Further Information: Send large SASE for samples.

EWE & EYE
P.O. Box 646
Mahopac, NY 10541
(800) 220-YARN

Offers: Supplies and yarns for hand/machine knitting. Also offers knitting machines, sweater kits (including features from Vogue), accessories, instructional videos and books.
For Further Information: Catalog, $4 (refundable).

FARMYARD FIBERS
3655 Jacob Rd. Ste.B
Grass Lake, MI 49240

Offers: Line of yarns, including chenille in 101 colors, alpaca/wool blends and mohair.
For Further Information: Send large SASE for samples.

THE FIBER SHOP
22183 11th St.
Davenport, IA 52803
(319) 322-3535

Offers: "Knit Kit" service by subscription; members get packet each month with yarn, photo, samples, descriptions and bonus discounts. Yarns may include Prism Wildstuff and others.
For Further Information: Call or send SASE.

THE FIBER STUDIO
9 Foster Hill Rd.
P.O. Box 637 CSS
Henniker, NH 03242

Offers: Natural yarns and equipment for knitting, crocheting (also for weaving and spinning) with cottons, wools, mohairs. Also offers close-out yarns.
For Further Information: 60 yarn samples, $4; equipment catalog, $5.
Discounts: Quantity.
Accepts: MasterCard, Visa

FIBERS & MORE
Box 636
Camas, WA 98607
(360) 834-4426

Offers: "Projects-to-Go" kits—designs for knitting, handweaving (placemats, scarves, blankets, sweaters, dye proj-
ects, others). Also offers a line of doll hair in a variety of styles and materials.
For Further Information: Catalog of kits, $2.
Accepts: MasterCard, Visa

FIBRES
P.O. Box 135
Osterville, MA 02655
(508) 428-3882

Offers: Current yarns: Silk City, Aarlen, Brentwood, Classic Elite, Melrose, Plymouth, Reynolds, Valentino, Flatura de Crosa, Scotts Woolen Mill, Knitting Fever and Schaffhauser.
For Further Information: Price list, order data, $2.50 (refundable).
Accepts: MasterCard, Visa

THE FIFTH STITCH
300 Clinton St.
Defiance, OH 43512
(419) 782-0991

Offers: Line of domestic and imported yarns with dimension and texture, for designer work.
For Further Information: Call or send SASE.
Store Location: At above address.

FINGERLAKES WOOLEN MILL
1193 Stewarts Corners Rd.
Genoa, NY 13071
(800) 441-WOOL

Offers: Fingerlake yarns: wools, angora/wool and silk/wool blends and Unspun in 23 colors. Spinning kits and fulled kits for felting also available.
For Further Information: $4 for samples.
Discounts: Sells wholesale to yarn stores and professional designers.

FRY DESIGNS
515 NW Wide Ave.
Roseburg, OR 97470

Offers: Patterns (original) for tissue box covers, toothpick holders, wallsamplers, and monthly/seasonal designs, including lighthouses, snowmobiles, trains, Indians, animals, Christmas and others.
For Further Information: Send large SASE.

GOSSAMER THREADS & MORE
575 4th Ave.
Durango, CO 81301
(970) 247-2822

Offers: Knitting yarns: wools, linens, cottons, silks, alpaca and cashmere, plus lace knitting items, including some hard to find.

For Further Information: Send SASE.
Accepts: MasterCard, Visa

TERESA DANE GOTO
6740 Samuel Ct.
Anchorage, AK 99516
(907) 345-2031

Offers: Fashionable Beginnings machine-knitted garment patterns for mothers-to-be, nursing mothers and children: sweaters, skirts, jogging pants. Patterns include hidden-zippered outfits and baby and older boy and girl patterns.
For Further Information: Send SASE for list.
Discounts: Sells wholesale.

GRAND VIEW COUNTRY STORE
U.S. Rt. 2
Randolph, NH 03570
(800) 898-5715

Offers: Hundreds of yarns, original knitting kits, patterns and basket kits. Also offers a line of wool yarn from self-grown sheep. Holds "Weekend knit ins."
For Further Information: Call or write for newsletter.

HANDIWORKS
P.O. Box 13482
Arlington, TX 76094
(817) 277-1250

Offers: "Rag Elegance" (fabric strip) knitting and crochet patterns, including sweatshirt with knit/crochet yoke, unattached collars, crochet vest, others.
For Further Information: Color cards (15) and price list, $3.
Discounts: Sells wholesale.

JANKNITS
1500 Cohagen Rd.
Ingomar, MT 59039
(406) 354-6621
Fax: (406) 354-6721

Offers: Line of knitting books by Janet Mysse, including *Affordable Furs*, featuring working with fur and leather. Also offers books on Fisherman knits and knitting for soft sculptured dolls. A line of yarns is also available.
For Further Information: Send SASE.
Discounts: Sells wholesale.

KATHE'S KITS
1505 Mayfair
Champaign, IL 61821
(217) 355-5400
Fax: (217) 356-0624

Offers: Knitting machine kits: chenille rayon, angora, cotton, wool—includes designer coats and jackets, children's designs, others. Also offers Knitpicky knitting machines—computer interface models. A book called *Kathe's Knits for Passap Babies* also available.
For Further Information: Call or send SASE.

KENCO
2531 N. 85th St.
Omaha, NE 68134
(800) 228-6633

Offers: Rag crochet fabric by the pound; wood and plastic hooks, patterns, supplies and books. Also offers fabric paints and other products.
For Further Information: Free catalog.
Accepts: Discover, MasterCard, Visa

KNIT KNACK SHOP, INC.
Rt. 3
P.O. Box 104
Peru, IN 46970
(317) 985-3164
Fax: (317) 985-3164

Offers: Extensive line of machine knitting books, Hauge D100 Linker for knitting machine, others.
For Further Information: Send SASE for price list.
Store Location: At above address. Hours: M-F, 9-5.
Discounts: Sells wholesale.
Accepts: MasterCard, Visa

KNIT-O-GRAF PATTERN CO.
958 Redwood Dr.
Apple Valley, MN 55124
(612) 432-5630

Offers: Pictoral knitting patterns for 4-ply yarns: cardigan and pullover sweaters, puppet mittens, afghans, socks, others.
For Further Information: Color catalog, $1.25.

KNITTING BASKET V.I.P. GUILD
P.O. Box 5367
Tahoe City, CA 96145
(800) 252-YARN

Offers: Subscribing members receive promotions of color pictures and yarn samples, with discounts. Enroll yearly with fee.
For Further Information: Call or send SASE.

KNITTING CIRCLES
2530A Cedar Beach
Charlotte, VT 05445
(802) 425-3208

Offers: Circular knitting patterns.
For Further Information: Send SASE.

KNITTING MACHINES OF FLORIDA
1428 E. Semoran Blvd., Suite 108
Apopka, FL 32703
(800) 346-2311

Offers: Cone yarns, Brother Knitting machines, weaving looms. Also offers Craft Cascade acrylics, others.
For Further Information: Send SASE for yarn sample sheets.
Discounts: Sells wholesale.
Accepts: Discover, MasterCard, Visa

KRUH KNITS, MERCHANTS TO THE MACHINE KNITTER
P.O. Box 1587
Avon, CT 06001
(860) 651-4353

Offers: Knitting machines and machine accessories, computer programs, video tapes, electronic patterns. Also offers finishing tools, furniture, lamps, aids, videos, yarn winders, motors, gauge helps, punchcards, ravel cords, sewing aids. Carries a full line of yarns. Offers frequent Buyer's Club and Video Rental Club.
For Further Information: 168-page catalog, $5. Includes discount coupons.

JEAN LAMPE-DESIGNS IN FIBERS
1293 NW Wall St., #1501
Bend, OR 97701

Offers: Luxury handspun yarns for socks and sweaters: "Snug buggies" knit kits for children's slippers; mini-filling boards for felting. Also offers custom-made, mini-yarn swifts of cherry wood.
For Further Information: Send SASE.
Discounts: Teachers, institutions and professionals; sells wholesale to businesses.

LOST ART YARN SHOPPE
123 E. Front St.
Traverse City, MI 49684
(616) 941-1263
Fax: (616) 941-8815

Offers: Yarns/kits: Skacel, Rowan, Brown Sheep, Elite, Manos, Pingouin, Reynolds, Renaissance, others. Also offers knitting needles, accessories, patterns, books and rug braiding items, needlepoint.
For Further Information: Send for catalog; price lists and samples, $4 (refundable).
Store Location: At above address. Hours: M-F, 10-5, Sat, 10-4.

THE MANNINGS
1123 Green Ridge Rd.
P.O. Box 687
East Berlin, PA 17316
(717) 624-2223

Offers: Yarns of most major manufacturers, mill ends and books. Also offers spinning and weaving products.
For Further Information: Catalog and yarn style card, $2.50.

MARTHA JEAN'S
P.O. Box 347
Chewelah, WA 99109

Offers: Early 1900s crochet camisole patterns, chart for lily, iris, rose or other yokes, plus camisoles, baby items and household accessories.
For Further Information: List, $2.

MOUNTAIN COLORS
Box 156
Corvallis, MT 59828
(406) 777-3377

Offers: Hand-painted yarns, including multicolored wool and mohair in variety of colors. Patterns and kits for socks, vests, hats, mittens and others.
For Further Information: Color card, $5.

N.S.D. PRODUCTS
P.O. Box 880
Brandon, MS 39043
(601) 825-6831 or (800) 514-9210

Offers: Camel crochet (uses crochet hooks but looks like knitting)—wooden and other hooks, hard-to-find accessories, instruction patterns, videos and books.
For Further Information: Free catalog request line. Call (800) 524-9210.
Discounts: Sells wholesale.
Accepts: MasterCard, Visa

THE NEEDLEWORK ATTIC
4706 Bethesda Ave.
Bethesda, MD 20814
(301) 652-8688 or (800) 654-6654 for orders

Offers: Sweater kits in a variety of color choices for selected styles, plus Rowan yarns and kits, and books.
For Further Information: Send SASE for information.
Store Location: At above address. Hours: T, W, F, 10-5:30. Th, 10-9. Sat, 10-4.
Accepts: MasterCard, Visa

NEWTON'S KNITS

2100 E. Howell, Sp. 209
Anaheim, CA 92806
(714) 634-0817

Offers: Toyota knitting machines and Yarn Country cone yarns in a range of colors.
For Further Information: Contact your dealer, or send SASE for nearest location.
Discounts: Sells wholesale.

NORTHEAST KNITWORKS

P.O. Box 109
Freeport, ME 04032
(207) 865-1939
Fax: (207) 865-3418

Offers: Natural fiber yarns on cones and in balls imported from New Zealand, England and Peru, including wool, alpaca, llama/wool, mohair, and alpaca/mohair types.
For Further Information: Call, fax or write for yarn card costs.

PASSAP—U.S.A.

271 W. 2950 S.
Salt Lake City, UT 84115
(800) PASS-301

Offers: Passap knitting machines, including the Electronic and other models. Also offers steam presses and irons. Manufacturer.
For Further Information: Write for nearest dealer; free brochures.

PATTERNWORKS

P.O. Box 1690
Poughkeepsie, NY 12601
(914) 438-5464 or (800) 462-8000
Fax: (914) 462-8074

Offers: Knitting and yarn accessories and kits, including line of needles (Turbo, Brittany, Inox), bamboo, interchangeable and flex. Aids include needle cases, ball winders, guides, calculators, rulers, graphs, gauges, finishing items, counters. Also offers knitting patterns, full line of buttons, books, videos, software for Dos/Windows.
For Further Information: Free catalog.
Discounts: Teachers and institutions.

PENELOPE CRAFT PROGRAMS, INC.

P.O. Box 1204
Maywood, NJ 07607
(201) 368-8379
Fax: (201) 712-9601

Offers: Software (for IBM or compatible PC/XT/AT or PS/2 with at least 19K and PC/MS-DOS 2.11 or higher): Knit

One adjusts knitting patterns to specified gauge and size.
For Further Information: Write or call.
Discounts: Sells wholesale.
Accepts: American Express

ROCLITH CREATIONS

15510 Riding Stable Rd.
Laurel, MD 20707
(800) 240-5484

Offers: Keyto "Knitlite" knitting machine light, adjustable clamp-on, with triphosphor fluorescent tube the length of machine with output the equivalent to a 250W incandescent bulb.
For Further Information: Call or send SASE.

SCHOOLHOUSE PRESS

6899 Cary Bluff
Pittsville, WI 54466
(715) 884-2799 or (800) YOU-KNIT

Offers: Handknitting tools, wool yarns, over 100 books and videos, complete knitter's supplies.
For Further Information: Wool samples and catalog $3.
Accepts: MasterCard, Visa

THE SEWING CENTER

2581 Piedmont Rd. NE
Atlanta, GA 30324
(404) 261-5605 or (800) 241-4646
Fax: (404) 261-0162

Offers: Singer embroidery and monogram machines.
For Further Information: Send SASE.
Accepts: American Express, Discover, MasterCard, Visa

SEW-KNIT DISTRIBUTORS

9789 Florida St.
Baton Rouge, LA 70815
(504) 923-1260 or (800) BUY-KNIT
Fax: (800) 866-1261

Offers: Knitting machines and accessories by Brother Knitking, Singer (fits Studio). Also offers videotapes, ribbers, winders, hobbys, laces, hand punches, transfers, strippers, tools, bed extensions, Dazor lamp, tilt stand metal, Susman irons, Jiffy steamers, Baby Lock sergers, Read Pleaters, Stanley Pleaters, Baby Lock models. Carries dress forms, blocking cloth.
For Further Information: Send SASE for accessory price lists and product brochures.
Accepts: American Express, Discover, MasterCard, Visa

SKACEL COLLECTION, INC.
224 SW 12th St.
Renton, WA 98055
(206) 255-3411

Offers: Knitting yarns, patterns and books: Schaffhauser Wolle, Scholler Wolle, Austermann Wolle, Mondail, and effect and jewelry yarns. Knitting and crochet yarns, patterns and books by Schaffhauser Wolle, Shoeller Wolle, Mondial and Skacel. Also offers Addi Turbo needles.
For Further Information: Write.

STEPHANIE'S STUDIO & YARN
1637 Appian Rd.
Bybee, TN 37713

Offers: Cone yarns for knitting machines, including Jade, spiral twist cottons, ravel cord, acetate, acrylics, blends, wools, mohair, metallics—by the pound or cones. Also offers a yarn club: on payment of fee, members receive a yarn catalog, newsletter, patterns and discounts.
For Further Information: Send SASE for list.
Discounts: Quantity.
Accepts: MasterCard, Visa

STONEBRIER YARN & DESIGN CO.
7900 E. Princess Dr. #2141
Scottsdale, AZ 85255
(602) 502-0800

Offers: Designer yarns and accessories by Lane Borgosesia, Di Crosa, Melrose, Vendome, Anny Blatt, Shewe and other name brands.
For Further Information: Price list, $3.

THE STRING SLINGER
P.O. Box 23272
Chattanooga, TN 37422
(815) 843-0272
Additional address:
P.O. Box 5232, Station B
Victoria, British Columbia V8R 6N4
Canada

Offers: Instructional knitting machine videos (and workbooks): *Machine Knitting* series—for Japanese machines—and the *Passap Tutorial Series.*
For Further Information: Send SASE.

STUDIO LIMESTONE
253 College St.
P.O. Box 316
Toronto, Ontario M5T 1R5
Canada
(416) 864-0984

Offers: Yarns/kits: Rowan, Annabel Fox, Fox Fibre, Vaturu-

guai. Also offers patterns, bond knitting frames, buttons (pewter, earth), Britany and Addi Turbo needles and needlepoint kits.
For Further Information: Shade cards set, $25 (refundable); price list, $2.

STUDIO PRODUCTS, INC.
10002 14th Ave. SW
Seattle, WA 98146
(206) 433-8405

Offers: Line of designer electronic knitting machines.
For Further Information: See your dealer, or send SASE.

TD CREATIONS
421 Horn Ave. S.
Moorhead, MN 56560
(218) 236-7987

Offers: Crochet patterns for 15″ doll bodies and 15″ fashion dolls: old-fashioned dresses and matching hats in ruffled, striped, hoop or straight styles with a lacy look.
For Further Information: Send SASE for list.
Accepts: MasterCard, Visa

TESS' DESIGNER YARNS
33 Strawberry Point
Stenben, ME 04680
(207) 546-2483

Offers: Designer yarns and silk fabrics, including crepe de chine, china and broadcloth silk, raw, suede charmeuse; dyed-to-match yarns.
For Further Information: Send SASE.

BONNIE TRIOLA
343 East Rd.
Erie, PA 16509
(814) 825-7821

Offers: Cone yarns for machine knitters, weavers: wool/rayon, cotton/rayon, ribbon, cable cotton. Also offers yarns by Tamm, Millor, and odd-lot and/or designer yarns.
For Further Information: Catalog and mailings, $10.
Discounts: Quantity; wholesale to legitimate businesses, teachers and schools.

THE WEAVER'S LOFT
308 S. Pennsylvania Ave.
Centre Hall, PA 16828
(814) 364-1433 or (800) 693-7242

Offers: Full line of knitting yarns and supplies.
For Further Information: Free catalog; sample set, $18.

WESTRADE SALES, INC.
8571 Bridgeport Rd.
Richmond, British Columbia V6X 1R7
Canada
(604) 270-8737

Offers: Cone knitting yarns from Forsell and Bramwell in 30 styles and a full line of colors, plus blends and Shetland-type mixtures.
For Further Information: Call.

THE WOOL CONNECTION
Rt. 10 Riverdale Farms
Avon, CT 06001
(203) 678-1710

Offers: Line of machine and hand knitting yarns—most types, colors and textures.
For Further Information: 20-page color catalog, $3 (refundable with $25 order).

WOOL SHOP VIDEO, INC.
25 The Plaza
Locust Valley, NY 11560
(800) 771-WOOL

Offers: Instructional video of basic knitting techniques with Bobby Groome. Video includes over 25 stitches and techniques with instruction booklet.
For Further Information: Call or send SASE.
Accepts: MasterCard, Visa

YARN BARN
918 Massachusetts St.
Laurence, KS 66044
(913) 842-4333

Offers: Line of knitting and crochet products, yarns, dyes and books. Also offers spinning and weaving equipment.
For Further Information: Knitting/crochet catalog, $1.
Store Location: At above address.
Discounts: Quantity.

YARN FOR EWE
2720 Crown Point Ct.
Sidney, OH 45365
(513) 492-3315

Offers: Knitting yarns, supplies, books.
For Further Information: Send SASE for list.

YARN GALLERY
1509 Burning Lantern Ln.
Kannapolis, NC 28081
(704) 933-5559
Fax: (704) 938-5809

Offers: Natural fiber and novelty yarns, kits, patterns, accessories and books by Dale, Cynthia Helen, Tahki, Stahl, Idiecity, Plymouth, Cleckheaton, Gedifra, Llena and Junhans.
For Further Information: Catalog and color cards, $4 (refundable with $30 order).
Accepts: MasterCard, Visa

YARN-IT-ALL
2223 Rebecca Dr.
Hatfield, PA 19440
(215) 822-2989
Fax: (215) 822-6394

Offers: Brother knitting machines—electronic fine needle, bulky punch card and all accessories. Also offers Brother stands/tables, accessories. Yarns: Sunray, Mayflower, Joggerspun, Fosell, Phentex, Millor, others. Videos, patterns and books are also available.
For Further Information: Free catalog.
Store Location: At above address. Call for appointment.
Discounts: Quantity.
Accepts: MasterCard, Visa

YARNARTS
59 Palmer Ridge
Gansevoort, NY 12831

Offers: Kathleen Early designer original crochet patterns, including picture cover sheets, diagrams and graphs that allow detail in crochet for doll hands, arms, fingers, toes, ears, nose. Patterns include fully posable dolls and doll clothing—16″ Elvis, babies, animals, unicorn, and others.
For Further Information: Free brochure.
Discounts: On 2 or more patterns.

Lace Making

Also see General Needlecraft Supplies, Knitting and Crochet, Yarns and other related categories.

CARPENTERS' CRAFTS
P.O. Box 1283
Alton, IL 62002
(618) 462-1768

Offers: Instructional videos, including *How To Tat* and *Fun With Tatting*, as well as videos on crazy quilts, quilling, chair weaving and more.
For Further Information: Send for free details.
Accepts: MasterCard, Visa

CRAFT GALLERY
P.O. Box 8319
Salem, MA 01971
(617) 744-6980

Offers: Tatting cotton threads and patterns, Battenberg orna-ment kits, Tatsy patterns and threads, plus imported and other threads in cotton, linen, others. Also offers lace bobbins (including antique English style), lace pins, shuttles (imported, rosewood, board and flat types, others), blank napkins, handkerchiefs and lace sets. Aids include wrist ball holders and other needlecraft helps. Books include a full line of lacemaking techniques and titles.
For Further Information: Catalog, $2.

VICTORIAN VIDEO PRODUCTIONS
1304 Scott St.
Petaluma, CA 94954
(707) 762-3362 or (800) 346-8887

Offers: Instructional videos: (1) *Needlelace Medallions*—basics; (2) *Bobbin Lace*—covering graduated levels of instruction in basic twist, cross, Torchon ground and others, including finishing. Offers many other craft and needlecraft videos.
For Further Information: Free catalog.
Discounts: Schools and libraries; sells wholesale to businesses.

Macrame

Also see General Needlecraft Supplies, Knitting and Crochet, Yarns and related categories.

AL CON ENTERPRISES
P.O. Box 429
Hickory, NC 28603
(800) 523-4371
Fax: (704) 328-1700

Offers: Al Con brand macrame braid/cord—full line of colors (6mm to 8mm). Also offers patterns.
For Further Information: Free catalog and sample.
Discounts: Quantity; sells wholesale.

BRIAN'S CRAFTS UNLIMITED
1421 S. Dixie Freeway
New Smyrna Beach, FL 32168

Offers: Macrame supplies: synthetic cords (indoor/outdoor), Maxi twist in solids and blends, metallics, braid/tube (2mm to 6mm). Accessories: rings (brass, bamboo, Dee, split key, metal rectangles, plastic), purse snaps, owl eyes, box wreath frames, pre-drilled Marbella beads and wood blocks. Also offers chair frames, ceramic and wood beads, fusing tools, books and other craft supplies.
For Further Information: Catalog, $1 (refundable).
Accepts: MasterCard, Visa

MUNRO CRAFTS
3954 W. Twelve Mile Rd.
Berkley, MI 48072

Offers: Line of macrame supplies and craft jewelry.
For Further Information: Catalog, $5, refundable.

SUNCOAST DISCOUNT ARTS & CRAFTS
9015 U.S. 19 N.
Pinellas Park, FL 34666
(813) 572-1600

Offers: Maxi-Cord macrame cord (6mm polypropylene) in over 28 solid colors and over 18 mixed color rolls. Also offers cord color chart and other craft supplies.
For Further Information: Full crafts catalog, $2.

TEXTILE ENTERPRISES, INC.
216 Main St.
P.O. Box 154
Whitesburg, GA 30185
(770) 834-2094
Fax: (770) 834-2096

Offers: Macrame supplies: cords (twists, braids in colors, heathers, mixed), wire braid, fancy cords, waxed linens, jute, braided metallics, cotton cables. Accessories: purse closures, full line of rings (wood, bamboo, rattan, others), purse handles, metal rings/frames (holiday and other shapes), lampshades (Tiffany style and others), plus table frame kits, wall brackets, ceiling hook sets, others.
For Further Information: Catalog, $5.
Discounts: Quantity; sells wholesale.

Needlepoint

Also see General Needlecraft Supplies, Embroidery and Cross-Stitch, Yarns and related categories.

ARTS ARRAY
P.O. Box 546
Cottage Grove, OR 97424
(541) 942-8070

Offers: Line of European "tapestries" (hand-silkscreened color on Penelope double-weave) and kits: over 500 motifs by Royal Paris, Tapex, Margot Seg, Rico, others in traditional and classic designs—religious, Renaissance, florals, wildlife, seasonal, masterpieces, whimsical subjects, others. Also offers petit point kits (over 26) in classic designs.
For Further Information: Catalog, $2.
Discounts: May run sales.

CAMAS INTERNATIONAL
222 Gulf Rd., Suite 605
Lansing, NY 14882
(800) CAMUS

Offers: "Tartan Point" pillow kits, including authentic Scottish tartans interpreted in needlepoint; in all popular tartans; 14" pillow kit includes Patermayan yarn, Zweigert canvas and instructions.
For Further Information: Send SASE.
Accepts: MasterCard, Visa

GITTA'S CHARTED PETIT POINT
289 Lakeshore Rd. E.
Port Credit, Ontario L5G 1H3
Canada
(905) 274-7189

Offers: Needlepoint/petit point (and cross-stitch) charts/kits in over 62 traditional motifs: Victorian, Renaissance, Eskimo, florals, fowl, others. Fabrics: linens and others. Brand name threads: wools, cottons. Also offers canvases, silkscreen mesh and custom needlework framing.
For Further Information: Catalog, $5.
Discounts: Teachers and institutions; sells wholesale to businesses.

MAGGIE CO.
309 Chestnut St.
San Francisco, CA 94133

Offers: Needlepoint kits, including contemporary and Inuit collectors series hand adapted from original art. Also offers kits on needlepoint canvas including Persian yarn.
For Further Information: Full color brochure, $3.

JEAN MCINTOSH LTD.
P.O. Box 232
Pembina, ND 58271
or 1115 Empress St.
Winnipeg, Manitoba R3E 3H1
Canada
(204) 786-1634 or (800) 665-1361 for customer orders
Fax: (204) 774-4159

Offers: Needlepoint and petit point kits and charts: traditional and classic designs in a wide range of motifs, including florals, scenic tapestries, others. Also offers cross-stitch materials.
For Further Information: Catalog, $5.
Store Location: At above address. Hours: M-F, 9-5.
Discounts: Sells wholesale to legitimate businesses.

STUDIO LIMESTONE
253 College St.
P.O. Box 316
Toronto, Ontario M5T 1R5 Canada
(416) 864-0984
Fax: (416) 864-0984

Offers: Rowan and Ehrman needlepoint kits. Yarns: Rowan, Annabel Fox, Fox Fibre, Valuruguai and others. Also offers books and knitting supplies.
For Further Information: Sample shade cards, $25 (refundable); price list, $2.

Outdoors and Outerwear

Also see Clothing and Accessories, Fabrics and Trims, Knitting and Crochet, Quilting, Sewing and other specific categories.

FROSTLINE KITS
2525 River Rd.
Grand Junction, CO 81505
(970) 241-0155
E-mail: http:www.backboard.com/~frostline

Offers: Precut outerwear kits (coats, jackets, baby wear, others) for adults, children: robes, comforters, others—ready-to-sew.
For Further Information: Write for catalog.
Accepts: American Express, Discover, MasterCard, Visa

THE GREEN PEPPER
1285 River Rd.
Eugene, OR 97404
(541) 689-3292

Offers: 85 outerwear clothing patterns for adults and children, including suits, pants, jackets, tops, mittens, booties, vests and others. Also offers patterns for carriers/equipment, including garment and other bags, fanny pack, sleeping bag quilts, ponchos, horse blanket, wind socks. Fabrics also available, including nylon/lycra, waterproof and water repellent selections. Polartec fleece, insulations, heavy ribbing, Neoprene. Also offers YKK zippers, buckles, hooks, hardware, webbing and thread.
For Further Information: Catalog, $2.
Discounts: Bulk prices offered.
Accepts: MasterCard, Visa

HANG-EM HIGH FABRICS
1420 Yale Ave.
Richmond, VA 23224
(804) 233-6155

Offers: Fabrics: ripstop nylons, dacron (and adhesive). Supplies: webbing, repair tapes, swivels, tubing and tubes (fiberglass, carbon, vinyl), tapes, eyelet tools and more.
For Further Information: Free catalog.

KARLIN OF QUAKERTOWN
420 East Broad St.
Quakertown, PA 18951
(800) 828-7798

Offers: Flag and banner fabric—200 denier nylon in 60″ width, 39 colors; ¼ yard-plus purchase.
For Further Information: Call or send SASE.

MARINE SEWING
6801 Gulfport Blvd.
St. Petersburg, FL 33707
(813) 345-6994 or (800) 713-8157
Fax: (813) 347-1424

Offers: Line of outdoor fabrics: canvas, vinyls, others (for boating/camping and outdoor items). Also offers notions for outdoor-fabric sewing.
For Further Information: Catalog, $3 and SASE.

OUTDOOR WILDERNESS FABRICS
16195 Latah Dr.
Nampa, ID 83651
(708) 466-1602

Offers: Outdoor fabrics: Polartec, Ultrex, Taslan, Supplex, Ballistics, Cordura, others. Also offers insulations, no-see-um netting mesh, hardware, supplies.
For Further Information: Free price list; full samples, $5.
Accepts: Discover, MasterCard, Visa

QUEST OUTFITTERS
2590 17th St.
Sarasota, FL 34234
(941) 378-1620

Offers: Line of outdoor fabrics, including Polartec, Ultrex Thinsulate, Cordura, pack cloth, Supplex and more. Also offers wear and gear patterns, fasteners, zippers and other hardware.
For Further Information: Free catalog.
Accepts: MasterCard, Visa

RAIN SHED
707 NW 11th St.
Corvallis, OR 97330
(503) 753-8900

Offers: Outerwear patterns/kits/supplies. Brand patterns by Sew Easy, Daisfiber by Kingdom, Coat Craze, Four Seasons,

Green Pepper, Stretch'N Sew, Suitability, Travel Pals. Patterns: parkas, pants, vests, jackets, coveralls, suits, gaiters, caps, nightshirts, rompers, robes, swimsuits, riding outfits, totes, caddies, comforters, windsocks. Luggage: daypacks, cases, bags (ski, duffle, flight, diaper, thermal bottle). Fabrics: coated/uncoated nylons and Taslan, Supplex, Techtile, cordura, vinyls, packcloth, waterproof/breatheables, wicking knits, mesh, fleece, lycra, blends/cottons, camouflage, insulations. Also offers reflective tapes, webbings, cords, repair tapes, velcro, notions, tools (snaps/setters, eyelets, hot tips, cutters, scissors) and hardware.

For Further Information: Catalog, $1.

Store Location: At above address. Hours: T-Sat, 9:30-5:30.

Accepts: Discover, MasterCard, Visa

SEATTLE FABRICS

3876 Bridge Way N.
Seattle, WA 98103
(206) 632-6022
Fax: (206) 632-0881

Offers: Outdoor/recreational fabrics: Ultrex, Gore-Tex, lycra, taffeta, ripstop, oxford, packcloth, cordura, Sunbrella, Textilene, closed cell foam, mosquito netting, heat-seal packcloth, others. Also offers hardware, sewing notions, webbing. Custom orders.

For Further Information: Price list, $3 (refundable).

SHARLAINE PRODUCTS

104 Washington St.
Auburn, ME 04211

Offers: Outdoor and marine fabrics including acrylic and cotton canvas, Pac cloth, Ripstop nylon and vinyls. Also offers zippers, webbing, fasteners and hardware.

For Further Information: Samples and data, $2 (refundable).

THORBURN'S

123 Nashua Rd. Suite 128
Londonberry, NH 03053
(603) 437-4924

Offers: Line of polar fleece fabrics in prints and solids. Also offers kits, patterns and threads.

For Further Information: 35 swatches and brochure, $5.

TIMBERLINE SEWING KITS

P.O. Box 126-CS
Pittsfield, NH 03263
(603) 435-8888

Offers: Outerwear kits: jackets, vests, parkas, foot mittens, gaiters. Luggage kits: cargo bags, travel bags, totes, bike bags, logs. Comforter patterns also available. Fabrics: nylons, Cordura, taffeta, ripstop, water-repellent types. Also offers goose and duck down.

For Further Information: Brochure, $1; fabrics list on request.

Discounts: Teachers and institutions.

WY'EAST FABRICS

1345 19th St. NE
Salem, OR 97301

Offers: Full service supplier of outdoor fabrics including polar fleece, Ultrex, Cordura and others. Also offers patterns, buckles and other hardware.

For Further Information: Catalog, $2.

Quilting

Also see General Needlecraft Supplies, Fabrics and Trims, Sewing and other related categories.

ANGIE'S

P.O. Box 968
Frisco, TX 75034

Offers: Cotton print fabrics from known manufacturers, including fat quarter and yardage assortments for quilting and other uses. Also offers the octascope—dragon's eye—for creating multiple images of one quilt block.
For Further Information: Send SASE for list.

ART-IN-A-PINCH

7738 Davenport Rd.
Princeton, MN 55371
(320) 369-4500

Offers: "Art-In-A-Pinch" wooden hangers for quilts, without pressure points to damage the piece. Also offers rugs, weavings, etc.
For Further Information: Free brochure.

THE CALICO CAT

204 E. Main
Auburn, WA 98002
(800) 908-0885

Offers: Block-of-the-Month fabric kits; members pay modest fee and receive "makes-12″ block" fabric monthly; in Christmas, pastel, cozy flannel or soft-edge piecing categories.
For Further Information: Call or send SASE.

JAMES CARROLL ANTIQUES

P.O. Box 239
Franconia, NH 03580

Offers: Vintage fabric collection—1930s through 1950s cotton prints (plaids, paisleys, florals, juveniles); fat quarter assortments.
For Further Information: Catalog and color-photocopied swatches, $3.

CLOTH OF GOLD

1220 Spartanburg Highway
Hendersonville, NC 28792
(800) 316-0947
Fax: (704) 697-7651

Offers: Cotton fabrics in calicos, geometrics, solids, florals and more, including muslin in up to 108″ widths. Also carries Concord, Marcus Brox, South Seas, RJR, Hoffman and others. Long and fat quarter assortments and 6″ squares and assorted flag gold remnants also available.
For Further Information: Call, or send $3 for more than 300 swatches.
Accepts: MasterCard, Visa

COCHENILLE DESIGN STUDIO

P.O. Box 4276
Encinitas, CA 92023
(619) 259-1698

Offers: Computer software, including for quilting, Stitch Painter; and other sewing topics. Books, including Designing Repeat Patterns and others.
For Further Information: Catalog, $1.

COLONIAL PATTERNS

340 W. 5th St.
Kansas City, MO 64105
(816) 471-3313
Fax: (816) 842-1969

Offers: Aunt Martha's transfer patterns, ball-point tube paint, flour sack towels, pillowcases, quilt kits and quilt design books. Also offers "Uncle Bud's Yard Buddies" wood cutouts and patterns.
For Further Information: See your dealer, or write.

CONNECTING THREADS

P.O. Box 8940
Vancouver, WA 98668
(800) 574-6454

Offers: Extensive collection of quilt patterns and instruction books. Quilting tools; threads, tools, notions, cutters, markers, batting (cotton, polyester, wool), Q-snap lap and floor frames.
For Further Information: Call or write for free catalog.

THE COTTON PATCH

1025 Brown Ave.
Lafayette, CA 94549
(800) 835-4418

Offers: Wide range of cotton fabrics, including authentic African and Japanese cotton. Sulky rayon and metallic threads, silk ribbon; quilting and sewing notions, patterns, 300 quilt related and sewing books also available.
For Further Information: Catalog and fabric swatches, $8 ($5 refundable).

EXTRA SPECIAL PRODUCTS CORP.

P.O. Box 777
Greenville, OH 45331
(513) 548-9388
Fax: (513) 548-9580

Offers: Quilting aids—rulers, seamers, templates, grids, stenciling and other tools. Also offers plans for build-your-own quilt frames, Dream Seamer, learn-to-appliqué sets.
For Further Information: See your dealer, or write for catalog.

FABRIC SHACK STORES

995 Marvin Ln.
Waynesville, OH 45068
(513) 897-0092

Offers: Full line of name brand quilting materials, including home spuns and others.
For Further Information: Call or send SASE.

FAIRFIELD PROCESSING CORP.

P.O. Box 1157
Danbury, CT 06813
(203) 744-2090

Offers: Poly-fil, fiber fill, Extra-Loft, Traditional Low-Loft Cotton Classical, and Ultra-Loft battings. Also offers Soft Touch and pop-in pillow inserts. Manufacturer.
For Further Information: Contact dealer.

THE GIBBS CO.

606 6th St. NE
Canton, OH 44702
(216) 455-5344 or (800) 775-4424

Offers: Gibbs quilting, embroidery and framing hoops in oak, hickory and black walnut. Also offers basketry supplies.
For Further Information: Free catalog/brochures.
Discounts: Quantity; teachers, institutions and professionals; sells wholesale to legitimate businesses.

GINGER'S NEEDLEWORKS

P.O. Box 92047
Lafayette, LA 70509
(318) 232-7847

Offers: Cotton fabric collections/squares in designer prints, solid shades (30-plus piece assortments).
For Further Information: Catalog, $2; over 400 samples, $6.
Accepts: American Express, Discover, MasterCard, Visa

GUTCHEON PATCHWORKS, INC.

917 Pacific Ave., #305
Tacoma, WA 98402
(206) 383-3040

Offers: 100 percent cotton fabrics in over 200 prints and coordinating solids. Manufacturer.
For Further Information: Fabric samples, $3.
Accepts: MasterCard, Visa

HAPCO PRODUCTS

210 N. Central
P.O. Box 150
Rocheport, MO 65279
(573) 698-2102

Offers: Quilting accessories, including needles for quilting, appliqué and hand piecing, Hapsco quilting frame, Majestic 88 coated needles that glide through cotton batting, carousel mat holder for rotary cutting. Quilter's Helper thread holder.
For Further Information: See your dealer, or write.

HINTERBERG DESIGN, INC.

2805 E. Progress Dr.
West Bend, WI 53095
(414) 338-0337 or (800) 443-5800

Offers: Quilting frames and hoops, including floor-standing, no-baste types, variety of sizes.
For Further Information: Send SASE for details.
Accepts: MasterCard, Visa

THE HOWELL HOUSE

201 N. Main
Churuvusco, IN 46723
(219) 693-2438

Offers: Quilter's quarters in cotton name brands, including 18″×22″ in assortment bundles.
For Further Information: Call or send SASE.

INNOVATIVE IMPRINTS
10264 Beecher Rd.
Flushing, MI 48433
(810) 659-9606

Offers: Imprinting service for photographs to fabric, in color or black and white, with seam allowance.
For Further Information: Send SASE.

JASMINE HEIRLOOMS
500 Fairview Dr.
Greenville, SC 29609
(803) 292-0735

Offers: "Frugal Frame" quilting frame, including no-baste floor model in 2 width frame-head sizes. Upgrading to heirloom furniture style also available.
For Further Information: Send large SASE for brochure.

KEEPSAKE QUILTING
Route 258
P.O. Box 1618
Centre Harbor, NH 03226

Offers: Quilting supplies: Patterns, stencils, a variety of aids, fabric medleys, quilting kits, over 600 cotton fabrics (solids, plaids, patterns, textures, others), specialty fabric assortments, batting and muslin.
For Further Information: Free 128-page color catalog (or $1 by 1st class mail).

KEN QUILT MANUFACTURING CO.
113 Pattie St.
Wichita, KS 67211
(316) 262-3438
Fax: (316) 262-3455

Offers: Professional model quilting machines, variable speed to full 3500 RPM; four-way quilting operations.
For Further Information: Send stamp for literature and prices.
Accepts: Discover, MasterCard, Visa

LA MAISON PIQUEE
P.O. Box 1891
Milwaukee, WI 53201
(414) 332-4590

Offers: Quilting patterns: Set of nineteenth-century designs, bicentennial sampler of colonial America. French quilting explained in *Quiltbroidery*.
For Further Information: Send SASE for pattern list.
Discounts: Quantity; teachers and institutions; sells wholesale to legitimate businesses.

MAGIC NEEDLE
Rt. 2
Box 172
Limerick, ME 04048

Offers: Quilting kits, patterns, crazy-quilt items, threads, including silk, metallics, hand-dyed; pre-cut fabrics and fabric packages. Also publishes newsletter.
For Further Information: Catalog, $1.

MOUNTAIN MIST
100 Williams St.
Cincinnati, OH 45215
(513) 948-5276

Offers: Cotton and polyester quilt batting, cotton-covered pillow forms, polyester stuffing. Line of quilt patterns with templates in florals, inspirational and other designs. Manufacturer.
For Further Information: Contact your dealer, or send SASE.

NOLTING'S LONGARM MANUFACTURING, INC.
Rt. 3
Box 147
Highway 52 E
Stover, MO 65078
(573) 377-2713

Offers: Nolting's longarm quilting machines in 4 sizes (18″ to 36″) and a computerized quilting machine. Manufacturer.
For Further Information: Send SASE.

PATCHWORK PLEASURES
2394 Double Church Rd.
Stephens City, VA 22655

Offers: Hand-dyed cotton fabrics, including "Fiber Fantasies" color variegated designs, available in 100 colors. Also offers quilting supplies, silk ribbons, specialty threads, notions, kits, patterns and books.
For Further Information: Catalog with swatches and supplements, $4.

QUILT IN A DAY
1955 Diamond St.
San Marcos, CA 92069
(800) 777-4852
Fax: (619) 591-4424

Offers: Instructional videos and books by Eleanor Burns. Supplies: threads, patterns, others.
For Further Information: Free catalog.
Discounts: Teachers and institutions; sells wholesale to legitimate businesses.

THE QUILT PATCH

208 Brigham St.
Marlborough, MA 01752
(508) 480-0194

Offers: Quilting supplies, including a full line of threads, stencils, aids, others. Fabrics: cotton prints and solids, designer fabrics. Also offers books, instructional videos and handcrafted quilts.
For Further Information: Catalog, $2; with swatches, $5.

THE QUILTING BEE

357 Castro Street
Mountain View, CA 94041
(415) 969-1714 or 1-888-QUILTER
Website: http://www.quiltingbee com

Offers: Largest selection of printed and hand-dyed cottons in contemporary and traditional prints. Over 1,000 book titles. Will special order any item available in the market. Viking, White, Bernina, EuroPro and Baby Lock machines, sergers and all feet and accessories. Over 800 classes per year on all aspects of quilting, art, crafts and sewing for children and adults. Men's Clubs and computer user groups specializing in designing on the machines. Something for everyone. See our "Crafts for Kids" pages on the World Wide Web.

QUILTING BOOKS UNLIMITED

1911 W. Wilson
Batavia, IL 60510
(708) 406-0237

Offers: Over 1,400 quilting book titles—classic, contemporary and other motifs for quilts, clothing and home accessories; covers a variety of techniques/methods. Also offers sewing notions, over 2,000 bolts of 100 percent cotton fabrics.
For Further Information: Catalog, $1.
Store Location: At above address.
Discounts: Quantity; teachers and institutions.

QUILTS & OTHER COMFORTS

1 Quilters Lane
P.O. Box 4100
Golden, CO 80402
(800) 881-6624
Fax: (303) 277-0370

Offers: Quilting patterns/precut kits: designer, classics, heirloom, contemporary, old favorites, children's and others—all bed sizes. Also offers pillow kits, easy-patchwork kits. Fabrics: solid cottons by the yard, muslins, color packets. Aids: templates, patterns, frames (hoops, stands), notions, cutters, threads, bindings, linings. Carries quilt clothing patterns and books.
For Further Information: Catalog, $2.50.
Discounts: Teachers and institutions; sells wholesale to legitimate businesses.

QUILTWORK PATCHES

209 SW 2nd St.
Corvallis, OR 97333
(541) 752-4820

Offers: Cotton fabrics, including pre-cut assortments, squares, and coordinated pieces; foundation piecing supplies, watercolor squares, cutting scraps, and a Designer Fabric Club. Also has Q-Snap PVC quilt frames and quilting accessories.
For Further Information: Free brochure.

THE QUILTWORKS

Division of R&Z
1055 E. 79th St.
Minneapolis, MN 55420

Offers: Quilting fabrics: Concord, Marcus, Wamsutta, Peter Pan, Bernartex, Hoffman, Dan River, Mission Valley, RJR, South Seas and VIP. Full line of supplies.
For Further Information: Contact a dealer.
Discounts: Sells wholesale.

ST. PETER WOOLEN MILL

101 W. Broadway
St. Peter, MN 56082
(507) 931-3734
Fax: (507) 931-9040

Offers: Natural wool batting, custom wool, recarding service. Also makes comforter, pillow and mattress pads.
For Further Information: Free brochure.
Discounts: Sells wholesale.
Store Location: At above address. Hours: M,T,W,F, 9-5:30. Th, 9-8. Sat, 9-5. Sun, 12-4.

SALLY GOODSPEED

2318 N. Charles St.
Baltimore, MD 21218

Offers: 1920s-1940s quilting patterns, including Sunbonnet figures, Mother Goose, traditional, "Grandmother's," Primer and Dutch. Designs by Nancy Cabot, Ruby Short McKin, Bertha Corbett and others available.
For Further Information: Catalog, $2.95.

THE SEWING ROOM

320 Harmon Dr.
Lubbock, TX 79416

Offers: Quilting stencils (precut, clear plastic) in over 600 designs: geometrics, florals, borders, classics, animals, storybook, vehicles, old-fashioned motifs, alphabets, others. Marking tools are also available.
For Further Information: Catalog, $3 (refundable).
Discounts: Sells wholesale.

JANE C. SMITH, QUILTMAKER
RFD 1, P.O. Box 518A
South Berwick, ME 03908
(207) 676-2209
Fax: (207) 676-5567

Offers: Custom machine quilting services for customers; holds quiltmaking classes.
For Further Information: Free brochure.
Discounts: Quantity; teachers, institutions and professionals; sells wholesale to legitimate businesses.

SPILLER DYEWORKS
2524 Pine Bluff Rd.
Colorado Springs, CO 80909

Offers: Hand-dyed fabrics, including cotton, silk, velvet, linen and rayon in multiple colors.

For Further Information: Color card and ⅓ yard of usable sample, $5.

THE STEARNS TECHNICAL TEXTILES CO.
100 Williams St.
Cincinnati, OH 45215
(513) 948-5271
Fax: (513) 948-5281

Offers: Mountain Mist cotton batting (no prewashing), with Glazene finish, plus Gray poly-batting.
For Further Information: See your dealer, or write.
Accepts: MasterCard, Visa

Rug Making

Also see General Needlecraft Supplies, Knitting and Crochet, Spinning and Weaving, Yarns and other related categories.

ANDERSON HANDCRAFTED PRODUCTS

18962 McKays Cove Ln.
Leonardtown, MD 20650

Offers: Rug-hooking frames: Hardwood, adjustable (height/angle), portable; with guards; 9″ × 22″ working area; floor model. Optional lap stand.
For Further Information: Send SASE.

BAR-B WOOLIES

5308 Roeding Rd.
Hughson, CA 95326
(209) 883-0833

Offers: Lines of custom hand-spun and commercial hand-dyed yarns for rug hooking. Also offers dyes, including chushing, Coik, Classics, Gay World, Jacob Fleeles, mohair (natural, dyed and wool blends), silk, llama, linen, alpaca and various other fibers also available. Also offers weaving supplies and equipment.
For Further Information: Samples, $4 and SASE.

PATSY BECKER

18 Schanck Rd.
Holmdel, NJ 07733
(908) 946-3485

Offers: Line of Patsy rug-hooking designs in whimsical/folk art style motifs.
For Further Information: Catalog, $5.

JEANNE BENJAMIN

RR #1, Box 93 Lake Rd.
Brookfield, MA 01506

Offers: Line of "New Earth" rug hooking designs.
For Further Information: Swatch "Spot, Dip and Sky" catalog, $2; with addendum, $6.

NANCY BLAIR: TOMORROW'S HEIRLOOMS

11310 Prairie
Allendale, MI 49401
(616) 895-6378

Offers: Rug hooking supplies, including wools/tweeds in wide range of colors, dyed wool, kits, dyes, cutters, frames, bindings, hooks. Also offers ready-to-cover footstool of finished or unfinished oak.
For Further Information: Call or send SASE.
Discounts: Sells wholesale.

BRAID-AID

Rt. 53
Pembroke, MA 02359
(617) 826-2560

Offers: Rug-making/weaving supplies: Hooking/braiding wools by yard, primitive and Scotch burlaps, monk's cloth, cottons, homespuns, rug warp. Wool remnants available by pound. Kits: Rug-braiding, accessory kits. Tools/equipment: Cutter units, hooks, shears, magnifiers. Also offers patterns, shirret items, Braid-Klamp and Braid-Aids, dyes, yarns.
For Further Information: Color catalog, $4; free price lists.
Store Location: At above address. M-Sat, 9-5. Sun, 1-5.
Discounts: Teachers.
Accepts: MasterCard, Visa

BURLAP'N RAGS

52 Courtland St.
Rockford, MI 49341
(616) 866-4260

Offers: Line of rug hooking supplies and small kits.
For Further Information: Catalog, $2.
Store Location: At above address.
Discounts: Teachers.

COUNTRY BRAID HOUSE

462 Main St.
Tilton, NH 03276
(603) 286-4511

Offers: Line of rug braiding supplies including kits, wool. Also offers videos and books.
For Further Information: Send for brochure.

W. CUSHING & CO.

P.O. Box 351
Kennebunkport, ME 04046
(800) 626-7847
Fax: (207) 967-8682

Offers: Rug-hooking swatches: Perfection, Jacobean, spot dyed, studio, plus Dorr background wools, plaids and tweeds. Lines of rug designs: Joan Moshimer, Frost, Edward Sands,

Ruth Hall, Pearl K. McGown, others. Also offers known-brand frames, acid dyes for wool, rug hooks and books.
For Further Information: Catalog of rug hook patterns, $6 + postage.
Accepts: Discover, MasterCard, Visa

DIFRANZA DESIGNS
25 Bow St.
North Reading, MA 01864
(508) 664-2034

Offers: Hooked rug patterns/kits (burlap, precut wool fabrics): traditional and contemporary designs (for brick covers, tapestries, chair seats, pillows) including unusuals, florals, special occasion/personalized, New England motifs, others.
For Further Information: Catalog, $5.
Discounts: Teachers; sells wholesale to legitimate businesses.

THE DORR MILL STORE
P.O. Box 88
Guild, NH 03754
(603) 863-1197 or (800) 846-DORR

Offers: Wool fabric (exclusive decorator colors for hooking, braiding, quilting) and tweeds. Also offers hooking kits in a variety of traditional designs.
For Further Information: Free supply list; swatches, $3 (collection of 166 shades).

KIM DUBAY
37 Bow St.
Freeport, ME 04032
(207) 865-0512

Offers: "Primitive Pastimes" line of original primitive hooked rug kits and patterns.
For Further Information: send large SASE for price list; $3 for color photos.

EARTH GUILD
33 Haywood St.
Asheville, NC 28801
(800) 327-8448

Offers: Rug punches: old style, heavy-duty, punch needle. Hooks: latch, traditional types. Rug braiding: Braid-Klamp, Braidkin, Vari-Folder Braid Aid braiders. Yarns: cottons, linens, wool, rug wools, heavyweight, Berbers, Navajo wool, others. Also offers primitive and Scotch burlap, cutters, dyes, equipment, others. Supplies for fabric decorating, leather work, basketry, candlemaking, papermaking and other crafts also available.
For Further Information: Free catalog, or complete 100-page catalog, $1.

Discounts: Quantity; teachers and institutions; sells wholesale to legitimate businesses.
Accepts: American Express, MasterCard, Visa

EHB DESIGNS
132 Rosedale Valley Rd.
Toronto, Ontario M4W 1P7
Canada
(416) 964-0634

Offers: Acid dyes for wool, silk, mohair, angora, nylon yarn or fabric. Also offers fiber reactive dyes for cotton, linen, rayon and basketry materials and auxiliary chemicals and instructions for dye, paint and print work. Cotton quilt fabric, silk and wool merino yarns and hand-dyed and hand-painted yarns also available. Also offers technical assistance.
For Further Information: Free price lists. Acid color chart, $1. Fiber reactive chart, $2.50

EMMA LOU'S HOOKED RUGS
8643 Hiawatha Rd.
Kansas City, MO 64114
(816) 444-1777

Offers: Original Heartland hooked rug designs on monk's cloth or burlap. Rug-hooking kits.
For Further Information: Catalog, $4.50.

FKS DESIGNS
18 Brotherton Rd.
Vincentown, NJ 08088

Offers: Looper rug kits, including pre-looped cotton loopers and wound warp.
For Further Information: Send large SASE for brochure.

JANE MCGOWN FLYNN, INC.
P.O. Box 1301
Sterling, MA 01564
(508) 365-7278

Offers: Over 500 rug-hooking designs—traditional, classic, others (on burlap or cotton). Hooks: Pearl K. McGown, pencil. Frames: Puritan, hoops. Cutters: Frazaer, Rigby. Supplies/aids: binding, shears. Also offers Dorr wool backgrounds/swatches, colors by Maryanne, burlap (Scottish, primitive) and cotton, books, custom stamping on backing or odd/large sizes.
For Further Information: Catalog, "Designs to Dream On," $10.
Discounts: Teachers and institutions.

FORESTHEART STUDIO
200 S. Main St., Box 112
Woodsboro, MD 21798
(301) 845-4447

Offers: Belgian linen backing fabric—by yard, 15-yard lot

or bolt. Also offers rug wools, dyes, rug-hooking frames and cutters.
For Further Information: Send SASE for list.
Discounts: Quantity.

CONNIE E. FORNERIS FIBER DESIGNS
2446 NW 35th Terrace
Gainesville, FL 32605
(904) 373-0681

Offers: Hand-dyed wool rug yarns in gentle grading colors. Holds classes.
Discounts: Sells wholesale to qualified buyers.

HARRY M. FRAZIER CO.
433 Duggins Rd.
Stoneville, NC 27048
(910) 573-9830
Fax: (910) 573-3545

Offers: Supplies for hooking and braiding, and shirred-wool fabric by the yard or pound, plus others. Also offers rug hooks, braiding sets, cloth slitting machines, and others.
For Further Information: Patterns and supplies catalog, $6.

FREDERICKSBURG RUGS
P.O. Box 649
Fredericksburg, TX 78624
(210) 997-9440

Offers: Line of rug hooking and braiding kits, including contemporary and others. Also offers patterns and supplies and holds classes.
Accepts: MasterCard, Visa

GINNY'S GEMS
5167 Robinhood Dr.
Willoughby, OH 44094
(216) 951-1311

Offers: Full line of patterns (burlap, monk's cloth) for hooked rugs: Navajo, other Indian and Southwestern designs (kachinas, pottery, symbolic, others), Oriental and Eastern patterns. Dry dyes and dye formula books available.
For Further Information: Catalog, $4.
Discounts: Teachers and institutions; sells wholesale to legitimate businesses.

GREAT NORTHERN WEAVING
P.O. Box 462
Kalamazoo, MI 49004
(616) 341-9752

Offers: Braid-Aid braiding tools, reel aid, Fraser cutters, palm looms. Yarns/threads: linens, cottons, cotton rags (on coils), rug roping and filler cotton, fuzzy loopers, warps.
For Further Information: Catalog, $1.

Discounts: Quantity.
Accepts: MasterCard, Visa

THE HOOK NOOK
1 Morgan Rd.
Flemington, NJ 08822
(908) 806-8083

Offers: Lib Callaway Collection of rug hooking patterns.
For Further Information: Catalog, $5.50.

JACQUELINE DESIGNS
237 Pine Point Rd.
Scarborough, ME 04074
(207) 883-5403

Offers: Rug-hooking patterns in traditional and primitive designs (on cotton, homespun, linen, wool, burlap with precut wool strips): florals, fruits, pictorals, scenics, Christmas motifs, others. Also offers bliss cutters, wool yardage, custom-dyed swatches, precut stripettes, frames (Puritan, hoops), others.
For Further Information: Catalog, $8 post paid.
Discounts: Teachers and institutions; sells wholesale to legitimate businesses.

KINDRED SPIRITS
115 Colonial Ln.
Dayton, OH 45429

Offers: Rug hooking designs for small primitive and manageable projects which incorporate appliqué, quilt blocks and stitcheries.
For Further Information: Catalog, $3.

MAJIC CARPET
205 Locke St. S.
Hamilton, Ontario L8P 4B5
Canada
(416) 522-8669

Offers: Rug hoops (hardwood), plus hooking supplies and patterns.
For Further Information: Price list, $1.

MANDY'S WOOL SHED
Rt. 1
P.O. Box 2644
Gardiner, ME 04345
(207) 582-5059

Offers: Wool fabric (for hooking, braiding, weaving): Tweeds, plaids, solids in pastels, white wool.
For Further Information: Samples set (100), $3.
Discounts: Quantity.

MAYFLOWER TEXTILE CO.
305 Union St.
Franklin, MA 02038
(508) 528-3300

Offers: Puritan lap frame (to stretch rug, smooth onto frame sides, tighten; removable) and frame stand.
For Further Information: Order from dealer or teacher.
Store Location: At above address. Hours: M-F, 9-9. Sat, 9-5.

MILLER RUG HOOKING
248 Brentwood Ave.
Sacramento, CA 95825
(916) 428-1234

Offers: Traditional rug-hooking kits (with hand-dyed wool fabrics).
For Further Information: Color flyer, $4.

MISTY MOUNTAIN FIBER WORKSHOP
814 Annapolis Rd.
Gambrills, MD 21054
(410) 923-3852

Offers: Wool: Tahki, Plymouth, Dyed in the Wool, others. Also offers designer kits, fibers, accessories and books, plus looms and spinning wheels. Basic lessons with purchase of wheel or loom at no charge.
For Further Information: Free catalog.

MORTON HOUSE PRIMITIVES
9860 Crestwood Terrace
Eden Prairie, MN 55347
(612) 936-0966

Offers: Primitive rug-hooking designs printed on monk's cloth or rug warp.
For Further Information: Catalog, $4.50 prepaid.
Discounts: Teachers.

PAT MOYER
308 W. Main St.
Terre Hill, PA 17581
(717) 445-6263

Offers: Rug-hooking (wool strips) kits/patterns on burlap: traditionals—scenes and florals, abstracts, children's, geometrics, Indian/Southwest, others. Also offers kits/patterns for chair pads, rounds, hearthsidings. Dial-a-Harmony color wheels available. Also offers catalog/workbook of 200 original full-page designs.
For Further Information: Send SASE.

NEW EARTH DESIGNS
Beaver Rd.
Lagrangeville, NY 12540
(914) 223-2781

Offers: Rug-hooking designs (silkscreen printed) in Oriental, primitive and traditional motifs, with color photos.
For Further Information: Catalog, $6 (refundable)

OAK SPRING INTERNATIONAL
1000 Benson Rd.
Green Oaks, IL 60048
(708) 816-5969

Offers: Custom fish patterns for rug hooking by licensed taxidermist, including "trophy rug" of fish chosen and fish stair treads in 3 Series—salt water, cold water and warm water.
For Further Information: Call with inquiry; catalog and flyer, $3.

JANE OLSON RUG STUDIO
5400 W. 119th St.
Inglewood, CA 90304
(310) 643-5902
Fax: (310) 643-7367

Offers: Rug-hooking patterns (burlap or monk's cloth and rug warp), McLain and Potpourri swatches, Cushing dyes, frames (Bliss, Puritan Lap, portable wood frame) and hoops. Also offers Braid Klamp aid set and other aids, PB braid clamp plus scissors, hooks, needles, cutters (Fraser, Bliss), linen, and other cords and books. Publishes bimonthly instruction sheets. Service: Custom dyeing.
For Further Information: Catalog, $4.
Discounts: Teachers and institutions; sells wholesale to legitimate businesses.

PENNY RUGS & RUNNERS
P.O. Box 105345
Jefferson city, MO 65110

Offers: Rug hooking kits and eighteenth-century vintage designs. Custom-dyed wool felts also available.
For Further Information: Brochure, $2 and large SASE.

POLKA'S YARN FARM
Rd. #2 Box 312
Vandergrift, PA 15690
(412) 845-6883

Offers: Complete line of locker-hooking supplies, including hooks, kits, backing. Also offers instructional videos.
For Further Information: Call or send SASE.

RED CLOVER RUGS
84554 Parkway Rd.
Pleasant Hill, OR 97455
(800) 858-YARN
(541) 744-5934

Offers: Over 130 Shelbourne Museum and original Red Clover patterns for both punch needle and traditional rug hooking. Over 325 colors of wool rug yarn. Punch needle rug kits, books and the Oxford Punch needle also available. Also offers custom designing of punch-hooked rugs.
For Further Information: 40-page color catalog, $4.

RIGBY CLOTH STRIPPING MACHINES
P.O. Box 158
Bridgton, ME 04009
(207) 647-5679

Offers: The original cloth-stripping machine which cuts wool into narrow strips for hooking or wider strips for braiding or weaving. Available in 4 models and 10 sizes of cutter heads. Offers cutter regrinding service. Manufacturer.
For Further Information: Send SASE for catalog.
Discounts: Teachers and suppliers.

RITTERMERE-HURST-FIELD
Box 487
Aurora, Ontario L4O 3L6
Canada

Offers: Rug-hooking designs: wide array of traditional, classic and other designs, plus scenics, florals, animals, geometric motifs, many others. Also offers rug kits, rug hooks, wools, other supplies and aids and knitting kits.
For Further Information: 110-page catalog, $6.

THE RUGGING ROOM
P.O. Box 824
Westford, MA 01886
(508) 692-8600 or (800) 822-2957

Offers: 200-plus rug hooking patterns, including pictorals, primitives, animals, geometrics, others. Service: custom designing and repairs.
For Further Information: Catalog, $3.50.
Discounts: Quantity; teachers, institutions and professionals; sells wholesale to legitimate businesses.

RUMPLESTILTSKIN'S
20360 NW Phillips Rd.
Hillsboro, OR 97124
(503) 629-2174
Fax: (503) 690-0744

Offers: Tuft-hooking needles (eggbeater type)—electric and hand models. Also offers frames and rug backing.
For Further Information: Send SASE.

SCOTT GROUP
5701 S. Division Ave.
Grand Rapids, MI 49548
(616) 531-6400

Offers: Discounted rug yarns—wools (cones, skeins and by the pound). Full range of colors.
For Further Information: Send SASE with inquiry (send sample or requirements).

SEA HOLLY HOOKED RUGS
1906 M. Bayview Dr.
Kill Devil Hills, NC 27948
(919) 441-8961

Offers: Traditional rug-hooking kits/patterns. Wools by the yard or pound and hand-dyed wool. Also offers hooks, rug shears, cutters and frames including Heritage lap frame with gripper strips. Also offers burlap, rug binding, and other aids and supplies. Books are also available.
For Further Information: Send SASE for brochure.
Discounts: Teachers and institutions; sells wholesale to legitimate businesses.

SHILLCRAFT
8899 Kelso Dr.
Baltimore, MD 21221
(410) 682-3060

Offers: Latchhook kits (for rugs, pillows)—designs stenciled on canvas with precut wool or acrylic yarn (interchangeable colors available), traditional and contemporary motifs: Kamariah and Persian, florals, animals, Southwestern, children's, patriotic, inspirational, Christmas, others. Tools and aids, cross-stitch, and other needlecraft kits.
For Further Information: Catalog, $1.
Discounts: Sells wholesale to legitimate businesses.

SUSAN SMIDT
97 Freedom Hollow
Salem, MA 01970
(508) 741-6620

Offers: Illusion metallic wools—two-sided fabric with hooking wool on one side and metallic finish on the other.
For Further Information: Double set of samples, $3.

SPINDLE HILL
3251 Main St.
Coventry, CT 06238
(203) 742-8934

Offers: Mill end hooking wools—random colors, by pound (5 lb. minimum). Also offers hooked rug repair service (for clean rugs).
For Further Information: Send SASE.

SWEET BRIAR STUDIO
P.O. Box 731
Hope Valley, RI 02832
(401) 539-1009

Offers: Traditional and primitive supplies for rug making, custom designs and designer patterns.
For Further Information: Send for catalog.

TRIPLE OVER DYE
187 Jane Dr.
Syracuse, NY 13219
(315) 468-2616

Offers: TOD dye formulas books (over 100 formulas per book)—*TOD Book I* and *TOD Book II* by Lydia Hicks, *TOD Book III* by Janet Matthews. Includes TOD snips (8 shade samples to put with each formula in TOD books). Also offers measuring spoons—¼ tsp. to ¹⁄₃₂ tsp.
For Further Information: Free brochure.
Discounts: Quantity; teachers and institutions.

VERMONT RUGS
P.O. Box 485
Johnson, VT 05656
(802) 635-2434

Offers: Cotton denim strips with chenille edge, rug strips (blends)—by 25 lb.-and-up lots.
For Further Information: Send SASE and $1 for sample.
Discounts: Quantity

WHISPERING HILL FARM
Rt. 169
P.O. Box 186
South Woodstock, CT 06267

Offers: Rug-hooking supplies, including backing fabrics (primitive and fine burlap, linen), others. Specializes in out-of-print rug hooking books.
For Further Information: Catalog, $2.75.

THE WHITE HOUSE
653 E. Russell Lake Dr.
Louisville, IN 46077

Offers: Primitive hooked rug kits in a variety of designs, including animals, scenics and others.
For Further Information: Send $3 for information.

THE WOOL WINDER
RR 1
Manilla, Ontario K0M 2J0
Canada
(705) 786-1358

Offers: Line of rug-hooking and braiding supplies, including Woolrich and primitive wools.
For Further Information: Price lists, $1.

WOOL WORKS, PLUS
1246 Oak Ridge Dr.
South Bend, IN 46617
(219) 234-2587

Offers: Line of rug-hooking and braiding supplies and accessories.
For Further Information: Catalog, $1 (refundable).
Discounts: Teachers and dealers.

YANKEE PEDDLER HOOKED RUGS
57 Saxonwood Rd.
Fairfield, CT 06430
(203) 255-5399

Offers: Rug-hooking wool by yard or pound, line of other supplies including hooks, frames, new designs for spot-dyed wools, others.
For Further Information: Catalog, $5; send large SASE for flyer.

YESTERYEARS RUG HOOKING STUDIO
Rt. 1
Meaford, Ontario N0H 1Y0
Canada
(519) 538-2425

Offers: Ash hoops in three sizes, plus rug hooks and other supplies.
For Further Information: Write.

Sewing

Also see other categories of Section II.

A.C.S.
447 West 36th St.
New York, NY 10018

Offers: Sewing supplies, including cutting tools, notions, matched thread, linings, tapes and zippers pattern-making products, fasteners and other products also available.
For Further Information: Catalog, $5 (refundable).

ALL BRANDS
9789 Florida Blvd.
Baton Rouge, LA 70815
(504) 923-1285
Fax: (800) 866-1261

Offers: Sewing machines, sergers and embroidery machines: Bernina, Pfaff, New Home, Juki, Elna, Viking, White, Necchi, Riccar, Brother, Simplicity, Singer; commercial brands—Johnson, Thompson, Singer, Juki, others. Monogrammers—Toyota, Brother, Melco, others. Also offers smocking pleaters, machine accessories, cabinets, tables, pressing equipment, warehouse locations.
For Further Information: Send SASE for list (specify product, brand and price levels).
Accepts: American Express, Discover, MasterCard, Visa

AMAZON DRYGOODS
2218 E. 11th St.
Davenport, IA 52803
(319) 322-6800
Fax: (319) 322-4008

Offers: Nineteenth-century-inspired products: over 700 historic/ethnic clothes patterns, up to the 1950s, with emphasis on the 1800s: men's and women's clothing including corsets, military uniforms. Supplies/aids: hoop wire, boning, stays, feathers. Fabrics: Nainsook, batiste and other cottons, flannels, taffeta, satins, gold "bouillon" frieze, tradecloth. Also offers hat veilings, trims, military buttons and yard goods (blue, butternut, gray wool, etc.). Books available on costuming, fashions, accessories and lace making, Victorian and Indian clothing. Carries ready-made historic clothes, shoes, hats, accessories, plus washboards, buckets, washtubs, others.

For Further Information: General catalog, $3; pattern catalog, $7, shoe, $5
Accepts: American Express, MasterCard, Visa

AMERICAN & EFIRD, INC.
P.O. Box 507
Mount Holly, NC 28120
(704) 827-7556

Offers: Maxi-Lock polyester cone threads (for sergers and other sewing machines) in a full line of colors.
For Further Information: Contact your dealer, or send SASE.

ATLANTA THREAD & SUPPLY CO.
695 Red Oak Rd.
Stockbridge, GA 30281
(404) 389-9115

Offers: Sewing supplies/aids (some known brands): cone threads, closures, markers, linings/pockets, interfacings, shoulder pads. Also offers pliers, measurers, dress forms, hampers, caddys, gauges, notions, pleaters, cords, weights, pressing aids (irons, machines, steamers). High-speed sewing machines: Tacsew, Singer, Pfaff, Consew. Racks: counter, spiral, adjustable, garment, others. Also offers cutting machines.
For Further Information: Free catalogs.
Discounts: Quantity.

THE BEE LEE CO.
P.O. Box 36108
Dallas, TX 75235
(214) 351-2091

Offers: Sewing supplies: threads, buttons, zippers, laces, trims, Western trims, snap fasteners (pearl, others).
For Further Information: Free catalog.

BERNINA
3500 Thayer Ct.
Aurora, IL 60504

Offers: Bernina brand sewing machines, sergers, embroidery machine and scanners.
For Further Information: Send SASE.

BERNINA SEWING CENTER

660 Denison St.
Markham, Ontario L3R 1C1
Canada
(905) 475-9365

Offers: Bernina sewing machines and serger machines.
For Further Information: Send SASE.

BIRCH STREET CLOTHING, INC.

P.O. Box 6901
San Mateo, CA 94403

Offers: Pattern for children's travel pillow that converts to rest mat, plus patterns for children's clothing. "Suspender-alls," pants, sunsuits, crawlers, reversible blazers and vests also available. Also offers patterns for pop-up hat, robes, poncho, jackets, spiral and painted skirts, and others. Reversible zippers, snaps and snap kits also available.
For Further Information: Catalog, $1.

BOXWOOD ROAD DESIGNS

11307 Boxwood Rd.
Fredricksburg, VA 22408

Offers: Line of flag patterns and kits with fabric.
For Further Information: Catalog $2.
Accepts: MasterCard, Visa

THE BUTTON SHOP

7023 Roosevelt Rd.
Berwyn, IL 60402
(847) 795-1234

Offers: Sewing supplies: line of zippers, bindings, interfacings. Threads: Mercerized, specialty, invisible, machine, carpet, metallics, including Talon American and others. Buttons: usuals, military, decoratives. Also offers trims, elastics, tapes, cords, bra parts, pockets, ribbons, knit cuffs, measurers, closures, buckles, markers, notions. Carries old treadle and other sewing machine parts, plus new parts. Also offers scissors.
For Further Information: Free catalog.
Discounts: Quantity; sells wholesale.

BUTTONS BY MAIL

Rd. 3, Box 375
Georgetown, DE 19947
(302) 856-7569

Offers: Line of designer buttons for variety of garment styles.
For Further Information: Call or send SASE.

BUTTONS UNLIMITED

205 E. Casino Rd., Suite B20-28
Everett, WA 98204

Offers: Line of buttons—classic and unusual designs, shapes, styles.
For Further Information: Catalog, $3 (refundable).

CALICO CUPBOARD

P.O. Box 245
Rumney, NH 03266
(800) 348-9567

Offers: Patterns and sewing kits (precut, ready-to-sew): baby quilts, table runners, placemats, others.
For Further Information: Catalog, $2.

COATS & CLARK, INC.

Consumer Service Dept.
30 Patewood Dr., #351
P.O. Box 27067
Greenville, SC 29616
(803) 234-0331

Offers: Dual-Duty plus and specialty threads, tapes and trims, sewing aids, Talon zippers, Red Heart yarns, J&P Coats and Anchor embroidery floss and crochet threads. South Maid and Aunt Lydia crochet threads.
For Further Information: Contact your dealer, or send for free order form.
Discounts: Educators and institutions; sells wholesale to legitimate businesses.

CREANATIVITY

P.O. Box 335
Thiensville, WI 53092
(414) 242-5477

Offers: Nativity patterns/kit of soft figures: Holy Family, angel, kings, sheep, camel, donkey; starter set includes stable; Noah's Ark patterns.
For Further Information: Send SASE.
Accepts: American Express, Discover, MasterCard, Visa

CREATIONS

Box 59, Bldg. 1
Olde Lafayette Village Route 15
La Fayette, NJ 07848
(201) 209-8573

Offers: Custom-fitted fashion patterns drawn to measurements, with standard and couture instructions and embellishment suggestions included. Also carries line of fabrics, beads and yarns.
For Further Information: Free bimonthly newsletter and full color catalog.

CSZ ENTERPRISES, INC.
1288 W. 11th Street, Suite 200
Tracy, CA 95376
(209) 832-4324

Offers: Dress forms and pants forms kits: exactly duplicates body (make own or custom made). Also offers instructional videos and form stands.
For Further Information: Send SASE.

C. CUMMINGS
67 De Row Ct.
Sacramento, CA 95833

Offers: Publications on writing and marketing pattern designs, selling original designs to magazines, others.
For Further Information: Send SASE.

THE CUTTING EDGE
P.O. Box 430
Perryville, MO 63775
(314) 547-7562

Offers: Serger cone threads: metallics, colors, wooly nylon, Sulky rayon, ribbon floss, synthetic ribbons, packs. Aids: threader, totes, irons, neck lamps, others. Also offers cone stands, trees and serger books.
For Further Information: Send SASE for brochure.
Discounts: Quantity; teachers and institutions; sells wholesale to legitimate businesses.

DELECTABLE MOUNTAIN CLOTH
125 Main St.
Brattleboro, VT 05301
(802) 257-4456

Offers: Buttons in a variety of sizes, styles, colors.
For Further Information: Send $1 and SASE for list.

DOGWOOD LANE
P.O. Box 145
Dugger, IN 47848
(800) 648-2213

Offers: Handmade porcelain buttons (folk shapes), classic clothing and patterns.
For Further Information: Catalog, $2.50.

DRESS RITE FORMS
3817 N. Pulaski
Chicago, IL 60614
(312) 588-5761

Offers: Dress forms for all sizes and shapes; male and female.
For Further Information: Send for custom forms.

DRITZ CORP.
P.O. Box 5028
Spartanburg, SC 29304
(800) 845-4948

Offers: Dritz sewing aids: cutting mats and rotary cutters, measuring devices, grommets/kits, rivets, snaps, tools. Other aids available include grippers, holders, seam hams, press items, weights, notions, metallic threads and thread sets, machine accessories, belt/buckle kits, line of scissors, shears and snips, line of elastics, trims, cords.
For Further Information: Contact your dealer, or send SASE.

EASTMAN MACHINE CO.
779 Washington St.
Buffalo, NY 14203
(716) 856-2200

Offers: Chickadee professional electric rotary shears that cut material to ½″ thick, wheel cutters and sets, line of shears, scissors and nips; cutting mats, cleaners and sprays. Manufacturer.
For Further Information: Send SASE.

EASTMAN SEWING RESOURCES
3250 Peachtree Corners Cir.
Norcross, GA 30092

Offers: Sewing supplies including tools, gadgets, scissors, cutting tools, clamps, tapes and rules, pens and pencils, pins, sprays. Ergonomic work aids and other products also available.
For Further Information: Free catalog.

ELNA, INC.
7642 Washington Ave. S.
Eden Prairie, MN 55344
(612) 941-5519 or (800) 848-ELNA (in the U.S.)
or (416) 856-1010 (in Canada)

Offers: Sewing machines, including budget-priced sergers, others, plus machine accessories and attachments. Also offers ironing presses and sewing notions.
For Further Information: Contact dealer, or send SASE.

FASHION FABRICS CLUB/NATURAL FIBER FABRICS
10490-10512 Baur Blvd.
St. Louis, MO 63132
(314) 993-4919 or (800) 468-0602

Offers: Fabrics from clothing lines of designers like Liz Claiborne, Jones New York and Leslie Fay. Natural synthetic fibers including silks, wools, cottons, linens, rayons and blends.
For Further Information: Send SASE for brochure.

Discounts: Club plan offers fabric at reduced cost on payment of modest fee.

VICTORIA FAYE
P.O. Box 640
Folsom, CA 95763
(916) 983-2321

Offers: Imported sewing supplies: French and English laces, Swiss embroideries, silk fabrics and ribbons, other ribbons. Also offers sewing kits and other trims, lace motifs, jabots and collars (Swiss, English, French), plus original design patterns for dolls, teddies.
For Further Information: Catalog, $5 (refundable); silk ribbon color guide, $2.50.
Accepts: MasterCard, Visa

SHERMANE FOUCHE
P.O. Box 410273
San Francisco, CA 94141
(415) 550-0254

Offers: Designer pattern collection of women's jackets, trousers, others.
For Further Information: Send SASE.

GREENBERG & HAMMER, INC.
24 W. 57th St.
New York, NY 10019
(212) 246-2836 or (800) 955-5135

Offers: Interfacings, sewing notions, accessories and supplies for dressmakers, costumers, milliners, others. Also offers professional steamers.
For Further Information: Free catalog and swatchbook.
Discounts: Sells wholesale.

HANCOCK FABRICS
3841 Hinkleville Rd.
Paducah, KY 42001
(800) 845-8723

Offers: Fabrics: Drapery, upholstery, quilting, dress/fashion, others. Line of quilting supplies and general sewing supplies, including scissors, rotary cutters, rulers, mats, other notions nd other products.
For Further Information: Free catalog.
Discounts: Quantity; sells wholesale.

HOME-SEW
P.O. Box 4099, Dept. CSS
Bethlehem, PA 18018
(610) 867-3833

Offers: Sewing supplies: aids, ribbons, laces, threads, buttons, elastics, barrettes, web belting, poly boning, fringes, bindings, tapes, scissors, cutters, bridal appliqués, others.

For Further Information: Catalog, 50¢.
Discounts: Quantity; sells wholesale.

ISLANDER—VIDEO DIVISION
P.O. Box 66
Grants Pass, OR 97526
(503) 479-3906, (800) 944-0213

Offers: Sewing instructional videos, by Margaret Islander: Industry shortcuts, shirt making, skirts, others—industrial techniques adapted to home sewing.
For Further Information: Send SASE for brochure.
Accepts: MasterCard, Visa

JUKI AMERICA
14518 Best Ave.
Santa Fe Springs, CA 90670
(310) 483-5355

Offers: Juki Lock server, models for 1-, 2-, or 3- to 4-thread convertible overlock machines.
For Further Information: Contact your dealer, or send SASE.

LIFE INDUSTRIES
205 Sweet Hollow Rd.
Old Bethpage, NY 11804
(516) 454-0055

Offers: Remay pattern cloth: heavy-duty stabilizer sold by 6-yard lot.
For Further Information: Send SASE.
Accepts: MasterCard, Visa

LIFETIME CAREER SCHOOLS
101 Harrison
Archbald, PA 18403
(717) 876-6340

Offers: Dressmaking home-study course—speed-up methods and factory shortcuts included—for home sewers and professionals.
For Further Information: Free booklet.

LIVE GUIDES
10306 64th Place W.
Mukilteo, WA 98275
(206) 353-0240

Offers: Generic serger instructional video—all aspects of serger sewing on nine models of sergers (purchase or rent).
For Further Information: Send SASE.
Accepts: MasterCard, Visa

MARY'S PRODUCTIONS

217 N. Main
P.O. Box 87, Dept. CSS
Aurora, MN 55705
(218) 229-2804

Offers: Sewing books: appliqué, accents, sweatshirts, travel gear/gifts, squeakers, others. Videos: Designer Sweat.
For Further Information: Send SASE for free brochure.
Discounts: Sells wholesale.

MELCO EMBROIDERY SYSTEMS

1575 W. 124th Ave.
Denver, CO 80234
(800) 366-3526

Offers: Melco Embroidery Systems line of computerized embroidery equipment. Systems are modular to allow expansion. A computer with EDS III software can control from 1 to 768 sewing heads; the premier controller controls up to any 4 embroidery machines. Also offers Wilcom Digitizing Systems.
For Further Information: Send SASE.

NANCY'S NOTIONS

P.O. Box 683
Beaver Dam, WI 53916
(414) 887-0391 or (800) 833-0690

Offers: Sewing Aids/Notions: scissors, cutters, measurers, third hand, weights, markers, papers, machine accessories, hoops, charted designs/kits, laces, appliqué press sheets and fusibles, interfacings, reflective tape/material, serger aids, rag rug items. Threads: Mettock, wooly nylon, rayon, metallics, Sulky rayon. Patterns: quilted clothes, larger-women fashions (sizes 38 to 60). Video series, with Nancy Zieman—sewing, altering, tailoring, home decor, art, monogram, quilting techniques.
For Further Information: Free catalog.
Discounts: Teachers, institutions and professionals.

NATIONAL THREAD & SUPPLY CO.

695 Red Oak Rd.
Stockbridge, GA 30281
(800) 331-7600 ext. 230

Offers: Sewing threads—over 40 types, including Coats & Clark serging thread (in 250 colors). Also offers Wiss and Gingher scissors, Sussman irons, Dritz notions, others.
For Further Information: Free catalog.
Accepts: American Express, MasterCard, Visa

112 SEWING SUPPLIES

142 Medford Ave.
Patchogue, NY 11772
(516) 475-8282

Offers: Sewing machine parts, attachments, accessories for home/commercial models, hard-to-find items.
For Further Information: Catalog, $3 (refundable).
Store Location: At above address.
Discounts: Teachers and institutions.

PFAFF AMERICAN SALES CORP.

610 Winter Ave.
Paramus, NJ 07652
(201) 262-7211

Offers: Pfaff brand sewing machines including electronic models. European manufactured.
For Further Information: See your dealer or write.

PROFESSIONAL SEWING SUPPLIES

P.O. Box 1427
Seattle, WA 98111
(206) 324-8823

Offers: Sewing supplies including original heart-shaped Chakoner marker, fine silk pins, needles, thimbles, cutting tools, Also offers silk-weight iron-on interfacing and iron-on tapes and other hard-to-find supplies.
For Further Information: Send 25¢ and SASE for catalog.
Discounts: Sells wholesale; quantity discounts.

PURCHASE FOR LESS

231 Floresta Way, CSS
Portola Valley, CA 94028

Offers: Books on quilting—appliqué, patchwork, foundation method, samplers, imagery, modular, traditional and contemporary, basics, advanced, shortcuts, others. Sewing subjects include clothing/quilting, serging, cutting, colors, couture, embroidery, other fiber arts.
For Further Information: Catalog, $2.
Discounts: Offers percentage off cost.

RANITE CORPORATION/SURE-FIT DESIGNS

P.O. Box 5698
Eugene, OR 97405
(541) 344-0422

Offers: Personal fitting system, including starter package: dress kit with master pattern, templates, book, designing stylus, tracing vellum, instructional video. Also offers *Wrapped in Fabrique* about machine embroidery, embellishment and applique.
For Further Information: Send SASE.

ROSEMARY'S SEWING SUPPLY

2299 Duncan Rd.
Midland, MI 48640
(517) 835-5388

Offers: 100 percent cotton flannel (by yard): solids, prints, children's, double-napped, diaper. Also offers quilt bundles,

patches, receiving blanket flannel, muslin, pellon. Threads: cone and others. Carries aids, accessories, quilt batts, scissors, measuring tools.
For Further Information: Send SASE with 2 stamps.
Discounts: Quantity.

SARAH'S SEWING SUPPLIES
7267-A Mobile Highway
Pensacola, FL 32526
(904) 944-2960

Offers: Sewing notions: zippers, adjustable patterns, pins, needles, threads, aids, others.
For Further Information: Free catalog.

SCISSORS & SNIPS
P.O. Box 90147
Nashville, TN 37209

Offers: Scissors/shears by Wiss, Mundial, Gold Seal, Fiskars, Clauss and others. Also offers parts and supplies for cut and sew operations.
For Further Information: Free catalog.

SEW FANCY
Unit 23, RR #1
Beeton, Ontario L0G 1A0
Canada
(905) 775-1396
Fax: (905) 775-0107

Offers: Specialty sewing supplies including fabrics, heirloom sewing items, and supplies for smocking, quilting and fine sewing. Also carries patterns, including Stretch & Sew and others.
For Further Information: Catalog, $5.
Discounts: Sells wholesale.

SEW/FIT CO.
5768 W. 77th St.
Burbank, IL 60459
(708) 458-5600 or (800) 547-4739

Offers: Cutting mats in 2 types and sizes. Quilting templates, rulers, T-squares. Also offers Sew/Fit manual.
For Further Information: Free catalog.
Discounts: Quantity; teachers and institutions; sells wholesale to legitimate businesses.

SEWING LIBRARY
231 Islamorada Ln.
Naples, FL 33961

Offers: Sewing instruction books including books on puff quilts, mock appliqu , serger techniques, Sashiko, couture, pieced clothing, alteration business, fabric origami, you-make patterns and others.

For Further Information: Send large SASE for complete list.

SEWIN' IN VERMONT
84 Concord Ave.
St. Johnsbury, VT 05819
(802) 748-3803, (800) 451-5124

Offers: Singer brand sewing machines and sergers, irons, presses and accessories.
For Further Information: Free brochures.
Store Location: At above address.

SIERRA OAKS
2475 Fawn Hill
Auburn, CA 95603
(206) 251-9345

Offers: Igloo pet bed patterns—3 sizes.
For Further Information: Send SASE.

SILKPAINT CORP.
18220 Waldron Dr.
P.O. Box 18
Waldron, MO 64092
(816) 891-7774

Offers: Fiber-Etch fabric remover cellulose dissolving medium (removes plant fibers within embroidered area for "instant cutwork"). Also offers silk-painting items.
For Further Information: Free catalog.
Discounts: High and middle schools; sells wholesale to legitimate businesses.

SINGER SEWING CENTER
1669 Texas Ave. S.
College Station, TX 77840
(409) 693-6592

Offers: Singer, Necchi, Pfaff, Elna and other sewing machines, plus serger attachments. Sewing equipment: flower-stitch attachment, embroiderer's delight, spiral stitch attachment, automatic buttonholer (with 5 templates). Also offers Stitch'N'Trim overlock attachments.
For Further Information: Send SASE for list.
Accepts: American Express, Discover, MasterCard, Visa

THE SMOCKING BONNET
16012 Frederick Rd.
Lisbon, MD 21765
(800) 524-1678

Offers: English smocking/French hand sewing: Patterns, smock gathering machines. Fabrics: broadcloth, batiste, others. Threads: DMC, Swiss-Metrosene. Also offers a variety of laces, other aids.
For Further Information: Catalog, $3.

Store Location: At above address.
Discounts: Teachers and institutions; sells wholesale to legitimate businesses.

SOLO SEWING SUPPLIES
P.O. Box 378-D
Foxboro, MA 02035

Offers: Line of sewing supplies including zippers, threads, buttons, scissors, notions, irons and others.
For Further Information: Catalog, $1 (refundable).

SOUTHWEST SAVVY
P.O. Box 136
Apple Valley, CA 92307

Offers: Southwestern soft accessories patterns: cactus varieties, cactus-shaped potholder/mitts, pillows, wreaths. Southwest placemat patterns, roadrunner, quail and hummingbirds. Also offers Southwestern folk art woodcrafts plans and kits.
For Further Information: Send SASE for list.

SPEED STITCH
3113-D Broadpoint Dr.
Punta Gorda, FL 33983
(813) 629-3199

Offers: Sewing threads: sulky rayon, machine cottons, basting, metallics, wooly nylon, Metrocor, rayon ribbon floss. Patterns/kits: pillows, vests, others. Patterns: quilts, clothing, patchwork, others. Handbag items: frames, clasps, snaps. Kits and books: charted needlework, cutwork, quilting, others; fabric paints/dyes. Also offers battings, cutters, boards, hoops, stabilizers, machine attachments, magnifiers, and *Sewing With Nancy* videos.
For Further Information: Catalog, $3 (refundable).
Discounts: Quantity; teachers, institutions and professionals.

SUBURBAN SEW 'N SWEEP, INC.
8814 Ogden Ave.
Brookfield, IL 60513
(708) 387-0500

Offers: Singer Sewing machines, pressers, others.
For Further Information: Call or write for models available.
Accepts: MasterCard, Visa

THINGS JAPANESE
9805 NE 116th St., Suite 7160
Kirkland, WA 98034
(206) 821-2287

Offers: Silk notions, including thread, ribbon, bias tape and instant set fabric dyes and paints to "color" and embellish silk fibers. Also offers instructional guides and kits for coloring, stenciling and stamping silks.

For Further Information: Catalog, $1.
Discounts: Teachers and institutions; sells wholesale to legitimate businesses.

THE THREAD BARE PATTERN CO.
P.O. Box 1484
Havelock, NC 28532
(800) 4-PATTERN

Offers: Line of sewing supplies.
For Further Information: Catalog, $2.

THREAD DISCOUNT SALES
10222 Paramount Blvd.
Downey, CA 90241
(310) 928-4029
Fax: (310) 928-1064

Offers: Singer and White sewing machines, sergers, overlock machines. Also offers coned thread-spun polyester, super rayon embroidery, wooly nylon, novelty metallics and assorted others in a full range of colors.
For Further Information: Catalog, $2.
Discounts: On Singer and White sewing machines and overlocks.

TIMBERLINE SEWING KITS
Clark St., P.O. Box 126
Pittsfield, NH 03263

Offers: Sewing kits: totes, garment and cargo bags, packs, bike bags, drawstring sacks, billfolds, wallets, accessory pouches, ski bags, gaters. Also offers comforter kits (4 bed sizes) and outerwear clothing kits (jackets, vests, others). Manufacturer.
For Further Information: Catalog, $1.
Discounts: May run sales. Teachers and institutions.

TREADLEART
25834 Narbonne Ave.
Lomita, CA 90717
(310) 534-5122

Offers: Sewing threads, including Sulky rayon (35 variegated colors), DMC machine embroidery threads. Also offers sewing machine accessories: Walking foot (quilting). Carries fusible interfacings, stabilizers, needles, hoops, scissors, cutters, patterns, books. Also offers a rotary blade sharpener.
For Further Information: Catalog, $3.

VAN EPS
312 Willow Dr.
Little Silver, NJ 07739
(800) 382-5130

Offers: Swatch service (3 mailings per year) for couture fabrics (yearly fee), imported/domestic: cottons, silks, linens,

woolens. Also offers patterns, trims, others.
For Further Information: Send SASE.
Store Location: At above address.

VIKING SEWING MACHINE CO.
22760 Berea Rd.
Cleveland, OH 44111
(800) 358-0001

Offers: Viking Husqvarna sewing machines and other models.
For Further Information: Send SASE for nearest dealer.

WELLSPRING GALLERY
3330 S. Robertson Blvd.
Los Angeles, CA 90034
(310) 441-4204
Fax: (310) 470-6424

Offers: Art/specialty sewing products, including threads—tire silk, Sulky metallic, rayon and hand embroidery types. Also offers stabilizers, including interfacing, iron-ons and liquids. Specialty books including technique, art sewing, beading, design, paper and basketry titles available. Also carries other supplies.
For Further Information: Call or send SASE.

WHITE SEWING MACHINE CO.
11750 Berea Rd.
Cleveland, OH 44111
(216) 252-3300

Offers: Elna sewing machines.
For Further Information: See your dealer, or write.

WONDERFUL WORLD OF HATS
897 Wade Rd.
Siletz, OR 97380
(503) 444-2203

Offers: Hatmaking/Designer Home Study courses, including 15 study units with videos of classic style.
For Further Information: Catalog, $3.

YLI CORP.
P.O. Box 109
Provo, UT 84601
(800) 854-1932

Offers: Silk embroidery products, including ribbons in 185 colors, thread, floss, kits, patterns, videos and books. Also offers serging threads, including Wooly Nylon, Candlelight Metallic, monofilament, lingerie/bobbin, Wool embroidery yarn and fabric also available.
For Further Information: Catalog and Candlelight color chart, $2.50.

Spinning and Weaving

Also see General Needlecraft Supplies, Knitting and Crochet, Lace Making, Rug Making, Yarns and other related categories.

AVL LOOMS
601 Orange St.
Chico, CA 95928
(916) 893-4915
Fax: (916) 893-1372

Offers: Weaving looms: Baby Wolf portable, Baby Dobby to dobby loom. Also offers computer software for IBM, MAC and Apple II, plus weaving equipment/aids.
For Further Information: Catalog, $2.
Discounts: Quantity; teachers and institutions; sells wholesale to legitimate businesses.

AYOTTES' DESIGNERY
Maple St.
P.O. Box 287
Center Sandwich, NH 03227
(603) 284-6915

Offers: Home-study course in handweaving: series of lessons—beginner to professional levels. Also offers yarn club membership and yarn sales: cottons, wools, mohairs, linens, silks, novelties, close-outs reduced. Weaving looms and equipment also available.
For Further Information: Catalog, $1.
Store Location: At above address.
Discounts: Quantity.

BECK'S WARP 'N WEAVE
2815 34th St.
Lubbock, TX 79410
(806) 799-0151 or (800) 658-6698

Offers: Supplies/equipment/tools and looms for weaving, plus Ashford spinning wheels. Yarns: cottons, wools, mill ends, others. Also offers supplies for lace making, basketry, silk/metallic embroidery, cross-stitch.
For Further Information: Catalog and yarn samples, $2.
Discounts: Quantity discounts on yarns.
Accepts: MasterCard, Visa

BLUSTER BAY WOODWORKS
P.O. Box 1970
Sitka, AK 99835

Offers: Line of weaving shuttles, including 31 styles of hard-woods and custom designed shuttles to specification.
For Further Information: Send SASE for brochure.

BOUNTIFUL
125 Moraine, P.O. Box 1727
Estes Park, CO 80517
(970) 586-9332

Offers: Spinning wheels and weaving looms by Schacht, Norwood, Cranbrook, Harrisville, Louet, Glimakra, AVL, Ashford, Heritage, Lcclerc, Navajo. Also offers tapestry looms, parts and accessories, yarns, videos and books. Has layaway service.
For Further Information: 70 page catalog, $5.
Accepts: American Express, Discover, MasterCard, Visa

MAURICE BRASSARD ET FILS, INC.
1972 Simoneau, CP 4
Plessisville, Quebec G6L 2Y6
Canada

Offers: Weaving yarns: cottons, polyester, Orlon, linen, boucle, silk—all in several colors. Also offers Lamieux yarn (wool) and Nilus Leclerc looms.
For Further Information: Free price list; list with samples, $9.95.

CAROL LEIGH'S SPECIALTIES
7001 Hill Creek Rd.
Columbia, MO 65203
(573) 874-2233

Offers: Spinning and weaving tools, equipment, supplies and books. Line of natural dyes and kits, and permanent mothproofing. Triangular frame looms that weave in 6 sizes. Holds classes in spinning, natural dyeing, weaving and felting.
For Further Information: Product catalog, $2. Free workshop brochure.
Accepts: MasterCard, Visa

CASTLEGATE FARM
424 Kingwood-Locktown Rd.
Flemington, NJ 08822
(908) 996-6152

Offers: Romney fleece—greased and washed; plus handspun and millspun yarns.
For Further Information: Brochure, fleece samples, $2.50.
Store Location: At above address.

COBUN CREEK FARM
Rt. 10
P.O. Box 15
Morgantown, WV 26505
(304) 292-1907

Offers: Coopworth wool fleece—colored, white.
For Further Information: Send 25¢ and SASE for wool sample.
Discounts: Quantity.

COTTON CLOUDS
5176 S. 14th Ave. CS
Safford, AZ 85546
(520) 428-7000 or (800) 322-7888

Offers: Cotton yarns, kits, solid and variegated rayon chenille yarns; cotton spinning fibers, spinning wheels, looms, patterns, knitting machines, books.
For Further Information: Catalog and yarn, $6.50 ($5 refundable).
Discounts: Quantity; sells wholesale to legitimate businesses and production artists.

COYOTE PINES RARE BREED
P.O. Box 487
Balgonie, Saskatchewan S0G 0E0
Canada
(306) 771-2797

Offers: Karakul roving, handspun, natural-colored yarns.
For Further Information: Sample kit, $3.

CREEK WATER WOOL WORKS
P.O. Box 716
Salem, OR 97308
(503) 585-3302

Offers: Weaving looms by Norwood and Cranbook, cotton warp and rug filler, linen warp and weft, natural dyes and mordants, chemical dyes, drum and hand carders.
For Further Information: Call or send SASE.

CUSTOM COLORS
1221 S.W. Maple St.
Dallas, OR 97338
(503) 623-3404

Offers: Custom color cottons, blends (spinning), and quilt fabric. Pima cotton and silk, cotton/ramie and other cotton blends. Also offers cotton roving. Spinning equipment including Schacht, Ashford, plus spindles also available.
For Further Information: Samples, $5.
Discounts: Sells wholesale.
Accepts: MasterCard, Visa

CUSTOM HANDWEAVING
P.O. Box 477
Redondo Beach, CA 90277

Offers: Exotic yarns, including silk and blends, cashmere, camel, mohair, cottons, Spinning fibers, cut silk top; spinning equipment and books. Also offers handle wheels and looms of Ashford, Clemes & Clemes, Lendrum, Louet and Schacht.
For Further Information: Samples of exotic yarns, $6. Spinner's samples and prices, $1.50.
Accepts: MasterCard, Visa

CYREFCO
P.O. Box 2559
Menlo Park, CA 94026
(415) 324-1796

Offers: Cyrefco weaving looms—counter balance, counter march looms; Pegasus dobby system—for Cyrefco, Glimakra and other looms.
For Further Information: Catalog, $2.

DAFT DAMES HANDCRAFTS
P.O. Box 148-B
Akron, NY 14001
(716) 542-4235

Offers: Yarns, including pearl and mercerized cottons, cotton flake, silks, Shetland wool/polyesters and rayon chenille. Natural cotton warps.
For Further Information: Send 75¢ for each sample.

DORSET LOOMS
413 Lake Rd.
Mechanicsville, NY 12118
(518) 664-3668

Offers: Dorset looms—crossbuck design, folding floor models.
For Further Information: Write or call.
Discounts: Sells wholesale.

DUNDAS LOOM CO.
P.O. Box 7522
Missoula, MT 59807
(406) 728-3050
Fax: (406) 728-4695

Offers: Floor and table looms in 3 sizes each; spinning wheels, tapestry looms, weaving and spinning accessories.
For Further Information: Brochure, $2.50.
Discounts: Sells wholesale through dealers.

EARTH GUILD
33 Haywood St.
Asheville, NC 28801

Offers: Spinning wheels including Country Craftsman,

Reeves, Louet, Schacht, Norwood, Glimakra. Weaving looms: Rigid-Heddle, Tapestry, table, folding, floor (Schacht, Louet) and children's. Yarns: warps, wefts—cotton, linen, Euroflax, Marysville, Ironstone, metallics, Wilde, Elute, Harrisville, Christopher, others. Dyes: Natural Procion, Lanaset acid wool. Also offers spinning wheel construction plans, wheel accessories, loom accessories/tools, fibers, netting/knotting, rug making and other crafts supplies. Books are also available.
For Further Information: Free catalog of starter sets, samples and basic books, or 100-page complete catalog, $3.
Accepts: American Express, Discover, MasterCard, Visa

EARTHSONG FIBERS
Rt. 3, Box 108
Westby, WI 54667
(800) 473-5350

Offers: Line of yarns, fibers, dyes, spinning and weaving equipment, videos and books. Also offers herbs and essential oils.
For Further Information: Catalog and newsletter, $5.

EATON YARNS
P.O. Box 665
Tarrytown, NY 10591
(914) 631-1550

Offers: Finnish weaving yarns; wools, cottons and seine twines. Also offers Poppena Strips and two and line linens.
For Further Information: Color cards, $1.50 each.
Discounts: Sells wholesale.

EDGEMONT YARN SERVICE, INC.
P.O. Box 205
Washington, KY 41096
(606) 759-7614 or (800) 446-5977

Offers: For weaving: Maysville carpet warp, fillers, yarns, including cottons, wools, plus rags, loopers, jazz strings. Weaving looms and loom parts: Schacht table, Lil Bea 2-harness and Orco models floor looms. Also offers loom parts.
For Further Information: Free price list. Samples $5.
Discounts: Quantity; sells wholesale to legitimate businesses.

THE EWE TREE
61 Geoppert Rd.
Peninsula, OH 44264
(216) 650-6777

Offers: Fabric rolls, 6″-12″ wide, for rug weaving, rug and basket crochet and other crafts; 40 lb. minimum.
For Further Information: Send SASE for samples.
Accepts: Discover, MasterCard, Visa

FAIRMOUNT FARM FLEECES
Fairmount Farm, Thomas Rd.
Rindge, NH 03461
(603) 899-5445

Offers: Fleece for spinning and weaving: natural colors—white, cream, light/dark grays, browns, blacks. Also offers Finnsheep and Finnsheep Xs.
For Further Information: Send SASE.
Store Location: At above location.

FIBER LOFT
Rt. 111, P.O. Box 327
Harvard, MA 01451

Offers: Weaving/spinning equipment by Leclerc, Schacht, Harrisville, Ashford, Louet yarns, including natural fibers/blends such as alpaca wools, cottons, mohairs, rayons by Harrisville, Elite, Tahki, Plymouth, Crystal Palace, others. Exotics, fibers such as silks, angora, ribbon, cashmere, others.
For Further Information: Yarn samples, $5.25; fiber samples, $2.75.
Discounts: Quantity; sells wholesale to businesses.

THE FIBER SHOP
Rt. 2
P.O. Box 290
Farmland, IN 47340
(317) 468-6134

Offers: Spinning/weaving equipment, including Charkha wheels, Gaywood dyes, knitting and crochet accessories. Fibers: wools, blends, cottons, exotics, flax, others.
For Further Information: Free catalog.
Accepts: MasterCard, Visa

THE FIBER STUDIO
Foster Hill Rd.
P.O. Box 637-CSS
Henniker, NH 03242
(603) 428-7830

Offers: Yarns: novelties, Shetlands, rug wools, chenilles, cottons, silks, brushed mohair, perle cottons (3/2 to 5/2), Berber wool, 10/6 rug linen, Tahki wools. Spinning fibers: New Zealand fleeces, yak, mohair, camel hair, alpaca, silk rovings, flax. Also offers weaving looms and spinning wheels, studio knitting machines, exotic wood buttons, mill ends and closeouts.
For Further Information: Catalog, $1; yarn samples, $5; fibers samples, $4.
Discounts: Quantity.
Accepts: MasterCard, Visa

FIRESIDE FIBERARTS

P.O. Box 1195
Port Townsend, WA 98368
(360) 385-7505

Offers: Weaving looms: floor, tapestry and other types. Also offers weaving accessories. Benches with moving seats and display fixtures.
For Further Information: Catalog, $3.

FLEECE & FROMAGE FARMS

Siam Rd.
Windham, NY 12496
(518) 734-4952

Offers: Chemical-free yarns, exotic blends of kid mohair and silk, Rambouillet raw fleece, ready-to-spin roving and batting, and washable lambskins.
For Further Information: Samples, $1 (specify interest).

FLOCK OF MANY COLORS

2100 Swan Highway
Bigfork, MT 59911
(406) 837-4294

Offers: Montana wools: Raw, natural-colored fleece (black, grays, white). Specializes in long fleeces.
For Further Information: Samples, $3.

FORT CRAILO YARNS CO.

Broadway & Wisner Aves.
P.O. Box G
Newburgh, NY 12551
(914) 562-3623

Offers: Crailo handweaving yarns: full line of wools (worsted, rya, spun and lite spun), cottons (8/1 to 8/6).
For Further Information: Samples and list, $2.
Store Location: At above address.
Discounts: Quantity.

FRICKE ENTERPRISES

8702 State Rd. 92
Granite Falls, WA 98252
(360) 691-5779

Offers: Wool carders—chain-drive drum carders, metal and wood frames, motorized and manual models, bench carders. Also offers cotton and wool hand cards, batt picker, spinning wheels and accessories.
For Further Information: Send SASE for catalog.

FROM THE FARM/HEIRLOOMS KITS

Rt. 2
P.O. Box 239
Milton-Freewater, OR 97862

Offers: Pre-wound warp kits for wool scarves, garlic basket

kits, angel kits and others. Also offers herbal products.
For Further Information: Brochure, $2.

GAYWOOD DYES

P.O. Box 88952
Seattle, WA 98138
(206) 395-0327

Offers: Australian spinning/weaving supplies. Offers dyes for wool, mohair, silk, fur, nylon and cashmere. Also offers Gaywood sliver in a variety of shades, covered Correidale wool fiber, nooramunga spinning wool (Merino cross).
For Further Information: Contact your supplier, or send SASE.

GILMORE LOOMS

1032 N. Broadway Ave.
Stockton, CA 95205
(209) 463-1545

Offers: Handweaving looms: 4/8 harness types to 54″ sizes, flat heddles. Also offers Little Gem 18″ (4-harness) and 23″ 8-harness looms for weaver chair use; folds, with back wheels. Inkle loom also available.
For Further Information: Free brochure.

THE GLEANERS YARN BARN

P.O. Box 1191
Canton, GA 30114
(404) 479-5083

Offers: Mill end yarns and threads in natural, synthetic and blends, in a variety of sizes and types. Wool rug yarn by the pound also available.
For Further Information: Sample catalog and mailing list (1 year), $3. Wool yarn samples, $1.

GOOD WOOD

Rt. 2
P.O. Box 447A
Bethel, VT 05032
(802) 234-5534

Offers: "Good Wood" frame and slant weaving looms in small sizes; small frame loom kit. "Magic Heddle" lets weaver warp looms without threading warp through holes or slots. Also offers wood "inchworms" for making knitted cord and weaving project kits with natural fibers to use with Good Wood looms.
For Further Information: Call or write.
Accepts: MasterCard, Visa

DIANA HARDY: SPINNING & WEAVING

315 Washington St.
Lake Charles, LA 70601
(318) 478-9867

Offers: Line of spinning wheels and looms, fibers, yarns,

dyes, rug hooking and knitting supplies. Also offers books.
For Further Information: Call or send SASE.

LOUISE HEITE, ICELANDIC WOOL
P.O. Box 53
Camden Wyoming, DE 19934
(800) 777-9665

Offers: Icelandic wool for spinning and weaving (also knitting and felt work).
For Further Information: Write.

HERITAGE LOOMS
Rt. 6, P.O. Box 731
Alvin, TX 77511
(409) 925-4161
Fax: (409) 925-4506

Offers: Looms: table and inkle types. Also offers shuttles, weaving supplies and loom repair service.
For Further Information: Catalog, $1.50.

HUNT VALLEY CASHMERE
6747 White Stone Rd.
Baltimore, MD 21207

Offers: Cashmere fiber and yarn in skeins or cones.
For Further Information: Send SASE for brochure.

IN SHEEP'S CLOTHING
(800) 484-7133

Offers: Home-grown angora, fiber and yarn—specify preference. Also offers angora rabbits and supplies, custom knitting service.
For Further Information: Free catalog; samples, $1.

J-MADE LOOMS
P.O. Box 452
Oregon City, OR 97045
(503) 631-3973

Offers: Standard and computer-aided weaving looms: floor and table models (4-, 8-, 12- and 16-harness). Accessories and aids: warp beam kits, shuttles, raddles, warping frame, heddles, reeds, loom parts, weaving tools, others.
For Further Information: Catalog, $3.
Discounts: Quantity; teachers and institutions; sells wholesale to legitimate businesses.

JAGGER SPUN
Water St.
P.O. Box 188
Springvale, ME 04083
(207) 324-4455

Offers: Coned wool yarns (worsted, Merino). Also offers

"Superlamb" merino lambswool heather in 16 colors (washable), and wool/silk blends for weaving and machine knitting.
For Further Information: Catalog, $6.
Discounts: Teachers and institutions; sells wholesale to legitimate businesses.

JANE'S FIBER WORKS
604 Franklin St.
Greenville, TN 37745
(423) 639-7919

Offers: Spinning wheels and looms by Louet, Schacht, Toika, Glimakra and Beka. Also offers Gaywood and natural dyes, fibers, yarns and others; Interweve, Unicorn and Dos Teyedoras books.
For Further Information: Call or write for price list.

KESSENICH LOOMS
P.O. Box 156
Allegan, MI 49010
(616) 673-5204

Offers: Looms: four table models (10″ to 25″) and four floor models (30″ to 46″).
For Further Information: Brochure, $1.

KINGS VALLEY ANIMAL FAMILY
39968 Ward Rd.
Monmouth, OR 97361
(503) 929-2100

Offers: Fleece, including Romney, all-natural colors and white. Also offers processing service by special order and by pound.
For Further Information: Send SASE for fleece list; samples, $1.50 page.

KNOTS & TREADLES
P.O. Box 394
Delmont, PA 15626
(412) 468-4265

Offers: Video rental library—via UPS. Also offers weaving/spinning supplies and equipment, sheep motifs (on fabrics, ribbons, stickers, others), plus books and yarns.
For Further Information: Send 3 stamps for catalog. Sheep fabric swatches. $5.

LA LANA WOOLS
136 Paseo Norte
Taos, NM 87571
(505) 758-9631

Offers: Handspun yarns (plant-dyed and textured), carded blends, fleeces. Also offers Schacht equipment.
For Further Information: Sample card set, $20.

LAMBSPUN BULKY SAMPLE CLUB

Box 320
Fort Collins, CO 80522
(800) 558-LAMB

Offers: Yarns and fibers by the pound: cashmere, silk, alpaca, kid mohair, merino, others.
For Further Information: Send $5 for six list mailings.
Discounts: Sells wholesale.

LEESBURG LOOMS AND SUPPLY

201 No. Cherry St.
Van Wert, OH 45891
(419) 238-2738
Fax: (419) 238-2963

Offers: Leesburg line of looms and supplies, including two-harness and four-harness floor models.
For Further Information: Call for free brochure.

LOOM EXCHANGE

P.O. Box 9937
Seattle, WA 98109
(206) 782-6083

Offers: Used looms listings.
For Further Information: Publication, $1 and SASE ($4.50 in Canada).

THE LOOMPAL

4223 Lost Lane
Las Cruces, NM 88005
(505) 523-9039

Offers: Line of loom covers for variety of brands and models.
For Further Information: Send large SASE for brochure and price list. Indicate loom model.

LOUET SALES

P.O. Box 267
Ogdensburg, NY 13669
(613) 925-4502

Offers: Spinning wheels—9 sizes and accessories; carding equipment; floor looms with various weaving widths, featuring countermarche system; 24-harness table "Magic" dobby loom. Also offers a variety of natural fibers, dyed merino and corriedale for felting. British mohair and Merino yarns, Euroflak wetspun, dyed linen and silk embroidery yarns, including hand-dyed with natural dyes. Also lace making and felting equipment, range of dyes, patterns and books.
For Further Information: Catalog and list of dealers, $1.

THE LUNATIC FRINGE

161 Ave. C
Apalachicola, FL 32320
(904) 653-8747

Offers: The tubular spectrum color gamp kit—brilliant colors by the ounce, pound or ton. (Also has handmade jewelry, including shuttle pendant.)
For Further Information: Write.

MACOMBER LOOMS

Beech Ridge Rd.
P.O. Box 186
York, ME 03909
(207) 363-2808

Offers: Macomber handweaving looms: traditional Ad-A-Harness Looms and Ad-A-Cad/Cam Systems; also offers floor models and accessories.
For Further Information: Write or call for catalog.

THE MANNINGS

P.O. Box 687
1132 Green Ridge Rd.
East Berlin, PA 17316
(717) 624-2223

Offers: Weaving looms by Schacht, Norwood, Gilmakra, Cranbrook, Louet, Harrisville, LeClerc, and Gallinger. Spinning wheels by Ashford, Louet, Lendrum, Schacht and Rick Reeves. Wide variety of yarns from most major manufacturers and mill end yarns. Books for knitters, weavers, spinners, dyeing and felt making also available. Also holds classes.
For Further Information: Catalog and yarn style card, $2.50.

MOUNTAIN LOOM CO.

P.O. Box 509
Vader, WA 98593
(800) 238-0296 or (360) 295-3856

Offers: Looms: 12″ to 28″ table models; 4-, 8-, 12- and 16-harness models. Also offers transportable floor, tapestry and countermarch floor-style looms. Carries Maru Dai for Kumihimo, plus accessories and books.
For Further Information: Color catalog, $2.
Accepts: MasterCard, Visa

NORSK FJORD FIBER

P.O. Box 271
Lexington, GA 30648
(706) 743-5120

Offers: Norwegian, Swedish supplies/yarns for spinning, weaving and knitting. Also offers felting supplies, Norwegian pewter buttons and clasps; plus fleece and rovings in a variety of animal shades. Also offers portable tapestry looms.

NORTHWEST LOOMS

P.O. Box 1854
Ridgecrest, CA 93556
(619) 375-3179

Offers: Handweaving looms and equipment, including

Pioneer open-heddle/reed and traditional weaving looms, double-beam hardwood beam looms, shuttles, warping boards and related equipment.
For Further Information: Write.

NORWOOD LOOMS
P.O. Box 167
Fremont, MI 49412
(616) 924-3901

Offers: Weaving looms: workshop, folding, floor models—4-, 8- and multiple-harness. Also offers loom benches, shuttles, warping boards, other equipment, plus quilting frames and hoops. Manufacturer.
For Further Information: Brochure, $2.
Discounts: Sells wholesale to legitimate businesses.

OCTAVIA'S JEWELS
P.O. Box 308
Gladwyne, PA 19035
(610) 941-3508

Offers: Line of cotton yarns—10/2, 16/2, 20/2 and finger styles; variety of colors. Also offers sewing patterns in children's sizes, and fabric by the yard.
For Further Information: Send SASE for samples, information.

OLD MAN WOOL FARM
40350 Xeon St., NW
Stanchfield, MN 55080
(612) 396-2106

Offers: Handspinning fleeces in natural colors from romney-cross sheep. Available in grease, washed to processed and mohair.
For Further Information: Send large SASE with 2 stamps for samples and catalog.

OREGON WORSTED COMPANY
P.O. Box 82098
Portland, OR 97282
(503) 786-1234

Offers: Line of wool handweaving yarns, including Wilamette 2-ply, and Nehalem 3-ply; 12 basic and 30 promotional colors. Sold in cones.
For Further Information: Send $3 and SASE for color card.

PINE CREST ANGORA RANCH
P.O. Box 3867
Prescott, AZ 86302
(602) 776-0505

Offers: Mohair (long staple, no second cuts): raw and hand scoured/carded, by the pound.
For Further Information: Send SASE for prices.

PINTLER SHEEPCAMP
530 Faucher
Moxee, WA 98936
(509) 453-0183

Offers: Roving: Romney, mohair, Lincoln and blends in white and natural shades, plus Lincoln silver fleeces.
For Further Information: Send SASE for list.

RAREBRIAR SHETLAND SHEEP
Rt. 3, Box 317
Walla Walla, WA 99362

Offers: Line of yarns and clean fleeces from Shetland sheep.
For Further Information: Yarn samples, $1.

THE RIVER FARM
P.O. Box 895, New Market
Fulks Run, VA 22844
(800) USA-WOOL

Offers: Fleece—black, brown, gray, white Corriedale (skirted, sorted). Weaving looms and spinning wheels: Schacht, Ashford, Country Craftsman, Louet.
For Further Information: Catalog, $1.
Accepts: MasterCard, Visa

RIO GRANDE WEAVER'S SUPPLY
216 Pueblo Norte Rd.
Taos, NM 87571
(505) 758-0433, (800) 765-1272

Offers: Rio Grande weaving loom and spinning wheel. Rio Grande yarns: hand-dyed wool rug/tapestry/apparel types. Also offers Glimakra and Schacht equipment, wool warp yarns, natural and synthetic dyes, books.
For Further Information: Full color catalog, $5.
Discounts: Quantity.

SUZANNE RODDY—HANDWEAVER
1519 Memorial Dr.
Conroe, TX 77304
(409) 441-1718

Offers: Weaving and spinning equipment/supplies, including looms by AVL, Glimakra, Harrisville, Louet, Norwood.
For Further Information: Catalog, $3; free price list.

SAJAMA ALPACA
P.O. Box 1209
Ashland, OR 97520
(800) 736-0949

Offers: Line of alpaca yarns on cones in variety of colors.
For Further Information: Call for free samples.

ST. PETER WOOLEN MILL

101 W. Broadway
St. Peter, MN 56082
(507) 931-3734

Offers: Wool batting, wool roving, alpaca roving, curly mohair. Service: custom scouring and carding of new and used wool.
For Further Information: Free brochure.
Store Location: At above address.
Discounts: Quantity; teachers and institutions; sells wholesale to legitimate businesses.

SCANDINAVIAN DESIGNS

607 E. Cooper St.
Aspen, CO 81611
(970) 925-7299
Fax: (970) 925-7299

Offers: Prism mohair yarn dyed in five values; mohair cones (15 colors).
For Further Information: Dye color cards, $5.
Store Location: At above address. Hours: M-Sat. 10-7.
Accepts: American Express, MasterCard, Visa

SCARBROUGH

125 Moraine
P.O. Box 1727
Estes Park, CO 80517
(303) 586-9332

Offers: Equipment: Schacht, Ashford, Louet, Lendrum, Jensen, Norwood, Cranbrook, Harrisville, AVL, LeClerc, Clemes. Also offers natural dyestuffs, Meck wool combs, accessories, spinner's sample pack, plus instructional videos and books.
For Further Information: Fiber samples, $3.50; catalog, $2.50.
Accepts: MasterCard, Visa

LOIS SCARBROUGH

125-B Moraine
P.O. Box 1727
Estes Park, CO 80517
(303) 586-9332

Offers: Looms and wheels: Schacht, Harrisville, Louet, Norwood, Cranbrook, AVL, LeClerc, Ashford, Glimakra, Dundas, Jensen, Friendly, Inkle, rigid heddle, cardweaving, tapestry, Navajo and 4-harness styles. Harrisville yarns, kits, supplies and folkwear patterns also available.
For Further Information: Catalog, $5.
Accepts: American Express, Discover, MasterCard, Visa

SCHACHT SPINDLE CO., INC.

6101 Ben Place
Boulder, CO 80301
(800) 228-2553

Offers: Spinning wheels for fine/medium/heavy weight yarns. Weaving looms: floor models, table, tapestry and rigid-heddle type table models, plus inkle looms, rope machines. Accessories and tools: winders, shuttles, beaters, heddles, spindles, umbrella swift, others.
For Further Information: See your spinning supply shop; or send $2.50 for catalog and address of nearest dealer.

SCHOOLHOUSE YARNS

P.O. Box 1152
Worland, WY 82401
(800) 452-8813

Offers: Finnish weaving yarns: wool blanket type and other wools, worsted, plus linens and linen warp, seine twines and cotton Pilvi. Also offers cotton bias strips, and Toika looms and loom equipment.
For Further Information: Toika catalog, $2; sample cards, $2 each, plus 75¢ shipping.

SHADEYSIDE FARMS

P.O. Box 48
Chenango Bridge, NY 13745

Offers: Fibers, including "luxury" dyed or undyed; spun or unspun. Also offers dyes and tools.
For Further Information: Send SASE.

SHANNOCK TAPESTRY LOOMS

10402 NW 11th Ave.
Vancouver, WA 98685
(360) 573-7264

Offers: Shannock tapestry looms—high-tension, heavy-duty, professional type, with roller beams and weaving accessories.
For Further Information: Write.

SILK CITY FIBERS

155 Oxford St.
Paterson, NJ 07522
(201) 942-1100

Offers: Cone yarns (color coordinated, over 1,000 shades) including Contessa, Avanti, Majesty, Chenille, Katrinka, Slinky, Soie Rustique. Also offers cottons: Stonewash, lace, perle, stripe, fancy, others. Carries Metallique, Prima Donna, English wool, Montego, others.
For Further Information: Send SASE for introductory material.

SILK FOR LIFE YARNS

Box 4, 1300 S. Layton Blvd.
Milwaukee, WI 53215

Offers: Silk yarn handspun or hand-reeled, wool/silk or wool/silk/cotton blends.
For Further Information: Samples and prices, $2.

THE SILK TREE

1551 Johnston Street, #15
Vancouver, British Columbia V6H 3R9
Canada
(604) 687-7455
Fax: (604) 465-0976

Offers: Line of silk yarns and fibers, natural and dyed silk batting for quilting and spinning.
For Further Information: Samples, $5.

SILVER CLOUD FARM

1690 Butler Creek Rd.
Ashland, OR 97520
(503) 482-5901

Offers: Romney sheep and Angora goat fleeces for hand-spinning.
For Further Information: Send SASE for prices.

SPIN 'N WEAVE

2801 West TNA Road
Tucson, AZ 85716
(602) 321-0588

Offers: Supplies, fibers and yarns for weaving, spinning, dyeing (also crochet and basketry).
Store Location: At above address. Hours: M-Sat, 10-5.

STEEL HEDDLE

P.O. Box 550
Greenville, GA 30222
(706) 672-4238

Offers: Reeds: Steel Heddle brand, in standard and pattern reeds. Also offers custom-made reeds.
For Further Information: Send for order information/prices.
Discounts: Sells wholesale.

STONY MOUNTAIN FIBERS

939 Hammocks Gap Rds.
Charlottesville, VA 22911
(804) 295-2008

Offers: Spinning wheels, carders, combs, fibers, dyes and books.
For Further Information: Catalog, $2 (refundable).

STRAW INTO GOLD

3006 San Pablo Ave.
Berkeley, CA 94702
(510) 548-5241

Offers: Ashford spinning wheels, plus yarns by Crystal Palace, Chanteline and Villawool. Also offers coned yarns, wheel accessories, knitting needles and books.
For Further Information: Send SASE (52¢ postage) for lists.
Store Location: At above address.
Discounts: Quantity.

TREENWAY CRAFTS LTD.

725 Caledonia Ave.
Victoria, British Columbia V8T 1E4
Canada
(604) 383-1661
Fax: (604) 383-0543

Offers: Silk yarns in 15 weights/sizes; hand-dyed yarns in 70 colors; Ashford product line. Publishes newsletter.
For Further Information: Complete samples and price list, $5; complete samples with alpaca and merino wool, $8.

VICTORIAN VIDEO PRODUCTIONS, INC.

P.O. Box 1540
Colfax, CA 95713
(916) 346-6184
Fax: (916) 346-8887

Offers: Over 150 instructional videos on traditional and contemporary techniques for spinning, feltmaking, weaving, dyeing, and other needlecrafts and crafts.
For Further Information: Call or send SASE.
Discounts: Sells wholesale to legitimate businesses.
Accepts: Discover, MasterCard, Visa

THE VILLAGE WEAVER

5609 Chaucer
Houston, TX 77005
(713) 521-0577

Offers: Weaving and spinning equipment: Norwood, Schacht, LeClerc, Cranbrook, Glimakra, Harrisville, Ashford, Louet, Brother. Also offers weaving and spinning accessories and machine knitting equipment.
For Further Information: Catalog, $2 (with classes information).

VILLAGE WOOLS, INC.

3801 San Mateo NE
Albuquerque, NM 87110
(800) 766-4553

Offers: Line of Brown Sheep yarns and supplies for Navajo

weaving. Original patterns and kits for weaving and knitting also available.
For Further Information: Free catalog.

VRESEIS LTD.
P.O. Box 87-T
Wickenburg, AZ 85358

Offers: Cotton yarns, sliver and fabrics—naturally colored.
For Further Information: Samples, $8.

THE WEAVER-ARTISANS OUTLET
Clarion St.
P.O. Box 80
Smicksburg, PA 16256
(814) 257-8891

Offers: Line of looms, yarns and book. Also holds classes.
For Further Information: Call or send SASE.
Discounts: Sells wholesale.

WEAVER'S CABIN
20578 317th St.
Avon, MN 56310
(612) 845-7115

Offers: Spinning wheels by Rick Reeves, Ashford, Louet, Schacht, Pioneer and Chakkhas, Great Wheel Miner heads and spinning tips. Selection of woolcombing and carding equipment and fibers. Weaving products by Schacht, Harrisville, Norwood and Glimakras. Also offers heavy rug looms and electric rag rug cutters. Yarns also available, including linens, pearl cotton and marino wool. Dyes by Graywool and Procion.
For Further Information: Catalog, $3; wool roving 14 color sample card, $1.50; yarn samples, $5.

THE WEAVER'S LOFT
308 S. Pennsylvania Ave.
Centre Hall, PA 16828
(814) 364-1433 or (800) 693-7242

Offers: Weaving and spinning supplies and yarns.
For Further Information: Free catalog; sample set, $18 (refundable).

THE WEAVER'S PLACE
75 Mellor Ave.
Baltimore, MD 21228
(410) 788-7262

Offers: Line of Japanese braiding equipment, capped hardwood bobbins and fibers. Also offers braiding pattern and other books. Holds classes.
For Further Information: Catalog, $2.

THE WEAVER'S SHOP & YARN CO.
39 Courtland St.
P.O. Box 457
Rockford, MI 49341
(616) 866-9529

Offers: Weaving looms from Glimakra, Schacht, Norwood, Cranbrook, Harrisville. Also offers yarns, fibers, spinning equipment. Also holds classes.
For Further Information: Catalog, $3.

WEAVER'S WAY
P.O. Box 70
Columbus, NC 28722

Offers: Yarns, including mercerized Perle cottons, natural and novelty cottons and other name brands. Alternatives, Weaver's Way Wool and equipment also available.
For Further Information: Catalog and sample cards, $3.

THE WEAVING EDGE
3107 Franklin Rd. SW
Roanoke, VA 29014
(540) 982-0970

Offers: Complete source of supplies for knitting, weaving, crochet, quilting and spinning.

WEAVING WORKS
4717 Brooklyn Ave. NE
Seattle, WA 98105
(206) 524-1221

Offers: Weaving looms, spinning wheels and accessories, plus traditional and fashion yarns in a variety of fiber types. Also offers dyes, books, basketry supplies, and hand and machine knitting supplies.
For Further Information: Catalog, $1 (refundable).

WEBS
Service Center Rd.
P.O. Box 147
Northampton, MA 01061
(413) 584-2225

Offers: Namebrand yarns, close-outs, mill ends, and Webs lines in rayon, chenille, cottons, mohair, linen and wools on cones and skeins for knitters, machine knitters and hand weavers. Also has looms, spinning wheels, knitting supplies and books.
For Further Information: Samples, $2. Equipment brochure, no charge.
Discounts: Quantity; institutions. Discounts on yarn to all.

WHEELS BY VAN EATON

711 S. 70th Ave.
Yakima, WA 98908
(509) 966-1696

Offers: 18″ model "Fold 'N 'TOTE" handcrafted spinning wheels with Scotch tension, ratios of 15:1 and 10:1.
For Further Information: Send SASE.

THE WOOLERY

Rt. 1
Genoa, NY 13071
(315) 497-1542

Offers: Weaving looms: Glimakra, Harrisville, LeClerc, Schacht, Norwood/Cranbrook. Also offers accessories, spinning wheels, hand-spinning equipment and supplies, dyes, Fingerlakes yarns (wools/blends), kits.
For Further Information: 20-page catalog, $2 (cash/check) or $3 (MasterCard/Visa).
Discounts: On spinningwheels and looms.

YARN BARN

918 Massachusetts St.
Lawrence, KS 66044
(913) 842-4333

Offers: Line of weaving yarns, looms, spinning wheels, dyes and books.
For Further Information: Weaving, spinning and dyeing catalog, $1; looms and spinning wheels catalog, $1.

YOLO WOOL PRODUCTS

41501 County Rd. 27
Woodland, CA 95776
(916) 666-1473

Offers: Sliver for spinning, weaving yarns, plus wool batting and knitting yarns.
For Further Information: Flyers, samples, $2.
Discounts: Quantity; sells wholesale to legitimate businesses.

Yarns—Multipurpose

Also see General Needlecraft Supplies, Knitting and Crochet, Spinning and Weaving and other related categories.

BLACK SHEEP WOOLS
P.O. Box 9205
Lowell, MA 01853
(508) 937-0320

Offers: Line of natural-fiber yarns.
For Further Information: Samples, $3.

BROADWAY YARN CO.
P.O. Box 1467
Sanford, NC 27331
(919) 774-6331

Offers: Yarns for weaving, crochet, knitting, macrame: Poly/cottons, nylon, wools and blends, polyester. Also offers loom selvage, others.
For Further Information: Swatch cards, $3 (refundable).
Discounts: Sells wholesale.

CREATIVE YARNS
9 Swann St.
Asheville, NC 28803
(704) 274-7769

Offers: Knitting yarns: Towan, Plymouth, Tahki, Brown Sheep. Also offers handpainted needlepoint canvas, silks, Paternaya, metallics.
For Further Information: Catalog, $3.50.
Accepts: MasterCard, Visa

DAVIDSON'S OLD MILL YARNS
P.O. Box 8
Eaton Rapids, MI 48827
(517) 663-2711

Offers: Mill end yarns: variety of types and colors.
For Further Information: Catalog, $3.

ERDAL YARNS, LTD.
303 Fifth Ave., Suite 1104
New York, NY 10016
(800) 237-6594 or (212) 725-0162

Offers: Yarns for knitting and weaving, including a wide range of high fashion yarns, regular and mill end yarns.
For Further Information: Yarn samples and colors, $2.50.

FIESTA YARNS
P.O. Box 2548
Corrales, NM 87048
(505) 897-4485

Offers: Hand-dyed yarns—mohair, rayon, cotton, silk, wools—in a variety of plies, colors, textures.
For Further Information: Color cards, $10.

FILATURE LEMIEUX, INC.
Box 250, 125 Rte. 108
St. Ephrim, Beauce S. Quebec, G0M 1R0
Canada
(418) 484-2169
Fax: (418) 484-5561

Offers: Line of La-Mieux yarn wool in over 100 colors for knitting, weaving, carpets and rugs.

THE GLEANERS YARN BARN
P.O. Box 1191
Canton, GA 30114
(404) 479-5083

Offers: First-quality mill end yarns: cottons, rayons and blends, cotton/nylon, acrylics, wools, polyesters, orlon, lyrux, angora blends, wool rug, boucle and novelty types. Available by the pound.
For Further Information: Current samples (year's mailing), $3.
Discounts: Quantity.

MARTHA HALL
462 Main St.
Yarmouth, ME 04096
(207) 846-9746

Offers: Hand-dyed yarns: mohair, silks, linens, cottons, cashmere, alpaca, natural Maine wools. Also ribbons, totes, baskets and books.
For Further Information: Catalog, $2; yarn sample set (230), $12.

HANEKE MERINO WOOL

630 North Blackcat Rd.
Meridian, ID 83642
(800) 523-WOOL

Offers: Merino wool yarn, naturally processed; and alpaca/wool blends.
For Further Information: Free sample cards.

JAMIE HARMON

RR 3, Box 464
Jericho, VT 05465

Offers: Handspun and naturally dyed wool yarn, worsted weights, others. Also offers Rainbow Ridge children's sweater kits.
For Further Information: Samples and brochure, $4.

MARR HAVEN

772 39th St., Dept CSS
Allegan, MI 49010
(616) 673-8800

Offers: Wool yarn, including merino-Rambouillet, by skeins or cones in natural and dyed colors. Supplies for hand and machine knitters. Locker hooks and spinning supplies also available.
For Further Information: Send large SASE.

DEBBIE HAZY

607 Seabrook Dr.
Indiana, PA 15701
(412) 349-4899

Offers: Knit roping yarn for placemats, rug weft or braiding.
For Further Information: Sample pack, $2.

HUMMINGBIRD FIBERS

431 Seaview Dr.
Aptos, CA 95003
(408) 689-0434

Offers: Yarns for knitting and weaving—cottons, rayons, synthetics—allergy-free types.
For Further Information: Samples, $3 (refundable).

CHERYL KOLANDER'S AURORA SILK

5806 N. Vancouver Ave.
Portland, OR 97217
(503) 286-4149

Offers: Line of silk yarns, naturally hand-dyed, in 4 sizes and 180 colors for weaving, knitting, crochet and needlework. Also offers hemp spinning fiber, including 5 yarns for knitting, weaving and needlework in 24 naturally hand-dyed col-ors and a book on hemp. Also offers natural dyes and custom dyeing service.
For Further Information: Samples, $2.

MOUNTAIN COLORS

P.O. Box 156
Corvallis, MT 59828
(406) 777-3377

Offers: Hand-painted yarns and multi-color painterly yarns in 14 shades inspired by the Rocky Mountain West, available in wool, mohair and novelty types.
For Further Information: Color card and brochure, $5.

OGIER TRADING CO.

410 Nevada Ave.
P.O. Box 686
Moss Beach, CA 94038
(415) 728-8554
Fax: (415) 728-8539

Offers: Line of imported fashion and novelty yarns—variety of weights, colors, styles. Knitting needles and accessories; books.
For Further Information: Color card subscription, $12 for 4 mailings; $20 for 8 mailings.

PERSONAL THREADS BOUTIQUE

8025 West Dodge Rd.
Omaha, NE 68114
(800) 306-7733

Offers: 800 yarns in all colors by Vittadini, Jaeger, Tahki, Classic Elite, Brown Sheep, Colinette, Misoni, Cynthia Helene, Annabell Fox and others. Also carries full range of needlework supplies.
For Further Information: Call for newsletter and prices.

QUALITY YARNS

570 Westbank Rd.
Glenwood Springs, CO 81601
(800) 845-YARN

Offers: Variety of yarns including wools, cottons, linens, metallics, silks.
For Further Information: 64 sample cards, $20; selected samples, $5.

SCHAEFER YARNS

(800) FOR-YARN

Offers: Line of hand-dyed yarns, including designer, wools, novelties and others.
For Further Information: Call.

SILK FOR LIFE YARNS

Box 4F, 1300 S. Layton Blvd.
Milwaukee, WI 53215

Offers: Silk yarn handspun or hand-reeled, wool/silk and wool/silk/cotton blends.
For Further Information: Samples and prices, $2.

THE UNIQUE

11 E. Bijou St.
Colorado Springs, CO 80903
(719) 473-9406

Offers: Line of Rauma yarns; close-out yarns
For Further Information: Color cards, $3.50 each.
Store Location: At above address. Hours: M-Sat, 10-5:30.
Accepts: American Express, Discover, MasterCard, Visa

WEAVER'S WAY

P.O. Box 70
Columbus, NC 28722

Offers: Mercerized/Perle, natural and novelty cotton yarns, wools. Also offers weaving equipment.
For Further Information: Catalog, sample cards set, $3 (cash).
Discounts: On volume orders.

WILDE YARNS

3737 Main St.
P.O. Box 4662
Philadelphia, PA 19127
(215) 482-8800

Offers: Wool yarns for weaving and knitting in variety of weights and colors. Carded wool in natural and dyed colors for hand spinning and feltmaking.

For Further Information: Sample pack, $7.50.
Store Location: At above address.
Discounts: Available to retailers, institutions, and production crafts people.

THE WOOLERY

R.D. 1, Stewarts' Corners
Genoa, NY 13071
(315) 497-1542

Offers: Yarns: Soft wools and angoras in 29 colors. Un-Spun yarns also available.
For Further Information: Samples, $3.
Discounts: Sells wholesale.

YARN BARN

918 Massachusetts St.
Lawrence, KS 66044
(913) 842-4333

Offers: Weaving and knitting yarns, and weaving and spinning equipment, dyes and books.
For Further Information: Catalog, $1.
Store Location: At above address.
Discounts: Quantity.

YARNS BY MAIL

2215 Louise Lane
Norman, OK 73071
(405) 360-0140

Offers: Yarns, including Green Mountain Spinnery wool, silk, mohair, cotton; sport, DK, worsted; skeins and cones. Fingerlakes Woolen Mill merino, silk, angora; DK, worsted, bulky types. Un-spuns also available, skeins winding service, no charge.
For Further Information: Call or send $6 for color samples.
Accepts: MasterCard, Visa

Resources

Associations

Also see General Craft Supplies and Publications.
Include a business-size, stamped, self-addressed envelope with inquiries to associations.

AMERICAN ASSOCIATION OF WOODTURNERS

3200 Lexington Ave.
Shoreview, MN 55126
(612) 484-9094
Fax: (612) 484-1724

This International non-profit association is dedicated to providing education and information to those interested in this craft. Members get a quarterly journal, American Woodturners, and annual resources directory and other benefits.

AMERICAN CRAFT COUNCIL

72 Spring St.
New York, NY 10019

This nonprofit educational organization promotes excellence in contemporary craft (clay, fiber, glass, metal, wood and other media) through a variety of programs. Publishes *American Craft*, a bimonthly magazine and holds juried craft fairs annually across the country. Also offers a research library.
For Further Information: Send SASE.

AMERICAN QUILTER'S SOCIETY

P.O. Box 3290
Paducah, KY 42002
(502) 898-7903
Fax: (502) 898-8890

Members of this society of professional and amateur quilters join to carry on this American tradition. They receive *American Quilter* magazine 4 times yearly, the *Update* bimonthly newsletter, discount admission to the Annual National Quilt Show and Contest (that awards over $80,000 in cash prizes), receive member discounts of up to 20 percent on books and other resources. They also share experiences, ideas and advice with other members nationwide.

AMERICAN SEWING GUILD

1341 Highcrest Dr.
Medford, OR 97504
(503) 772-4059

Membership includes a quarterly notion newsletter and discounts. Regional groups hold meetings.

AMERICAN SOCIETY OF ARTISTS, INC.

P.O. Box 1326
Palatine, IL 60078

This is a professional service organization for artists and artisans; membership is juried. Membership benefits include access to a health insurance program, art shows and art/craft shows. Those qualified may participate in lecture and demonstration services. Alsooffers *A.S.A. Artisan*, a quarterly publication.

AMERICAN SOCIETY OF GEMCUTTERS

P.O. Box 9852
Washington, DC 20016

Members of this association receive *American Gemcutter* magazine monthly, plus gem cutting evaluations and instructions with regional and national awards for excellence. Also offers marketing assistance through participation in a national marketing plan to sell cut stones. Offers other educational and supplemental services, design library supplements, access to the Gemcutters National Library, others.

AMERICAN SOCIETY OF MARINE ARTISTS

1461 Cathy's Ln.
North Wales, PA 19454

This is a national organization formed to promote marine art for all interested in ship, shore or sea. Members take part in national exhibitions, educational exchange, informative newsletters and social gatherings.

ASSOCIATION OF TRADITIONAL HOOKING ARTISTS

1360 Newman Ave.
Seekonk, MA 02771

This rug-hooking association of guilds (ATHA) has a publication issued bimonthly—with news, views, tips and techniques on the craft.

THE FRIENDS OF THE ORIGAMI CENTER OF AMERICA

15 W. 77th St.
New York, NY 10024
(212) 769-5635

This is an organization of those interested in the paper folding art of origami. Members have use of a lending library, receive a newsletter and get a free folding session and may attend conventions.

HANDWEAVERS GUILD OF AMERICA, INC.

2402 University Ave., Ste. 702
St. Paul, MN 55114
(612) 646-0802
Fax: (612) 646-0806

This is a nonprofit organization dedicated to bringing together weavers, spinners, dyers, basket weavers, patrons and educators interested in the fiber arts. HGA offers members educational opportunties, a subscription to *Shuttle, Spindle & Dyepot*, a quarterly magazine, and discounted rates to the biennial conference and annual exhibit. Also offers slide kits, textile sample kits and videos for rental; videos, books and manuals for sale.
Accepts: MasterCard, Visa

INTERNATIONAL GUILD OF MINIATURE ARTISANS

P.O. Box 71
Bridgeport, NY 13030
(315) 699-3903

The IGMA was founded to establish a standard of quality and promote excellence in the field of artistic miniatures; individuals may join as general members and after six months may apply for Guild Artisan Membership (by submitting samples of their work). Pays an initiation fee if accepted. Among the primary goals of the association: encouragement, education. Events: exhibits, shows—with awards for excellence.

INTERNATIONAL SCULPTURE CENTER

1050 Potomac St. NW, #250
Washington, DC 20007
(202) 785-1144
Fax: ((202) 785-0810

A subscription to *Sculpture Magazine* automatically entitles one to a membership in this nonprofit organization devoted to professional development of sculptors, and an appreciation of sculpture worldwide. Among other member benefits: Free registration in Sculpture Source (a computerized slide registry linking sculptors with purchasers; non-artists get a discount on first-time use), group health and fine arts insurance rates, discounts, priority registration to events, use of a resources library. (Professional level memberships receive additional benefits.)

THE KNITTING GUILD OF AMERICA

P.O. Box 1606
Knoxville, TN 37901

This is an association of those who love to hand or machine knit and knitting teachers, designers, manufacturers and shop owners, etc., that offers members a master knitter program, correspondence courses, a national design competition and national convention; also offers the bimonthly magazine, *Cast On*, with designs and how-to information, and product

and other news. Local guilds meet and share educational programs.

THE KNITTING GUILD OF CANADA

P.O. Box 549
St. George, Ontario N0E 1N0
Canada
(519) 442-4150
Fax: (519) 942-4673

This guild of machine and hand knitters connects knitters from coast to coast in Canada. It offers a quarterly magazine, teacher registry, information and a library on all aspects of knitting.

MARITIME SHIP MODELERS GUILD

1675 Lower Water St.
Halifax, Nova Scotia B3J 1S3
Canada

This guild is dedicated to sharing expertise in ship model construction. Monthly meetings are held, along with monthly workshops. Club members are interested in a wide range of styles and types of model construction.

NATIONAL ASSOCIATION OF MINIATURE ENTHUSIASTS

P.O. Box 69
Carmel, IN 46032
(317) 571-8094

Members of this miniatures crafting organization network with others and receive the *Miniature Gazette* quarterly.

NATIONAL CLOTH DOLLMAKERS ASSOCIATION

1601 Provincetown Dr.
San Jose, CA 95129
(317) 571-8094

This association whose members love and make cloth dolls is open to any who shares that experience.

NATIONAL INSTITUTE OF AMERICAN DOLL ARTISTS

77 Cornell St.
Kingston, NY 12401
(914) 687-7949

This is an organization of professional doll artists and its devoted patrons. For patrons membership information, contact: Kathie Van Winkle, 12730 Shadowline St., Poway, CA 92064. For artist membership information, contact Lisa Lichtenfels, P.O. Box 90537, Springfield, MA, 01139.

NATIONAL MODEL RAILROAD ASSOCIATION

4121 Cromwell Rd.
Chattanooga, TN 37421
(423) 892-2846
Fax: (423) 899-4869

Membership to this national group is open to all age groups—

youth to elders—who are interested in model railroading. These members receive the NMRA bulletin of news, events and related information.

NATIONAL SOCIETY OF TOLE AND DECORATIVE PAINTERS
P.O. Box 808
Newton, KS 67114

Since its inception in 1972, this nonprofit organization has grown to approximately 30,000 members, including students, teachers, designers and the business community. It has chapters in the U.S, Canada and 35 foreign countries (each chapter sponsors workshops and holds meetings). Members receive a bimonthly publication and are entitled to attend the convention and events.

THE PROFESSIONAL ASSOCIATION OF CUSTOM CLOTHIERS
P.O. Box 8017
Medford, OR 97504
Fax: (503) 770-7041

This is a sewing industry association (ACCI), that includes primary and secondary resources uniting all facets of industry under various membership divisions. The association holds the largest trade show in the country in the spring and fall.

Their "Statement and Object" to members: to create a greater appreciation among the public for craft, needlework and other related products; to educate and foster cooperation among both the public and industry. A bimonthly newsletter disseminates news and events data to members.

SOCIETY OF CRAFT DESIGNERS
6175 Barfield Rd. NE, Suite 220
Atlanta, GA 30328
(404) 252-2454

Members of this society are designers, editors, manufacturers and others who are involved in the crafts industry and who hold an annual convention and other noteworthy events for the promotion of excellence of design. It also fosters professionalism in the marketplace, education for its members, and conducts seminars and a referral service listing. A bimonthly newsletter and other reference material is offered.

SURFACE DESIGN ASSOCIATION
P.O. Box 20799
Oakland, CA 94620
(510) 841-2008

This is a nonprofit, educational association. Members receive a quarterly journal with surface design data, news, and technical and business information.

Books and Booksellers

Also see specific categories throughout the book.

BETTERWAY BOOKS
NORTH LIGHT BOOKS
F&W Publications
1507 Dana Ave.
Cincinnati, OH 45207
(513) 531-2222
(800) 289-0963 for book orders

Offers: Publisher of a variety of woodworking and craft titles.

Woodworking titles include project books, how-to books and informational titles such as *The Woodworker's Sourcebook*, by Charles Self; *The Woodworker's Guide to Pricing Your Work*, by Dan Ramsey; *Good Wood Handbook*, by Jackson Day; *Making Elegant Gifts From Wood*, by Kerry Pierce; *100 Keys to Preventing and Fixing Woodworking Mistakes*; and *Measure Twice, Cut Once*, by Jim Tolpin.

Craft titles include *The Teddy Bear Sourcebook*; *The Doll Sourcebook*; *How to Start Making Money with Your Crafts*, by Kathy Ruzek; *Crafts Marketplace: How and Where to Sell Your Work*; and several others.

For Further Information: Request a free catalog from the above address.

CRAFTER'S CHOICE
Book of the Month Club
Camp Hill, PA 17012
(717) 697-6443

Offers: Members of this book club choose 3 introductory books at nominal cost, agree to purchase 2 more books within the year at member prices; crafts and needlecraft titles are chosen from brochures printed 15 times yearly.
For Further Information: Send SASE with inquiry.

CREATIVE NEEDLECRAFTS CLUB
Rodale Press Inc.
P.O. Box 10220
Des Moines, IA 50381-0220

Offers: New members choose 1 book for $1 plus postage and

handling and agree to buy 2 books within the next year; they offer many craft and needlecraft titles.
For Further Information: Write.

DOVER PUBLICATIONS, INC.
31 E. 2nd St.
Mineola, NY 11501
(516) 294-7000

Offers: Craft/needlecraft books including a series of copyright-free design books, and cut-and-use stencil books. Craft books include glass crafts, silkscreen, paper, woodworking, needlecrafts (quilt, knit, crochet, lace, cross-stitch, others). Also offers textiles, photography, architecture, art instruction, children's activities, Indian crafts and designs, stencil books, plus non-art/craft titles.
For Further Information: Free catalog.

BETTE S. FEINSTEIN
96 Roundwood Rd.
Newton, MA 02164
(617) 969-0942

Offers: Books, both out of print and new; including needle and fiber crafts (quilting, customers, textiles, dress making, patchwork, cutwork, stamp work, ethnic and historic clothing, others), needlecraft and sewing booklets and old magazine issues. Service: Free book searching.
For Further Information: Lists, $1.
Accepts: Discover, MasterCard, Visa

LARK BOOKS
50 College St.
Asheville, NC 28801
(704) 253-0467

Offers: Arts, crafts and needlecraft books: woodworking, kaleidoscopes, paper, gold leaf, eggs, nature, ceramics, basketry, others. Needlecrafts: embroideries, art, quilts, textiles, silk painting, knitting, rug making, weaving, lace making, doll making, others.
For Further Information: Free catalog.

MEREDITH BOOKS
Locust at 17 St.
Des Moines, IA 50309-3023

Offers: Publishers of a variety of craft titles.
For Further Information: Send for catalog.

NORTH LIGHT BOOK CLUB

P.O. Box 12171
Cincinnati, OH 45212-0411
(513) 531-8250

Offers: Each month you'll get a free issue of *North Light Magazine*, offering 100 or more books on all areas of fine art—each book discounted at least 20 percent off the retail price. North Light also provides book excerpts, step-by-step lessons, tips from renowned art instructors, and devotes a full page to a club members' work in each issue. Drop them a note or call to find out what the latest new member offer is. Currently, it's a book of your choice free with another one for just half price.
For Further Information: Call or write.

NORTH LIGHT BOOKS

1507 Dana Ave.
Cincinnati, OH 45207

Offers: Arts/crafts how-to books. Fine art titles include watercolor, pastel, oil, acrylic, airbrush, screen printing, design, graphics, drawing, perspective, pencil, others. Crafts titles include decorative painting, gift making, silk painting, dough craft, paper sculpture, nature projects, home building, log homes, play houses, masonry, woodworking, furniture making, molding and others.
For Further Information: Free catalog.
Discounts: Quantity; teachers and institutions; sells wholesale to legitimate businesses.

PUBLISHERS CENTRAL BUREAU

1 Champion Ave.
Avenel, NJ 07001

Offers: General book categories, but has some arts/crafts/needlecrafts/hobbies titles: woodworking, paper and artists' titles, folk art, needlecrafts, plus armor, railroads, anatomy, books useful for designs.
For Further Information: Write for catalog.

RODALE PRESS INC.

33 E. Minor St.
Emmaus, PA 18098

Offers: Publishers of craft titles.
For Further Information: Request catalog from above address.

STERLING PUBLISHING CO. INC.

387 Park Ave. S
5th Floor
New York, NY 10016-8810

Offers: Publishers of various craft titles.
For Further Information: Request catalog from above address.

STOREY PUBLISHING

Schoolhouse Rd.
Pownal, VT 05261
(800) 441-5700

Offers: Over 130 country skills booklets, including: rug making, furniture, stencils, curtains and quilts, insulated window shutters, homemade wine, clay flowerpots, canoes, solar heated pit greenhouse, chair caning, hearth and root cellar construction, pole woodshed, cold frame construction and other country booklets.
For Further Information: Free catalog.
Discounts: Quantity; sells wholesale to legitimate businesses.
Accepts: MasterCard, Visa

WOODWORKER'S BOOK CLUB

P.O. Box 12171
Cincinnati, OH 45212-0171
(513) 531-8250

Offers: A free monthly issue of the club newsletter, describing the main selection and dozens of other selections. You have at least 10 days to make up your mind. Drop a note to find out about the latest membership opening offer.
For Further Information: Call.

General Craft Business

Also see Supportive Materials and Aids. This category aids those who have gone from hobby status to professional with crafts work—those who are suppliers, service providers or otherwise in business, and those who desire to be in business.

AMERICA ONLINE
(800)827-6364

Offers: Computer bulletin board service: on-line data communications, marketing or information resource, technical assistance. Charged by month; has trial membership.
For Further Information: Call.

ARTIST CREATED
(303) 442-2148

Offers: Listings of over 1,400 craft galleries and gift shops; cost depends upon specified area (all or state/region).
For Further Information: Call.

BOARDWATCH
8500 W. Bowles Ave., Suite 210
Littleton, CO 80123
(800) 933-6038

Offers: Monthly publication listing computer bulletin board services.
For Further Information: Send SASE.

BARBARA BRABEC PRODUCTIONS
P.O. Box 2137
Naperville, IL 60567

Offers: Crafts marketing reports and books by Barbara Brabec (a home-based business authority): *Homemade Money* (5th Edition), *How to Select, Start, Manage, Market and Multiply the Profits of a Business at Home, Creative Cash, How To Sell Your Crafts, Needlework, Designs & Know-How*, and *Handmade for Profit*.
For Further Information: Send for free brochure.

CARRIS POTTERY
105 Monticello Rd.
Oak Ridge, TN 37830
(615) 483-7167

Offers: Computer program for display-items method of marketing crafts.
For Further Information: Free brochure.

COMPUSERVE
(800) 848-8990

Offers: Computer service including bulletin board that serves as a communication, data and marketing resource. Provides crafts (and other) forums, technical assistance. Has trial membership.
For Further Information: Call.

CULTURAL CENTERS OF COLOR/NEA
1100 Pennsylvania Ave.
Washington, DC 20335
(202) 682-5400

Offers: Report on national survey (1990); lists culturally oriented arts organizations.
For Further Information: Send SASE.

CUSTOM DATA SOLUTIONS
P.O. Box 1002
Fort Lee, NJ 07024
(201) 224-3336

Offers: Computer software: craft mall operations, vendor lease/business, reports totals, rental income, check printing, customer database, mailing labels.
For Further Information: Call or send SASE.

FEDERAL TRADE COMMISSION
Enforcement Div., B.C.P.
600 Pennsylvania Ave. NW
Washington, DC 20580
(202) 326-2222

Offers: Data on the legalities of mail-order operations.
For Further Information: Contact with inquiry.

THE FRANCISCO ENTERPRISE
572 143rd St.
Caledonia, MI 49316
(616) 877-4185

Offers: *The Craftmarket Listing*: market of crafts to best prospects—over 2,000 active craft gallery, gift shop and boutique buyers who appreciate direct mail marketing. Includes: mailing labels, sourcebook, card decks, disks, tapes sequenced in alphabetical order and/or zip code order.
For Further Information: Send SASE.

THE FRONT ROOM PUBLISHERS

P.O. Box 1541
Clifton, NJ 07015

Offers: Publications on marketing/home business: *Directory of Craft Shops, Directory of Wholesale Reps for Artisans, Pattern Designer Directory . . ., Market Your Handcrafts to Shops/Galleries*, and *How to Purchase Supplies Wholesale*. Also offers special reports on selling, debts, credit, crafter's directory, others.
For Further Information: Free *Learning Extension* Catalog.

MINORITY BUSINESS DEVELOPMENT

Hoover Blvd., 14th/Constitution NW
Washington, DC 20230
(202) 482-1936

Offers: Provides Commerce Department with advice and funding for minority businesses.
For Further Information: Write or call.

THE NATIONAL DIRECTORY OF ARTISTS & CRAFTSMEN

P.O. Box 424
Devault, PA 19432
(610) 640-ARTS

Offers: Frequently updated Resource Publication of Artist and Craftsmen of the 20th & 21st centuries. For Further Information, send SASE; and/or send for forms.

NORTHWOODS TRADING CO.

13451 Essex Ct.
Eden Prairie, MN 55347

Offers: *Directory of Wholesale Reps for Craft Professionals* lists sales reps selling to department stores, gift shops, museums and galleries, with descriptions of each company, and tips and data on presenting crafts work. An aid to making the right connections.
For Further Information: Catalog, $16.95.

THE REP REGISTRY

P.O. Box 2306
Capistrano Beach, CA 92624
(714) 240-3333

Offers: Registry service. Over 4,000 gift industry sales representatives who work for professional craftspeople. Also offers *Working with Wholesale Reps, A Beginner's Handbook*.
For Further Information: Send SASE for details.

REVENUE SERVICE CO., INC.

P.O. Box 200205
Denver, CO 80220
(800) 453-1127
Fax: (303) 355-5338

Offers: Nationwide collection service for crafts accounts collecting.
For Further Information: Send SASE.

SILVER LINING

(800) 828-4143

Offers: Business computer software for consignment shops, craft malls, other professional use. Covers sales, accounts receivable, inventory tracking, wholesale/retail pricing, consignment inventory—for IBM compatibles.
For Further Information: Call.

SYLVIA'S STUDIO

1090 Cambridge St.
Novato, CA 94947
(415) 883-6206

Offers: Publications by Sylvia Landman. Books include *Make Your Quilting Pay For Itself* and *Crafting For Dollars*. 28-page business reports on operating a teaching studio, writing for the crafts market, marketing crafts, and mail order selling. Audio tapes of small business college classes, including arts/crafts marketing, mail order, starting a home business, couples in business and time management.
For Further Information: Send SASE.

Publications

Publications in your areas of interest can be treasures of source information, technical inspiration and networking cooperation. Check a newsstand or library for a single issue of a publication that interests you. If you inquire regarding subscriptions to publications, include a business-size, stamped, self-addressed envelope, or, try requesting a current single issue of the publication and include a check or money order of at least $6.00 to cover cost and postage.

AIRBRUSH ACTION MAGAZINE
P.O. Box 3000
Denville, NJ 07834

This magazine, published 6 times yearly, presents color illustrated airbrushing articles, projects, resources, regional stores listings and other data.

AIRBRUSH MAGAZINE
3676 Cosby Hwy.
Cosby, TN 37722

Articles in this airbrushing publication feature color step-by-step instruction from known instructors.

AMERICAN INDIAN ART MAGAZINE
7314 E. Osborn Dr.
Scottsdale, AZ 85251
(602) 994-5445

This is a quarterly magazine fostering Native American art, with features on all aspects, historic and contemporary.

THE AMERICAN NEEDLECRAFTER
23 Old Pecan Rd.
Big Sandy, TX 7575

This is the official newspaper of American Needlecraft Association. It is published quarterly, with articles of interest to neeldecrafters from members and manufacturers, special savings for members, calendar of nationwide stitching events, pattern book review and Needlepals—pen pals with needlecrafting interests.

AMERICAN PATCHWORK & QUILTING
1912 Grand Ave.
Des Moines, IA 50309

This is a magazine published 6 times yearly with instructions and inspiration for quilters. It features instructions and tested full-sized patterns, tips, editorial reviews of latest quilt products, profiles of quilters, designers and shops.

AMERICAN QUILTER
P.O. Box 3290
Paducah, KY 42002
(502) 898-7903

This official magazine of the American Quilter's Society displays quilts and techniques that promote the art form and preserve the craft. Among the features: Who's who, historical notes, show listings and events, more.

AMERICAN WOODWORKER
P.O. Box 139
Emmaus, PA 18049
(610) 967-5171

This home woodworking project magazine presents techniques and how-to's from the masters, with detailed instructions and in-depth buyer's guides.

THE ARTISTS' MAGAZINE
1507 Dana Ave.
Cincinnati, OH 45207

This monthly magazine features step-by-step art instruction in a variety of media, from oil and watercolor to acrylic and colored pencil. Each issue presents tips and techniques from professional artists, plus complete listings of markets to show and sell your work.

ART CALENDAR
P.O. Box 199
Upper Fairmount, MD 21867

This monthly publication connects artists with exhibition and income opportunities and includes over 5,000 listings of shows and other possibilities for exhibiting. It is verified and published yearly, with news on legislation, professional opportunities and others.

ART/QUILT MAGAZINE
9543 Meadowbriar
Houston, TX 77063

This is a quarterly magazine devoted to art quilts. It features artists and includes shows, symposia, quilter's issues, reviews and other topics.

BEAD & BUTTON
P.O. Box 56488
Boulder, CO 80323

This bimonthly magazine is meant for those interested in beads and buttons. It includes product information, craft projects and innovative ideas.

BEARHUGS
300 E. 40th St.
New York, NY 10016
(212) 717-1514

Distributed internationally, this monthly bear-lovers publication shows, features and informs about—bears.

BETTER HOMES AND GARDENS CRAFT & WEAR
1716 Locust St.
Des Moines, IA 50309
(515) 284-3000 or (800) 374-4244

Send SASE.

BLACK SHEEP NEWSLETTER
25455 NW Dixie Mountain Rd.
Scappoose, OR 97056

This quarterly newsletter is meant for growers, spinners and textile artists interested in black sheep wool and other animal fibers. Upcoming events and book reviews are included. Advertising.

THE BUSINESS OF HERBS
Rt. 2,
P.O. Box 246
Shevlin, MN 55676

This bimonthly newsletter reports trade news, market tips, grower resources, sources and more. Herbal facts, interviews, ideas, forums, book reviews, events and business ideas round out issues. Advertising.

CERAMIC ARTS & CRAFTS
30595 W. Eight Mile Rd.
Livonia, MI 48152

This monthly magazine focuses on how-to's in hobby ceramics, with color projects, materials list and instructions. A variety of techniques are given in each issue, as are "See What's New" and "Worldwide Shows." Advertising.

CERAMICS MAGAZINE
30595 Eight Mile Rd.
Livonia, MI 48152

This ceramics publication presents mold designs and products from known manufacturers, decorating techniques, contributions by world famous ceramic artists, articles by profes-

sionals, tips and shortcuts. Includes paper patterns on clay carbon graph paper. National show listings. Advertising.

THE CLOTH DOLL
P.O. Box 2167
Lake Oswego, OR 97035

This quarterly magazine serves the interest of cloth doll makers and collectors. Issues provide at least 3 doll and clothing patterns, articles on techniques, accessories, new products, feature artists, book reviews and doll show reviews. Advertising.

COLOR TRENDS
5129 Badland Ave. NW
Seattle, WA 98117

This magazine is devoted to color and dyes, with actual dyed fabric, yarn and paper samples included, plus dye instructions, yarn painting, designer fabrics data, color innovations, more; published twice yearly.

COTTAGE CONNECTION
P.O. Box 14460
Chicago, IL 60614
(312) 939-6490

This is a newsletter of the National Association for the Cottage Industry. It provides news and information on general business and laws, advertising, copyrights and more; includes book/video reviews and calendar—for professionals, suppliers and distributors.

COUNTRY CRAFTS
P.O. Box 1790
Peoria, IL 61656

This publication is available quarterly.

THE CRAFT MARKETING NEWS
P.O. Box 1541
Clifton, NJ 07015

This monthly is published for all wanting to market their talent—with listings of shops wanting handcrafts and reports on business, plus wholesale suppliers, profiles. Advertising.

THE CRAFT SHOW CALENDAR
P.O. Box 424
Devault, PA 19432

This publication provides listings and information on craft shows in the mid-Atlantic region of the U.S.

CRAFTING TRADITIONS
P.O. Box 996
Greendale, WI 53125

Published six times a year, this publication features more than 40 craft projects per issue. Full size patterns and instructions for variety of crafts, including holiday and family oriented crafts, are included.

CRAFTS
News Plaza
P.O. Box 1790
Peoria, IL 61656

How-to techniques and full-sized, fold-out patterns are included in colorful monthly issues of this magazine that presents an array of crafts/needlecrafts techniques. Advertising.

THE CRAFTS FAIR GUIDE
P.O. Box 5508
Mill Valley, CA 94942
(415) 332-7687

This quarterly publication covers in detail, and through reviews, over 1,000 fairs throughout the West. Fairs are rated for sales/enjoyment. Invaluable for show marketing. Shows listed by dates/town/state. Advertising.

CRAFTS 'N THINGS
2400 Devon, Suite 375
Des Plaines, IL 60016

This magazine carries a variety of general craft projects, craft ideas, how-tos and tips for beginner and advanced craftspeople. Single-sided full-size patterns and step-by-step instructions are offered. Published 10 times yearly.

CRAFTS PLUS
130 Spy Ct.
Markam, Ontario L3R 0W6
Canada

Published 8 times yearly, this crafts magazine provides a wide variety of crafts and needlecrafts projects. Columns include "Coming Events in Canada" listings, plus product and Canadian dealers information. Advertising.

CROCHET HOME
23 Old Pecan Rd.
Big Sandy, TX 75755

An assortment of crochet patterns with instructions and diagrams make up this bimonthly magazine, including projects for personal and home decor; women's and children's clothing and others. Also features letters, articles, pictures and directions and regular features.

CROCHET WITH HEART
P.O. Box 5595
Little Rock, AR 72215

This magazine features crochet projects, including afghans, baby items and keepsakes, clothing and accessories. It includes gift suggestions, designer profiles, buyer's guide, advice, letters and reviews of Leisure Arts and Coats & Clark leaflets.

CROCHET WORLD
306 E. Parr Rd.
Berne, IN 46711

This bimonthly crochet magazine presents illustrated project patterns for adult and children's apparel, dolls and doll clothes, toys and home decor items. Projects are marked for level of ability, easy to advanced. "Potpourri," reader-trades/wants, and "Show-It-Off" are among regular features. Advertising.

CROSS COUNTRY STITCHING
P.O. Box 710
Manchester, CT 06045

This counted cross-stitch magazine is published 6 times yearly, with 20 to 25 design projects per issue, in color, with clear charts. Designs include country motifs, scripture, others.

CROSS-STITCH & COUNTRY CRAFTS
3000 Walnut St.
P.O. Box 52416
Boulder, CO 80302
(303) 678-8747

Every bimonthly issue of this magazine has at least 23 original cross-stitch patterns and designs with color photos (close-up, hands-on) as aids, plus chart ratings and skein data; includes heirloom and country motifs. "Finish It Tonight" projects and designer originals are included.

CROSS-STITCH! MAGAZINE
23 Old Pecan Rd.
Big Sandy, TX 75755
(903) 636-4011

Bimonthly magazine gives stitch basics and projects for many cross stitch items, each with stitch and color charts, materials lists and instructions. Readers' letters with hints and getting started columns are in each issue, along with patterns for everyone, from wall hangings to wearables.

THE CROSS STITCHER MAGAZINE
701 Lee St., Dept. CSS2
Des Plaines, IL 60016

This bimonthly magazine is devoted to cross-stitching, providing a variety of pattern illustrations, features and other information.

DECORATIVE ARTIST'S WORKBOOK
1507 Dana Ave.
Cincinnati, OH 45207

This bimonthly magazine is for decorative painters and crafters. Each issue features new designs to paint on walls, furniture, T-shirts, wood cutouts and more. All projects are complete with materials lists, full-size patterns, step-by-step instructions and color photos to show the way.

THE DOLL ARTISAN
9 River St.
Oneonta, NY 13820
(607) 432-4977

This is a bimonthly magazine for production doll makers (and those interested in doll making); a publication of the Doll Artisan Guild.

DOLL CRAFTER
30595 W. Eight Mile Rd.
Livonia, MI 48152

This is a bimonthly magazine for creators and collectors of dolls. Each issue contains a free clothing pattern and features collectible dolls.

DOLL DESIGNS
306 E. Parr Rd.
Berne, IN 46711

This bimonthly magazine is meant for doll and toy craftspeople. Includes features on composition, cloth, soft-sculpture, ceramic and other dolls, technical how-to's, styles and trends of today and vintage toys. Houses, furniture and clothing are covered, and profiles of doll artists included. Columns: Letters, shows, tips, questions/answers. Advertising.

DOLLMAKING PROJECTS & PLANS
169 5th Ave.
New York, NY 10010
(212) 989-8700

Magazine of crafting techniques and plans, data and sources for dolls—cloth, ceramic, vinyl and others. Includes directions for projects with diagrams, patterns, illustrations. Features include trends, news, calendar of events and collector's data. Advertising.

THE DOLLREADER
900 Frederick St.
Cumberland, MD 21502

This publication appears 8 times yearly, with a sister publication (*The Teddy Bear and Friends*).

DOLLS IN MINIATURE
1040 Bentoak Ln.
San Jose, CA 95129

This quarterly magazine is concerned with making and collecting miniature dolls. Sample issue, $5. ($9 outside U.S.)

EARLY AMERICAN LIFE
P.O. Box 8200
Harrisburg, PA 17105
(717) 657-9555 or (800) 435-9610 for subscriptions

This magazine on early America offers crafts, examples of quality craftsmanship, building, decorating and renovation ideas; gives source data and a calendar of events (arts/crafts and folk festivals, historic exhibits).

FIBERARTS, MAGAZINE OF TEXTILES
50 College St.
Asheville, NC 28801
(704) 253-0467

This magazine showcases contemporary and historical fiber, with articles on quilting, weaving, stitchery, soft sculpture surface designing and more. Also includes educational and travel listings and show opportunities and data. Advertising.

THE FIBERFEST MAGAZINE
P.O. Box 112
Hastings, MI 49058

Published quarterly, this magazine includes fibers from natural source (plants, animals) to finished, features on spinning, dyeing, felting and others.

FINE PRINT
1610 Bush St.
San Francisco, CA 94109
(415) 543-4455

The artistry of book printing and binding are presented in this quality magazine.

FINE TOOL JOURNAL
27 Fickett Rd.
Pownal, ME 04069

This quarterly magazine on tools for craftspeople and collectors features absentee auctions, tools for sale, technical and historical information, coming events calendar and other topics.

FINESCALE MODELER
P.O. Box 1612
Waukesha, WI 53187
(414) 796-8776

This magazine, issued nine times yearly, aids readers with

crafting skills on all levels by presenting tips, projects and instructions in the realms of ships, cars, dioramas, military vehicles and others. Advertising.

FLYING MODELS

P.O. Box 700
Newton, NJ 07860

Model aircraft is the main feature of this magazine. It is meant for enthusiasts of all ages, levels of skill and interest.

FOR THE LOVE OF CROSS STITCH

P.O. Box 5595
Little Rock, AR 72215

This is a magazine for cross stitch lovers. Each issue is devoted to cross stitch, with new projects and techniques, designs for every skill level.

GARDEN RAILWAYS

P.O. Box 61461
Denver, CO 80206

This magazine, published 6 times yearly, features large scale railroad building articles on track, road building structures & rolling stock. Gives full G-scale coverage and data on electric steam & battery operations. Product reviews are also presented.

HAND PAPERMAKING

P.O. Box 77027
Washington, DC 20013

Semi-annual journal and quarterly newsletter with information on the art and craft for western and eastern papermaking.

HANDCRAFT ILLUSTRATED

P.O. Box 7450
Red Oak, IA 51591

Quarterly published crafts. Project and resources magazine, with decorating ideas, quick projects, field guide and reader's notes.

HANDWOVEN

201 E. 4th St.
Loveland, CO 80537

This weaving magazine is issued 5 times yearly, with photographed weaving projects to provide ideas, inspiration and instruction to handweavers of all skill levels, plus articles of lore, history, techniques, profiles and functional pieces for the home. Includes woven fashions, accessories, fabrics. Advertising.

THE HERB COMPANION

201 E. 4th St.
Loveland, CO 80537

This bimonthly magazine for herb growers and enthusiasts presents herbs and their uses—culinary, in crafts, potpourris—plus growing, cultivating, drying and other herbal topics. Regular features include "In Basket" (letters), a calendar of events and book reviews.

THE HERB QUARTERLY

P.O. Box 689
San Anselmo, CA 94960
Published quarterly. Includes articles on herb crafting; also medicinal, gardening, culinary, folklore.

HERBALGRAM

P.O. Box 201660
Austin, TX 78720
(512) 331-8868

This quarterly journal is published by the American Botanical Council and the Herb Research Foundation. Includes reviews, media coverage, herb data, updates, legalities, conference data, book reviews and an events calendar—all edited by an advisory board.

THE HOME SHOP MACHINIST

P.O. Box 629
Traverse City, MI 49685

This bimonthly magazine provides expert guidance, information and resources to all who enjoy working with metal for pleasure or profit in their home shops.

HOOKED ON CROCHET

23 Old Pecan Rd.
Big Sandy, TX 75755

An assortment of crochet projects with instructions and diagrams make up this bimonthly magazine, including projects for home decor and gifts; women's and children's clothing, and home decorator items. Letters and "stitches" are regular features.

HOW MAGAZINE

1507 Dana Ave.
Cincinnati, OH 45207

The focal point for this bimonthly magazine is graphics—design, technique and concepts as given by contemporary art directors, production people, computer-graphics professionals and others—with coverage of techniques, tools, problem solving, color separations, papers, computer systems, business, legalities, PR, more.

INTERNATIONAL SCULPTURE
1050 17th St. NW, #250
Washington, DC 20036
(202) 785-1144

Members of this organization receive a magazine of information on business, projects, exhibits and more.

KIT CAR
8490 Sunset Blvd.
West Hollywood, CA 90069
(213) 782-2000

Specialty cars constructed from kits is this bimonthly magazine's focus. Each issue illustrates and details a showcase of models. Technical features aid car builders in installation and operation. Regulars: news, assembler's guide and swaps. Advertising.

KITELINES
P.O. Box 466
Randallstown, MD 21133

This is the comprehensive international journal of kiting and a major source of news, plans, techniques, reviews of new kites and books, profiles of kiting personalities, in-depth features. With event and supplier lists. Advertising.

KNITTERS MAGAZINE
P.O. Box 1525
Sioux Falls, SD 57101

This magazine includes several knitting projects.

KNITTERS NEWS
Box 65004
358 Danforth
Toronto, Ontario M4Y 3Z2
Canada

This knitting newsletter, published 5 times yearly, includes patterns, techniques, projects and more.

LAPIDARY JOURNAL
60 Chestnut Ave., Suite 201
Devon, PA 19333-1312
(610) 293-1112
Fax: (610) 293-1717

For 50 years, Lapidary Journal has been the premier source of information about the gem, bead, jewelry-making, mineral and fossil fields. Spectacular full-color photography of beads and jewelry and the sensational "Jewelry Journal" section inspire thousands of advanced readers to try new easy-to-follow gemstone and jewelry-making projects. Special editions include the Bead Annual, the Annual Buyers' Directory,

and the Fossil, Gemcraft, and Design Editions. Glossy, 180 pages monthly, $4.95 cover price.
For Further Information: For subscriptions call 1-800-676-4336 or request the free *Lapidary Journal Book & Video Catalog* by calling (610) 676-GEMS.

LEATHER CRAFTERS & SADDLERS JOURNAL
331 Annette Ct.
Rhinelander, WI 54501

This bimonthly leather working publication with how-tos, step-by-step instructional articles, including full-sized patterns of leather craft, leather art, custom saddle and boot making; all skill levels. It covers leather, tools, machinery and allied materials, plus leather-craft industry news.

LEISURE ARTS-THE MAGAZINE
P.O. Box 5595
Little Rock, AR 72215

LET'S TALK ABOUT DOLLMAKING MAGAZINE
300 Nancy Dr.
Point Pleasant, NJ 08742

Current materials, techniques, products and resources for doll-making are included in the four issues that are published irregularly.

LETTER ARTS REVIEW
1624 24th Ave. SW
Norman, OK 73072

This publication features calligraphy and other lettering forms.

MCCALL'S NEEDLEWORK
P.O. Box 5063
Harlan, IA 51537

This bimonthly magazine presents readers with professional projects that are diagrammed or charted and color illustrated for easy crafting. Emphasis: needlecrafts, basics and innovations for fashions and accessories. Features books, buyer's guide, shows. Advertising.

MIND YOUR OWN BUSINESS AT HOME
P.O. Box 14850
Chicago, IL 60614

This newsletter of the National Association for the Cottage Industry presents aspects of home-based business.

MINIATURE COLLECTOR
170 5th Ave.
New York, NY 10010

This magazine gives readers a look into the world of dollhouses and other scale miniatures, with professional articles, "Projects & Plans" and "Showcase" features. Household furnishing, houses, buildings and architectural details are illustrated. Departments: auctions, news, calendars, new products. Advertising.

MODEL AIRPLANE NEWS
P.O. Box 428
Mount Morris, IL 61054

Model aircraft is this monthly magazine's focus—carried through step-by-step projects (illustrated, diagrammed and described), articles on products/use, and "Field and Bench Review" of aircraft. Regulars: "Clubs," "Plans Mart," others. Advertising.

MODEL RAILROADER
P.O. Box 1612
Waukesha, WI 53187

This monthly magazine presents inspirational tours of the world's layouts including prototype data and how-to information. Also included are tips, projects and photographs. Advertising.

MODERN MACHINE KNITTING
264 H St.
P.O. Box 110
Blaine, WA 98230

This monthly machine-knitting magazine features illustrated project patterns and sources of supplies.

THE NATIONAL DIRECTORY OF ARTISTS & CRAFTSMEN
P.O. Box 424
Devault, PA 19432
(610) 640-ARTS

Offers: Frequently updated Resource Publication of Artist and Craftsmen of the 20th & 21st centuries. For Further Information, send SASE; and/or send for forms.

NATIONAL STAMPAGRAPHIC
1952 Everett St.
North Valleystream, NY 11580

This quarterly magazine is about rubber stamps of the artistic kind. It presents the creations of stamp artists throughout, with technical features, personal profiles and more. Features: exchanges, hints. Advertising.

THE NEEDLECRAFT SHOP, INC.
23 Old Pecan Rd.
Big Sandy, TX 75755

Send SASE.

NEEDLEPOINT NEWS
1041 Shary Circle
Concord, CA 94518

This is a bimonthly magzine of how-to's, designs, profiles and technical data—all related to needlepoint. Business-related information may be included.

NEEDLEPOINT PLUS
P.O. Box 5986
Concord, CA 94524

This bimonthly publication is written by and for needlepointers. Newest trends and designs are presented with diagrams, charts, photos, book reviews.

NEEDLEWORDS
306 E. Parr Rd.
Berne, IN 46711

Published quarterly, this publication abounds with counted cross-stitch graphed patterns (some in color), trends, techniques. Features: finishing, primers, "World of Stitches" projects and basics. Advertising.

NUTSHELL NEWS
21027 Crossroads Circle
P.O. Box 1612
Waukesha, WI 53187

This is a monthly magazine of miniatures that offers reports on shows, profiles of craftspeople and displays of their work, plus how-to tips and techniques, visits to museums/collections and more. Miniature projects are diagrammed and directed. Regulars: shows, letters, reviews, mini-market, others. Advertising.

OLD-TIME CROCHET
306 E. Parr Rd.
Berne, IN 46711

This quarterly crochet magazine features patterns from cover to cover—classic and traditional apparel, accessories and home decor. Advertising.

ORNAMENT
P.O. Box 2349
San Marcos, CA 92079

Ornaments of the ancient, contemporary and ethnic kind are the focus in this quality magazine that presents jewelry and clothing. Original designs are beautifully photographed. Includes: news, features, galleries and shops data, collecting, resources. Advertising.

OUTDOOR & TRAVEL PHOTOGRAPHY
1115 Broadway, 8th Floor
New York, NY 10010

This photography magazine focuses on the outdoors, nature and travel. Published quarterly, it presents topics unique to this specialty; adds a "Readers Portfolio" for submission of work and resume.

PAINTING MAGAZINE
2400 Devon Ave. Dept. 49126
Des Plaines, IL 60018

This bimonthly magazine is devoted to painting throughout and includes instructions on basic shapes, mixing/blending and other techniques on wood, fabric, metal, rocks and other surfaces with all kinds of paints. Ideas, hints, and book and video reviews compliment the issues.

PHOTO OPPORTUNITY
P.O. Box 838
Montclair, NJ 07042

Profiles of professionals, strategies for studios and business places, promotions are given in this bimonthly magazine. Regularly featured: success pointers and resources, events calendar and profiles. Advertising.

PHOTO TECHNIQUES
7880 Merrimac
P.O. Box 48312
Niles, IL 60648

This is a bimonthly magazine.

PHOTOGRAPHER'S FORUM
614 Santa Barbara St.
Santa Barbara, CA 93101

Send SASE.

PHOTOGRAPHIC MAGAZINE
8490 Sunset Blvd.
West Hollywood, CA 90069

This is a monthly how-to magazine that features techniques and special effects (darkroom, lighting, tools, equipment, others). Presents/reviews cameras and video products. Has advertising.

PIECEWORK
201 E. 4th
Loveland, CO 80537

Piecework is meant for those who love handwork, and those who value its past and present role—exploring historic and ethnic, fabric-related needlework in articles and selected projects. The bimonthly magazine presents handwork to inspire both novice and advanced creators in quilting, knitting, crochet, basketry, appliqué and lacemaking.

PINE MEADOW KNITTING NEWS
490 Woodland View Dr.
York, PA 17402

Knitting newsletter with emphasis on knitting for charity, published every 8 weeks.

PLASTIC CANVAS CORNER
P.O. Box 5595
Little Rock, AR 72215

Created for plastic canvas lovers, this magazine offers 6 issues yearly with quick and easy projects, including original designs, tips, color charts with instruction for home accessories of every kind for variety of skill levels and styles, traditional to contemporary. Letters and hints, book reviews and a buyer's guide, contests and designers interviews are also featured.

PLASTIC CANVAS! MAGAZINE
23 Old Pecan Rd.
Big Sandy, TX 75755

Bimonthly magazine gives stitch basics and projects for many plastic canvas needlepoint items, each with stitch and color charts, materials lists and instructions. Typical patterns, include wall hangings, baskets, boxes, tissue holders, organizers, banks, vases and others.

POPULAR PHOTOGRAPHY
1515 Broadway
New York, NY 10036

This monthly magazine includes techniques and equipment, innovations, workshops listings, problem solving and new products. Advertising.

POTPOURRI FROM HERBAL ACRES
P.O. Box 428-MB
Washington Crossing, PA 18977

This networking publication is issued quarterly. Features ideas, tips, recipes, crafts and news in herbs.

THE PROFESSIONAL QUILTER
P.O. Box 1628
Wheat Ridge, CO 80034

From a pro/business standpoint, this quarterly magazine offers features on management and marketing; organization of studio, home, business; teaching, designing; issues of ethics, economics and more. Includes valuable input from professionals. Regulars: reviews, resources, competitions/shows, news, computer data. Advertising.

PROFITABLE CRAFT MERCHANDISING

News Plaza
P.O. Box 1790
Peoria, IL 61656

This monthly magazine is published for retailers, manufacturers, publishers, importers, distributors and designers; presents product information from a craft merchandising level, with new trends, projects, news and views in crafts, needlecrafts and creative sewing. Reports trade shows, events, reviews, news. Includes Retailer Assistance Cards and an Annual Craft Market Handbook with subscription. Advertising.

PROJECTS IN METAL

P.O. Box 629
Traverse City, MI 49685

This bimonthly magazine is meant for those serious about shopwork and includes complete plans for valuable tools and accessories which are presented to prepare the home metalworker for hobby projects offered in every issue.

QUICK & EASY PLASTIC CANVAS!

23 Old Pecan Rd.
Big Sandy, TX 75755

This bimonthly magazine presents easy projects with stitch and color charts, materials lists, and instructions for a wide range of home decor items, from baskets to hangings, organizers, cubes and others.

QUICK & EASY QUILTING

306 E. Parr Rd.
Berne, IN 46711

This is a bimonthly magazine with a comprehensive selection of quilting projects.

QUILT WORLD

306 E. Parr Rd.
Berne, IN 46711

This bimonthly magazine presents full-sized patterns throughout—motifs, diagrams, photographs for a variety of quilts—from heritage to contemporary style. Includes international news, "Notes & Quotes," "Pieces and Patches" rundown, book reviews, "Quilters Queries & Quotes," "Show Directory" and "Classifieds."

QUILTER'S NEWSLETTER MAGAZINE

741 Corporate Circle, Suite A
Golden, CO 80401

Each issue of this magazine is packed with 50 to 100 quilt photos, plus news, lessons, features, hints, contests. Project how-to's are diagrammed, with full-size patterns for 5 to 15

quilts. Features: noted quilters, show calendars, club/guilds, more. Advertising.

R/C MODELER MAGAZINE

144 Sierra Madre Blvd.
P.O. Box 487
Sierra Madre, CA 91024

This is a magazine devoted to radio control models.

RADIO CONTROL CAR ACTION

251 Danbury Rd.
Wilton, CT 06897

This R/C car magazine features the newest models and trends, plus photo features on cars, bodies, accessories, driver models. Includes information on engines, parts, pit tips, plus articles, product news and advertising.

RAILFAN & RAILROAD

P.O. Box 700
Newton, NJ 07860

This monthly railroad magazine puts emphasis on the contemporary scene with coverage of trains, railroads and facilities, runs and developments. Features on traction and light rail, narrow gauge, railroadiana, video and book reviews and coming events, trips and all for the dedicated rail enthusiast.

RAILROAD MODEL CRAFTSMAN

P.O. Box 700
Newton, NJ 07860

Model railroads—actual lines, and modeling kits and scratch-building protypes—are covered in this monthly magazine. Model landscaping and kit hints are given. Departments: Letters, exchanges and dealer directory.

RUBBERSTAMPMADNESS

408 SW Monroe, #210
Corvallis, OR 97333

A world of rubber stamping is represented in this bimonthly publication that is color-covered; includes reviews of catalogs, news, mail art, how-to's, letters and trends. Advertising.

RUG HOOKING

500 Vaughn St.
Harrisburg, PA 17110

This magazine is published 5 times per year and is devoted to all aspects of rug hooking, including pictured projects (4 to 5 per issue) from hooking experts to instruct and inspire. Features techniques, beginnner and pro designs, preparing and dyeing wools, ideas, profiles of professionals, and photographs. Advertising.

SAC

P.O. Box 159
Bogalusa, LA 70429

This monthly publication gives nationwide listings and articles for art and craft show opportunities. Includes details on place, time, deadline and fees involved. Has display and classified advertising.

THE SCALE CABINETMAKER

P.O. Box 2038
Christiansburg, VA 24073

This is a quarterly magazine for those who build miniatures. Includes how-to features with directions and other data useful to scale crafters.

SCALE SHIP MODELER

7950 Deering Ave.
Canoga Park, CA 91304

Covering all aspects of model boating, this magazine gives informative articles, with color photos—techniques, kit reviews, showcases, events. Features: product/book reviews, letters, museums/clubs, wants and product news. Advertising.

SCULPTURE

P.O. Box 91110
Washington, DC 20090

This is the magazine of the International Sculpture Center (a nonprofit organization devoted to the advancement of contemporary sculpture). Examples of superb sculpture abound throughout each issue. "News Commissions," "Exhibitions" and "Reviews" are included. Advertising.

SEW BEAUTIFUL

518 Madison St.
Huntsville, AL 35800

Magazine of sewing projects and features, suppliers guide, answer column.

SEW NEWS

P.O. Box 1790
Peoria, IL 61656

This sewing publication appears monthly, reporting on fashions, fabrics, sewing savvy and projects. Features projects and suggestions (illustrated) on color, dyeing, coordinating, others. Sewing patterns reviewed, hints given; includes resources, product data, book reviews, tips, latest products, videos, shoppers. Advertising.

THE SEWING UPDATE

P.O. Box 1790
Peoria, IL 61656

This bimonthly newsletter features fashion sewing how-tos by professionals Jan Saunders, Marla Kazell, Mary Mulari and Janet Klaer. Also offers innovative ideas, techincal data, questions/answers, and product, equipment and pattern news.

SHUTTLE, SPINDLE & DYEPOT

2402 University Ave. W., Suite 702
St. Paul, MN 55114

This is the official magazine of the Handweaver's Guild of America (see Associations). Issues have technical data, illustrations and descriptions of the finest examples of weaving, spinning and dyeing. Issues also have guild news, product coverage and advertising.

SIDELINE BUSINESS

P.O. Box 351
Emmaus, PA 18049

This monthly publication guides those with at-home businesses to market craftswork and ideas.

SIGN CRAFT MAGAZINE

P.O. Box 60031
Fort Myers, FL 33906
(941) 939-4644

Recognizing sign making as an art, this bimonthly magazine presents photos, ideas, data on design, materials, business. Includes photo displays of signs, and newest products are shown. Regulars: letters, tips and news. Advertising.

THE SILKWORM

12213 Distribution Way
Beltsville, MD 20705

A networking newsletter for the silk and fabric painter, textile/fiber artist and the creative sewer and quilter. Published 6 times yearly.

SIMPLY CROSS STITCH

23 Old Pecan Rd.
Big Sandy, TX 75755

Cross-stitch projects in this bimonthly magazine are shown with stitch and color charts, instructions and materials lists, including patterns for home decor and wearables, letters, hints and a getting started column are in each issue.

SPIN-OFF
201 E. 4th St.
Loveland, CO 80537
This quarterly magazine is meant for hand spinner enthusiasts. It is a resource for information on fibers, spinning and dyeing techniques, project ideas and equipment. Feature topics have included hand-spun yarns and fiber, equipment and other data. Advertising.

STITCHER'S SOURCELETTER
P.O. Box 575749
Salt Lake City, UT 84157

Send SASE.

STRATEGIES
P.O. Box 838
Montclair, NJ 07042

Subtitled the *Self-Promotion Newsletter for Photographers*, this business newsletter is geared to it as fine art. Careers, exhibitions, portfolios, grants and other data is given in all bimonthly issues.

STREET ROD ACTION
7950 Deering Ave.
Canoga Park, CA 91304

This hot rod magazine is geared to hot rod kits and building—with features, product information and resources, plus events, NSRA news, book reviews, tips, showcases, color photos. Advertising.

SUNSHINE ARTISTS U.S.A.
1736 N. Highway 427
Longwood, FL 32750

This monthly magazine is a calendar of art/craft shows and events nationwide. Listings given by state are definitive. Advertising.

TEDDY BEAR REVIEW
170 5th Ave.
New York, NY 10010

This quarterly publication on teddy bears presents teddy history; projects are shown, as are profiles, holiday topics, collections and more.

THE TEDDY TRIBUNE
254 W. Sidney St.
St. Paul, MN 55107

This magazine is published 5 times yearly, and features "news and views of the bear world," articles, trends, events, reviews. Advertising.

THREADS MAGAZINE
P.O. Box 5506
Newtown, CT 06470

Much that can be created with threads is presented in this quality magazine. Design, details and techniques for art wear, needlecrafts and related topics are given and illustrated. Regular features: letters, answers, technical tips, calendars, conferences, workshops, competitions, book reviews, suppliers and more. Advertising.

TOLE WORLD
P.O. Box 5986
Concord, CA 94524

This bimonthly painting magazine is project-packed with presentations of well-known artists, an array of technical aids and features.

TOY SOLDIER REVIEW
127 74th St.
North Bergen, NJ 07047

This is a quarterly international magazine for toy soldier enthusiasts—craftspeople, collectors, others.

TRAINS
P.O. Box 1612
Waukesha, WI 53187

This monthly magazine gives model railroad enthusiasts contemporary in-depth editorial features in steam, diesel, passenger and freight operations. Industry reports and features round out with photographs of past and present railroading. Advertising.

TREADLEART
25834 Narbonne Ave.
Lomita, CA 90717

This bimonthly magazine is geared to sewing embellishment—projects, hints, topics—illustrated, diagrammed and described.

THE WATER COLOUR GAZETTE NEWSLETTER
619 Hamilton Ave., Unit 1
Winnipeg, Manitoba R2Y 1Z3
Canada

Send SASE.

WESTART
P.O. Box 6868
Auburn, CA 95604

This semi-monthly tabloid has a readership of artists, craftpeople and students. It features current reviews and listings of fine art competitions and arts and crafts fairs and festivals.

MARTHA WETHERBEE BASKET SHOP NEWS
171 Eastern Hill Rd.
Sanfornton, NH 03269

This publication is a quarterly newspaper that features premier basket making classes nationwide.

WILDLIFE PHOTOGRAPHY
P.O. Box 224
Greenville, PA 16125

As the title suggests, this is a publication for those who photograph in the wild.

WOMEN ARTIST NEWS
P.O. Box 3304, Grand Central Station
New York, NY 10164

This bimonthly magazine may profile artists/craftspeople who work in crafts and fiber crafts. Published for critics, museums, galleries, teachers, other enthusiasts. Shows articles on history, opinions and related. Reviews exhibitions/events, books. (Supported in part by funds from the New York State Council on the Arts.)

WOOD
1912 Grand Ave.
Des Moines, IA 50309

This is a bimonthly woodworking magazine featuring projects and new products from cover to cover—with specifications, directions, diagrams and illustrations. Data is presented for woodworkers of all levels, novice to professional. Other features include in-depth articles on accomplished craftspeople, new products and techniques information. Advertising.

WOOD STROKES
33 Centernial Pkwy.
P.O. Box 58377
Boulder, CO 80323

This magazine gives paint and design projects for wood.

WOODSHOP NEWS
35 Pratt St.
Essex, CT 06426

Monthly newspaper of craft people and product, features, tips, letters and craft fairs schedules.

WOODWORK
P.O. Box 1529
Ross, CA 94957

This bimonthly magazine covers woodworking today, with topics for all skill levels. Presents cabinetmaking design and how-to's, profiles of professionals and their work, and technical theory. Includes quality photography and diagramming throughout for projects and other features—on contemporary and other furnishings. Regular features include techniques, questions and answers. Advertising.

THE WORKBASKET
700 W. 47th St., Suite 310
Kansas City, MO 64111

This home magazine presents features on knitting, crochet, sewing, embroidery, quilting, other needlecrafts and crafts. Projects are diagrammed. Included are projects for home, decor, wearables and accessories for all. Advertising.

WORKBENCH
700 W. 47th St., Suite 310
Kansas City, MO 64112

This do-it-yourself woodworking magazine covers projects for home improvement, furniture and accessories making/repair and more—with detailed directions and photographs. Regular features include "Product News," "Equipment Guide," "Calendar of Woodworking Shows," "Letters," "Workbench Solver," "Carpenter's Apprentice" and resources. Advertising.

Supportive Materials and Aids

Also see General Craft Supplies.

A.I.M. DISPLAYS

P.O. Box 718
Franklin, NC 28734
(800) 524-9833

Offers: Aluminum display panels with mest inserts, folding hinges and leveler feet in a variety of sizes. Open bar units for hanging items, fabric covered foam boards and shelving units.
For Further Information: Free brochure.
Discounts: Quantity; teachers and institutions.

ACTION BAG CO.

501 N. Edgewood Ave.
Wood Dale, IL 60191
(708) 766-2881 or (800) 824-2247
Fax: (800) 400-4451

Offers: Bags: Ziplock and other plastic bags in a variety of sizes, including Floss-A-Way and bolt bags for fabrics, plus cotton drawstring bags, retail shopping bags and shipping supplies. Manufacturer.
For Further Information: Free catalog.
Discounts: Sells wholesale.

ADLER SALES, INC.

P.O. Box 8317
Richmond, VA 23226
(804) 288-4480

Offers: Custom-built display cases (for miniatures and others): Walnut bases, optional mirror-backed, multi-sizes.
For Further Information: Free list.

AFFORDABLE DISPLAYS

2030 Calumet St.
Clearwater, FL 34625
(813) 443-3469
Fax: (813) 443-3068

Offers: Custom designed point-of-purchase wood and Plexiglas displays. Slatwall and grid accessories also available.
For Further Information: Call or send SASE.

ALPHA IMPRESSIONS

4161 S. Main St.
Los Angeles, CA 90037
(213) 234-8221

Offers: Labels—woven and custom printed.
For Further Information: Free brochures.
Store Location: At above address.
Discounts: Quantity.

ALLYSON'S

21 Cote Dr.
Eppling, NH 03042

Offers: Engraved title plates, in 7 styles, 5 type styles.
For Further Information: Free brochure.

ALUMA PANEL, INC.

2410 Oak St. W.
Cumming, GA 30131
(800) 258-3003

Offers: Sign blanks and stands: Aluminum, styrene and D-board types, variety of sizes. Also offers flexible magnetic sheeting, sparcal vinyl, corrugated plastic, blank banners, sandblast stencil, chromatic paints.
For Further Information: Send SASE for list.

ARMSTRONG PRODUCTS

P.O. Box 979
Guthrie, OK 73044

Offers: "Ultra-System" display panels including portable style, perforated to allow hanging shelves and items; interchangeable with other System panels.
For Further Information: Call or write for free catalog.

JERRY ANTHONY PHOTOGRAPHY

3952 Shattuck Ave.
Columbus, OH 43220
(614) 451-5207
Fax: (614) 457-8381

Offers: Color printing for the arts, postcards, catalog sheets and fine art prints.
For Further Information: Free packet.
Accepts: American Express, Discover, MasterCard, Visa

BADGE-A-MINIT
348 N. 30th Rd.
P.O. Box 800
La Salle, IL 61301
(815) 224-2090

Offers: Badge-A-Minit Starter kit: you-make, with original design fronts, others. Kit features machine, supplies, directions.
For Further Information: Free color catalog.

BAGS PLUS
640 Country Club Ln., Suite 201
Itasca, IL 60143

Offers: Bags, including poly-zip close, heavy weight and with hand holes. Also offers cellophane in 11 sizes, with a cloth drawstring. Shopping bags and gift totes, T-shirt bags also available. Handles small orders.
For Further Information: Send SASE.

THE BOTTLE SOLUTION
P.O. Box 3562
Boone, NC 28607
(704) 262-5810

Offers: Bottles, including vinegar, corked, vials and other containers.

CHARM WOVEN LABELS
P.O. Box 30027
Portland, OR 97230
(503) 254-2645

Offers: Personalized woven labels with stock phrases: From the Needles of, Custom Made by, Original, Handmade by, Hand Knit by, Made Especially for You, Fashioned by or blank (you choose). Care instruction labels.
For Further Information: Free brochure.

CHIMERA STUDIOS, INC.
3708 E. Hubbard St.
Mineral Wells, TX 76067

Offers: "Flame Pruf" additive, by quart.
For Further Information: Send SASE.

COLLECTOR'S HOUSE
704 Ginesi Dr., Suite 11
Morganville, NJ 07751
(908) 972-6190 or (800) 448-9298

Offers: Displays—jewelry tray, bracelet T-bar, necklace stand/easel, Allstate portable table top showcases, Riker Mount display boxes (butterfly cardboard with glass top, variety of sizes, with cotton, velvet). Fittable covers, price tags, bags, boxes and bubble wrap.

For Further Information: Send for catalog.
Discounts: Quantity.

CRAFT KREATIONS
P.O. Box 6152
Columbia, MD 21045

Offers: Craft tags, including personalized styles for pricing, wash/care and shows.
For Further Information: Catalog, $2.
Discounts: Sells wholesale.

CREATIVE ENERGIES, INC.
1607 N. Magnolia Ave.
Ocala, FL 34475
(800) 351-8889

Offers: Display systems—Public Hanging stackable panel unit (indoor/outdoor), Earth Mounds collapsible pedestable for 3D, staking/weight systems for all canopies. Also offers triple truck dolly, Light-Dome waterproof canopy and zippered side curtains for all canopies.
For Further Information: Free brochure, video, $5.

DANA LABELS, INC.
7778 SW Nimbus Ave.
Beaverton, OR 97005
(503) 646-7933

Offers: Custom-printed labels—garment labels, size tabs, tags, care and content labels. Also offers paper shipping, embossing and cosmetic labels, pressure sensitive and others.
For Further Information: Brochure, $1.

DEALERS SUPPLY
P.O. Box 717
Matawan, NJ 07747
(800) 524-0576
Fax: (908) 591-8571

Offers: Display supplies—fire-retardant fitted table covers, showcases, display grid modules, KD Kanopies, folding tables, lighting, booth signs, black lights, alarms and security aids, display risers and others.
For Further Information: Free catalog.
Accepts: MasterCard, Visa

DESIGNER PAPER PRODUCTS
45 Prospect St.
Yonkers, NY 10701
(800) 831-7791

Offers: Packaging—boxes for apparel, jewelry, gifts, plus paper bags, shopping bags, tissue, wrapping papers, patterned bags, printing.
For Further Information: Free catalog.

DIANNA TZARINA
1099 Atlantic Dr., Bldg. 4
West Chicago, IL 60185
(800) 932-1099

Offers: Display cases, including mirror-back doll (and other) cases in standard and custom sizes.
For Further Information: Free list.
Accepts: MasterCard, Visa

DISPLAYBRIGHT
108 Echo St.
Santa Cruz, CA 95060
(800) 995-1723

Offers: Portable halogen display lighting (use with Abstracta and other systems).
For Further Information: Send SASE for list.

DOVER PUBLICATIONS, INC.
31 E. 2nd St.
Mineola, NY 11501
(516) 294-7000

Offers: Copyright-free design books—black on glossy white, clip/use: borders, holiday motifs, seasons, art nouveau/deco, contemporary motifs, patriotic, sports, office, children's, silhouettes, old-fashioned, travel, transportation, health, symbols, florals, ethnic, early ads, calligraphy.
For Further Information: Free catalog.

ESSENTIALS & SUCH
4746 W. Jennifer Ave., Suite 107
Fresno, CA 93722
(209)277-4747
Fax (209) 277-9755

Offers: Containers, including bottles, jugs, jars, vials, boxes, cans; glass, plastic, tin, metal, others. Also offers caps, lids, droppers, sprayers, sealants, Excelsior and poly and cotton bags. Also has naturals.
For Further Information: Call or write for general catalog.
Discounts: Sells wholesale.

EVERGREEN BAG CO.
990 Main St.
East Hartford, CT 06108
(800) 775-3595

Offers: Paper and plastic packaging, including retail containers, poly bags. Also offers shipping supplies, including cord-handled shopper bag, white T-shirt bags, textured and other gift boxes and others.
For Further Information: Free catalog.

FLOURISH CO.
5763 Wheeler Rd.
Fayetteville, AR 72703
(501) 444-8400 or (800) 296-0049

Offers: White tarps—standard and custom sizes—and Protector canopies. Protector canopy that converts to indoor booth, and Archtop skylight canopy with zippered sides and wind vents.
For Further Information: Free brochure.

THE GLASS PANTRY
231 Cherry Alley
Maysville, KY 41056

Offers: Line of bottles, including a variety of types and sizes for cosmetics and liquids.
For Further Information: Free catalog.

GRAPHCOMM SERVICES
P.O. Box 220
(360) 331-5668 or (800) 488-7436

Offers: Custom labels and hangtags, tagging equipment, self-inking stamps. Service: Design.
For Further Information: Free catalog
Discounts: Quantity

HEIRLOOM WOVEN LABELS
P.O. Box 488, Grand Central Station
Moorestown, NJ 08057
(609) 722-1618
Fax: (609) 722-8905

Offers: Woven labels—wide range of colors/styles, personalized. Name tapes, care, size and content labels.
For Further Information: Call or write.

HOLLAN CRAFT
3 Ann St.
Succasunna, NJ 07876

Offers: Custom banners, including hand-sewn banners for display of company name and log, or other.
For Further Information: Call or write.

IDENT-IFY LABEL CORP.
P.O. Box 140204
Brooklyn, NY 11214

Offers: Personalized labels on white cotton woven labels, custom labels and name tapes, with stock phrases: Original by, Handmade by, Made Especially for You by, Hand Knit by, Made With Love by Mother (Grandmother), Made With Tender Loving Care, Hand Woven by, Fashioned by and blank style (you-add). Name tapes (1 line).

For Further Information: Send SASE for list.
Discounts: Quantity.

INTERNATIONAL PRINTING ACCESS

251 Main St.
Old Saybrook, CT 06475
(203) 388-0419
Fax: (203) 388-6754

Offers: Custom printing of color glossy postcards in 200-plus runs available on all 12 point card products.
For Further Information: Call or write for sample package and price list.

JEFF'S DECAL COMPANY

1747 Selby Ave.
St. Paul, MN 55014
(612) 646-5069
Fax: (612) 644-2695

Offers: Custom water-slide decals and labels for all crafts. Minimum orders are 25 sheets or more for single-color decals and one thousand sheets or more for multi-color. Labels start at a press run for 250 minimum.
For Further Information: Sample and listing, $1 or fax ideas on amounts, colors and sizes.

JENKINS

3950 A Valley Blvd.
Walnut, CA 91789
(909) 594-1349/1471

Offers: Canopies for indoor/outdoor use, canopy connectors, hardware, sawhorses, signs and sign frames, racks, other accessories.
For Further Information: Send SASE for list.

K.I.A. PHOTOGRAPHY

453-5 Main St.
Nashua, NH 03060
(603) 888-0357

Offers: Promotional items—color postcards, business cards, catalog sheets, brochures, others in a variety of sizes, from photo to slide. 1-5 week production, 1,000 minium.
For Further Information: Call or send $3 for 36-page catalog.

KIMMERIC STUDIO

P.O. Box 3586
Napa, CA 94558

Offers: Decorative craft hand tags in over 240 designs for craft show invitations, price and personalized use, including 2-color, bulk combinations. Also offers colored string.
For Further Information: Catalog and samples, $2.

L&L STITCHERY

P.O. Box 43821
Atlanta, GA 30336
(404) 691-2239

Offers: Personalized woven labels: Fabric sew-ons, name tapes.
For Further Information: Free brochure.

M.D. ENTERPRISES DISPLAY SYSTEMS

9738 Abernathy
Dallas, TX 75220

Offers: Display systems for the professional artist. KD Kanopy Shelters.
For Further Information: Call or write for brochure.

MADE IN THE SHADE E-Z UP

P.O. Box 231
Cool, CA 95614
(800) SHADE-2-U

Offers: E-Z Up portable shelters—canopies and accessories in a variety of sizes, basic units and others.
For Further Information: Free brochure and list.

ELAINE MARTIN, INC.

P.O. Box 674
Deerfield, IL 60015
(800) 642-1043
Fax: (708) 945-9573

Offers: Show/display equipment—snap joint canopies in 3 standard colors, with slant, flat or peak roof models. Also E-Z Up and KD Canopies, display booth, side panels, display grids and panels, display pedestals, folding tables. Director chair and accessories.
For Further Information: Free catalog.
Accepts: American Express, Discover, MasterCard, Visa

JOHN MEE CANOPIES

P.O. Box 11220
Birmingham, AL 35202
(205) 967-1885

Offers: KD Majestic canopies, 3 sizes. EZ-UP 500 canopies, 4 sizes with double truss frame and polyester top. Also offers package specials, and items from Show-off, Graphic Display Systems, Armstrong, including replacement tops, chairs, others.
For Further Information: Write or call for free catalog.
Accepts: MasterCard, Visa

MEGAWORKS

P.O. Box 341, 13 Summit St.
East Hampton, CT 06424

Offers: Line of jewelry display cases and inserts, variety of sizes and types.

MITCHELL GRAPHICS

2363 Mitchell Park Dr.
Petosky, MI 49770
(800) 583-9401

Offers: Printing of full-color postcards on recycled paper with soy ink.
For Further Information: Free product and sample package.

NAME MAKER, INC.

P.O. Box 43821
Atlanta, GA 30336
(800) 241-2890

Offers: Fabric labels (small quantities, up), plus retail program for craft and fabric shops.
For Further Information: Send SASE for list.

NEW VENTURE PRODUCTS

1411-B 63rd Way N.
Clearwater, FL 34620
(800) 771-SHOW

Offers: The Showoff Line of canopy and display systems—portable, easy-set-up displays in a variety of sizes and types.
For Further Information: Call or write.

NEWSTECH

12447 Pinebrook
South Lyon, MI 48178

Offers: Hand tags, business cards and self-stitch labels in a variety of orginal designs to-be-personalized, plus tying yarns and cords.
For Further Information: Catalog, $2.
Discounts: Quantity.
Accepts: MasterCard, Visa

NORTHWEST TAG & LABEL, INC.

110 Foothills Rd., Suite 243
Lake Oswego, OR 97034

Offers: Labels on satin, nylon, polyester: care content, size tabs, in stock, and custom labels, size stickers. Also offers hang tags in a variety of types, and custom-made labels to specification.
For Further Information: Brochure, $1.

ON DISPLAY

P.O. Box 42007
Richmond, VA 23225
(804) 231-1942
Fax: (804) 232-5906

Offers: Bases for display of items, including plug-in and battery powered models lighted for effects with glass or crystal

in 24 stock shapes/sizes, revolving and custom-made solid bases for awards or special projects.
For Further Information: Call or write.

PACKAGING UN-LIMITED INC.

1121 W. Kentucky St.
Louisville, KY 40210
(502) 584-4331, (800) 234-1833

Offers: Boxes—corrugated, gift, hat, jewelry, custom-sized, others. Also offers bags, bubble and foam wraps, tissue, foam peanuts, tape, mailing tubes, folders (optional printing).
For Further Information: Free brochure.

PANELS BY PAITH, INC.

2728 Allensville Rd.
Roxboro, NC 27573
(800) 677-2484

Offers: Plaques in over 5 shapes/sizes of bases for display.
For Further Information: Free catalog.

THE PLASTIC BAG OUTLET

190 W. Passaic St.
Rochelle Park, NJ 07662

Offers: Plastic bags—hi-density T-shirt handle bags (4 sizes), loop handle bags, tote handle bags (3 sizes), and super reinforced tote handle bags.
For Further Information: Send SASE for list.
Accepts: MasterCard, Visa

PLASTIC BAGMART

554 Haddon Ave.
Collingswood, NJ 08108
(800) 360-BAGS

Offers: Plastic bags—clear, zip-lock, carryout types—plus shipping tapes, bubble pack bags, tissue, others.
For Further Information: Send for free catalog.
Discounts: Quantity; sells wholesale to legitimate businesses and professionals.
Accepts: MasterCard, Visa

POLYBAGS PLUS

P.O. Box 3043
Port Charlotte, FL 33949

Offers: Polybags, zipclose bags, cotton drawstring bags, floss organizers, heavy-duty piece bags selection. Others.
For Further Information: Send SASE for brochure.

SAKET CO.

7249 Atoll Ave.
North Hollywood, CA 91605
(818) 764-0110

Offers: Plastic bags in all sizes, small and large quantities, for crafts/hobbies, commercial and office use, industry. Cellophane bags.

For Further Information: Free catalog.

Store Location: At above address.

Discounts: Quantity; teachers and institutions; sells wholesale to legitimate businesses and professionals.

STERLING NAME TAPE CO.

P.O. Box 939
Winstead, CT 06098
(800) 654-5210
Fax: (860) 379-0394

Offers: Custom labels printed with name, logo, artwork, etc., in one or more ink colors with care or content information on back.

For Further Information: Sample kit, $1.

T.S.I. WHOLESALE MFG. JEWELERS AND REFINERS

2875 Morris Rd.
Lapeer, MI 48446
(810) 644-8291
Fax: (810) 664-9780

Offers: Custom casting service for medals, paper weights with embedded medal, charms and small jewelry from customer's wax molds. Also offers jewelry repair and stone setting.

For Further Information: Call or send SASE.

THE WOOD FACTORY

1225 Red Cedar Circle
Fort Collins, CO 80521
(970) 224-1949 or (800) 842-9663

Offers: Wood displays and accessories, including trees, shelving, cabinets, contemporary designs. Custom designed portable wood displays and accessories, including arches, revolving panel displays, shelving and crates.

For Further Information: Free catalog.

YAZOO MILLS, INC.

305 Commerce St.
New Oxford, PA 17350
(717) 624-8993

Offers: Mailing tubes—in a full line of lengths and any quantity, with end plugs for most standard sizes; sold by carton.

For Further Information: Free catalog.

Index

A

A La Art Stamp Crafters, 122
A.A. Clouet, 62
AAA Camera Exchange, Inc., 114
A&I Camera Classics Ltd., 114
Aardvark Adventures, 191
Abby Yarns 'N Kits, 199
Abe's Cameras & Electronics, 114
Ace R/C, 92
Acey Deucy, 120
Ackley's, 62
Acme Electric, 148
ACP Inc., 10
A.C.S., 224
Action Bag Co., 266
Adams Wood Products, 148
Adirondack Seatweavers, 10
Adjustable Clamp Co., 148
Adler Sales, Inc., 266
Adopt-A-Doll, 36
Advance Scientific, 127
Advanced Machinery, 148
Adventures in Crafts, 135
Aegean Sponge Co., Inc., 19
Aerospace Composite Products, 92
Affordable Displays, 266
Aftosa, 19
Aiko's Art Materials Import, 5
A.I.M. Displays, 266
Aim Kilns, 19, 36
Airbrush Action Magazine, 254
Airbrush Magazine, 254
A.J. Fisher, Inc., 92
Al Con Enterprises, 209
Alberta's Molds, Inc., 19
Albums Inc., 114
Aldea's, 199
Alden Company, William, 148
Aleta's Rock Shop, 62
Alexander Art Corporation, 5
Alice's Stained Glass, 14, 57
Aljo Manufacturing Co., 160
All About Dolls, 169
All Brands, 199, 224
All Night Media, Inc., 120
All Street Camera, 118
Allen's Basketworks, 10
Allyson's, 266
Alpel Publishing, 52, 161, 165
Alpha Faceting Supply, Inc., 62
Alpha Impressions, 266
Alteryears, 165
Aluma Panel, Inc., 266
Amazon Drygoods, 165, 224
America Online, 252
American & Efird, Inc., 224
American Art Clay Co., Inc., 19, 52, 78, 103, 129

American Association of Wood-turners, 247
American Blind & Wallpaper Factory, 196
American Coaster, The, 36
American Craft Council, 247
American Craft Products, 80
American Frame Corp., 48
American Handicrafts/Merribee, 191
American Indian Art Magazine, 254
American Mineral Gift, 28
American Needlecrafter, The, 254
American Patchwork & Quilting, 254
American Quilter, 254
American Quilter's Society, 247
American Science and Surplus, 127
American Sewing Guild, 247
American Society of Artists, Inc., 247
American Society of Gemcutters, 247
American Society of Marine Artists, 247
American Woodworker, 254
America's Hobby Center, Inc., 92, 99
Analytical Scientific, 127
& Everything Nice, 36
Anderson Handcrafted Products, 218
Angel Stitch, 174
Angie's, 213
Anglers Art, The, 46
Angler's Workshop, 46
Anne-Made Designs, 120
Annie's Attic, 199
Ann's Ceramics, 19
Ann's Doll Things, 36
Anthony Photography, Jerry, 266
Anything in Stained Glass, 57
A-1 Racing Parts, Inc., 33
Apache Canyon Mines, 62
APC Hobbies, 92
APL Trader, Inc., 62
Apollo Knitting Studio, 199
Applied Design Corp., 92
ARA Imports, 62
Archer's Hobby World, 92
ARE, Inc., 62
Arise, 183
Arizona Gems & Minerals, Inc., 63
Arizona Z Car, 33
Armor, 148
Armstrong Products, 266
Arnel's, Inc., 19
Arnhild's Knitting Studio, 199
Arnold, Noel, 99
Aron's, 165

Art by God, 106
Art Calendar, 254
Art Decal Co, 19
Art Essentials of New York Ltd., 111, 131
Art Express, 5
Art Impressions, 120
Art Quilters Studio, 179
Art Store, The, 52, 179
Art Supply Warehouse, 5
Art Tech Casting, Co., 63
Art to Wear, 14
Art Video Library, 2, 52
Art-Video Productions, Inc., 2
Artery, The, 120
Artful Illusions, 161
Artgems Exporters, Inc., 63
Art-In-A-Pinch, 213
Artisan Design, 174
Artistan/Santa Fe, Inc., 5
Artist Created, 252
Artistically Inclined, Inc., 179
Artist's Club, The, 5
Artists' Magazine, The, 254
Autograph, Inc., 141
ART/QUILT MAGAZINE, 254
Arts Array, 210
ASF (All Sisters Fabrics), 183
Ashlandbarns, 30, 99
ASLI Arts, 183
Association of Traditional Hooking Artists, 247
Astro Flight, Inc., 88
ASW Express, 5
Atelier de Paris, 179
Atira's Fashions, 165
Atlanta Puffections, 169
Atlanta Thread & Supply Co., 224
Atlantic Mold Corp., 20
Atlantic Spice Co., 106
Atlas Metal Sales, 78
Auntie Knits, Inc., 199
Australian Opal Imports, 63
Auto-Etch, 93
AV Productions, 20
Avenrich, 183
Aviation Industrial Supply Co., 148
AVL Looms, 232
Ayottes' Designery, 232

B

Backdrop Outlet, 114
Badali: Jewelry & Prospecting Supplies, 63
Badge-A-Minit, 267
Badger Air-Brush Co., 5
Badger Hardwoods of Wisconsin, 148
Baer Fabrics, 165, 183
Bags Plus, 267

Baldwin Fine Porcelain, 36
Balloons, 110
Bally Bead Co., 14
Balsa USA, 88
Baltazor's, 166, 191
B&B Publishing, Inc., 135
B&H Photo, 114
B&J, 28
B&J Rock Shop, 63
Banwell Designs, Tom, 36
Bar-B Woolies, 218
Barbara's Playhouse, 36
Barbeau Fine Fabrics, 183
Barclay Leaf Imports, Inc., 131, 135
Bare Hill Studios/Fiber Loft, 200
Barington, Sonya Lee, 183
Barker Company, 103
Barkim, Ltd., 200
Barletta's, 165
Bartley Software, Inc., 161
Barton's Barnwood, 30
Basket Beginnings, 10
Bates, Inc., Susan, 191
Batiks Etcetera, 183
Bay Country Boutique, 200
Bead & Button, 255
Bead Boppers, 14
Bead Broker, 14
Bead Directory, The, 14
Bead Lady Designs, 14
Bead Shop, The, 14
Beada Beada, 14
Beadbox, Inc., 63
Beadniks, 63
Beads From Around the World, 15
Beadworks, 15
Beadzip, 15
Bear Woods Supply Co., Inc., 135
Bearhugs, 255
Beautiful Bride Pattern Co., 166
Because You Count, Inc., 174
Becker, Patsy, 218
Beck's Warp 'N Weave, 191, 232
Bee Lee Co., The, 224
Bee Paper Co., 112
Beebe Hopper, 3
Beer & Wine Hobby, 144
Bell Ceramics, 37
Bellous, Gina C., 80
Bemidji Woolen Mills, 169
Benbow Chemical Packaging, Inc., 111
Bendigo Woolen Mills, 200
Benjamin, Jeanne, 218
Benson Hobby Products, 93
Bergmann, Bernie, VW Engine Spec., 33
Berman Leathercraft, 75
Bernadine's Needle Art, 174

Bernina, 224
Bernina Sewing Center, 225
Better Built Corp., 30
Better Homes & Gardens Crafts Club, 255
Betterway Books, 250
BFK, 73
Binding Stitch, The, 184
Birch Street Clothing, Inc., 166, 225
Bizarro, 120
Black Sheep Newsletter, 255
Black Sheep Wools, 200, 243
Blackman Productions, Wm., 2
Blair: Tomorrow's Heirlooms, Nancy, 218
Blick, Dick, 6, 52, 129, 131
Blue Diamond Kiln, 20
Blue Ridge Machinery & Tools, Inc., 141
Bluejacket Ship Crafters, 93
Blueprints-Printable, 179
Bluster Bay Woodworks, 232
Boardwatch, 252
Bob Ross TV Art Club, 2
Bobel Bros., 37
Bodkin Craft, 80
Bogen Photo Corp., 114
Bogert & Hopper, Inc., 149
Boise Kites, 73
Bolek's Craft Supplys, Inc., 52
Bombay Bazaar, 63
Bonfit America, Inc., 161
Bookbinder's Warehouse, The, 112
Boone Trading Co., 15, 128
Bottle Solution, The, 267
Bountiful, 232
Bourget Bros., 64
Boutique Trims, Inc., 53
Bovis Bead Co., 15
Boxwood Road Designs, 225
Boyd's, 53
Brabec Productions, Barbara, 252
Braid-Aid, 218
Bramsch Video Group, 80
Bramwell Yarns, U.S.A., 200
Brandmark, 141
Brassard et Fils, Inc., Maurice, 232
Brewery, The, 144
Bri Metal Fabricators, 129
Brian's Crafts Unlimited, 53, 209
Brickyard Ceramics & Crafts, 20
Bridals International, 166
Brides 'N Babes, 166
Bridgewater Scrollworks, 135
Britex-By-Mail, 184
Broadway Yarn Co., 243
Brodnax Prints, 80
Bromwell Marketing, 114
Brook Distinctive Fabrics, Sawyer, 184
Brown Engineering, 30
Brown House Dolls, 37
Bryant Laboratory, Inc., 129
Bryne Ceramics, 20
Buck Run Carving Supplies, 146
Buckaroo Bobbins, 166
Buffalo Batt & Felt, 191

Buffalo Tipi Pole Co., 60
Burda Patterns, 161
Burl Tree, 149
Burlap'N Rags, 218
Bushfield, Ann C., 200
Business of Herbs, The, 255
Button Emporium, The, 184
Button Factory, 184
Button Shop, The, 225
Buttons by Mail, 225
Buttons Unlimited, 225
By Diane, 169
By Jupiter!, 179
By Shirley McKibben, 200
Byron Originals, Inc., 88

C

Caboose Hobbies, 99
Cadillac Mountain Farm, 106
C.A.I.-Ming, 20
Calico Cat, The, 213
Calico Cupboard, 225
Calumet, 115
Camas International, 210
Cambridge Camera Exhange, Inc., 115
Camera World of Oregon, 115
Campbell Bosworth Machinery Co., 75
Campvill Hill Crafts, 37
Canadian Craft Supplies, 37
Candlechem Co., 103
C&R Loo, Inc., 57
Caning Shop, The, 10, 106
Canterbury Designs, Inc., 174
Cantrell, Mary, 169
Canyon Records & Indian Arts, 15
Cape Cod Cooperage, 135
Caravan Beads, 15
Carbone, Inc., Martin C., 112
Carbone, Inc., Martin R., 53
Cardin Originals, 161
Cardinal Engineering, 141
Carlisle Restoration Lumber, 30
Carlson Engine Imports, 88
Carodan Farm Wood Shop, 200
Carol Leigh's Specialties, 232
Carolina Mills, 184
Carpenters' Crafts, 208
Carris Pottery, 252
Carroll Antiques, James, 213
Carter Products Co., Inc., 149
Cartoonerama, 2
Carvers' Eye Company, 37, 169
Casey's Wood Products, 149
Caspar, Charles A., 20, 60
Castcraft, 103
Castings, 103
Castlegate Farm, 232
Castolite, 103
Cat's Paw, 80
Cayce Co., The, 149
Cellar Homebrew, The, 144
Cementex Latex Corp., 103
Center for the Study of Beadwork, 15
Central Camera Co., 115
Central Model Marketing, 93

Central Valley, 99
Century Leather, 184
Cer Cal, Inc., 20
Ceramic Arts & Crafts, 255
Ceramic Bug Supplies, 20
Ceramic Creations, 21
Ceramic Restoration, 21
Ceramicorner, Inc., 21
Ceramics Magazine, 255
Certainly Wood, 149
Charles Publishing, 200
Charlotte's Hobbies & Crafts, 53
Charm Woven Labels, 267
Charmor's, 200
Chartru Enterprise, 161
Chase Taxidermy Supply Co., Dan, 134
Chatham Art Distributors, Inc., 6
Cheap Joe's Art Stuff, 6
Cheetah Model, 88
Cherry Tree Toys, 149
Chester Book Co., 53
Chicago Latex Products, Inc., 37, 104
Chimera Studios, Inc., 267
Chris Rossbach, 96
Christie Designs, Victoria, 120
Chroma, Inc., 6
Cinema Leathers, 184
Circustamps, 120
Cir-Kit Concepts, Inc., 80
Clarkcraft, 33
Classic Colonial Homes, 30
Classic Instruments, PK, 33
Classic Roadsters, Ltd., 33
Clay Magic, Inc., 21
Cleveland Model & Supply Co., 88, 93
Cloth Doll, The, 255
Cloth of Gold, 213
Coastal Enterprises, 104
Coats & Clark, Inc., 225
Cobun Creek Farm, 233
Cochenille Design Studio, 162, 213
Cochran's Crafts, 16
Code Felt Ltd., 184
Coherent Visual, 174
Collectible Doll, 37
Collector's House, 267
Collins Creations, 179
Colonial Hardwoods, Inc., 149
Colonial Patterns, 213
Colophon Book Arts Supply, Inc., 112
Color Trends, 255
Colorado Doll Faire, 37
Colorcraft, Ltd., 179
Colourfields, 201
Columbine Beads, 16
Co-Motion Rubber Stamps, 121
Compleat Sculptor, Inc., The, 129
Compu Stitch, 174
Compucrafts, 174
CompuServe, 252
Concept Research and Development, Inc., 93
Con-Cor, 99
Concord Miniatures, 80

Condon Company, Inc., M.L., 149
Conklin's, 30
Connecticut Cane & Reed Co., 10
Connecting Threads, 213
Conrad Machine Co., 6
Constantine & Son, Inc., Albert, 149
Cookie Mold Carver, 104
Coronet China & Decal Co., Inc., 21
Cottage Connection, 255
Cotton Clouds, 201, 233
Cotton Patch, The, 214
Cotton Shoppe, The, 185
Couch, Tony, 2
Country Accents, 78
Country Baskets, 11
Country Braid House, 218
Country Crafts, 255
Country Hearts & Stars, 196
Country Seat, Inc., 11
Covington Engineering Corp., 57, 64
Coxe Blocks, 146
Coyote Pines Rare Breed, 233
CPM, Inc., 115
Craft Catalog, 53
Craft Gallery, 191, 208
Craft Industries Limited, 179
Craft King, 53
Craft Kreations, 267
Craft Makers, 53
Craft Marketing News, The, 255
Craft Show Calendar, The, 255
Craft Supplies 4 Less, 64
Craft Supplies USA, 150
Craft Time, 104
Crafter's Choice, 250
Crafters Mart, 150
Crafting Traditions, 256
Crafts, 256
Crafts By Donna, 175
Crafts Fair Guide, The, 256
Crafts Just for You, 135
Crafts 'N Things, 256
Crafts Plus, 256
Crafts Unlimited, 54
Craftsman Wood Service Co., 150
Craftsmen's Studio, 175
Crafty Cut-Outs, 150
Cranberry Painter, 135
Crazy Crow Trading Post, 60
Creanativity, 225
Create an Heirloom, 37
Create Something Beautiful, 201
Create-A-Tie, 161
Createx Colors, 111
Creations, 225
Creations By Erline, 38
Creative Catalyst Productions, 2
Creative Ceramics, 21
Creative Clock, 28
Creative Corner, 21
Creative Craft House, 54, 191
Creative Energies, Inc., 267
Creative Handcrafts, 201
Creative Needlecrafts Club, 250
Creative Paperclay Co., 38, 104

Creative Yarns, 243
Creek Water Wool Works, 233
Creek-Turn, Inc., 57
Crescent Bronze Powder Co., 111
Cridge, Inc., 21
Criss-cross, 80
Crochet Home, 256
Crochet With Heart, 256
Crochet World, 256
Croffwood Mills, 150
Crooked-River, 64
Cross Country Stitching, 256
Cross Stitch, The, 175
Cross-Stitch & Country Crafts, 256
Cross-Stitch! Magazine, 256
Cross Stitcher Magazine, The, 256
Crown City Hardware Co., 150
Crown Plane Co., 150
CR's Crafts, 38
CRS's Crafts, 169
Crysbi Crafts, Inc., 54
CS Flight Systems, 88
CSZ Enterprises, Inc., 226
Cultural Centers of Color/NEA, 252
Cummings, C., 226
Cupboard Distributing, 136
Cushing & Co, W., 218
Custom Ceramic Molds, 21
Custom Colors, 233
Custom Data Solutions, 252
Custom Handweaving, 233
Custom Knits & Manufacturing, 201
Custom Tackle Supply, 46
Custom Wood CutOuts Unlimited, 136, 150
Cutawl Co., The, 131
Cutting Edge, The, 226
Cyrefco, 233

D

D & J Electronics, 88
D & J Hobby & Crafts, 93
Daft Dames Handcrafts, 233
Daisy Chain, 175
Dallas, Mr. & Mrs. of, 24
Dana Lables, Inc., 267
Dan-Sig Co., The, 141
D'Anton Leather Company, 185
D'Argenzio's, 201
Darkroom Aids Company, 115
Dar's Quite Corner, 169
Davic Computer Services, Inc., 175
David A. Leffel, 3
Davidson's Old Mill Yarns, 243
Davis Wholesale, Lou, 21, 54
Dawn for New Directions, 64
Dealers Supply, 267
Dear Dolly, 38
Debcor, 22
Decart, Inc., 180
Decor Time, 28
Decorative Artist's Workbook, 257
Deer Creek Products, 150
Dee's Delights, Inc., 81
Delafield Stamp Co., 121
Delectable Mountain Cloth, 226

Delta 1 Custom Photo Manufacturing, 115
Delta Technical Coatings, Inc., 111, 180
Dember Arts, 2
Dendritics, Inc., 64
Depot Dollhouse Shop, The, 81
Design Consulting Service, 129
Design Preservation Models, 99
Design Technics Miniatures, 81
Design Works, Inc., 30
Designer Furniture Plans, 50
Designer Paper Products, 267
Designer Secrets, 196
Designs by Bentwood, Inc., 136
Designs By Cynthia Wise, 201
Designs By Debbie Mitchell, 180
Designs By Judi, 81
Designs by Roberta, 201
Desktop Images, 2
DGA Designs, 89
Dharma Trading Co., 180
Dial-A-Photo, Inc., 115
Diamond Enterprises, 93
Diamond "M" Brand Mold Co., 81
Diamond Pacific Tool Corp., 64
Diana's Treasures, Inc., 38
Diane's Beads, 16
Dianna Tzarina, 268
Difranza Designs, 219
Diminutive Specialties, 81
Dimity, 201
Dimples, 185
Discount Agate House, 64
Discount Arts and Crafts, 54
Discount Bead House, 16
Discount Hobby Center, 93
Displaybright, 268
Diva Rubber, 121
Dixie Art & Airbrush Supplies, 6
Dobry Enterprises, 196
Documounts, 48
Dodd: Marble & Granite, 129
Dody Lyness Co., 106
Dogwood Lane, 226
Doll Adventure, The, 38
Doll Annex, 38
Doll Artisan, The, 257
Doll Crafter, 257
Doll Designs, 257
Doll Emporium Pattern Col., 170
Doll Gallery, Inc., 39
Doll House, The, 39
Doll Majik!, 39
Doll Sculpting Videos, 39
Dol-lee Shop, The, 38
Dollhouse Factory, The, 81, 170
Dollmakers, The, 39
Dollmaking Projects & Plans, 257
Dollreader, The, 257
Dolls And Treasures, 39
Dolls, Bears & Surprises, 39
Dolls Delight, Inc., 170
Dolls, Etc., 39
Dolls in Miniature, 257
Dollspart Supply Co., 39
Dolly Delites, 39
Dongo Molds, 22

Donna's Molds, 22
Don's Hobby Shop, Inc., 89
Doran Enterprises, 115
Dorothy Biddle Service, 106
Dorr Mill Store, The, 219
Dorrance Co., Gregory D., 146
Dorset Looms, 233
Dos De Tejas, 162
Double D Productions, 162
Double D Rubber Stamps, Inc., 121
Double Joy Beads, 16
Dove Brush Mfg., Inc., 54
Dover Publications, Inc., 54, 250, 268
Dowering Designs, 166
Dremel, 151
Dremel, Inc., 141
Dress Rite Forms, 226
Dritz Corp., 226
Dromedary, The, 94
Dubay, Kim, 219
Duckwork's Woodcrafts, 81
Dundas Loom Co., 233
Duralite, Inc., 22
Durham, 129
Durham Co., The, 111, 131
Durstenfeld, Ligia, 81
Dux' Dekes Decoy Co., 136
Dwyer's Doll House, 82

E

Eagle America Corp., 151
Eagle Coach Work, Inc., 33
Eagle Feather Trading Post, 60
Eagle Woodworking, 50
E&B Marine, 33
Early American Life, 257
Earth Art, 65
Earth Guild, 192, 219, 233
Earthsong Fibers, 201, 234
Earthworks, 60
East West Dye Co., 78
Eastern Art Glass, 57
Eastgem, Ltd., 65
Eastman Machine Co., 226
Eastman Sewing Resources, 226
Easy Leaf, 136
Eaton Yarns, 234
Ebac Lumber Dryers, 31
Ebersole Lapidary Supply, Inc., 65
Econ Abrasives, 151
Econo Craft, 202
Edgemont Yarn Service, Inc., 234
Edmund Scientific, 78, 127
Educational Lumber Co., 151
Egger's, 46
EHB Designs, 219
Elan Pattern Co., 162
Elbridge Company, The, 136
Elect-a-Lite, Inc., 82
Ellis Peeples Dolls, 172
Elna, Inc., 226
Eloxite Corp., 65
Embossing Arts Co., 121
Embroidery Machine, 175
Emerald City Stamps, 121
Emma Lou's Hooked Rugs, 219
Emperor Clock Co., 28, 50

Enchanted Attic, The, 170
Enchanted Doll House, The, 82
Engelhard Corp., 22
England Things, 82
Engraving Arts, 65
Enterprise Art, 54
Erdal Yarns, Ltd., 243
Eric Clutton, 93
Ericson, Lois, 162
Essentials & Such, 104, 268
Eva Sportscars, 34
Evenheat Kiln, Inc., 22
Evening Star Designs, 185
Everett-Morrison Motorcars, 34
Evergreen Bag Co., 268
Evergreen Scale Models, 94
Everlastings, 106
Ewe & Eye, 202
Ewe Tree, The, 234
Executive Photo & Supply Corp., 116
Exquisite Images, 121
Extra Special Products Corp., 78, 180, 214

F

Fabric Center, 196
Fabric Fancies, 166
Fabric Gallery, 185
Fabric Outlet, The, 196
Fabric Shack Stores, 214
Fabrics Unlimited, 185
Factory Direct Craft Supply, 55
Fairfield Processing Corp., 214
Fairmount Farm Fleeces, 234
Famous Labels Fabric Outlet, 185
Fancy Stitches, 175
Fancywork, 175
Fancywork and Fashion, 170
Fantasy Craft, 82
Farmyard Fibers, 202
Farris Machinery, 151
Fash-en-hues, 22
Fashion Blueprints, 162
Fashion Fabrics Club, 185
Fashion Fabrics Club/Natural Fiber Fabrics, 226
Fashion Touches, 162
Favor-Rite Mold Co., 22
Faye, Victoria, 227
Fay's Fashion Fabrics, 162, 185
FC&A's Transfer Patterns, 180
Fears, Jackie, 162
Feather Craft Fly Fishing, 46
Federal Trade Commission, 252
Feibing Company, Inc., 75
Feinstein, Bette S., 192, 250
Fell & Company, Inc., David H., 65
Fern Vasi Dolls, 82
Fernwood Miniatures, 82
Fiber Loft, 234
Fiber Shop, The, 202, 234
Fiber Studio, The, 39, 202, 234
Fiberfest Magazine, The, 257
Fiberarts, Magazine of Textiles, 257
Fibers & More, 170, 202
Fibres, 202

Fida Studio, The Robert, 130
Field's Fabrics, 185
Fieldwood Co., Inc., The, 82
Fiesta Yarns, 243
Fifth Stitch, The, 202
Filature Lemieux, Inc., 243
Fine Print, 257
Fine Tool Journal, 257
Finescale Modeler, 257
Fingerlakes Woolen Mill, 202
Firefly Embroideries, 16
Fireside Fiberarts, 235
Fishman's Fabrics, 186
5 T's Embroidery Supply, 175
FKS Designs, 219
Fleece & Fromage Farms, 235
Fletcher-Lee & Co., 6
Fletcher-Terry Co., The, 48
Flex Eyes, 146
Flock of Many Colors, 235
Flora & Company Multimedia, 3
Flora, J., 186
Flora Multimedia & Co., 40, 180
Floral Decor, 106
Flourish Co., 268
Flying Models, 258
Flying Things, 73
Flynn, Inc., Jane McGown, 219
FOB Village Originals, 65
Focus Camera, Inc., 116
Folkwear, 166
Follansbee Dock Systems, 31
For the Love of Cross Stitch, 258
Ford Trunks, Charlotte, 136
Foredom Electric Co., The, 141
Forestheart Studio, 219
Forever Timeless, 166
Formby's Workshop, 151
Formula 1, 94
Forneris Fiber Designs, Connie E., 220
Fort Crailo Yarns Co., 235
Forté Industries, 136
Fouche, Shermane, 227
Frame Fit Co., 48
Frame Strips, 48
Frame Wealth, Inc., 6
Francisco Enterprise, The, 252
Franken Frames, 48
Franklin Art Glass, 57
Franklin Distributors Corp., 116
Frank's Cane & Rush Supply, 11
Frank's Hobby House, 89
Frantz Bead Company, 16, 58
Frazier Co., Harry M., 220
Fredricksburg Rugs, 220
Fred's Dollhouse & Miniature Center, 82
Free Trade Photo, 116
Freed Co., The, 16
Freeman, L., 82
Freestyle, 116
Fricke Enterprises, 235
Friends of the Origami Center of America, The, 247
Friends Patterns, 162
Frog Tool Co. Ltd., 151

From The Farm/Heirlooms Kits, 235
Front Room Publishers, The, 253
Frostline Kits, 211
Fruit Basket Upset, 121
Fry Designs, 202
Fuji Photo Film, U.S.A., Inc., 116
Fun Stuff, 40
Furniture Designs, Inc., 50

G

G Street Fabrics, 186
Gabriel's, 65
Galastic Trade Commission, 94
Galloway, Adola, 40
Gameplan/Abstract, 16
GamePlan/ArtRanch, 130
Garden of Beadin', The, 16
Garden Railways, 258
Garden State Camera, 116
Gare, Inc., 22
Garrett Wade Co., Inc., 151
Gastonian Detail, The, 136
Gaywood Dyes, 235
Gemco International, 65
Gemini Inc., 131
Gemmary, The, 66
Gemstone Equipment Manufacturing, 66
Generations Brewing, 144
Gennie Shifter, 34
Gerlachs of Lecha, 112
GH Productions, 11
GHA, The Jewelry Mold Co., 22
Ghee's, 163
G.H.T.A. Co., 180
Gibbs Co., The, 214
Gilliom Manufacturing, Inc., 152
Gilmer Wood Co., 146
Gilmore Looms, 235
Ginger Tree, The, 106
Gingerbread House of Miniatures, 82
Ginger's Needleworks, 214
Ginny's Gems, 220
Gitta's Charted Petit Point, 210
Glass Craft, Inc., 58
Glass House, 40
Glass Pantry, The, 268
Glass Workbench, The, 58
Gleaners Yarn Barn, The, 235, 243
Glen-L Marine, 34
Global Dolls Corp., 40
Global Village Imports, 186
Globe Union International, Inc., 66
GM Plastics, 89
Gnomebodies & Somebodies, 40
Godin Art, Inc., 136
Gold Leaf & Metallic Powders, Inc., 111, 131, 137
Goldberg & Co., Inc. H.E., 186
Golden Fun Kits, 170
Golden West Motorsport, Inc., 34
Goldenwest Manufacturing, Inc., 40
Goldline Ceramics, 23
Gold's Artworks, Inc., 112
Good Impressions, 121

Good Stamps—Stamp Goods, 112, 121
Good Wood, 235
Good-Krüger Dolls, 40
Goodman, A., 66
Goodspeed, Sally, 170
Goodwin's Kites, 73
Gossamer Threads and More, 202
Gotto Teresa Dane, 203
Gramma's Graphics, 180
Granberg International, 31
Grand View Country Store, 203
Granny's Quilts Sewing Center, 192
Graphcomm Services, 268
Graphic Chemical & Ink Co., 6
Graphic Dimensions Ltd., 48
Graphic Media Co., 7
Graphic Rubber Stamp Co., 121
Gratiot Lake Basketry, 11
Graves, Co., 66
Great American Sewing Factory, 186
Great Aunt Victoria's Wicker, 11
Great Copy Patterns, 163
Great Fermentations, 144
Great Northern Weaving, 220
Great Planes Model Manufacturing, 94
Great Winds Kite Co., 73
Greatwood Log Homes, Inc., 31
Green Frog Productions Ltd., 99
Green Pepper, The, 211
Greenberg & Hammer, Inc., 227
Greenbert's Great Train, Dollhouse & Toy Shows, 83
Grey Owl Indian Craft Co., Inc., 60
Grieger's, 66
Grizzly Imports, Inc., 152
Grizzly Peak Kiteworks, 73
Grumbacher, 7
Gryphon Corp., 66
Gumbo Graphics, 122
Gutcheon Patchworks, Inc., 214

H

Hagstoz & Son, Inc., T.B., 66
Hall, Martha, 243
Hamilton Eye Warehouse, 40
Hancock Fabrics, 196, 227
Hand Papermaking, 258
H&B Precision Card Models, 100
Handcraft Designs, 40
Handcraft Illustrated, 258
Handiworks, 203
Handweavers Guild of America, Inc., 248
Handworks, 192
Handwoven, 258
Haneke Merino Wool, 244
Hang-Em High Fabrics, 73, 211
Hannily Patterns, 170
Hansa, 17
Hapco Products, 214
Happy Hearts, 170
Harbor Freight Tools, 141
Hard-To-Find Needleworkbooks, 192
Hardwoods, DJ, 151

Hardy Patterns, Jean, 163
Hardy: Spinning & Weaving, Diana, 235
Harmon, Jamie, 244
Harriet's, 163
Harriet's TCS-Patterns, 166
Harris Engineering, 34
Harris Enterprises, 152
Hartco, 131
Haskell's, 28
Haus of Dolls, 40
Haynes Sign Co., 132
Hazy, Debbie, 244
Heartfelt, 171
Heartwarmers, 41
Heaven & Earth, 67
Heavenly Dolls, 41
Heirloom Toys, 41
Heirloom Woven Labels, 268
Heite Icelandic Wool, Louise, 236
Hello Dolly, 41
Herb Basket, The, 11
Herb Companion, The, 258
Herb Quarterly, The, 258
Herb Shoppe, 107
Herbalgram, 258
Herbally Yours, 107
Heritage Craft Studio, Inc., 137
Heritage Looms, 236
Heritage Saw Co., 137
Hermes, J., 83
Hermes Leather, 186
Herrills Execuform, 89
Herrschers, 192
Hesson Collectables, 163
HH Designs, 175
High Country West Needlework Shop, 192
High Fly Kite Company, 73
Highwood Bookshop, 146
Hill Decal Co., 23
Hinterberg Design, Inc., 214
Hippo Heart, 122
His & Her Hobbys, 83
HK Holbein, 7
Hobbies & Helis International, 89
Hobby House, Inc., 94
Hobby Lobby International, Inc., 94
Hobby Shack, 89
Hobby Surplus Sales, 100
Hobbyland, 89
Hofcraft, 137
Hoffman Hatchery, 107
Hogue, 152
Hollan Craft, 268
Holland Mold, Inc., 23
Hollaway, Judy, 171
Home Craft Express, Inc., 137
Home Fabric Mills, 196
Home Lumber Co., 152
Home Shop Machinist, The, 258
Home-Sew, 227
Homespun, 196
Hong Kong Lapidaries, Inc., 67
Hood Finishing Products, Inc., 152
Hook Nook, The, 220
Hooked on Crochet, 258
Hope-Franklin, Inc., 67

Horsley Publications, Peter, 132
Horton Brasses, 152
Horween Leather Co., 75
Hotglass, 58
House of Caron, 83
House of Miniatures, The, 83
House of Onyx, 67
Houston Art & Frame, Inc., 137
Houston Stained Glass Supply, 58
How Magazine, 258
Howee's Inc., 152
Howell House, The, 214
Hoy's Stained Glass Distributors,
    Ed, 58
HTC, 142, 152
Hubers, 67
Hudson Glass Co., Inc., 58
Hummingbird Fibers, 244
Hunt Valley Cashmere, 236
Huston's, 41

I

Ident-Ify Label Corp., 192, 268
Illusions of Grandeur, 167
Imagination Station, 181
Imperial Picture Frames, 48
In Sheep's Clothing, 236
In Stitches, 176
Indian Store, The, 60
Indoor Model Supply, 89
Inkadinkado, 122
Inkers-A-Way, 122
Innovative Imprints, 215
Innovative Model Products, 89
Innovative Photography, 83
Instant Interiors, 197
International Guild of Miniature
    Artisans, 248
International Hobbies, 100
International Hobby Corp., 100
International Hobby Supply, 94
International House Of Bunka, Inc.,
    176
International Printing Access, 269
International Sculpture, 259
International Sculpture Center, 248
International Tool Corp., 153
International Violin Co., 153
Interweave Press, 192
Into The Wind, 73
I/R Miniatures, Inc., 94
Irene's Dolls, 41
Iron Shop, The, 31
Islander—Video Division, 227
Italian Art Store, The, 7
It's Sew Easy Home Video, 197
Ivy Imports, Inc., 160, 181

J

J & T Imports Dried Flowers, 107
Jackite, Inc., 74
Jackson Marking Products, 122
Jacobs, Ed, 122
Jacqueline Designs, 220
Jacqueline's, 83
Jagger Spun, 236
Jam Creations, 11
Jamestown Distributors, 34
J&L Casual Furniture Co., 50

Jane's Fiber Works, 236
Janice Naibert, 42
Janknits, 203
Janna Joseph Designs, 83
Jann's, 46
Jansen, Joan, 171
Jantz Supply, 146
Jasmine Heirlooms, 215
Jax Chemical Co., Inc., 58
Jay-Kay Molds, 23
Jay's of Tucson, 67
Jeff's Decal Company, 269
Jehlor Fantasy Fabrics, 186
Jenkins, 269
Jennell's Doll House, 41
Jennings Decoy Co., 137, 146
Jerry's Artorama, 7
Jerry's Tackle, 46
Jewel Sommars, 44
J-Made Looms, 236
Joan Adams, 80
Joann Bentson, 37
Joe Kubert Art & Graphic Supply,
    7
Johnson's Custom Models, 90
Joppa Glassworks, Inc., 17
Joseph's Coat, 171, 186
Judi's Dolls, 171
Juki America, 227
Jurak, 3
Jurgen Craft Products, 107
Just Needlin', 176

K

K & B Manufacturing, 90
K & S Engineering, 95
K-Ceramic Imports, 23
Kais, Inc., 41
Kalabash Kites, 74
Kalish Brushes, 7
K&S Tole Craft Supply, 137
Karen's Crafting Accessories, 55
Karin's Mini Garden, 83
Karlin of Quakertown, 211
Kart World, 34
Kathe's Kits, 203
Kathryn Luna, 104
Katrina's Bits & Bobs, 176
Kaune, Bob, 153
Kayne & Sons Custom Hardware,
    153
Keepsake Quilting, 215
Kelly's Ceramics, Inc., 23
Kemper Doll Supply, 41
Kemper Enterprises, 23
Kemper Manufacturing Co., 104
Kemp's Krafts, 176
Ken Hankinson Associates, 34
Ken Quilt Manufacturing Co., 215
Kenco, 203
Kennebec Wool & Fur, 187
Kennedy, F.G.A., Esther, 67
Kessenich Looms, 236
Key Dome, 31
Keystone Wood Specialties, Inc.,
    153
K.I.A. Photography, 269
Kilkenny Miniatures, 84

Kimmeric Studio, 269
Kindred Spirits, 220
King Foundry, Paul, 130
Kings Valley Animal Family, 236
Kingsley North, Inc., 67
Kins Rubber Stamps, Judi, 122
Kirchen Bros., 55
Kit Bunker, The, 95
Kit Car, 259
Kite Sails, 74
Kite Studio, 74
Kitelines, 74, 259
Kiyo Design, Inc., 192
Klear Copy Design Rubber Stamps,
    122
Kline Carving Shop, J.H., 147
Klockit, 28
Knight's, 67
Knit Knack Shop, Inc., 203
Knit-O-Graf Pattern Co., 203
Knitters Magazine, 259
Knitters News, 259
Knitting Basket V.I.P. Guild, 203
Knitting Circles, 203
Knitting Guild of America, The,
    248
Knitting Guild of Canada, The, 248
Knitting Machines of Florida, 204
Knots & Treadles, 236
Kolander's Aurora Silk, Cheryl,
    244
Kraus, 144
Kreinik Manufacturing Co., Inc.,
    176
Krona International, 68
Kruh Knits, Merchants to the
    Machine Knitter, 204
Kubert Art & Graphic Supply, Joe,
    55
Kuempel Chime, 28
Kwik-Sew Pattern Co., The, 163
Kyle, Enterprises, Inc., Carolyn,
    181

L

La Lana Wools, 236
La Maison Piquee, 215
L.A. Stampworks, 123
Lace Heaven, 187
Lace Land, 163
LACIS, 193
Laguna Clay Co., 23
Laila's, 137
Lake City Craft Co., 112
Lambspun Bulky Sample Club, 237
Lamp Shop, The, 197
Lamp Specialties, Inc., 23
Lampe-Designs in Fibers, Jean, 204
Lampen, Betty, 84
L&L Stitchery, 269
Laney Co., 68
Lapcraft, Inc., U.S.A., 68
Lapidabrade, Inc., 68
Lapidary Journal, 259
Lark Books, 250
Lasting Impressions, 123
Lauratex Fabrics, 181
Laurel Street Studio, 171

Lavina Interiors, 75
*Leather Crafters & Saddlers
    Journal,* 259
Leather Factory, Inc., The, 75, 187
Leather Unlimited, 76
Leather Unlimited Corp., 187
Leesburg Looms and Supply, 237
Lehman, 24
Leichtung Workshops, 153
Leisure Arts—The Magazine, 259
Lencraft, 90
Les French Wigs, 41
*Let's Talk About Dollmaking
    Magazine,* 259
Letter Arts Review, 259
Life Industries, 227
Lifetime Career Schools, 41, 227
Light Impressions, 116
Lightsheet, 95
Liliedahl Publications, 3
Lily of the Valley, 107
Lily Pond Products, 24
Lindal Cedar Homes, 31
Linda's Specialty Fabrics, 187
Little Goodies, 84
Little House of Miniatures on
    Chelsea Lane, 84
Little Joys Dolls, 171
Little Red House at Beauvais
    Castle, 84
Little Something for Everyone, A,
    84
Live Guides, 227
LJ Book & Video Sellers, 68
LJ Originals, Inc., 176
Lobo Power Tools, 153
Locomotive Workshop, 100
Logan Kits, 163
Lomoriello, Marje, 197
Long Creek Products, 107
Loom Exchange, 237
Loomis, Mary Wales, 163
Loompal, The, 237
Lord Perry Historical Fashions, 171
Lortone, Inc., 68
Lost Art Yarn Shoppe, 204
Louet Sales, 237
Love You to Bits, 123
Loving Little Rubber Stamps, 123
Loyel Enterprises, 151
Luci's Dolls, 42
Lunatic Fringe, The, 237

M

Macbeath Hardwood Co., 153
MacNeil, Sylvia, 171
Macomber Looms, 237
Made in the Shade E-Z Up, 269
Mafell North America, Inc., 153
Maggie Co., 210
Magic Brush, Inc., The, 137
Magic Cabin Dolls, 171
Magic Needle, 193, 215
Magic Threads, 171
Magnolia, 113
Mahamadon Sumarch, 167
Maine Street Stamps, 123
Mainline and Siding, 100

Mainline Hobby Supply, 100
Maitland Hines, Fred, 3
Majic Carpet, 220
Majic of Maine, 3
Mamiya America Corp., 116
M & M Trims, 181
M&R Technologies, Inc., 176
Mandy's Wool Shed, 220
Mangum's Western Wear, 17
Manlick, MMR, Donald B., 100
Mannings, The, 204, 237
Manny's Woodworkers Place, 153
Manor House Designs, 138
Mantua Industries, 100
Manzanita Decorative Wood, 154
Marauder & Co., 34
Marilyn's Needlework & Frames, 176
Marine Sewing, 211
Maritime Ship Modelers Guild, 248
Marjon Ceramics, 24
Marlene's Decorative Fabrics, 197
Marling Lumber Co., 154
Marr Haven, 244
Martha Jean's, 204
Martin, Inc., Elaine, 269
Mary Jane's Cross 'N Stitch, Inc., 176
Marydoll's Molds, 84
Maryland China Co., 24
Mary's Productions, 228
Ma's Body Shop, 42
Master Stitch Designs, Inc., 177
Mastercraft Plans, 154
Masterpiece Eye Co., Inc., 42
Masterpieces In Miniature, 84
Material Memories, 171
Material World, The, 187
Maxant Industries, 68, 104
Maxim, Inc., Mary, 193
Maybelle's Dollworks, 42
Mayco Colors, 24
Mayflower Textile Co., 221
McCall's Needlework, 259
McGuire, John, 11
McIntosh Ltd., Jean, 210
Mckenzie Taxidermy Supply, 134
Mcron Ceramic Molds, 24
M.D. Enterprises Display Systems, 269
MDI Woodcarvers Supply, 147
Meadow Everlastings, 107
Mediascape Inc., 123
Medieval Miscellanea, 167
Mee Canopies, John, 269
Megaworks, 269
Meisel Hardware Specialties, 154
Meistergram, 177
Melco Embroidery Systems, 228
Melind Co., Louis, 123
Mens Sana, 177
Meredith Books, 250
Merit Albums, Inc., 116
Metalliferous, 68
Mettle Co., The, 48
MFD Enterprises, Inc., 55
M.G. Lighthouse, 84
Mich, Co., Earl, 132

Michiko's Creations, 187
Micro-Mark, 95
Microstamp Corp., 142
Mid-Continent Leather Sales Co., 76
Midland Tackle, 46
Midwest Dowel Works, Inc., 154
Midwest Products Co., Inc., 90
Mill End Store, 187
Miller Rug Hooking, 221
Mimi's Books & Patterns for the Serious Dollmaker, 172
Mind Your Own Business at Home, 259
Mini Graphics, 84
Miniatronics, 101
Miniature Aircraft USA, 90
Miniature Collector, 259
Miniature Corner, The, 85
Miniature Image, 85
Miniature Lumber Shoppe, 85
Miniature Maker's Workshop, 85
Miniature Wood Productions, 85
Minnesota Clay USA, 24
Minnesota Lapidary Supply Corp., 68
Minolta Corp., 117
Minority Business Development, 253
Miroscale Industries, Inc., 84
Misty Mountain Fiber Workshop, 221
Mitchell Co., E.C., 154
Mitchell Graphics, 270
MLCS, Ltd., 154
M-M Videos, 3
Model Airplane News, 260
Model Expo, Inc., 95
Model Railroader, 260
Model Shipways, 95
Modern Machine Knitting, 260
Moe Wubba, 123
Monterey, Inc., 187
Montoya/Max, International, Inc., 130
Morning Glory Products, 193
Morning Light Emporium, 17
Morton House Primitives, 221
Mostly Animals, 123
Mountain Colors, 204, 244
Mountain Loom Co., 237
Mountain Mist, 215
Mountain Woodcarvers, Inc., 147
Mountain-Mark Trading, 69
Moyer, Pat, 221
MTA Hobbies, 90
Mueller, Edwina L., 172
Muffys Boutique Muffy's Boutique, 172
Muller Studios Sign Co., 132
Munro Crafts, 209
Murielle Roy & Co., 167
Murray Clock Craft Ltd., 29
Museum of Modern Rubber, 123
My Sister's Shoppe, Inc., 85
Mythical Reflections, 58

N

Name Brand, 124
Name Game, The, 17
Name Maker, Inc., 270
Nancy's Notions, 193, 228
Napa Valley Art Store, 7
National Artcraft Co., 24, 55
National Association of Miniature Enthusiasts, 248
National Cloth Dollmakers Association, 248
National Instititute of Artists & Craftsmen, The, 253, 260
National Instititute of American Doll Artists, 248
National Model Railroad Association, 248
National Nonwovens, 188
National Society of Tole and Decorative Painters, 249
National Stampagraphic, 260
National Thread & Supply Co., 228
Natural Fiber Fabric Direct, 188
Nature's Finest, 107
Nature's Herb Co., 107
Nature's Holler, 108
Nature's Treasures, 69
NCE Enterprises, 69
Neal, Bookseller, John, 113
Neale, Typecraft, Nancy, 55
Needlecraft Shop, Inc., The, 260
Needlepoint News, 260
Needlepoint Plus, 260
Needlework Attic, The, 204
Needlewords, 260
New Earth Designs, 221
New England Country Designs, 138
New Mexico Bead and Fetish, 17
New Venture Products, 270
New York Central Art Supply, 7
New York Institute of Photography, 117
Newark Dressmaker Supply, 167, 193
Newstech, 270
Newton's Knits, 205
NGraver Co., 69
Nikon Consumer Relations, 117
Nischke Ribbonry, 188
NK Products, 95
No Starch Press, 193
Nocera Miniatures, Joseph F., 85
Nolting's Longarm Manufacturing, Inc., 215
Nonferrous Metals Co., 78
Noonmark, 85
Noresta Cane & Reed, The, 12
Norsk Fjord Fiber, 237
North Carolina Basket Works, 12
North Country Outfitters, 46
North Light Art School, 3
North Light Book Club, 251
North Light Books, 3, 251
Northeast Knitworks, 205
Northeastern Scale Models, Inc., 85
NOrthern, 142
Northwest Hobby Shop, 90
Northwest Looms, 237

Northwest Tag & Label, Inc., 270
Northwind Farm Publications, 108
Northwoods Trading Co., 253
Norwood Looms, 238
Nova Tool Co., 142
Nowell's Molds, 25
NRI School of Photography, 117
N.S.D. Products, 204
Nudo Products, Inc., 132
Nutshell News, 260

O

Oak Leaf Wood 'N Supplies, 154
Oak Spring International, 221
Oakridge Hobbies, 85
O'Brien Manufacturing, 69
O'Briens Cellar Supplies, 144
Octavia's Jewels, 238
Ogier Trading Co., 244
Old Man Wool Farm, 238
Old Time Plan Service, 90
Old-Time Crochet, 260
Olson Rug Studio, Jane, 221
Olympic Enterprises, Inc., 25
Omni Models, 95
On Board Fabrics, 197
On Display, 270
On My Goodknits Inc., 188
On the Fly, 46
100 Proof Press, 124
112 Sewing Supplies, 228
Opitmagem, 69
Oppenheim's, 188
Optional Extras, 69
Oregon Dome, Inc., 31
Oregon Worsted Company, 238
Oriental Silk Co., 188
Ornament, 260
Ornamental Resources, Inc., 17, 69, 188
Ornaments Unlimited, 138
Orton, Ceramic Foundation, Edward, Jr., 25
Osborne & Co., C.S., 75
Ott's Discount Art Supply, 8
Our Nest Egg, 108
Out on a Whim, 17
Outdoor & Travel Photography, 261
Outdoor Wilderness Fabrics, 211
Overseas Publishers Representatives, 194
Owen Publishing Co., 50
Oxford Craft Software, 177
Ozark Basketry Supply, 12

P

P & D Hobby Shop, 101
Paasche Airbrush Co., 8
Pacific Front Hobbies, 96
Pacific Weave, 12
Painter's Corner, Inc., 3
Painting Magazine, 261
Pakaging Un-Limited Inc., 270
Panels by Paith, Inc., 270
Panter Lodges, 31
Panther Primitives, 61
Pantograms Manufacturing Co., Inc., 177

Paragon Industries, Inc., 25, 58
Paragraphics Corp., 142
Park Bench Pattern Co., 163
Parker, Joy, 85
Parser Minerals Corp., 69
Passap—U.S.A., 205
Past Patterns, 167
Patchwork Pleasures, 215
Patterncrafts, Inc., 55
Patterns of History, 167
Patternworks, 205
Patterson, 117
Paw Prints, 164
P.C. English, 138
PDI, Inc., 69
Peace Resource Project, 124
Pear Blossom Patterns, 172
Pearl, 8
Pearl Moon Fibers, 42
Peck-Polymers, 90
Peddler's Wagon, 194
Pegee of Williamsburg, 167
Pelham Tool, Inc., 154
Pellon Division, 188
Penelope Craft Programs, Inc., 205
Penn State Industries, 154
Penny Rugs & Runners, 221
Pentel of America, Ltd., 8, 181
Perfect Palette, 3
Perfect Touch, 42
Perkins, Co., H.H., 12
Perkins Miniatures, Don, 86
Perma Color, 8
Permofax Products, Inc., 155
Personal Threads Botique, 244
Peruvian Bead Co., The, 69
Pfaff American Sales Corp., 228
Philips Boyne, 188
Phoenix Model Co., 96
Photo Opportunity, 261
Photo Scope, 117
Photo Techniques, 261
Photographer's Formulary Co.,
    117, 181
Photographer's Forum, 261
Photographer's Ware House, 117
Photographic Magazine, 261
Photography Book Club, 117
Photo-Therm, 117
Pieces of Olde, 167
Piecework, 261
Pierce Co. The, 118
Pilgrim Shoe & Sewing Machine
    Co., 76
Pine Crest Angora Ranch, 238
Pine Meadow Knitting News, 261
Pinocchio's Miniatures, 86
Pintler Sheepcamp, 238
Pioneer Gem Corp., 70
Pipe Dreams, 124
Pippin's Hollow, 42
Pixation, 8
Plaid Enterprises, 138
Plastic Bag Outlet, The, 270
Plastic Bagmart, 270
Plastic Canvas Corner, 261
Plastic Canvas! Magazine, 261
Plastruct, 96

Plateau, The, 164
Platypus, 172
Play Dolls, 172
Pleasure Crafts, 42
Plymouth Reed & Cane Supply, 12
PNTA, 118
Pocahontas Leather, 76
Polifor-Form Industries, 35
Polka's Yarn Farm, 221
Polybags Plus, 270
Polyform Products Co., 56
Popular Photography, 261
Porta-Nails, Inc., 155
Posh Impressions, 124
Posy Patch Originals, 86
Potpourrie from Herbal Acres, 261
Pourette Mfg. Co., 104
Powell, Ltd., Anne, 177
Powers, Beverly, 172
Prairie Designs of California, 59
Prairie Ranch, 108
Precise Clock, Inc., 29
Precision Enterprises Unlimited, 90
Precision Movements, 29
Preemie-Yums, 164
Premier Wax Co., Inc., 130
Premium Products of Louisiana,
    Inc., 59
Prime Publishing, Inc., 36
Print Play, 124
Printmakers Machine Co., 8
Pro Chemical & Dye, Inc., 181
Professional Association of Custom
    Clothiers, The, 249
Professional Quilter, The, 261
Professional Sewing Supplies, 228
Profitable Craft Merchandising,
    262
Projects in Metal, 262
Promenade's LE Bead Shop, 17
Provincial Ceramic Products, Inc.,
    43
PSMC, Inc., 29
PTNA, 110
Publishers Central Bureau, 251
Pueblo Trading, 70
Purchase for Less, 228
Pure China Silk Co., 177
Pyramid Products, 78
Pyrotex, 127

Quadrotech, 91
Qualin International, Inc., 181, 189
Quality Upholstery, 50
Quality Yarns, 244
Quest Outfitters, 211
Quick & Easy Plastic Canvas! 262
Quick & Easy Quilting, 262
Quill-It, 113
Quilt in a Day, 215
Quilt Patch, The, 216
Quilt World, 262
Quilter's Newsletter Magazine, 262
Quilting B, The, 172
Quilting Bee, The, 216
Quilting Books Unlimited, 216
Quilts & Other Comforts, 216

Quiltwork Patches, 216
Quiltworks, The, 216

Radio Control Car Action, 262
Raheb, Barbara J., 86
Rail Graphics, 101
Railfan & Railroad, 262
Railroad Model Craftsman, 262
Rails 'N Shafts, 101
Rain Shed, 211
Rainbow Opals & Gems, 70
Rainbow Woods, 138
Ranite Corporation/Sure-Fit
    Designs, 228
Rarebriar Shetland Sheep, 238
Raum's Fantasy Dolls, Karen, 43
Rayco Paint Co., 132
Rayer's Bearden S.G. Supply, Inc.,
    59
Razertip Industries, 147
RB Industries, Inc., 155
R/C Modeler, 91
R/C Modeler Magazine, 262
Reactive Metals Studio, Inc., 70
Realistic Backdrops, 101
Red Beans & Rubber Stamps, 124
Red Caboose, The, 101
Red Clover Rugs, 222
Red Hot Rubber, Inc., 124
Redline Raodsters, 35
Reed & Cane, V.I., 12
Reinert Ceramics, Carol, 25
Reja Dolls, 43
Remarkable Rubber Stamps, 124
Renegade, 168
Rep Registry, The, 253
Repcon International, Inc., 197
Revenue Service Co., Inc., 253
Rex Graphic Supply, 8, 142
Ribbon Factory, The, 189
Ribbons & Roses, 177
Ridge Carbide Tool Corp., 155
Rigby Cloth Stripping Machines,
    222
Rimer, Gold And Betty, 86
Rio Grande Weaver's Supply, 238
Riordan, Brynn, 43
Ritter Carvers, Inc., 147
Rittermere-Hurst-Field, 222
Rivendell, Inc., 43
River Farm, The, 238
River Gems and Findings, 70
River View Molds, 25
R-Molds, 25
Ro Supply Company, Charles , 101
Robbie's Doll Creations, 172
Roberti, Daughters and Sons,
    Barney, 138
Robison-Anton Textile co., 177
Rocking B Maufacturing, 25
Rocking Horse Farm, 168
Roclith Creations, 205
Rodale Press Inc., 251
Roddy—Handweaver, Suzanne,
    238
Rollerwall, 197
Roman's, 43

Ronan Paint Corp., T.J., 132
Rondel Wood Products, 86
Rosebar Textile Co., Inc., 168
Rosemary's Sewing Supply, 228
Rosemont Hobby Shop, 91
Rosen Studio, Seth, 59
Rosenstand, Eva, 177
Roudebush Co., The, 51
Roussels, 70
Rowan Replicars, 35
Royal Findings, Inc., 70
Royal Products Corp., 96
Royalwood Ltd., 12
Rubber Duck Stamp Co., 125
Rubber Poet, 125
Rubber Railroad Stamp Works, 125
Rubberstampede, 125
Rubberstampmadness, 262
Rug Hooking, 262
Rugging Room, The, 222
Rumplestiltskin's, 222
Rupert, Gibbon & Spider, Inc./Jac-
    quard Products, 160
Russell, Sharon E., 86
Rynne China Co, 25

SAC, 263
Saf-T-Pockets, 164
St. Peter Woolen Mill, 216, 239
Sajama Alpaca, 238
Saket Co., 270
Sally Goodspeed, 216
Salter Industries, 31
San Francisco Herb Co., 108
Sandcastle Creations, 43
Sandeen's, 177
Sandeen's Scandinavian Art, Gifts
    & Needlecraft, 138
S&G, Inc., 138
S&S Arts and Crafts, 56
S&S Arts & Crafts, 194
Sandy Pond Hardwoods, Inc., 31
Sarah's Sewing Supplies, 229
Saratoga Sodlier Shop & Military
    Bookstore, 96
Satellite City, 96
Sav-Mor Leather & Supply, 76
Sawdust And Paintings, 138
Sax Arts & Crafts, 8, 56, 113
SB Power Tools, 155
Scale Cabinetmaker, The, 263
Scale Ship Modeler, 263
Scandinavian Designs, 239
Scarbrough, 239
Scarbrough, Lois, 239
Schacht Spindle Co., Inc., 239
Schaefer Yarns, 244
Schaifer's Enameling Supplies, 79
Schoepfer, Inc., G., 43, 147
School of Clock Repair, 29
Schoolhouse Ceramics, 26
Schoolhouse Press, 205
Schoolhouse Yarns, 239
Scientific Models, Inc., 86
Scioto Ceramic Products, Inc., 26
Scissors & Snips, 229
Scott Group, 222

Scott Publications, 26, 43
Sculpture, 263
Sculpture Studio & Foundrey, 130
Sea Holly Hooked Rugs, 222
Seattle Fabrics, 212
Seeley Doll Center, 43
Semplex, 144
Sepp Leaf Products, Inc., 111, 132
Serrao, Rene D., 96
Seven Corners Ace Hardware, Inc., 155
Sevtec, Inc., 35
Sew Beautiful, 263
Sew Fancy, 229
Sew Far, Sew Good, 189
Sew Little Pattern Co., 164, 172
Sew Natural, 189
Sew News, 263
Sew Original Needleart, 178
Sew Sassy Lingerie, 164
Sew Special, 173
Sew Sweet Dolls From Carolee Creations, 173
Sew/Fit Co., 229
Sewin' in Vermont, 229
Sewing Center, The, 205
Sewing Library, 229
Sewing Room, The, 216
Sewing Update, The, 263
Sew-Knit Distributors, 205
Shadeyside Farms, 239
Shaker Workshops, 50
Shannock Tapestry Looms, 239
Sharlaine Products, 212
Sharma Trading Co., 160
Shaw Mudge And Co., 108
Shaw Studio, Jackie, 139
Shear Delight Fibers, 44
Sheffield School of Interior Design, 197
Sheldon Designs, 32
Sheltech, 79
Shelter Systems, 32
Shelton's Hobbies, 91
Shep, R.L., 168
Shillcraft, 222
Shipwreck Beads, 17, 70
Shoff Tackle, 46
Shooters of USA Lab, 118
Shopsmith, Inc., 155
Shuttle, Spindle & Dyepot, 263
Side Door, The, 86
Sideline Business, 263
Siegel Co., Inc., M., 76
Sierra Oaks, 229
Sig Manufacturing Co., Inc., 91
Sign Craft Magazine, 263
Signilar Art Videos, 4
Sign-Mart, 132
Silk City Fibers, 239
Silk for Life Yarns, 240, 245
Silk Tree, The, 240
Silkpaint Corp., 181, 229
Silkworm, The, 263
Silver Armadillo, 70
Silver Cloud Farm, 240
Silver Lining, 253
Silver's Wholesale Club, 197

Simmons, Inc., Robert, 9
Simply Cross Stitch, 263
Simply De-Vine, 108
Simply Elegant Designs, 113
Singer Sewing Center, 229
Sioux Ceramic Supply, 26
Skacel Collection, Inc., 206
Skutt Ceramic Products, 26
Skytech Models, 91
Small Houses, 86
Small World, 96
Smidt, Susan, 222
Smile Photo and Video, Inc., 118
Smith, Inc., Daniel, 9
Smith, Don, 91
Smith Equipment, 70
Smith, Quiltmaker, Jane C., 217
Smith's Beads, L.C., 18
Smithy, 142
Smocking Bonnet, The, 229
Society of Craft Designers, 249
Soho South, 182
Solmon Brothers, 76
Solo Sewing Supplies, 230
Something Special, 173
Source Marketing Ltd., 194
South Forty Farms, 44
South Westamps, 125
Southern Oregon Scientific, 127
Southwest America, 71
Southwest Savvy, 230
Sparkle!, 168
Sparkling City Gems, 71
Spaulding & Rogers, 110
Spaulding Trading and Shipping, 96
Specialties, 189
Specialty Products International, 144
Speed Stitch, 230
Speedotron Corp., 118
Spiller Dyeworks, 217
Spin 'N Weave, 240
Spindle Hill, 222
Spin-Off, 264
Sportscraft, 35
Springtime Design, 173
S-T Leather Co., 76
Stafford, Phyllis, 86
Stahl, Janet, 164
Stained Glass Superstore, The, 59
Stamp Addiction, 125
Stamp Antonio, 125
Stamp in the Hand Co., A, 125
Stamp of Excellence, Inc., 125
Stamp Pad Co., Inc., The, 125
Stampendous!, 126
Stampinks Unlimited, 126
Stampourri, 126
Stan Brown's Arts & Crafts, Inc., 6
Standard Doll Co., 173
Standard Doll Supply House, Inc., 44
Standard Hobby Supply, 101
Star Stilts Co., 26
Starr Gems, Inc., 71
Stearns Technical Textiles Co., The, 217

Steatite of Southern Oregon, Inc., 130
Steebar, 29
Steel Heddle, 240
Steel Master, 32
Stencil House of N.H., Inc., 139
Stephanie's Studio & Yarn, 206
Sterling Name Tape Co., 271
Sterling Publishing Co., Inc., 251
Stetkewicz, Ron, 87
Stewart-Superior Corp., 126
Stitch In Time, 178
Stitcher's Sourceletter, 264
Stone Age Industries, Inc., 71
Stonebrier Yarn & Design Co., 206
Stony Mountain Fibers, 240
Storey Publishing, 251
Strategies, 264
Straw Into Gold, 240
Strawberry Sampler, The, 178
Street Rod Action, 264
Street Specialties, 35
Stretch & Sew Fabrics, 189
String Slinger, The, 206
Strings 'N Things, 178
Stu-Art, 49
Studio Books, 194
Studio Limestone, 206, 210
Studio Products, Inc., 206
Studio Word Processing, Ltd., 194
Suburban Sew 'N Sweep, Inc., 230
Such a Deal Tulle, 189
Sugar Creek Industries, Inc., 26
Suitability, 164
Suitables, 164
Sun Designs, 155
Sun Ray Products Corp., 35
Suncoast Discount Arts & Crafts, 209
Sunfeather Herbal Soap Co., 108
Sunflower Studio, 189
Sunshine Artists U.S.A., 264
Superior Aircraft Materials, 91
Sureway Trading Enterprises, 182
Surface Design Association, 249
SURMA, 139
Sweet Briar Studio, 223
Sweet Celebrations, 104
Sweet Medicine, 61
Swiss Box, Ltd., 139
Sylvia's Studio, 253

T

Tackle Shop, The, 47
Tallina's Doll Supplies, Inc., 44
Tallix, 130
Tampa Bay Mold Co., 26
Tandy Leather Co., 77, 189
Tara Materials Inc., 132
Taunton Press, The, 155, 168, 194
Taylor Bedding Manufacturing Co., 194
Taylor Design Group, 155
Taylor, Linda, 87
Taylor's Cutaways & Stuff, 194
TBR, Inc., 26
TD Creations, 206
TDI Doll Co., 44

Tech-Toys, 96
Teddy Bear Review, 264
Teddy Tribune, The, 264
Teleflite Corp., 97
Tennessee Moulding & Frame Co., 49
Terry Craft, 51
Tess' Designer Yarns, 206
Testfabrics, Inc., 189
Testrite Instrument Co., Inc., 142
Texas Dory Boat Plans, 35
Textile Colors, 182
Textile Enterprises, Inc., 108, 209
Textile Reproductions, 194
Thai Silks, 190
Theo-Stitch, 178
Things Japanese, 230
32nd Parallel, 97
Thomas Instrument Co., Inc., 118
Thorburn's, 212
Thread Bare Pattern Co., The, 164, 230
Thread Discount Sales, 230
Threads at Gingerbread Hill, 190
Threads Magazine, 264
Thrifty Needle, The, 164
Thumb Workshops, Tom, 109
Thumbelina Needlework Shop, 178
Thur Fabrics, L.P., 190
Timberline, 71
Timberline Geodesics, 32
Timberline Sewing Kits, 212, 230
Tip Sandblast Equipment, 133
T.L.C. Doll Hospital, 44
TM Porcelain Co., 44
Toft's Tole House, 139
Tole World, 264
Tool Crib of the North, The, 142, 156
Tool Factory, 156
Toolmark Co., 156
Toomuchfun Rubberstamps, 126
Total Nonsense Ceramics, 44
Total Shop, 156
Touch the Earth, 18
Tower Hobbies, 97
Toy Soldier Co., The, 97
Toy Soldier Review, 264
Trademark Sign Systems, 133
Trafton Thompson Publishing, 139
Train Master Ltd., The, 102
Train World, 102
Trains, 264
Traintown of Canada, 102
Treadleart, 230, 264
Trear Designs, J., 182
Treasures, 139
Treasures From Heaven, 173
Treenway Crafts Ltd., 240
Tremont Nail Co., 156
Trend-Lines, Inc., 156
Trenton Mold, 26
Triola, Bonnie, 206
Triple Over Dye, 223
Tripp's Mfg., 71
Trow and Holden Co., 130
Troy-Built Manufacturing Co., 32
Tsi, 71

T.S.I. Wholesale Mfg., Jewelers and Refiners, 271
Turncraft Clocks, Inc., 29
Twelve Squared, 97
Twilight Designs, 178
Twinrocker Handmade Paper, 113

U

Uhlfelder, Co., Leo, 133
Ultimate Collection, Inc.,The, 44
Ultimate Herb & Spice Shoppe, The, 109
Ultramouse Ltd., 190
Ultrascraps/D.M. Designs, 190
Ultravision, 143
Uncle Rebus Stamp Co., 126
Unicorn Studios, 173
Unicorn Universal Woods, 156
Unique Place/World of Kites, The, 74
Unique Spool, The, 190, 195
Unique, The, 245
United Art Glass, Ltd., 59
United States Pearl Co., Inc., 71
Universal Hovercraft, 97, 98
Universal Synergetics, 18
Universal Wirecraft Co., 71
U.S. Bronze Powders, Inc., 111
UTEX Trading, 190
Utrecht Manufacturing Corp., 9

V

Valley Model Trains, 102
Val's Naturals, 109
Van Dyke's, 45, 51, 105, 134
Van Eps, 230
Vanguard Model Marine, 97
Vantec, 97
Vaughn & Bushness Manufacturing Co., 156
VC Photographic Art Supplies, 118
V.E.A.S., Inc., 59
Veas Productions, 4
Vega Enterprises, Inc., 156
Verilux, 9
Vermont Rugs, 223
Veteran Leather Co., 77
Vibra-Tek Company, 72
Vickie's Anguish Original Molds, 45
Vicki's Original Designs, 45
Victorian Craftsman, Ltd. The, 87
Victorian Times, 87
Victorian Video Productions, 13, 208, 240

Viking Folk Art Publications, 139
Viking Sewing Machine Co., 231
Viking Woodcrafts, Inc., 139
Village Miniatures, 87
Village Originals, 29
Village Weaver, The, 240
Village Wools, Inc., 240
Vintage Wood Works, 32
Vinylwrite Custom Lettering, 98
Virginia Basket Supply, 13
Visual Image Printery, 126
Vito's Ceramic Supply, 27
Vitrex Ceramics, Ltd., 27
Viv's Ribbons & Laces, 173
Vixen Hill, 32
Vreseis Ltd., 241
V.U.E., 51

W

W & D Mini Homes, 87
Wakeda Trading Post, 61
Walden Woods Designs, 87
Wall Lumber Co., Steve, 157
Walters Basket Willow Craft, 13
Warling Miniatures, 87
Warm Products, Inc., 197
Watch Parts, 72
Water Colour Gazette Newsletter, The, 264
Weaver Leather, Inc., 77
Weaver-Artisans Outlet, The, 241
Weaver's Cabin, 241
Weavers Loft, The, 206, 241
Weaver's Place, The, 241
Weaver's Shop & Yarn Co., The, 241
Weaver's Way, 241, 245
Weaving Edge, The, 241
Weaving Works, 241
Web of Thread, 182
Webs, 241
Webster Co., Kate, 173
Wee World of Dolls, Inc., 45
Weefoke Empire, 45
Wellspring Gallery, 195, 231
Wensco Sign Supply, 133
Wescraft, 91
West Mountain Gourd Farm, 109
Westart, 264
Westbank Doll Supply, Inc., 45
Westcott, Co. F.J., 118
Westcott, Peter, 87
Westcroft Beadworks, 18
Western Trading Post, 61
Western Woodworks, 139
Westrade Sales, Inc., 207

Westwood Ceramic Supply, 27
Wetherbee Basket Shop, Martha, 13
Wetherbee Basket Shop News, Martha, 265
Wheels by Van Eaton, 242
Whispering Hill Farm, 223
White House, The, 223
White Pine Designs, Inc., 140
White Sewing Machine Co., 231
Whittemore-Durgin, 59
Whole Customer's Catalogue, The, 168
Whole Earth Access, 157
Wiener Wood Carver, Ron, 157
Wild Woman Artworks, 9
Wilde Yarns, 245
Wildlife Photography, 265
Wilke Machinery Co., 157
William's, 145
Williams & Hussey Machine Co., Inc., 157
Wilson's Ladybug Art Center, Shirley, 140
Wilton Enterprises, 105
Wind Under Your Wings, 74
Winfield Collection, The, 157
Wings 'N Things, 98
Winsor & Newton, 9
Wise Screenprint, Inc., 27
With Heart & Hand, 198
Wizards Of Wood, 140
Women Artist News, 265
Wonder Punch, 178
Wonderful World of Hats, 231
Wood, 265
Wood Carvers Supply, Inc., 147
Wood Cellar, The, 140
Wood Factory, The, 271
Wood Mizer Products, 32
Wood Molding & Millwork Producers Association, 157
Wood N' Things, Inc., 147
Wood Strokes, 265
Wood to Paint, 140
Woodartist, 157
Woodcraft Supply Corp., 157
Woodcrafts and Supplies, 158
Wooden Heart, The, 140, 182
Wooden Memories, 45
Wooden Porch Books, 195
Woodland Scenics, 102
Woodmaster Tools, Inc., 158
Wood-Met Services, 79
Wood-N-Crafts, Inc., 56

Wood-Ply Lumber Corp., 157
Woodshop News, 265
Woodturner's Catalog, The, 158
Woodwork, 265
Woodworker's Book Club, 158, 251
Woodworkers Source, 158
Woodworkers' Store, The, 158
Woodworker's Supply, 158
Woodworks, 158
Wool Connection, The, 207
Wool Shop Video, Inc., 207
Wool Winder, The, 223
Wool Works, Plus, 223
Woolery, The, 242, 245
Worden's World of Crafts, Inc., 140
Workbasket, The, 265
Workbench, 265
World Beads USA, 18
World Frame Distributors, 49
World Of Trains, 102
World Trading, Inc., 77
Woven Spirit Baketry, 13
WSC, 195
Wy'East Fabrics, 212

Y

Yankee Ingenuity, 29
Yankee Peddler Hooked Rugs, 223
Yarder Manufacturing Co., 133
Yarn Barn, 207, 242, 245
Yarn for Ewe, 207
Yarn Gallery, 207
Yarnarts, 207
Yarn-It-All, 207
Yarns by Mail, 245
Yazoo Mills, Inc., 271
Yesterday's Children, 45
Yesterday's Children Pattern Co., 45
Yesterdays, 182
Yesteryears Rug Hooking Studio, 223
YLI Corp., 195, 231
Yolo Wool Products, 242
Yozie Mold Co., 27

Z

Zanotti, Alan, 128
Zembillas Sponge Co., Inc., 27
Zip Manufacturing, 27
Zona Tool Company, 98
Zone VI Studios, Inc., 119
Zum Bali Bali Rubber Stamps, 126

More Great Books for Crafters!

The Doll Sourcebook—Bring your dolls and supplies as close as the telephone with this unique sourcebook of retailers, artists, restorers, appraisers and more! Each listing contains extensive information—from addresses and phone numbers to business hours and product lines. #70325/$22.99/352 pages/176 b&w illus./paperback

Painting Houses, Cottages and Towns on Rocks—Turn ordinary rocks into charming cottages, country churches and Victorian mansions! Accomplished artist Lin Wellford shares 11 fun, inexpensive, step-by-step projects that are sure to please. #30823/$21.99/128 pages/398 color illus./paperback

Handmade Jewelry: Simple Steps to Creating Wearable Art—Create unique and wearable pieces of art—and have fun doing it! 42 step-by-step jewelry-making projects are at your fingertips—from necklaces and earrings, to pins and barrettes. Plus, no experience, no fancy equipment and no expensive materials are required! #30820/$21.99/128 pages/126 color, 30 b&w illus./paperback

The Teddy Bear Sourcebook: For Collectors and Crafters—Discover the most complete treasury of bear information stuffed between covers. You'll turn here whenever you need to find sellers of bear making supplies, major manufacturers of teddy bears, teddy bear shows, auctions and contests, museums that house teddy bear collections and much more. #70294/$18.99/356 pages/202 illus./paperback

How to Start Making Money with Your Crafts—Launch a rewarding crafts business with this guide that starts with the basics—from creating marketable products to setting the right prices—and explores all the exciting possibilities. End-of-chapter quizzes, worksheets, ideas and lessons learned by successful crafters are included to increase your learning curve. #70302/$18.99/176 pages/35 b&w illus.

The Art of Painting Animals on Rocks—Discover how a dash of paint can turn humble stones into charming "pet rocks." This hands-on easy-to-follow book offers a menagerie of fun—and potentially profitable—stone animal projects. Eleven examples, complete with material list, photos of the finished piece and patterns will help you create a forest of fawns, rabbits, foxes and other adorable critters. #30606/$21.99/144 pages/250 color illus./paperback

Stencil Source Book 2—Add color and excitement to fabrics, furniture, walls and more with over 200 original motifs that can be used again and again! Idea-packed chapters will help you create dramatic color schemes and themes to enhance your home in hundreds of ways. #30730/$22.99/144 pages/300 illus.

Decorative Wreaths & Garlands—Discover stylish, yet simple-to-make wreaths and garlands. These 20 original designs use fabrics and fresh and dried flowers to add color and personality to any room, and charm to special occasions. Clear instructions are accompanied by step-by-step photographs to ensure that you create a perfect display every time. #30696/$19.99/96 pages/175 color illus./paperback

The Complete Flower Arranging Book—An attractive, up-to-date guide to creating more than 100 beautiful arrangements with fresh and dried flowers, illustrated with step-by-step demonstrations. #30405/$24.95/192 pages/300+ color illus.

The Complete Flower Craft Book—Discover techniques for drying fresh flowers and seedheads, creating arrangements to suit all seasons and occasions, making silk flowers, potpourri, bath oil and more! This guide is packed with photographs, tips and step-by-step instructions to give you a bouquet of ideas and inspiration! #30589/$24.95/144 pages/275 color illus.

Jewelry & Accessories: Beautiful Designs to Make and Wear—Discover how to make unique jewelry out of papier maché, wood, leather, cloth and metals. You'll learn how to create: a hand-painted wooden brooch, a silk-painted hair slide, a paper and copper necklace and much more! Fully illustrated with step-by-step instructions. #30680/$17.99/128 pages/150 color illus./paperback

Dried Flowers: Colors for Every Room in the House—Create exquisite arrangements to match any room or color scheme! With this versatile and easy-to-use reference, you'll discover the full range of available flower types, as well as step-by-step projects and a gallery of arrangements to inspire your work! #30701/$27.99/144 pages/4-color throughout

Decorative Boxes To Create, Give and Keep—Craft beautiful boxes using techniques including embroidery, stenciling, lacquering, gilding, shellwork, decoupage and many others. Step-by-step instructions and photographs detail every project. #30638/$15.95/128 pages/color throughout/paperback

Elegant Ribboncraft—Over 40 ideas for exquisite ribbon-craft—hand-tied bows, floral garlands, ribbon embroidery and more. Various techniques are employed—including folding, pleating, plaiting, weaving, embroidery, patchwork, quilting, applique and decoupage. All projects are complete with step-by-step instructions and photographs. #30697/$16.99/128 pages/130+ color illus.

Paint Craft—Discover great ideas for enhancing your home, wardrobe and personal items. You'll see how to master the basics of mixing and planning colors, how to print with screen and linoleum to create your own stationery,

how to enhance old glassware and pottery pieces with unique patterns and motifs and much more! #30678/$16.99/144 pages/200 color illus./paperback

Nature Craft—Dozens of step-by-step nature craft projects to create, including dried flower garlands, baskets, corn dollies, potpourri and more. Bring the outdoors inside with these wonderful projects crafted with readily available natural materials. #30531/$14.95/144 pages/200 color illus./paperback

Paper Craft—Dozens of step-by-step paper craft projects to make, including greeting cards, boxes and desk sets, jewelry and pleated paper blinds. If you have ever worked with or wanted to work with paper you'll enjoy these attractive, fun-to-make projects. #30530/$16.95/144 pages/200 color illus./paperback

The Complete Book of Silk Painting—Create fabulous fabric art—everything from clothing to pillows to wall hangings. You'll learn every aspect of silk painting in this step-by-step guide, including setting up a workspace, necessary materials and fabrics and specific silk painting techniques. #30362/$26.99/128 pages/color throughout

Fabric Sculpture: The Step-By-Step Guide & Showcase—Discover how to transform fabrics into 3-dimensional images. Seven professional fabric sculptors demonstrate projects that illustrate their unique approaches and methods for creating images from fabric. The techniques—covered in easy, step-by-step illustration and instruction—include quilting, thread work, applique and soft sculpture. #30687/$29.99/160 pages/300+ color illus.

Everything You Ever Wanted to Know About Fabric Painting—Discover how to create beautiful fabrics! You'll learn how to set up work space, choose materials, plus the ins and outs of tie-dye, screen printing, woodgraining, marbling, cyanotype and more! #30625/$21.99/128 pages/color throughout/paperback

Master Strokes—Master the techniques of decorative painting with this comprehensive guide! Learn to use decorative paint finishes on everything from small objects and furniture to walls and floors, including dozens of step-by-step demonstrations and numerous techniques. #30347/$29.99/160 pages/400 color illus.